Praise for 'The Complete Walt Disney World'

"Julie Neal's a real expert." —*Richard Qu...*

"It's so well done... If you are going to W
this book you're making a mistake." —*R...*

"Seriously thorough." —*Family Circle*

"Highly recommended." —*New York Dail...*

"Should leave fans of Mickey smiling from ear to ear." —*Chicago Tribune*

"A thorough overview, with inside tips. Also makes a nice souvenir." —*Boston Globe*

"Far and away the best guide to Disney World... Refreshing in its honest opinions."
—*St. Louis Post-Dispatch*

"A fantastic planning tool... A guidebook series marked by stunning photography and
depth of information... Unusual details that matter to families... So beautifully illustrated,
vacationers will want to save it as a keepsake." —*Orlando Sentinel*

"Our favorite Disney guidebook." —*Ft. Worth Star Telegram*

"Endless tips." —*Knoxville News-Sentinel*

"Stunning photos... Looking through this book is simply fun. It will make you more
knowledgeable, while immersing you in the magic of Disney World." —*Kirkus Reviews*

"In-depth insider knowledge... The magic of Disney radiates from the pages... All the
information needed to ensure your vacation is the experience of a lifetime... Definitely the
book to purchase to help plan out your trip." —*Midwest Book Review*

"The ultimate Walt Disney World guidebook... Everything you could possibly need to
know to plan and pull off the best Disney trip ever... Colorful, easy-to-navigate... Leaves
no stone unturned." —*Writer's Digest*

"Visually engaging... What sets apart the Neals' book are the color photographs of rides,
rooms and characters." —*Library Journal*

"In this case, 'complete' is not hyperbole, it is a fact... Makes a trip to Disney seem more
like an adventure full of surprises, instead of a whine-filled money drain."
—*MomMostTraveled.com*

"The best reference available for planning a Disney vacation." —*Orlando Vacation Rentals*

"Well-written and illustrated, with sumptuous colour photographs." —*Florida Review
and Travel Guide (United Kingdom)*

Awards and honors

Outstanding Family Product. Disney's iParenting Media Awards.*

Travel Guide of the Year. 2012 ForeWord Reviews Awards; 2012 Next Generation Indie
Book Awards; 2012, 2011, 2010 International Book Awards; 2011, 2010, 2009, 2008 National
Independent Excellence Awards; 2012, 2010 Benjamin Franklin Awards (silver medalist);
2009 ForeWord Reviews Awards (silver medalist); 2009 Living Now Book Awards (silver
medalist); 2008 National Best Book Awards (finalist)

Travel/Family Activity Book of the Year. 2010 Living Now Book Awards; 2009 Living Now
Book Awards (silver medalist)

Nonfiction Book of the Year. 2009 National Independent Excellence Book Awards; 2008
Writer's Digest International Book Awards

Book of the Year. 2012 Eric Hoffer Book Awards (finalist)

Best Interior Design. 2010 International Book Awards (finalist)

Reference Book of the Year. 2009 Writer's Digest Int'l Book Awards (silver medalist)

Best Southeast Nonfiction. 2008 Independent Publisher Book Awards (silver medalist)

* The Complete Walt Disney World is the only guidebook ever honored by the Walt Disney Co.

The Complete Walt Disney World 2017

ISBN 978-0-9903716-4-9

Writing and research: Julie Neal
Photography: Mike Neal
Additional photography and research: Micaela Neal

Produced by Coconut Press Media Inc.
Published by AdventureKEEN
Manufactured in the United States of America
Distributed by Publishers Group West

Acknowledgments

Our thanks to Craig Dezern, Yolanda Cade, Rick Sylvain, Jason Lasecki, Jonathan Frontado, Bebee Frost, Darrell Fry, Matt Gottfried, David Hillstrom, Charles Stovall and the late Dave Herbst for a variety of assistance, and: Ngonba Anadou, Mandee Andrichyn, Odalys Aponte, Kevin Baker, Richard Bogart, David Brady, Juliana Cadiz, Mike Colangelo, Michael Colavolpe, Brian Cotten, Jason Dobbins, Todd Ferrante, Andrea Finger, John Frost, Jay and Kisha Garcia, Phran Gauci, Lorraine Gorham, Matt Hathaway, Jamie-Lyn Hawkins, Holland Hayes, David Hobart, Walter Iooss, Rob Iske, Eric Jacobson, Kristie A. Jones, Kristine Jones, Chris Kraftchick, Kathy Mangum, Roberto Martinez, Bob Miller, Tony Morreale, Doobie and Rebekah Moseley, Nenette Mputu, Charles Ridgway, Kathy Rogers, Joe Rohde, Debbie Sacleux, Susan Schofield, Steve Schussler, Theron Skees, Laura Spencer, Rheo Tan, Benjamin Thompson, Paul Tomayko, Alicia Vaughn, Jenn and Jay Wakelin, Terry Ward, Chris Weaver, John Wetzel, Kevin Yee and all the Disney resort and duty managers.

To Micaela. Put on your Sunday clothes. There's lots of world out there.

#OrlandoUnited

The Complete Walt Disney World® 2017

Julie and Mike Neal

Contents

6 **A World of Its Own**
And how it came to be

8 **Magic Kingdom**
The world's most popular theme park

124 **Epcot**
Disney's World's Fair

172 **Disney's Hollywood Studios**
A tribute to Tinseltown

214 **Disney's Animal Kingdom**
Lions, tigers and thrill rides

298 **Water Parks**
Blizzard Beach and Typhoon Lagoon

310 **Disney Springs**
Disney calls it The Place to Be

330 **ESPN Wide World of Sports**
The country's top spot for amateur athletics

336 **Accommodations**
Insight and information on every Disney hotel

374 **Planning Your Trip**
FastPass+, involving your children, much more

408 **Telephone Directory**

410 **Index**

415 **About the Authors**

SYMBOLS USED IN THIS BOOK

★ **STARS.** Attractions, food locations and hotels are rated from one to five stars, based on how well they live up to their promise.

✔ **CHECKMARKS.** Indicate author personal favorites.

$00 **DOLLAR AMOUNTS.** When shown before a food location indicates the average price of an adult dinner or snack, including soft drink, tax and tip.

DDP **DISNEY DINING PLAN.** Marks a participating food spot. **DDP** indicates it charges one credit, **DDP2** two credits, **DDPq** a quick-service credit, **DDPs** a snack credit.

00m **AVERAGE WAIT TIMES.** These show the hourly Standby wait times of an attraction on random days in the first half of 2016, including peak periods.

Illustration © Disney

Confirming the news. An Orlando press conference in 1966.

A World of Its Own

TWICE THE SIZE OF MANHATTAN, Walt Disney World is the world's largest collection of theme parks, water parks and resorts. A world of its own, it's unlike anywhere else.

A trip to Disney is not just a way to spend time with your kids, nor merely an escape from day-to-day doldrums. If you do it right it can be a reawakening of that free-spirited, good-natured soul who lives deep inside you. The one your spouse married, the one you want your kids to emulate. Yes, it's crowded. Expensive. And you have to plan it. But no other man-made vacationland so embraces a sense of wonder about the world.

Populated daily by more than 100,000 visitors as well as 65,000 employees (or as Disney calls them, "cast members"), Walt Disney World is the No. 1 vacation destination on the planet. It includes four theme parks, two water parks, a sports complex, shopping and entertainment districts and 20 resort hotels.

Project X. In 1964 the Disney Co. began secretly buying up parcels of land southwest of Orlando, using false names and dummy corporations to keep prices low. In October 1965, the Orlando Sentinel-Star identified the buyer. A month later Walt Disney, his brother Roy and the governor of Florida confirmed the existence of their "Project X." It was a plan for a futuristic city—the Experimental Prototype Community of Tomorrow (EPCOT)—a place to explore solutions to urban problems of the day. It would include a theme park to pay its bills, a version of California's Disneyland.

Walt dies. After Walt Disney's sudden death a year later, Roy decided to go ahead with the idea, at least the theme park portion, but changed its name to Walt Disney World to honor his brother. The largest private construction project in the history of the United States, it broke ground in 1969. Two military men led its development. Army General Joe Potter had overseen operations at the Panama Canal and the 1964 World's Fair; Navy Admiral Joe Fowler had supervised the building of Disneyland. Nine thousand workers moved 8 million cubic yards (6 million cubic meters) of dirt, built 47 miles (76 km) of canals, 22 miles (35 km) of levees, dredged a lake and lagoon. They built roads, shops, a phone company, power plant, sewage plant and tree farm.

Walt Disney World opened on Oct. 1, 1971.

Photo above: Florida State Archives. Opposite page: © Disney

Roy Disney dedicates Walt Disney World. October 1971.

Magic Kingdom

"Partners"

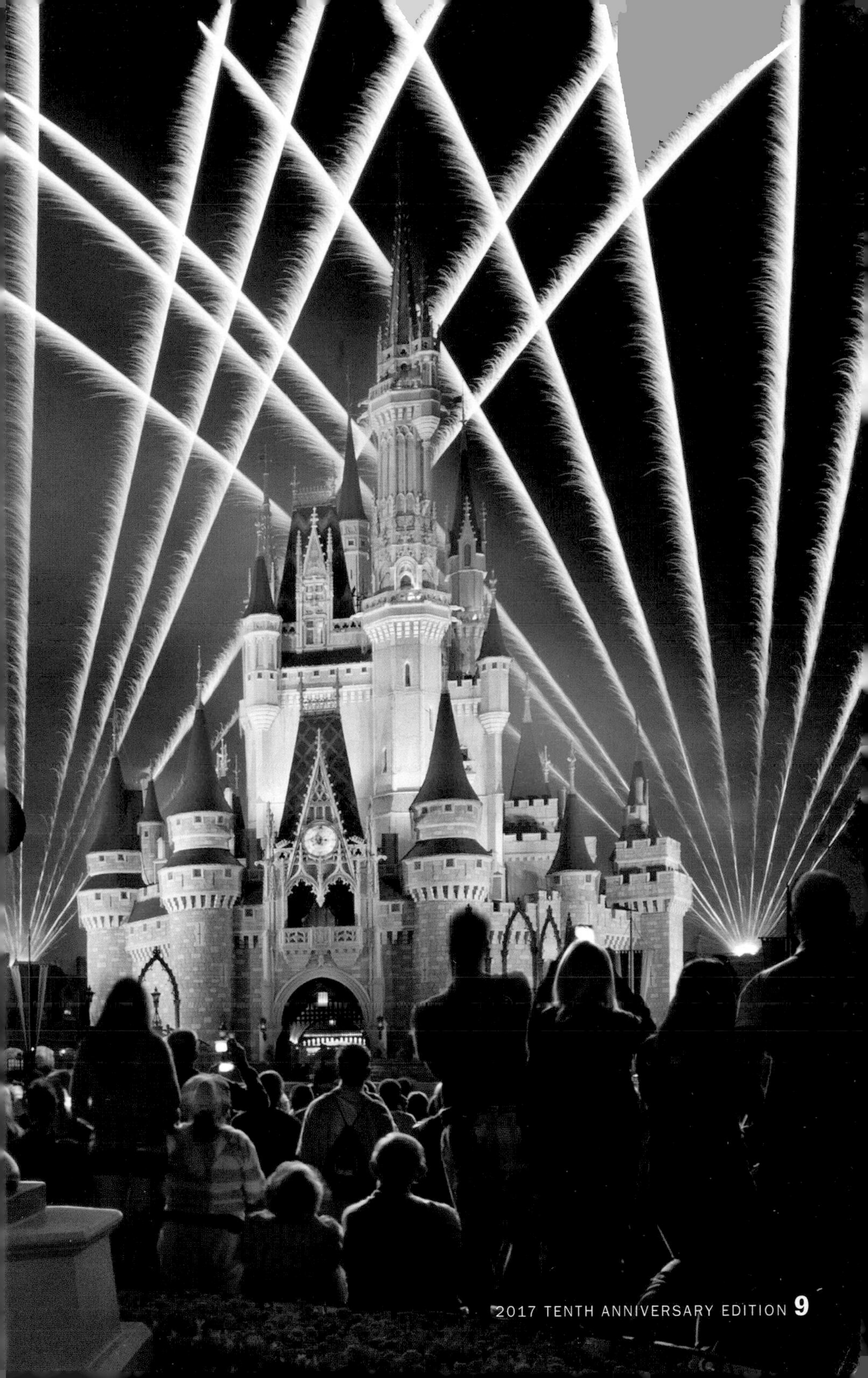

The Dapper Dans.

A PLACE FOR ADVENTURE, FANTASY and nostalgia; a site to celebrate "Once upon a time..." and "...happily ever after," the world's most popular theme park appeals to childhood dreams, memories and imagination, the wish to be the prettiest girl at the ball. Its idealized world includes the friendliest small town ever, an achingly beautiful castle, flying elephants and pirate ships, and mountains of space, splashes and big thunder.

Best of the park. ❶ Disney's most child-focused park, it's easy to navigate, with attractions placed closely together. ❷ It has lots of rides and shows, more than twice that of any other Disney World park. ❸ There's a cornucopia of characters—in parades, shows and attractions, a street party, character meals, and at many meet-and-greet spots. ❹ A small-town American boulevard from a century ago, Main Street U.S.A. is the heart of all things Disney, a dreamlike lane that's lovingly detailed, from its architecture and ambient music to the costumes of its citizens. ❺ Finally, the park has the master's touch. Although he didn't live to see it completed, Walt Disney was deeply involved in its planning and several of its attractions. His spirit lives in the Carousel of Progress, Enchanted Tiki Room, It's a Small World, Peter Pan's Flight, Pirates of the Caribbean and the Walt Disney World Railroad.

Worst of the park. Among its issues: ❶ Attraction capacity 9,750. Park capacity 60,000. You do the math. ❷ Inconvenience. Getting to the park can be an adventure in itself, as its parking lot is a mile away. ❸ And oh that bright future of ours! Tomorrowland has little shade but lots of hot asphalt.

If it rains. Ducking out of the rain is pretty easy, as stores and fast-food spots line most walkways. Big Thunder Mountain Railroad and the Seven Dwarfs Mine Train close when it rains; parades, street parties, outdoor shows and fireworks shortened or cancelled. Eleven attractions close when lightning is in the area: Astro Orbiter, Dumbo, Jungle Cruise, Liberty Square Riverboat, Magic Carpets of Aladdin, Main Street Vehicles, Splash Mountain, Swiss Family Treehouse, the Tomorrowland Speedway, Tom Sawyer Island and the Walt Disney World Railroad.

Family matters. Several rides have height minimums: 44 inches (112 cm) for Space Mountain, 40 (102 cm) for Big Thunder Mountain Railroad and Splash Mountain; 38 (97 cm) for the Seven Dwarfs Mine Train; 35 (89 cm) for Barnstormer. Tomorrowland Speedway drivers need to be 54 inches (137 cm) tall; riders 32 (81 cm). Stitch's Great Escape has a minimum height of 40 inches (102 cm). Except for the Speedway all of these attractions could frighten children. Others that might: Astro Orbiter, The Haunted Mansion and Pirates of the Caribbean.

Where to meet characters. More than 50 characters appear at the park. You can use FastPasses to meet Mickey Mouse and Tinker Bell at the Town Square Theater (Mickey may talk to you!) and a gaggle of princesses at Princess Fairytale Hall in Fantasyland, as well as Ariel in her grotto. Dressed as circus performers, Daisy and Donald Duck, Goofy and Minnie Mouse greet you at Pete's Silly Sideshow in Fantasyland. Characters dance with you in the Move It Shake It Dance & Play It Street Party at the Cinderella Castle hub and at the #IncrediblesSuperDanceParty in Tomorrowland. Main Street U.S.A.'s Crystal Palace and Cinderella Castle's Cinderella's Royal Table host character meals; the former has Pooh characters, the latter princesses.

Aladdin. Near Magic Carpets of Aladdin, Adventureland.

Alice. At the Mad Tea Party, often with the Mad Hatter or White Rabbit, Fantasyland.

Anastasia and Drizella. Behind Cinderella Castle, Fantasyland.

Ariel. Ariel's Grotto, Cinderella's Royal Table (often); Fantasyland.

Aurora. Princess Fairytale Hall (often), Cinderella's Royal Table (often); Fantasyland.

Baloo. Move It Shake It (no autographs).

Beast. Be Our Guest restaurant (dinners).

Belle. Enchanted Tales with Belle (doesn't sign autographs, but hands out bookmarks), Cinderella's Royal Table; Fantasyland.

Buzz Lightyear. Outside the Carousel of Progress, Tomorrowland.

Chip 'n Dale. Tomorrowland Rocketeer Plaza; Move It Shake It (no autographs).

Cinderella. Princess Fairytale Hall, Cinderella's Royal Table; Fantasyland.

Country Bears. Frontierland Hoedown.

Daisy Duck. Pete's Silly Sideshow, as Daisy Fortuna.

Donald Duck. Pete's Silly Sideshow, as The Amazing Donaldo.

Eeyore. The Many Adventures of Winnie the Pooh, Fantasyland; Crystal Palace.

Fairy Godmother. Behind Cinderella Castle, Fantasyland.

Frozone. Incredibles Dance Party.

Jasmine and Aladdin.

Big Thunder Mountain Railroad.

Gaston. Near his Tavern, Fantasyland.

Genie. Near Magic Carpets of Aladdin, Adventureland.

Goofy. Pete's Silly Sideshow, as the Great Goofini; Move It Shake It (no autographs).

Jack Sparrow. Capt. Jack's Pirate Tutorial, Adventureland.

Jasmine. Near Magic Carpets of Aladdin, Adventureland; Cinderella's Royal Table (often); Fantasyland.

Jessie. At the Rivers of America Crossing between Liberty Square and Frontierland.

NEW! Judy Hopps. Move It Shake It.

King Louie. Move It Shake It.

Lady Tremaine. Behind Cinderella Castle, Fantasyland.

Mad Hatter. At the Mad Tea Party, often with Alice or White Rabbit, Fantasyland.

Marie. Town Square (sporadically).

Mary Poppins. Plaza Gardens, Main Street U.S.A.

Merida. Fairytale Garden to the right of Cinderella Castle, Fantasyland.

Mickey Mouse. Town Square Theater.

Minnie Mouse. Town Square; Pete's Silly Sideshow as Minnie Magnifique.

Mr. Incredible. Incredibles Dance Party.

Mrs. Incredible. Incredibles Dance Party.

NEW! Nick Wilde. Move It Shake It.

Penguins. Plaza Gardens, Main Street U.S.A. (sporadically, with Mary Poppins).

Peter Pan. Peter Pan's Flight, Fantasyland.

Phineas and Ferb. Move It Shake It.

Piglet. At the Many Adventures of Winnie the Pooh, Fantasyland; Crystal Palace.

Pluto. Town Square.

NEW! Rafiki. Adventureland Veranda.

Rapunzel. Princess Fairytale Hall.

Snow White. Next to City Hall, Town Square; Cinderella's Royal Table (often).

Tiana. Princess Fairytale Hall.

Tigger. At the Many Adventures of Winnie the Pooh, Fantasyland; Crystal Palace.

Tinker Bell. Town Square Theater.

Tweedledee, Tweedledum. Mad Tea Party, Fantasyland (occasionally).

Wendy. Peter Pan's Flight, Fantasyland.

White Rabbit. At the Mad Tea Party, often with Alice or the Mad Hatter, Fantasyland.

Winnie the Pooh. At the Many Adventures of Winnie the Pooh, Fantasyland; Crystal Palace.

Woody. At the Rivers of America Crossing between Liberty Square and Frontierland.

Know before you go. Need a stroller? Cash? A FastPass fix? Here's where to find it:

ATMs. Park entrance, near the lockers; inside City Hall, Main Street U.S.A.; breezeway between Adventureland and Frontierland; near the Pinocchio Village Haus restrooms, Fantasyland.

Baby Care Center. Changing rooms, nursing areas, microwave, playroom. Sells diapers, formula, pacifiers, over-the-counter meds. Left of Crystal Palace, Main Street U.S.A.

FP+ kiosks. Cast members help you book and reschedule FastPasses. *Main Street U.S.A.:* City Hall. *Adventureland:* Jungle Cruise; breezeway between Adventureland and Frontierland. *Fantasyland:* Mickey's PhilharMagic. *Tomorrowland:* At Buzz's Space Ranger Spin; at Stitch's Great Escape.

First aid. Registered nurses treat minor emergencies, call EMTs for serious issues. To the left of Crystal Palace, Main Street U.S.A.

Guest Relations. Cast members answer questions, reserve restaurants, exchange currency, have maps and times guides for all parks, store items found in the park that day. Walk-up windows are outside park entrance (on the far right); a walk-in lobby is inside the park at City Hall on Main Street U.S.A.

Locker rentals. $7 a day, $5 deposit. Park entrance, at the right.

Package pickup. Disney will send anything you buy to the park entrance to pick up later at no charge. Allow three hours for it to get there. Packages can also be delivered to Disney hotels or shipped nationally.

Parking. Cars $20 a day; free for Disney hotel guests and annual passholders. Preferred parking adds $15 and gives everyone in your car a bottle of water.

Stroller rentals. At the Stroller Shop, inside the park entrance on the right. Single strollers are $15 a day ($13 length of stay), doubles $31 ($27 length of stay). Get replacements at the Frontierland Trading Post or at the Tomorrowland Terrace.

Disney transportation. Monorail trains run to the Contemporary, Grand Floridian and Polynesian Village Resort Hotels and the Transportation and Ticket Center (TTC) where they connect to an Epcot line. Buses serve all Disney resort hotels and theme parks as well as the Blizzard Beach water park; there's no direct bus service from Magic Kingdom to Disney Springs, Typhoon Lagoon or the ESPN Wide World of Sports complex.

Wheelchair and scooter rentals. The Stroller Shop, at the park entrance, rents wheelchairs for $12 a day; $10 a day for length-of-stay rentals). EVCs are $50 ($20 deposit).

Outside Gaston's Tavern.

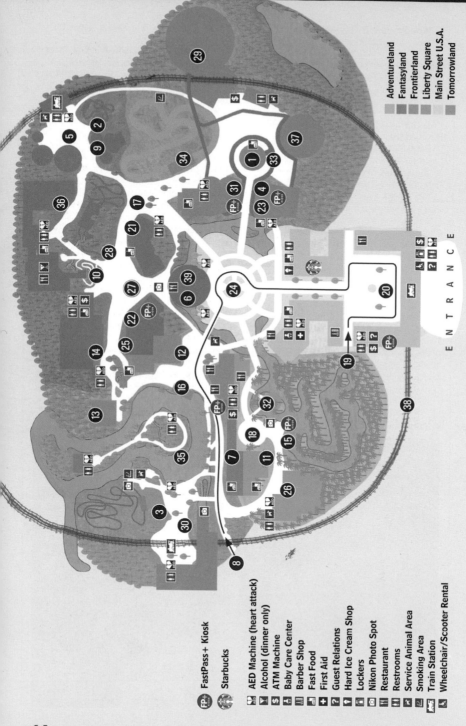

FP+ FastPass+ Kiosk

☆ Starbucks

🔌 AED Machine (heart attack)
🍷 Alcohol (dinner only)
$ ATM Machine
🍼 Baby Care Center
💈 Barber Shop
🍴 Fast Food
✚ First Aid
? Guest Relations
🍦 Hard Ice Cream Shop
🔒 Lockers
📷 Nikon Photo Spot
🍽 Restaurant
🚻 Restrooms
🐾 Service Animal Area
🚬 Smoking Area
🚂 Train Station
♿ Wheelchair/Scooter Rental

Adventureland
Fantasyland
Frontierland
Liberty Square
Main Street U.S.A.
Tomorrowland

ENTRANCE

Map art: Micaela Neal

Attractions at a glance

Here's a quick look at the park's attractions, each of which is reviewed in detail later in this chapter. Each is rated from one to five stars (★), a checkmark (✓) indicates an author favorite; the FastPass+ logo (FP+) appears if it can be reserved in advance. Numbers in red circles match those on the map at the left.

❶ Astro Orbiter. ★★★★ ✓ Hub-and-spoke rockets circle high over Tomorrowland at a 45-degree angle. Tomorrowland.

❷ The Barnstormer. ★★★★★ ✓ FP+ Zippy kiddie coaster offers real but brief thrills; stars Goofy. Fantasyland.

❸ Big Thunder Mountain Railroad. ★★★★★ ✓ FP+ Runaway train coaster is all curves all the time. Frontierland.

❹ Buzz Lightyear's Space Ranger Spin. ★★★ ✓ FP+ Ride-through sci-fi shooting gallery uses laser beams. Tomorrowland.

❺ Casey Jr Splash 'n' Soak Station. ★★★★ Splash zone. Fantasyland.

❻ Celebrate the Magic. ★★★★ Creative light show projects on Cinderella Castle.

❼ Country Bear Jamboree. ★★ Comedic bears sing cornball songs. Frontierland.

❽ Disney's Festival of Fantasy Parade. ★★★★★ ✓ FP+ Creative afternoon procession features characters, dancers, Maleficent as a fire-breathing dragon.

❾ Dumbo the Flying Elephant. ★★★★★ ✓ FP+ Two-seat baby elephants soar in a circle. Indoor playground. Fantasyland.

❿ Enchanted Tales with Belle. ★★★★ ✓ FP+ Volunteers help heroine tell her story. Magical effects. Fantasyland.

⓫ The Enchanted Tiki Room. ★★★ ✓ Vintage revue stars Audio-Animatronic birds, flowers and tikis. Adventureland.

⓬ The Hall of Presidents. ★★★★★ ✓ Widescreen documentary followed by robotic U.S. presidents. Liberty Square.

⓭ The Haunted Mansion. ★★★★★ ✓ FP+ Tour a ghostly retirement home filled with spooky, silly spirits. Liberty Square.

⓮ It's a Small World. UPDATED! ★★★★★ ✓ FP+ Slow boats tour world cultures. Singing dolls, whimsical animals. Fantasyland.

⓯ Jungle Cruise. ★★★★ ✓ FP+ Exotic river tour with a mad skipper. Adventureland.

⓰ Liberty Square Riverboat. ★★★ Mark Twain narrates steamer tour. Liberty Square.

⓱ Mad Tea Party. ★★★★ ✓ FP+ The classic spinning teacups. Fantasyland.

⓲ Magic Carpets of Aladdin. ★★★ ✓ FP+ Four-seat hub-and-spoke ride. Adventureland.

⓳ Main Street Electrical Parade. ★★★★ ✓ FP+ Retro Lite Brite night procession.

⓴ Main Street Vehicles. ★★★★ ✓ Retro vehicles shuttle you to and from Cinderella Castle. Main Street U.S.A.

㉑ The Many Adventures of Winnie the Pooh. ★★★★ ✓ FP+ Dark ride with Tigger, Piglet, Heffalumps, Woozles. Fantasyland.

㉒ Mickey's PhilharMagic. ★★★★★ ✓ FP+ Donald Duck stumbles through classic Disney films in 3-D movie. Fantasyland.

㉓ Monsters Inc Laugh Floor. ★★★★ FP+ Interactive video improv show stars witty, animated monsters. Tomorrowland.

㉔ Move It! Shake It! Dance & Play It! ★★★★ ✓ Street party with characters, dancers. Castle hub, Main Street U.S.A.

㉕ Peter Pan's Flight. ★★★★★ ✓ FP+ Vintage dark ride has aerial views of London, Never Land. Fantasyland.

㉖ Pirates of the Caribbean. ★★★★★ ✓ FP+ Classic dark indoor boat ride is filled with rowdy pirates. Adventureland.

㉗ Prince Charming Regal Carrousel. ★★★★★ ✓ Pretty canopy-covered antique merry-go-round. Fantasyland.

㉘ Seven Dwarfs Mine Train. ★★★★ ✓ FP+ Indoor–outdoor coaster has swaying cars, Audio-Animatronic dwarfs. Fantasyland.

㉙ Space Mountain. ★★★★★ ✓ FP+ The world's first indoor roller coaster is very dark, simulates space flight. Tomorrowland.

㉚ Splash Mountain. ★★★★ FP+ Indoor-outdoor log flume. Frontierland.

㉛ Stitch's Great Escape. ★ Experiment 626 is a prisoner in this in-the-round prequel to "Lilo & Stitch." Tomorrowland.

㉜ Swiss Family Treehouse. ★★★ Climb-thru "Swiss Family Robinson" home. Shows its age, wears OK. Adventureland.

㉝ Tomorrowland PeopleMover. ★★★ ✓ Elevated tour enters Space Mountain.

㉞ Tomorrowland Speedway. ★★★ ✓ FP+ Kiddie race cars. Tomorrowland.

㉟ Tom Sawyer Island. ★★★ Two connected isles have cave, fort, mine. Frontierland.

㊱ Under the Sea. ★★★ FP+ Dark musical ride tells Ariel's story. Fantasyland.

㊲ Walt Disney's Carousel of Progress. ★★★ ✓ Robotic family marvels at 20th-century electrical advances. Tomorrowland.

㊳ Walt Disney World Railroad. ★★★ ✓ Steam train circles the park.

㊴ Wishes. ★★★★★ ✓ FP+ Emotional fireworks shows syncs with music.

Victorian architecture.

Main Street U.S.A.

You enter the park with a stroll back in time, to a small county seat at the turn of the 20th century. The past made perfect, Main Street U.S.A. recalls a vibrant town on the Eastern seaboard. A world of barbershop singers and homemade fudge, a Victorian streetscape of horse trolleys and early automobiles.

You start off in Town Square, a green surrounded by the town's civic structures—its city hall, firehouse, train station and exhibition hall. In the center of the square (or during peak periods, off to the side) is a statue of the town's founding father. In this case that's Roy Disney, Walt's brother, who supervised the creation of Walt Disney World after his brother's death. Roy is posed sitting on a bench, chatting with Minnie Mouse.

Next comes Main Street itself.

Back where you belong. The look of the boulevard comes from, of all things, the 1969 20th Century Fox movie "Hello Dolly!," a turn-of-the-century musical based in New York City. Built on that studio's California backlot by longtime Fox production designer John DeCuir, its Main Street used huge facades, cutouts, and scenery backdrops to create a time gone by. DeCuir designed the Magic Kingdom Main Street at the same time, using similar methods and styles. His work on "Hello Dolly" was honored with an Oscar for Best Art Direction. Decuir also created the sets for the 1956 movie "The King and I," 1958's "South Pacific" and 1963's "Cleopatra." His son became a Disney imagineer.

Imagineer John Hench helped design the street. "Main Street," he told the Orlando Sentinel, "has the Victorian feeling, which is probably one of the great optimistic periods of the world. When we thought progress was great and we all knew where we were going… It reflects that prosperity, that enthusiasm. There's some nostalgia involved, of course, but nostalgia for what? There was never a Main Street like this one. But it reminds you of some things about yourself that you've forgotten about."

'The optimism of America.' In many ways the boulevard replicates Walt Disney's first Main Street U.S.A., at California's Disneyland. On the day that park opened in 1955, he told reporters it represented "a gentle transition from the hustle and bustle of the modern real world to the timeless worlds of fantasy and adventure. Main Street retains some of the superficial aspects of modern cities that guests had struggled through just moments before arriving, like a somewhat familiar landscape of buildings and streets. However, there is no garbage, no funeral parlor, no pool hall, no chaos and confusion. And everything is scaled down in size like a toy.

"Here is the America of 1890 to 1910, at the crossroads of an era. Where the gas lamp is gradually being replaced by the electric lamp; the plodding horse-drawn street car is giving way to the chugging horseless carriage. America was in transition; the discoveries of the late 19th century were beginning to affect our way of life. Main Street represents… the optimism of America."

Second Empire Victorian. That's the architectural style of Main Street U.S.A., a distinctive look of the era that mixed together Cape Cod clapboarding, mansard roofs with colored shingles, bay and dormer windows, and wrought-iron balconies of every color. Gingerbread accents include decorative brackets, fancy frieze trim, crowns of ornate molded cornices. Every building is different. Fronted with flowers and trees, most of the 51 structures have their own individual color schemes and window framing.

The Industrial Revolution is just taking hold. Some buildings display prefabricated metalwork, an Industrial Age invention. Interiors have tin ceilings, as well as brick floors and huge chandeliers.

Some buildings replicate actual structures. The train station is based on an upscale turn-of-the-century station in Saratoga Springs, N.Y. The Town Square Theater channels the look of the 1877 Adelphi Hotel in nearby Saratoga, N.Y. The Crystal Palace uses styles from outside the East, combining the glass dome of San Francisco's 1879 Conservatory of Flowers with the greenhouse interior of London's 1851 Crystal Palace exhibition hall.

You're at… a movie theater. Your Main Street experience begins outside the street, indeed outside the park, as you step off a bus or monorail at an anachronistic wrought-iron depot, and approach a turn-of-the-20th-century train station. It completely blocks your view. That's on purpose, as entering the Magic Kingdom is meant to replicate the experience of going to a movie theater.

View from a double-decker bus.

Julie Neal

The train station acts as a curtain, hiding your view of the park in the same way a theater's curtain "hides" your view of its film. The Magic Kingdom curtain opens as the lights dim as you walk under the station into a tunnel. Passing some posters that highlight Coming Attractions, you soon notice the aroma of popcorn in the air.

As you emerge into daylight, the projector shines its light over your head and your movie begins. Its story gets underway, and before you know it you've lost yourself in a fantastical fictional world.

Florida's Main Street complements the original one in California. It re-creates a midwestern town, a mix of Fort Collins, Colo., and Walt Disney's hometown of Marceline, Mo. Taken together, the two antique avenues symbolize an All-American rivalry that still exists today: East versus West.

Fun fact. Building facades use the motion-picture technique of forced perspective to appear larger than they are. First floors are at full scale, second floors are at 80 percent of full size, third floors 80 percent of that.

Fun finds. ❶ The stars of Disney's 1955 film "Lady and the Tramp" have pressed their paws in pavement in front of Tony's Town Square Restaurant, just as they did in the movie. **❷** Inside Tony's, a window in the back right corner looks into the alley where their iconic "spaghetti kiss" took place. **❸** Inside the Chapeau you can eavesdrop on an 1890s conversation between a mom and daughter by picking up the earpiece of an old wall phone. The two complain about the price of hamburger and discuss how to attract a man. **❹** Main Street vehicle license plates read "1915," the year the state of Florida first issued plates. **❺** A vintage U.S. mailbox hangs from a lamppost in front of the Emporium. It's fully functional; mail from it is collected six days a week. A similar mailbox is next to the News Stand gift shop outside the park. **❻** Often you can hear the sounds of a singer and dancer from two windows on West Center Street, a small court halfway down Main Street. Lettering on the windows reads "Voice and Singing Private Lessons" and "Music and Dance Lessons, Ballet, Tap & Waltz." **❼** A cigar-store Indian stands in front of the Crystal Arts shop. It's there because a store in that spot sold cigars and other tobacco products during the 1980s and 1990s. Earlier the Indian stood across the street, in a front of a dedicated tobacco store. **❽** The Starbucks logo on the Main Street Bakery replicates the original 1971 Starbucks logo with two exceptions—its lower words read "Fresh Roasted Coffee" instead of the original's "Coffee Tea Spices," and its mermaid's longer hair lays over her breasts.

No-charge snapshot.

RAILROAD OFFICE

Keeping Dreams on Track

WALTER E. DISNEY
CHIEF ENGINEER

POPULATION
600,000,000

THE MAGIC KING

DISNEY WORLD

Walt Disney World Railroad station.

Hidden Mickeys. ❶ In Tony's Town Square restaurant, as bread loaves in a basket on a server. ❷ Outside the eatery, the shape hides in plain sight on a wooden access panel of the back of its hanging sign, the center of a filigreed Victorian design. It's tiny, but obvious once you spot it. ❸ A "Steinmouse & Sons" piano hides Mickey's shape above its keys, in a logo shaped like a sheet music stand. The piano appears in a window to the left of the main entrance to the Emporium Gallery, just below a sign that reads "Collectibles."

Live entertainment

Main Street U.S.A. bursts at the seams with quality live entertainment:

★★★★ ✔ **Casey's Corner Pianist.** A skilled player bangs out honky tonk, rag and Disney tunes on a white upright. *Seven 20-min. shows 12:30p–7:45p Sun–Mon; noon–7p Tue–Sat. Casey's Corner patio.*

★★★★★ ✔ **Citizens of Main Street.** A troupe of improvisational actors portray the boulevard's vintage townsfolk, strolling the street to chat, dance, joke, sing and pose for photos. Characters include Mayor Weaver, Fire Chief Smokey Miller, voice instructor Victoria Trumpetto, Main Street Gazette reporter and avid pin-trader Scoop Sanderson and socialite suffragettes Hildegard Olivia

Harding and Bea Starr. *20-min. sets hourly 9:45a–1:45p. Roaming Main Street.*

★★★★★ ✔ **Dapper Dans.** This barbershop quartet mixes a harmonically perfect old-time repertoire with chimes, tap dancing and corny humor. Want to make them smile? Point it out to them: they're "5-Star Rated"! *20-min. sets 11a–3:30p Sun; 8a–3:30p Mon; park open–3:30p Tue–Sat. Roaming Main Street, sometimes riding the trolley.*

★★★★ ✔ **Electrical Water Pageant.** This classic light parade roams the waters of the Seven Seas Lagoon and Bay Lake. So uncool it's cool. *Nightly; passes Polynesian Village Resort at 9p, Grand Floridian at 9:15p, Wilderness Lodge at 9:30p, Fort Wilderness at 9:45p, the Contemporary at 10:15p and Magic Kingdom at 10:30p. On nights with later park hours, the appearance near Magic Kingdom is delayed until after the Wishes fireworks. Outside the park, on Seven Seas Lagoon.*

★★ **Flag Retreat.** A security color guard lowers the park's U.S. flag, often with a visiting vet. Sincere. *20 min. 5p. Town Square.*

★★★★★ ✔ **Magic Kingdom Welcome Show.** The park opens with a song-and-dance hello from Main Street residents, who usher in a train-full of characters. *10-min. show 15 min. before park opens. Entrance plaza.*

★★★★ ✔ **Main Street Philharmonic.** This 12-piece comedic brass and percussion

Singing with the Citizens of Main Street.

Main Street Trolley Show.

ensemble plays Disney hits and Americana favorites. *Two 20-min. sets 12:30p–1:30p Sun–Mon; 3 sets noon–4p Tue–Thur. On Main Street; also in Storybook Circus, Fantasyland.*

★★★★ ✔ **Main Street Trolley Show.** Gay '90s couples hop off a horse trolley to perform a soft-shoe pantomime with lots of lip-syncing. The troupe changes its show for every season. So strange, but so Disney. *Three 5-min. shows per 20-min. set, 9a–10:30a Sun–Mon; 9a–noon Tue–Sat.*

Scavenger hunt

Sorcerers of the Magic Kingdom. You play this game on video screens that hide throughout the park. Recruited by Merlin the Magician, the wizard of the Arthurian legend portrayed in Disney's 1963 movie "The Sword in the Stone," the goal is to stop Hades (from Disney's 1997 movie "Hercules") from making the Magic Kingdom his summer home. You achieve this by casting spells on Disney villains, who appear on the screens and react when you hold up an RFID-embedded card, a packet of which you get when you sign up. Play

the game long enough (think a full day) and you'll send Hades back to H-E-double-hockey sticks. The cards are free, and Pokémon quality. The video animation, however, is beneath Disney's standards, and some characters don't have their well-known voices. Though it has little repeat value, the game offers families a way to play together, and there is never a wait. Get your cards as soon as you enter the park, while it's convenient. Play game as it fits into your attraction schedule. *Duration: Allow 5 min per portal or effect. Debuted: 2012. Access: Wheelchairs, ECVs OK. Disability services: Video captioning. Sign-up location: Main Street firehouse.*

Restaurants and food

Lots of choices here, including good Italian and burger restaurants, a mediocre character buffet and the world's busiest Starbucks:

★★ **$45 DDP Crystal Palace.** Even adorable Winnie the Pooh, Eeyore, Piglet and Tigger can't redeem this character buffet. It's just too crowded, overpriced and loud. High ceilings and marble tabletops make

Roy Disney with Minnie Mouse.

for a pretty decor, but amplify the noise. Tables are packed together, with little room between them, which makes it a chore to squeeze back and forth to the food lines, where there are decent meats and salads but salty soups and vegetables. Characters often can't linger at your table, so when you meet one it's just for a moment. For the most time with them reserve a table for the first or last breakfast seating or the first dinner seating. *Breakfast 8a–10:45a, $30 (children $18); lunch, dinner 11:30a–park close, $42 (children $25). Seats 400.*

★★★ ✔ **$26 DDP The Plaza.** The food at this Victorian café screams diner—good hamburgers, sandwiches and sundaes—but the quiet atmosphere fits a more upscale eatery. Carpeted floors, padded wrought-iron chairs and faux-marble tabletops add to the charm. Hand-dipped ice cream treats come from the adjacent parlor. *11a–9:30p; $14–$21 (children $9–$11). Seats 94.*

★★★★ ✔ **$34 DDP Tony's Town Square.** Fans of 1955's "Lady and the Tramp" may not recognize this comfortable café as the Tony's from that film—it's not overly themed—but

that's about its only weakness. The menu offers generous portions of Italian comfort food; the shrimp scampi has roasted tomatoes. A lovely glass-ceiling solarium can be too sunny but there are many other indoor tables; ask for one by the fountain. The authors eat lunch here often. *11:30a–9:30p; $18–$34 (children $9–$11). Seats 286.*

★★★ ✔ **$15 DDPq Casey's Corner.** The hot dogs and fries are decent, satisfying and overpriced; the small dining area is clean and peaceful. *11a–park close; $8–$13. Seats 128, including 80 outdoors.*

★★★ **$8 DDPq Main Street Bakery.** Redone in 2013 as a Starbucks, this former Disney-run bakery still has a Disney touch to its decor, but other than that it's the same as any other Starbucks anywhere. Except for two things. First, there's no place to sit. And second, this is the busiest Starbucks in the world. Not Disney World, the world world. The line, therefore, is often insane. On New Year's Eve it can stretch all the way down to Tony's, almost to the train station. *$2–$6. No seats.*

★★★ ✔ **$8 DDPs Main St. Confectionery.** Apples dipped in candy or chocolate, cake pops, cotton candy and house-made fudge are a few treats you can watch being made at this candy store. Also here: packaged candy and treats, some kitchen items, mugs. You want the fudge—at least share a piece. *$4–$12. No seats.*

★★★ ✔ **$5 DDPs Plaza Ice Cream Parlor.** Hand-dipped real ice cream treats. *11a–park close; $3–$6 (children $3). Seats 128 outside at umbrella-covered tables.*

Shops and merchandise

Stores line Main Street U.S.A., offering a smorgasbord of Disney souvenirs. You can get your first haircut here, too.

The Art of Disney. In the Main Street Cinema. The usual arty and home decor stuff, all with Disney themes—oil paintings, prints, figurines, big figs and the like. Always something interesting though. Some Vinylmation figures.

The Chapeau. Mickey ears, novelty caps.

Crystal Arts. Arribas Bros. shop has glass and crystal pieces, glass-blowing demonstrations. To the right of the Main Street Bakery.

Curtain Call Collectibles. Apparel, toys, Disney souvenirs, many Mickey items. At the exit of the Town Square Theater.

The Emporium. Though it looks like a line of little stores from the outside, The Emporium is really one big long shop that takes up nearly the entire left side of Main Street. Inside is a huge selection of all kinds of merchandise. It's Magic Kingdom's biggest store, with a little of everything. Usually packed with people at the front where the more obvious souvenirs are, less crowded in back with the fashion apparel.

Harmony Barber Shop. This iconic old-fashioned barber specializes in a child's first haircut. Its package includes a commemorative pair of Mickey ears and a certificate. Other services include adult cuts and beard and mustache trims. There's no shampooing here; come with clean hair. A potbelly stove adds to the illusion of timelessness, as does the pleasant unhurried banter of your barber. The Dapper Dans sometimes stop by, just like they should. Between the Car Barn and the Emporium in Town Square. *9a–5p. First haircuts $25, other services $18–$19. Reservations: 407-939-7529. Walk-ins welcome.*

Newsstand. Disney souvenirs and sundries outside train station, open early so you can get your autograph books and caps before the park opens. On the left side of the train station, inside the touch-point entry poles.

Uptown Jewelers. Fine Pandora jewelry; also costume jewelry, purses, scarves. A nice variety of items, many with Disney themes.

The world's busiest Starbucks.

Blowing off steam.

Walt Disney World Railroad

Open-air steam-train rides circle park

★★★ ✔ A relaxing way to travel around the Magic Kingdom, this authentic narrow-gauge railroad circles the park. Antique steam locomotives pull trolley-style passenger cars down a track lined with bamboo, palms, pines and live oaks. Two or three trains run continuously, so there's rarely much of a wait at any station.

It's a nice ride, pleasantly breezy and shaded from the sun. Unlike when you're walking, you can't get lost—hop on a train at Frontierland and you will go directly to Dumbo and his circus even if you have no idea how to get there. But it's not perfect; a hokey pre-recorded narrator drops every "G" as if he's ridin' the rails at Dollywood. Alongside the track, obviously fake deer and other creatures rarely have a hankerin' to move.

Tips. *When to go:* Anytime. *Where to sit:* On the right for the best views, though riders on the left sometimes spot live alligators in a canal behind Fantasyland.

Fun finds. ❶ Mutoscopes and a few other antique amusements line the waiting room of the Main Street station; some of them still work. ❷ Inside the train station's second-floor ticket booth, an early-1900s scissor phone extends from a wall, its handset beneath it. ❸ Several authentic copies of Harper's Weekly lay under the phone on a desk. They're dated 1862, the second year of the U.S. Civil War, a time when the magazine was the most-read publication in the country.

A closer look. Disney acquired the four steam locomotives from the United Railway of the Yucatán in the late 1960s. Built by Baldwin Locomotive Works of Philadelphia between 1916 and 1928, they had hauled passengers, jute, sisal and sugar cane through Mexico for decades. Disney had the engines restored at the Tampa Shipbuilding and Dry Dock Company in 1971. They take on water at the Fantasyland station every third loop and get serviced every few hours.

Key facts. *Duration:* 20-min round trip. *Capacity:* 360. *Queues:* ● outdoor, covered. *Service stops:* Idle during parades, fireworks. *Weather issues:* Closed during thunderstorms. *Debuted:* 1971. *Access:* Wheelchairs, ECVs ● K; no Disney strollers. *Disability services:* Handheld captioning. *Stations:* At Town Square, Frontierland, Fantasyland.

Main Street fire truck.

Main Street Vehicles

Just hop on one of these quaint replicas and feel special

★★★★ ✔ It's too bad they're usually out only in the mornings, because these old-fashioned vehicles are a true Disney treasure. Shuttling passengers either way between Town Square and Cinderella Castle, they offer old-school fun. Just hop on and off you go—no FastPass required. The rides are free, and there's never a line to get on one.

Traveling in one gives you a taste of a bygone era. The vehicles look completely authentic, with their uncushioned metal dashes, worn leather and wood benches, and their sounds only reinforce that notion. Bells ding. Engines chug. Horns honk. Horses clop.

You also feel special. As you are driven down Main Street the masses part for you, then smile and wave as you pass.

The fleet consists of four horse trolleys, three horseless carriages, two jitneys, a miniature fire truck and a double-decker bus. The trolley runs on a track embedded in the street; its driver operates a set of reins, a brake pedal and a foot bell. The Dapper Dans barbershop quartet often hops on to serenade riders.

Tips. *When to go:* Immediately after you enter the park. *Where to sit:* Up front, for the best view and to chat with your driver. *For families:* Ask ahead of time and your child might be able to honk a horn, ring the trolley's bell or crank the fire truck's siren. *For the best time:* If a woman named Barbara is driving it, ride the fire truck. Perhaps the happiest person on earth, she often sings as she steers, and her unabashed joy makes it impossible not to join in. That's her in the photo above.

Fun facts. ❶ Built for Disney, the vehicles debuted at the Magic Kingdom the day it opened. ❷ They run on natural gas. ❸ When the Magic Kingdom opened in 1971, the only two attractions taking an "A" ticket were the Main Street Vehicles and Fantasyland's carousel. Both are still as popular as ever.

Hidden Mickey. Small brass three-circle shapes adorn the harness and leather straps of the horses that pull the trolleys.

Key facts. *Duration:* 3-4 min. *Capacity:* 6-40 depending on the vehicle. *Operating hours:* Park open—late morning. *Weather issues:* Closed during rain. *Debuted:* 1971. *Access:* Must be ambulatory. *Location:* Boards at Town Square and the hub in front of Cinderella Castle.

Park open.

Adventureland

The sound of beating drums introduces you to this exotic land, a blend of African jungles, Arabian nights, British explorers, Caribbean architecture and South Seas landscaping as seen through a 1950s American lens. Australian tree ferns, banana palms, bougainvillea and hibiscus line walkways. Disney's "True-Life Adventure" documentaries of the era provided the spark for the land's emphasis on jungles and wild animals.

Hidden Mickeys. ❶ A smiling Mickey face graces a Tiki in front of the Adventureland entrance, in some tropical landscaping in a small plaza on the right (lately a designated smoking section). **❷** The three-circle shape appears on the top portion of two shields on the entrance bridge, the first shield on the right and **❸** the second shield on the left. **❹** In the Agrabah Bazaar open-air shop it hides as three tiny round concave ceramic tiles embedded in the floor, in front of a door that reads "Elephant Tales" (the store's former name).

Live entertainment

Kids participate in an interactive show.

★★★★★ ✔ **Capt. Jack Sparrow's Pirate Tutorial.** Comical Jack and first mate Mack recruit young pirates from the crowd—teaching them the Pirate Oath, how to be rescued from a desert island, how to distract and flee from an enemy and how to sing the Pirates of the Caribbean theme song "Yo Ho (A Pirate's Life for Me)." *Typically 6 25-min. shows 1:30p–7:30p Sun–Mon; 10:30a–4:30p Tue–Sat. Across from Pirates of the Caribbean.*

Scavenger hunt

A Pirate's Adventure. You trigger special effects throughout Adventureland in this game, as you use a treasure map to help Capt. Jack Sparrow lift a curse. There are five maps, each with a different mission. There's never much of a line to play, and the effects are pretty cool—you may fire a cannon, or raise a sunken skeleton out of its water. At the completion of each map's mission, you collect a treasure finder card from a cast member; after getting all five, you earn a grand finale card signed by Capt. Jack. Your MagicBand triggers the effects; if you don't have one, pick up a "magic talisman" when you get your map. Play the game during the morning or late afternoon, when the weather is relatively cool. If you get lost, touching your MagicBand to any game station will tell you where you should be. *Duration: Allow 5 min per portal or effect. Debuted: 2013. Access: Wheelchairs, ECVs ●K. Sign-up location: Next to Pirates of the Caribbean, Adventureland.*

Restaurants and food

The Jungle Cruise inspired a very good new restaurant here; this is also the home of Walt Disney World's famous Dole Whip.

NEW! ★★★★★ ✔ $36 DDP Skipper Canteen. Wise-cracking Jungle Cruise skippers are your servers at this new restaurant, which serves its "World Famous Jungle Cuisine" in several unique dining rooms, including the crew mess hall and a once-hidden secret meeting area of the Society of Explorers and Adventurers. The Asian, South American and African cuisine

is near-gourmet, with tasty signature dishes such as Trader Sam's head-on shrimp, tossed in a chili-garlic sauce, and a grilled steak marinated in sofrito and served with house-made chimichurri. Green-apple boba balls top the refreshing Schweitzer Slush, made with frozen apple and passion fruit juices. Get a tour of the place before leaving; funny punny jokes are plastered everywhere; ask to see the Great Wall of China. *11:30a–9p; $17–$34 (children $10–$13). Seats 222.*

UPDATED! ★★★ ✔ $16 DDPq Tortuga Tavern. This breezy outdoor café now features three different barbecue sandwiches, served between slices of Texas toast with sides of beans and coleslaw. A roasted corn and vegetable salad can optionally include chicken or barbecue beef brisket. It will be open only when crowd levels demand. The best tables are those on a back patio that's sheltered by tropical foliage. Ambient fiddle music adds some life, as do signs and posters that reveal a backstory: the place is run by a teenage girl, Arabella Smith from the young-adult book series "Pirates of the Caribbean: Jack Sparrow." And she has her rules. *Seasonally 11a–4p; $10–$13 (children $6–$7). Seats 240, including 12 at bar and 28 at umbrella-covered tables.*

★★★ ✔ $5 DDPs Aloha Isle Refreshments. Dole Whip soft-serve; pineapple floats;

A Pirate's Adventure.

Skipper Canteen.

pineapple spears; pineapple juice. Near the exit of the Enchanted Tiki Room. *Park open–10p; $4–$6. Seats 72 at umbrella-covered tables.*

★★★ **$8 DDPs Egg Roll Cart.** Egg rolls (cheeseburger spring rolls, vegetable rolls); chips, chocolate-chip cookies. Outdoor stand. *Near the Magic Carpets of Aladdin. 9a–9p; $3–$5.*

★★★ ✔ **$7 DDPs Sunshine Tree Terrace.** Dole Whip soft-serve, slushies, coffee. *Park open–10p; $4–$10.*

Shops and merchandise

Bounties of pirate booty. It's here, along with some interesting non-Disney merchandise.

Agrabah Bazaar. Shirts, hats, sandals; warm-weather fashion apparel, accessories; Quiksilver, Roxy, Billabong brands.

Bwana Bob's. Sundries. Outdoor stand.

Island Supply. Sunglass Hut sunglasses.

La Princesa de Cristal. Arribas Bros. jewelry and glass figurine cart. *To the right of Pirates of the Caribbean.*

Plaza del Sol Caribe Bazaar. This sprawling open-air shop offers pirate booty galore, including fashion apparel, toys and a bunch of Jake and the Never Land Pirates stuff. Also some Peter Pan merchandise. *At the exit of Pirates of the Caribbean.*

Zanzibar Trading Co. Tam-tam drums, "thumb pianos," other simple instruments; rubber toy snakes and tarantulas; exotic animal plushies; children's apparel, accessories; sundries. *Connected to Agrabah Bazaar.*

Makeover salon

Shyin' away from a lil' makeup, ye scallywag? What kind of pirate ye be?

Pirates League. This salon transforms adults and children into swashbucklers, swashbucklerettes and, of course, mermaids. Packages include facial effects, bandanas, false earrings, eye patches, swords, temporary tattoos, an official pirate name and personalized oath. Costumes, headwear and photo packages too. New recruits can join an Adventureland Pirate Parade daily at 4 p.m. *At the exit of Pirates of the Caribbean. Packages $30–$75. Ages 3 and up. Reservations up to 180 days in advance: 407-939-2739.*

Couples sit side-by-side, families of four can ride together.

Magic Carpets of Aladdin
Colorful carnival ride is simple, satisfying

★★★ ✔ FP+ Inspired by Disney's 1992 animated feature "Aladdin," this carnival-style hub-and-spoke ride is a fun diversion. Circling around a giant genie bottle, you fly a magic carpet which climbs, dips and dives at your command. It's a nice use of 90 seconds, especially early in the morning or late at night when its waiting line is short.

Just another Dumbo? Not really. Each carpet seats four, not two, so small families can ride together. Tall palms lend a tropical air. The carpets ride rougher than Dumbo, too.

Tips. *When to go:* At night, when lines are short and the weather cool. *Where to sit:* In front, so you can control the height of your carpet. The back seat controls the pitch. *While you fly:* Flip the front-seat lever up and down to bounce your carpet. Fly about halfway up to be in the line of fire of a spitting golden camel.

Fun finds. ❶ Aladdin and Jasmine stroll into the boarding area, choose a small family and go for a ride with it on many mornings around 9:30 a.m. ❷ Camel heads drool water into the pool. ❸ Aladdin's pet monkey Abu cartwheels around the genie-bottle hub in a sequence of images which recalls early zoetrope animation. ❹ A second camel statue spits water at you as you fly.

Hidden Mickeys. ❶ Mickey appears as three tiny yellow dots on a small, faded four-piece bracelet, which is embedded in a walkway behind the camel statue that faces the ride. It's very faded ❷ He also hides nearby as three circles on a small teardrop-shaped silver charm in the walkway, between the ride exit and a pole outside the Agrabah Bazaar open-air shop.

Key facts. *Duration:* 90 sec. *Capacity:* 64. *Queue:* Outdoor, shaded. *Weather issues:* Closed during thunderstorms. *Debuted:* 2001. *Access:* ECV users must transfer. *Location:* In front of the Enchanted Tiki Room.

Average wait times (standby line)

9a	10a	11a	12p	1p	2p	3p	4p	5p	6p	7p	8p	9p	10p	11p
10m	20m	20m	20m	20m	20m	15m	20m	25m	20m	20m	20m	15m	10m	5m

Hidden Mickey. A profile, high in the tree.

A young woman climbs toward the living room.

Swiss Family Treehouse

There's never a wait to tour this dated but detailed home

★★★ You'll climb six stories at this outdoor attraction, a self-guided tour through the improvised home of a shipwrecked dad, mom and three sons that's based on the 1960 Disney movie "Swiss Family Robinson." Ingenious contraptions include a plumbing system that uses a water wheel, bamboo buckets and troughs. The tree's 62 steps can challenge adults but give kids an easy way to burn off energy. Though the tree pales as an attraction based on modern standards, from a 1960s perspective it's pretty cool. Remnants of the ship are everywhere. Ropes from it hold the home together, rooms adapt found objects into everyday effects. Giant clamshells serve as sink basins.

Tip. *When to go:* At night, when the heat's died off and the tree looks the most realistic.

Fun finds. ❶ Prehistoric drawings decorate volcanic rocks near the entrance. ❷ Cannons sit at the ready throughout the grounds. In the movie the family used them to fight off pirates. ❸ Lush flowers attract real wild hummingbirds and butterflies around the base of the tree. ❹ Huge bullfrogs often live under its bridges. ❺ The boat's oars and sails cover the entranceway. ❻ The ship's bell hangs beneath you to your right as you climb the first staircase. ❼ A Bible lays on a table in the living room. ❽ A cask of rum sits in rafters above it. ❾ The room's pull-stop organ is a true antique. ❿ The song it plays is "Swisskapolka," a lively tune heard in the movie as family members race each other riding wild animals. During November and December the organ plays "❶ Christmas Tree" and "Deck the Halls." ⓫ The ship's sails provide cover for the library and kitchen.

Hidden Mickeys. ❶ The mouse appears as a spiral and two small holes in the lava rock to the left of the attraction, facing the Adventureland entrance. ❷ On the tree itself, a right-facing profile of him is formed within a patch of green moss on the trunk. Tough to see on a sunny day, it's on your right just after you leave the tree's second room and go down some stairs.

Key facts. *Duration:* Unlimited, allow 20 min. *Capacity:* 300. *Queue:* Outdoor, shaded. *Debuted:* 1971 (Disneyland 1962). *Access:* You must be ambulatory. *Location:* Just past the Adventureland entrance sign.

Crowds fill almost every Jungle Cruise boat.

Jungle Cruise

Vintage boat ride goes overboard with jokes and puns

★★★★ ✔ FP+ Lampooning British efforts to colonize remote areas of the world in the early 1900s, this tongue-in-cheek outdoor boat ride threatens you with peril at every turn—snakes, cannibals, head-hunters, hungry hungry hippos. None of them are scary. But they're all fodder for jokes thanks to your crazed Jungle Cruise skipper. She fears only one thing: her destiny of never being anything more than a crazed Jungle Cruise skipper. "I think I'll go again," she'll probably declare at the end of your trip. "And again. And again. Every 10 minutes. For the rest of my life."

Is it worth your time? Yes if you get a good skipper. No if you don't, except for its historic value. The original serious version of this ride was Walt Disney's pride and joy. You start your adventure at a 1930s jungle outpost. From there you board a canopied tramp steamer for a trip down some of the world's most treacherous rivers—the Amazon, Congo, Nile and Mekong, your guide pointing out sights along the way. He or she speaks from a script that includes far more jokes than can be used in one trip, creating an improvised routine that is often hilarious. Once out of sight of their managers, some skippers slyly sneak in other material (for example, channeling Ariel in the temple, singing *"Look at this stuff, isn't it neat..."*). The comedic skills of your skipper greatly affect your experience. It's a four-star ride if you get a witty guide with good timing.

Tips. *When to go:* At night. A spotlight on the boat adds to the fun. *Where to sit:* On the left for the best views, ideally next to the skipper. *For families:* Ask as you board and your child may be able to "steer" the boat.

A closer look. Disney's oldest major attraction, the Jungle Cruise debuted at California's Disneyland in 1955. For its first seven years it was a serious ride, an educational journey

Average wait times (standby line)

9a	10a	11a	12p	1p	2p	3p	4p	5p	6p	7p	8p	9p	10p	11p
15m	50m	50m	60m	60m	55m	50m	55m	45m	55m	40m	40m	40m	30m	10m

Wild-eyed skipper.

Ambushing native.

into exotic areas of the world most Americans had never seen, even in photographs. Inspired by the 1951 movie "The African Queen" and created at the same time as Disney's "True-Life Adventure" nature films, the ride was Disneyland's signature attraction.

Scholastic it stayed until the early 1960s, when Walt began to hear of returning park visitors not going on it anymore, since it wasn't all that much fun and never offered anything new. So in 1962 its skippers became slightly sarcastic with their shtick and soon some lighthearted new scenes were added. One showed a rhino using its horn to poke a cartoonish safari party up a pole. A second took boats through a playful pool of cute

Hungry hippo; crocodiles Old Smiley and Ginger.

"My previous crew."

bathing elephants threatening to squirt the boats with water. By the 1970s the entire thing was played for laughs. Today humorous props and a silly radio broadcast add a lighthearted touch to the waiting area, and the boats include details such as cooking gear hanging from roof nets.

Fun facts. ❶ It was a manly cruise. Its skippers were exclusively male until May, 1995. A year later, half were female. **❷** It changed its pole climbers. For 25 years the safari party being chased up a pole consisted of four black porters in khaki uniforms and red hats—the implied guides of a hunting expedition. In 1996 they were changed to Caucasians, their outfits and gear switched to that of a film crew. **❸** A native is famous. The face and body of a dancing tribesman were formed from molds of Woody Strode. One of the first non-white college and professional football stars and later an accomplished actor, Strode posed for a nude painting that was displayed briefly at

Dock signs.

CRew MesS
LUNCH MeNU

MONDAY
Fricasse of
Giant Stag Beetle
(taste a bit like chicken)

TUESDAY
Barbecued
Three-Toed Skink
(has a chickeny flavor)

WEDNESDAY
Consomme of
River Basin Slug
(poultry like)

THURSDAY
Fillet of Rock Python
(chicken-esque)

FRIDAY
CHICKEN (REALLY!!)

Everything tastes like chicken.

the 1936 Berlin Olympics until Nazis discovered it. Known for his stunning good looks, Strode came from parents who each had black and American Indian ancestors. "Toy Story" character Sheriff Woody is named after him. ❹ Some former skippers are famous. They include comedian Steve Martin, Disney-Pixar animation guru John Lasseter, actor Kevin Costner and Ron Ziegler, the straightlaced press secretary of President Richard Nixon during the Watergate scandal. ❺ One of the Disney World boats sank. It happened in 2004, directly in front of the dock as guests waited to board it. The only person aboard the boat was its skipper, on his first day on the job. He had put the engine in reverse and accidentally broken off the piece of the boat's hull that connects to an underwater track. ❻ There's a song about it. Comedic songwriter "Weird Al" Yankovic parodied the ride in a 2009 tune, "Skipper Dan." Based on Weezer's 2008 song "Pork and Beans," it tells the tale of a failed actor who is stuck working as a Jungle Cruise skipper. "Look at those hippos! They're wigglin' their ears!" he tells his crew. "Just like they've done for the last 50 years!"

Fun finds. ❶ At the entrance, a missing search party sent to find a previous Jungle Cruise boat is identified by six skulls on a poster. ❷ "Danger! Please contact Wathel Rogers, animal handler, to enter live cargo holding area" reads a sign on a cage. One of the original Disney imagineers, Rogers designed the mechanical systems used to make the animals move. ❸ The Adventurers Club—an innovative longtime comedy spot at Downtown Disney (today's Disney Springs) that closed years ago—is the destination of a few items in a large wire cage. ❹ The office of Albert Awol, the disc jockey for the Jungle Cruise company's radio network, sits alongside the standby queue. The "Voice of the Jungle" broadcasts period news, bulletins, music and quizzes on the DBC (Disney Broadcasting Company). ❺ "Fishing in the Jungle Cruise waters is prohibited," he warns, "unless you're fishing a relative out of the water." ❻ Dr. Winston Hibler, the narrator of Disney's "True-Life Adventure" movies, is the intended recipient of a barrel. His address is Outpost 71755, a belated acknowledgment that Hibler wrote the speech Walt Disney gave at the dedication of California's Disneyland on July 17, 1955. ❼ Near the end of the queue, a crate of Goff-brand "crocodile-resistant pants" is a reference to Harper Goff, an imagineer who helped Walt Disney plan the Disneyland ride as well its Main Street U.S.A. The crate lists the Goff company address as 1911 Main Street, Fort Collins, Colorado. Goff was born in 1911, and used the buildings of his Fort

Hidden Mickey. On the side of crashed plane.

Collins hometown as the basis of his Main Street work. Goff was also the set designer for the classic 1942 film "Casablanca." ❽ The use of the ride's boats for "daredevil trips over Schweitzer Falls is strictly prohibited," warns a poster in the queue. ❾ A giant black tarantula periodically jerks and rears up in a small cage near the dock. ❿ "Recent events have created a number of openings" at the company, announces an ominous poster at the loading area. ⓫ E.L. O'Fevre is the Jungle Navigation Co.'s latest employee of the month, a sign announces over the boarding area. ⓬ Every exotic dish the crew mess serves for lunch tastes like chicken, reports a menu board. ⓭ Boat names include Amazon Annie, Congo Connie, Wamba Wanda and Zambesi Zelda. ⓮ On the ride, signs of your impending doom include what your skipper may say are "the remains of my last Jungle Cruise crew"—some painted skulls mounted on trophy poles in the Congo. ⓯ Behind them, gorillas have sacked the crew's camp. One of them stares down the barrel of a rifle, a pose re-created by an ape in the 1999 Disney movie "Tarzan." ⓰ A nearby crate is labeled Ammo 717, a reference to the July 17, 1955 opening date of California's Disneyland. ⓱ As the rhino chases the lost safari party up a pole, does the man on the bottom look familiar, foolish mortal? He's the caretaker

of the graveyard at the Haunted Mansion. ⓲ "I love disco!" secretly shouts one of the ride's headhunters just after the start of his chant, though the panicked patter of your skipper may drown it out. A mischievous Disney audio engineer added the phrase in the late 1970s. ⓳ One of Trader Sam's shrunken heads bears a resemblance to Katharine Hepburn, the co-star of "The African Queen." ⓴ According to a chalkboard in the exitway, previous Jungle Cruise passengers who have gone missing include "Ilene Dover," "Ann Fellen," "Al Belaite," and "B.N. Eaton." ㉑ "This end up… or was it this end up… or maybe this end up" read the sides of a square box below the chalkboard. ㉒ Another one warns "Fragile! Handle with care!" but then in small print acknowledges "Who's kidding who? Contents probably already broken." ㉓ Two roped crates pay homage to the 1960 Disney movie "Swiss Family Robinson." One, addressed to the film's director Kenneth Annakin, lists his address as "W\SS Supply Company, Colony of New Guinea"—a reference to "Swiss Family Robinson" book author Johann Wyss and the intended destination of the Robinson family before its ship broke up. ㉔ A second crate is headed to "Thomas Kirk Esq." at the Field Office of "M. Jones Cartographers Ltd." on the island of "Bora Danno." Thomas Kirk

Jingle Cruise. Trader Sam-ta, holiday boat names.

played middle son Ernst in "Swiss Family Robinson" and was the lead character in Disney's 1964 film "The Misadventures of Merlin Jones." James McArthur was oldest son Fritz in "Swiss" and later Danny "Danno" Williams in the 1968–1980 television series "Hawaii Five-O." The two crates initially sat alongside the entrance to the adjacent Swiss Family Treehouse. ㉕ Reindeer heads hide in tropical wreaths during November and December, as the ride transforms itself into the "Jingle Cruise." Other holiday finds include: ㉖ gift tags on items inside crates that indicate that the skippers are giving passenger possessions to each other as presents just inside the entrance, ㉗ a can of Ethanol that's been turned into eggnog on the dock, and along the exitway skippers' New Year's resolutions written on a chalk board that include ㉘ a "75% passenger return rate" and "❷vercome fear of passengers."

Hidden Mickeys. ❶ "You're a Bendel bonnet, a Shakespeare sonnet, you're Mickey Mouse!" croons singer John Hauser on the radio broadcast, performing a 1934 version of the Cole Porter standard "You're the Top." ❷ Lichen patches create Mickey's iconic three-circle shape on a tree across the river from the boarding dock. Small but impossible not to notice once you spot it the first time, it appears on a trunk that rises and splits to the right, above and behind the crew's shack. ❸ Formed by stamped circles surrounded by rivets, the three circles appear on the ride between and below the windows of the back end of a crashed airplane, which rests in overgrowth on your right just after you pass Schweitzer Falls. The front of the plane, a period-correct Lockheed Model 12 Electra Junior, is also at Walt Disney World. Robotic versions of Humphrey Bogart and Ingrid Bergman stand in front of it in the "Casablanca" set on The Great Movie Ride at Disney's Hollywood Studios. ❹ Three gray stones form Mickey's shape on the ground in front of the rhino poking the safari party up a pole. ❺ The mouse in also hiding in the temple, on your right as three yellow dots on the back of a giant spider.   •

Key facts. *Duration:* 10 min. *Capacity:* 310. *Queue:* Outdoor, covered. *Weather issues:* Closed during thunderstorms. *Debuted:* 1971 (Disneyland 1955). *Access:* Wheelchairs, ECVs OK. *Disability services:* Assistive listening, handheld captioning. *Location:* Across from the Magic Carpets of Aladdin.

American tiki architecture. Celebrated to its fullest.

Walt Disney's Enchanted Tiki Room

Slow-paced blast from past celebrates historic Disney show

★★★ ✔ "I heard there's gonna be birds in here," said the 9-year-old girl, waiting for the preshow to start. "I hate birds."

Sorry, it's 'cho time!

"All the birds sing words and the flowers croon" in this sweet yet woefully dated musical revue, a 1960s Disney icon which stars over 2⊙⊙ robotic birds, flowers and carved tikis. Young children may or may not like the show's vintage songs and corny jokes; others might yawn at the slow pace. Still, it's a Disney classic, and worth a look. The performance takes place in-the-round in an air-conditioned theater. You sit on a bench.

Perched above you, birds sing "Let's All Sing Like the Birdies Sing," "The Hawaiian War Chant" and "The Tiki, Tiki, Tiki Room." Flowers warble from hanging baskets; tikis chant on the walls. Four macaws host the revue—German Fritz, Mexican José, Irish Michael and French Pierre. José is stereotyped to a ridiculous extent; the show begins with him waking up and complaining "my siestas are getting *chorter* and *chorter*."

In a preshow, two toucans recall how they migrated to the show from the Jungle Cruise.

As stuffy Claude tells the tale, downhome Clyde accents it by imitating an elephant, lion and lurking crocodile ("Lurk! Lurk!").

A closer look. Conceived by Walt Disney as a restaurant with a coffee bar in its center, the Tiki Room became a show before it debuted at California's Disneyland in 1963. Its then-brand-new Audio-Animatronic technology stunned audiences. Hundreds of tiny movements in its birds, flowers, and tiki idols synchronized to 22 minutes of chatter, chirps, chants and croons, triggered by pneumatic valves that opened and closed at exactly the right times, creating movements that seemed almost real. Proud of the fact that unseen cables connected everything to a backstage control system much like Cape Canaveral cables connected Mercury space capsules to distant blockhouses, Walt boasted that the show used "the same scientific equipment that will guide rockets to the moon."

A clone of the attraction opened at the new Walt Disney World in 1971. After attendance waned, the Disney company redid the show in 1998, creating a sarcastic new version starring wisecracking parrot Iago from the 1992

All the birds sing words and the flowers croon. And the tikis chant.

Disney movie "Aladdin" and stuffy hornbill Zazu from 1994's "The Lion King." The new show made fun of its predecessor, as new Tiki Room owner Iago interrupted its opening performance of "The Tiki, Tiki, Tiki Room" by yelling "Stop the music! I said, stop the music! What is that? I'm gonna toss my crackers!"

After a 2010 fire burnt the bitchy bird to a crisp, Disney restored the show to an edited version of its original 1963 version (albeit with modern audio and lighting) and replaced its preshow with an edit of its first Florida take.

Tips. *When to go:* In the afternoon when other attractions have long lines, or during a rain. There's never a crowd. *Where to sit:* Halfway down on the left side of the room; the host birds will often face you.

Fun facts. ❶ Preshow toucan Claude is voiced by English actor Sebastian Cabot, best known to American audiences as Mr. French the butler on the 1960s sitcom "Family Affair." **❷** The preshow makes reference to three aspects of the original attraction that are no longer there. Clyde says listening to

Walt Disney inside California's Enchanted Tiki Room in 1963.

some rhythmic drumming is "almost as much fun as New Year's Eve in the orange groves" (a reference to the show's original sponsor, the Florida Citrus Growers) and refers to the building by its original name, the Sunshine Pavilion. Claude calls the attraction by its original title, the Tropical Serenade. ❸ The main show's bird calls and whistles were all voiced by one man. A. Purvis Pullen was also the voice of the birds in Disney's 1937 movie "Snow White and the Seven Dwarfs" as well as those in 1959's "Sleeping Beauty," Cheetah the chimp in the 1930s Johnny Weissmuller Tarzan films and Bonzo the chimp in the 1951 Ronald Reagan flick "Bedtime for Bonzo." Using the stage name Dr. Horatio Q. Birdbath, he performed with novelty band Spike Jones and His City Slickers, providing its bird calls and dog barks. Despite all that, Pullen called his Tiki Room work "my favorite accomplishment... The one that's gonna last."

Fun finds. ❶ "I wonder what happened to Rosita?" José asks as female cockatoos begin to sing "Let's All Sing Like the Birdies Sing," though a bird with that name has never been in the show. ❷ Though they don't mention it, during that song José and the three other host macaws parrot vintage crooners. José mimics Bing Crosby, ❸ Irish Michael channels Jimmy Durante, ❹ German Fritz scats like Louis Armstrong and ❺ Frenchman Pierre becomes—but of course!—Maurice Chevalier. ❻ When the flowers croon, their petals form lips and their stamens form tongues. ❼ Some orchids have babies who sing along with them. ❽ Tikis carved into the walls move their eyes and mouths as they chant. ❾ Upside-down masks on the walls depict Negendei, the Earth Balancer, who is always portrayed standing on his head. ❿ The "phew! phew!" sounds of the pressurized air that animates the birds and flowers are easy to hear. Though modern Audio-Animatronic figures use hydraulic oil-filled valves, those in the Tiki Room still use their original air-valve tech, to ensure they can't possibly leak on their audience.

Hidden Mickeys. ❶ On the theater's entrance doors, formed by berries on a stem underneath a bird's tail, about 4 feet (1.5 meters) off the ground. ❷ On the side of the building facing the Magic Carpets of Aladdin, as the center of an elaborate stone pillar.

Key facts. *Duration:* 13 min. *Capacity:* 250. *Queue:* Outdoor, shaded. *Showtimes:* Continuous. *Operating hours:* Typically opens at 10a. *Fear factor:* A simulated thunderstorm outside the room's windows can startle timid toddlers. *Debuted:* 1971 (Disneyland 1963); updated 2011. *Access:* Wheelchairs, ECVs OK. *Disability services:* Audio Description, assistive listening, handheld captioning. *Location:* Behind the Magic Carpets of Aladdin.

The exterior recalls El Morro, a 16th-century fortress in San Juan, P.R.

Pirates of the Caribbean

Plastered privateers pillage, plunder, promote pictures

★★★★★ ✔ FP+ Disney didn't invent the idea of the fantasy pirate, but it may have perfected it. Drunken Caribbean pirates "pillage and plunder... rifle and loot... kidnap and ravage and don't give a hoot" in this rowdy, rum-soaked attraction, a dark indoor boat ride which takes you through the Audio-Animatronic ransacking of a Spanish port.

There's plenty to catch your eye, as you pass dozens of vignettes filled with sight gags and details. Special effects simulate fire, lightning, wind and, best of all, splashing cannonballs. Designed in part by the same artists who created the goofy Country Bear Jamboree, the ride keeps a lightweight tone; its pirates have such caricatured features they seem straight out of a cartoon.

The attraction later became the inspiration for Disney's "Pirates of the Caribbean" film series, and has since been updated to include Capt. Jack Sparrow and other characters from those movies. Its cool, dim queue winds through a stone fort.

Storied it be. Pirates of the Caribbean tells two distinct stories, which somewhat contradict each other. The first is a morality tale, told in flashback form. It begins in the present day, as your boat passes through a watery grotto lined with skeletons of pirates, many of whom met their fate by being stabbed and left to die. Then, as your boat drops down a short waterfall, you travel back in time to see what led those pirates to their doom—an irresponsible life of debauchery.

Scenes after the waterfall tell their own story, one worked into the ride after the success of the "Pirates" movies. In this tale, Capt. Hector Barbossa and his crew have tracked Capt. Jack to the port and are desperate to find him. But they never do, leaving him to claim the town's riches for himself. You witness the pirates' attack on

Average wait times (standby line)

9a	10a	11a	12p	1p	2p	3p	4p	5p	6p	7p	8p	9p	10p	11p
5m	50m	35m	40m	50m	30m	25m	40m	35m	20m	30m	25m	20m	10m	5m

A stalemate.

the port, interrogation of the port's officials, auctioning of the women and burning of its buildings—all of which is celebrated and set to music. Toward the end, some pirates have been locked in a dungeon and are trying to get a dog to bring them the key to their cell. Meanwhile, draped over an ornate throne in the town's vault, Capt. Jack toasts his success by singing to a parrot.

Historic it be. The last attraction that Walt Disney personally helped design, Pirates of the Caribbean combines a Missouri farm boy's view of adventure with a Hollywood showman's use of theatrics. He originally planned it as a walk-through exhibit, with non-moving figures like those in a wax musuem. After the success of two Disney efforts at the 1964 New York World's Fair (General Electric's Carousel of Progress, with its life-like Audio-Animatronic characters, and United Way's It's a Small World, with its high-tech water jets that propelled boats of guests through

Entrance detail.

"Strike yer colors, ye bloomin' cockroaches."

its scenes), he changed it over to a boat ride with robotic figures. It debuted at California's Disneyland on March 18, 1967, three months after his death.

Expanding it be. Over the years Disney has filled the area around the attraction with other Pirates-themed offerings. Across the Adventureland walkway from the ride's entrance, the intimate live stage show **Captain Jack Sparrow's Pirate Tutorial** teaches kids how to be rescued from a desert island, use swordplay to flee an enemy, and sing the ride's theme song. Next to it, the **Tortuga Tavern** snack bar is based on the young-adult book series "Pirates of the Caribbean: Jack Sparrow." Set in a time before the first "Pirates of the Caribbean" movie, its story includes the character Arabella Smith, an adolescent barmaid who takes over the Tavern after her drunken dad and pirate mom disappear. Living above the tavern, Arabella flirts with fellow teenager Jack Sparrow and dates young Bootstrap Billy Turner. Near the ride exit, the **Pirates League** makeover salon transforms adults and children into swashbucklers, swashbucklerettes and mermaids. Finally, players of the interactive scavenger hunt **A Pirates Adventure** help Capt. Sparrow lift a curse by using a treasure map to find hidden objects throughout Adventureland, many of which come to life.

PC it be not. The ride's scenes are all in good fun, of course, but parents may wonder if portraying the joys of torture, heavy drinking and the selling of women into slavery send the best messages to a wide-eyed young child. "There is nothing politically correct about Pirates of the Caribbean," admits Disney Imagineer Eric Jacobson. "In fact, much of it is patently offensive."

In fairness, the attraction does imply the consequences of such behavior. Its first scene has always shown that its pirates end up murdered, and over the years the ride's caveman view of women has certainly been toned down.

A barrel that today hides Capt. Jack originally hid a titillated young woman who was nearly naked. Holding her lacy pink petticoat, a drunken pirate in front of her looked at riders passing by in front of him and asked, "Say, have you set your eyes on the bewitched maiden in your travels? Oh she be a lively lassie she were. Oh I tell you true, it's all right to hoist me colors on the likes of that shy little wench! Favor—keep a weathered eye open, mateys. I be willing to share I be!"

Responding to rider complaints, Disney replaced the petticoat with a treasure map in 1997, and changed out the pirate's dialogue to "this map says X marks the spot, but I be seein' no X's afore me." As for the girl, Disney dressed her and gave her a small treasure

Brides to be.

chest to hold, hoping to convey that she was hiding not to protect her virtue but her valuables. (In California Disney removed the woman from the scene completely, replacing her with a cat and the pirate's lust with gluttony, as he now told passersby "I be looking for a fine pork loin, I be!")

Though the complaints died down, the changes didn't please everyone. In an interview in the Los Angeles Times after, an imagineer who helped create the original ride bitterly referred to the updated one as "Boy Scouts of the Caribbean."

Disney changed the scene again in 2006, replacing the woman (in California, the cat) with a spying Capt. Jack Sparrow and giving the pirate yet another monologue and prop. Now he can read his map just fine, and desires neither flesh nor food, only Mr. Sparrow. "What I wouldn't give to see the look on Capt. Jack's face when he hears tell 'tis only me that gots the goods," he says, holding a key to the town's treasure room that Jack's about to nab.

The company redid a second scene that year too. Originally, just past the bridal auction a group of pirates continually chased slim young women in circles, the conquests-to-be giggling as they ran. Then came the gag: an older, overweight woman chasing a pirate.

At first Disney tried to convey that the pirates were merely hungry by having the young women hold pies. As for the old woman, she wasn't lustful, simply angry, since now she had a rolling pin in hand and her pirate a stolen ham. Today all the women chase the pirates, angry at them for stealing all kinds of things. Listen closely, however, and you'll notice that the young women are still giggling.

Tips. *When to go:* Early in the morning or late at night, when lines are short. *Which line to pick:* The right one. Its sights include some chess-playing skeletons. *Where to sit:* Ask for the front row. You'll have a clear view of everything, and lots of legroom.

Fun facts. Aye, there be a treasure trove of trivia at this attraction. Such as: ❶ It was fashionably late. When Walt Disney World opened in 1971 it didn't include a Pirates of the Caribbean ride, as Disney bigwigs reasoned that since the real Caribbean was so close to Florida nobody would be interested in a pretend version of it. They soon saw the error of their ways, however, and a Florida version of the ride debuted at the Magic Kingdom in 1973. ❷ It holds a Disney 'first.' Pirates of the Caribbean was the first Disney attraction to exit through a gift shop. Most still don't do it today. ❸ It had bona fide bones. When it first opened at California's Disneyland, the ride's skeletons were real—actual human remains from the UCLA Medical Center. ❹ It has a famous ghost. The voice of the cryptic

© Disney

Micaela Neal

Johnny Depp! Or at least reasonable facsimiles, using molds of Depp's face.

warning "dead men tell no tales," the auctioneer and every member of the band in the subsequent scene (including the donkey and the dog) come from the Haunted Mansion's Ghost Host, voice talent Paul Frees. ❺ Some of it's gone Hollywood. Many of the attraction characters appear in the "Pirates" movies, among them the magistrate, the redhead, the snoring pirate with the pigs and the jailed prisoners with their dog. In 2011 the bridal auction was expanded into a live-action short, "Tales of the Code: Wedlocked." In it, after a feisty blonde and a flirty redhead have both been left at the altar by Jack Sparrow, the two suddenly find themselves in an auction competing against each other. Angered by the higher bids for the redhead, the blonde accuses her of not only coloring her hair, but also enhancing her breasts. Still, the pirates shout "We wants the redhead!" ❻ The faces of the Audio-Animatronic Jack Sparrows were created using molds of Johnny Depp's face. He voiced their dialogue, too.

Fun finds. ❶ Cannonball holes mar the attraction's sign, which is a sail on a mast. ❷ Broken oars support the sail. ❸ Pressing a telescope to an eye socket, the skeleton of a pirate peers down at park guests from a crow's nest atop the mast. ❹ Unseen Spanish guards shout commands amid cannon fire along the left entrance line, though both are nearly drowned out by the ride's theme music. ❺ Shackled in chains, two pirate skeletons play chess along the right entrance line, in a dungeon cell behind some wall slits and jail bars. Remnants of their clothes hang from their bones, as if they started their game when they were alive. Chess players will note that the skeletons have reached a stalemate. During busy periods an extension of the left entrance line also passes by them. ❻ At the ride's boarding dock, a pirate ship appears off in the distance through an archway on your right. Cannons are aimed at it. ❼ A huge human skull hides in plain sight in the rocky wall in front of you as you near a small beach. Obvious once you see it, it's formed by large rocks in the wall just to the left of the beach, and has no lower jaw. ❽ Mermaids swim next to your boat, appearing on both sides as faint glimmers of light. The creatures' tails sometimes break the surface, creating small ripples. Their siren songs waft through the air. ❾ The skeleton of a mermaid lies in a fishing net of a small boat on the beach, next to some pirate skeletons. ❿ Still

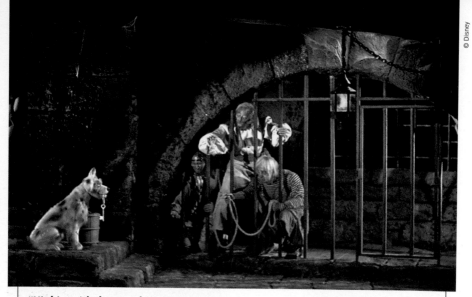

© Disney

"Hit him with the soup bone!"

gripping its sword, one pirate skeleton is standing, pressed against a wall. A seagull nests in its hat. ⓫ Just past the beach, a crazed pirate skeleton stands at the remains of a wooden helm, steering its ship's wheel during a violent storm, unaware that the wheel is not attached to a ship. ⓬ The Wicked Wench is the name of the attacking pirate ship to your left in the battle scene, identified by a nameplate on its stern that's barely visible in the darkness. ⓭ "Strike yer colors ye bloomin' cockroaches," Capt. Barbossa commands his crew, repeating an order yelled by the boat's original captain from 1971 to 2006. ⓮ Speaking in Spanish, the fort's soldiers bark orders to each other and shout threats at the pirates. ⓯ The pirate interrogating officials at the village well has a hook for a hand. ⓰ When he commands that the village magistrate tell him "Where be Captain Jack Sparrow? Speak up! Or do you fancy a swim with Davy Jones?" the magistrate's wife pleads from a window: "Don't tell him Carlos! Don't be chicken!" ⓱ "I am no chicken! I will not talk!" Carlos calls back to her, just before getting dunked. ⓲ Waiting to be questioned, a second town official shivers in fear. ⓳ Near the well, Capt. Jack hides among some female dressmaking forms, his fingers pinching a derriere. ⓴ At the bridal auction, the first woman in line is beaming,

happy to be sold. Referring to her as "stout-hearted and corn-fed" the auctioneer gently orders the portly woman to "shift yer cargo, dearie. Show 'em yer larboard side." ㉑ "Are you selling her by the pound?" one of the bidding pirates jokes. ㉒ Second in line, an impatient redhead lifts the hem of her corseted red dress to coyly flash her leg, petticoat and red heels. "Strike yer colors ye brazen wench!" the auctioneer barks. "No need to expose yer superstructure!" ㉓ When a pirate on your left fires his pistol, its bullet "pings" a hanging sign on your right, making it sway. ㉔ Dressed in a bridal gown and veil, another women in line clasps her hands hopefully. ㉕ A crying woman is consoled by a spinster, who also wears a veil. ㉖ One of the pirates is Abraham Lincoln—or at least his scruffier identical twin. Appearing in plain sight near the right side of your boat, he joins with the others to shout "We wants the redhead! We wants the redhead!" Disney officials confirm to us off the record that the figure—who unlike his fellow buccaneers has slow, graceful arm movements and no caricatured facial features—is the same Audio-Animatronics character seen as Lincoln for decades at the nearby Hall of Presidents. Begging you to notice him, Disney has topped off its Pirate Abe with a tall stovepipe-like hat. ㉗ One pirate tries to

Hidden Mickey. Tilted, on her left shoulder.

Rookie raiders. Pirates League mannequins.

get a cat to drink with him. "Here kitty, kitty, kitty," he slurs. "Have a little 'ol tot of rum with ol' Bill, aye?" ㉘ A dog and a donkey bark and bray in rhythm as a cantina band performs the attraction's theme song, "Yo-Ho (A Pirate's Life for Me)." ㉙ ⃝One pirate nearly topples over as he steps into a boat, struggling to steal a towering amount of loot. ㉚ To your right, another pirate snores as he sleeps in a puddle of mud, with pigs oinking behind him. ㉛ As you reach a small bridge, a grossly hairy leg of a pirate dangles off an archway above your head. ㉜ "A parrot's life for me!" sings the parrot next to that pirate. ㉝ Frustrated that a dog nearby has the key to their dungeon in his mouth but won't bring it them, one jailed pirate suggests to his cell mates, "Hit him with the soup bone!" ㉞ As the dog glances at your boat, a captive calls "Rover, it's us what needs yer ruddy help, not them blasted lubbers!" ㉟ Actually the prisoners could easily escape the cell, as its bars are widely spaced. ㊱ Across from the dungeon in the treasure room, the key that was held by the earlier pirate in front of a barrel pokes out from the unlocked door. ㊲ Basking among the riches in the room, Capt. Jack drunkenly declares "I shall take this paltry sum as a stipend to cover my expenses. My reward for a life of villainy, larceny, skullduggery and persnickety." ㊳ As he breaks into the ride's theme song, a parrot interrupts him after the words *"maraud and embezzle and even hijack"* to squawk "Hi Jack! Hi Jack!" ㊴ Jack refers to the colorful bird as "my chromatic winged beast." ㊵ A peg-leg mark appears repeatedly on the ride's exit ramp, as part of the safety graphics that show you where to step.

Hidden Mickeys. Mickey's three-circle silhouette appears ❶ as marks in a plaster wall in the left queue, above and to the right of a fireplace mantel; ❷ as coins on a scale on your right in the gift shop, just after you exit the ride, ❸ and again in that shop as angled golden circles near the left shoulder of a woman's tunic, in a colorful painting in the room's far back corner.

Key facts. *Duration:* 9 min. *Capacity:* 330 (15 per boat). *Queue:* Indoor, air-conditioned. *Fear factor:* Spooky opening scenes, short dark drop, realistic cannon fire. *Debuted:* 1973, revised 2006, 2012 (Disneyland 1967). *Access:* ECV and wheelchair users must transfer. *Disability services:* Handheld captioning, Audio Description. *Location:* At the back entrance to Adventureland.

The Liberty Bell. Cast from the same mold.

Liberty Square

Honoring our Colonial heritage and those patriots who broke away from England to form the United States, this land's Federal and Georgian architecture brings back the time of the Revolutionary War.

Fun finds. ❶ The rousing theme song to the BBC television show "Monty Python's Flying Circus" plays as ambient music. That's because it's actually a John Philip Sousa tune, "The Liberty Bell." ❷ Snaking down the center of the main walkway, a curved squiggle of brown pavement symbolizes sewage that flowed on 18th-century streets. It leads to restrooms. ❸ Cast in 1987 from the same mold as the original, a replica of The Liberty Bell hangs in a small plaza in front of the Hall of Presidents. ❹ A version of Boston's historic Liberty Tree elm looms nearby. Disney's tree is a 160-year-old Southern live oak, transplanted in 1971 from its original location 8 miles away. Its acorns have spawned 500 additional trees. ❺ Thirteen lanterns hang from its branches, representing the 13 colonies that formed the United States. ❻ Their flags circle the Liberty Bell. ❼ Perfect for photos, stocks for adults and children stand in front of the riverboat dock. ❽ Along the left side of the building that holds The Hall of Presidents, a rag doll in a window is a Colonial-era signal to firefighters that the room belongs to a child. ❾ A rifle in a second-story window sends a message that the owner is home and ready to fight. ❿ Nearby, two lanterns in a window recall the "two if by land, one if by sea" phrase from the 1860 Longfellow poem "Paul Revere's Ride." ⓫ Beyond the building, a plaque of interlocked hands tells arriving firefighters that the building's firemans-fund fee has been paid.

Hidden Mickeys. ❶ In the Columbia Harbour House restaurant, as circular wall maps in a room across from the order counter, and ❷ as painted grapes atop a spice rack in the lobby, to the right of a fireplace.

Live entertainment

NEW! Great Moments in American History. Historical tales as told by the Muppets— Kermit the Frog, Miss Piggy, Fozzie Bear, the Great Gonzo and of course Sam Eagle—who join a town crier in a live show. *Debuts Oct. 2016 outside The Hall of Presidents.*

Restaurants and food

Both a table-service restaurant and a fast-food spot dish up hearty, all-American fare:

★★★★ ✔ **$35 DDP Liberty Tree Tavern.** Hearty comfort food and a cozy atmosphere make this unpretentious New England eatery a relaxing break. Resembling a large, Colonial house, it has six separate little dining rooms, which keeps its noise level low. Despite its name, no liquor flows. Best choice for lunch: the tender pot roast. Dinner is a fixed-price, family-style Thanksgiving feast. *Lunch 11:30a–3p, $14–$23 (children $10–$11); dinner 3:15p–9.30p, $33 (children $19). Seats 250.*

★★★★★ ✔ **$17 DDPq Columbia Harbour House.** This fresh, healthy eatery focuses on chicken and seafood. It straddles the border between Liberty Square and Fantasyland; sit upstairs over the walkway to people-watch. I like the salmon and chicken pot pie. *11a–9p; $10–$14 (children $6–$7). Seats 593.*

★★★★ ✔ **$8 DDPs Liberty Square Market.** Outdoor stand with hot dogs, baked potatoes and sweet potatoes, whole fruit. *9a–9p; $2–$6. Seats 104 at umbrella-covered tables.*

★★★★ ✔ **$11 DDPs Sleepy Hollow.** Waffles and funnel cakes. *9a–park close; $4–$8. Seats 164 outdoors, plus 24 around the corner in the air-conditioned Heritage House.*

Shops and merchandise

The standout here is a Haunted Mansion-inspired shop with distinctive merchandise.

Memento Mori. No princess dresses here; this spooky store is totally dedicated to The Haunted Mansion. Shelves are packed with more than 100 items based on the attraction—action figures of its hitchhiking ghosts, tombstone-shaped coasters, fashion apparel inspired by its demonic wallpaper. You can buy a ghostly portrait of yourself taken in a Spirit Photography studio. Disney lore says the shop is the mortal home of Mansion spiritualist Madame Leota; her spirit visits from time to time. *In front of The Haunted Mansion.*

Ye Olde Christmas Shoppe. This cute spot offers oodles of ornaments, nutcrackers, stockings and other festive gear. A section of the store is set aside for the current or upcoming holiday, such as 4th of July or Halloween. *Across from The Hall of Presidents.*

Liberty Square entrance.

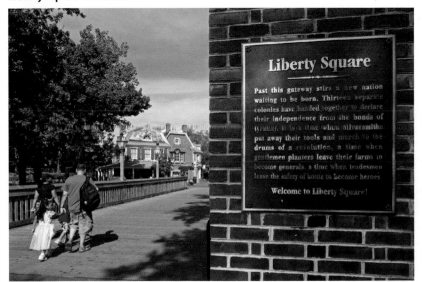

The Liberty Belle.

Paddle power.

Liberty Square Riverboat

Real paddlewheeler is more interesting than its trip

★★★ "Steady as she goes!" Narrated by Mark Twain, a ride on the three-tiered Liberty Belle steamship offers a taste of life on the Mississippi. Circling Tom Sawyer Island on what Disney calls the Rivers of America, its peaceful half-mile journey passes scenes that depict the rural America of the 1800s. Unfortunately the sights, for the most part, are nothing special: a wilderness cabin, an old grandpappy on a dock, few remarkably stoic woodland creatures, a cave where you hear something. The highlight is a small Native American camp, which has animated figures and smoke effects.

Voyages at dusk offer a pleasant diversion, but afternoon trips can be hot and crowded. The craft has only a handful of seats.

Despite its flaws as a ride, the boat itself offers a look at a forgotten aspect of American history. Though guided by an underwater rail, it's a real steam wheeler. Before each trip, cast members pump a diesel boiler full of river water, which it turns to steam and pipes it to an engine which drives a giant wheel—as well as the boat's electrical system. Atop the ship: a working smokestack and steam whistle.

Tips. *Where to stand:* On mild days head to the top deck for the best view; on hot days try the covered second floor. *Want to sit?* A second-floor lounge has cushioned benches, as well as antique maps, etchings, photos and a display of playing cards and poker chips. *What to notice:* The lovely wildflowers that border Tom Sawyer Island; the respectful talk about Native Americans. *Family matters:* Show your children the steam engine. It's on the lower deck, in front of the paddle-wheel. Where else will they see one?

A closer look. Much like railroads, paddle steamers were a principal means of transporting goods and passengers in the 1800s. Boiler explosions destroyed many of the wooden vessels, which led to their demise. Invented by the Romans, the paddlewheel was the first practical form of mechanical boat propulsion.

Key facts. *Duration:* 13 min. *Departures:* Typically every 30 minutes between 10a and dusk. *Capacity:* 400. *Queue:* Outdoor, covered. *Debuted:* 1971, updated 2007. *Access:* Wheelchairs, ECVs OK. *Location:* To the left of the Hall of Presidents.

Independence Hall. Disney's version.

The Hall of Presidents

A civil civics lesson with robotic commanders-in-chief

UPDATED! ★★★★★ ✔ Expect a new version of this uplifting theatrical presentation to premiere in 2017, as Disney adds an Audio-Animatronic version of our new president to its stage as its featured speaker—just as it always has since 1971.

The show begins with a large-format film. Starting with Washington's struggle to build a new nation, it scans our country's history. That's followed by the opening of a curtain that reveals a 100-foot-wide (30-meter) stage lined three-deep with every U.S. president—nearly four dozen life-sized animated figures—and a roll-call introduction of them one-by-one. George Washington speaks, as does Abraham Lincoln and our current commander-in-chief.

Fans of American history, parents wanting to inspire their children or perhaps just anyone longing for a return to civility in American politics should love every minute.

Tips. *When to go:* In the afternoon. Rarely crowded, the show offers a great way to beat the heat. *Where to sit:* Front row center. The closer you are to the presidents, the more you can catch their gestures and expressions.

Fun facts. ❶ The widescreen projection system was invented by Ub Iwerks, the original animator of Mickey Mouse. ❷ Disney's first Honest Abe didn't work that well when it debuted at the 1964 New York World's Fair. With any spike in current, it would flail its arms, hit itself repeatedly in the head and then slam itself down in its chair, confusing audiences who wondered if the bizarre routine was part of the show. ❸ Now retired, a Disney publicist tells us that he often told visiting reporters that some of the on-stage presidents were played by real people—that since there were always at least one Audio-Animatronic figure out for repairs, each show had at least one human stand-in. When he asked Walter Cronkite to spot the live actor, the veteran newsman just laughed. A moment later he turned to the publicist and said, "Jefferson?"

Key facts. *Duration:* 20 min. *Showtimes:* Typically every half hour. *Capacity:* 740. *Queue:* Indoor. *Debuted:* 1971, revised 2017. *Access:* Wheelchairs, ECVs OK. *Disability services:* Assistive listening, reflective captioning. *Location:* Just past the Liberty Square entrance off the park's central hub.

A foggy evening.

The Haunted Mansion

A charmingly creepy tour of a ghostly retirement home

★★★★★ ✓ FP+ Ghosts dance, duel, sing, play music, sip tea, guzzle booze, even hitchhike in this dark indoor ride, which is so tongue-in-cheek that it's never truly scary. Sitting comfortably in an open "Doom Buggy," you creep through it room-by-room passing hundreds of ghosts, most of which are brought to life by age-old visual tricks.

Welcoming foolish mortals for more than four decades, this ghostly retirement home serves as a supernatural senior center, sort of a nursing home for ghosts who by their nature have no need for nurses.

Like similar places in the mortal world, its goal is to increase its number of residents through the use of a strong marketing effort. Just like at a timeshare complex—and many senior living centers—your "tour" of it is a sales pitch. "There are several prominent ghosts who have retired here from creepy old crypts from all over the world," your unseen ghost host boasts. "Actually, we have 999 happy haunts… but there's room for a thousand. Any volunteers?" Highlights include Madame Leota (a head in a crystal ball), a murderous bride in the attic, and hundreds of ghosts celebrating "a swinging wake."

At the end, a doll-sized bride perched up on a wall whispers "hurry back… hurry back…" Then she giggles, mischievously. "Be sure to bring your death certificate, should you decide to join us."

Whew! She always gets to me.

Tips. *When to go:* Often. There's no way you can take everything in on one visit.

Key facts. *Duration:* 11 min. *Capacity:* 320. *Queue:* Outdoor, covered. *Fear factor:* Dark; some sudden screams and pop-up faces. *Restraint:* Lap bar. *Debuted:* 1971, revised 2007. *Access:* Must be ambulatory. *Disability services:* Handheld captioning, Audio Description. *Location:* Next to Fantasyland.

Average wait times (standby line)

9a	10a	11a	12p	1p	2p	3p	4p	5p	6p	7p	8p	9p	10p	11p
10m	40m	40m	50m	55m	30m	30m	35m	25m	20m	15m	10m	10m	5m	---

The tombstone of Master Gracey. Cast members often top it with a rose.

The Haunted Mansion: A Closer Look

By Micaela Neal. Walt Disney first pondered building a haunted house in the early 1950s as he was planning his first theme park, California's Disneyland. He imagined it as a walk-through tour, led by live butlers and maids. For a storyline, he considered Washington Irving's spooky 1820 tale "The Legend of Sleepy Hollow," which his company had just included in its 1949 compilation movie "The Adventures of Ichabod and Mr. Toad." But he also flirted with two other stories, one of a sea captain who kills his nosy bride and then hangs himself; another of a wedding party attended by villains such as Captain Hook, the bad guy of his then-current film project "Peter Pan." Distracted by more-finished Disneyland concepts such as Main Street U.S.A. and the Jungle Cruise, Disney didn't have time to flesh out his haunted house thoughts and the project stagnated.

Nevertheless, in 1961 Disneyland passed out handbills to guests announcing that it was about to build a haunted house. Two years later the exterior facade was done; a sign out front referred to it as a "haunted mansion" and promised that its interior would include a scary portrait gallery and a "Museum of the Supernatural."

Delays. The attraction, however, still wasn't built for years, as Walt Disney was again sidetracked by other projects. First he focused on the 1964 New York World's Fair, which would introduce his attractions Carousel of Progress and It's a Small World as well as his robotic Abraham Lincoln. When the fair closed, he obsessed on EPCOT, his planned Experimental Prototype Community of Tomorrow in Florida which he felt could solve the problems of America's inner cities.

Without Walt's leadership, the creative crew in charge of the Haunted Mansion lacked a cohesive vision. It developed conflicting ideas for it, some scary, some silly, some strange. By the time some of its members appeared with Walt to introduce it to the public on a 1965 episode of the television series "Walt Disney's Wonderful World of Color," no one was on the same page. Walt secmed unfamiliar with the ride, referring to it as "The House of Illusions." When an imagineer sheepishly corrected him with "The Haunted Mansion," Walt added "of the Supernatural." Later, when he again called the ride "The House of Illusions," another imagineer corrected him by calling it "The Museum of the Weird" and going on to explain how it would have man-eating plants.

Finally, a ride. After Walt Disney died in 1966, imagineers decided the ride would be a hodgepodge of nearly all of their ideas, everything but man-eating plants. Disneyland's Haunted Mansion opened in August, 1969, almost two decades after Walt Disney's first haunted-house thoughts. The mishmash of scenes left many riders less than thrilled. Even some of its imagineers openly disliked it; one summed it up as having "too many cooks."

Soon, though, a special quality of the mansion came to light: it had so many details that no matter how often someone rode it they always saw something new. A second version premiered at Walt Disney World's Magic Kingdom when that park opened in 1971.

Updates. Disney revamped the ride a few years ago. It expanded the standby queue, adding a side plaza filled with busts, tombstones and interactive crypts. It enhanced the seance, upgrading the spiritualist's crystal ball so that instead of sitting on a table it floats in the air. The hitchhiking ghosts gained the power to pull pranks, such as removing your head and blowing it up like a balloon. Imagineers replaced portraits that followed you with their eyes with ones that changed when flashed by lightning, swapped some huge rubber spiders for a roomful of odd staircases, and added a story of a murderous bride to the attic. They also overhauled the mansion's audio, adding three-dimensional sounds to its stretching room.

Inspirations. Disney scrapped its "Legend of Sleepy Hollow" idea early on, but revived its New England setting for Disney World's Haunted Mansion. The exterior resembles the Harry Packer Mansion, an 1874 estate in rural Jim Thorpe, Penn. Other influences:

"The Cask of Amontillado." A bricklayer trowels a man into a brick crypt, leaving him to die with his arm sticking out in this 1846 novel by Edgar Allen Poe. In the final gag in the mansion's graveyard, a human arm trowels itself into a brick crypt.

The dune buggy. A modified Volkswagen Beetle, this open-chassis vehicle gained popularity during the surfer craze of the 1960s. It gave rise to the term Doom Buggy.

"Haunted House." The lyrics (and music) of this 1931 novelty tune by Ray Noble and his New Mayfield Orchestra (*"When the doors all squeak and the windows creak, and the ceilings leak 'cause the roof's antique..."*) are eerily similar to those of "Grim Grinning Ghosts" (*"When the crypt doors creak and the tombstones quake, spooks come out for a swinging wake..."*). Noble also wrote the pop standard "The Very Thought of You."

"The Haunting." Walls stretch, doors breath, tap and thump as a haunted house comes to life in this 1963 British horror film.

"The Hitch-Hiker." A hitchhiking ghostly man follows a woman in this 1960 episode of the television series "The Twilight Zone." At one point he gets into her car. Eventually she learns she has died, and that the hitchhiker is an angel sent to escort her to heaven.

"The Hitch-Hiker."

The Hatbox Ghost.

"La Belle et la Bête." Busts track visitors with their eyes and human arms hold wall torches in this 1946 French version of the Beauty and the Beast fairytale. On the ride library busts track you and human arms hold wall torches in the de-boarding area.

"Nosferatu." A shadowy clawed figure reaches out to seize a young woman's heart in this 1922 German version of "Dracula." Later a death clock startles a young man. In the ride's corridor of doors, the shadow of a grasping claw passes over a demonic clock.

"The Phantom of the Opera." A troubled ghost plays the organ of an opera house he haunts in this 1910 novel, which led to a 1925 movie as well as later films and stage shows. On the ride, a ghost plays a ballroom organ and opera singers perform in the graveyard.

"The Picture of Dorian Gray." In this 1890 novel by Oscar Wilde, a young man sells his soul to the devil in exchange for a future where a portrait of him ages but he does not, leaving him youthful forever. In the mansion, a foyer portrait similarly ages its young man.

"The Raven." A narrator accuses this black bird of stealing people's souls in this 1845 Poe poem. Robotic versions of it flap their wings and glare at you throughout the ride. Originally it was to chide the Ghost Host for hanging himself ("Caw… caw… he took the coward's way!") and the conservatory's piano player for playing too loud ("Caw… caw… you've disturbed another guest!").

"Relativity." Each on its own plane and with its own source of gravity, three stairways interlock in this 1953 illustration by Dutch artist M.C. Escher, the basis of the ride's similar staircases.

William Shakespeare. He coined the phrase "grim grinning ghost" in his 1592 poem "Venus and Adonis." After Death kills her lover Adonis (the Greek god of beauty), Venus (the goddess of love) cries "Grim-grinning ghost, earth's worm, what dost thou mean? To stifle beauty and to steal his breath?"

Characters. Though the ride doesn't tell a story, it does have some key characters:

Constance Hatchaway. This menacing bride and her wedding memorabilia haunt the attic. Her name tells her story: she constantly used her hatchet to do away with her husbands. She's fond of money and fine jewelry.

The Ghost Host. This gleeful pun-loving spirit introduces himself in the portrait gallery, reveals he hung himself to escape it, and then repeatedly tempts you to join him.

Madame Leota. The floating head of a psychic medium appears in a hovering crystal ball halfway through the ride. She sends "sympathetic vibrations" to the mansion's ghosts, who materialize for you from then on.

Master Gracey. Supposedly the owner and main resident of the mansion, this character originated in fan fiction written by cast members which went viral online. The mansion has no character by this name; a tombstone bearing the inscription "Master Gracey" refers to Disney imagineer Yale Gracey. Still, Disney included a Master Gracey character in its 2003 movie "The Haunted Mansion" and sells Master Gracey merchandise.

The Hatbox Ghost. A fan favorite who barely exists, this elderly cloaked figure with stringy hair and a gold tooth has gained a cult following among Haunted Mansion

Madame Douglas. When she recorded the voice of Madame Leota, actress Eleanor Audley (lower right) was appearing in the sitcom "Green Acres" as the mother of Oliver Douglas.

enthusiasts. He debuted with the original attraction at California's Disneyland in 1969, standing across from the bride in the attic. Decked out with a top hat and a huge grin, he clutched a cane with one hand and held a translucent hatbox in the other. Thanks to some lighting tricks, as riders passed him his head disappeared from his body and reappeared in the box in time with the bride's beating heart. Or at least it was supposed to. Unfortunately, the trick didn't work. Since the attic wasn't completely dark, its ambient light prevented his head from completely disappearing. So as riders passed by he looked like he was simply standing there, holding a flashing box with his face in it. The gag was quickly removed. A year later Disney built a second Hatbox Ghost for its Disney World mansion but so far hasn't used it. It has, however, snuck images of him into the corridor of doors, and sells Hatbox Ghost merchandise.

The Hitchhiking Ghosts. A hunchbacked top-hatted carpetbagger, a thin dapper skeleton in a long coat and a hairy little prisoner shackled to a ball and chain hitch rides near the end of the tour. Thanks to a mirror, you see yours travel with you; the Ghost Host claims he follows you home. Fan fiction has given the hitchhikers names which Disney itself has embraced: the carpetbagger is Phineas, the skeleton Ezra, the prisoner Gus.

Voices. Tony the Tiger? Gumby? Ripper Roo? You hear them all, or at least their voices, as you travel through the mansion. Even Mickey Mouse shows up.

Xavier ("X") Atencio. This famed Disney imagineer is the man trapped in the coffin ("Let me outta here!").

Eleanor Audley. A top character actress of her day, Audley is spiritualist Madame Leota. The voice of stepmother Lady Tremaine in Disney's 1950 movie "Cinderella" and evil fairy Maleficent in 1959's "Sleeping Beauty," she appeared in many 1960s sitcoms, including "The Beverly Hillbillies" (private-school headmistress Mrs. Millicent Schuyler-Potts), "The Dick Van Dyke Show" (Parents Council President Mrs. Billings), "Green Acres" (Eunice Douglas, the disapproving mother of

Courtyard busts. Forsythia and Wellington Dread, with clues on how they killed their victim.

liver Douglas) and "My Three Sons" (Mrs. Vincent, the disapproving mother-in-law of Steve Douglas). She had a bit part in "The Hitch-Hiker" episode of "The Twilight Zone."

Kat Cressida. Attic bride Constance Hatchaway, she's ditzy Dee Dee in Cartoon Network's 1990s series "Dexter's Laboratory."

Paul Frees. The Haunted Mansion's Ghost Host, he was villain Boris Badenov in the 1959-1964 television series "The Adventures of Rocky and Bullwinkle," Disney character Professor Ludwig Von Drake and, in falsetto, Pillsbury Doughboy Poppin' Fresh.

Dallas McKennon. The bearded ghost in the graveyard who struggles to understand a mummy ("What's that? Louder! I can't hear you! Eh?"), McKennon worked in Hollywood for five decades. He voiced animated stars Archie Andrews and Gumby, and late in life provided the insane laugh of Ripper Roo in the video game series "Crash Bandicoot." Disney fans know him for his safety spiel at Big Thunder Mountain Railroad ("This here's the wildest ride in the wilderness!"), his banjo player Zeke at Country Bear Jamboree and his Ben Franklin in The American Adventure.

Jimmy Macdonald. This Disney sound-effects man does the shrieks and screams heard in the corridor of doors. After World War II he voiced Mickey Mouse, Pluto, Chip 'n Dale and "Cinderella" mice Jaq and Gus.

The Mellomen. This harmonizing quartet provided the voices of the graveyard's singing busts. It performed on Rosemary Clooney's 1954 snappy hit "Mambo Italiano" and was Elvis Presley's backup group in the movies "It Happened at the World's Fair" (1963), "Roustabout" (1964) and "Paradise Hawaiian Style" (1966) and, as the Bible Singers, "The Trouble with Girls" (1969). Only one of the group's faces appears on the busts; that of bass singer Thurl Ravenscoft (see below).

Loulie Jean Norman. The voice of the graveyard's female opera singer, Norman sang the high background melody of the Token's 1961 hit "The Lion Sleeps Tonight" ("Ah...ah... ah... AHHH!") as well as the signature accompaniment to the theme song of the 1960s television series "Star Trek" (ooh-OOH... oh-oh-oh-oh ooh..."). For her Haunted Mansion recording Walt Disney asked her to sing as if she was possessed.

Thurl Ravenscoft. The bass singer of the Mellomen leads the singing busts, his head broken off from its pedestal. Ravenscoft sang "You're A Mean One, Mr. Grinch" in the 1966 Dr. Seuss television special "How the Grinch Stole Christmas!" and was the longtime voice of Kellogg's Frosted Flakes mascot Tony the Tiger. At Disney he's also buffalo head Buff at the Country Bear Jamboree and German macaw Fritz at the Enchanted Tiki Room.

Fun facts. As you might expect, the Haunted Mansion has more than its share of nonessential but interesting facts. Some of the best:

Musical crypt detail.

It holds two firsts. The Haunted Mansion was the first Disney attraction created after Walt Disney died. It debuted at California's Disneyland in 1969, three years after his death. It was also the first Walt Disney World attraction completed in 1971.

It held a world record. The Mansion was in The Guinness Book of World Records—for one year. Named the World's Largest Dark Ride in 1999, it lost that title in 2000 to Valhalla, an indoor log flume in England.

It has two antiques. The hearse outside the mansion was built during the Civil War. It was later used in Hollywood movies, including the 1965 John Wayne Western "The Sons of Katie Elder." The piano in the conservatory was built by Philadelphia's Schomacker Piano Co. in the late 1800s.

It has two tunes. Nearly all the music in the ride is the same song—"Grim Grinning Ghosts (The Screaming Song)." It's performed in eight styles, everything from a sluggish instrumental dirge to a zippy barbershop harmony. Musicians will note that its tension comes from sharps or flats that aren't part of its key signature. The ballroom version sounds so strange because sound engineers had an organist play it backward and then reversed the recording; the sound of the flute in the graveyard band was created that way too. Gaylord Carter—the house organist during the 1920s at Grauman's Metropolitan Theatre, the largest movie palace in Hollywood—recorded the takes heard in the foyer and corridor of doors. An off-key dirge of Wagner's Bridal Chorus ("Here comes the bride") adds ambience to the attic.

It's prepared for your cat. Kitty Litter is the main product made from fuller's earth, the substance used to create the mansion's dust and cobwebs. A light tan dust made from clay, it's also used by Hollywood set dressers to make scenes look dusty or dirty.

It's one of a kind. The Haunted Mansion is the only Disney ride that suggests you kill yourself, which its Ghost Host does after he asks you to find a way out of its windowless, doorless art gallery. "Well, there's always my way," he coos, as the lights go out to reveal his hanging, swinging corpse high above you.

It stars Sister Sunshine. Julia Lee appears as the attic bride, Constance Hatchaway. Lee played Anne Steele (also known as "Sister Sunshine") in the 1990s television series "Buffy the Vampire Slayer."

They're all heathens! None of the tombstones include a cross or any other type of religious symbol.

There's plenty of pepper. The ballroom scene contains the largest implementation of Pepper's Ghost, a theatrical illusion from the Victorian era in which objects appear to fade in or out of existence or transform into other objects. Employed at theme parks and museums throughout the world, the trick

Madame Leota tombstone.

usually uses two rooms, only one of which its audience can see. Thanks to a large angled mirror, objects in the second room reflect into the first, appearing or disappearing as lights on them turn on and off. At the mansion, robotic figures reflect into its 90-foot-long (27-meter) ballroom from multiple rooms above and below its passing Doom Buggy audience. The effect is named after John Henry Pepper, a scientist who gained fame with it in 1862.

You never go in the home. The entire ride takes place in a nondescript warehouse building behind the mansion's facade.

Fun finds. To quote an unrelated song, the Haunted Mansion has "more to see than can ever be seen," more fun little things to look for than any other attraction at Walt Disney World. Here are more than 300 of them:

Grounds. ❶ A bronze bat peers down on you from the mansion's wrought-iron gate, above the clock of its FastPass+ entrance. The bat's tail is forked. ❷ Satan's horned head decorates the top of oval signs on either side of the entrance gate. Snakes slither around his neck. ❸ The howl of a wolf wafts through the air. ❹ The mansion's weathervane is a bat, its wings outstretched. ❺ Though chess-piece-like chimneys and trim details were common on 19th-century Gothic rooftops, Disney says those atop the mansion were intentionally designed to resemble pieces of the game. Every piece is represented except

the knight, "because it's always night at the Haunted Mansion." ❻ Columns alongside its front door resemble coffins. ❼ A black wreath decorates the door. ❽ Human figures top some metal railings and stand within others. ❾ Stone-faced cast members dress as butlers and maids. They often speak in a glum monotone. ❿ At night the lights around the Haunted Mansion flicker. ⓫ Lightning flashes on it at night, accompanied by cracks of thunder. ⓬ Holding a lantern, a shadowy figure wanders behind the mansion's windows at night. ⓭ Out front, dead roses lay in a horse-drawn hearse. ⓮ A bridle and tack hang in front of the hearse, but hold no visible horse. ⓯ Lanterns on the hearse glow at night. ⓰ Horseshoe and wheel tracks lead to the hearse from a nearby barn. ⓱ Next to the barn is a boathouse. Oars are stored inside. ⓲ Signs inform you that children under the age of 7 must ride with a "mortal" who is at least 14 years old. ⓳ Mortals are restricted to three per Doom Buggy. ⓴ Near the end of the FastPass+ queue, a second touchpoint makes a theremin sound as it reads your MagicBand or park ticket. ㉑ During Mickey's Not-So-Scary Halloween Parties a ghostly storyteller often sits on the lawn telling jokes. She'll chat with you. ㉒ Party cast members wear ghoulish makeup that includes cobwebs.

Dread family busts. In the standby queue, a murder mystery similar to those in the game of Clue hides on a collection of busts that arc

Outdoor graveyard.

around a small enclave. Dread family members Bertie, twins Forsythia and Wellington, Aunt Florence, Uncle Jacob and Cousin Maude have, for most the part, killed each other (though one killed no one, and one accidentally killed herself) and it's your job to figure out who did who in. Hints appear on the busts and on tarnished plaques beneath them. ❶ A snake around Bertie's neck hints how he killed his victim. A vial of poison on his plaque gives you another clue. His victim is revealed on a nearby inscription that includes the phrase "...the poison he had swallowed." ❷ A pistol on the plaque of Florence divulges her weapon of choice. Her victim's inscription describes its subject as an "expert shot" and closes with "in the end that's what he got." ❸ A dead bird on the plaque of the twins hints how they killed their victim. A small bag of bird seed between them offers a further clue. Their victim "was found face down in canary seed." ❹ A tiny hammer on Maude's plaque makes her weapon known. Her victims' inscription reveals they died from "bumps." ❺ Matchsticks in Maude's hair foretell her fate. Her inscription reveals that her "dreams went up in smoke."

Musical crypt. ❶ "Grim Grinning Ghosts" plays when you touch embossed images of musical instruments on the side of this Standby queue crypt. Each plays the tune separately. A band plays these instruments in the ride's graveyard scene. ❷ "He's gone from this world of trouble and strife," reads an inscription. "But a touch of your hand brings his music to life." ❸ "Grim Grinning Ghosts" also plays when you touch the keys of a pipe organ, itself an homage to the mansion's ballroom organ. ❹ Sculpted banshees fly from its pipes. ❺ Play the keys dramatically for a dramatic rendition. ❻ Play them too long and the banshees blow air and spit at you. ❼ A huge red-eyed raven peers down from atop the pipes, its wings spread open. ❽ The brand of the organ—Ravenscroft—is a shout-out to Thurl Ravenscroft, the singing bust in the ride's graveyard. ❾ On the right side of the crypt, a horn with tentacles is among the supernatural instruments that play when you touch them. ❿ Touch a one-eyed cat and it will meow angrily. ⓫ "A composer of note and renown here reposes," an inscription on this side of the crypt reads. "His melodies fade as he now decompooos."

Sea captain's crypt. ❶ "Here floats Captain Culpepper Clyne, allergic to dirt so he's pickled in brine," reads the inscription on this Standby queue crypt. "He braved the sea and all her wrath, but drowned on land while taking a bath." ❷ Atop it, bubbles billow over the sides of an open bathtub which holds Clyne's body. ❸ His waterlogged fingers grip the tub's edge. ❹ He sometimes sneezes, spraying water at those nearby. ❺ He slurs the shanty "Drunken Sailor" (*"What shall we do with a drunken sailor, early in the* *morning?"*) ❻ Water squirts from barnacles. ❼ Cover the barnacles with your hands and sculpted golden-eyed fish on the crypt spit at you. ❽ Foggy portholes dot the back of the crypt. ❾ Far to the right, a wedding ring of the bride in the attic sets in the concrete plaza.

Writer's crypt. Books pop in and out by themselves on this Standby-queue crypt, the home of poetess Prudence Pock. ❶ Push in one, another pops out. ❷ The books group in collections of 13. ❸ A secret coded message—a cryptogram (ha!)—hides in symbols on their spines. Each symbol represents a letter of the alphabet. ❹ Monstrous faces decorate the crypt. ❺ Nibs of ink pens border its top. ❻ "Writer's block" killed the poetess, according to its epitaph. ❼ Speaking from within it, she asks you for help with her writing efforts. "In the swamp, poor Sally Slater was eaten by an… what rhymes with 'Slater'?" ❽ She can hear your response if you answer in front of the Spectrecom, a small microphone gadget on the front of her crypt. ❾ Answer correctly and she responds with delight. ❿ The Spectrecom's small print shows it was patented by "R.H. Goff." A key Mansion concept artist, Ralph Harper Goff also did the layout of Epcot's World Showcase and concepts of its Japan, Italy and United Kingdom pavilions. Outside of Disney, he designed the sets for the classic 1942 Warner Brothers movie "Casablanca" and was the art director of the 1971 Paramount film "Willy Wonka and the Chocolate Factory." ⓫ As Prudence composes her poems, they appear in a book in her handwriting.

Back wall crypt. More mansion creators are honored in a Standby crypt that's not interactive: ❶ Paul Frees, the voice of the Ghost Host ("Farewell forever, Mister Frees; Your voice will carry on the breeze."); ❷ Ken Anderson, concept artist ("Drink a toast to our friend Ken. Fill your glass and don't say 'when.'"); ❸ Rolly Crump, key developer ("While Brother Roland here reposes, his soul's above, one supposes."); ❹ and Blaine Gibson, character sculptor ("A train made a stain of absent-minded Uncle Blaine. Rest in pieces."). ❺ A gate to the graveyard stands ready for the graveyard caretaker, a character seen later on the ride at the gate of the back graveyard, cowering with his dog. ❻ A small door in the gate provides for it. ❼ The caretaker's shoe prints lead to and away from the gate. ❽ So do the dog's paw prints.

Tombstones. A graveyard sits to the left of the Haunted Mansion entranceway. Seen from the Standby queue, its tombstones hide tributes to the imagineers who designed and built the attraction. ❶ Xavier ("X") Atencio's headstone stands in a sliver of land within the standby queue. Atencio wrote the mansion's script, created the lyrics to "Grim Grinning Ghosts" (see Inspirations) and coined the term "Doom Buggy." He also wrote the script of the original Pirates of the Caribbean attraction, the lyrics to its theme song "Yo Ho (A Pirate's Life for Me)" and the lyrics to "The Bear Band Serenade" at the Country Bear Jamboree. A key Disney staffer for decades, Atencio also helped animate the 1940 movie "Fantasia." (His inscription reads "Requeisat Francis Xavier. No time off for good behavior.") ❷ Dave Burkhart built mansion architecture and show models. The Haunted Mansion was one of his biggest projects. ("Dear departed Brother Dave. He chased a bear into a cave.") ❸ Harriet Burns, Disney's first female imagineer, built mansion models, finished figure models and designed sets for the attraction. Her tall obelisk is themed to the opera, and includes a tiny horned Viking helmet near its top. ("First Lady of the opera, our haunting Harriet. Searched for a tune but could never carry it.") ❹ Collin Campbell created concept art for all of Walt Disney World. Ironically, he died just a few days after his obelisk debuted in 2011. It stands in a paved portion of the standby queue. ❺ Claude Coats championed the mansion's scary elements. ("At peaceful rest lies Brother Claude. Planted here beneath this sod.") ❻ Marc Davis masterminded the ride's silly elements, including its cartoonish faces and sight gags. One of Disney's legendary "Nine Old Men," he was a key company artist. His characters included Cruella De Vil, Maleficent and Tinker Bell. His tombstone stands in a sliver of land within the standby queue. ("In memory of our patriarch. Dear departed Grandpa Marc.") ❼ Yale Gracey developed nearly all of the mansion's special effects. His tombstone—which is in its own small plot in the standby queue, surrounded by crypts—refers to him as "master" as a tribute to his mastery of his craft, though many fans mistake the word to mean that "Gracey" is the head of the mansion household. ("Master Gracey, laid to rest. No mourning please at his request.") ❽ Placed there by cast members playfully paying their respects to both the character and the person, a real red rose often rests atop Gracey's grave. It's picked from roses that grow on the

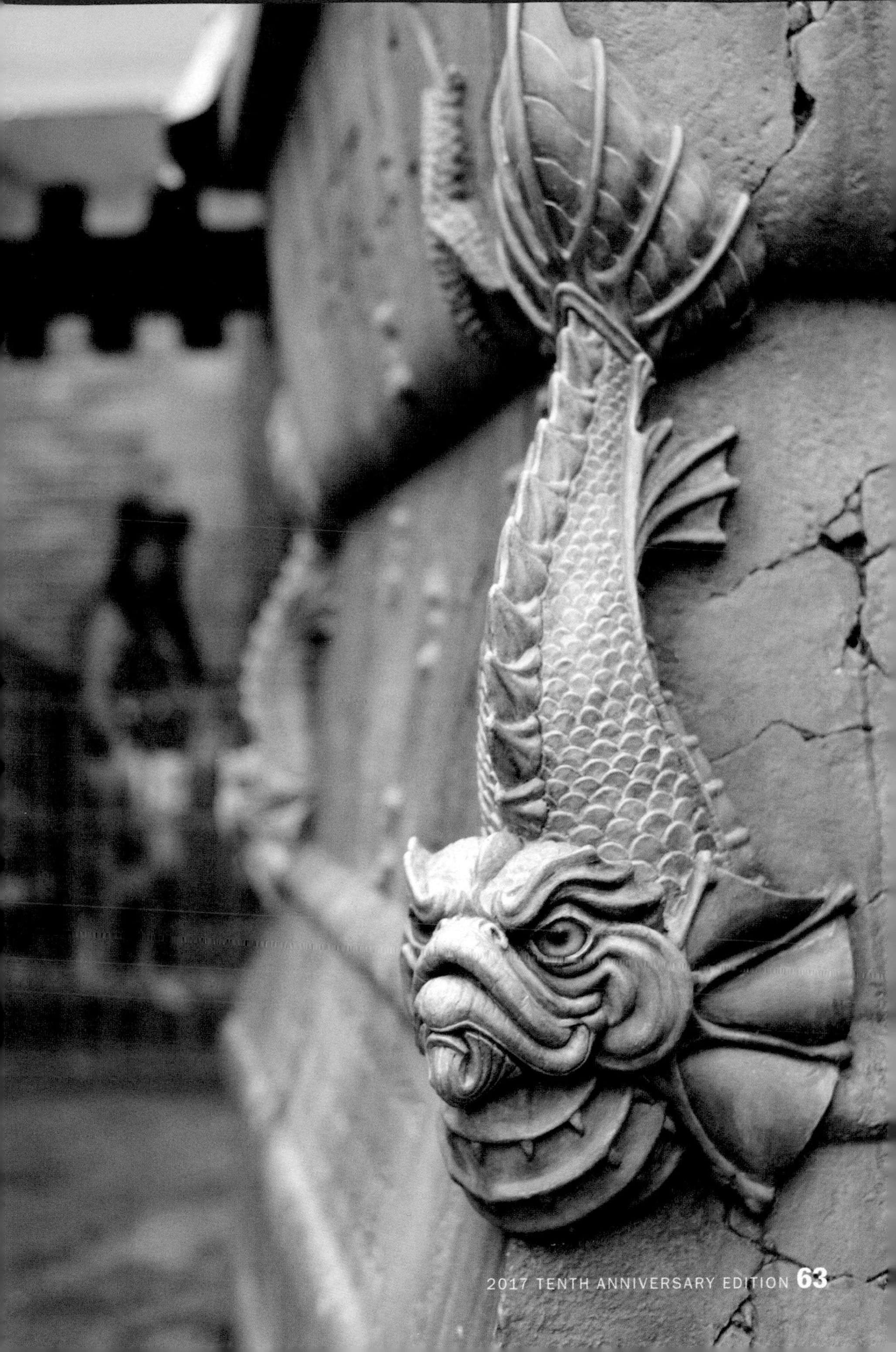

Foyer portrait.

grounds. ❾ Cliff Huet designed the building's interior. ("Rest in peace Cousin Huet. We all know you didn't do it.") ❿ Fred Joerger designed all the original rock work at Walt Disney World, including that of the mansion's exit crypts. ("Here lies good old Fred. A great big rock fell on his head.") ⓫ Bud Martin designed the mansion's lighting. ("Here lies a man named Martin. The lights went out on this old spartan.") ⓬ Chuck Myall was a Walt Disney World master planner. ("In memoriam Uncle Myall. Here you'll lie for quite a while.") ⓭ Artist Dorothea Redmond painted mansion concept art. She also did the concepts of the mosaic murals of Cinderella Castle. The first female production designer in Hollywood,

Redmond designed the sets for more than 30 movies, including 1939's "Gone With the Wind" and many Alfred Hitchcock films. Her obelisk has no epitaph. ⓮ Wathel Rogers helped pioneer Disney's Audio-Animatronics technology, which is used throughout the mansion. His earlier work included Disney's robotic Abraham Lincoln figure and Carousel of Progress family. He later became the art director of the Magic Kingdom. ("Here rests Wathel R. Bender. He rode to glory on a fender.") ⓯ Robert Sewell led Disney's model makers. ("R.I.P. Mister Sewell. The victim of a dirty duel.") ⓰ Disney artist Leota ("Lee") Toombs posed for the mansion's disembodied head that speaks from inside a crystal ball, a

Library.

spiritualist who became known as "Madame Leota." Chosen for the part because her eyes were the right distance apart to fit a test model, she also provided the face and voice of "Little Leota," the eerie bride at the end of the ride. Toombs' stone (ha!) is the only one with an embossed face, and the only one that's animated. Its face tilts forward and back, its closed eyelids open and its green eyes shift from side to side. The movements occur about once a minute. Children often notice them first. Born Leota Wharton, Toombs married Disney animator Harvey Toombs in 1947. Her daughter Kim Irvine animated the face of the bride in the attic. The marker's epitaph ("Dear sweet Leota, beloved by all. In regions beyond now, but having a ball.") recalls one of Madame Leota's incantations ("Creepies and crawlies, toads in a pond; let there be music, from regions beyond."). ⑰ Audio engineer Gordon Williams created the attraction's sound effects. ("R.I.P. Good friend Gordon. Now you've crossed the river Jordan.")

Hilltop tombstones. Tough-to-see stones honor fictional mansion characters, some of which existed only in unused concepts for it. ① One marks the grave of Bartholomew Gore, a ghostly pirate captain featured in the very first story treatment for The Haunted Mansion, written in 1957. ② Another honors Gore's bride Priscilla, whom he murdered in that tale. ③ A third is for Beauregard, the name proposed for a live butler who would have guided guests through the Gore mansion. ④ Five markers up high on the hill mark the graves of the singing bust characters seen later in the ride's graveyard: Cousin Algernon (a moniker that comes from the 1895 Oscar Wilde play, "The Importance of Being Earnest"), ⑤ Ned Nub, ⑥ Phineas Pock, ⑦ Rollo Rumkin, ⑧ and Uncle Theodore (the broken bust). Disney identified the names of the bust in 1960s concept art but doesn't on the ride. ⑨ Hidden under trees on the hill in overgrowth, two tombstones honor two of the ride's hitchhiking ghosts: Gus, the short bearded prisoner ⑩ and Ezra, the lanky, bug-eyed skeleton. ⑪ Two gravedigger shovels are thrust into the bottom of the hill. Vines curl up their shafts.

Mansion foyer. ① As you enter an unseen owl hoots and flaps away. ② A cross-eyed, arrow-tongued face appears in the pattern of the fireplace grate. ③ In a portrait above the fireplace, a young debonair man morphs into an old man who turns bug-eyed and bony as he transforms into a skeleton.

Portrait gallery. ① Monstrous faces appear in patterns in floor grates. ② Bat-eared gargoyles on the walls hold flickering candles. ③ The voice of the Ghost Host circles the gallery. ④ Creaks fill the air as the chamber begins to stretch. ⑤ In one portrait, a widow who sits on the tombstone of her husband is Constance Hatchaway, the bride in the attic. ⑥ Unseen bones clatter to the floor after the Ghost Host reveals his hanging corpse. ⑦ Unseen bats flap away after the exit door opens. ⑧ Gargoyles whisper "stay together" after the Ghost Host urges groups to "all stay together, please." ⑨ The gargoyles giggle. ⑩ Linger too long in the gallery and they hiss "Get out!"

Boarding area. ① A distant wolf howls. ② Grinning skulls frame doors. ③ Screaming skulls top woodwork. ④ Toothy brass bats top chain stanchions. ⑤ A bat-shaped lamp to the left of the Doom Buggy track illuminates the ride's safety warnings. ⑥ Hung on the walls are seven portraits that have appeared in the mansion since it opened. Among the subjects are an arsonist in front of a burning building; ⑦ Capt. Culpepper Clyne, a ghostly seafarer who holds a harpoon; ⑧ the mansion's Ghost Host, a tall, ghoulish man who clutches a hatchet and has a severed noose hanging from his neck; ⑨ Rasputin, an ominous, bearded man with clasped hands; ⑩ Jack the Ripper, a mustachioed man with a top hat and a disturbing grin, who grips a knife; ⑪ Dracula, a smiling pale man who wears a cape and holds a lantern aloft; ⑫ and the Witch of Walpurgis, a black-haired woman who holds a black cat.

On the ride. ① Half eagle and half lion, a rearing griffin appears on your left at the base of a candelabrum. ② A second candelabrum floats above you. ③ A wrinkled crone ④ and a stern upper-class couple who stands in front of a painting of the Haunted Mansion are among the subjects of wall portraits.

Portrait hall. Everyday subjects transform into extraordinary ones when flashes of lightning illuminate a line of paintings on the wall. ① A reclining young woman holding a rose turns into a snarling white tiger holding a bone. ② A knight and rearing horse turn skeletal. ③ A stately sailing ship changes into a ghost ship. ④ A woman's hair turns into snakes, her body gets covered by snake bites as she morphs into Medusa. Her necklace turns into a serpent.

Library. ① Glowing marble busts between the bookshelves seem to turn their heads

Passed performers. Left: "The Phantom of the Opera," 1925. Right: The mansion organist.

and follow you with their eyes. ❷ Carved bats leer at you from the library's paneling. ❸ A ladder teeters as an unseen ghost atop it shuffles between the shelves. ❹ An abstract image of Donald Duck appears in a rope-like pattern on a red velvet chair. Similar chairs appear later in the mansion. ❺ The chair rocks by itself. ❻ Snarling beast heads extend from columns. Similar columns appear in the upcoming corridor of doors and ballroom.

Music room. ❶ Sheet music on the floor has staff lines but no notes, implying the composer died before completing his work. ❷ Behind the piano, a storm brews outside a window. ❸ Upright coffins top the sides of the window frame. ❹ Other instruments in the room include a violin on a settee to the left of the piano, and an ornate cello to the right. ❺ Sheet music for a "Vocal Concert in the Open Air" foreshadows the ride's graveyard scene. It's on a music stand. ❻ A large griffin forms the base of a banister.

Staircases. ❶ Ghostly glowing footprints climb the stairs.

Endless hallway area. ❶ Small demons hiss at you from the wallpaper. ❷ Their eyes blink and glow. ❸ A suit of armor subtly moves. It holds a shield and an elaborate axe.

❹ Carved fang-baring serpents hang from crown molding.

Conservatory. ❶ The coffin's handles look like bats. ❷ Withered plants and rotting flowers remain from a funeral. ❸ Perched on a wilted wreath, the mansion's raven glares at you with glowing red eyes.

Corridor of doors. ❶ The Hatbox Ghost appears in framed sketches on the walls. In one, a crown tops his head. ❷ A cut noose hangs from the Ghost Host in another sketch. His shadow raises an axe. ❸ Clangs, knocks, moans and laughter fill the air. ❹ Doorknobs turn, their knobs snarling serpents. ❺ Mace knockers bang. ❻ Some doors appear to breathe. ❼ Menacing faces hide in transom patterns above the doors. ❽ Green light leaks out from the last door on each side of the corridor. ❾ "Tomb Sweet Tomb" reads a sampler. ❿ A grandfather clock channels a demon. Its casing forms hair and eyes, its face a fanged mouth, its pendulum is a tail. ⓫ Spinning backward, the clock's glowing dial marks the hour "13." ⓬ The shadow of a giant clawed hand passes in front of the clock.

Seance room. ❶ Lit candles and tarot cards top Madame Leota's table. ❷ The ride's raven settles on her velvet chair. ❸ A harp, tambourine and trumpet are among the instruments that float around the room. ❹ Other flying objects include a bullfighter's red cape and a flickering Tiffany lamp with its table. ❺ A green orb leaves a glowing trail as it wanders along a back wall.

Ballroom. ❶ Ripped drapes flutter in a breeze. ❷ An old woman knits in a rocking chair in front of a fireplace. She appears in the same pose as the grandmother in the Tomorrowland attraction Walt Disney's Carousel of Progress. ❸ The ballroom's blazing fire is a ghostly green. ❹ A ghost on the mantle wears a top hat, and has his arm around a bust of a stern old woman (a bust once planned to sing along with the five male busts in the graveyard). ❺ The fireplace grate forms black-cat silhouettes. ❻ A hearse is backed up to an opened door. A coffin has fallen out of it. ❼ Five ghosts float out of the coffin. ❽ The female dancers lead the males, due to an oversight in Disney's Pepper's Ghost design. Since the figures are actually reflected into the ballroom, their images are reversed. ❾ At the banquet table, a female ghost has been presented a "death-day" cake, topped by 13 candles. ❿ Each time she blows out the candles, she also blows out the apparitions of the ghosts around her. ⓫ One of the ghosts is a dead-ringer for a Pirate of the Caribbean: the sprawled-out blubbery buccaneer who blathers on about his treasure map. ⓬ A drunken ghost has slid under the table and passed out. ⓭ Julius Caesar ("Great Caesar's ghost!") sits at the end of the table. ⓮ His lover Cleopatra perches above him on the chandelier. ⓯ She's with her later conquest, Marc Antony. ⓰ Mr. Pickwick, from the Charles Dickens 1836 novel "The Pickwick Papers," swings from the chandelier. ⓱ Banshees rise out of the pipes of the ballroom organ. ⓲ Its music stand forms a leering bat. ⓳ Appearing in separate portraits on the back wall, two ghosts duel above a balcony. Painted with their backs to each other, they emerge from their paintings to turn and fire pistols. ⓴ In another portrait, a blonde's opera glasses have eyes of their own. It's left of the balcony, obscured by shadows.

Attic. ❶ "Here Comes the Bride" (Wagner's "Bridal Chorus") wafts through the air, its chords melancholy and off-key. ❷ A heart thumps in the background. ❸ Props from earlier versions of the ride hide in the bric-a-brac: ❹ the red carpet which lay under the previous bride (beneath the first wedding portrait); ❺ a candelabrum that once sat atop the music room piano (near the third wedding portrait); ❻ a carpet bag that previously held a pop-up ghost in the attic (to the right of Constance); ❼ and an old lamp that originally hung over Leota's crystal ball (across from Constance). ❽ The bride's marriage certificates of bride Constance Hatchaway are scattered throughout the attic. ❾ The heads of her grooms fade and disappear from her wedding portraits. ❿ The bride's expression changes from portrait to portrait. At first she's grimacing, as she poses with a short humble country boy, Ambrose Harper, who wears an ill-fitting suit. ⓫ A nearby wedding album reads "Our Wedding Day." ⓬ After her second marriage—to banker Frank Banks—she looks bored. ⓭ A hanging banner reads "True Love Forever." ⓮ In her third portrait, after hooking Chinese diplomat Marquis de Doome, she hides a smile. Her husband wears military regalia, including a sash, medals and a plumed hat. ⓯ For her fourth wedding portrait Constance is pleased, after marrying spiffy if stocky Reginald Caine, a gambling railroad tycoon who sports a gem in his lapel and a ring on his little finger. ⓰ The spoils of his globe-trotting adventures litter the floor. ⓱ After her fifth wedding, the bride is smiling and satisfied, having snagged wealthy George Hightower. ⓲ She holds a rose in this final portrait, just like she does in her stretching-room portrait. ⓳ A suit of armor and a harp are among the couple's many wedding gifts, which surround the portrait's ornate frame. ⓴ Constance wears the same dress in each portrait, but always another string of pearls. ㉑ The hatchet she used to behead her grooms rests on the floor to the right of a wedding cake. ㉒ Her ghost brandishes a glowing version of the weapon, and giggles sinister variations on classic wedding vows—"In sickness and in wealth!" ㉓ The hats of her grooms hang on a rack across from her. ㉔ Hatboxes behind it allude to the Hatbox Ghost, the character originally intended for the spot. ◆

Graveyard. ❶ A raven caws from a branch to your right. ❷ The archway of the graveyard's gate forms a monstrous face. ❸ A golden hoop earring adorns one of the ghouls who pop up behind the tombstones after each chorus of "Grim Grinning Ghosts." ❹ Some of the stones "quake," just as the lyrics of the song say they do. ❺ A medieval minstrel band consists of a flutist emerging from his crypt, ❻ a drummer beating bones against it, ❼ a kilt-wearing bagpiper, ❽ a soldier playing a small harp ❾ and a trumpeter wearing pajamas. ⑩ When the trumpeter rears up with a flourish, two owls above him do too. ⑪ Sitting on tombs to the right of the band, some cats hiss and yowl to its beat. ⑫ A skeletal dog howls on a hill. ⑬ A king and queen ride a makeshift seesaw—a board balanced on a tombstone. ⑭ Their princess daughter swings from a nearby tree branch, sipping tea. ⑮ A British duke and duchess toast at a candle-lit table. ⑯ Bicycling ghosts circle behind them. ⑰ A skeletal corpse raises a teacup behind a grave. ⑱ Sometimes he raises his head. ⑲ A floating teapot pours tea into a cup. ⑳ Tracks veering off your path lead to a hearse stuck in mud. ㉑ Its driver chats with a duchess sitting atop the hearse sipping tea. ㉒ A ghost sits up from a coffin that's fallen out of the back of the hearse. ㉓ He chats with a sea captain. ㉔ A skinny dog sniffs an Egyptian sarcophagus. ㉕ As it stirs its tea, the mummy mumbles through its bandages. ㉖ "What's that? Louder! I can't hear you! Eh?" cries an old bearded man leaning toward the mummy, holding a horn to his ear. ㉗ The Grim Reaper hovers in a tomb, his beady eyes staring at you from inside a dark hood. ㉘ Opera-singing ghosts in Viking gear belt out solos. ㉙ Holding his severed head, a decapitated knight stands alongside his executioner. ㉚ The executioner cheerfully sings a duet with a pint-sized prisoner, who just around the corner has escaped to become a hitchhiking ghost. ㉛ As you leave the graveyard, the raven appears above you.

Mausoleum. ❶ A portrait of Cousin Maude Sweeny lays next to the hitchhiking ghosts. A member of the Dread family, Maude appears on a bust in the standby queue. ❷ In the reflection of your Doom Buggy, your hitchhiker may stretch your face, place a hat on your head, blow your head up like a balloon, or switch heads with you. ❸ "Hurry back... hurry back..." a miniature bride beckons from above, in the attraction's creepiest moment. "Be sure to bring your death certificate if you decide to join us." ❹ The little bride clutches a dead bouquet. ❺ Her veil flutters in a breeze.

Exitway. ❶ Yellow bat silhouettes replace the typical safety shoe prints on the moving walkway. ❷ Human arms hold up wall sconces. ❸ As you leave the ghosts make one last pitch for you to join them, singing an a cappella dirge of "Grim Grinning Ghosts" (*"If you would like to join our jamboree, there's a simple rule that's compulsory. Mortals pay a token fee. Rest in peace, the haunting's free. So hurry back, we would like your company."*)

❹ Valet bells hang in one of the exitway's "Servant's quarters," an area that's closed to most visitors. Again honoring imagineers, each is for a mythical room: Ambassador Xavier's Lounging Lodge (Xavier Atencio), ❺ Colonel Coats' Breakfast Berth (Claude Coats), ❻ Uncle Davis' Sleeping Salon (Marc Davis), ❼ Master Gracey's Bedchamber (Yale Gracey), ❽ Grandfather McKim's Resting Room (a tribute to Sam McKim, a mansion concept artist), ❾ Professor Wathel's Reposing Lounge (Wathel Rogers), ❿ and Madame Leota's Boudoir (Leota Toombs).

Outdoor crypts. Occupants of crypts outside the exit have puns for names: ❶ Asher T. Ashes, ❷ Bea Witch, ❸ C. U. Later, ❹ Clare Voince, ❺ Dustin T. Dust, ❻ Hail N. Hardy, ❼ Hal Lusinashun, ❽ Hap A. Rition, ❾ I. Emma Spook, ❿ I. M. Ready, ⓫ I. Trudy Dew, ⓬ Love U. Trudy, ⓭ M. T. Tomb, ⓮ Manny Festation, ⓯ Metta Fisiks, ⓰ Paul Tergyst, ⓱ Pearl E. Gates, ⓲ Rustin Peece, ⓳ Rusty Gates and ⓴ Wee G. Bord. ㉑ "The seventh did him in" explains the inscription on a large crypt that holds Bluebeard and six of his seven wives. In the folktale, after his seventh spouse Lucretia discovers that the French aristocrat had murdered each of his previous wives, she had her brothers kill him.

Pet cemetery. ❶ Mr. Toad rests at the back left corner of this small wooded hillside. His grave is an inside joke, Disney toying with the idea that it killed the character in 1997 when it converted the raucous Mr. Toad's Wild Ride to the Many Adventures of Winnie the Pooh. Other pet cemetery residents: ❷ Eric, a snake named for Disney Imagineer Eric Jacobson, who led the mansion's 2007–2012 refurbishment (the snake "met his fate at the hands of a garden rake"); ❸ Little Maisy, a poodle ("So prim and proper and never lazy. All you do now is push up daisies."); ❹ Rover, a dog ("Every dog has his day. Too bad today was your last."); ❺ a duck ("Little Waddle saw the truck. But Little Waddle didn't duck.") ❻ and a cat ("Nine lives always go so fast. Poor Whiskers couldn't make them last."). ❼ A small circular plaque lists how the cat lost his lives—"bad catnip," "a shoe at two," "sour milk," "hairball," "one bad year," "same year," "local dog," and "fell off limb." ❽ Faux bird chatter comes from the trees. ❾ Red-eyed dogs and grape-eating snakes appear in the wrought-iron frames of nearby benches.

Memento Mori gift shop. ❶ The eye on the store's main sign follows you. ❷ Madame Leota's face hides in a pupil on a sign facing

Cast member. Wearing special makeup for Mickey's Not-So-Scary Halloween Party.

Fantasyland. ❸ In the shop her face materializes in a mirror, accompanied by a snippet of "Grim Grinning Ghosts." ❹ Roses and a raven trim the mirror's frame. ❺ Holding a skull, the mortal Leota appears in a wall portrait, with her tarot cards and crystal ball. ❻ The portrait changes when her spirit visits the shop. The skull's eye sockets shine orange, a green-eyed black cat appears at her feet, and a red-eyed raven spreads its wings behind her. ❼ Eyes of demons appear in the shop's wallpaper at that time. ❽ "The Old Curiosity Shop," an 1841 Charles Dickens novel about how death transforms living angels into heavenly ones, lays on a bottom shelf to the right of Leota's portrait. ❾ Her face appears on brooches worn by female sales clerks. ❿ Atop merchandise shelves are potion ingredients, ⓫ flickering candles and ⓬ raven-adorned candelabra. ⓭ Spiderwebs decorate the woodwork of merchandise racks. ⓮ A flaming red ghost light hovers in a jar on the far left of a shelf on the wall with Leota's portrait. ⓯ A sparkly blue ghost light floats in a jar on a shelf on the right side of the store, near a small window. ⓰ A fiery blue ghost light appears to the left of the shop's small Spirit Photography image studio, in a jar on a high shelf. ⓱ Complete with a wooden frame and a crank, the studio's huge camera resembles a 19th-century antique. ⓲ Skeletons wear Victorian attire on the studio's linen wallpaper. ⓳ Have your ghostly picture taken and a cast member will inform you that your impression will be ready when "the spirits ring the bell"—an allusion to one of Madame Leota's incantations in the mansion's seance room. ⓴ A bell eventually rings.

Nightmare nods. The ride hides seven shout-outs to the 1993 movie "The Nightmare Before Christmas." ❶ Jack Skellington's face is in the library, on the spine of a book on a table. ❷ His image is on a red book on the floor below that table. ❸ As you enter the attic, a Jack doll sits on a far-right shelf. ❹ His face is on a red book on the attic floor, near the bride's second wedding portrait. ❺ A Jack snowglobe sits on a shelf in the attic's back right corner. ❻ The black-and-white-striped limbs of a Jack plush stick out from behind the hatboxes. ❼ A doll that looks like Sally hides on a nearby shelf, under a table.

Hidden Mickeys. ❶ Three barnacles form a cockeyed Mickey on the crypt of Capt. Culpepper Clyne, just under and between the "R" in "Culpepper" and the "C" in "Clyne." ❷ The mansion's circular foyer and two stretching rooms inadvertently form the three circles. ❸ Mickey appears twice in the music room, in the metal loops of the music stand. ❹ In the ballroom he's formed by the left-most place setting on the near side of the banquet table. ❺ In the attic he's created by plates on the floor near the third wedding portrait. ❻ In the graveyard he's held aloft by the silhouette of the Grim Reaper.

Early in the morning.

Frontierland

Twangin' banjo and fiddle music—and cast members clad in gingham and denim—welcome you to this lighthearted look at 19th-century rural America.

Fun finds. ❶ Texas John Slaughter's Academy of Etiquette "will make 'em do what they oughta," vows a poster left of the Frontierland Shootin' Arcade. That's a shout-out to the theme song of the 1950s Disney television serial "Texas John Slaughter"—*"Texas John Slaughter made 'em do what they oughta, and if they didn't, they died."* ❷ Another sign feigns Public Outrage over the opening of a saloon, between the Frontier Trading Post and Frontier Mercantile. ❸ At Pecos Bill Tall Tale Inn and Café, "Diarrhoea or worms" are solved by Herrick's vegetable pills, according to a poster outside the main entrance. ❹ The legend of Pecos Bill—the toughest cowboy who ever lived—hangs inside on the right. ❺ Display cases hold artifacts of Bill's famous friends Johnny Appleseed, Buffalo Bill, Paul Bunyan, Davy Crockett and the Lone Ranger. ❻ "Respect the land, defend the defenseless... and don't ever spit in front of women and children." That's Bill's Code of the West. It hangs on a wall just inside the middle entrance.

Hidden Mickey. Loops of rope form the shape above a cash register at the Frontier Trading Post, to the left and above a sign that explains "How to Pin Trade."

Live entertainment

Your choice: square dancin' or toe-tappin':

★★★ **Frontierland Hoedown.** Spoons and washboards are played by the Country Bears—OK, not my first choice—but the square dancing is the real thing and friendly country couples show you how to do it. Just in case you never much cottoned to it in 5th grade. *20-min shows typically Tue–Sat afternoons. In front of the Country Bear Jamboree.*

★★★★ ✔ The Notorious Banjo Brothers and Bob. Two pickers and a tuba player play Disney tunes, bluegrass, cowboy melodies. *20-min. shows typically 11a–5:30p Tue, Thur–Sat; 1:30p–5:30p Wed. Roaming Frontierland.*

Restaurants and food

A formerly seasonal-only spot is the best bet: **UPDATED! ★★★ $35 DDP The Diamond Horseshoe.** Now open year-round, this saloon and dance hall serves food from the nearby Liberty Tree Tavern kitchens. There's no drinkin' or dancin', but for Frontierland vittles it can't be beat. Lunch is a buffet. Dinner is all-you-can-eat, brought to your table: cornbread, salad, meats, potatoes, veggies, dessert. *11:30a–8:30p; $33 (children $19). Seats 190.*

UPDATED! ★★★ $19 DDPq Pecos Bill Tall Tale Inn and Café. A new Tex-Mex menu at this fast-food spot has burritos, fajitas, nachos, a taco burger. The fixins' bar has salsa. Dessert? Churros. Back dining rooms are the quietest. *10:30a–park close; $12–$16 (children $5–$6). Seats 1,107.*

★★ $15 DDPs Golden Oak Outpost. Chicken nuggets. *Outdoor stand. Walkway to Adventureland. 11a–5p; $10. Seats 99 outdoors.*

★★★ $8 DDPs Westward Ho. Corn dogs, chocolate-chip cookies, frozen lemonade. *Outdoor stand. 9a–park close; $3–$5.*

Shops and merchandise

Some unique plushies, pins and Splash Mountain merchandise top the list here:

Big Al's. Character plushies, Jessie and Woody dolls, raccoon-tail hats, other novelty caps, sundries. *Outdoor stand. Across from the Country Bear Jamboree.*

Briar Patch. Kitchen housewares; packaged food and candy; mugs; souvenirs; children's apparel, infantwear; plushies (notably Thumper from "Bambi" and Tod the fox from "The Fox and the Hound"); Goat Mountain soaps; young children's toys; tees; caps, novelty caps, Mickey headbands; sundries. *In front of Splash Mountain.*

Frontier Trading Post. Many pins, pin sets, lanyards; MagicBands; unusual character plushies; some other plushies; rock specimens; hats, novelty caps, Mickey headbands; sundries. *On the main walkway, across from Tom Sawyer Island.*

Prairie Outpost & Supply. Confectionery counter, candy dispensers. Also packaged candy and foods; kitchen items. *On the main walkway, across from Tom Sawyer Island.*

Splashdown Photos. Splash Mountain souvenirs (photo frames, shirts, mugs, plastic plates); Thumper dolls; beach towels; packaged foods; hats; sundries. *At the exit of Splash Mountain.*

Frontierland Shootin' Arcade. Targets move when hit, $1 gets you 25 shots.

The Five Bear Rugs. The house band.

Country Bear Jamboree

Corny, classic musical revue stars robotic bears

★★ It helps to have a good attitude at this musical revue, where goofy-faced robotic bears sing tidbits of old-time country and cowboy songs. It's as cornball as a "Hee-Haw" rerun, true, but in an endearing sort of way.

On one hand, the show takes place in a friendly hall where everyone is welcome. The Audio-Animatronic bears are pretty impressive, particularly the one who lowers from the ceiling on a swing, then sways back and forth, especially when you consider that the show debuted decades ago, when computers were barely a thing. Each of the 18 life-sized bears has a distinct personality and appearance. Some song lyrics invariably make people laugh—"every guy who turns me on turns me down;" "mama, don't whip little Buford, I think you should shoot him instead." Along with the nearby Hall of Presidents, the show is a rare way for people who can't go on rides to see vintage Disney Audio-Animatronic figures.

On the other hand—the sexism. For the most part male bears are presented as skilled performers, likeable good 'ol boys. Females, however, are always emotional, fat, flirtatious, needy, randy or outright drunk.

Tips. *When to go:* Mid-afternoon, when other lines are lengthy, and you want to get out of the sun. *Where to sit:* In the middle of a middle row. You'll be able to see the bears' faces well, and hear the songs clearly.

Fun facts. ❶ Two songs come from legendary cowboy star Tex Ritter: 1950's "My Woman Ain't Pretty (But She Don't Swear None)" and 1937's "Blood On the Saddle," known as the goriest country song of all time during its heyday. ❷ Legendary Disney animator Marc Davis—he drew Cruella De Vil, Maleficent and Tinker Bell—designed the bears' faces; he also did those of the Pirates of the Caribbean and the animals in It's a Small World. ❸ Disney designed the show in the 1960s for a never-built resort in California's Sequoia National Forest. ❹ It was said to be Walt Disney's favorite attraction.

Key facts. *Duration:* 11 min. *Capacity:* 380. *Queue:* Indoor. *Showtimes:* Continuous. *Operating hours:* Opens 10a. *Debuted:* 1971, revised 2013. *Access:* Wheelchairs, ECVs OK. *Disability services:* Assistive listening, reflective captioning. *Location:* Next to Pecos Bill Tall Tale Inn.

Tom needs a spell checker.

Tom Sawyer Island

Caves, forts, trails offer safe, old-fashioned experience

★★★ This small wooded island is rarely crowded, a definitive break from theme-park madness. Meant to recall the classic 1876 novel by Mark Twain, "The Adventures of Tom Sawyer," its shady sidewalks are studded with small adventures, none of which are dependent on a video screen or any modern tech. You can explore Injun Joe's Cave, Old Scratch's Mystery Mine, a windmill and a charming watermill. Atop a hill are a brook, duck pond, playground and two picnic tables.

Across a suspension footbridge, a second island holds frontier outpost Fort Langhorn, complete with a snoring sentry and robotic horses. Toy rifles in its towers can fire at Big Thunder Mountain trains and the riverboat.

While the idea of the island is charming, the reality of it may prove on the dull side for modern kids. You get to the islands on a powered raft and return that way too, which can take awhile.

Tips. *When to go:* In the morning or about 90 minutes before dusk, when it's not so hot out. *Hidden things to do:* Play checkers at various tables. Cross over a bouncy barrel bridge. Worm your way through a "secret" escape tunnel at the very back of the fort.

Fun fact. The bird trapped in the mill's cogs re-creates a scene from the landmark 1937 Disney short "The Old Mill."

Fun finds. ❶ The mill's various creaks and groans subtly create the tune "Down By The Old Mill Stream." ❷ The women's restroom at Fort Langhorn is labeled "Powder Room."

Key facts. *Duration:* Give it 1–2 hrs. *Capacity:* 400. *Queue:* Outdoor, covered. *Fear factor:* Toddlers can get lost in the cave's side niches. *Operating hours:* Typically 10a–dusk. *Weather issues:* Rafts don't run in thunderstorms. *Debuted:* 1973. *Access:* Must be ambulatory. *Location:* The raft dock is across from the entrance to Splash Mountain.

Average wait times (for raft trips, each direction)

9a	10a	11a	12p	1p	2p	3p	4p	5p	6p	7p	8p	9p	10p	11p
---	5m	5m	15m	20m	20m	20m	15m	5m	5m	5m	5m	---	---	---

Splashdown.

Splash Mountain

Elaborate log flume recalls forgotten Disney film

★★★★ FP+ You plunge 52 feet (16 meters) into a soaking splashdown during this half-mile flume ride, which recalls Disney's 1946 film "Song of the South." A hollowed-out log takes you through bayous, swamps, a cave and a flooded mine as you witness a fox and bear's attempts to snare a sly rabbit. The ride's bright colors, Audio-Animatronics characters and peppy music will appeal to children; its many false drops and big fall to thrill-seekers.

Based on folk tales popular with slaves in the antebellum South, a vague storyline portrays how tiny Brer ("brother") Rabbit is continually threatened by Brer Fox and Brer Bear, but always outsmarts them. In his final escape, the hare tricks the fox into tossing him safely back home, where he is welcomed by his friends.

Tip. *Where to sit:* The front seat for the best view and to get soaked, the back seat to stay relatively dry.

Fun finds. ❻ "FSU!" cheer two gophers who pop down from the ceiling as you enter the flooded Laughing Place. That's a literal shout-out to Florida State University, the alma mater of one of the ride's imagineers.

Hidden Mickeys. ❶ As stacked barrels on the right side of the second lift. ❷ Inside the mountain as a bobber left of a picnic basket. ❸ As a hanging rope in the flooded cavern, just past a turtle. ❹ In the riverboat scene, as a full-figure Mickey reclining in a cloud.

Key facts. *Duration:* 12 min. *Capacity:* 440. *Queue:* Indoor. *Fear factor:* A small drop is completely dark; the big one can scare adults. *Restraint:* Lap bar. *Weather issues:* Closed during thunderstorms. *Debuted:* 1992 (Disneyland 1989). *Health advisory:* You should be free from motion sickness; pregnancy; high blood pressure; heart, back or neck problems. *Access:* Height min 40 in (102 cm); must be ambulatory.

Average wait times (standby line)

9a	10a	11a	12p	1p	2p	3p	4p	5p	6p	7p	8p	9p	10p	11p
20m	50m	55m	70m	70m	65m	65m	70m	65m	60m	50m	40m	40m	20m	5m

All curves all the time.

Big Thunder Mountain Railroad

Runaway mine train has super swerves, scant scares

★★★★★ ✔ FP+ Full of fun, this rollicking roller coaster is ideal for those who like fast turns but not big drops. All curves all of the time, it's exciting but never scary. Meant to be a trip through Utah's Monument Valley, the track takes you around and through a realistic mountain that's filled with detail. Sights include swarming bats inside a watery cave, hot springs, a flooded town, a collapsing mine shaft, even some dinosaur bones. Scattered throughout the landscape are live cactus, as well as hundreds of pieces of authentic mining gear, which Disney scoured from ghost towns during the 1970s. There are also about 20 fairly realistic animals, including big-horned sheep, bobcats and javelinas.

Like many coasters, it runs faster late in a day, after its track grease fully melts.

In 2013 the attraction was spiffed up with an interactive queue that's packed with hundreds of little things to look for.

Tips. *When to go:* At night. Every swerve comes as a surprise, as the scenery is lit but not the track. *Where to sit:* For the truly wildest ride, the back seat.

Hidden Mickeys. ❶ The shape appears on your right on the first chain lift, formed by stalagmites on the floor of the cave. ❷ Again on your right at the end of the ride as rusty gears on the ground; easy to see, as it comes up when your train has slowed to a crawl.

Key facts. *Duration:* 4 min. *Capacity:* 150. *Queue:* ●utdoor, covered. *Fear factor:* Jerky, violent turns toss riders in their seats. *Restraint:* Lap bar. *Top speed:* 36 miles per hour (58 kph). *Weather issues:* Closed during thunderstorms. *Debuted:* 1980 (Disneyland 1979). *Health advisory:* Disney advises that riders should be free from motion sickness; pregnancy; high blood pressure; heart, back or neck problems. *Access:* Height min 40 in (102 cm); must be ambulatory.

Average wait times (standby line)

9a	10a	11a	12p	1p	2p	3p	4p	5p	6p	7p	8p	9p	10p	11p
15m	40m	40m	45m	50m	45m	40m	40m	35m	35m	40m	30m	30m	20m	5m

Utah's Monument Valley.

Big Thunder Mountain Railroad: A Closer Look

By Micaela Neal. Big Thunder Mountain Railroad is the rare roller coaster that tells a story, a tale of a frontier mining town with such a relentless pursuit of riches that it upset the spirits of nature.

According to Disney lore, during the Gold Rush men from the Utah town of Tumbleweed were prospecting on a nearby mountain, a Native American burial ground. Though the ridge rumbled when mining took place— the Apache called the peak "Big Thunder"—the gold diggers were persistent. Adding insult to injury, they partied hard at night, drinking, playing poker and dancing with parlor girls.

Eventually the spirits had enough. Miners began to hear ghostly sounds, cave-ins became frequent and equipment mysteriously failed. One day a train suddenly spun out of control, and flew around the mountain like a bat out of hell. More desecration of the mountain led to a devastating flood—though some miners were too drunk to notice as they partied hearty at the Gold Dust Saloon. Moments later an earthquake struck. Word

of the mine's troubles eventually got out, and soon it, its trains and the little town of Tumbleweed were all abandoned.

Thirty years later, as eyewitness accounts of the incidents have faded into folklore, mining tycoon Barnabas T. Bullion has resurrected the company and is blasting into the mountain once again. He comes from a wealthy and powerful East Coast family, and considers the gold in the mountain to be his birthright by virtue of his odd name.

Bullion has discovered new veins of gold. He's revamped the rails and retooled some mine shafts to create a tourist attraction, giving sightseers a chance to tour his facility and ride the legendary trains. But as those riders will soon learn, some legends are true.

Fun facts. ❶ The 1984 movie "Indiana Jones and the Temple of Doom" used the sounds of the Big Thunder trains in its mine cart sequence. **❷** It was the first Walt Disney World attraction designed with computers. **❸** Bossman Bullion is a fraud! The portrait of

You light 'em, you hide.

Big Thunder Mining Co. President Barnabas T. Bullion hanging in the queue portrays Disney Imagineer Tony Baxter, the chief designer of the attraction.

Fun finds. ❶ Marked "Today's rain forecast," a measurement bar points to "40 inches," the ride's height minimum. ❷ Sticks of dynamite are strapped to the clock of the FastPass+ sign. A black fuse leads away from them. ❸ Lanterns throughout the grounds continuously dim and flicker. ❹ Crates and boxes of Lytum & Hyde brand explosives scatter throughout the landscape. The company is based in Sparks, Nev. ❺ A crate of Widowmaker explosives rests between the ride's entrance and exit. ❻ Recalling the toast *"Through the lips and over the gums, look out stomach here it comes!"* a crate of O'verdigums Irish Blend whiskey is nearby. ❼ According to a sign in the queue, Costas A. Lott is the manager of the B.T. Bullion Co. Store, where "all sales are mandatory" and "all sales are final." ❽ "Meal provided daily, baths weekly" reads a sign for the Big Thunder Boarding House. ❾ Its proprietress is Mrs. Liddy Stockley, the character who ran the boarding house in Disney's 1975 live-action comedy about the Gold Rush, "The Apple Dumpling Gang," the company's most successful movie of the 1970s. ❿ther nods to the film hide throughout the queue. ⓿ At the company's office, a list of pay rates on the wall reveals

the name of the mine's foreman: G. Willikers. ⓫ In an open safe, gold bars and ore sparkle (and rumble) whenever someone nearby in the queue uses a Remote Distance Blasting Machine (see below). ⓬ Bullion's land grant notes the mine sits in "the Western River Valley" and includes "Thunder Mesa"—a never-built area of Magic Kingdom that the ride was meant to be a part of, and a Western River Expedition boat ride it would also have included. ⓭ Tommy knockers (mischievous leprechaun-like creatures) are in one of the Big Thunder mines, according to a large Assay Report board. ⓮ Pinned on a bulletin board is a letter from "E.Z. Marks" to Professor Cumulus Isobar, a self-proclaimed "Rainmaker and Purveyor of Medicines and Elixirs" seen later on the ride. E.Z. asks for an alternative medicine for his bunions, explaining that the professor's last cure actually worsened his health. Marks' address is 1313 Gullible Way. He mentions his children, Patsy and Rube. In a postscript, he adds that *"The entire Marks clan is planning a trip back east in order to see the bridge you so graciously sold me!"* ⓯ A note on a second bulletin board identifies Chase M. Downs as the Tumbleweed sheriff. ⓰ *"Dear Barney…"* writes Jason Chandler, founder and president of The Society of Explorers and Adventurers, in a letter to Bullion posted at the top right of the board. *"I took the liberty of consulting with Madame Larhou at the Museum of the*

Weird, and it is her considered opinion that you should consider abandoning this entire operation at once... some forces simply are not to be trifled with." The Society of Explorers and Adventurers once ran the Adventurers Club at Downtown Disney (today's Disney Springs). During the 1960s, the Museum of the Weird was one of many Disney concepts for an attraction that became the Haunted Mansion. ⓱ *"Ready to head West, even if there are reports of Tommy-knockers and cave-ins in the mine,"* reads a yellowed telegram to Tumbleweed resident K. Derreis. In real life, Katy Harris is a Disney artistic director known for her willingness to travel. She's worked at theme parks around the world. ⓲ *"I've got men here ready to go dig gold. Didn't tell them about the troubling problems you have,"* reads a telegram from Ruthless Pete. That's a reference to Disney's cartoon cat Pete, the shady long-time nemesis of Mickey Mouse and host of the Magic Kingdom attraction, "Pete's Silly Sideshow." More signs and notices: ⓳ A sign for the Butterfly Stage Line notes it connects to the Carolwood Pacific Railroad Co. Carolwood Pacific was the name Walt Disney gave a miniature railroad he built in his backyard. ⓴ Clearly labeled "Do Not Store With Any Explosives," ⓵ Faithful-brand blasting caps are stored in the rafters, as is a bucket filled with dynamite sticks. Powder kegs are nearby. ㉑ Remote Distance Blasting Machines let you blast new mine shafts. You crank a contraption to prime it, then push a nearby plunger to trigger an explosion. ㉒ Steampunk "subterrascopes" let you look into shafts and spy on miners who aren't exactly working hard, using a complex series of lenses and mirrors. ㉓ To their left, a log by foreman Willikers reveals that he's been spying on the miners for a week and a half. ㉔ Next to a map, sketches of a can-can girl lifting her leg illustrate that "wounds, illnesses or missing limbs are not acceptable excuses to miss a work shift." ㉕ *"All friends, come celebrate my marriage to the prettiest lady in Tumbleweed, my wife Sue, at the Gold Dust Saloon. Drinks are on you!"* invites a yellowed note from "Bill." That's nearby fast-food proprietor Pecos Bill, with news regarding his gal Slew Foot Sue. ㉖ *"Looking for a new roommate who doesn't snore or eat beans,"* solicits a second note. ㉗ *"Missing: One gold tooth and one non-gold tooth. Last seen in my mouth at the Gold Dust Saloon. Reward 5¢"* offers a third note. ㉘ Equipment

in a ventilation room supposedly ensures that the miners' air is safe. Crank some huge fans to life and images on them animate like those of an old mutoscope. ㉙ You can check the air in the mine shafts by turning cranks on Autocanary Air Quality Analyzers and seeing how birds respond. ㉚ "Formulated to keep your canary alert," sacks of "Cheep Cheep Cheep" Alarm Bird Seed pile nearby. ㉛ Hanging above the machines, empty bird cages are those of feathered volunteers who have met their fate. ㉜ One cage is labeled "Rosita." At the Enchanted Tiki Room, co-host José has pondered "I wonder what happened to Rosita?" for decades. ㉝ Another cage nameplate reads "X. Benedict." ㉞ "Belly up to the world famous 'mile long' bar!" promotes a poster for the Pecos Bill Tall Tale Inn and Café, the nearby fast-food spot that once had a Mile Long Bar. ㉟ Miner's Hall is the intended destination of a nearby crate of mining equipment. That's the building that houses the ride's Gold Dust Saloon. ㊱ As your train pulls out, sounds of working miners echo from your right. ㊲ Speakers hidden throughout the ride play the sounds of a train with a steam whistle, even though your train doesn't have one. ㊳ As you enter the town of Tumbleweed, a sign reports that its population has dropped from 2015 to "dried out." ㊴ Wearing red long johns, prospector Cousin Elrod has washed into town in his bathtub. Hands behind his head, he leans back and savors the moment. ㊵ On your left, rainmaker Professor Cumulus Isobar bails himself out of his flooded wagon. ㊶ Atop the wagon, twirling windmill, honking horns and whistling steam vents form a makeshift weather machine. ㊷ "Dogs" is the amount of rain present at the time, according to the wagon's moisture gauge. That's its highest reading, beyond "drizzle" and "cats." ㊸ D. Hydrate and U. Wither are the proprietors of the nearby Superior Mercantile dry goods store. ㊹ An alcohol-fueled poker game has been flooded out at the adjacent Gold Dust Saloon. Cards rest on a table behind an open door. ㊺ Just above the saloon, carousing miners fire pistols in the air, toss laughing women off their feet and lift mugs of sudsy beer. ㊻ "Dave V. Jones Mine" is the short tunnel you enter as you exit Tumbleweed. According to legend Davy Jones is the devil of the seas. Being consigned to his locker means drowning at sea. ㊼ "Flooded Out" reads a Flood-ometer on your left as you round a bend. ㊽ "Furniture, Upholstery &

Flooded frolics.

Embalming" are offered by the Tumbleweed Cabinet & Casket Co., according to words on a gray coffin atop a storage shed on your right after you pass through some hot springs. ㊾ Büme, Büme & Büme dynamite (and Lytum & Hyde dynamite) is stacked in open boxes in front of the shed. ㊿ The ride's trains are named I.B. Hearty, I.M. Brave, I.M. Fearless, U.B. Bold, U.R. Courageous and U.R. Daring. (51) Back in the boarding area, Morris Code is the mining company's telegraph manager. His office is alongside the exit walkway of the left-side track. (52) The cage of a canary hangs above the exit for the right-side track. The bird inside isn't moving; sometimes it's not even there. (53) Outside the ride just to the right of a Nikon Photo Spot, a small geyser erupts every few minutes. Stand too close and you'll get sprayed. (54) "Tumbleweed Boat Tour" reads the back of a small rowboat resting upside-down on the mountain's muddy riverbank. Impossible to spot from the coaster's grounds, it's easy to see from the Liberty Square Riverboat.

Cinderella Castle.

Fantasyland

The park's largest land, Fantasyland appeals to young children and their families. The land has attractions that aren't very scary, don't have huge height minimums and don't have violent storylines. The land has four distinct areas. Its original space—the Castle Courtyard—resembles a Renaissance fair. An Enchanted Forest section is themed to three classic Disney movies—"Beauty and the Beast," "The Little Mermaid" and "Snow White and the Seven Dwarfs." A Storybook Circus area focuses on attractions themed to "Dumbo." A small space—just a small garden and a restroom—is themed to "Tangled."

One of the most photographed buildings in the world, Cinderella Castle has its picture taken at least 50,000 times a day. And no wonder. An icon of imagination, innocence and romance, it's not only a famous landmark but also quite a piece of fantasy architecture.

Its design combines the look of a medieval fortress and a Renaissance castle. The heavy lower walls have saw-toothed battlements like those used to hide artillery atop 11th-century stone forts. The top has the turrets, spires and Gothic trim of French castles built in the 14th, 15th and 16th centuries. Accents include 13 winged gargoyles and a portcullis, an iron gate over the entrance that appears ready to drop at a moment's notice.

Though it's really a 189-foot-tall (58-meter) steel frame covered in fiberglass, it appears to be a 300-foot (90-meter) stone fortress. Disney designed it to be seen from a mile away, so visitors arriving on ferries and monorails could spot it with anticipation.

The mosaic. Inside is a more traditional piece of art. Along the central hall, 500,000 bits of glass—in 500 colors—tell the tale of Cinderella in a five-panel mosaic. The 15-by-10 foot (5-by-3 meter) arches were crafted by a team led by artist Hanns-Joachim Scharff, based on concept art by Disney's Dorothea Redmond, who designed Fantasyland itself.

Castle photo © Disney

The mosaic took two years to make. Scharff redrew Redmond's art to life-size proportions on heavyweight brown craft paper, which he cut up into 50 or so puzzle-like pieces. He used both smooth and uneven glass pieces, a third of them fused with silver and gold. Scharff cut many by hand, shaping them with a power grindstone. He used thin strips of glass strip to outline hands and faces, and chopped multihued rods crosswise for other effects.

Scharff was a fascinating man and played a significant role in world history. Born in Germany in 1907, he became a Luftwaffe interrogator of captured American Air Force senior officers and ace pilots during World War II. Considered one of the best interrogators in the history of armed combat, he treated his prisoners with kindness and respect, which led them to reveal key pieces of military information without even knowing it. At one time the Gestapo investigated him for suspected collaboration with the United States because of his then-unusual technique. Scharff saved the lives of six U.S. prisoners from execution, by proving their innocence to the German secret police. After the war, he moved to New York and befriended many of his former captives. Changing careers, he indulged in a pre-war hobby and started a small mosaic studio. A Neiman Marcus order of 5,000 tables gave him the funds to set up a larger studio in California, where he introduced the smooth-surface Venetian glass form of mosaic art to this country in 1952. Scharff died in 1992, but his studio continues under the stewardship of his daughter-in-law, Monika, who started her apprenticeship on these five Cinderella murals and did much of the work on the ones outside The Land pavilion at Epcot.

Hanns-Joachim Scharff is widely respected today, especially by U.S. military veterans who argue against torturing terror suspects.

Also inside. The castle also includes a restaurant and makeover salon, security rooms, three elevators and an apartment that, though once planned for the use of the Disney family, remained unfinished until

Castle mosaic.

2006. Today it's the Cinderella Castle Suite, a fourth-floor foyer, salon, bedroom and bath that's sometimes offered to guests. The 650-square-foot (198-square meter) suite combines Renaissance style with modern conveniences. Above a fireplace, a portrait of Cinderella magically changes into a television. The bedchamber includes a 17th-century desk with inlaid computer hookups. Bathroom sinks resemble wash basins; faucets look like hand pumps. A cut-stone floor recalls the castle mosaic. If you're invited, you access the suite through a door in the breezeway. An elevator takes you to a foyer decorated with original "Cinderella" concept art by the famed Mary Blair and a display case holding, of course, a glass slipper.

Fun finds. ❶ In the mosaic Drizella's face is green with envy, Anastasia's red with anger. ❷ Cinderella's wishing well sits to the right of her castle, on a walkway to Tomorrowland. ❸ A statue of the princess stands in a small fountain behind the castle to the left. Thanks to a sketch of a crown on a wall behind it, toddlers who stand in front of the fountain see Cinderella wearing her crown. ❹ Luggage carts outside the Storybook Circus train station include bags for Hyacinth Hippo from 1940's "Fantasia," ❺ the Big Bad Wolf from Disney's 1933 cartoon "The Three Little Pigs" and ❻ Red's Amazing Juggling Unicycles, a shout-out to Pixar's 1987 short "Red's Dream," the story of a circus clown who rides a red unicycle in a juggling act. ❼ Another bag marked "Melody Time Brand Brass Horns" refers to Disney's 1948 animated movie "Melody Time." ❽ Hat boxes are from Ten Schillings and Sixpence Ltd., a nod to the number on the Mad Hatter's hat brim in the 1951 movie "Alice in Wonderland."

Hidden Mickeys. ❶ In Fairytale Garden, the three-circle shape hides in etchings in the base of axe blades scattered throughout the area. ❷ In Ariel's Grotto, a side profile of Mickey's face is sculpted in relief, in the queue just after you take the last right turn before entering Ariel's chamber, on the lower part of the left rear wall near the floor. ❸ Outside Gaston's Tavern it's on the statue of Gaston, formed by dark impressions in the rock below his left leg near the water line. ❹ At the Be Our Guest restaurant the three circles appear as a tattered hole in the fabric hanging from the ceiling in the West Wing dining room. You'll spot it if you stand directly in front of the rose at the rear of the room, then turn around and look up to your right. ❺ The shape also shows up as textured swirls in a rock on

Creating the mosaic. Artist Hanns-Joachim Scharff in his California studio, 1969.

Mickey's Royal Friendship Faire.

top of a low wall to the left of the outdoor check-in area. ❻ ❶n the Pete's Silly Sideshow tent the circles hide on a Daisy Fortuna poster in Daisy Duck's blouse, just beneath her face. ❼ Mickey's predecessor ❶swald the Lucky Rabbit hides as three pebbles in the walkway in front of Enchanted Tales with Belle.

Live entertainment

Fantasyland features an elaborate castle show and a lively troupe of street performers.

★★★★ ✔ **Main Street Philharmonic.** This 12-piece comedic brass and percussion ensemble plays Disney hits and Americana favorites. *20-min. shows most days 11:15a–4p; also performs on Main Street U.S.A.*

NEW! ★★★★★ ✔ **Mickey's Royal Friendship Faire.** "Hiya Toots!" says a "Tangled" ruffian to Minnie Mouse. That's just one of the surprisingly delightful moments in this new castle show, which showcases stars from 2009's "The Princess and the Frog," 2010's "Tangled" and 2013's "Frozen." Sassy flapper Tiana cuts a rug and channels a fan dancer while her sweetie Naveen plays a ukulele. Snowman ❶laf

doesn't recognize Mickey Mouse. ❶ueen Elsa belts out "Let It Go." Well, that last bit isn't much of a surprise, but it is appropriately melodramatic and beautifully done. The pl❶t of this snappy show doesn't matter; the stars and music do. *Typically 5–6 20-min. shows 10a–5:15p. Cinderella Castle stage.*

★★★★ ✔ **Royal Majesty Makers.** A retired knight, etiquette diva, squire and lady-in-waiting conduct Knight School, deliver ball invitations, solicit volunteers for a Sword in the Stone ceremony and lead dances. *20-min. sets 9:30a–3:30p. Castle Courtyard, Fantasyland.*

Restaurants and food

Fantasyland is home to two of the toughest reservations on Disney property:

★★★★★ ✔ **$34 DDP Be Our Guest.** Boasting a stunning dining hall that recalls the one in the 1991 movie "Beauty and the Beast," this contemporary French-American restaurant is beautiful, and filled with lovely effects. A prix-fixe breakfast debuted in 2015; a fast-food lunch is mostly sandwiches and salads. Dinner is an enchanting experience

Rapunzel's tower from "Tangled."

with a creative menu, an inspired wine list and impressive service. Some dishes are prepared tableside; the Beast himself greets guests in a side chamber. Special decor effects add charm throughout the day. *Breakfast 8a–10a, $24 (children $14); lunch 10:30a–2:30p, $13–$17 (children $7–$9); dinner 4p–10p, $21–$35 (children $10–$13). Seats 754. Enchanted Forest.*

★★★★ **$75 DDP2 Cinderella's Royal Table.** Snow White, Jasmine and other Disney princesses greet guests at their tables at this regal restaurant, which hides up on the second floor of the iconic Cinderella Castle. No one comes for the food; the ridiculously overpriced prix-fixe menus offer French-American fare that's worth about half its tab. Instead, the draw here is location, location, location—your child will never forget that you ate inside this world-famous landmark—as well as the bevy of impossibly poised young women who usually embody their princess roles to perfection. The medieval dining hall seems authentic; its stone walls, sky-high ceiling and stained glass windows fit for royalty. Unlike the other princesses, Cinderella does not appear in the dining room. She's in the lobby. Note: Cinderella's Royal Table is the toughest restaurant reservation to nab in all of Disney World; its tables often book to capacity 190 days early, on the first day they're available to Disney-hotel guests. Meals are paid for at the time they're reserved. Prices include trinkets for children and a photo of each diner with Cinderella. *Breakfast one hour before park open–10:30a, $60 (children $36); lunch 11:45a–2:45p, $68 (children $41); dinner 3:50p–park close, $75 (children $44). Seats 184. A Disney Signature Restaurant. Inside Cinderella Castle.*

★★ **$12 DDPq Friar's Nook.** It's mostly mac and cheese at this outdoor fast-food window—you can get it on a hot dog, pot roast, a bacon cheeseburger or all by itself. *11a–9p; $4–$10. Seats 88 at umbrella-covered tables shared with Storybook Treats. Castle Courtyard.*

★★★ ✔ **$11 DDPs Gaston's Tavern.** This little spot has the mark of its buffoonish owner (the villain of 1991's "Beauty and the Beast") all over it. It uses antlers in all of its decorating, serves beer (or at least a sweet slushy kids' drink that looks like beer) and features a huge gooey cinnamon roll perfect for those not on a diet. Fans of the film love the decor; few leave without taking a selfie or two in a fireside faux-fur chair. It's the only indoor fast-food spot in the park that's open in the morning and has seats. *$4–$8. Seats 102, including 32 outside. Enchanted Forest.*

★★ **$15 DDPq Pinocchio Village Haus.** Right in the middle of Fantasyland just behind the castle, this Italian-themed spot is as unreliable as its namesake's ability to tell the

Bonjour Village Gifts.

truth. Sometimes its generous flatbreads are full of sharp flavor; other times they're barely cooked. Lined with murals that depict scenes from Disney's 1933 movie "Pinocchio," its Old World interior is charming as long as it's vacant; unfortunately it's often packed with, for some reason, very unhappy kids. To avoid the ruckus come very early or very late. Nab a window-side table in the far left dining room and you'll look down into the boarding area of It's a Small World. *11a–park close; $10–$11 (children $6–$7). Seats 400. Castle Courtyard.*

★★★★★ ✔ **$12 DDPs Big Top Treats.** Creating temptations before your eyes, this sweet shop serves up concoctions that are fresher and more varied than those on Main Street. Bakers stroll through the store with free samples. Visitors rave about Big Top's chocolate-covered bananas; I love the elaborate caramel apples and the caramel corn, especially when it's fresh. *$4–$11. No seats; outdoor shaded tables nearby. Inside Big Top Souvenirs, Storybook Circus.*

★★★ **$8 DDPs Cheshire Café.** Cereals with milk, muffins, fresh fruit. Also coffee, hot tea, lemonade, orange juice. Near Mad Tea Party. Outdoor window. *$2–$5. Seats 40 at mostly-covered tables. Castle Courtyard.*

NEW! ★★★ **$11 DDPs Prince Eric's Village Market.** Turkey legs; also assorted fresh fruit, vegetables; frozen lemonade. Outdoor stand.

11a–6p; $2–$11. No seats. Across from Under the Sea, Enchanted Forest.

★★★ **$9 DDPs Storybook Treats.** Soft-serve ice cream. Outdoor window. *11a–park close; $4–$5. Seats 88 at umbrella tables shared with Friar's Nook. Castle Courtyard.*

Shops and merchandise

Top of the heap is the wonderful Big Top Souvenirs in Storybook Circus:

Bibbidi Bobbidi Boutique. If your little girl is into the princess look you just might spend a good chunk of her college savings at this makeover salon. Depending on how much you'd like to draw out of that account, she can get her hair and nails done, her cheeks and lips made up, a princess costume and sash, even a photo session. The room is a shrine to princess glamour. Elaborate tiaras sparkle in glass domes; frothy princess gowns hang on the walls as if they're works of art. Boys can get their hair glittered and spiked; those who do get a toy sword and shield. *Girls $65–$195 and up; boys $20. Ages 3–12. 8a–7p.; allow 30–60 min. Reservations at 407-939- 7895 6 months in advance. Inside Cinderella Castle.*

Big Top Souvenirs. A hidden oasis at the back of Fantasyland, this big circus tent offers a huge variety of merchandise, features a watch-them-make-it sweet shop right in the

Outside Dumbo the Flying Elephant.

Storybook Circus.

middle and has a terrific atmosphere—cast members often juggle scarves, spin plates or play games with kids as they work the floor. The merch includes Storybook Circus souvenirs; a side station embroiders Mickey ear hats. The heavenly aroma, jaunty circus music and cool air-conditioning tempt you to stay forever. Disney geeks will drool over hidden tributes to obscure Disney characters such as Salty the Seal. *Storybook Circus.*

Bonjour Village Gifts. This upscale boutique sells china, dolls, housewares and other high-end stuff themed to "Beauty and the Beast." Stone arches and a wood-beamed ceiling add a rustic feel. *Enchanted Forest.*

Castle Couture. Young princesses squeal over the sparkly gowns at this little shop, which specializes in princess costumes and accessories. It's supposedly the dressmaker's shop for the adjacent castle's royalty; sewing materials fill top shelves. An antechamber serves as a princess Photopass studio though anyone who asks can have their picture taken in it at no extra charge; a professional backdrop and overhead soft boxes help create a perfect portrait. *Castle Courtyard.*

Fantasy Faire. An angry Donald Duck glares down at you from the ceiling of this small store. Underneath him are some unique Donald T-shirts (an author favorite) and impulse items, as well as Mickey Mouse ear hats. Orchestral ambient music adds to a relaxing atmosphere. *At the exit of Mickey's PhilharMagic, Castle Courtyard.*

Hundred Acre Goods. Head to this teeny shop for cute-as-a-button Pooh toddler and infant apparel, plush and toys. The cute storybook-page decor has shelves that look to drip honey. *At the exit of The Many Adventures of Winnie the Pooh, Castle Courtyard.*

Sir Mickey's. Despite its name, this one-time menswear shop has responded to the Princess Fairytale Hall character spot next door by going gaga for gals. Now its more-or-less filled with clothing for girls and women, most of it themed to princesses, much of it unexpectedly creative. The holdover dude decor is based on two classic cartoons, "The Brave Little Tailor" and "Mickey and the Beanstalk." It includes many tailoring references, large vines and the "Beanstalk" giant peeking in from outside. *Castle Courtyard.*

A child can ride with a parent.

Prince Charming Regal Carrousel

Charming antique merry-go-round recalls forgotten era

★★★★★ ✔ It's a basic pleasure, but one children today rarely get to enjoy: the fun of straddling a big pretend horse which glides up and down as it circles, a breeze on your skin, calliope notes in the air. Designed for adults as well as kids, this antique merry-go-round has five sizes of horses. Each one is unique.

Tips. *When to go:* After dark when the ride's 2,300 tiny white lights cast a charming glow. *Where to sit:* ⬤n the outside for the fastest ride, on the inside for the slowest.

Fun facts. ❶ Selling hand-carved merry-go-rounds on the side, The Philadelphia Toboggan (i.e., roller coaster) Co. built the ride in 1917 ⬤riginally red, white and blue and called the Miss Liberty Merry-Go-Round, it's one of only four five-row carousels the company ever made. ❷ Created for Detroit's Palace Garden Park, it later spent time in ⬤lympic Park in Maplewood, N.J. ❸ Disney bought it in 1969, repainting it purple and

pink and replacing its wooden horses with fiberglass replicas. ❹ Though Walt Disney had died, the company honored his wish that it repaint all the horses white, so that all of their riders would be heroes. ❺ The ride's original wooden trim boards and chariot remain.

Fun finds. ❶ Some steeds carry medieval weapons—a battle axe, lance, war hammer and a one-handed flail with a spiked steel ball. ❷ The original namesake of the carousel, dignified blonde Miss Liberty adorns the side of its chariot. Her face appears in the outer rounding board. ❸ Eighteen hand-painted illustrations recount the story of Cinderella on the inner rounding board. ❹ Disney added a golden tail ribbon to a horse in the second row. It's now known as Cinderella's steed.

Key facts. *Duration:* 90 sec. *Capacity:* 91 (87 horses, 1 chariot). *Queue:* ⬤utdoor, shaded. *Restraint:* Belt. *Debuted:* 1971. *Access:* Must be ambulatory. *Location:* Castle Courtyard.

Average wait times

9a	10a	11a	12p	1p	2p	3p	4p	5p	6p	7p	8p	9p	10p	11p
5m	5m	5m	5m	5m	10m	10m	10m	5m	5m	5m	5m	5m	5m	5m

No wait... for the first five minutes.

Peter Pan's Flight

Vintage flying pirate ships take you off to Never Land

★★★★★ ✔ FP+ You'll fly over London and swoop through Never Land on this indoor dark ride, which uses an overhead track to suspend two-seat pirate ships. Designed 60 years ago and essentially unchanged since, the attraction has a throwback charm that just gets sweeter with age.

The ride depicts key moments of Disney's 1953 movie "Peter Pan." You start off in the Darling nursery, then fly over night-time London—its roads filled with moving vehicles—as you head off to Never Land. Passing the Lost Boys, Princess Tiger Lily and a trio of mermaids, you eventually sail through Capt. Hook's ship, and witness his battles with Peter and a ticking crocodile.

A new interactive queue gives you something to do if you pick the standby line. And wait you will, unless you rush here at 9 a.m.

Tips. *When to go:* First thing in the morning or anytime with a FastPass. *Where to look:*

Up and down. You fly through the scenes, so there are sights all around you.

Fun finds. ❶ In the queue, a bedside calendar from December 1904 has the 27th circled, the date of the first stage performance of J.M. Barrie's novel "Peter Pan." ❷ Nearby, your shadow can ring the shadow of a bell, be landed on by the shadow of a butterfly, tap the shadow of Tinker Bell which will cause her to take flight; be topped by the shadow of a top hat or Capt. Hook's feathered hat—and if that last one happens the shadow of your hand will become a hook. ❸ On the ride, one of the mermaids inadvertently resembles Ariel, the Little Mermaid.

Key facts. *Duration:* 3 min. *Capacity:* 60. *Queue:* Indoor, covered. *Restraint:* Safety bar. *Debuted:* 1971 (Disneyland 1955). *Access:* Must be ambulatory. *Disability services:* Handheld captioning, Audio Description. *Location:* Castle Courtyard.

Average wait times (standby line)

9a	10a	11a	12p	1p	2p	3p	4p	5p	6p	7p	8p	9p	10p	11p
60m	70m	70m	55m	75m	75m	75m	65m	70m	75m	80m	45m	40m	40m	10m

"Beauty and the Beast."

Mickey's PhilharMagic

Delightful 3-D tribute to Disney musicals stars Donald Duck

★★★★★ ✓ FP+ Donald Duck steals a smooch from Ariel (or at least tries to), battles the brooms from "Fantasia" and causes chaos in the dining room from "Beauty and the Beast" in this delightful 3-D movie. Action-packed yet never scary, funny but also touching, it's a treat for any age. The plot? When Maestro Mickey Mouse runs late for a performance of his magical musician-free orchestra, Donald attempts to replace him. His failure leads to a madcap adventure, as he gets swept into key moments of six Disney musicals.

The show plays on one of the world's widest 3-D screens. Some objects appear to leave the screen and hang directly in front of the audience. Hidden odorizers, air guns and water misters immerse you in the action, as do innovative lighting effects and a wrap-around sound system. The 3-D images aren't razor sharp but plenty bright. Scene transitions are terrific.

Tips. *When to go:* In the afternoon when other attractions have long lines. *Where to sit:* In the middle of a back row, where the 3-D effects have the most impact.

Déjà Donald. For the most part, the words spoken by Donald Duck come from original audio recordings of old Disney cartoons and are voiced by the authoritative voice of Donald, the late Clarence "Ducky" Nash. A few examples: ❶ Shouted at an unruly flute the duck then tosses into the audience, "I'll show you who's boss!" is from a moment in the 1941 cartoon "Early to Bed" when Donald yells at a noisy alarm clock he then tosses across his bedroom. ❷ After pixie dust gives him the ability to fly, the duck proclaims "Nothin' to it!" That's from a scene in the 1944 cartoon "Commando Duck" when, as he learns to parachute, he masters bending his knees when he lands. ❸ One line of the duck's dialogue isn't Donald at all. When he orders

Average wait times (standby line)

9a	10a	11a	12p	1p	2p	3p	4p	5p	6p	7p	8p	9p	10p	11p
5m	10m	10m	10m	10m	15m	15m	15m	15m	10m	10m	10m	10m	5m	5m

"Aladdin."

his magic carpet to fly "Faster! Faster!" the character speaking is *Donna Duck*, an early version of Daisy. In 1937's "Don Donald," speed-loving Donna says the words to Donald while riding in his car.

Fun finds. ❶ There's always a murmur in the theater before the show begins, as faint audience noise plays from hidden speakers. ❷ As stage manager Goofy walks behind the curtain, he hums the "Mickey Mouse March" and steps on a cat ("Sorry little feller!"). ❸ In the movie, when Lumiere rolls out toward the audience he's on a tomato that wasn't there a moment earlier. It arrived when Donald briefly blocked the view to ask, "Where's my hat?" ❹ Ariel giggles as she swims onscreen. ❺ Strobes in the ceiling flash when Donald kisses an electric eel. ❻ When a crocodile sends the duck flying during "I Just Can't Wait to be King," you hear him circle behind you. ❼ When Simba sings that he's "in the spotlight," so are some members of the audience. ❽ When a pull chain falls into view, Zazu turns off Simba's light and responds, "Not yet!" ❾ Jasmine waves to an audience member as she starts to sing "A Whole New World." ❿ When she and Aladdin wave goodbye to Donald, so does their carpet. ⓫ Once Mickey regains control of his orchestra, the flute wakes up the tuba and trips Donald into it, paying him back for earlier

tossing it into the audience. ⓬ As you leave the theater, you hear the voice of Goofy saying goodbye to you in five languages ("Sigh-a-NAIR-ee!"). That's a sly shout-out to the glittery farewell offered by the attraction across the walkway: It's A Small World.

Hidden Mickeys. ❶ In the lobby mural, as seven 1-inch-wide white paint splotches. From the right, they appear between the third and fourth bass violin, between the second and third clarinet, above the second trumpet, below the second trumpet, to the left of the fourth trumpet, and twice to the left of the sixth clarinet. ❷ On the theater's right stage column, in the French horn tubing. ❸ In the film's "Be Our Guest" scene, as brief shadows on the dining table, visible as Lumiere sings the word "it's" in "Try the gray stuff, it's delicious!" Lumiere's hands cast Mickey's ears; his base Mickey's face. ❹ As a hole made in a cloud as Aladdin's carpet flies through it. ❺ When the carpets dive toward Agrabah, as three domes atop a tower on the left. ❻ In the gift shop, as music stands along the top of the walls.

Key facts. *Duration:* 12 min. *Capacity:* 450. *Queue:* Indoor, air-conditioned. *Fear factor:* Sudden images, briefly totally dark. *Debuted:* 1971. *Access:* Wheelchairs, ECVs OK. *Disability services:* Assistive listening, reflective captioning. *Location:* Castle Courtyard.

Illustration © Disney

Scandinavia.

it's a small world

Colorful classic boat ride offers hope of world peace

UPDATED! ★★★★★ ✔ FP+ Promoting world harmony with dolls that sing in unison, this indoor boat ride takes you on a colorful, cultural trip around the globe. Abstract sets, whimsical animals and hundreds of singing dolls fill your field of vision.

"The happiest cruise that ever sailed" starts off in Europe. It crosses through Asia, Africa, Latin America and Polynesia, then heads back to Europe to Copenhagen's Tivoli Gardens—Walt Disney's inspiration for the look of California's Disneyland and hence the Magic Kingdom—where all the world's children come together to celebrate the "world that we share" by dressing in white, singing in unison and enjoying the carnival together.

Not everyone loves the ride, of course, and for good reason. The dolls barely move their lips, and their song repeats too often for an 11-minute ride (though usually as an instrumental, sometimes just a rhythm track, and

when dolls do sing, half the time they're doing so in Italian, Japanese, Spanish or Swedish). The Latin American and South Pacific scenes are skimpy, and the ride concludes with some glitter-board good-byes that must have cost all of $1.98. In a 2016 update, digital displays alongside them bid farewell to riders by name—at least to those wearing MagicBands.

You can enjoy it in at least four ways:

As a ride. To infants, the ride is a wide-eyed journey filled with happy faces, funny animals, gentle music and the largest crib mobiles they've ever seen. To older children, it's a place to bond with their parents, as there's no narration and lots of time to chat. ("Where are we now, mom?" "Hawaii!").

As a political statement. It's a Small World argues that you can honor diversity while still celebrating the commonality of mankind. Though the dolls speak different languages, they all sing the same song.

Average wait times (standby line)

9a	10a	11a	12p	1p	2p	3p	4p	5p	6p	7p	8p	9p	10p	11p
10m	25m	25m	25m	30m	30m	30m	25m	25m	25m	15m	15m	10m	0m	0m

The rainforest.

As a piece of art. Just like a painting in an art museum, the attraction has a sophisticated sensibility that is often overlooked. As designed by illustrator Mary Blair—she did the backgrounds of the Disney movies "Cinderella" (1950) and "Alice in Wonderland" (1951)—the modernist sets form a playful pop-art collage that combines both organic and geometric shapes as well as classic cultural motifs (for ideas, Blair tried out combinations of wallpaper cuttings, cellophane and acrylic paint). As for color, Blair again thought like a child, leaving no hue unused and using no shading within one.

As a piece of history. The ride was initially created for the UNICEF pavilion at the 1964 New York World's Fair. One of 50 attractions that charged a fee, It's a Small World accounted for 20 percent of paid admissions, more than any other attraction. It also inspired some political merchandise, as The Women's International League for Peace and Freedom sold It's a Small World-style dolls to help fund protests against the Vietnam War. The ride also debuted a new way to transport guests through a ride, using a new flume system that employed tiny water jets to propel free-floating, open-topped boats.

Tips. *Where to sit:* Ask for the front row of the first boat in a group for the best view and the most legroom. *Where to look:* Up.

Lots of stuff hangs from the ceilings. *Tips for families:* Compete with your kids: Who can identify the most countries? Who can spot the most animals?

Fun facts. ❶ Jungle Cruise skippers tell their passengers that children left on their boats will wind up in It's a Small World, their feet glued to its floor, forced to sing its theme song "over and over for the rest of their lives." ❷ During the finale of Jim Henson's MuppetVision 3-D, Small World dolls join in to help destroy the theater.

Fun finds. ❶ In the boarding area, a giant clock comes to life every 15 minutes. ❷ In the first room a pink poodle ogles the can-can girls, a crazy-eyed Don Quixote tilts at a windmill while Sancho Panza looks on in alarm, and a Swiss yodeler wields an ax. ❸ In the Middle Eastern room, one of the flying carpets has a steering wheel. ❹ In the African room, Cleopatra winks at you.

Hidden Mickey. ❶ The three-circle shape appears as purple flower petals in Africa, along a vine between the giraffes on your left.

Key facts. *Duration:* 11 min. *Capacity:* 600. *Queue:* Indoor. *Debuted:* 1971, renovated 2010, updated 2016 (New York World's Fair 1964, Disneyland 1966). *Access:* ECV users must transfer. *Disability services:* Handheld captioning, Audio Description. *Location:* Castle Courtyard.

A ride for nearly everyone.

Seven Dwarfs Mine Train

Delightful indoor-outdoor coaster has absurd waits

★★★★ ✔ FP+ This musical indoor-outdoor coaster is ideal for families. It gives just the right amount of thrills—more than Barnstormer, less than Big Thunder Mountain Railroad—making it a perfect fit for kid-friendly Fantasyland. Better still, even though it's based on a princess story it appeals to both sexes, as it focuses its attention on the dwarfs. Snow White appears only at the end of the ride, and only if you look for her.

As for downers, it's short. And not really worth its often ridiculous standby wait.

Tips. *When to go:* Anytime with a FastPass. *Where to sit:* In the front seat for the best views and the mildest ride; in back for a more thrilling experience.

Fun find. ❶ The image of Walt Disney's first makor cartoon character, Oswald the Lucky Rabbit, appears on a beam to your left past the crest of the second lift hill. Think Mickey with long floppy ears.

Hidden Mickeys. You'll find Mickey as a three-circle shape ❶ on the loading area on the back wall above the podium, and three times inside the mine: ❷ just to the left of Dopey (level with his head, on a support beam), ❸ as three jewels slightly to the right of Grumpy, and ❹ as a full-bodied figure atop the second lift down low on your right, across from the hidden image of Oswald, holding a pickaxe.

Key facts. *Duration:* 3 min. *Capacity:* 20 (4 per mine cart, 2 per row). *Queue:* Outdoor, tree-lined path leads into an indoor queue. *Fear factor:* Tight speedy turns may frighten preschoolers, especially in the back rows. *Restraint:* Lap bar. *Weather issues:* Closed during thunderstorms. *Debuted:* 2014. *Health advisory:* Expectant mothers should not ride. *Access:* Height min 38 in (97 cm); wheelchair and ECV users must transfer. *Location:* Enchanted Forest.

Average wait times (standby line)

9a	10a	11a	12p	1p	2p	3p	4p	5p	6p	7p	8p	9p	10p	11p
65m	70m	80m	120m	110m	95m	100m	110m	80m	70m	100m	110m	110m	80m	30m

Heffalumps and woozles!

The Many Adventures of Winnie the Pooh

Charming dark ride tells tale of chubby little cubby

★★★★ ✔ FP+ You bounce with Tigger, float in a flood and see Pooh drift off to dreamland on this dark indoor ride, which uses imaginative effects to create a memorable experience. Traveling in a four-person "Hunny Pot," you enter a storybook to witness the weather woes and heffalump-and-woozle nightmare of the 1968 featurette "Winnie the Pooh and the Blustery Day," which in 1977 became part of the movie "The Many Adventures of Winnie the Pooh." Hidden behind swinging doors, each scene comes as a surprise. A standby queue has an interactive playground; children (and adults) can draw on video walls that appear to drip honey.

Tips. *Where to sit:* The front seat of your Pot has the best view. Children in back can't see over adults in front of them. *For families:* The ride gives parents a chance to talk to kids about fear. Scenes depict the Pooh characters afraid of two things they should be (a windstorm and flood) and one thing they shouldn't (rumored truths).

Fun finds. ❶ A mirror in the boarding area makes riders appear to disappear into a storybook. ❷ Words on its first page blow off of it. ❸ Words on its Floody Place page wash off.

Hidden Mickeys. ❶ Mickey hides at the ride's entrance, on the transom of the door inside Mr. Sanders' treehouse. ❷ On the ride he's on the radish marker in Rabbit's garden.

Key facts. *Duration:* 3 min 30 sec. *Capacity:* 48. *Queue:* Outdoor, covered. *Fear factor:* A clap of thunder and an odd dream sequence may startle timid toddlers. *Restraint:* Lap bar. *Debuted:* 1999. *Access:* ECV users must transfer. *Disability services:* Audio Description. *Location:* Castle Courtyard.

Average wait times (standby line)

9a	10a	11a	12p	1p	2p	3p	4p	5p	6p	7p	8p	9p	10p	11p
30m	35m	40m	30m	40m	35m	30m	30m	35m	35m	30m	30m	20m	10m	0m

Micaela Neal

A perfect ride for couples.

Mad Tea Party

Simple spinning teacups leave you giddy and grinning

★★★★ ✔ FP+ "If I had a world of my own, everything would be nonsense," says schoolgirl Alice, in Disney's 1951 movie "Alice in Wonderland." "Nothing would be what it is because everything would be what it isn't. And contrary-wise; what it is it wouldn't be, and what it wouldn't be, it would. You see?"

You'll be as confused as Alice as you leave this classic carnival ride, which puts you in an oversized teacup that spins as it circles on a floor that circles too.

Most guests get dizzy, and most love it. "My favorite Disney World ride has always been the teacups," NASCAR driver Kyle Petty tells us. "From the time I was little I've loved to jump in and make people sick." My husband lost his ability to go on rides like this a few years ago, and I miss riding it with him.

A wheel in the center of your cup lets you control how fast you spin, and which direction. Covered by a huge canopy, the Mad Tea Party operates in any weather. Getting a FastPass will save you a few minutes, but you may regret using one on such a slight ride.

Tips. *When to go:* Morning, late afternoon or evening... anytime it's not crowded. *Where to sit:* Pick a cup. Any cup. *How to get really dizzy:* Spin your wheel first one way, then the other, as fast as you can. *How not to get dizzy:* Don't spin the wheel. Instead, hold onto it tightly so it doesn't move, and stare at it as the ride itself rotates and turns. *For families:* The cups give you a chance to get silly with your children. Most kids love it when mom or dad slides into them or playfully twirls the wheel.

Fun finds. ❶ The movie's soused mouse pops out of the ride's central teapot. **❷** The film's Japanese tea lanterns hang overhead.

Key facts. *Duration:* 2 min. *Capacity:* 72 (18 4-person teacups). *Queue:* Outdoor, shaded. *Debuted:* 1971 (Disneyland 1955). *Access:* Must be ambulatory. *Location:* Castle Courtyard.

Average wait times (standby line)

9a	10a	11a	12p	1p	2p	3p	4p	5p	6p	7p	8p	9p	10p	11p
5m	10m	15m	15m	20m	20m	15m	20m	15m	10m	10m	10m	5m	0m	0m

Belle and her knights. See the Hidden Mickey?

Enchanted Tales with Belle

Audience volunteers help the princess act out her story

★★★★ ✔ FP+ This wonderful little attraction is Disney's ultimate character meet-and-greet. with a live show tossed in to boot. Engaging and lovely in her golden gown, the heroine from 1991's "Beauty and the Beast" is just a few feet from the audience in this cozy indoor show. With the help of enchanted candlestick Lumiere as well as child and parent volunteers, she shares a lively re-telling of her "tale as old as time." The show takes place in the library of the Beast's castle, which you reach with help of a magical mirror. The queue takes you through Belle's cottage and Maurice's workshop.

Tips. *When to go:* In the morning, as soon as the park opens. Disney needs at least 20 people to present a show, so you might wait a few moments. But you'll avoid having to wait outside—and you'll get a fresh, lively Belle. *Where to sit:* Front and center if you can. *For families:* Encourage your children

to volunteer. Everyone who wants to be in the show can be, and usually they're the only ones who get a photo with Belle. *Have your own princess?* In the first room of the cottage, take a photo of her in front of little Belle's height chart. It's on the right wall.

Fun finds. ❶ A French book telling the Cinderella tale lies open on a table in Belle's cottage. ❷ A book near the door to Maurice's workshop is titled "La Belle au Bois Dormant." In other words, Sleeping Beauty. ❸ Maurice's blueprints for the wood-chopping machine seen in "Beauty and the Beast" hang on his workshop's wall.

Hidden Mickey. The three circles appear as roses at the neckline of Belle's gown.

Key facts. *Duration:* 20 min. *Capacity:* 45. *Queue:* Unshaded, outdoor. *Debuted:* 2012. *Access:* Wheelchairs, ECVs OK. *Disability services:* Assistive listening, handheld captioning. *Location:* Enchanted Forest.

Average wait times (standby line)

9a	10a	11a	12p	1p	2p	3p	4p	5p	6p	7p	8p	9p	10p	11p
15m	25m	40m	30m	30m	45m	20m	25m	25m	40m	10m	15m	20m	10m	---

Kiss her, you fool!

Under the Sea

Slow-moving musical ride tells Ariel's tale

★★★ **FP+** This ride wisely features the charming songs from Disney's 1989 hit "The Little Mermaid" to retell its story. After your ride vehicle—a clamshell which resembles a Haunted Mansion Doom Buggy—turns backward to (virtually) sink underwater, you meet Ariel and her fishy friends dancing and playing instruments to "Under the Sea." Subsequent scenes show evil octopus Ursula singing "Poor Unfortunate Soul" and Prince Eric balking at giving our girl a smooch to "Kiss the Girl." Kiss her, you fool! He never does, at least not while you're watching. The sound quality is excellent. In one scene you hear separate instruments as you pass them.

The ride takes you past many characters from the movie, including Flounder, Scuttle, Flotsam and Jetsam. Unfortunately it skims over the climactic battle where Ursula gets her comeuppance, suffers from a lack of detail and some uninspired hard-plastic figures.

Tips. *For families:* Be sure to play the crab game in the standby queue; it's a great way to pass the time. Wave your hand to help the crustacean sort Ariel's gadgets and gizmos.

Fun find. An image of the Nautilus submarine from the movie "20,000 Leagues Under the Sea" hides on the left side of the queue, in rocks alongside a pool. That's a tiny tribute to an iconic Disney submarine ride that originally was in this area of the park.

Hidden Mickey. The three circles appear in the queue as sunlight on a wall past a carved ship's figurehead, from holes in a rock above—only on Nov. 18, Mickey's birthday.

Key facts. *Duration:* 7 min. *Capacity:* 4 per clamshell. *Queue:* Indoor. *Fear factor:* Ursula may scare toddlers. *Restraint:* Lap bar. *Debuted:* 2012. *Access:* ECV users must transfer. *Disability services:* Handheld captioning, Audio Description. *Location:* Enchanted Forest.

Average wait times (standby line)

9a	10a	11a	12p	1p	2p	3p	4p	5p	6p	7p	8p	9p	10p	11p
10m	20m	20m	25m	20m	30m	30m	35m	25m	25m	25m	15m	10m	5m	0m

Sure it's for kids.

Dumbo the Flying Elephant

Recently improved carnival ride is better than ever

★★★★★ ✓ FP+ Flying baby elephants become cozy ride vehicles on this classic hub-and-spoke ride. Since the attraction's move to Storybook Circus in 2012 it's gotten much better—it now has two Dumbo rides, one that moves clockwise, the other counterclockwise. Each has a pool for Dumbo to fly over and multi-colored, changing lights that, at night, make the water glow. The queue includes an indoor playground. When there's a wait to ride Dumbo, parents sit on benches while children play. When it's time, a restaurant-style pager sounds an alert.

Couples will enjoy the ride almost as much as children; its small seat requires scootching together and sharing one big seatbelt.

Tips. *When to go:* Before 11 a.m. for the shortest lines of the day, or use a FastPass. If you can, ride at night, when the attraction glows with brilliant lights. *For families:* Snap a pic of your children in a stationary Dumbo

between the two rides. *Other tips:* Ask for the Dumbo on the right (i.e., the one closest to the rest of the park) to get a terrific view of Magic Kingdom. The Dumbo on the left mostly just views the adjacent Barnstormer ride.

Fun finds. ❶ Flying storks deliver baby Dumbos along the top of each hub. ❷ Golden peanuts adorn the hubs, almost as if the legume was an object of worship.

Hidden Mickey. Elephant tracks form the three-circle shape in the walkway just in front and to the left of the FastPass entrance.

Key facts. *Duration:* 2 min (6 revolutions). *Capacity:* 64 (32 per ride, in 16 2-seat vehicles); play area capacity 175. *Queue:* Indoor, includes large, elaborate play area; leads to outdoor shaded queue. *Restraint:* Seatbelt. *Weather issues:* Closed in thunderstorms. *Debuted:* 1971, redone 2012 (Disneyland 1955). *Access:* Wheelchair and ECV users must transfer. *Location:* Storybook Circus.

Average wait times (standby line)

9a	10a	11a	12p	1p	2p	3p	4p	5p	6p	7p	8p	9p	10p	11p
10m	20m	30m	30m	20m	30m	35m	35m	20m	20m	20m	20m	15m	10m	5m

An old-fashioned family coaster.

The Barnstormer

Brief, cheerful kiddie coaster packs a punch

★★★★★ ✔ FP+ A perfect first coaster for kids, this little biplane is also fun for couples and friends. Though it lasts only 20 seconds, its planes zip around a tight track at 25 mph (40 kph), about as fast as the rockets inside Space Mountain. Constantly leaning into each other, riders sit two abreast in a cozy seat.

The Great Goofini. Adding to the fun is a witty backstory—the tale of an aerial mishap of the Great Goofini, the stage name Goofy gave himself during his stint as a circus daredevil. Taxiing a crop duster out of a barn, he climbed up in the air perfectly straight... into a signal tower. Immediately losing control, he swooped and swayed back to the barn, crashing through his billboard on the way.

Tips. *When to go:* First thing in the morning; when cast members will often let you stay in your seat for multiple flights. *Where to sit:* For the wildest ride ask for the back seat (Row 8); for the best view the front seat.

Fun finds. ❶ Definitely *not* the star of the circus, Goofy has put together his act on the cheap. His entrance is a hodgepodge of Dumbo leftovers, rusting metal and scrap wood. The back of his sign reveals it's made from the one of his old coaster, The Barnstormer at Goofy's Wiseacre Farm. ❷ When seen together, the numbers of his planes—5, 19 and 32—form the date of his first cartoon appearance: May 1932.

Hidden Mickey. On the right of the billboard, in the blades of an airplane propeller.

Key facts. *Duration:* 1 minute. *Capacity:* 16 per plane. *Queue:* Outdoor, mostly unshaded. *Fear factor:* Tight turns, one steep turning drop. *Restraint:* Lap bar. *Top speed:* 25 mph (40 kph). *Track:* Steel. *Weather issues:* Closed during thunderstorms. *Debuted:* 1996, revised 2012. *Health advisory:* Expectant mothers should not ride. *Access:* Height min 35 in (89 cm); ECV and wheelchair users must transfer. *Location:* Storybook Circus.

Average wait times (standby line)

9a	10a	11a	12p	1p	2p	3p	4p	5p	6p	7p	8p	9p	10p	11p
5m	15m	15m	20m	30m	30m	30m	20m	20m	20m	15m	20m	10m	5m	5m

Not much to it, but kids love it.

Casey Jr. Splash 'n' Soak Station

Beat the heat at this jolly splash zone

★★★★ It's more soak than splash, but that's part of the fun. Kids have a blast trying to dodge the intermittent sprays, especially if parents join in. Surrounding little locomotive Casey Jr. from Disney's 1941 film "Dumbo" are several boxcars holding faux circus animals that shoot, spit and squirt water. Oddly, the pavement is brick, not the squishy soft ground water-play areas usually have. Few kids seem to have trouble with it, though.

Tips. *When to go:* Anytime. *Where to play:* If your youngsters want a light spray instead of a drench, have them play in front of the boxcar with the monkeys on top. *Other tips;* To dry off, a cart just out of range of the water sells $20 beach towels.

Fun finds. Numbers on the train cars and clown wagon refer to the opening years of the four Walt Disney World theme parks. ❶ A "71" on the elephant car refers to 1971, the year Magic Kingdom debuted. ❷ An "82" on the clown wagon refers to 1982, the year Disney added Epcot. ❸ On the giraffe car, "89" refers to the 1989 debut of Disney's Hollywood Studios, then known as Disney-MGM Studios. ❹ On the camel car, "98" refers to 1998, the opening year of Disney's Animal Kingdom. Numbers on ❺ the nearby merchandise cart ("7") and ❻ locomotive ("9") are those of the engines of the Casey Jr. Circus Train ride at California's Disneyland. ❼ Mrs. Jumbo (Dumbo's mom) peeks out of the elephant car. ❽ The locomotive has "a smoky stack" and sounds "his funny little whistle," just like his theme song ("Casey Jr.") says he does when it's sung the park's opening welcome show.

A closer look. The splash zone and its adjacent restroom are a 1940s railroad turntable and roundhouse storage shed. Surrounded by his animal-filled boxcars waiting to be unloaded, Casey Jr. sits on the turntable, tracks from the Walt Disney World railroad leading up to him. Why? Because for most of their history locomotives did not have a reverse gear, so in order to turn around one had to pull onto a piece of side track that was mounted on a circular turnabout, and twirled around to face the other way.

Key facts. *Duration:* Allow about 15 min. *Weather issues:* Closed during thunderstorms. *Debuted:* 2012. *Access:* Wheelchairs, ECVs OK. *Location:* Storybook Circus.

MONSTERS INC.
Laugh FLOOR
NOW PLAYING

THE LU

TOMORROWLAND
TERRACE
NOODLE STATION

To the future... of the past!

Tomorrowland

An intergalactic spaceport, today's Disney view of tomorrow is the future of the 1930s—the Buck Rogers and Flash Gordon world of machine-age rockets and flying saucers and aliens out to take over everything. Except for some of it, which is the tomorrow of today as seen from the 1990s. Or the future of the 1970s as seen from today. Confused? By all means, commander. It's best appreciated by not thinking about it. Or at night, when bright beacons and colorful neon light its buildings' brushed metal curves.

Fun finds. ❶ "Extry! Extry! Read all about it!" calls a New Yawk newsboy of the future near the PeopleMover ride. If you listen closely, you can hear him talk to you. "Your face looks familiar, let me check my scanner," he may say. "That's it! I've seen youse in the funny papers!" ❷ Alien Coca-Cola logos mark crates in front of a drink stand.

Hidden Mickeys. The three-circle shape hides in a mural inside Mickey's Star Traders as ❶ loops of a highway, ❷ train headlights, ❸ glass domes, ❹ satellite dishes, ❺ clear domes covering a city and ❻ Mickey ears on top of two windows.

Live entertainment

Crowds gather for the sole entry, a street party starring characters from the 2004 movie "The Incredibles."

★★★ **#IncrediblesSuperDanceParty.** Join a conga line formed by Mr. Incredible, with the missus bringing up the rear and Frozone egging you on. A high-energy dance party with a DJ playing catchy hits, with often not much of a crowd. *Intermittently 2p–9p Sun–Mon; 5p–10p Tue–Sat. Rockettower Plaza stage.*

Restaurants and food

Apparently the future has no tipping; there are only fast-food spots in this land:

★★ **$17 DDPq Cosmic Ray's Starlight Café.**
This sprawling spot has dumped most of its
interesting choices. No more ribs, no more
deli sandwiches on whole-grain bread. Now
the menu's pedestrian—burgers, chicken, hot
dogs and barbecue pork. A condiment bar is
expansive. The ordering system requires you
to wait in different lines to order different
items. A cheap 1970s Six Flags decor features
tiresome robotic lounge singer Sonny Eclipse.
Usually pretty calm, though a midday rush
can quickly turn it into a madhouse. *10a–park
close; $10–$15 (children $6–$7). Seats 1,162.*

★★ **$16 DDPq Tomorrowland Terrace.** This
perfect outdoor location has so many menu
changes it's hard to keep up; lately the offerings haven't been that great. At presstime it
served burgers, chicken and smoked sausage
sandwiches. *11a–9p; $10–$13 (children $6–$7).
Seats 500 in sheltered, open-air area.*

★★★ **$8 DDPs Auntie Gravity's Galactic
Goodies.** This outdoor stand sells soft-serve
ice cream treats, smoothies, assorted cereals
with milk, muffins, whole fruit. *$2–$5. Seats
30 at umbrella-covered tables.*

★★★ **$11 DDPs The Lunching Pad.** Hot
dogs, ham and cheese pretzels. *Outdoor
stand. 11a–9p; $4–$8. Seats 83 outdoors.*

★★ **$10 DDPs Cool Ship.** Mickey pretzels,
soft drinks. *Outdoor stand. 10a–10p; $5. Seats
25 at nearby umbrella-covered tables.*

Shops and merchandise

Sadly there's nothing machine-age for sale
in Tomorrowland, nothing at all that looks
like the place. Instead it's mostly routine stuff
you can easily find elsewhere, along with a
few Space Mountain souvenirs.

**Buzz Lightyear's Space Ranger Spin
Photos.** Toy Story toys, Disney Infinity figures, souvenir photos from the ride. *At the
exit of Buzz Lightyear's Space Ranger Spin.*

Buzz's Star Command. Toy Story plushies, T-shirts, toys. An outdoor stand topped
with the little green aliens. *In front of Buzz
Lightyear's Space Ranger Spin.*

Merchant of Venus. Currently Star Wars
action figures, apparel, books, comic books,
lightsabers, Princess Leia costumes, toys,
T-shirts. A custom photo spot uses a green
screen to put your face on the body of a
Star Wars character. *At the exit of Stitch's
Great Escape.*

Mickey's Star Traders. Disney souvenirs,
sundries. *Near Merchant of Venus.*

Tomorrowland Light & Power Co. Space
Mountain souvenirs and T-shirts; toy rocket
ships; packaged astronaut food. A D-Tech-
On-Demand station lets you customize and
buy your own MagicBand, phone case or
tablet case. No longer has an arcade. *At the
exit of Space Mountain.*

Cool Ship.

An alien encounter.

Stitch's Great Escape

Cheap, confusing theatrical show is only for Stitch fans

★ A low-budget makeover of the attraction that preceded it (The ExtraTERRORestrial Alien Encounter), this in-the-round theatrical show is geared to those familiar with the early moments of the 2002 movie "Lilo & Stitch." It includes a cool Experiment 626 robot, but spends most of its time showing TV-quality animated videos.

The story takes place before the film. When 626 is held at a Planet Turo jail, he's guarded by cannons that track genetic signatures. Then the creature spits on the floor, the power shorts out and he escapes. Thanks to some hidden devices in your seat harness, it sounds, feels and smells as if 626 lingers near you.

Eventually making his way to Earth, the monster woos a very famous young woman at her Florida castle. He's rejected.

The Audio-Animatronics tech is impressive. His ears have simultaneous movements just like those of a dog, and his eyes, arms, fingers and spine move fluidly.

The host of the preshow is great. Training you how to guard prisoners as he chats with his wife on the phone, a sarcastic skinless sergeant shifts his weight from foot to foot and counts down on his fingers. It's Jim Carrey, doing his Fire Marshall Bill from the 1990s television series "In Living Color."

Tips. *Where to stand for the preshow:* Front row center (as you leave the indoor queue, choose the door to the left); the cop will look right at you. *Where to sit:* In the back for the best view. Stitch sits high off the floor.

Key facts. *Duration:* 18 min. *Capacity:* 240 (2 120-seat theaters). *Queue:* Indoor. *Fear factor:* Ominous harnesses, dark periods scare some children. *Restraint:* Shoulder harness. *Debuted:* 2004. *Access:* Height min 40 in (102 cm); ECV users must transfer. *Location:* Across from Monsters Inc Laugh Floor.

Average wait times

9a	10a	11a	12p	1p	2p	3p	4p	5p	6p	7p	8p	9p	10p	11p
10m	15m	15m	20m	20m	25m	15m	15m	15m	15m	10m	10m	10m	10m	10m

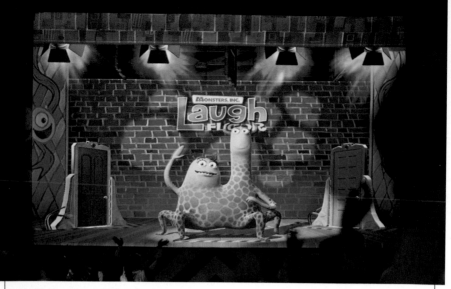

Comic duo Sam 'n' Ella.

Monsters Inc. Laugh Floor

Animated creatures joke with their audience

★★★★ FP+ An animated monster may pick you out of the crowd to chat with or might tell your joke during this high-tech improvisational comedy show. Three large video screens front a club-style theater, where characters from the "Monsters Inc." world tease and talk with audience members in real time. The host is Mike Wazowski, who wants to generate electricity for his utility company by gathering laughter in bulk.

The show pulls off its magic using hidden cameras, real-time animation software and talented backstage improv actors, much like Epcot's Turtle Talk with Crush.

Most shows are surprisingly funny. Every one is different, as the characters base much of their humor (and anti-humor) on audience members. You can text a joke to the performers ahead of time from the waiting area.

Tips. *When to go:* In the middle of day, so you see a show with a full house. The actors feed off the audience. *How to have a character talk to you:* Wear a colorful shirt or a big hat. *How to get your texted joke read:* Make it simple and Disney-based. "Where did Captain Hook get his hook? The second-hand store!"

Fun finds. ❶ Just inside the second queue room on the left, a vending machine offers treats such as Sugar Salt & Fat, Same Old Raccoon Bar and a Polyvinyl Chloride candy bar, which small print on its wrapper notes is artificially flavored. ❷ In that room's pre-show video, the first child Mike Wazowski makes laugh has a poster of Tomorrowland on his bedroom wall.

Key facts. *Duration:* 15 to 20 min. *Capacity:* 400. *Showtimes:* Continuous. *Queue:* Indoor. *Operating hours:* Closes one hour before Magic Kingdom does. *Debuted:* 2007. *Access:* Wheelchairs, ECVs OK. *Disability services:* Reflective captioning, assistive listening. *Location:* Across from Stitch's Great Escape.

Average wait times (standby line)

9a	10a	11a	12p	1p	2p	3p	4p	5p	6p	7p	8p	9p	10p	11p
20m	10m	20m	20m	20m	25m	20m	20m	20m	15m	20m	10m	10m	10m	---

Rock 'Em... Sock 'Em... Blast 'Em.

Buzz Lightyear's Space Ranger Spin

Ride-through laser-gun game is a blast if you aim well

★★★ ✔ FP+ You use a laser gun to shoot at over a hundred cartoon targets at this video arcade, which turns the idea of a shooting gallery inside out: here the targets stay in one place while you move on a track. Riding in a two-seat space cruiser, you fire at silly cartoon aliens, black-lit targets that often move, light up or make noise if you hit them. A dashboard display tracks your score. Though the ride is low-tech by today's standards, kids and gamers should still enjoy it.

Everything takes place in a world of toys. Buzz gets his information from a giant Viewmaster; your Space Cruiser gets its power from a backpack of double-A batteries. The ride depicts an epic battle between Buzz and the Evil Emperor Zurg, who's out to become all-powerful by stealing all of the toy world's power—its batteries.

Though it is fun, the ride does have drawbacks. Every player's laser light is the same color (red), which makes it tough to get feedback on your aim. Targets are not labeled with point values, so serious gamers waste a lot of shots. And instead of being rewarded by working together—as players are at Toy Story Mania at Disney's Hollywood Studios—here you compete against each other. Whoever controls your Space Cruiser's joystick gets a huge advantage, as they can line up the vehicle with whatever they want.

Tips. *Where to sit:* On the right. You'll face the most targets. *For Buzz fans:* The space ranger often meets guests nearby, in front of Walt Disney's Carousel of Progress.

How to get a high score. The maximum point total possible on the ride is 999,999. Here's how your score can get close to that:

1. Call dibs on the joystick, so you can keep your vehicle facing the right targets.

2. Sit on the right side of your vehicle. That side has two-thirds of the targets.

Average wait times (standby line)

9a	10a	11a	12p	1p	2p	3p	4p	5p	6p	7p	8p	9p	10p	11p
5m	35m	35m	45m	50m	50m	45m	30m	40m	35m	25m	20m	20m	10m	5m

Evil Emperor Zurg. "Guards! Seize them! And their little green friends too!"

3. Once your gun is activated, pull the trigger and hold it in for the entire ride. The flashing laser beam will help you track your aim. It will fire about once a second.

4. Aim only at targets with big payoffs: As you enter Room 1, aim for the left arm of the left robot (each hit is 100,000 points).

5. As you pass that robot, turn your vehicle to the left and hit the other side of that same arm (25,000 points).

6. As you leave the first room, turn backwards and aim at the overhead claw of the other robot (100,000 points).

7. As you enter the second room, aim at the top and bottom targets of the large volcano (25,000 points).

8. As soon as you see Zurg, hit the bottom target of his space scooter (100,000 points) by firing early and late; you can't aim low enough to hit it straight on.

9. As you enter the third room, aim about six feet to either side of the top of the exit to hit an unmarked target in the middle of a rectangular plate (25,000 points).

10. If the ride stops, find a high-value target and keep firing. You'll rack up points.

Fun fact. ❶ The track layout is unchanged from the ride's days as "If You Had Wings," a 1970s attraction that took passengers through a series of sets that portrayed Caribbean and Latin American countries served by Eastern Airlines. One area created the sensation of speed by combining wraparound point-of-view video clips with a slight breeze. As the ride didn't require one of the park's various "A" through "E" tickets, it was a guest favorite.

Fun finds. ❶ As you enter Planet Z the bendy snake from the "Toy Story" movies appears in front of you. ❷ Man-eating plant Audrey 2 from the 1986 movie "Little House of Horrors" circles to your right. ❸ "Guards! Seize them! And their little green friends, too." Zurg orders as you cruise through his spaceship. ❹ As you exit the ride, the spaceship of Stitch flies on the first mural on your right. It's tiny.

Hidden Mickeys. ❶ A green land mass forms a Mickey profile on the planet Pollost Prime. It appears four times: on a poster in the queue, to the left of the Viewmaster in the queue, on the ride in front of you as you fight the video version of Zurg and to your left in the final battle scene. ❷ Another Mickey profile appears on your left as you enter Zurg's spaceship, under the words "Initiate Battery Unload."

Key facts. *Duration:* 5 min. *Capacity:* 201. *Queue:* Indoor. *Debuted:* 1998. *Access:* ECV users must transfer. *Disability services:* Audio Description, handheld captioning. *Location:* Near Carousel of Progress.

"I'm on top the world!"

Tomorrowland PeopleMover

Breezy tour offers a nice way to unwind

★★★ ✔ Zip around Tomorrowland on this breezy and relaxing tour. An elevated track snakes you alongside, around and through four buildings. It's a great escape from a rain since the entire track is under roof. When Space Mountain shuts down you get a peek at it with its work lights on. It's shocking.

Tips. *When to go:* At night, when red lights illuminate your path. There's rarely a wait, so you can hop on whenever you like. *Want to go twice?* Just ask. *What to do:* Take photos of each other. It's one of the few Disney attractions where riders face each other.

A closer look. While planning his dream city of EPCOT, Walt Disney thought a system of small electric trains would give people an efficient, pollution-free way to run errands or get to work, as it wound alongside or circled over convenience stores, offices and mass-transit stations. He formed a separate company—Community Transportation Services (CTS)—to sell them to cities, and designed this ride as the demonstrator. But without his leadership (he died during development) the idea bombed. CTS sold only one train—in 1981, to the George Bush Intercontinental Airport in Houston. It's still running, under that airport's main terminal.

Easy to maintain, the train's power system has no moving parts except its wheels. Every six feet or so a magnetic coil in its track pulses with electricity in a carefully timed rhythm, turning on to pull a car to it, off to let it roll over it, creating a near-silent glide of linear induction. The idea won a design achievement award from the U.S. Dept. of Transportation.

Fun find. A page asking Mr. Tom Morrow to "contact Mr. Johnson in the Control Tower to confirm your Flight to the Moon" refers to the original 1971 show in the theaters that today hold Stitch's Great Escape, its host and the host of its replacement show.

Hidden Mickey. In a window, a beauty salon belt buckle displays the shape.

Key facts. *Duration:* 10 min. *Capacity:* 900 (4 per car). *Queue:* Outdoor, covered. *Fear factor:* A stretch through Space Mountain is pitch dark. *Top speed:* 7 mph (11 kph). *Debuted:* 1975, revised 1996, 2009. *Access:* Must be ambulatory. *Disability services:* Audio Description, handheld captioning. *Location:* Loads beneath Astro Orbiter.

Disney's smallest ride vehicle.

Astro Orbiter

Thrilling retro rockets fly twice as fast as Dumbo

★★★★ ✔ Fast, high and a little bit scary, open-air rockets twirl five stories above Tomorrowland on this hub-and-spoke ride. Perched atop the boarding station of the already-elevated PeopleMover ride, Astro Orbiter lifts you 55 feet (17 meters) off the ground. Guests take an elevator to reach it. But there's more to this ride than height. Top speed is 20 mph (32 kph)—plenty zippy when you're in a tight circle and your rocket tilts at 45 degrees. Flying within a huge kinetic model of rings, planets and moons, riders make about 20 revolutions around a Buck Rogers-style antenna. At night the rockets' nose cones glow green, their exhaust fires red. The ride was dismantled and refurbished in 2014; it's now much more colorful.

Unfortunately, Disney put no effort in the waiting area. You simply stand beneath the ride, waiting to board its elevator. The line moves slowly. There's nothing to do.

Tips. *When to go:* First thing in the morning. You'll get right on and can ride two, sometimes even three times in a row. Or after dark, when all the lights are on. *It's a must for:* Young thrill-seekers who are too short for the roller coasters. Astro Orbiter is Walt Disney World's only thrill ride that doesn't have a height minimum.

Fun fact. The ride's orange steel-mesh elevator is a shout-out to the rocket gantries used at launchpads in early 1960s manned space missions at nearby Cape Canaveral, Fla.

Key facts. *Duration:* 2 min. *Capacity:* 32. *Queue:* Outdoor, partially shaded. *Fear factor:* Height, angle can bother all ages. *Restraint:* Safety belt. *Top speed:* 20 mph (32 kph). *Weather issues:* Runs during light rains; grounded by downpours, lightning. *Debuted:* 1971; updated 1994, 2015 (Disneyland 1955). *Access:* Must be ambulatory. *Location:* Above the Tomorrowland PeopleMover.

Average wait times

9a	10a	11a	12p	1p	2p	3p	4p	5p	6p	7p	8p	9p	10p	11p
15m	25m	35m	30m	40m	30m	30m	30m	30m	40m	30m	15m	15m	10m	10m

Micaela Neal

A 1900s Valentine's Day.

Walt Disney's Carousel of Progress

Yesterday's great big beautiful tomorrow

★★★ ✓ Disney's first Audio-Animatronic family—father John, his wife Sarah, their children Patricia and Jimmy, Grandma and Grandpa, and grouchy Cousin/Uncle Orville welcome you into their home as they live through a hundred years of history, from the Gay '90s to the 1990s. This vintage theatrical show demonstrates how electricity has improved everyday life, and in particular reduced the wife's burden of housework (products of their time, none of the characters realize that her burden could also be eased if her husband and kids would pitch in more).

Four scenes depict the 1900s, 1920s, 1940s and 1990s. First presented at the 1964 New York World's Fair, the attraction uses a unique circular theater in which the seating area rotates from scene to scene. In each one, the family marvels about how great things are in "today's world," and John concludes that "life couldn't get any better." Last updated in 1994, the show is woefully out-of-date but still offers a charming look at the optimism of the past. It's also a historic Disney artifact.

'Don't bark at him, Rover.' The attraction has a fascinating pedigree. Disney created it

for the fair's General Electric pavilion, which in keeping with that company's slogan at the time—"Progress Is Our Most Important Product"—was called Progressland. The show demonstrated how GE appliances had a history of helping families and, in a futuristic finale set in 1966, pitched a modern "GE push-button kitchen that all but runs itself" as the family celebrated Christmas in their stylish all-electric GE Medallion home, opening presents such as a GE portable television. The sponsor's name was woven through the script. "Don't bark at him, Rover," the dad told the dog when it barked at a stranger. "He might be a good customer of General Electric."

Walt Disney wrote much of the dialogue himself, and insisted his Audio-Animatronic people perform not only basic movements but also "business" small supplemental actions that would make them seem more like real actors on a stage. Thanks to Walt, when 1920s house guest Cousin Orville relaxes in a bathtub, he also wiggles his toes.

To bridge the scenes, Disney songwriters Robert and Richard Sherman ("It's a Small World") wrote "There's a Great Big

Micaela Neal

A 1940s Halloween.

Beautiful Tomorrow." Its lyrics captured the blind optimism of the fair: *"There's a great big beautiful tomorrow, shining at the end of every day. There's a great big beautiful tomorrow, just a dream away!"*

After the World's Fair closed Disney moved the show to California's Disneyland. A revamped finale featured a home video-cassette recorder, a product that wouldn't appear in stores for more than a decade.

That '70s show. A third script tied the show into the women's movement when the attraction moved again in 1975, this time to Walt Disney World. In a new 1920s scene, the daughter searched Help Wanted ads though her father warned "It's a man's world out there." The 1940s wife demanded equal pay for wallpapering the rumpus room, asking her husband "If you hired a man to do this, wouldn't you pay him?"

A new finale showed dad cooking the Christmas turkey. To meet General Electric's new demand that the show focus on the present—"We're trying to sell light bulbs today, not tomorrow," one reportedly told Disney—the Shermans wrote a new theme song. Dissing the future as "still but a dream," it proclaimed *"Now is the time! Now is the best time! Now is the best time of your life!"*

Though the show rotated clockwise in its earlier incarnations, it switched directions for the Florida setup. It also returned to using wigs made from human hair. Nylon versions had been used at Disneyland, but over time klieg lights above the father had melted his hair into what one Disney imagineer described as "a sticky pile of goo."

Lumbago and laser discs. After losing General Electric as the show's sponsor, in 1994 Disney created a fourth version of the attraction, one which still plays today. Though it keeps much of its 1970s banter, its script is also peppered with old-fashioned sayings—the wife "gets to the core of the apple"; the husband knows it won't rain because "my lumbago isn't acting up." Peering into his dad's stereoscope, the son exclaims "Ooh la la! So that's Little Egypt doing the hoochie-koochie!" a reference to an exotic dancer at the 1893 Chicago World's Fair. The finale takes place in the great big beautiful tomorrow of, well, 1994. While mom stays busy with a laptop computer, Grandpa longs for the days before "car phones and laser discs."

Tips. *When to go:* During a hot afternoon. *Where to sit:* Second or third row center. Any farther back and the dialogue from the stage will be too faint and the background music (from the back of the room) will be too loud. *For families:* Children love watching Rover, the family dog. He appears in every scene, listening and reacting to the action.

Micaela Neal

A 1990s Christmas.

Occasionally he glances at the audience, wags his tail and barks.

Cousin Bugs. Mel Blanc, the long-time voice of Bugs Bunny and other Warner Bros. cartoon characters, provides the voice of Uncle Orville. Other voice talents include Jean Shepherd (narrator of 1983's "A Christmas Story") as the dad, Debi Derryberry (voice of Nickelodeon's Jimmy Neutron) as the daughter, Janet Waldo (daughter Judy in the 1960s cartoon series "The Jetsons" and Josie in the 1970s "Josie and the Pussycats") as the Christmas grandma and 1950s singing cowboy (and voice of the original Carousel of Progress dad) Rex Allen as the Christmas Grandpa.

'Bigger than Toad!' In the fall of 2001, less than a month after Disney World started a 15-month celebration of Walt Disney's 100th birthday, it closed his beloved Carousel of Progress. The reason: dwindling attendance. Within days, fans organized a protest. "Let's make this bigger than Toad!" wrote one blogger, referring to an earlier failed attempt to save the attraction Mr. Toad's Wild Ride. This time, however, the protest worked. Disney reopened the attraction a few months later.

Fun facts. ❶ The six auditoriums rotate at 2 feet (0.6 meters) per second on large steel wheels and tracks, just like railroad cars. **❷** The show's grandma also rocks in front of the Haunted Mansion ballroom fireplace. (Grandma is one cool old lady—early on she watches a boxing match on television and really gets into it; in the finale she beats her grandson at a video game.) **❸** Though General Electric no longer sponsors the show, it still contains its 1920s and 1940s GE appliances. **❹** The Carousel of Progress is the only Walt Disney World attraction that was touched by Walt Disney himself.

Hidden Mickeys. ❶ In the first scene, a cloth decoration forms Mickey's shape. It's above a mirror in daughter Patricia's bedroom. **❷** In the 1940s scene, the sorcerer's hat from 1940's "Fantasia" sits near an exercise machine. Mickey items in the finale include: **❸** a nutcracker on the mantel, **❹** a plush under a Christmas tree, **❺** a salt shaker on the bar, **❻** an abstract painting on the wall and at the start of a video game the son and grandma play, **❼** the engines of a spaceship **❽** and a hand-drawn shape on a pink note tacked to a bulletin board on the far right wall.

Key facts. *Duration:* 21 min. *Capacity:* 240 per theater, 6 theaters. *Queue:* Outdoor, uncovered. *Debuted:* 1964 World's Fair, Walt Disney World 1975. *Access:* Wheelchairs, ECVs OK. *Disability services:* Assistive listening, handheld and activated video captioning. *Location:* Between Buzz Lightyear's Space Ranger Spin and Space Mountain.

Standby on the left, FastPass on the right.

Space Mountain

Walt Disney World's first roller coaster is still its best

★★★★★ ✔ FP+ "Daddy, did you hear me scream?!" beamed the 6-year-old girl, hopping out of her rocket. "That! Was! Cool!" said her 10-year-old brother. The parents shared a look. "Let's ride again!" exclaimed the wife.

Open-air rockets zoom through a dark universe inside this circular building, which holds the world's oldest, and arguably still best, roller coaster in the dark. Sitting in low-slung ride vehicles that are just a single seat wide, guests hurtle through an inky abyss filled with shooting stars. Every dip, drop and turn comes as a surprise. Top speed is 28 miles per hour (45 kph), plenty fast in the dark.

Have a nice flight. The ride's story begins as you enter the building, a futuristic space-port and repair center that's orbiting above the earth. Passing the departure board, a long tunnel leads to a launch platform. Once you board a rocket, a sign urges you to "Check Invisible Oxygen Dome," another flashes

"Have a Nice Flight" and then off you go—into the flashing blue "energizing portal" that powers your machine. Climbing the launch tower (the chain lift), you pass under a large ship that's in for service. Then you blast off, on a journey through what an early Disney press release called "the void of the universe." As you come back to earth, you trigger a sonic boom in a red "de-energizing" tunnel.

A few years ago Disney made the ride darker and smoother and added ambient techno music and sound effects. It also added a bank of video games to its standby queue as well as a few knowing references to the 1970s.

'Where's Mr. Smee?' With astronauts Scott Carpenter, Gordon Cooper and Jim Irwin as its first passengers, Space Mountain opened on Jan. 15, 1975. Though Disney promoted it as "the nation's most breathtaking thrill ride," not every guest got the message. As they climbed in their rockets many expected

Average wait times (standby line)

9a	10a	11a	12p	1p	2p	3p	4p	5p	6p	7p	8p	9p	10p	11p
30m	85m	95m	70m	90m	95m	75m	80m	65m	65m	70m	65m	55m	40m	20m

Energizing portal.

something along the lines of Peter Pan's Flight, since back then Disney parks didn't have roller coasters. Moments later, up came their lunches and out flew their hats, purses, eyeglasses and, more than once, false teeth. Disney's response included discreetly ironing out some of the most violent jerks and jolts.

Though it opened during a recession, Space Mountain was an instant smash. When summer came, families with teens, many of whom would not have considered a Disney vacation before, began crowding Magic Kingdom turnstiles early each morning. The recession, in ●rlando at least, ended.

Tips. *Where to sit:* The front row of a front rocket gives you the most immersive experience, the most breeze and the most surprises, Row 1 on the boarding platform. *Long legs?* You'll prefer Row 1 or 4. *Need speed?* Back seats fly faster through turns and down drops.

Fun facts. ❶ Space Mountain's blue "energizing portal" has a practical function: its flashing lights shrink your pupils so your flight seems darker than it really is. ❷ Why do the docked ship's engine nozzles look like the plastic caps of spray-paint cans? Because they are. Used by an artist on a small concept model, the caps were accidentally reproduced perfectly on the full-scale prop. ❸ The ride has 30 rockets, numbered 1 through 31. There is no rocket 13.

Fun finds. ❶ Panels just inside the building refer to it as Star Port Seven-Five, a nod to the ride's opening year. ❷ The attraction has four tributes to the Discovery One spacecraft seen in the 1968 movie "2001: A Space ●dyssey." The angled clapboard walls of the ride's entrance tunnel are those of its transport interior. In the boarding area, the spool-like corners the rockets pass by are the axles of the ship's rotating living quarters. The blue strobe tunnel recalls its hexagonal corridor that leads to its EVA pods. The docked ship at the lift hill has Discovery ●ne's unique head-spine-and-hip shape. ❸ Intergalactic route maps along the queue hide references to the Little Mermaid, Mickey's pet dog and the 1937 movie "Snow White and the Seven Dwarfs." ❹ The ship at the chain-lift is labeled MK-1, a hint that Magic Kingdom's Space Mountain is the original version of the ride; similar versions have since been built in four other Disney parks around the world.

Key facts. *Duration:* 2 min 30 sec. *Capacity:* 180. *Queue:* Indoor. *Restraint:* Lap bar. *Top speed:* 28 mph (45 kph). *Fear factor:* Surprising drops, turns. *Debuted:* 1975, revised 2009. *Access:* Height min 44 in (112 cm); wheelchair, ECV users transfer. *Health advisory:* Avoid if claustrophobic, pregnant or have back, blood pressure, heart, motion sickness or neck problems. *Location:* Back of Tomorrowland.

A rule to live by: never let your sister drive.

Tomorrowland Speedway

Slow smelly race cars are horribly dated, surprisingly fun

★★★ ✓ FP+ Sounding and smelling like Harleys that desperately need tune-ups, small-scale race cars rumble down a half-mile track at this vintage attraction, children behind their wheels. Meandering past beautiful live oaks and magnolias, riders wind around five turns and under and over a bridge. Some cars are left-hand drive, some right.

Straight out of a Six Flags park, the ride's sun-baked waiting line is one of Disney's worst. Umbrellas offer some shade; a covered grandstand gives those not riding a way to sit down in the shade.

Tips. *When to go:* First thing in the morning, or after dark with a FastPass when the ride is breezy. *Where to sit:* In the passenger seat if you have a child, or aren't as child-like as your companion. *Want to race?* Ask for two cars side by side. *Not riding?* Take a starting-line snapshot from a footbridge above the track, just past the boarding area.

Fun facts. ❶ Why is this old-time attraction in Tomorrowland? For a reason that could only make sense in the world of Disney: When it opened in 1971, the track was a version of Autopia, an attraction in California's Disneyland which when it opened in 1955 represented the interstate highways of that era's future. ❷ Today's attraction also has remnants of a 1994 redo. It turned the ride into a Indianapolis 500-style event that included outer-space aliens among its drivers.

Key facts. *Duration:* 5 min. *Capacity:* 292 (146 cars). *Queue:* Outdoor, partially shaded. *Restraint:* Lap belt. *Top speed:* 7 mph (11 kph). *Weather issues:* Closed during thunderstorms. *Debuted:* 1971 (Disneyland 1955). *Revised* 2011. *Access:* Height min 54 in (137 cm) to take car out alone, 32 in (81 cm) to ride; must be ambulatory. *Location:* To the left of Space Mountain, next to Fantasyland.

Average wait times (standby line)

9a	10a	11a	12p	1p	2p	3p	4p	5p	6p	7p	8p	9p	10p	11p
20m	30m	30m	35m	40m	40m	30m	35m	40m	40m	30m	25m	20m	10m	5m

Phineas leads a conga line.

Move It! Shake It! Dance & Play It!

Shake your groove thing with Disney characters

★★★★ ✔ You can dance with a Disney character in this colorful street party, which takes place a few times a day in front of Cinderella Castle. If you're not shy about dancing in public, it's an easy way to have a fun character experience. Beginning in Town Square as a five-float parade, the procession turns into an interactive party when it reaches the Cinderella Castle hub, as hosts Mickey Mouse, Minnie Mouse, Donald Duck, and Goofy invite you to snap a few selfies of yourself dancing. Soon you're urged into the street to dance with other characters, and perhaps join in a conga line. Finally, you and the rest of the crowd choose a current pop tune to be the show's finale.

Dancing characters include Baloo and King Louie (from 1967's "The Jungle Book"), cartoon chipmunks Chip 'n Dale, Woody and Jessie from the Toy Story films, Disney Channel stars Phineas and Ferb and Nick Wilde and Judy Hopps, the stars of 2016's "Zootopia." The show is an update of the former Move It! Shake It! Celebrate It! show.

The street party takes place in direct sunlight, and the asphalt really reflects the heat; privately some performers refer to the show as "Shake It Bake It." Whenever the heat index is above 105 degrees—that's nearly every afternoon between May and September—Disney cuts the conga line.

Tips. *Which show to see:* The first one or the last one, when the weather's cooler. *How to get your selfies on the floats:* Post them to Twitter or Instagram. #moveitshakeitpics.

Key facts. *Duration:* 12 min. *Weather issues:* Cancelled during rain; shortened when the heat index is above 105 degrees. *Debuted:* 2009. *Access:* Special areas for guests in wheelchairs, ECVs. *Location:* Proceeds down Main Street, stops at the Cinderella Castle plaza for the show, then returns.

Typical show times

9a	10a	11a	12p	1p	2p	3p	4p	5p	6p	7p	8p	9p	10p	11p
---	---	11:00	12:30	---	---	---	---	5:45	---	---	---	---	---	---

Disney's Festival of Fantasy Parade.

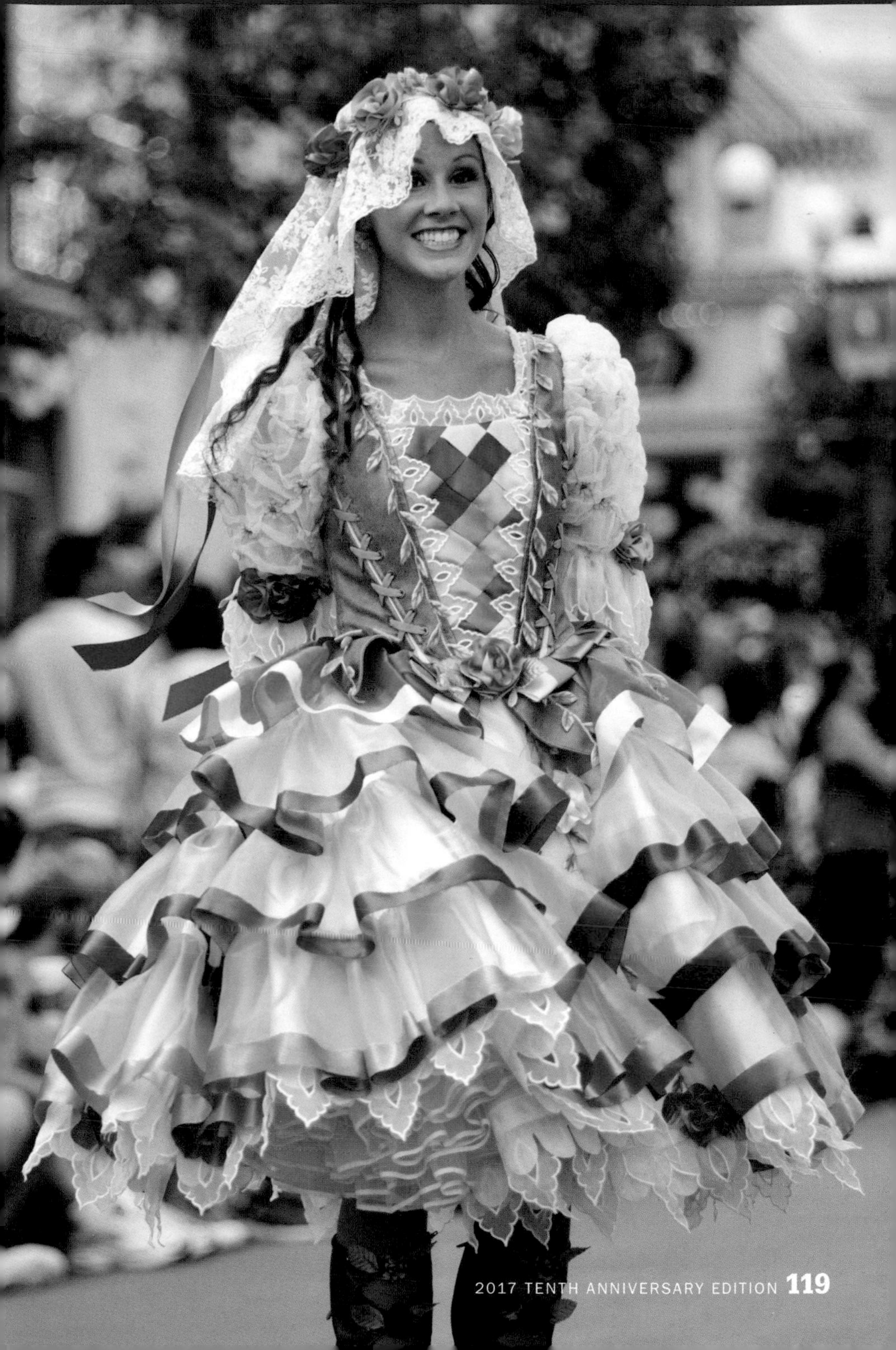

© Disney

Ariel flips her tail.

Disney's Festival of Fantasy Parade

Disney's best parade has beautiful floats, costumes, music

★★★★★ ✔ FP+ Magic Kingdom's new-for-2014 parade is truly new—nothing is re-used from past parades, nothing has been patched together. The performers wear fantastic costumes, bursting with color. Floats celebrate Disney princesses, "Tangled," "The Little Mermaid," "Peter Pan" and "Brave." The eye-popper is the "Sleeping Beauty" segment, which stars the evil Maleficent as a giant fire-breathing Steampunk dragon. Unfortunately, some characters (including Mickey Mouse) are high in the air, making it tough for children to interact with them.

The park's sound system was upgraded for this parade, adding more musical zones and improving the equipment. The procession's music was composed by Mark Hammond, who also wrote the score for the popular Mickey's Soundsational Parade at California's Disneyland. Regal trumpet riffs give the parade a celebratory feel.

On rainy days Disney runs an alternate procession, the brief Rainy Day Cavalcade. It consists of an assortment of characters waving from a few Main Street Vehicles.

Tips. *When to go:* Arrive 45 minutes early to get a great viewing spot (with a FastPass, 20 minutes). *Where to stand:* The best spot is now the FastPass spot: in front of the Emporium in Town Square, in the middle of Main Street U.S.A., facing the castle. Another good choice: the inner circle of the castle hub, again facing the castle; the parade will arc around you.

Hidden Mickeys. ❶ The three-circle shape appears as balloons in the upper left corner of the parade banner, ❷ as a blue jewel and two smaller white jewels in the center of a large snowflake above "Frozen's" Queen Elsa, ❸ as indentations on a gear on the belly of the dragon Maleficent ❹ and as three bolts on the elbow of its left foreleg.

Key facts. *Duration:* 12 min. *Fear factor:* The dragon occasionally breathes plumes of fire. *Showtime:* Daily at 3p, peak days add an earlier parade at noon. *Weather issues:* During rain replaced by short procession. *Debuted:* 2014. *Access:* Reserved area for wheelchair viewers. *Location:* Travels through Frontierland, then Liberty Square and finally down Main Street U.S.A.

Funhouse face. From "Pinocchio."

Main Street Electrical Parade

Lite-Brite floats create cheesy, charming time trip

★★★★ ✔ FP+ Shimmering with light, everything—floats, characters, twirling snails—is covered with tiny bulbs in this Moog-music marathon, which is either wonderful, weird or wonderfully weird, depending on your point of view. Most people love it, clapping along to its "electro-synthomagnetic musical sounds" and applauding its floats, most of which pay tribute to classic Disney movies.

Tinker Bell (1953's "Peter Pan") kicks things off, sprinkling pixie dust that swirls over every float that follows. Goofy's is first, a train with Mickey and Minnie Mouse. Next comes Alice (1951's "Alice in Wonderland"), who chats with guests from atop a giant mushroom, that film's hookah-smoking caterpillar behind her. Dopey (1937's "Snow White and the Seven Dwarfs") drives a gem-filled mine train. Dancing donkey-eared boys lead in a decadent carnival float (1940's "Pinocchio"), a giant funhouse face backed by huge cigar-store Indians. Anastasia and Drizella (1950's "Cinderella") steal the spotlight from their stepsister, awkwardly holding up their legs as they beg Prince Charming to let them try on his glass slipper. One float honors 1977's

"Pete's Dragon," the latest Disney movie at the time this parade debuted. Oddly appropriate, a red-white-and-blue finale salutes the United States, as high-stepping chorus girls line a long American flag.

One downside: The parade's song, a manic version of the 1966 synthesizer ditty "Baroque Hoedown," repeats.

And repeats.

And repeats.

Tips. *When to go:* Arrive 30 minutes early to get a decent viewing spot. *Where to stand:* On Main Street to see the parade with a great backdrop of either Cinderella Castle or Main Street facades, and if you're leaving the park afterward a short walk to the exit.

Fun fact. The parade is a sequel of sorts to the Electrical Water Pageant, 14 floats with an equally electro vision. Around since 1971, it travels the Seven Seas Lagoon nightly.

Key facts. *Duration:* 20 min. *Weather issues:* Canceled during rain. *Debuted:* 1977, revised 2010 (Disneyland 1972). *Access:* Reserved areas for wheelchair viewers. *Location:* Starts on Main Street U.S.A., then travels Liberty Square and Frontierland.

Bright lights, moving images.

Celebrate the Magic

High-tech light show transforms Cinderella Castle

★★★★ Using projected animated images and video, Cinderella Castle appears to transform during this nighttime show; the building becomes, in essence, a three-dimensional movie screen. Some of the visuals are bizarre. At one point the star of the 2012 movie "Wreck it Ralph" appears on the structure, which morphs it into an 8-bit brick version of itself that Ralph proceeds to wreck until hero Fix-It Felix saves the day. Later the castle becomes Buzz Lightyear's rocket ship and appears to blast off above itself—a tough thing to do.

Most scenes feature songs from Disney movies, including "I Want to Be Like You," from the 1967 film "The Jungle Book" and "I Just Can't Wait to Be King" and "Hakuna Matata" from 1994's "The Lion King." Delicate snowflakes swirl up the castle walls in a frosty segment from the movie "Frozen," complete with Queen Elsa belting out the Academy Award-winning song "Let It Go."

Disney updates Celebrate the Magic a few times each year.

Tips. *When to go:* Show up in front of the castle about 15 minutes before the show begins to get a good spot to watch it (however you may already be there, as this projection show is sandwiched between the end of the Main Street Electrical Parade and the start of the Wishes fireworks show. Celebrate the Magic sometimes plays twice a night, before the parade and then again before Wishes). *Where to stand:* In the center of the castle hub, no closer than the statue of Walt Disney. From this spot, you'll be far enough away to see the front of the castle and its angled sides, all of which have different images and special effects projected onto them, but be close enough to see all of the details. If viewed from an angle, the projections become distorted and skewed. *For families:* The segment featuring Maleficent could frighten your toddlers; you may want to distract yours from the villain's appearance.

Key facts. *Duration:* 10 min. *Fear factor:* The Maleficent moment has scary music and images. *Showtimes:* Once or twice a night; before Wishes, sometimes before the nighttime parade. *Weather issues:* Canceled during rain. *Debuted:* 2012 (revised often). *Access:* Wheelchairs, ECVs OK. *Location:* Projected onto the front of Cinderella Castle.

Seven hundred explosions, 12 minutes.

Wishes

Synchronized fireworks are breathtaking, inspiring, touching

★★★★★ ✔ FP+ Tinker Bell flies from Cinderella Castle in Disney's signature fireworks show. It starts with a lone glowing star arching through the night sky. After narrator Jiminy Cricket (from 1940's "Pinocchio") talks about wishing on a star, $200,000 worth of pyro explode in sync with the voices of beloved Disney characters and the beats and rhythms of classic songs.

Far more sophisticated than you might expect, Wishes paints delicate strokes as well as bold. Sometimes the sky sparkles, sometimes it flashes. The show packs an emotional punch too, as it teaches a heart-tugging lesson about believing in yourself. Parents often tear up during the finale.

Tips. *When to go:* 20 minutes before showtime. *Where to stand:* On the crest of the Main Street U.S.A. bridge, between the ice cream parlor and the castle hub. You'll be far enough away to see all the fireworks, but also close enough to see the castle's lighting effects. *For families:* Instead of fighting the huge crowd that leaves the park right after the show, get some ice cream and ask your children about their dreams and wishes. Tell them yours.

Fun fact. Tinker Bell is sometimes a man. The role's physical requirements are only that "she" weigh less than 105 pounds (48 kg) and be shorter than 5 foot 3 inches (160 cm).

Fun finds. ❶ Fireworks form stars during the opening verse of "When You Wish Upon a Star." ❷ Hearts appear at the end of a "Beauty and the Beast" segment; ❸ a frowning face during the villains portion. ❹ As each Disney character says their wish, the accompanying fireworks are the color of his or her signature wardrobe. ❺ During the "Sorcerer's Apprentice" sequence, the castle is lit to resemble the blue hat Mickey Mouse wore in that segment from 1940's "Fantasia," with its white stars and moons. ❻ Images of the Evil Queen's mirror appear on the castle as she commands "Slaves in the magic mirror, come from the farthest space..."

Key facts. *Duration:* 12 min. *Fear factor:* Loud noises. *Weather issues:* Cancelled for thunderstorms. *Debuted:* 2003. *Access:* Reserved areas for wheelchair viewers. *Location:* The fireworks explode far behind and alongside the castle; the best viewing spots, by far, are in front of it.

Epcot

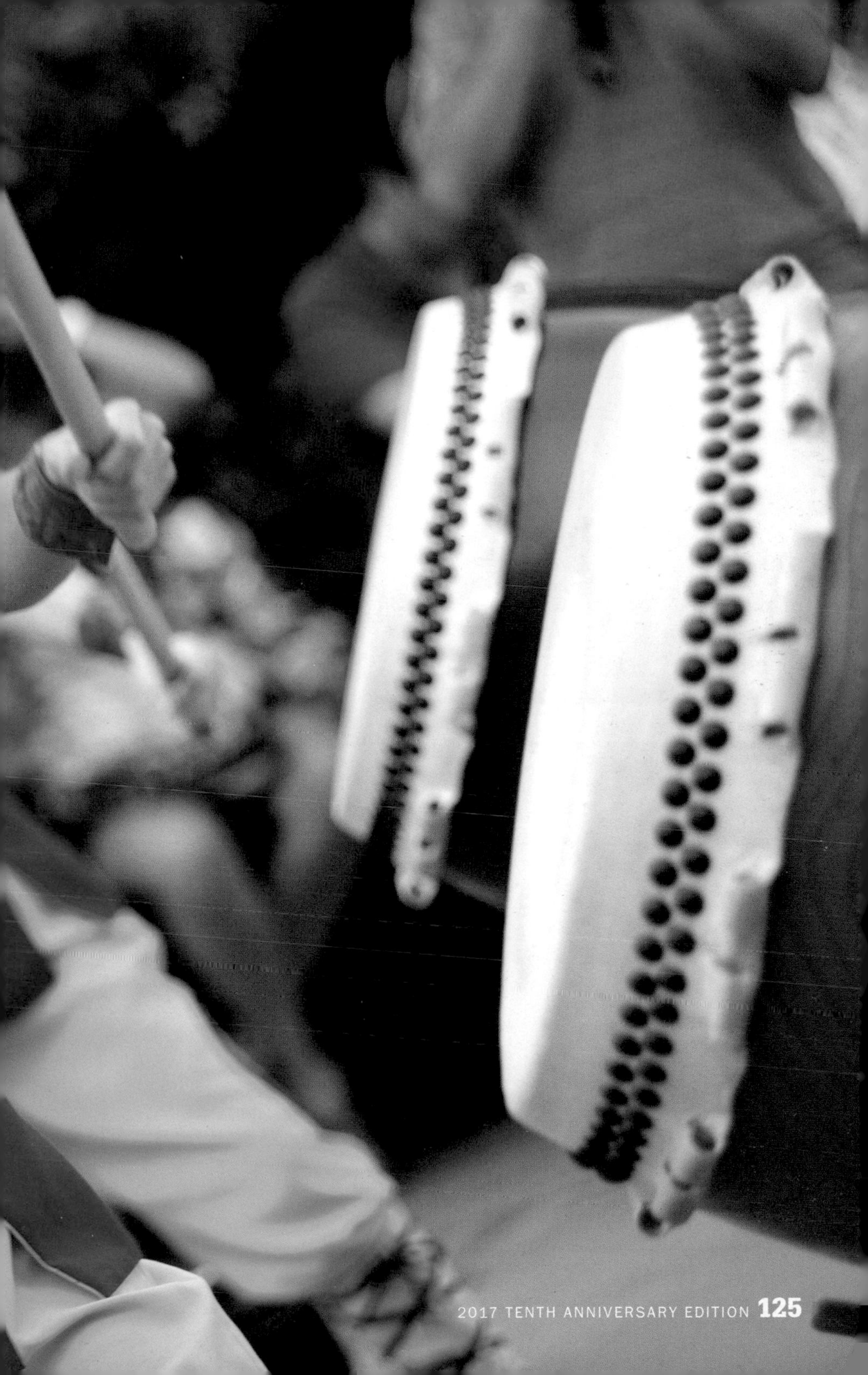

Spaceship Earth.

HUMAN ACHIEVEMENT RULES at this park, which celebrates science, technology and diversity. Like a World's Fair, it's grouped into pavilions, and its experiences are more interesting than thrilling, more inspiring than exciting.

Divided into two sections, Epcot has a split personality. With its abundance of scientific themes, Future World is a logical thinker, a corporate nerd with a pocket protector. Emphasizing culture, World Showcase is a people person, a music-loving shopaholic with a margarita in her hand.

The park forms a Figure 8. The bottom circle is Future World, with six pavilions and a central plaza. The top loop is World Showcase with 11 pavilions on a central lake. The two areas keep separate hours. In general Future World opens at 9 a.m. and closes at 7 p.m.; World Showcase is open from 11 a.m. to 9 p.m.

Best of the park. Three must-do attractions: ❶ Soarin' Around the World, ❷ Turtle Talk with Crush and ❸ The American Adventure. The best restaurants: ❹ Via Napoli, ❺ Monsieur Paul and ❻ Spice Road Table. ❼ Happiest Place on Earth: La Cava del Tequila. Other Epcot highlights: ❽ Outdoor areas aren't as crowded as those at other Disney parks, thanks to the many plazas and pavilions. ❾ The variety of attractions. Nowhere else can you talk to an animated turtle, train to be an astronaut and have Ben Franklin and Mark Twain teach you the true meaning of being an American—all in the same day. ❿ The extreme variety of food, alcoholic drinks and candy. ⓫ The native young adults in each World Showcase country, who love to chat. ⓬ The wares of the World Showcase, especially those in the Japan, Mexico and Morocco pavilions. ⓭ The live entertainment. Each act is something different. ⓮ Only at Epcot can you meet characters such as Joy and Sadness from "Inside Out," the Three Caballeros version of Donald Duck or Launchpad McQuack from "Ducktales."

Worst of the park. Attractions: ❶ Ellen's Energy Adventure, ❷ Journey Into Your Imagination with Figment, and though we hate to say it, ❸ Frozen Ever After. As for restaurants: ❹ Nine Dragons and ❺ the Lotus Blossom Café. ❻ The scarcity of Disney smiles in the public spaces of Future World, which are oddly lacking in cast members. ❼ Beyond some coloring stations, Agent P's World Showcase Adventure and the Frozen ride, Epcot has few child-focused experiences. ❽ Many attractions and pavilions have blatant corporate sponsorships, which may make you wonder why Disney's charging you if it's also charging them. ❾ The walking. Hike through Future World and you've still got 1.3 miles to go to get around the World Showcase. Hard to do on a hot day.

The World Showcase.

Opposite page photo © Disney

If it rains. Epcot is a mixed blessing on wet days—though it's mostly comprised of indoor pavilions with multiple activities, those pavilions are spread out—walking between them will get you soaked. Test Track closes when lightning is nearby. IllumiNations can get cancelled due to rain, as can all the park's outdoor concerts and street entertainment.

Family matters. Four rides have height minimums—Mission Space (44 in, 112 cm), Soarin' Around the World and Test Track (40 in, 102 cm) and Innoventions' The Sum of All Thrills (48 in, 122 cm). Other attractions that might scare children include Ellen's Energy Adventure, Journey Into Imagination with Figment and the evening IllumiNations spectacle. Every restaurant has a children's menu. Most pavilions have Kidcot Fun Stops, which let children progressively decorate a free cutout of Duffy the Disney Bear.

Where to meet characters. Nearly two dozen characters appear at Epcot. It's the only place at Disney to meet Mulan, Baymax or Joy and Sadness. Many characters are at the Epcot Character Spot in Innoventions Plaza; FastPasses are available for Mickey and Minnie Mouse and Goofy. The Garden Grill in Future World and the Norway Akershus Royal Banquet Hall in the World Showcase

host character meals; the latter gathers a gaggle of princesses. Random characters pop up to the left of the American Adventure and near the International Gateway.

Aladdin. Morocco.
Alice. U.K. garden; Norway meals (often).
NEW! **Anna and Elsa.** Norway pavilion.
Ariel. Norway meals (often).
Aurora. Norway meals (often).
NEW! **Baymax.** Character Spot.
Belle. France along the World Showcase walkway; Norway meals (often).
Chip 'n Dale. Garden Grill.
Cinderella. Norway meals (often).
Daisy Duck. Main entrance plaza.
Donald Duck. Mexico, in garb from the 1944 movie "The Three Caballeros."
Goofy. Character Spot.
Jasmine. Morocco; Norway meals (often).
NEW! **Joy and Sadness.** Character Spot.
Marie. France (sporadically).
Mary Poppins. U.K. in front of the tea garden; Norway meals (often).
Mickey Mouse. Character Spot; Garden Grill (in farmer garb).
Minnie Mouse. Character Spot.
Mulan. China; Norway meals (often).
Pluto. Garden Grill; World Showcase gazebo in front of Disney Traders East.
Snow White. Germany wishing well; Norway meals (often).

Joy and Sadness.

World Showcase rain.

Know before you go. Need a stroller? Cash? A FastPass fix? Here's where to find it:

ATMs. *Park entrance (far left), bridge between Future World and World Showcase, near the American Adventure restrooms; International Gateway entrance.*

Baby Care Center. Changing rooms, nursing areas, microwave, playroom. Sells diapers, formula, pacifiers, OTC meds. *Odyssey Center, between Test Track and Mexico.*

FastPass+ kiosks. Cast members help you book and reschedule FastPasses. *Future World East and West breezeways, center of Innoventions Plaza, International Gateway.*

First aid. Registered nurses treat minor emergencies, call EMTs for serious issues. *Next to the Baby Care Center, Odyssey Center.*

Guest Relations. Cast members answer questions, reserve restaurants, exchange currency, have maps and times guides for all parks, store items found in the park that day. *Walk-up windows outside park entrance (far right); walk-in lobby left of Spaceship Earth.*

Locker rentals. $7 a day, $5 deposit. *At the Camera Center near Spaceship Earth; International Gateway.*

Package pickup. Disney will send anything you buy in the park to either park main entrance to pick up later at no charge. Allow three hours. Packages can also be delivered to Disney hotels or shipped nationally.

Parking. Cars $20 a day. Preferred parking adds $15, gives everyone in car bottle of water.

Stroller rentals. Outside the front entrance on the far left, also at the International Gateway. Single strollers are $15 a day ($13 length of stay), doubles $31 ($27 length of stay). Get replacements at the Germany pavilion.

Disney transportation. Monorails run to the Transportation and Ticket Center (TTC), connect to the Contemporary, Grand Floridian, Polynesian Village resorts and the Magic Kingdom park. Buses serve all other Disney resorts and theme parks as well as the Blizzard Beach water park; there's no direct service to Disney Springs, Typhoon Lagoon or ESPN Wide World of Sports. Boats serve Disney's Hollywood Studios and Epcot resort hotels from the park's International Gateway.

Wheelchair and scooter rentals. Each entrance rents wheelchairs for $12 a day ($10 length of stay). EVCs are $50 ($20 deposit).

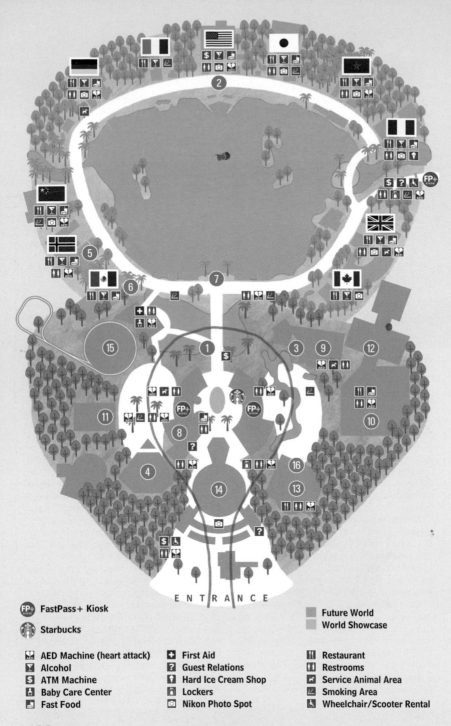

Art: Micaela Neal

Attractions at a glance

Numbers in orange circles correspond to those shown on the map at the left.

① Agent P's World Showcase Adventure. UPDATED! ★★★★★ ✔ Now you can use your phone to stop Dr. Doofenshmirtz from taking over the World Showcase. This interactive scavenger hunt triggers hidden actions and effects throughout the land's pavilions. It's based, of course, on the Disney Channel series "Phineas and Ferb." *World Showcase.*

② The American Adventure. ★★★★★ ✔ Audio-Animatronics figures tell the story of this country, warts and all, with help from elaborate stage sets and interesting film segments. Moving. *The American Adventure pavilion, World Showcase.*

③ Disney & Pixar Short Film Festival. NEW! ★★★★★ ✔ **FP+** Three cartoons show off the state of 3-D animation—Pixar's 2001 "For the Birds" and 2012 "La Luna," and Disney's 2013 "Get a Horse!" In-theater effects enhance each short. "Get a Horse!" is so good you can't tell what's real. Replaced Captain EO in 2016, with an upgraded theater. *Imagination Pavilion, Future World.*

④ Ellen's Energy Adventure. ★★ Before she was Dory, comedian Ellen DeGeneres briefly became a corporate shill for Exxon-Mobil and starred in this elaborate 45-minute infomercial for fossil fuels. Includes a blast of a Big Bang and some cool dinosaurs. *Universe of Energy pavilion, Future World.*

⑤ Frozen Ever After. NEW! ★★★ FP+ The Audio-Animatronic versions of Anna, Elsa and other characters are outstanding at this indoor boat ride; the rest isn't much. *Norway pavilion, World Showcase.*

⑥ Gran Fiesta Tour. UPDATED! ★★★ You love the history of Mexico. You adore Disney's 1944 movie "The Three Caballeros." Or you've just had too many margaritas and will giggle at anything. That's why you'll love this bizarre, confusing, insulting yet somehow addictive attraction, an indoor boat ride that's one long strange trip. Now with an Audio-Animatronics finale. *Mexico pavilion, World Showcase.*

⑦ IllumiNations. ★★★★ ✔ **FP+** Nightly fireworks and laser show abstractly portrays the history of the world. *World Showcase.*

⑧ Innoventions. UPDATED! ★★★ ✔ Hands-on corporate exhibits showcase science and technology. You design then ride a virtual roller coaster at Raytheon's Sum of All Thrills; explore the importance of color at Glidden's new Colortopia. Now just one building. *Innoventions Plaza, Future World.*

⑨ Journey Into Imagination with Figment. ★★ FP+ Monty Python's Eric Idle takes you on a tour of the stuffy Imagination Institute on this dark special-effects ride. Few people like it, fewer care. *Imagination pavilion, Future World.*

⑩ Living with the Land. ★★★★ ✔ **FP+** Odd plants and farming techniques highlight this indoor boat tour through greenhouses. *The Land pavilion, Future World.*

⑪ Mission Space. ★★★★ FP+ Choose from two types of flight simulators to fly off to Mars. A hardcore version secretly spins you on a NASA-designed centrifuge that provides intense G forces. A sissy substitute secretly doesn't do anything but keeps you from throwing up. Take the warnings seriously. Min. height 44 in. (112 cm). *Future World.*

⑫ Soarin' Around the World. UPDATED! ★★★★★ ✔ **FP+** Simulated hang-glider trip now travels the world, flying over natural and manmade landmarks. State-of-the-art video definition will defy your expectations; breezes, scents, and gentle swooping movements make it all seem pretty real. There's no narration, just dramatic music. The most popular ride in the park, with the wait times to prove it. Now with a third theater to lessen that load. Min. height 40 in (102 cm). *The Land pavilion, Future World.*

⑬ The Seas with Nemo & Friends. ★★★★ ✔ **FP+** An excellent collection of sealife fills these marine exhibits, which lack Disney's usual creative treatment. A gentle entrance ride retells the story of 2003's "Finding Nemo." *The Seas pavilion, Future World.*

⑭ Spaceship Earth. ★★★★ ✔ **FP+** Slow-moving dark ride uses Audio-Animatronic characters and elaborate sets to portray the history of communications. Better than it sounds. *Future World.*

⑮ Test Track. ★★★ FP+ You design a car then virtually test it on a real track; speeds reach 65 mph (104 kph). Min. height 40 in (102 cm). *Future World.*

⑯ Turtle Talk with Crush. UPDATED! ★★★★★ ✔ **FP+** New random cameo appearances by "Finding Dory" characters add even more surprises to this already superb theatrical show. An animated sea turtle engages in real-time conversations with his audience in ways you won't think are possible. *The Seas pavilion, Future World.*

Innoventions Plaza.

Future World

ACCORDING TO DISNEY'S PRESS RELEASES of the period, when it opened Epcot this land explored how "the wonders of enterprise" and "the innovative aspects of technology" would be used in a tomorrow that "promises new and exciting benefits for all." The land was "a showcase of discovery filled with new ideas," a corporate-sponsored world that brought technology and science to life.

But that didn't quite work out. Though companies did sign on as sponsors, many didn't see a large enough return on their investment. Over time many pavilions were redone as more traditional Disney attractions, or in some cases closed or torn down altogether. Today most of Future World isn't about the future, but when you visit it you may not care. Because much of what's left, and what's been added, is an innovative delight.

The land's layout mimics the left-right division of the human brain. As you enter the park, pavilions on the left focus on analytical, linear or engineering issues (i.e. energy, space travel, the automobile) and sit within a landscape of straight-lined walkways. Pavilions on the right cover more natural topics (the land, seas, human imagination) and rest in a hilly, meandering, watery landscape.

Fun finds. ❶ Every 30 minutes the central fountain performs a five-minute show choreographed to music. ❷ Fiber-optic lights hide in the sidewalks of Innoventions Plaza, pinpoints of shimmering stars in dozens of small squares. Colorful changing patterns appear in three 6-foot squares in front of the Epcot Character Spot. The lights are on all day, but only noticeable at night. ❸ Three drinking fountains imitate submarine sounds, sing opera and offer wisecracks such as "Hey, save some for the fish!" when water hits their drains. You'll find them in front of MouseGear along the east side of the Innoventions fountain, near the play fountain between Future

World and the World Showcase and close to the restrooms behind the Epcot Character Spot. ❹ Embedded in the walkway that leads from Innoventions Plaza to The Land pavilion, five rings of an Inventor's Circle honor 38 discoveries and inventions. Inventions listed in the inner ring lead to discoveries in the outer ring the inventions helped make possible. For example, the Alphabet leads to the "World Wide Web." ❺ Toss your trash at the Electric Umbrella fast-food spot and you may hear a voice inside your trash can talk back to you. Use the receptacle closest to the north-most entrance doors and a surfer dude may complain "Like, your trash just knocked off my shades!" or a Frenchman may cry "Zis ees my lucky day! French fries!"

Live entertainment

Future World only has one live performing group, a percussion trio:

★★★★★ ✔ **Jammitors.** Using trash cans and pails as instruments, janitors transform into witty drummers. *Innoventions Plaza.*

Restaurants and food

They're tough to find, but the land has two table-service restaurants as well as one of best fast-food spots in any Disney park.

★★★★★ ✔ **$37 DDP Coral Reef.** You'll eat fish while you watch fish at this dimly lit hidden treasure, where a long glass wall looks into The Seas aquarium. The signature appetizer is a creamy lobster bisque; entrees are consistently good. Brushed-metal tables are trimmed in light woods. Arrive at 11:30 a.m. and you may be able to walk right in; otherwise book lunch two weeks early; dinner at least 60 days out. When you arrive ask for an aquarium-front table on the floor; it's worth a longer wait. Amazed by the sharks, turtles and other sealife swimming inches away from them, tired children may forget they're tired. *11:30a–3:30p, 4p–9p; $20–$33 (children $10–$13). Seats 275. The Seas pavilion.*

NEW! ★★★★ ✔ **$51 DDP Garden Grill.** Now serving breakfast as well as lunch and dinner, this often-overlooked country restaurant offers Disney's most unusual character meals. Perched on the top floor of The Land pavilion, the circular Garden Grill is built like a merry-go-round, its open dining balcony slowly rotating around its kitchen once every two hours. Tables overlook the indoor portion of the Living with the Land attraction, which includes a rainforest and other landscapes. As you dine, cartoon chipmunks Chip 'n Dale, "farmer" Mickey Mouse and Pluto mosey up and sometimes sit a spell. Thanks to the restaurant's small size you see the characters

Coral Reef.

Jammitors.

often, maybe three times each if you stay an hour. Food is served "family style"—servers bring big platters and bowls to your table for your party to share, and replenish them as often as you like. Breakfast includes typical eggs, bacon and Mickey waffles but also a signature item unique to this spot, Chip's Sticky Bun Bakes. Lunch and dinner feature typical sliced beef and turkey, but also a Farmer's Salad that uses vegetables grown in the pavilion's greenhouses. Ask to sit on the balcony's outside ring and you'll get another benefit: your booth's high-backed seats will block your view of the rest of the restaurant, making each character's stop at your table a delightful surprise as you won't see him coming. *Breakfast 8a–10:30a; $30 (children $18). Lunch and dinner 11:30a–3p, 4p–8:30p; $42 (children $25). Seats 150. The Land pavilion.*

★★★ **$17 DDPq Electric Umbrella.** A new menu upgrades this sandwich spot, which serves burgers, a sausage and pepper sandwich, chicken salad, vegetarian flatbread and a veggie naan-wich. Kids meals include a flatbread. *11a–9p; $10–$14 (children $6–$7). Seats 426. Innovations Plaza.*

★★★ **$9 DDPq Starbucks Fountain View.** A Starbucks with a typical menu (with breakfast sandwiches) but no indoor seats. *9a–9p, $2–$6. Seats 68 outside. Innovations Plaza.*

★★★★★ ✔ **$16 DDPq Sunshine Seasons.** This excellent food court serves fresh grilled meats, noodles, salads, sandwiches, tasty soups; I recommend the chicken and salmon. There's breakfast too; the morning panini seems to be everyone's favorite. Nothing is fried. *Breakfast 9a–11a; $6–$10 (children $5). Lunch and dinner 11a–9p; $9–$14 (children $6–$7). Seats 707. The Land pavilion.*

★★★ **$8 DDPs Cool Wash.** Frozen slushies (Coca-Cola, raspberry lemonade and blue raspberry) with or without alcohol. No food. *Noon–7p; $5–$10. No seats, 6 stand-up tables, benches nearby. Near the Test Track exit.*

★★★★ ✔ **$8 DDPs Imagination Beverage.** Flavored popcorn (cheddar cheese, buffalo bleu cheese, sour cream and chive). Also regular popcorn, cotton candy, beer. *Noon–7p; $4–$5. Near the Imagination pavilion.*

★★★ **$11 DDPs Joffrey's.** Coffees, tea, hot chocolate, alcoholic coffees; pastries. *9a–9p; $4–$9. Near Universe of Energy.*

★★★ **$11 DDPs** **The Land Cart.** Pretzels, hummus, whole fruit, other healthy stuff. *10a–9p, $5–$7. In front of the Land pavilion.*

NEW! ★★★ **$11 DDPs** **Taste Track.** Soft-serve ice cream, root beer floats and sundaes make up the new offerings at this nondescript stand. Also hard root beer. It formerly sold grilled cheese sandwiches. *$4–$10. No seats, 6 stand-up tables, benches nearby. Near the Test Track exit.*

Shops and merchandise

Unique ride souvenirs stand out from the typical Disney items sold at these stores. And oh yeah, there's a place with free soft drinks.

After Market. Automotive apparel and toys; Test Track souvenirs. *Test Track exit.*

The Art of Disney. A gallery of lithographs, oil paintings, figurines. *Along the left side of Spaceship Earth.*

Camera Center. Camera equipment, picture frames, photo albums; MagicBands; phone, tablet cases. *Under Spaceship Earth.*

Cargo Bay. Space-themed apparel, toy rocket ships, packaged astronaut food, kid's astronaut costumes. Check out the toy X-2 rocket, from the ride. *Mission Space exit.*

Club Cool. This Coca-Cola shop is known throughout the Disney universe not for its Coke merchandise, but rather its unlimited free samples of soft drinks that the company sells in other countries. The best ones: Bibo from South Africa and Fanta Pineapple from Greece (mix them together). As a joke Disney has slipped in a bitter Italian apéritif: Beverly. *Innoventions Plaza.*

Gateway Gifts. Disney souvenirs, sundries. *Under Spaceship Earth.*

The Gift Stop. Disney souvenirs, sundries. *Outside the main gate at the far right.*

ImageWorks. Figment-themed merchandise, plushies. *At the exit of Journey Into Imagination with Figment.*

MouseGear. The main Epcot souvenir store, this huge place has all kinds of Disney items, the routine and the special. For the most part, however, it does not stock the international items sold in the World Showcase pavilions. *Innoventions Plaza.*

Pin Central. Assorted Disney collectible pins. Cast Members nearby are prepared to trade pins with guests. *Innoventions Plaza.*

SeaBase Gift Shop. "Finding Nemo" and "Finding Dory" apparel, toys, plushies, souvenirs. *At the exit of The Seas pavilion.*

Soarin' Gift Counter. Soarin' Around the World souvenirs, horticulture items (as this is the sign-up spot for Disney's Behind the Seeds greenhouse tour), Lion King merchandise (due to the nearby Circle of Life show). *Soarin' Around the World entrance, the Land pavilion.*

Club Cool.

Micaela Neal

A 1960s computer room.

Spaceship Earth

Slow ride through history is cooler than it sounds

★★★★ ✔ FP+ That huge silver sphere is more than the park icon. It's also a ride: a time trip through the history of communications. A four-seat vehicle spirals you slowly past detailed Audio-Animatronic scenes, starting with prehistoric cave-dwellers and continuing through the Dark Ages, Renaissance, Industrial Age and the start of the computer era. Narrating your trip is Dame Judi Dench, the English actress who played "M" in a series of James Bond films and Queen Elizabeth in "Shakespeare in Love."

The ride's 22 dioramas include a 1960s IBM computer room as programmers watch over a huge reel-to-reel mainframe; one tech sports an Afro that's bigger than her miniskirt yet smaller than her go-go boots. Next you pass through a 1976 Silicon Valley garage where a young Steve Wozniak creates the first personal computer, his storage shelf made of boards and concrete blocks. The ride's score features a 62-piece orchestra and 24-voice choir.

You shape your own future as the ride nears its finish. A touchscreen inside your ride vehicle lights up with a series of questions, asking how you'd like to live or work in the future. Then you're treated to a cartoon view of yourself a few decades from now, your face superimposed onto a silly animated body. Children in particular love this moment.

The exit of the ride is Project Tomorrow, a post-show area that features four interactive exhibits, all of which showcase the attraction's sponsor, Siemens. A giant globe in the room pinpoints the hometowns of all of that day's Spaceship Earth passengers.

Tips. *Just want to play the games?* The Project Tomorrow area has a separate entrance on the back sides of the building. *For couples:* This is Disney's best ride for snuggling; it's dark, slow and has bench seats.

Average wait times (standby line)

9a	10a	11a	12p	1p	2p	3p	4p	5p	6p	7p	8p	9p	10p	11p
10m	35m	40m	35m	30m	20m	15m	15m	10m	10m	10m	10m	5m	---	---

Fun facts. ❶ Famed science-fiction author Ray Bradbury ("Fahrenheit 451") helped design the ride, as did consultants from the Smithsonian Institution, the University of Southern California and the University of Chicago. ❷ It has 56 robotic figures. ❸ Its caveman speaks a Cro-Magnon language; cave drawings are based on images found in the Salon-Niaux cave in Ariège, France. ❹ Egyptian hieroglyphics replicate actual Middle Eastern designs. ❺ A pharaoh's words come from a real letter. ❻ Rewritten in 2008, the current narration has changed the meaning of a few scenes. The former Greek thespians are now teaching math. The burning of Rome is now a fire at the Library of Alexandria. And though they were once "debating ideas," Disney's medieval scholars are now "watching over books to save our dreams of the future." ❼ The family watching television first appeared in the RCA Home ❶f Future Living, the original post-show at Magic Kingdom's Space Mountain. ❽ Why is there a long pause after the questions about your future? Because that's where Disney originally planned a pop quiz. "While we're creating your future," Dench was to say, "let's see how much you remember about the past."

The Ball of Presidents. Many of the Audio-Animatronic figures in Spaceship Earth are duplicates of those who portray U.S. Commanders in Chief at Magic Kingdom's Hall of Presidents. Look carefully (and often beyond scruffy beards) to notice that the ride's Greek scholar is actually William Henry Harrison, its Roman soldier really Zachary Taylor, its Roman senator Theodore Roosevelt. Study two seated Islamic scholars to find Franklin Pierce and John Tyler; look at their leader and you'll see William Howard Taft. Later, a monk writing on parchment is John Adams. Is that Alexander Gutenberg inventing the printing press? Why no, it's James Buchanan! As you enter the Renaissance check out the lute player on your right—Dwight D. Eisenhower—and the sculptor on your left—Ulysses S. Grant. Three figures on your ride are duplicates of historical figures seen in an attraction at Epcot, the American Adventure. That show's Native American Chief Joseph is this ride's prehistoric shaman; its Andrew Carnegie is Gutenberg's pressman; its Matthew Brady Spaceship Earth's telegraph operator.

Other fun finds. ❶ At the telephone switchboard, two out of three callers are told "I'm sorry, that line is busy." ❷ The radio

A Greek scholar. President Harrison.

station's call letters "WDI" refer to Walt Disney Imagineering. ❸ A placard in the computer room states "Think," the slogan of IBM founder Thomas J. Watson that inspired Apple's "Think Different." ❹ Nearby is a 1960s IBM Selectric typewriter and a manual for the System 360 Job Control Language used on 1964 mainframes. ❺ "Coming Soon: Home Videoplayers" predicts the headline of a magazine article taped to the wall behind Woz. To his left is a pizza box with one slice left in it. Above him is a poster for Fleetwood Mac. ❻ Touchscreen "Work" futures always predict "a great big, beautiful tomorrow," the title of the theme song to Magic Kingdom's Carousel of Progress.

Hidden Mickeys. ❶ Mickey's three circles appear as parchment ink blots made by a sleeping monk and ❷ as bottle rings on the table of the first Renaissance painter.

Key facts. *Duration:* 14 min; allow up to 45 min for post-show activities. *Capacity:* 76 (19 Omnimover ride vehicles, each with two 2-person seats). *Queue:* Outdoor, partially covered. *Debuted:* 1982, revised 2008. *Access:* Must be ambulatory, stops to load mobility-impaired guests; narration in English, French, German, Japanese, Portuguese or Spanish. *Disability services:* Audio Description. *Location:* At the front of Future World, just inside the park entrance.

Caribbean aquarium.

The Seas with Nemo and Friends

Underrated pavilion displays odd sea life, trains dolphins

★★★★ ✔ Dolphins smile, sharks lurk, manatees float and sea turtles paddle at this pavilion, which is themed to the 2003 movie "Finding Nemo." To enter it you board a Clammobile (think Doom Buggy) which passes animated dioramas and video screens that re-create scenes from the film. Eventually the animated fish appear to swim with real ones.

Exhibits. On the first floor, **Bruce's Shark World** educates children about threats sharks face with interactive displays. A **Nemo & Friends** room contains live versions of "Finding Nemo" stars, including clownfish, blue tangs, Moorish idols and cleaner shrimp. Tanks also hold eels, frogfish, venomous lionfish, seahorses and live coral. On the second floor, a huge **Caribbean aquarium** is filled with angelfish, cobia, lookdown, rays, sharks, snapper, tarpon and turtles. An observation tunnel extends into it. Thrice a day **a herd of dolphins** shows off its skills in identity matching, rhythm identification and echolocation. An **aquaculture room** holds coral, cuttlefish, giant clams and clownfish.

In a small **manatee aquarium**, endangered Florida sea cows munch lettuce heads; you watch them from above the surface or through an underwater window. Docents give talks twice an hour.

Fun finds. ❶ Clinging to the aquarium glass as the fish around her continue to sing "Big Blue World," sea star Peach often begs "Hey wait! Take me with you! It's a nice song but they just never stop! Never, never, ever, ever, ever!" ❷ Rub Bruce's sandpapery skin and he'll respond "Oooooo! That's good!"

Key facts. *Fish feedings:* 10a, 3:15p. *Dolphin sessions:* 10:45a, 2:15p, 4:15p. *Queue:* Indoor. *Access:* Wheelchairs, ECVs OK. *Disability services:* Reflective captioning, assistive listening; Audio Description. *Debuted:* 1982, revised 2007. *Location:* The Seas pavilion.

Average wait times

9a	10a	11a	12p	1p	2p	3p	4p	5p	6p	7p	8p	9p	10p	11p
10m	15m	25m	30m	25m	20m	25m	20m	15m	15m	10m	10m	---	---	---

Destiny joins Dory and Crush.

Turtle Talk with Crush

Animated turtle jokes like an improv star in real time

UPDATED! ★★★★★ ✔ FP+ Thanks to some hidden cameras, real-time animation techniques and an talented improv performer backstage, children have real-time conversations with the animated surfer-dude sea turtle at this delightful show, which is based on the 2003 movie "Finding Nemo" and now the 2016 film "Finding Dory." Appearing on a viewing window that looks into his ocean, Crush addresses his subjects by name ("Elizabeth, your polka-dot shell is totally cool!"), asks specific questions ("Austin, is that your female parental unit in the fourth row? She's a total babe!") and reacts to their responses. His facial expressions are priceless.

Crush also works in some turtle trivia and conservation tips, and welcomes blue tang Dory, who can't speak whale perhaps a little too well. A 2016 update added characters from "Finding Dory," including Destiny the whale shark, Bailey the beluga whale and Hank

the octopus, and cameos from Nemo, Marlin or Crush's son Squirt. Different shows have different characters.

The theater is in the Seas pavilion. Seating is on backless benches; young children sit up front on a carpeted floor. The queue holds jellyfish, stingrays, eels and fish from the Great Barrier Reef. Getting a FastPass for the show guarantees you entry, but no special seating.

Tip. *To have Crush talk to your child:* Have her sit down front or along the theater's center aisle and wear a funny hat. *If your child is in a wheelchair:* If she would like to be near the screen, ask a cast member to arrange it before the show begins.

Key facts. *Duration:* 12 min; shows every 20 min. *Capacity:* 210. *Queue:* Indoor. *Access:* Wheelchairs, ECVs OK. *Disability services:* Reflective captioning, assistive listening; Audio Description. *Debuted:* 2004, revised 2016. *Location:* Seas pavilion.

Average wait times (standby line)

9a	10a	11a	12p	1p	2p	3p	4p	5p	6p	7p	8p	9p	10p	11p
10m	20m	20m	20m	15m	15m	15m	20m	20m	20m	15m	10m	10m	---	---

© Disney

High above Sydney.

Soarin' Around the World

Hi-def hang-gliding trip offers awe-inspiring ride

UPDATED! ★★★★★ ✔ FP+ "It's only a movie… it's only a movie…" That's what you'll say to yourself as you ride this updated hang-gliding experience. A poem to planet Earth, it takes you around the world, giving you the exhilarating sensation of flying over— sometimes through—places that no real hang glider could. Stunning scene transitions add to the thrills. A new super higher-definition screen makes some moments almost too real.

A wild fantasy. As you lift up to 40 feet (12 meters) into an 80-foot (24-meter) projection dome, from all sides your vision fills with natural landscapes and man-made wonders. Your glider tilts as it travels, your legs dangling free underneath. Hidden fans, odorizers, and surround-sound speakers subtly add to the experience.

Tips. *Where to sit:* In the center of the top row: Row 1, Gate B; views from the sides (Gates A or C) can skew the film's images.

Afterward: Consider taking a break at the pavilion's food court; the new film may be harder on your stomach than you expect.

Fun finds. ❶ Soarin' cast members may refer to your flight as "No. 5-5-0-5," a nod to the ride's opening date of May 5, 2005. ❷ The entire attraction resembles an airport. Cast members dress as airline employees, the gift stand looks like a ticket counter, the theater has runway lights, its gliders navigation lights. ❸ Manta rays swim in the water at Fiji.

Hidden Mickey. During the ride's finale, so big it's hardly hidden.

Key facts. *Duration:* 5 min. *Capacity:* 174 per each of 3 theaters (one new). *Queue:* Indoor. *Fear factor:* Gives a realistic sense of being in midair. *Restraint:* Seat belt. *Debuted:* 2005; redone 2016. *Access:* Height min 40 in (102 cm); wheelchair and ECV users must transfer. *Disability services:* Handheld captioning. *Location:* The Land pavilion.

Average wait times (standby line)

9a	10a	11a	12p	1p	2p	3p	4p	5p	6p	7p	8p	9p	10p	11p
20m	55m	90m	65m	50m	60m	75m	60m	55m	55m	50m	40m	20m	---	---

Tropical greenhouse.

Living with the Land

Slow boat ride takes compelling trip past exotic plants

★★★★ ✔ FP+ This indoor boat ride presents a subject that's usually dull as dirt—agricultural science—in an entertaining way. A calm float through four greenhouses, it's filled with weird plants and odd growing techniques you've never seen before. Nearly everything is interesting to look at, as are the fresh aromas of the leaves and fruit.

Crops include hanging bananas, coconuts, papayas; enormous nine-pound lemons and jackfruit weigh down their branches. Many plants hang from trellises, naked roots in the air. Some grow on overhead conveyor belts, touring their greenhouses like suits in a dry cleaner. You're bound to see a Mickey-shaped fruit or vegetable, grown in a plastic mold.

You also float through an aquaculture hut with young alligators, eels and sturgeon. The ride begins with a journey through a rainforest, desert and farm, each complete with Audio-Animatronic animals.

Tips. *When to go:* When you're already in the pavilion, waiting for your Soarin' FastPass time. *Where to sit:* In the front row, for the most legroom and best view.

Key facts. *Duration:* 14 min. *Capacity:* 20 per boat. *Queue:* Indoor. *Debuted:* 1982, last revised 2009. *Access:* ECV users transfer. *Handheld captioning. Audio Description. Location:* The Land pavilion, next to Soarin' Around the World.

★★ **The Circle of Life.** Though it's dated and badly faded, this short film stars Simba, Timon and Pumbaa from "The Lion King" and teaches an important lesson about protecting the environment. *Duration:* 13 min. *Capacity:* 482. *Queue:* Indoor. *Debuted:* 1995. *Access:* Guests may stay in wheelchairs, ECVs. Handheld, reflective captioning; assistive listening. *Location:* You enter the theater on the second floor of The Land pavilion, near its entrance.

Average wait times (standby line)

9a	10a	11a	12p	1p	2p	3p	4p	5p	6p	7p	8p	9p	10p	11p
10m	20m	20m	20m	20m	10m	10m	10m	5m	5m	0m	---	---	---	---

Figment's living room.

Journey Into Imagination with Figment

Tour the Imagination Institute. And turn into a zombie.

★★ FP+ You tour the stuffy Imagination Institute on this slow-moving dark ride. As director Dr. Nigel Channing (Eric Idle) demonstrates how he can "capture and control" imagination through the study of the human senses, he's continually interrupted by Figment, a free-spirited little dragon who soon takes over your tour and leads you into his home. It's upside-down, which proves, the creature says, that imagination comes "home" when it sees things from new perspectives.

"Huh?" you may ask. Exactly. Nothing makes sense and worse, you don't care. The last time I rode this ride, the family next to me consisted of a little girl who dozed off during it and her two parents, each of whom had the blank stare of a zombie. There is one nice effect. In a cage past the Sight Lab, a huge butterfly disappears as you pass it. In the original ride (1983–1999), Figment was the creation of Dreamfinder, a jolly wizard-like scientist.

Fun Finds. ❶ Hallway office doors show that the Institute employs professor Wayne Szalinski (of Disney's 1989 live-action comedy "Honey, I Shrunk the Kids"), ❷ inventor Phillip Brainard (1997's "Flubber") ❸ and principal Dean Higgins (1969's "The Computer Wore Tennis Shoes"). ❹ A page seeks student Merlin Jones (1965's "The Monkey's Uncle"). ❺ In another nod to Higgins, a pair of tennis shoes sits outside the ride's computer room.

Hidden Mickeys. ❶ A Mickey-eared pair of headphones sits in the Sight Lab, on top of a wheeled table. ❷ A toilet seat and two carpets form the three circles in Figment's bathroom.

Key facts. *Duration:* 6 min. *Capacity:* 224. *Queue:* Indoor. *Fear factor:* The last room has a sudden flash. *Debuted:* 1983, last revised 2001. *Access:* Guests may remain in wheelchairs, ECVs. *Disability services:* Handheld captioning, Audio Description. *Location:* The Imagination pavilion.

Average wait times (standby line)

9a	10a	11a	12p	1p	2p	3p	4p	5p	6p	7p	8p	9p	10p	11p
5m	20m	15m	15m	15m	15m	15m	10m	10m	10m	5m	5m	5m	---	---

© Disney

"Get a Horse."

Disney & Pixar Short Film Festival

Crisp 3-D showcases three stellar shorts

NEW! ★★★★★ ✔ FP+ The humor, the charm, the visual creativity of top-notch animation. You fully appreciate it when you see this trio of 3-D cartoons, especially when you see them here. In-theater effects add to the fun, but what stands out is the video. It's so clear.

The highlight is "Get a Horse," an excellent tribute to early Disney animation. Starring pie-eyed versions of Mickey, Minnie and the nefarious Peg-Leg Pete, it presents itself as a black-and-white short from the 1920s—an illusion that's tossed out the window once Mickey bursts through the screen. "Get a Horse" played in theaters in 2013, with "Frozen."

Next is "La Luna", a touching tale of a little boy who goes out to sea to learn what his father and grandfather do for a living, which is sweeping fallen stars off the moon. "La Luna" debuted with 2012's "Brave."

The trilogy wraps up with the lighthearted "For the Birds." When a funny-looking fowl tries to make friends with a flock of squeaky songbirds, they mock him. Bad idea. "For the Birds" debuted with 2001's "Monsters, Inc."

The theater's light crowds and cool air-conditioning make it perfect to visit during a hectic or hot day. Animation buffs will enjoy the preshow video. It offers a look at the history of Disney and Pixar shorts, presented through voice recordings of Walt Disney and interview clips of John Lasseter.

Fun Fact. In "Get a Horse" Mickey is voiced by Walt Disney. In fact, all the characters in that short are voiced by their original actors. Achieving that goal wasn't easy. Producers spent two weeks splicing together takes of Walt as Mickey to make the mouse say "red."

Fun Finds. All in "Get a Horse": ❶ When Horace Horsecollar walks onstage he's wearing a Captain America T-shirt and eating Milk Duds. ❷ A woman's voice yells "My nachos!" whenever a character crashes into the audience. ❸ Oswald the Lucky Rabbit pops up for a blink-and-you'll-miss-it cameo at the end.

Tip. *Where to sit:* In the center of a back rows for the most impressive 3-D effects.

Key facts. *Duration:* 18 min. *Showtimes:* Continuous. *Capacity:* 570. *Queue:* Indoor. *Debuted:* 2015. *Access:* Wheelchairs, ECVs ●K. *Disability services:* Handheld, reflective captioning; assistive listening. *Location:* Magic Eye Theater, Imagination pavilion.

A pointed lesson: Oil is good.

Ellen's Energy Adventure

Ellen DeGeneres, Bill Nye, a Big Bang, Big Oil... and dinosaurs

★★ An outdated attraction that has wit, robotic dinosaurs and a corporate take on the Universe of Energy. What is... Ellen's Energy Adventure? Correct!

This multimedia show starts off on a big video screen—with Ellen DeGeneres displaying the same loopy wit she used as Dory in 2003's "Finding Nemo" and 2016's "Finding Dory"—as her neighbor Bill Nye the Science Guy stops by her apartment to ask for some aluminum foil, a clothes pin and a candle.

Her reply: "Another hot date, huh?"

Watching as her snooty old college roommate (Jamie Lee Curtis) competes on the game show "Jeopardy," Ellen falls asleep and dreams that she's on the show too, and all of its categories deal with a subject she knows nothing about—energy. "Freezing" her nightmare, she asks Nye for help, and he takes her back in time for a crash course in Energy 101.

You go with her, and learn about it too.

Moving into a large theater, three huge screens dramatically portray the creation of the Earth: billions of years compressed into one stunning minute. Then the seating area breaks apart into trams, and you travel with Ellen through a swamp filled with dinosaurs—a close-up look at the beginning of fossil fuels. Eventually everyone returns to the present, and Ellen uses her new-found knowledge to become a "Jeopardy" champion.

Created before the tragic events of 9/11, the show totally ignores the problems of oil. There's no mention of the Middle East, no talk of global warming, oil spills or even fuel efficiency. The attraction was designed in part by Exxon-Mobil, its sponsor until 2004.

Tips. *When to go:* Anytime; there's never a crowd. *Where to sit:* In the left side of the auditorium, on the far right of a row about halfway back. You'll get close to the dinosaurs and still get a good view of each video segment.

Fun find. Michael Richards, who played Kramer in the television series "Seinfeld," cameos as a caveman who discovers fire.

Key facts. *Duration:* 45 min (shows every 17 min). *Capacity:* 582. *Queue:* Outdoor, unshaded. *Fear factor:* Loud Big Bang. *Debuted:* 1982, updated 1996. *Access:* ECV users transfer. *Disability services:* Assistive listening, handheld captioning. *Location:* Universe of Energy pavilion.

Heading to their training missions.

Mission Space

Designed with NASA, flight to Mars is almost too realistic

★★★★ FP+ So intense it includes motion-sickness bags, this flight simulator offers realistic sensations of space flight. It's set in the year 2036, as you and other astronauts are training for a mission to Mars. Though commander Gary Sinise reviews your duties carefully, as soon as you lift off everything goes wrong. You land on Mars, barely.

The ride has two versions. An "Orange" one gives you a real sense of a rocket launch, but can also make you dizzy, nauseated or worse. That's because, behind the scenes, its ride capsules sit on the spokes of a NASA-designed G-force creator, a rapidly rotating centrifuge. A "Green" ride gives you the same visual experience without the G-forces, as its capsules don't move. An elaborate post-show area has games, kiosks and a toddler area.

NEW! Your name and recommended job on Mars appear on a screen alongside the ride exit—if you're wearing a MagicBand.

Tips. *When to go:* Anytime except right after you've eaten. *How not to get sick on the Orange ride:* Stare straight at the video.

Fun finds. ❶ A prop from Disney's 2000 Sinise movie "Mission to Mars," a 35-foot (11-meter) Gravity Wheel borders the queue. ❷ Its hub includes the logo for Horizons, the original pavilion on this site.

Hidden Mickeys. ❶ In the attraction's courtyard as patio tiles and ❷ craters on the moon near the Luna 8 site, ❸ and in the queue as Mars craters on desk monitors.

Key facts. *Duration:* 6 min. *Capacity:* 4 per vehicle. *Queue:* Indoor. *Restraint:* Shoulder harness. *Debuted:* 2003, revised 2009. *Access:* Height min 44 in (112 cm); wheelchair, ECV users transfer. *Disability services:* Activated video captioning. *Health advisory:* Avoid if claustrophobic, pregnant or have back, blood pressure, heart, motion sickness or neck problems. *Location:* Behind MouseGear.

Average wait times (standby line)

9a	10a	11a	12p	1p	2p	3p	4p	5p	6p	7p	8p	9p	10p	11p
15m	30m	35m	40m	30m	25m	20m	25m	20m	15m	20m	25m	20m	---	---

Chevrolet concept vehicle.

Test Track

Virtually build a car, then virtually test it on a real ride

★★★ FP+ With 34 turns but no drops or loops, this mile-long thrill ride is ideal for those who like the speed of roller coasters but hate big drops—and don't mind a confusing storyline.

Using a touchscreen, you first choose your vehicle's strongest attribute (capability, efficiency, responsiveness or power) and create its shape, color and graphics. Then you board a real vehicle (not influenced by your design), and zoom down straightaways and through turns as it calculates how your design would have handled them. You begin on a dark track inside the building, as glowing light strips recall Disney's 1982 movie "Tron" and its 2010 "Tron Legacy." Then you head outside, where a speed loop whips you around the building at 65 mph. Post-show games link to your virtual car; a showroom displays real Chevys.

Tips. *Where to sit:* For the most legroom sit in the middle of a seat. *To fully experience it:* Help young children design their cars; it's a little complex. If you're with an older child, friend or spouse tell the cast member outside the design studio that each of you wants to create a car, that way you can virtually race them against each other. *About the Single Rider line:* If you use it you won't design a car, but rather pick from pre-made vehicles.

Hidden Mickeys. The shape hides on the right side of the Standby queue in photo collages ❶ of designers ❷ and concept artists.

Key facts. *Duration:* 5 min. *Capacity:* (6 per vehicle in two rows). *Queue:* Indoor, with Single Rider line. *Fear factor:* Intense speed. *Restraint:* Seat belt. *Weather issues:* Closed during thunderstorms. *Debuted:* 1999, revised 2012. *Access:* Height min 40 in (122 cm), must be ambulatory. *Disability services:* Activated video captioning. *Health advisory:* Avoid if claustrophobic, pregnant or have back, blood pressure, heart, motion sickness or neck problems. *Location:* Next to Mission Space.

Average wait times (standby line)

9a	10a	11a	12p	1p	2p	3p	4p	5p	6p	7p	8p	9p	10p	11p
55m	60m	75m	80m	60m	55m	70m	55m	50m	60m	55m	40m	40m	---	---

© Disney

Colortopia.

Innoventions

Corporate exhibits offer fun diversions, change often

★★★ ✔ This building houses sponsored displays with games or activities. Most are fun—the Sum of All Thrills and Colortopia exhibits especially so—but it's hard to feel you're on vacation while big corporate logos stare you in the face. For years, Innoventions was divided into two buildings, Innoventions East and Innoventions West. The latter closed in 2016; a portion of it has been redone as an addition to the Epcot Character Spot, with characters from the newest Disney or Pixar animated film, as well as a Photo Place for visitors with Disney Visa cards (1p–7p).

NEW! Colortopia. This Glidden Paint exhibit is all about the importance of color. You do three activities in order. First is the Power of Color Theater, where you learn "how every color tells a story" as colored lights shine on the white walls as a narrator explains how colors inherently associate with different ideas or moods. Next is the Color Lab, where multicolored discs spin side by side, appearing to mix colors together. You play a color game against the people around you; at the end you receive your "color ranking." Last, you use electronic paintbrushes with virtual paint to color in a picture on an interactive screen in the Color Our World Studio. Images change and react to the different colors you use; you can email the finished picture to yourself. Colortopia opened in 2016, replacing the Test the Limits Lab, a longtime Underwriters Laboratories exhibit.

StormStruck. This Federal Alliance for Safe Homes exhibit compares how different homes fare during a hurricane.

Sum of All Thrills. This Raytheon physics-based exhibit is the only Innoventions ride. After designing a roller coaster, jet plane or bobsled track, you experience it virtually in a small capsule that moves atop a robotic arm.

Take a Nanooze Break. Presented by Cornell University and National Science Foundation, this small interactive exhibit give you a feel for things that are too small to see. It's also a chance to get off your feet.

Key facts. *Duration per exhibit:* Avg 30 min. *Debuted:* 1994, revised 2016. *Access (Sum of All Thrills):* Height min 48 in (122 cm), wheelchair and ECV users transfer. *Disability services:* Audio Description. *Location:* Innoventions Plaza.

Canada pavilion.

World Showcase

THEY COME FROM ALL OVER THE WORLD, the young people who staff the pavilions of this special area. There's more than a thousand of them, most working as clerks and waiters, and nearly all are friendly, open and willing to chat. Recruited by Disney agents in their home countries, they come to the World Showcase for a year through the Disney Cultural Representative Program, using a special "Disney visa" the company persuaded the United States government to create just for this purpose.

They appear in pavilions that represent 10 countries: Canada, China, France, Germany, Italy, Japan, Mexico, Morocco, Norway and the United Kingdom. An eleventh one represents the United States. Each is meant to be a microcosm of its country, celebrating its architecture, culture and cuisine.

Originally planned to be a theme park of its own, the World Showcase has an odd shape. Round. Connected by a wide walkway, clusters of buildings circle a man-made 40-acre (16-ha) lake. Disney designed the area to hold 20 countries, almost twice the number it has, which inadvertently resulted in spacious gaps throughout the loop. In the 1980s the company announced it would add pavilions representing Israel, Spain and Equatorial Africa, but later canceled those plans.

The World Showcase has two entrances. A southern pedestrian bridge connects it to Epcot's Future World area, as do some small walkways off to its sides. Between the United Kingdom and France pavilions, a walkway also leads off to Epcot Resorts, a large hotel area that consists of Disney's BoardWalk Inn and Villas, Disney's Yacht and Beach Club and the Marriott-owned Walt Disney World Swan and Dolphin. Known as its International Gateway, this entrance offers complimentary water-taxi service to those hotels as well as Disney's Hollywood Studios theme park.

Pavilions. The architecture of each pavilion replicates vernacular styles of its country, and in some cases particular historic buildings. Few of these references are mentioned by Disney, however. Plaques pop up only occasionally. Most of the following details come from handouts Epcot's Guest Relations office gave to visitors back when the park opened in 1982. This survey of the pavilions tours them in a counterclockwise fashion, the direction most visitors walk through the area.

Canada. A Native Canadian Tsimshian carved one of the totems at the main entrance to this 3-acre (1-ha) version of our northern neighbor. Standing in front of a native log cabin, the 30-foot (9-meter) pole depicts the Raven folk bird releasing the sun, moon and stars from a carved cedar chest. Landscaping and architectural elements include allusions to all of the country's provinces and territories. A forced-perspective facade of the Hotel du Canada, a version of Ottawa's 1912 Chateau Laurier backs a flowery landscape based on Victoria's Butchart Gardens. Alongside the entrance courtyard, a trading post anchors a native village. Up the steps, a small stone building reflects the British influence on Canada's east coast.

The Canadian Rockies form the back of the area. A flowered path leads to a small canyon with a 30-foot (9-meter) waterfall. Pine-studded slopes surround a mine shaft trimmed with shoring and Klondike equipment.

The United Kingdom. Each building in this sprawling pavilion represents a different period in U.K. history. Approaching it from Canada, you first come to Hampton Court, the 16-century palace of King Henry VIII. It sits along the World Showcase walkway, its red brick walls topped by turrets and medieval crenelation. The white-stone side of the building is Abbotsford, the 19th-century Scottish estate where Sir Walter Scott wrote novels such as "Ivanhoe" and "The Lady of the Lake." Across a street is the 16th-century thatched-roofed cottage of Anne Hathaway, the wife of William Shakespeare. Farther down the street sits a half-timbered 15th-century Tudor leaning with age, a plaster 17th-century pre-Georgian, a stone 18th-century Palladian and a home built of angled bricks.

Alongside the lagoon, the Rose & Crown Pub is divided into three styles: a medieval rural cottage, a 15th-century Tudor tavern, and an 1890s Victorian bar.

France. It's Paris—the Paris of La Belle Époque, "the beautiful time" of optimism, elegance and progress from 1870 to 1910. You approach it by crossing the River Seine on the Pont des Arts footbridge (in other words, crossing the bridge over the canal that leads to Epcot's International Gateway

French cart manager.

entrance). Passing through a small park that, if you look at it right, recalls a key painting of the period—Georges Seurat's "A Sunday Afternoon on the Island of La Grande Jatte"—you enter a small vintage village, its three-story buildings topped with copper and slate mansard roofs, many with chimney pots; its town garden a manicured maze. Down a side street is Les Halles, an 1850 fruit and vegetable market built of iron and glass. Towering in the distance is the Eiffel Tower, with a period-correct tawny finish.

Morocco. Run by the Kingdom of Morocco, this World Showcase pavilion is the truest to its country and the most exotic, with food, music and wares that are little-known in the West. Meant to evoke a desert city, its walls are brick, tan plaster, and reddish sandstone. Each of the pavilion's intricate tiled rooms has at least one tiling mistake. Moroccan artists created deliberate flaws to reflect the Muslim belief that only Allah creates perfection.

Like traditional Moroccan villages, the pavilion is divided into two sections, the new (ville nouvelle) and old (medina). Out front, the new city recalls Casablanca and Marrakesh. It's anchored by the prayer tower of the Koutoubia Mosque, the largest religious structure in Marrakesh.

The medina of Fez lies in back, behind that city's 8th-century gate Bab Bou Jeloud. On the left of this walkway is the central courtyard of a traditional Moroccan home, complete with the sounds of the family. On the right is an open-air market, its bamboo roof lashed to thick beams. Wafting incense will remind baby boomers of a head shop. Behind the market, Restaurant Marrakesh sits within a southern Moroccan fortress.

Ancient cemeteries, in a theme park? Actually, Epcot has two of them: the Pyramid of Quetzalcoatl at the Mexico pavilion, and the Chellah Minaret, the tower of a 14th-century necropolis that rises above this pavilion's old town—as well as, in real life, Morocco's capital city of Rabat.

Japan. Founded in 1673, Japan's oldest retail business runs this pavilion. In Japan, Mitsukoshi is known for its department stores. In Epcot, it's known for a compound that symbolizes its country's culture through graceful architecture and landscaping.

The left side of the pavilion represents culture and religion. A pagoda recalls the 8th-century Horyuji Temple in Nara. Its five stories represent the five elements of creation—earth, water, fire, wind and sky. A hill garden's evergreens symbolize eternal life, its rocks the long life of our planet and its koi-filled water the brief life of animals and man. The rustic Katsura Grill channels the Katsura Imperial Villa, a 16th-century Kyoto palace.

Japan pavilion.

Italy pavilion.

Housing a store and two restaurants, the building on the right represents commerce. The structure recalls a ceremonial hall of Kyoto's 8th-century Gosho Imperial Palace.

The rear of the pavilion symbolizes Japan's formative political history. Sculptures of mounted samurai warriors guard the 17th-century wood and stone Nijo castle. Behind it is the 14th-century Shirasagijo (White Heron) castle, a moat-protected feudal fortress which in real life still overlooks the city of Himeji.

Out front, the "floating" red torii gate of the 16th-century Itsukushima Shrine stands in the World Showcase lagoon. A popular tourist site near Hiroshima, the actual gate can be approached only at low tide. The pavilion's shrine is always at low tide, thanks to its placement in shallow water and faux barnacles on its stained lower legs.

The Japan pavilion is the only Mitsukoshi business in the United States.

The American Adventure. One hundred and ten thousand hand-formed bricks form the facade of this English Georgian pavilion, which recalls the look of Colonial buildings at the time of the Revolutionary War. Its bricks line up in period-correct pattern, with each whole brick followed by a half brick. In a switch from typical Disney park architecture, the structure uses *reversed* forced perspective to make it appear *shorter* than actually is—just three stories tall, though it actually rises more than 70 feet (21 meters). The illusion only works from a distance; up close the second-story windows look huge.

Italy. An architectural tour of "the boot." That's what you'll get as you walk through this pavilion. With the World Showcase lagoon standing in for the Adriatic Sea, the front of the area is Venice, complete with a waterfront of bridges, gondolas and striped pilings. Two freestanding columns recall 12th-century monuments; one topped by the guardian of Venice, the winged lion of St. Mark the Evangelist; the other crowned by St. Theodore, the city's former patron saint who's shown killing a dragon, the act that gave him the courage to declare himself Christian. The 10th-century Campanile bell tower dominates the skyline; gold-leafed ringlets hang from an angel on top. Lining the plaza is the city's 14th-century Doge's (leader's) Palace; its first two stories resting on realistic marble columns that front leaded-glass windows, its third floor tiled and topped by marble sculptures, statues and filigree.

The pavilion's La Bottega shop is a Tuscany homestead; the Il Bel Cristallo shop the Sistine Chapel. A nearby stairway and portico reflect Verona. Beyond the plaza, a sculpture of Neptune and his dolphins recalls Bernini's 1642 fountain in Florence and the Trevi fountain in Rome. In back, the Via Napoli restaurant evokes the entire country, layering styles in a way that's common in Italian cities.

Germany. St. George slays his dragon in a statue in this pavilion's outdoor plaza. Beyond him, a clock comes to life at the top of each hour with a three-minute animated display. The facade of the Das Kaufhaus shop recalls the Kaufhaus, a 16th-century merchants' hall in the Black Forest town of Freiburg. Three statues on its second story honor Hapsburg emperors. The pavilion's rear facade combines the looks of two 12th-century castles, the Eltz and the Stahleck.

Roaming over the rivers and through the woods, four tiny trains run through a miniature outdoor village to the right of the pavilion, each on an individual track. Walkways extend over them and alongside the town, which has its own little live landscape. At Christmas some of the mini trees have lights, snow tops the homes and wreaths hang on their doors. Each spring the village participates in Epcot's Flower and Garden Festival, with tiny streetside banners and flower pots.

China. Surprising views appear in this pavilion's waterfront, as large boulders follow a Chinese tradition of being pockmarked with holes. Carefully maintained to look old and unkempt, a pond garden sits just beyond a triple-arched entrance gate, symbolizing nature's order and discipline in the convention of the eastern China town of Suzhou. The garden fronts the circular Hall of Prayer for Good Harvests, the main building of Beijing's 1420 Temple of Heaven, a summer retreat for emperors. Nearby are facades of an elegant home, a schoolhouse and stores that reflect European influences. The pavilion's gallery has a formal saddle-ridge roof.

Norway. A sod roof tops the bakery of this pavilion, reflecting a traditional way to insulate homes in Norway's rural valley of Setesdal that builders still use today. Nearby facades recall cottages of Setesdal, the seaside town of Bergen and the island communities of Alesund. The pavilion's restaurant and rear facade re-create Akershus, a 14th-century Oslo castle and fortress. Standing at the pavilion entrance is a

Germany pavilion.

China pavilion.

replica of the tiny 13th-century Gol Church of Hallingdal, one of Norway's stave ("wooden post") churches that played a key role in the country's movement to Christianity. A separate building where princess Anna and queen Elsa from the 2013 Disney movie "Frozen" greet fans, the new Royal Sommerhus is a replica of Detlistua, a colorful two-story cottage built in 1817 in the city of Trondheim, the capital of Norway during the Viking era and the inspiration for many locales in the film.

Mexico. A pyramid holds the bulk of this pavilion, in particular the ancient pyramid of feathered serpent god Quetzalcoatl in the city of Teotihuacan. Traditionally the god of the morning and evening star, Quetzalcoatl later became the patron of priests, the inventor of books and the calendar and the symbol of death and resurrection. His worship involved human sacrifice. The serpent's head repeatedly appears along the steps of Disney's structure. Inside the building, an entry portico of a mayor's mansion leads to an "outdoor" moonlit market set in the town of Taxco during its peak silver-mining days of the 16th century. Back outside, the Cantina

de San Angel looks similar to the San Angel Inn, a 17th-century Mexico City restaurant that's still operating today. It's owned by the same family that runs the pavilion's eateries.

Fun finds. ① Along the Canadian promenade, an odd carved bird head is split in two, with a hole for you to stick your face through. ② Atop the steps of the Canada pavilion and just to the right of the United Kingdom pavilion, old-fashioned British red telephone booths make cute photo props. ③ Huge wild bullfrogs often hide under lily pads in the China pond, and occasionally poke out their heads to look around. ④ In a nod to the history of the Norway pavilion, runestones from its original Maelstrom ride stand near its Royal Sommerhus. ⑤ Seen from the front of the World Showcase along the walkway toward the Mexico pavilion, the Morocco pavilion appears to include a tall reddish building far off in the distance. Actually, that's The Twilight Zone Tower of Terror at Disney's Hollywood Studios, an attraction that shares the Morocco pavilion's Spanish architectural influence.

xhibits and films

Most World Showcase pavilions include an exhibit or short travelogue. The exhibits change often; the films rarely do.

★★★ **O Canada.** You stand up to watch this tongue-in-cheek travelogue, which stars comedian Martin Short. Rocky crags, waterfalls and other sights project onto nine screens that wrap around you. In a way it's Soarin' over Canada, but without the ride. Developed in the 1950s by video engineer (and original Mickey Mouse animator) Ub Iwerks, Disney's CircleVision 360 theaters use nine projectors to project film from a nine-lens camera onto nine screens. Why nine? Because the idea requires an odd number of screens, so gaps between them can hide projectors that line up with screens across the room. Epcot has two such theaters, here and in the China pavilion. *Duration: 15 min; continuous shows. Capacity: 600. Queue: Outdoor, covered. Access: Wheelchairs, ECVs OK. Disability services: Reflective captioning, assistive listening; Audio Description. Debuted: 1982, revised 2012. Location: Canada pavilion.*

★★★ **Impressions de France.** Set to a score so ethereal it could put you to sleep, this lullaby of a travelogue fills your field of vision with fairy-tale grandeur. Its 200-degree screen packs 40 scenes in just 18 minutes. Starting off over the cliffs of Normandy, it stops at four chateaus, a church, market, vineyard, the gardens of Versailles, a rural bicycle tour and an antique Bugatti race through Cannes—just in the first five minutes. Still to come are hot-air balloons, fishing boats, a train, Notre Dame and the Alps. Produced for the opening of Epcot, the film has a timeless feel, evocative imagery and no sense of humor. Early on its narrator intones "My *Frahnce* awakens with the early dawn." Well, duh. Based on Napoleon III's royal theater in Fontainebleau, the intimate auditorium has padded yet petite seats; women larger than a size 16 won't be comfortable. *Duration: 18 min; continuous shows. Capacity: 325. Queue: Indoor. Access: Wheelchairs, ECVs OK. Disability services: Reflective captioning, assistive listening. Debuted: 1982. Location: France pavilion.*

★★★ **Moroccan Style.** Cases display traditional jewelry, clothing and accessories in the heavily tiled Gallery of Arts and History, a work of art in itself that's easy to overlook. Subtitled "The Art of Personal Adornment," it's to the left of its pavilion's front courtyard,

Re-Discovering America. "Untitled," Hughie Lee-Smith, 1951.

Moroccan Style.

behind closed doors. Once you're inside, look up. The ceiling is gorgeous. *Location: Morocco pavilion.*

NEW! ★★★★★ ✔ **Kawaii.** Kung fu? No. Pikachu. A floral kimono? No. A ruffled pink baby-doll dress. The word "kawaii" means "cute" in Japanese, but the term means more than that. It's the basis of a widespread change to the country's culture. With its roots in ancient Shinto art and traditions, the movement told hold after World War II and today is the dominant style among young adults. Subtitled "Japan's Cute Culture," this exhibit contrasts historic and modern items, and displays a modern Tokyo apartment filled with kawaii fashion, food and housewares. The exhibit presents characters such as Pikachu and Hello Kitty and plays J-pop, a candy-colored music that covers a range of genres and styles. And then there's "Melty-Go-Round (Harajuku Girl)," the centerpiece, a mixed-media sculpture of a pink schoolgirl. Resembling a pile of melty bubble gum, she's made from hundreds of little toys and trinkets. *Location: Bijutsu-kan Gallery, Japan pavilion.*

★★★★ **Re-Discovering America.** A 1832 bill of sale for a slave, a 1930 sign identifying Florida's American Beach as a "Negro Ocean Playground"... this display, subtitled "Family Treasures from the Kinsey Collection," exhibits oppression-related art and artifacts from a black family. Narrators such as Diane Sawyer and Whoopi Goldberg reflect on the concepts of Belief, Courage, Heritage, Hope and Imagination. The collection rotates 400 items. *Location: American Heritage Gallery, The American Adventure pavilion.*

★★ **Reflections of China.** Commie propaganda? Your grumpy old grandpa might call it that. And he'd have a point, as this CircleVision 360 film reflects reality like a fun-house mirror, excluding obvious elements of Chinese culture and history to show you the most trouble-free country on earth. You stand up for your indoctrination, as 30 vistas wrap around you, including those of the Great Wall, Forbidden City, rural areas such as Tibet and Inner Mongolia and modern cityscapes of Hong Kong and Shanghai. The host portrays 8th-century poet Li Bai. *Duration: 20 min; continuous shows. Capacity: 200. Queue: Indoor.*

Folk band Quickstep often performs at the United Kingdom pavilion.

Access: Wheelchairs, ECVs OK. Disability services: Reflective captioning, assistive listening; Audio Description. Debuted: 1982, revised 2003. Location: China pavilion.

NEW! ★★★ **Inside Shanghai Disney Resort.** A Disney ride focused on a cult movie, 1982's "Tron"? A castle devoted to *all* of the Disney princesses? No Main Street U.S.A.? This display explores how Disney thought outside the box for their latest theme park, which opened in 2016. Concept art, costumes, dioramas, models and maquettes give you a good sense of what it's all about; plaques explain core concepts. *Location: House of the Whispering Willows gallery, China pavilion.*

★★★ **Norsk Kultur.** Subtitled "Creating the World of Frozen," this small exhibit displays traditional Norwegian clothing, musical instruments, furniture and artifacts that relate to Disney's 2013 movie. A female figure wears an outfit similar to Anna's. Some items date back to the 1200s. *Location: Stave Church, Norway pavilion.*

★★★★ **La Vida Antigua.** Exhibits and artifacts give you a glimpse of ancient Maya, Aztec and Toltec civilizations. One diorama depicts athletes playing the first known team sport in history. Watch the replica of the central Aztec calendar stone; it slowly changes colors. *Lobby, Mexico pavilion.*

Live entertainment

The year 2017 is a pivotal year for the World Showcase—its Germany pavilion is finally going to get some outdoor entertainment. Many acts come and go throughout the circle, but the following ones have been here awhile and most likely will be performing throughout 2017. Showtimes are subject to change.

★★★★ **The British Revolution.** This cover band takes Baby Boomers back in time with hits of the Beatles, Clash, Led Zeppelin and The Who. *20-min. shows hourly 3p–8p, Sun.–Tue., Fri.–Sat. Location: Back green stage, United Kingdom pavilion.*

★★★★ ✔ **Rose & Crown pub musician.** Late in the day, a spirited piano player adds life to this tiny pub. Alas, only 12 seats offer views of her. *45-min. shows hourly 5p–9p. Location: United Kingdom pavilion.*

★★★ **Serveur Amusant.** A wine steward and "amusing server" mime a balancing act with a table, chairs and huge bottle of champagne. It's always a crowd-pleaser. *20-min. shows hourly noon–5p, Fri.–Tue. Location: World Showcase walkway, France pavilion.*

★★★★ **Matsuriza.** Intense drummers pound out propulsive beats on huge handmade instruments. *20-min. shows hourly noon–6p, Mon.–Thr., Sat. Location: ●n the pagoda, sometimes the plaza, Japan pavilion.*

★★★★★ ✔ **American Music Machine.** "Dream ●n"... "California Dreaming"... "Dream a Little Dream of Me"... "Teenage Dream"... the dreamy hits just keep on coming from this five-person a cappella ensemble, which despite its corny name is a talented group in which every member has terrific range and control. Led by a vocal percussionist, it tackles a tour of pop history, a medley of more than 30 tunes in 20 minutes. Tim Cook, the vocal arranger of the television series "Glee," created its harmonies. *20-min. shows hourly noon–5p, Wed.–Sun. Location: America Gardens Theatre, American Adventure pavilion.*

★★★★ ✔ **Voices of Liberty.** This stately a cappella group performs signature American tunes such as "America the Beautiful" and "This Land is Your Land" with a delicate passion. Rotunda shows are best, as the singers stand close to the audience. *15-min. shows hourly 11a–4p. Location: Mon.–Tue. at the America Gardens Theatre; Wed.–Sun. in the rotunda of the American Adventure pavilion.*

★★★★ **Sergio.** This funny mime pulls children into his show as he juggles soccer balls. If your child wants to be in it have him or her wear a distinctive outfit, smile and catch the tireless performer's eye. *20-min. shows hourly noon–7p, Sun.–Thr. Location: Plaza at the promenade, Italy pavilion.*

★★★★ ✔ **Sbandieratori Di Sansepolcro.** In medieval times, military standard bearers led their units into battle carrying flags, designed to be easily spotted and recognized by the troops behind them during the heat of the conflict. Leaders conveyed simple commands by pre-arranged signals, such as lifting the flags up and down or swaying them back and forth. ●ver time honor guards turned these routines into elaborate spectacles of color and precision. Formed in the small Italian town of Sansepolcro in 1953, this troupe keeps alive Italy's version of the art, using hand-painted flags and matching tunics and tights that recall the geometric patterns of its town's most illustrious citizen, Renaissance painter Piero della Francesca. Supporting trumpeters and drummers round out the act. The group appeared in the 2003 film "Under the Tuscan Sun." This offshoot came to the

Sbandieratori Di Sansepolcro.

World Showcase in 2014. *15-min. shows hourly noon-6p. Location: Plaza, Italy pavilion.*

★★ **Jeweled Dragon Acrobats.** The six young adults that make up this troupe perform feats of agility, balance and strength. But their pace can be slow; sometimes it seems you're watching little more than a warm-up for a yoga class. Too often the performers simply balance something on their heads or feet then present themselves for applause. Ta da! Years ago they were children; the act was cuter then. *20-min. shows hourly 4p–8p. Location: Courtyard, moved inside Hall of Prayer in bad weather, China pavilion.*

★★★★★ ✔ **Mariachi Cobre.** The best live band at Disney, this 11-piece group is a staple of Epcot, an example of the nuanced culture of our southern neighbor that often gets overlooked. Confident trumpets and vocals are backed up by harmonizing guitars and violins. Together 45 years, the band has played and recorded with Julio Iglesias and Linda Ronstadt, and has been appearing at Epcot since its opening day. Three members have been with it since its formation; eight have been part of it since its park debut. But all that's just facts and figures; the joy is in their sound. *25-min. shows hourly 11:30a–5p. Location: On the promenade next to the outdoor gift stand, moved inside the pyramid in bad weather, Mexico pavilion.*

Restaurants and food

Canada pavilion. For some reason this large pavilion only has one place to eat, the toughest reservation to nab in the park:

★★★ ✔ **$54 DDP2 Le Cellier.** This stone-walled eatery resembles a low-ceiling wine cellar. Alberta-beef steaks are aged 28 days. Made with Moosehead beer, a cheddar-cheese soup makes a great dip for complimentary bread. Le Cellier has the smallest dining area of any Epcot table-service restaurant and many fans; make your reservation early. *12:30p–9p; $28–$52 (children $9–$17). Seats 156. A Disney Signature Restaurant.*

★★★ **$9 Popcorn in Canada.** Cart offers popcorn, Canadian maple whisky, Canadian beer. *Noon–9p; $4–$10.*

United Kingdom pavilion. A jolly good indoor spot and waterside beer garden, a mediocre takeout window.

★★★★ ✔ **$35 DDP Rose & Crown.** It may not be the fanciest food in Epcot and it's pretty hearty, every time I eat here I want to come back. Maybe it's the potato soup, the most deliciously creamy I've ever had. Maybe it's the servers, a young bunch who exude British charm. Maybe it's the little covered patio, which on a nice day is one of Disney's best outdoor dining spots. The menu includes

Mariachi Cobre.

The American Adventure.

bangers and mash (good) and shepherd's pie (better) and a good selection of British beers. *Noon–9p; $17–$33 (children $9). Seats 242.*

★ **$13 DDPq Yorkshire County Fish Shop.** This walk-up window fries up average fish and chips. Better: a Victoria sponge cake filled with jam and buttercream. *11:30a–9p; $5–$11. Seats 30 outdoors, on covered tables.*

★★★ **$13 Beer Cart.** British beers, lagers, ales and cider pour from the taps of this outdoor stand. No food. *Noon–9p; $8–$15. Seats 40 outdoors in a shady waterside garden.*

France pavilion. Acclaimed French chefs are behind these restaurants:

★★★ **$38 DDP Chefs de France.** Generous with cream and cheese, this sophisticated spot offers entrees that are good but somehow rarely come off as all that special, though the smooth lobster bisque appetizer sure is. Tile floors and tin ceilings are nice but noisy. Founded by Paul Bocuse, Gaston Leôtre and Roger Vergé in 1982; managed today by Paul's son Jerome. *Noon–9p; $19–$36 (children $9–$10), a 3-course, prix-fixe meal is $40 without wine. Seats 266.*

★★★★★ ✔ **$55 DDP2 Monsieur Paul.** Can you imagine being awarded your nation's highest civilian honor because of the quality of your soup? That's what happened to French chef Paul Bocuse in 1975, who was placed into the French Legion of Honor for a black truffle soup he created for a state dinner. Once you taste the soup, the award will make sense. Crowned with a pastry dome to retain its truffle flavor, it exudes a steaming cloud of fragrance when you pierce its crust, then soaks its pastry into its broth, which hides a meticulous mix of carrots, chicken, duck, foie gras and, of course, black truffles, direct from the ground beneath French oaks and hazelnuts. Jerome Bocuse recently refocused this small spot into a tribute to his father, and a fine homage it is. Nearly everything is the same as that soup, an exquisite, heartfelt offering you'd never expect to find in a theme park, with a depth of flavor in its sauces only the French seem to understand. Friendly yet formal, the white-tablecloth spot expects you to dress up (no dress code is enforced) and your children to be well-behaved. As you arrive tuxedoed servers line up to greet

Via Napoli.

you, each offering a cordial *bonsoir* ("good evening"). ❶f course it's expensive, but portions are reasonable and some items are bargains. In the real France the soup is 85 euros, about $96. Here it's $29. *5:30p–8:35p; $39–$44 (children $13–$16), a 4-course, prix-fixe meal is $89 without wine. Seats 120. ❶n the second floor, above Chefs de France. A Disney Signature Restaurant.*

★★★★ ✔ **$12 DDPq Les Halles Boulangerie & Patisserie.** Lovely bakery serves pastries, quiche, sandwiches. *9a–9p; $5–$10. Seats 64.*

★★★ **$10 Aux Vins de France.** Store counter sells French wine. *By the glass $7–$11, flights $13. 11a–9p.*

★★★ **$10 DDPs Crêpes des Chefs de France.** Crêpes, soft-serve ice cream, coffee, French beer (Kronenbourg 1664). *9a–9p; $5–$6.*

★★★★ ✔ **$12 DDPs L'Artisan Des Glaces.** Parlor scoops up artisanal ice cream, sorbet and an "ice cream martini" with Grand Marnier and vodka. *Noon–9p; $4–$12. Seats 24 outside.*

★★★ **$10 Les Vins des Chefs de France.** ❶utdoor stand sells alcoholic slushies, beer, wine, champagne. *Noon–9p; $7–$18.*

Morocco pavilion. Though it sounds exotic, there's nothing scary about Moroccan cuisine. Flavors are mild; ingredients are the same as those in American cooking except have hints of French and Spanish influences.

★★★ **$35 DDP Restaurant Marrakesh.** The lamb shank couscous is like your mom's pot roast, complete with roasted carrots and meat that falls off the bone. Dinner adds sampler plates. ❶f course, mom's meals probably didn't include a belly dancer. Here, one shimmies in front of a small band, her moves more graceful than sensual. Children can join in. Ceilings are intricately decorated; walls are covered in tiles. Since Moroccan food is unfamiliar to many Americans, this is the least crowded Epcot eatery. Ask to sit by the dance floor. *Lunch 11:30a–3:15p; $16–$29 (children $9). Dinner 3:30p–9p; $21–$29 (children $9). Dancer hourly 1p–8p except 4p. Seats 255.*

★★★★★ ✔ **$39 DDP Spice Road Table.** Curse❶ with an accurate but misleading name—its dishes aren't hot, they're seasoned, with spices from the Mediterranean, Middle East and North Africa—this little waterfront restaurant often sits almost totally empty, though it's one of Epcot's best places to eat. A fusion of flavors, each dish wakes up your taste buds yet is amazingly balanced. Best bets include a creamy brie fondue served with apricots, walnuts and rosemary bread and a perfectly crusted yet tender rack of lamb. Drinks include Mediterranean beers and Moroccan wines. A three-hose hookah highlights the decor of the small dining room; an outdoor patio is nicely shaded. A step above the pavilion's other dining choices, Spice Road is a joint effort of Disney and its Moroccan management. Small tables are close together, so when the restaurant does fill up it's overcrowded. Reservations usually aren't needed until after 7 p.m. *11:30a–9p, $23–$33. Seats 172.*

★★★★ ✔ **$17 DDPq Tangierine Cafe.** This counter-service spot offers tasty chicken and lamb platters; a back counter serves baklava, tea, liqueur coffees and beer. *11a–9p; $10–$15 (children $9). Seats 100 on covered tables.*

★★★ **$9 The Oasis.** This outside stand sells slushies and smoothies (with or without alcohol), Mediterranean beers, sangria, baklava. *Noon–9p; $4–$12.*

Japan pavilion. Like the Moroccan pavilion this one's also not run by Disney, a fact which gives its food options a more authentic feel.

★★★ **$40 DDP Teppan Edo.** An entertaining tableside chef may juggle knives or make a "smoking Mickey train" out of onion stacks in these stunning red-and-black dining rooms. Using a grill set into your table, the chef's hands fly fast as they slice and dice and stir-fry beef, seafood or chicken. You share your table with other guests. *Noon–3:45p, 4p–9p; $22–$35 (children $14–$15). Seats 192.*

★★★★ ✔ **$41 DDP Tokyo Dining.** With good food and great service, this is what a World Showcase restaurant is supposed to be: a non-threatening way to fully experience a foreign cuisine. Traditional entrees include a tender chicken teriyaki and light shrimp tempura. A sushi menu has 50 choices. For dessert, the green tea mousse melts in your mouth. Diffused lighting, dark tables and a tile floor create a peaceful decor. The polite staff bows to you at every opportunity. *Noon–3:45p, 4p–9p; $26–$34 (children $12). Seats 116.*

★★★★ ✔ **$16 DDPq Katsura Grill.** The udon noodle soup. That's what you want at this comfortable counter-service spot. Or one of the subtle teriyaki dishes. *11a–9p; $9–$14 (children $8–$9). Seats 60 inside, 34 outside.*

★★★ **$12 DDPs The Garden House.** This outdoor stand sells Japanese beers, specialty cocktails, sake and plum wine. *Noon–9p; $6–$11. Nearby benches, seats outside the Katsura Grill.*

★★★★ ✔ **$12 DDPs Kabuki Cafe.** Kakigori (shaved ice) with a sweet milk topping. Blood orange, chocolate-cherry or coffee sake mist (alcoholic shaved ice). Sushi and edamame. Ramune (Japanese soda), Japanese beers, plum wine. Not bad for a tiny outdoor stand. *11:30a–9p; $4–$9.*

★★★ **$7 Mitsukoshi Department Store.** Hot or cold sake by the glass at a little bar in back. *11a–9p; $4–$8.*

The American Adventure. Think of all the amazing regional cuisine in the United States. And then forget it. Because for some reason this pavilion does. Why Disney, why?

★★★ **$14 DDPq Liberty Inn.** Cool air conditioning, clam chowder and peach cobbler elevate this comfortable yet nondescript fast-food spot. Burgers and hot dogs don't. *11:30a–8:30p; $8–$11 (children $6). Seats 710.*

★★★ **$8 DDPs Block & Hans.** American craft beers, cider and hard root beer from an outdoor stand. Mickey pretzels too. *3:30p–9p; $5–$9. Nearby benches.*

★★★ **$13 DDPs Fife & Drum Tavern.** Stand sells turkey legs; popcorn; slushies; soft-serve ice cream, root beer, alcoholic floats. *11:30a–9p; $4–$12. Nearby tables seat 125.*

★★★ **$14 DDPs Funnel Cake.** Powdered sugar and, if you'd like, vanilla ice cream, chocolate sauce or crushed cookies top the fried creations at this stand. *11a–9p, $7–$12. Nearby tables seat 125.*

Italy pavilion. Amazingly, the same New York company that runs these restaurants operates Morimoto Asia in Disney Springs. Yet you'd swear they're totally authentic.

★★★★★ ✔ **$41 DDP Tutto Italia.** Imported pastas and delicate sauces make this is the best fine Italian spot at Disney, though the sides for meat and fish entrees are optional at $9 each. Salads use ingredients like asparagus, curly endive and fava beans. An elegant decor has dark woods. *Lunch 11:30a–3:30p; $18–$34 (children $10); a 3-course, prix-fixe lunch is $27 without wine. Dinner 4:30p–9p; $24–$36 (children $10). Seats 300.*

★★★★★ ✔ **$34 DDP Via Napoli.** Disney's best pizza place, this might be the most satisfying restaurant in Epcot. True-Italian toppings and flavorful charred crusts are worth every penny it charges, which is about twice as much as your neighborhood Pizza

Hut. Individual pizzas are large enough to share if you add an appetizer, large pizzas are so humongous they're rolled out on carts. A secret: the pastas are even better than the pizzas—I love the decadently creamy paccheri. Ask to sit in the breezy main room; it's so relaxing you'll lose track of time. Just don't plan on any quiet conversations; tile floors and open wood-and-plaster ceilings amplify every sound. *11:30a–9p; $18–$30 (children $10). Seats 400, including 24 at a community table.*

★★★ **$12 Gelati.** This outdoor stand serves gelato cups, cones and creations (cookie sandwiches, sundaes), tiramisu, cannolis. *11a–9p; $5–$10.*

★★★ **$10 La Bottega Italiana.** Italian wine shop. *By the glass $7–$11, flights $13.* 11a–9p.

★★★ ✔ **$25 Tutto Gusto Wine Cellar.** Brick arches, wood beams and stone walls and floors make this tiny spot resemble a wine cellar. Small plates of cheeses, mini-panini, pasta and seafood complement nearly 200 wines—a nice way to get a taste of Italy without breaking the bank. *11:30a–9p; $8–$26. Seats 96.*

★★★ **$10 DDPs Via Napoli cart.** Period donkey cart offers wines, liquors; gelato, sorbet. *11a–9p; $5–$12.*

Germany pavilion. If you live in a city with a large German population you'll feel right at home here, where every day is Oktoberfest.

★★★★ **$46 DDP Biergarten.** A live band rolls out a barrel full of polkas and waltzes at this German buffet (kids love to get out on the dance floor), stopping now and then to demonstrate some strange instrument or lead a toast: *"Zicke zacke, zicke zacke, hoi! hoi! hoi!* Best bets include the schnitzel. The dining room looks like a medieval Rothenburg courtyard at night; the moon and stars glow overhead. Unless you're a party of eight you'll sit with others, sharing toasts and conversations. Young waiters wear Bavarian tracht wear—green lederhosen shorts and suspenders, white shirts, little black hats and teeny weeny ties. *Lunch noon–3p; $30 (children $16), Dinner 4p–9p; $38 (children $20). Band: 20-min. sets hourly 1p–8p. Seats 400.*

★★★ **$12 DDPq Sommerfest.** Outdoor walk-up window hands out bratwurst, frankfurters and hand-twisted pretzels, all begging to be washed down with beer. *11a–9p; $5–$10. Seats 24 on covered, sheltered patio.*

★★★ **$10 DDPs Germany cart.** Pretzels and beer. *11a–9p. $5.*

★★★★ ✔ **$12 DDPs Karamell-Küche.** Young German bakers make caramel treats before your eyes at this fragrant bakery. Long lines form all day long. *11a–9p. $4–$10.*

★★★ **$10 Weinkeller.** Schnapps and wine by the bottle or glass. *11a–9p. By the glass $7–$11, flights $13.*

China pavilion. Overall this is the worst pavilion for food, but it has a good snack stand:

★★ **$29 DDP Nine Dragons.** Though its green, yellow and blues highlight its serene decor and it has good teas, light desserts and a tiny cucumber stack appetizer direct from China's National Guest House, nearly everything else is straight outta food court. *Noon–9p; $16–$23 (children $8–$10). Seats 300.*

★★ **$15 DDPq Lotus Blossom Café.** Bland egg rolls, chicken, stir-fry. *11a–9p; $8–$12 (children $8). Seats 106 on covered patio.*

★★★★ ✔ **$11 DDPs Joy of Tea.** Bubble-milk tea and strawberry-red bean ice cream! Not as good: Small sandwiches, egg rolls. *11a–9p; $3–$10.*

Norway pavilion. A pricey princess palooza presents peppered mackerel; a bitty bakery brokers breads and baked goods:

★★★ **$67 DDP Akershus Royal Banquet Hall.** Disney princesses come to your table at this bustling Princess Storybook Dining Experience. Its American breakfast is family-style: all-you-can-eat but brought to your table. Lunch and dinner are Norwegian buffets. Some appetizers such as sliced fish jerky are acquired tastes, but the svinekotelett (pork chop) and kjøttkake (meatballs) will satisfy anyone raised on hearty fare. Kids can go healthy with grilled salmon but don't have to, there's always mac and cheese. Five characters may include Ariel, Aurora, Belle, Cinderella, Jasmine, Mulan and Snow White. *Breakfast 8a–11:10a; $47 (children $28). Lunch 11:55a–3:30p; $50 (children $29). Dinner 4:55p–8:35p; $55 (children $30). Seats 255.*

★★★★ ✔ **$13 DDPq Kringla Bakeri Og Kafe.** Tiny counter spot offers sandwiches, desserts and Norwegian pastries such as school bread and troll horns. *9a–9p; $8–$9 (children $6). Seats 50, outdoor but shaded.*

Mexico pavilion. Food that's better than you'd expect, with prices much higher.

★★★★ ✔ **$56 DDP La Hacienda de San Angel.** This inviting waterfront restaurant offers authentic fare and tasty drinks. Especially memorable are the fresh salsas, creative appetizers and flavorful margaritas—six varieties of which were developed

La Hacienda de San Angel.

with an "expert mixologist" the restaurant hired before it opened. A tequila ambassador helps you choose from among 17 choices. The restaurant emulates a cozy hacienda, with original artwork and unusual blown-glass light fixtures. Oversized windows provide a good view of the World Showcase lagoon. *4p–9p; $26–$58 (children $9–$10). Seats 250.*

★★★★ ✔ **$35 DDP San Angel Inn.** Good choices include a delicious *pollo a las rajas* grilled chicken dish, signature tortilla soup and a steak that tastes like it's straight off a backyard grill. Sitting on padded chairs and benches around a lantern-lit table, you dine in a dark moonlit courtyard. In the distance is a rumbling volcano that, depending on your margarita intake, may appear to be the most realistic effect Disney has ever created. The restaurant is run by the Debler family, the proprietors of the eatery's namesake restaurant in Mexico City. *11:30a–4p, 4:30p–9p, $19–$30 (children $9–$10). Seats 156.*

★★★ **$15 DDPq La Cantina de San Angel.** Lakeside fast-food spot sells churros, empanadas, nachos, tacos, beer, margaritas. *11a–9p; $8–$13 (children $8). Seats 150.*

★★★ **$10 Jardin de Fiestas.** Snack stand offers chilaquiles de pollo (layers of fried corn tortilla, seasoned chicken, green tomatillo sauce, topped with queso fresco, onions and sour cream), also a pork belly taco, margaritas, and beer. *11a–9p; $5–$6.*

★★★★★ ✔ **$21 La Cava del Tequila.** There's nothing Disney about this hole-in-the-wall tequila bar in the Mexican pavilion, except that perhaps it really is the Happiest Place on Earth. Serving margaritas, mezcal and shots of tequila, it's always packed, loud and an absolute delight. I prefer the $20 Dragones Top Shelf margarita, built from scratch using small batch blanco, organic agave and juice squeezed directly from limes. It's the best margarita I've had. If we sell a million copies of this book I'll celebrate by getting a $248 shot of Jose Cuervo 250 Anniversary, an añejo aged 8 years. On my last visit my waiter told me it's so popular that "the bottle's almost empty." A fascinating decor features a mural depicting the harvesting of agave; segments of it reappear on the backs of the bar's wooden chairs. One chair features a portrait of Mexican painter Frida Kahlo.

Thick wooden tables and tile floors add to the ambience and the din. Light comes from orange and green hanging globes. *11:30a–9p. Food $9-$16. Margaritas $13-$21, tequila shots $7–$248, mezcal shots $8–$44, tequila flights $23–$234. Children welcome. Seats 35.*

Other snack stands. At World Showcase Plaza **Joffrey's** (★★★ **$11 DDPs** 9a–9p; $4–$9) brews coffees and teas; **The Refreshment Port** (★★★★ **$12 DDPs** 11a–9p; $5–$10) serves croissant-doughnut "cronuts" tossed in cinnamon sugar and **Promenade Refreshments** (★★★ **$10 DDPs** 11a–9p; $3–$9) offers hot dogs and soft-serve ice cream. Between Germany and China, the **Refreshment Cool Post** (★★ **$11 DDPs** 11a–9p; $4–$8) has routine hot dogs and soft-serve ice cream.

Shops and merchandise

Except for The American Adventure, all pavilions sell goods rarely seen in the United States. Though the most touristy items come from China, each pavilion also stocks some things from the country it represents.

Canada. Offering playful products, two connected shops offer maple-syrup treats, dreamcatchers and hockey jerseys.

United Kingdom. The Beatles and Doctor Who merchandise, Guinness souvenirs, "Keep Calm and Carry On" items, pub and beer coasters and many Twinings teas crowd the shelves of cozy connected shops.

France. Small, elegant shops hold French wine, cosmetics and fragrance brands such as Chanel, Dior, Thierry Mugler and Guerlain, some in its signature bee bottles. Tiny La Signature is the only shop in the United States with the full line of Givenchy perfume; each year this Epcot boutique has a U.S. exclusive.

Morocco. Belly-dancing outfits, brass plates and platters, kaftans, carpets, lambskin lamps, rosewater bottles and aromatic bowls and boxes made of thuya (a burled-root wood grown only in Morocco) fill five incense-filled spaces. The shops are run by the Kingdom of Morocco, independently of Disney.

Japan. Bonsai trees, chopsticks, Hello Kitty toys, Mikimoto pearls, silk kimonos, tatami mats, quirky Pokémon toys and sake are just a few of the hundreds of products at a 10,000-square-foot Mitsukoshi store.

The American Adventure. Some fancy packaged foods are American-made, but most of the patriotic apparel and books at this small shop come from China.

Italy. Glass jewelry, Perugina candy and Puma sportswear stand out at this pavilion. Artisans create papier-mâché and fabric Carnivale masks in front of you. Two shops mark each side of the pavilion's entrance.

Germany. Beer steins, cuckoo clocks, nutcrackers, handmade glass pickle ornaments and Steiff stuffed animals highlight the German merchandise at this pavilion. Eight connected stores line its central courtyard.

China. A spacious main shop overflows with tons of Chinese merchandise, including Buddha and lucky cat figurines, incense, kimonos, teapots and panda plushies. Outside stands feature marionettes, hand-painted parasols and Lucky Buddha beer—a light beer that's worth buying just for its bottle.

Norway. Stylish apparel from Norwegian brands Helly Hansen and Dale of Norway, Geir Ness fragrances and silly plastic Viking helmets line the shelves of the main store. A shop at the Frozen meet-and-greet exit abounds with Frozen merchandise.

Mexico. Ceramic Day of the Dead skulls, piñatas, ponchos, salsa, sombreros and bottles of tequila are just a few of the plethora of products offered at an "open-air" market inside the pyramid. Artisans at a small table create exquisite wooden animals. Small shops sit on the outdoor walkway.

Elsewhere. At the World Showcase Plaza two stores sell Disney souvenirs and sundries; a third does at the International Gateway entrance. Tucked between the Germany and China pavilions, Village Traders sells African wood and stone craftwork (some created while you watch), musical instruments and colorful jewelry made from recycled Disney World guide maps that are shipped to Africa and hand-rolled into beads.

Sweets and treats

The authors' 23-year-old daughter has uncovered a treasure of treats in World Showcase, none of them more than a few dollars.

Canada. This one's easy: the pure maple-syrup lollipops at the Trading Post shop.

United Kingdom. Creamy Cadbury chocolate bars and other goodies at the Tea Caddy.

France. The bakery's créme brulee; top it off with cream and sugar, stir it up and head off to heaven. Also: the ice cream shop's chocolate macaroon ice cream sandwich.

Morocco. The walnut baklava from the bakery case of the Tangierine Café; cashew and pistachio varieties are also good.

Morocco pavilion.

Japan. Sweet watermelon Botan rice candy has a melt-in-your-mouth wrapper; an eight-piece package comes with a colorful sticker that's awesomely odd—one shows a smiling diva pickle wearing high heels and lipstick. Also worth checking out: semi-hard Sakuma strawberry milk candy.

Italy. A Baci Perugina hazelnut chocolate fortune ball, sold at La Bottega. Each ball has a different fortune inside.

Germany. A Werther's caramel apple oatmeal cookie at the Karamell-Küche shop. As wide as a large grapefruit, it's drizzled with caramel, and easily broken apart to share. You also can't go wrong with some fresh caramel popcorn.

China. The pavilion's creamy White Rabbit candy tastes like chewy vanilla taffy. Shaped like a Tootsie Roll, each piece has an edible inner wrapping made from a transparent sheet of rice. A bag gives you a few dozen individually wrapped pieces.

Norway. Made of almonds, Marabou chocolate and a brittle toffee center, Daim ("Dime") candy bars are lusciously sweet. Another must: the bakery's school bread, filled with custard and topped with coconut.

Mexico. A subtle, creamy treat that can get sticky once unwrapped, Glorias is a creamy goat's milk candy made with pecans. Five-piece packages are inside the pyramid.

Hidden Mickeys

❶ At the main entrance to the Canada pavilion, the three circles appear twice on a totem, under the top set of hands on your left. ❷ t the Le Cellier restaurant, another set is formed by the ends of wine bottles behind the check-in counter. ❸ At the U.K. pavilion, a sign for the Sportsman's Shoppe forms the shape from a soccer ball, a football and racket. ❹ Mickey hides within metal tree grates in the French courtyard, and in a bush in a nearby fleur-de-lis hedge garden. ❺ "Impressions de France" contains the world's first Hidden Mickey. It's in a house behind a wedding reception, the silhouette of a doll. ❻ Tree grates in the Japan courtyard form the three circles, as does the center of a drain cover in a koi pond. ❼ It appears as brass plates on a door of the Moroccan pavilion's waterside Souk-Al-Magreb shop and ❽ as a window in the dome of a minaret on the backdrop of Aladdin and Jasmine's meet-and-greet area (in the upper right-hand corner, next to a small ladder). ❾ At the German pavilion you'll find the shape in the center of the crown of the left-most Hapsburg emperor statue on the facade of the Das Kaufhaus shop. ❿ A small Mickey figurine often hides in the German train village, usually perched in a window of a little hilltop castle.

Mexico pavilion.

Finding Perry. You sign up for the game at carts throughout the World Showcase.

Agent P's World Showcase Adventure

'Phineas and Ferb' fans will love this scavenger hunt

★★★★★ ✔ This interactive game uses refurbished cellphones and hidden special effects to channel the comic sensibility of "Phineas & Ferb," the Disney Channel animated series about two brothers and their pet platypus, Perry. As fans of the show know, Perry has an alter ego as a secret agent—Agent P—and a nemesis—Dr. Doofenshmirtz, a bumbling mad scientist who for years has been out to take over his tri-state area. But now he has bigger plans. Off on a vacation to Epcot and its World Showcase, now he wants to take over the world. And what's worse, Agent P can't stop him. It's up to you.

As you sign up for the game, you become an agent of OWCA (the Organization Without a Cool Acronym) and are sent to a World Showcase pavilion to foil the scientist's plans. You receive instructions by using a FONE (Field Operative Notifications Equipment), which helps you defeat Doofenshmirtz as you search for particular landscape props and bring elements within them to life.

NEW! As of 2016 you can play the game on your smartphone, using a website that tracks your device and makes it interactive.

Where to sign up. There are four spots; one on the wide footbridge that connects Future World to the World Showcase, three others on the World Showcase walkway. The mission you get depends on where you sign up. *Odyssey Bridge:* Sign up here and you'll be sent to the Mexico, Norway or U.K. pavilion. *United Kingdom pavilion:* Off you'll go to the U.K., France, Japan, Mexico or Norway. *Norway pavilion:* Mexico, Norway or China. *Italy pavilion:* Germany or Japan. When you finish one mission, you can do another one.

By the way, you choose your agent name. When I play, I'm Agent J.

Tips. *When to play:* During the summer right when the park opens at 11 a.m., before the weather gets too hot or rainy.

Fun fact. "Phineas and Ferb" creators Dan Povenmire and Jeff "Swampy" Marsh spent many days at Epcot brainstorming ideas for the game and scouting locations.

Key facts. *Length:* Allow 25 min. per pavilion. *Capacity:* 100. *Hours:* 11a–8:15p. *Debuted:* 2012. *Access:* You can play the game from a wheelchair or an ECV. *Location:* Various World Showcase pavilions.

Ben Franklin and Mark Twain.

The American Adventure

Elaborate American history lesson is thoughtful, inspiring

★★★★★ ✓ The only World Showcase attraction that is critical of its country, this elaborate theatrical show embraces the triumphs of America and the optimism of its people, but doesn't shy away from our country's challenges and failures. Audio-Animatronic versions of Ben Franklin and Mark Twain tell the story, leading you from the time of the Pilgrims through World War II, with help from George Washington, Thomas Jefferson, Will Rogers, Rosie the Riveter and other historic figures. Chatting with Franklin after the Revolutionary War, Twain says "You Founding Fathers gave us a pretty good start… [but then] a whole bunch of folks found out that 'We the People' didn't yet mean all the people." Subsequent scenes cover slavery and the persecution of Native Americans.

At the end Franklin quotes "You Can't Go Home Again," a 1940 novel by Thomas Wolfe: "So, then, to every man his chance… the right to live, to work, to be himself, and to become whatever thing his manhood and his vision can combine to make him."

The figures move convincingly. For a moment Franklin appears to walk; Frederick Douglass sways on a raft. Braving Valley Forge, Washington shifts his weight in his saddle; his horse twitches like a real animal.

The scenes combine with a film, a mix of real and re-created images that pans across paintings and photos in a style that was later made famous by documentarian Ken Burns. A photomontage finale covers events of the past 50 years.

Fun facts. ❶ Just beneath your sight line is a mass of wiring and hydraulic cables which give movement to the figures, as well as a 175-ton (159,000 kg) scene changer that wheels in and raises 13 distinct sets. ❷ The show uses 35 Audio-Animatronic characters, including three Franklins and three Twains.

Hidden Mickey. As three rocks at the beginning of the first film in the show, behind and to the right of a kneeling Pilgrim woman.

Key facts. *Duration:* 30 min. *Showtimes:* Typically every 45 min. starting at 11:15a. *Capacity:* 1,024. *Queue:* Indoor. Debuted: 1982, revised 2007. *Access:* Wheelchairs, ECVs OK. *Disability services:* Audio Description, assistive listening, reflective captioning. *Location:* The American Adventure pavilion.

© Disney

Elsa, Anna and Olaf.

Frozen Ever After

Maelstrom makeover focuses on characters, music

NEW! ★★★ FP+ The Audio-Animatronic figures in this high-tech tour of Arendelle look like they stepped right out of the film. Projectors behind their faces pull off an impressive range of expressions, much like the dwarfs on Magic Kingdom's Seven Dwarfs Mine Train. And just what do these faces do? Sing! Topping off the ride is, of course, Queen Elsa. Floating into her ice castle, you watch her belt out the Academy-Award-winning "Let It Go." At the song's best moment—when she proclaims that the cold doesn't bother her anyway—your boat careens backward into swirling mist and fog.

Snowman Olaf shows up in three scenes. Other characters include Anna, Grandpappy Troll, Kristoff, Marshmallow, Sven and from the 2015 short "Frozen Fever," Snowgies.

On the downside there's no real story, the perfect video faces lack charm and much of the ride seems empty, almost unfinished.

Fun finds. ❶ The Standby line passes through Wandering Oaken's Trading Post and Sauna; the owner sporadically clears the steam off a window and utters a hearty "yoo-hoo!" ❷ Sometimes he traces Olaf or a snowflake with his finger on the steamy surface. ❸ A figurine of a three-headed troll sits on the counter of the Trading Post, an homage to the pavilion's original Maelstrom ride. ❹ Maelstrom puffins show up right after the drop, across from the fireworks.

Character greeting. Anna and Elsa greet guests nearby in a Royal Sommerhus cabin. When you meet Anna, break the ice (ha!) by asking about her boots. She'll show them off.

Key facts. *Duration:* 5 minutes. *Capacity:* 192. *Queue:* Indoor. *Fear factor:* Often dark, with one scary moment. *Debuted:* 2016. *Access:* Wheelchair and ECV users must transfer; assistive listening, reflective captioning. *Location:* Norway pavilion.

Average wait times (standby line)

9a	10a	11a	12p	1p	2p	3p	4p	5p	6p	7p	8p	9p	10p	11p
40m	80m	70m	60m	65m	60m	60m	60m	60m	60m	50m	35m	30m	---	---

Artwork © Disney

Where's Donald? José Carioca and Panchito Pistoles.

Gran Fiesta Tour

Donald Duck gets lost in Ol' Mexico

UPDATED! ★★★ On the day the World Showcase opened in 1982, it had one ride: El Rio del Tiempo. The River of Time. Riding in a slow-moving boat, you floated into a pyramid and met an ancient Aztec, an Audio-Animatronic warrior who welcomed you to his era. Floating deeper, you saw Aztec, Inca and Mayan cultures, all alive on video screens.

Then you moved forward in time, to modern Mexico. First floating through a Day of the Dead festival, then passing videos showing bars, beaches and cliff divers. A line of screens portrayed a market where vendors magically moved along with you from screen to screen, desperate to bargain with you.

This ride is an update of that one. A simple update really, as little has changed except the video screens. But what a difference! Now they focus not on Mexico, but instead on the Three Caballeros: suave Brazilian parrot José Carioca, pistol packing Mexican rooster Panchito Pistoles, and an insanely lecherous Donald Duck. They're about to serenade the masses in Mexico City. Only they can't, as Donald has gone off sightseeing and spied some señoritas who have stolen his heart.

Will José and Panchito find him in time? Yes. Will you care? No. But the trip is relaxing, and some clips are bizarre. Audio-Animatronic Caballeros now sing at the end, the same figures that once appeared in The Mickey Mouse Revue, an opening-day show at the Magic Kingdom. There's rarely a wait.

"Come here, my little enchilada." Donald Duck is a wild-eyed skirt chaser in 1944's "The Three Caballeros." Combining morphing sugar-rush animation with a storyline that redefines Donald as an unfettered philanderer, its Mexican segment sends the trio off on a flying serape tour of the country, where the duck goes ga-ga for dozens of live-action human women. Surreal animation includes illogical color changes and an overdose of morphing gags. Disney produced the movie as part of the U.S. Good Neighbor Policy, an effort to increase pro-American feelings in Latin America during World War II.

Key facts. *Duration:* 8 min. *Capacity:* 20 per boat. *Queue:* Indoor. *Debuted:* 1982, revised 2015. *Access:* ECV users must transfer. *Disability services:* Handheld captioning. *Location:* Mexico pavilion.

A fiery finale.

IllumiNations

Spectacle trumps story in nightly finale

★★★★ ✔ FP+ IllumiNations sets its sights high: to recount the history of Earth without narration. Synchronized to a symphonic score of world music, the nightly extravaganza uses the entire World Showcase to tell its tale its lagoon and its buildings—though it does that so abstractly you may not even notice the narrative. Strobes flash, laser beams dance, pavilions light up, fireworks burst, a huge Earth glides across the lagoon and shows moving images on its continents as it rotates, as you witness everything from the Big Bang to the present day. It's pretty impressive, even touching.

Tips. *When to go:* To nab a good spot, show up 20 to 30 minutes before the show starts at 9 p.m. *Where to watch it* Between the two gift shops at World Showcase Plaza. From there you'll see the show's symmetry as its designers intended; you'll also be relatively close to Epcot's front exit so you'll be ahead of the masses when the spectacle ends. Get a FastPass to ensure a spot here. *For families:* Work with your kids to identify the images on the globe; they change so quickly it's nearly impossible to catch them all.

Fun facts. ❶ Two-thousand eight-hundred fireworks launch from 750 mortar tubes in 34 locations; some explode 600 feet (183 meters) overhead. ❷ Wrapped in more than 180,000 LEDs, the 28-foot (9-meter) steel globe was the world's first spherical video display. ❸ The pavilions are outlined in 26,000 feet (8,000 meters) of lights. ❹ The Morocco pavilion does not participate in the show since some of its buildings represent religious structures. ❺ The show's music supervisor was Hans Zimmer, the composer for the 1994 Disney movie "The Lion King." ❻ Nineteen torches around the lagoon symbolize the first 19 centuries of modern history. The 20th torch, in the globe, represents our current century (don't think about that too much; the math doesn't exactly add up).

Key facts. *Duration:* 14 minutes. *Showtime:* 9p. *Fear factor:* Loud, bright explosions and fire (the authors' daughter hated this show when she was little). *Weather issues:* Cancelled during thunderstorms. *Debuted:* 1988; last revised 1999. *Access:* You can view the show from a wheelchair or ECV. *Location:* On and above the World Showcase.

Disney's Hollywood Studios

Park entrance.

A VALENTINE TO SHOW BUSINESS, Disney's Hollywood Studios is a theme park focused on movies and television shows. As such, it has something for nearly everyone. Fans of old Hollywood encounter Humphrey Bogart and James Cagney at the Great Movie Ride. Animation buffs relive the tales of "Beauty and the Beast," "Frozen" and "The Little Mermaid." Like action-adventure films? You want the Indiana Jones Epic Stunt Spectacular. Representing television is the park's iconic thrill ride, The Twilight Zone Tower of Terror, as well as a puppet show for toddlers, Disney Junior Live on Stage.

But more is coming. Much more.

Soon Disney will expand the park, replacing most of its old backlot and production areas with two major new lands.

Star Wars land. Focused on the Star Wars saga, what Disney press releases promise to be an "authentic, jaw-dropping" area will transport you "to a never-before-seen Star Wars planet." Specifically, you'll be at a remote trading port, one populated with aliens, droids and roaming beasts. Disney says the 14-acre (5.6-ha) land will open in 2018.

Two attractions will highlight the area. One will put you "in the middle of a climactic battle between the First Order and the Resistance." Another will take you on a "customized secret mission" behind the controls of the Millennium Falcon." Stores and dining areas will be run by "local inhabitants," and may include a Mos Eisley-style Cantina.

Fans of the Force, however, don't have to wait until the new land opens to get their Star Wars fix. The park already has its acclaimed Star Tours motion simulator. New smaller Star Wars experiences include character interactions and stage shows. And the park's new Star Wars night-time spectacle simply has to be seen to be believed.

Toy Story Land. Andy's backyard. That's the setting for this 11-acre (4.5-ha) land, which Disney says will also open in 2018. A larger-than-life version of the yard, Disney is building it to a giant scale, so that when you enter it you'll feel as though you're the size of a toy. A family-friendly Slinky Dog Dash roller coaster will "stretch Slinky's coils to the limit" as it coasts, plunges, zips and zooms through the land. A toy play set Andy bought from Pizza Planet, Alien Swirling Saucers spins you in a disc as Little Green Aliens try to capture you with a looming Claw. Special lighting, sound effects and "space jazz" music add to the fun. Like the Mad Tea Party at the Magic Kingdom, the attraction will be outside but under a roof, so you can ride it in the rain.

The land will also include a fast-food spot, a store (Al's Toy Barn) and a play area.

The park already has one Toy Story ride, the ever-popular Toy Story Mania 3-D video arcade. It's just added a third track, increasing its capacity by 50 percent.

Disney is building its Toy Story Land behind the existing theme park, against the back of the Toy Story Mania buildings. The area once contained the offices of Disney's East Coast Animation Studio and was seen on the Studios Backlot Tour.

Since the new lands will eliminate the studios area of Disney's Hollywood Studios, Disney will also be changing the park's name.

Best of the park. ❶ Disney's Hollywood Studios has exhilarating experiences—Rock 'n' Roller Coaster Starring Aerosmith and the Twilight Zone Tower of Terror both hurl you through the dark in ways that surprise you. ❷ The new nighttime fireworks show, Star Wars: A Galactic Spectacular, is a breathtaking, ground-breaking presentation.

❸ The park has a sense of humor. Many of its performers put a smile on your face—its Citizens of Hollywood, its hilarious Dr. Bunsen Honeydew and Beaker and Swedish Chef, its Arendelle historians, its sarcastic servers at its 50's Prime Time Café. ❹ The park's Disney Junior Live on Stage show speaks directly to young children without being condescending. ❺ And finally, it won't wear you out. Unlike most Disney theme parks, the Studios doesn't make you spend all day on your feet. It's quick to get around, and offers many ways to sit down and relax.

Worst of the park. ❶ For those visiting in 2017 the upcoming expansions don't mean much; what does is that right now there's not that much here. ❷ There's no place to have breakfast inside except a character meal.

If it rains. With its small size and plethora of indoor things to do, the park is easy to enjoy during a shower. There are many stores and dining spots to duck into. You can hang out in the Star Wars Launch Bay and the Walt Disney One Man's Dream exhibits for as long as you like. Rain cancels street entertainment; a light sprinkle shortens the Indiana Jones Epic Stunt Spectacular. Nearby lightning cancels that show as well as the nighttime spectacles Fantasmic and Star Wars: A Galactic Spectacular.

Bringing the funny. Princess Anna with an Arendelle historian.

A Stormtrooper interrogates.

Family matters. All thrill rides have height minimums—48 inches (122 cm) for Rock 'n' Roller Coaster Starring Aerosmith, 40 inches (102 cm) for Twilight Zone Tower of Terror and Star Tours. Four other attractions may be too much for toddlers: Fantasmic, The Great Movie Ride, Star Wars A Galactic Spectacular and Voyage of the Little Mermaid. Every restaurant offers a children's menu.

Where to meet characters. Over 20 Disney characters appear at the park. It's the only place to meet Star Wars stars like Chewbacca, Disney Junior characters such as Doc McStuffins, Olaf from "Frozen," the Green Army men from "Toy Story" and Goofy's son Max. The Hollywood & Vine restaurant in Echo Lake hosts character meals.

Buzz Lightyear. Woody's Picture Shootin' Corral, Pixar Place.

NEW! Chewbacca. Star Wars Launch Bay (does not sign autographs).

Chip 'n Dale. Across from the Sci-Fi Dine-In, Commissary Lane.

Daisy Duck. Chinese Theater, Hollywood Blvd.; Hollywood & Vine.

Doc McStuffins. Animation Courtyard; Hollywood & Vine breakfasts and lunches.

Donald Duck. Chinese Theater, Hollywood Blvd; Hollywood & Vine.

Goofy. Chinese Theater, Hollywood Blvd; Hollywood & Vine.

Green Army Men. Roaming Pixar Place.

Handy Manny. Hollywood & Vine.

Jake. Animation Courtyard; Hollywood & Vine.

NEW! Jawas. Star Wars Launch Bay (do not sign autographs).

NEW! Kylo Ren. Star Wars Launch Bay (does not sign autographs).

Lilo. Chinese Theater, Hollywood Blvd.

Mickey Mouse. Red Carpet Dreams, Commissary Lane (Sorcerer's Apprentice garb); Hollywood & Vine.

Minnie Mouse. Red Carpet Dreams, Commissary Lane; Hollywood & Vine.

Max. Chinese Theater, Hollywood Blvd.

NEW! Olaf. Celebrity Spotlight, Echo Lake.

Pluto. Animation Courtyard.

Sofia the First. Animation Courtyard; Hollywood & Vine.

Stitch. Chinese Theater, Hollywood Blvd.

NEW! Stormtroopers. Patrolling the Star Wars Launch Bay, Animation Courtyard; patrolling the park in front of the Chinese Theater, Hollywood Blvd. (do not sign autographs, usually don't stop for photos; however, may speak to you).

Woody. Woody's Picture Shootin' Corral, Pixar Place.

Know before you go.

Need a stroller? Cash? A FastPass fix? Here's where to find it:

ATMs. Right now there are two: at the park entrance on the left, and outside Keystone Clothiers on Hollywood Boulevard.

Baby Care Center. Changing rooms, nursing areas, microwave, playroom. Sells diapers, formula, pacifiers, over-the-counter meds. Just inside the park entrance on the left, next to the Guest Relations office.

FastPass+ kiosks. Cast members help you book and reschedule FastPasses. The corner of Hollywood and Sunset Boulevards; outside Jim Henson's MuppetVision 3-D; in front of Toy Story Mania; on Sunset Boulevard in front of The Twilight Zone Tower of Terror.

First aid. Registered nurses treat minor emergencies, call EMTs for serious issues. Just inside the park entrance on the left, next to the Guest Relations office.

Guest Relations. Cast members answer questions, reserve restaurants, exchange currency, have maps and times guides for all parks, store items found in the park that day. Walk-up windows outside the park entrance (far left); walk-in lobby inside the park.

Locker rentals. $7 a day, $5 deposit. Near the park entrance at Oscar's Super Service, Hollywood Boulevard.

Package pickup. Disney will send anything that you buy in the park up to its entrance to pick up later at no charge. Allow three hours. Packages can also be delivered to Disney hotels or shipped nationally.

Parking. Twenty dollars a day for cars; free for Disney hotel guests and annual passholders. Preferred parking adds $15, gives everyone in your car a bottle of water.

Stroller rentals. At Oscar's Super Service, inside the entrance on the right. Single strollers are $15 a day ($13 length of stay), doubles $31 ($27 length of stay). Get replacements at Tatooine Traders at the exit of Star Tours.

Disney transportation. Boats go to Epcot and Epcot resorts. Buses serve all Disney resorts and theme parks as well as the Blizzard Beach water park; there's no direct service to Disney Springs, Typhoon Lagoon or ESPN Wide World of Sports.

Wheelchair and scooter rentals. Oscar's Super Service, at the park entrance, rents wheelchairs for $12 a day ($10 length of stay). EVCs are $50 ($20 deposit).

Star Wars: A Galaxy Far, Far Away.

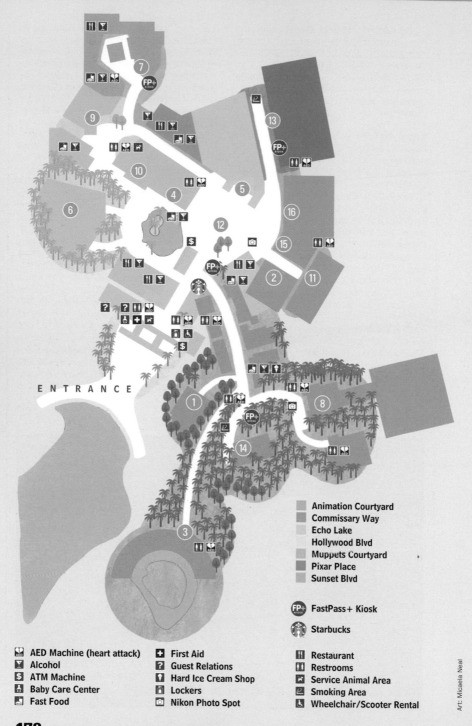

Animation Courtyard
Commissary Way
Echo Lake
Hollywood Blvd
Muppets Courtyard
Pixar Place
Sunset Blvd

FP+ FastPass+ Kiosk

Starbucks

AED Machine (heart attack)   First Aid   Restaurant
Alcohol   Guest Relations   Restrooms
ATM Machine   Hard Ice Cream Shop Service Animal Area
Baby Care Center   Lockers   Smoking Area
Fast Food   Nikon Photo Spot   Wheelchair/Scooter Rental

Art: Micaela Neal

Attractions at a glance

Here's a quick look at the attractions at Disney's Hollywood Studios, each of which is reviewed in detail later in this chapter. Each attraction is rated from one to five stars (★); a checkmark (✔) indicates an author favorite. The FastPass+ logo (FP+) appears if the attraction can be reserved in advance. Numbers in gold circles correspond to those shown on the map at the left.

① Beauty and the Beast Live on Stage. ★★★★★ ✔ FP+ Stage musical based on Belle's "tale as old as time" is fun and moving; its live singers, dancers and costumes dazzle. *Sunset Blvd.*

② Disney Junior Live on Stage. ★★★★★ FP+ Lively puppet show stars Disney Junior television characters from the programs "Mickey Mouse Clubhouse," "Doc McStuffins," "Jake and the Never Land Pirates" and "Sofia the First." Disney's best preschooler attraction if your kids know these shows. *Animation Courtyard.*

③ Fantasmic. ★★★ FP+ This evening spectacle stars a dreaming Mickey Mouse. Lasers, dancing fountains, water screens, fireworks; loud noises, bright flashes, scary villains abound when the dream becomes a nightmare. Many characters. *Sunset Blvd.*

④ For the First Time in Forever. ★★★★ ✔ FP+ Subtitled "A Frozen Sing-Along Celebration," this theatrical show combines humorous hosts with audience sing-alongs to musical clips from the movie. Includes all the hits, as well as live appearances—and singing—by Princess Anna and Queen Elsa. *Echo Lake.*

⑤ The Great Movie Ride. ENHANCED! ★★★★ ✔ FP+ Slow-moving indoor tram ride tours classic film scenes which Audio-Animatronic characters bring to life. A Turner Classic Movies sponsorship has greatly improved its queue, added Robert Osborne as its narrator and refreshed its film-clip finale. *Hollywood Blvd.*

⑥ Indiana Jones Epic Stunt Spectacular. ★★★★ ✔ FP+ Physical stunt show based on the original 1981 movie "Raiders of the Lost Ark." Hasn't changed much since that ancient tribesman placed that golden idol on the rock, but then again doesn't really need to. *Echo Lake.*

⑦ Jim Henson's MuppetVision 3-D. ★★★★ ✔ FP+ Kermit the Frog hosts this dated but funny movie, which is packed with vintage Muppet humor. The idea is that you're touring Dr. Bunsen Honeydew's lab, where he's just perfected the concept of 3-D. Quality video. *Muppets Courtyard.*

⑧ Rock 'n' Roller Coaster Starring Aerosmith. ★★★★★ ✔ FP+ Dark indoor roller coaster corkscrews, goes upside down, blares music by rock band Aerosmith. Listen for custom lyrics: "Love in a roller coaster! Livin' it up while you're upside down!" Min. height 48 inches (122 cm). *Sunset Blvd.*

⑨ Star Tours. UPDATED! ★★★★★ ✔ FP+ Wacky thrills aboard a Star Wars ship; routes vary with each ride, including some from the newest Star Wars movies. High-tech 3-D simulator can cause motion sickness. Min. height 40 inches (102 cm). *Just past Echo Lake.*

⑩ Star Wars: Path of the Jedi. NEW! ★ Narration-free short film compiles the most obvious Star Wars movie clips. The Force is weak with this one. *Echo Lake.*

⑪ Star Wars Launch Bay. NEW! ★★★★ ✔ Star Wars exhibits, character meet-and-greets and encounters, a behind-the-scenes film celebrating the saga. An attached shop offers elaborate costumes, toys, Aurabesh name tags, more. *Animation Courtyard.*

⑫ Star Wars: A Galactic Spectacular. NEW! ★★★★★ ✔ An amazingly awesome nighttime extravaganza that combines fireworks, lasers, pyrotechnics and high-tech projections onto the Chinese Theater and surrounding buildings. Laser duels in the sky? Check. Don't miss it. *Hollywood Blvd.*

⑬ Toy Story Mania. UPDATED! ★★★★★ ✔ FP+ Shoot at targets and rack up a high score in this ride-through series of 3-D video games starring "Toy Story" characters. Some new targets debuted in 2016, as did a second track that will increase capacity, should reduce Standby waits. *Pixar Place.*

⑭ The Twilight Zone Tower of Terror. ★★★★ ✔ FP+ Out-of-control elevator falls and ascends 13 stories in an unpredictable pattern. Sudden, swift drops and lifts. Min. height 40 inches (102 cm). *Sunset Blvd.*

⑮ Voyage of the Little Mermaid. ★★★ FP+ Musical stage show tells Ariel's story with fun puppets, a talented singer, nice effects... and too much video. *Animation Courtyard.*

⑯ Walt Disney: One Man's Dream. ★★★★ ✔ Walt Disney and Disney Company memorabilia and artifacts in a museum-style setting; a short biographical film narrated by Walt himself. *To the left of the Animation Courtyard, just outside Pixar Place.*

Sunset Boulevard.

Hollywood area

The front of the park channels the glory days of Tinseltown. Its Hollywood and Sunset Boulevard embody Los Angeles during the 1920s, '30s and '40s. Picturesque Echo Lake recalls Echo Lake Park in downtown Los Angeles, where silent movie czar Mack Sennett shot many of his Keystone Comedies. The real lake itself stood in for the lagoon in the 1960s television series "Gilligan's Island."

A loving look. The front of the park re-creates the look of Los Angeles during the mid-20th century. The turquoise entrance structures and their white-ringed pylons reflect 1935's Art Deco Pan Pacific Auditorium, a sports and music hall.

Disney's dreamlike 500-foot (152-meter) version of Hollywood Boulevard has 15 facades that replicate actual structures in Los Angeles. A Crossroads of the World gift kiosk is a Streamline Moderne stand at the 1937 Crossroads of the World shopping center. On the left side of the street,

Sid Cahuenga's is a tribute to 1930s and 1940s Craftsman bungalows that became Hollywood tourist shops. The Disney & Co. store brings back a Hollywood veterinary clinic and the black-marble-and-gilt Security Pacific Bank building (itself a copy of L.A.'s Richfield Oil Building, whose black and gold trim represented the "Black Gold" of the oil industry). Keystone Clothiers includes facades of the Max Factor Building and Jullian Medical Building. The right side of the street is equally inspired. The photo center is a clone of The Darkroom, a 1938 Hollywood photo shop known for its front window that looked like a camera. Celebrity 5 & 10 evokes an Art Deco building that housed a J.J. Newberry five and dime. The Hollywood Brown Derby looks like the 1929 second location of the eatery, a legendary dining spot for movie stars. Inside the buildings is a ceiling lover's paradise. Cover Story's film-roll theme recalls Frank Lloyd Wright.

At the end of Hollywood Boulevard is a full-scale replica of Grauman's Chinese Theatre built from the same 1927 blueprints.

In Disney's Echo Lake area, two snack stands honor 1920's programmatic architecture. A tramp steamer is Min & Bill's Dockside Diner, a nod to a 1930 pre-code comedy about Min Divot, a dockside innkeeper who has a love-hate relationship with Bill, a boozy fisherman. Having left its huge footprints in the walkway behind it, an apatosaurus is Dinosaur Gertie's Ice Cream of Extinction. In 1914 the childlike dinosaur starred in the earliest cartoon to be widely seen, the aptly named "Gertie the Dinosaur."

The nearby Hollywood & Vine restaurant evokes a cafeteria that stood on North Vine, near the actual Hollywood Blvd.

The Disney version of Sunset Boulevard begins with a replica of the 1940 Mulholland Fountain in Griffith Park. On your left, the Colony Sunset shop is New York City's Colony Theatre as it appeared in 1928, when it premiered the first Mickey Mouse sound cartoon, "Steamboat Willie." The Sunset Ranch Market recalls a 1934 Los Angeles Farmers Market where Walt Disney often had lunch. On your right, the Legends of Hollywood has the facade and corkscrew tower of the 1938 Academy Theater, a notable Los Angeles movie theater. The Once Upon a Time shop

is a dead ringer for the 1926 Carthay Circle Theatre, which hosted the premiere of "Snow White and the Seven Dwarfs" in 1937.

The entrance to Fantasmic's Hollywood Hills Amphitheater draws its design from the Ford Amphitheater in the Hollywood Hills. The stone entranceway to The Twilight Zone Tower of Terror replicates the Hollywood Gates, the 1923 entrance to the Hollywoodland real-estate development. The Hollywood Tower Hotel recalls the Spanish Revival look of the 1902 Mission Inn in Riverside, Calif.

Fun finds. ❶ Tailor Justin Stitches has an office above the Keystone Clothiers shop on Hollywood Boulevard ❷ as does Allen Smythee Productions. For years a Hollywood director would use the pseudonym "Allen Smythee" when he or she hated how a project turned out but was required to be listed in its credits. ❸ "We've Finished Some of Hollywood's Finest" proclaims the slogan of acting-and-voice studio Sights and Sounds. Located on the Echo Lake side of the Keystone Clothiers building, it's run by master thespian Ewell M. Pressum, voice coach Singer B. Flatt and account executive Bill Moore. ❹ Nearby is Holly-Vermont Realty, the name of an actual Hollywood business that in 1923 rented its back room to Walt and Roy Disney to use as their first office. ❺ The building directory shows that

Hollywood Boulevard.

dentists C. Howie Pullum, Ruth Canal and Les Payne share an office on the second floor. ❻ The office of Eddie Valiant—the grumpy gumshoe of the 1988 movie "Who Framed Roger Rabbit"—sits above the Hollywood & Vine restaurant. It has two windows, one of which Valiant's client Roger has crashed through. ❼ The office next door is available to rent, for 75 cents a day or $5 a week. ❽ A billboard for Roger's employer Maroon Studios tops Keystone Clothiers. Shipping crates to the left of Min & Bill's Dockside Diner reference three classic movies. ❾ One headed to "Scarlett O'Hara, Tara Plantation, 121539 Mitchell Lane, Jonesboro County, Georgia" from "Fleming Fashions Ltd., Atlanta" alludes to the lead character, main setting, premiere date, novelist, model city (Jonesboro, Ga.), director (Victor Fleming) and premiere city of the 1939 movie "Gone With the Wind." ❿ On its way to a Rick Blaine from Curtiz Wine & Spirits Ltd., a second crate refers to the main character and director (Michael Curtiz) of 1942's "Casablanca." ⓫ Addressed to "George Bailey, Bedford Falls," a crate from Wainwright Enterprises honors the main character, setting and a key secondary character (Sam Wainwright, the boyfriend of George's eventual wife) of the 1946 classic "It's a Wonderful Life." ⓬ "We're standing behind you" is the slogan of the International Brotherhood of Second Assistant Directors (say it slowly: IBSAD), which has an office above the Reel Vogue shop. During the Great Depression "Second Assistant Director" was a mercy title given to go-fers, who were often told "Get coffee and stand behind me."

Hidden Mickeys. ❶ The shape appears on Hollywood Boulevard on the Cover Story store, as a repeating pattern in the molding under second-floor windows. ❷ Curb stamps on Sunset Boulevard read "Mortimer & Co. Contractors 1928," a reference to Walt Disney's working first name for Mickey and the year he created him. ❸ At the Sunset Ranch Market the shape is formed by gauges on a welding torch behind the counter at Rosie's All-American Café. ❹ In Echo Lake, the shape appears in the napkin and utensil holders of the '50s Prime Time Café ❺ and as washers securing table tops at the adjacent Tune-In Lounge.

Live entertainment

The area has a terrific improv troupe and some "Star Wars"-themed entertainment.

★★★★★ ✔ **Citizens of Hollywood.** Impersonating showbiz stereotypes with unfettered glee, this improv troupe roams the park's Old Hollywood area as the living, breathing residents of a 1940s Tinseltown. The

Citizens of Hollywood.

The Twilight Zone Tower of Terror.

cast includes directors, divas, heartthrobs, has-beens, wannabes, starlets, inept public works employees, even a card shark. Most skits include audience "volunteers." To be one, wear something colorful, stand in front, smile and make eye contact. If you see script girl Paige Turner tell her the Neals say hello. *20- to 30-min. shows intermittently 9a–5:30p daily. Hollywood and Sunset Blvds.*

NEW! ★★★ **March of the First Order.** A Stormtrooper squad parades from Star Wars Launch Bay to Center Stage behind Captain Phasma. *20-min. shows hourly 10a–1p, 3p–4p.*

NEW! ★★★ **Star Wars: A Galaxy Far, Far Away.** Clips from iconic Star Wars moments play onscreen; key characters vamp onstage. *15-min. shows usually hourly 12:30p–2:30p, 4:30p–6:30p. Center Stage, Hollywood Blvd.*

Restaurants and food

A quick look: The best food is at the Brown Derby but it's pricey, the most fun is the 50's Prime Time Cafe. My top eats: the Derby Cobb salad and the Prime Time fried chicken.

★★★★★ ✔ **$29 DDP 50's Prime Time Cafe.** This retro experience is a hoot; servers hassle you if you don't keep your elbows off the table or eat your vegetables. Stage-set dinettes may remind baby boomers of grandma's house. Formica tables, sparkly vinyl chairs and black-and-white table TVs create a surreal atmosphere. The menu is comfort food—fried chicken, meatloaf, pot roast—and it's good. No reservations? If you need to, steal some seats at the bar. *11a–9:30p; $15–$25 (children $9–$11). Seats 225, 14 at the bar. Echo Lake.*

★★★ **$47 DDP Hollywood & Vine.** At dinner this crowded character buffet serves a wide variety of dishes, some quite good; coming to your table are Mickey and Minnie Mouse, Donald and Daisy Duck, and Goofy. The experience at breakfast and lunch is different: Disney Junior's Doc McStuffins, Handy Manny, Jake from "Jake and the Never Land Pirates" and Sofia from "Sofia the First" not only greet fans, they sing, dance and play with them, with a human emcee. Oddly the experience is not well known, so each child can get an enormous amount of time with the stars. *Breakfast 8a–10:20a, $27 (children $15); lunch 11a–2:55p, $34 (children $18); dinner 4:15p–8p, $47 (children $28). Seats 468. Echo Lake.*

★★★★★ ✔ **$46 DDP2 The Hollywood Brown Derby.** This fine-dining spot offers steaks, seafood and other American classics that are reworked to a modern standard. Especially good, however, is an original: the Hollywood Derby Cobb salad in all its chopped glory. New are a burger, noodle bowl and other less-expensive lunch options. The elegant eatery faithfully re-creates its namesake; to fully

Dinosaur Gertie.

50's Prime Time Cafe.

enjoy it take time to check out its hat-shaped brass table-side lamps, its gorgeous four-table Bamboo Room in the back corner (ask when you check in and you may get to sit there) and all the celebrity caricatures on the walls. Those in black frames re-create portraits at the original restaurant; those in gold frames are of singers and musicians of the era who had million-selling recordings. *Noon–9:30p; $18–$49 (children $7–$15). Seats 184. A Disney Signature Restaurant. Hollywood Blvd.*

NEW! ★★★★ $23 Hollywood Brown Derby Lounge. This pleasant outside spot serves the to-die-for Cobb salad from the restaurant, appetizers, a dessert trio and alcoholic drinks. *Noon–9:30p; $10–$20. Seats 40 outdoors, mostly covered. Hollywood Blvd.*

★★★★ ✔ $15 DDPq Starring Rolls Café. This tiny combination bakery and sandwich shop is packed during meal times, with a line spilling out the door. The cafe is recessed down a few steps, so a small wall separates diners from passersby. Breakfast offers fresh pastries, bagels and muffins. Lunch choices include a generous ham or turkey sandwich from the kitchens of the adjacent

Brown Derby. *Breakfast 8:30a–11:30a, $2–$6; lunch 11:30a–3p $9 $12 (children $6). Seats 60 outdoors, mostly covered. At the corner of Hollywood and Sunset Blvds.*

★★ ✔ $17 DDPq Sunset Ranch Market. Sitting on bustling Sunset, this outdoor food court can be a pleasant spot to people-watch. Food is nondescript but for the fruit and pretzels at the Anaheim Produce stand and the hand-dipped ice cream at the Hollywood Scoops stand out front. *Park open–park close; $4–$15 (children $5–$6). Seats 400 outdoors, mostly covered. Sunset Blvd.*

NEW! ★★★ $16 DDPs Docados del Lago Nachos y Empanadas. Chili-cheese nachos, beef empanadas, dulce de leche cookies, margaritas, beer. Outdoor stand. *Noon–6:30p; $11–$13. Echo Lake.*

★★★ $4 DDPs Dinosaur Gertie's Ice Cream of Extinction. Soft-serve cups and waffle cones, ice cream bars. Outdoor stand. *Noon–6:30p; $2–$5. Echo Lake.*

NEW! ★★★ $15 DDPs Hollywood Waffles of Fame. Turkey and gouda waffle, ham and cheddar focaccia sandwiches. Outdoor stand. *Noon–6:30p; $11. Echo Lake.*

★★ **$18 DDPq Min & Bill's Dockside Diner.**
You'll swear this outdoor counter-service
spot is a boat. There it is, apparently floating on Echo Lake. It serves… well the menu
changes constantly. *10:30a–9:15p; $10–$16
(children $14, comes with a Han Solo souvenir
bucket). Seats 140 outdoors. Echo Lake.*

★★★ **$14 DDPs Oasis Canteen.** Chicken
breast nuggets. Outdoor stand. *11a–6:30p;
$10–$11 (children $6). Echo Lake.*

★★★ **$3 DDPs Peevy's Polar Pipeline.**
Frozen soft drinks, with or without alcohol.
Whole fruit, ice cream bars. Outdoor stand.
11a–7p; $2–$4. Echo Lake.

NEW! ★★★ **$14 DDPs Sliders to the
Stars.** Pulled beef brisket sliders, barbe-
cued chicken sliders, beer. Outdoor stand.
Noon–6:30p; $11. Echo Lake.

★★★ ✔ **$11 DDPs Starbucks Trolley Car
Café.** The standard Starbucks menu. *Park
open–park close; $2–$9. Hollywood Blvd.*

Shops and merchandise

It's odd. Though most of the park's stores
are in its old Hollywood area, only a couple
of them—at most—sell any nostalgic or
Hollywood-oriented merchandise.

Adrian & Edith's Head to Toe. It will
only take 10 or 15 minutes to personalize
Mickey ears at this small shop. Towels can be
personalized, too. Built as a candy shop, the
store has the black and white tile common in
confectioneries. Tailoring and sewing equipment line upper shelves. *Hollywood Blvd.*

Celebrity 5 & 10. Kitchen items, housewares, packaged food. *Hollywood Blvd.*

Cover Story. Disney souvenirs, sundries.
Hollywood Blvd.

Crossroads of the World. Small kiosk has
Disney souvenirs, sundries. *Hollywood Blvd.*

The Darkroom. Disposable cameras,
picture frames, photo albums, MagicBands;
Disney movies and music. *Hollywood Blvd.*

Frozen Fractal Gifts. Frozen apparel,
toys; Anna, Elsa princess costumes; as much
Frozen stuff as can fit in an outdoor stand. *At
the exit of the Frozen sing-along, Echo Lake.*

Gem Creations. Every necklace, bracelet
and dreamcatcher is unique at this tiny
covered stand. The artist—the owner, the
woman who you'll probably meet behind the
counter—is an independent entrepreneur, not
a Disney employee. *Echo Lake.*

Indiana Jones Adventure Outpost. Hats,
shirts featuring the action hero. *Echo Lake.*

Indiana Jones Truck. Indiana Jones hats,
shirts; toy snakes. *Echo Lake.*

Keystone Clothiers. Upscale boutique has
upscale fashion apparel and accessories for
women, juniors, men. Includes items from the
Twenty-Eight & Main line. *Hollywood Blvd.*

Min & Bill's Dockside Diner.

Legends of Hollywood.

Legends of Hollywood. "Star Wars" merchandise, apparel, toys. *Sunset Blvd.*

Mickey's of Hollywood. Souvenirs, toys. The park's main store. *Hollywood Blvd.*

Mouse About Town. Graphic tees, hats, fashion apparel, sports apparel, jewelry, watches. *Sunset Blvd.*

Once Upon a Time. Children's shop has stylish kids' apparel, Belle costumes and accessories, casual shoes, plush, toys and other items. An homage to Hollywood's legendary Carthay Circle theater, its interior has an ornate arched ceiling and velvet drapes. Radio coverage of the 1937 premiere of "Snow White and the Seven Dwarfs," which was held at the Carthay Circle, fills the air. *Sunset Blvd.*

Planet Hollywood Super Store. Planet Hollywood items. *Sunset Blvd.*

Reel Vogue. Disney villains items, dolls; Nightmare Before Christmas apparel, Marvel merchandise; plush including tsum tsums. Formerly Villains in Vogue. *Sunset Blvd.*

Rock Around the Shop. Guitar-pick earrings? This shop has 'em, as well as Aerosmith items and a surprising variety of fashionable shirts for juniors. Wood floors, open ceilings and exposed lighting recall a backstage area; display stands look like instrument cases and trunks. *At the exit of Rock 'n' Roller Coaster, Sunset Blvd.*

Sunset Club Couture. Jewelry, watches, fashion accessories. *Sunset Blvd*

Sunset Ranch Pins and Souvenirs. What it says, plus caps and novelty hats. *Sunset Blvd.*

Sweet Spells. Bakers create candies, caramel apples and cookies in front of you at this small confectionery, which also sells packaged treats. *Sunset Blvd.*

Tower Gifts. The gift shop of the Hollywood Tower Hotel, in other words of The Twilight Zone Tower of Terror—Tower Gifts has fancy carpet, plaster walls with arches and elaborate ironwork. Keeping with its theme, it offers items from the hotel: door hangers, room key chains, front-desk bells, bathrobes, towels, mugs and glassware, all with the Hollywood Tower Hotel logo. Also has nice Tower of Terror-inspired fashion apparel; black-and-white Mickey, Minnie and Oswald the Lucky Rabbit plushies. *At the exit of the Tower of Terror, Sunset Blvd.*

"Casablanca."

The Great Movie Ride

TCM tie-in refreshes elaborate tribute to classic films

ENHANCED! ★★★★ ✔ **FP+** Gene Kelly "Singin' in the Rain"... Humphrey Bogart reminding Ingrid Bergman that "we'll always have Paris"... all those nearly naked showgirls twirling on the Tower of Beauty in "Footlight Parade"... OK, so you may not recognize everything you pass, but even so, this indoor tram trip is still worth your time.

A robotic tribute to Tinseltown, it takes you through soundstage sets that depict nearly every type of movie, with actors represented by Audio-Animatronic figures who sing, swing, fly, cower, sneer and threaten.

A new Turner Classic Movies sponsorship has refreshed the attraction's queue with different props and ever-changing posters, added a new interesting preshow documentary on the history of movies hosted by TCM's Robert Osborne, installed him as the tram's color man and updated the ride's film-montage finale.

The entrance facade is a reproduction of Grauman's Chinese Theatre. Like the plaza at that Hollywood landmark, this one is filled with more than 100 celebrity handprints (real ones). Front and center is the work of Warren Beatty, nearby are prints of Bob Hope, Jim Henson (and Kermit), Dustin Hoffman and Robin Williams (and their kids), George Burns, Tony Curtis and George Lucas.

Tips. *Where to sit:* In the second row of the tram's first car; you'll be right behind the driver (and later, a bad guy).

Key facts. *Duration:* 22 min. *Capacity:* 560. *Queue:* Indoor, overflows into covered outdoor area. *Fear factor:* Faux gunshots, sometimes real fire; the "Alien" creature and Wicked Witch threaten you. *Debuted:* 1989, revised 2015. *Access:* Wheelchairs, ECVs OK. *Disability services:* Assistive listening, handheld captioning. *Location:* At the end of Hollywood Blvd.

Average wait times (standby line)

9a	10a	11a	12p	1p	2p	3p	4p	5p	6p	7p	8p	9p	10p	11p
20m	25m	30m	35m	30m	25m	20m	15m	20m	20m	30m	20m	5m	0m	---

"Let It Go."

For the First Time in Forever

Sing along to all the hits at this witty stage show

★★★★ ✔ FP+ You'll be surprised who stars in this "Frozen Sing-Along Celebration." No, it's not Princess Anna or Queen Elsa, or even Kristoff, although all three appear, of course. Stealing the spotlight are two Arendelle historians, who retell the Frozen story with loads of sarcastic wisecracks.

Their narration punctuates musical clips from the film. The audience is encouraged to sing along, but no one needs persuading; audience members—mostly children and tweens—raise the roof as they sing their heads off. Lyrics appear on the screen karaoke-style, but few people need them.

The clips play out on enormous screens in high-definition, and their sound quality is crisp and clear. You'll remember why you liked the movie in the first place.

Instead of using excerpts from all the film's songs, the show features only its most popular tunes in their entirety. They're all here, including "Do You Want to Build a Snowman?" "For the First Time in Forever" and Olaf's hilarious "In Summer." Finally, Queen Elsa belts out "Let It Go" joined by her sister and swirling Disney snow. It's a breathtaking moment. Even if you've heard it many, many times, the song packs a wallop.

Tips. *When to go:* See the first show of the day or get a FastPass. *Where to sit:* As close to front center as you can get. FastPass holders get preferred seating near the front of the stage. *For families:* This cool, dark theater is a peaceful place to breastfeed, and the half-hour show gives you the time.

Fun find. Anna throws a snowball at Kristoff near the end of the show.

Key facts. *Duration:* 30 min. *Capacity:* 1,040. *Queue:* Outdoor, covered. *Showtimes:* Scheduled (see below). *Debuted:* 2014. *Access:* Wheelchairs, ECVs OK. *Disability services:* Assistive listening. *Location:* Echo Lake.

Typical show times

9a	10a	11a	12p	1p	2p	3p	4p	5p	6p	7p	8p	9p	10p	11p
---	10:30	11:30	12:30	1:30	2:30	3:30	4:30	5:30	6:30	7:30	---	---	---	---

Throwing a punch.

Indiana Jones Epic Stunt Spectacular
Special-effects show still entertaining after all these years

★★★★ ✔ FP+ Basically unchanged since its debut in 1989, this outdoor stage show is still entertaining, especially if you've never seen it before. Fireballs, gunshots, spears, swords, a great big boulder and a muscle-bound Nazi threaten Indy and his girlfriend Marion, as actors re-create physical stunts from the 1981 movie "Raiders of the Lost Ark." Between scenes you'll learn how backdrops can be quickly set up and dismantled, how heavy-looking props can be feather-light, and how stunt actors fake a punch. For flavor, Disney pretends the show is a real film shoot. Mock cameramen peer through mock cameras; a fake director barks out fake directions.

Tips. *Which show to see.* Either the first one or the last, when crowds are typically light and it's easy to get a good seat. The best show is at dusk, when fiery explosions pop against the sky. Avoid afternoon shows in the summer, when the poorly ventilated seating area can feel like a sweatbox. *Where to sit:* Front row center. To sit there you'll need a FastPass, as FastPass holders enter the theater first. *How to be in the show:* If you're seated close to the front, and jump up, wave and scream with wild abandon, the show's "casting director" will likely pick you as an extra.

Fun find. To the left of the show entrance, a British archeologist has dug a hole and lowered himself down into it. Pull on his rope and he'll get irritated—"I say! Stop mucking about up there!"

Key facts. *Duration:* 30 min. *Capacity:* 2,000. *Queue:* Outdoor, covered. *Fear factor:* Fire, simulated gunfire, explosions may upset toddlers. *Weather issues:* Canceled during rain. *Debuted:* 1989. *Access:* Wheelchairs, ECVs OK. *Disability services:* Assistive listening, handheld captioning, Audio Description. *Location:* Echo Lake.

Typical show times

9a	10a	11a	12p	1p	2p	3p	4p	5p	6p	7p	8p	9p	10p	11p
---	---	---	12:00	---	2:00	3:00	---	5:00	6:00	7:15	---	---	---	---

"Be Our Guest."

Beauty and the Beast Live on Stage

Nearly as old as time, musical stage show still enchants

★★★★★ ✔ FP+ As good as ever after a run of more than two decades, this lavish stage show re-creates the spirit of Disney's 1991 movie by focusing on its musical numbers. Choreographed productions of "Belle," "Gaston," "Be Our Guest," "Something There," "The Mob Song" and the title song form a condensed account of the tale as old as time. Portraying villagers and castle attendants, the supporting cast dances, faints, fights, jumps, kicks, swoons and twirls, often with skill usually seen only in Broadway performances. Colorful costumes and creative lighting lend a true theatrical feel.

Tips. *When to go:* See the first show of the day; it's the least crowded. During the summer avoid shows after noon; the theater is covered but otherwise open to heat, humidity and blowing rain. *Where to sit:* As close to front-row center as you can; you'll need a FastPass. You'll see every expression on the performers' faces and fully enjoy the many symmetrical dance numbers.

Fun finds. ❶ Thirty television stars have left their handprints in a small plaza behind the bleachers. ❷ The show begins with a pun: a ringing bell. ❸ The stage arch resembles the one at the Hollywood Bowl in Los Angeles. It lights up. ❹ During the curtain call keep an eye on Gaston. He stays in character, often flexing his biceps as he flashes the "call me" sign to females in the crowd.

Key facts. *Duration:* 25 min. *Capacity:* 1,500. *Queue:* Outdoor, unshaded. *Fear factor:* Little ones may be disturbed as Gaston stabs the Beast (the violence is not graphic). *Weather issues:* If it's raining bring your umbrella or poncho if you plan to get there early; the waiting area is a sidewalk. *Debuted:* 1991, revised 2001. *Access:* Wheelchairs, ECVs OK. *Disability services:* Assistive listening, Audio Description. *Location:* Sunset Blvd.

Typical show times

9a	10a	11a	12p	1p	2p	3p	4p	5p	6p	7p	8p	9p	10p	11p
---	---	11:00	---	1:00	2:00	---	4:00	5:00	---	---	---	---	---	---

Welcome to G-Force Records.

Rock 'n' Roller Coaster Starring Aerosmith

Rocketing launch highlights thrilling dark coaster

★★★★★ ✔ FP+ You go upside down twice on this dark, indoor roller coaster. The beginning is the scariest part: a powered launch that hurls you forward to a speed of 57 mph (92 kph) in just 2.8 seconds, then zooms through a half-mile of twists and turns, two loops and a tight corkscrew. A true rush, the ride re-creates a frantic Los Angeles freeway trip: As Aerosmith rock music pounds from speakers surrounding your seat in what looks like a Cadillac convertible limousine, you pass through two famous L.A. landmarks, the iconic "Hollywood" sign and the huge doughnut that in real life promotes Randy's Donuts near the Los Angeles airport.

"Make it a super stretch." The grins begin as you enter the building, the headquarters of mythical G-Force Records. Step through the lobby and you're off on a time-warp to

the 1970s. Along the walls are displays of real vintage recording and playback gear. Soon you come to Studio C, where you find the rock band Aerosmith (via video) mixing the rhythm tracks to their new number, "Walk This Way." Suddenly the guys have to leave; they're late for a show. But no worries: since the band members "can't forget our fans," they offer you—and everyone in line—backstage passes to their show. As the manager phones for a car she counts the crowd, then tells the limo company "We're going to need a stretch. In fact, make it a super stretch."

You're then ushered into a grimy back alley, where up pulls your ride. Moments later Aerosmith's Steven Tyler is screaming out a countdown, then a rubber-burning start squeals you off into the darkness. Eventually you arrive at the backstage entrance of an

Average wait times (standby line)

9a	10a	11a	12p	1p	2p	3p	4p	5p	6p	7p	8p	9p	10p	11p
45m	90m	80m	55m	70m	60m	40m	50m	55m	50m	50m	50m	50m	30m	---

L.A. arena, where a red carpet leads to (a video of) the band performing on-stage. **Tips.** *When to go:* During the first hour; you'll be able to ride it again before the hour's up. Later, use the Single-Rider line or get a FastPass, though if you do you'll bypass the lobby. *Where to sit:* For the most intense launch, ask for the front row. It will only add a couple of minutes to your wait, and it's worth it for its great view and most surprising ride—front-row passengers never know what scenery is coming up, as it lights up just as they reach it. Riders with long legs should ask for an odd-numbered row; those seats have far more legroom. Riders who use the Single-Rider line are not allowed to choose their seat. *For families:* Your child shouldn't be afraid to ride; the coaster starts fast but is always very smooth. Though children may have no idea who Aerosmith is, that won't diminish their fun. The thrills stand on their own. *Other tips:* In the pre-show room, stand to the left to be the first of your group in line for boarding when the door opens.

All-American Rock 'n' Roll. Known for its driving riffs and suggestive lyrics, Aerosmith formed in Boston in 1970. Its raunchy swagger, highlighted by Steven Tyler's prancing stage antics, drew comparisons to the Rolling Stones; Tyler and Stones singer Mick Jagger even looked similar. Early hits included 1975's "Walk This Way," which like the Stones' earlier "Satisfaction" used a groove so strong the words didn't matter. Aerosmith also created rock music's first power ballad, adding strings to 1973's piano-based "Dream On." Plagued by drug abuse in the late 1970s, the band got back on track in 1986, when Tyler and lead guitarist Joe Perry appeared on rap group Run D.M.C.'s cover of "Walk This Way." The video became an MTV staple. Later hits include "Love in an Elevator" and "Livin' on the Edge."

Fun facts. ❶ Unlike a regular coaster, the ride doesn't start off with a lift hill. Its launch is powered by a magnetic linear induction system imbedded in the track. Vehicles accelerate by being quickly pushed and pulled from one hidden magnet to another. An earlier, more primitive linear induction system powers Magic Kingdom's PeopleMover ride. ❷ When Disney agreed to the deal to feature Aerosmith on the ride, initially the company couldn't reach frontmen Steven Tyler and Joe Perry. Unbeknownst to Disney execs, the two were vacationing with their families at the time… at Walt Disney World.

Fun finds. ❶ The columns in the lobby mimic guitar necks, complete with frets and strings. ❷ The first display case holds a 1958 Gibson Les Paul Standard guitar ❸ as well as a disc cutter, a device that "cut records" by etching sounds from a mixing console onto a master disc. ❹ Record players in the second case range from a 1904 external-horn Edison Fireside to ❺ a 1970s Disc-O-Kid. ❻ Put your ear to doors marked "Studio A" or "Studio B" to hear Aerosmith rehearsing. ❼ Concert posters in the next room include one for a 1973 show from Aerosmith's first national tour, as the opening act for the New York Dolls. It's midway down on the right. ❽ An MC5 poster includes a still-visible marijuana leaf that Disney has covered with a small American flag. ❾ As you stand in the alley, signs on the rear of the G-Force building indicate that repair work has been done by Sam Andreas and Sons Structural Restoration, the garage is run by Lock 'n' Roll Parking Systems and that its dumpster is owned by the Rock 'n' Rollaway Disposal Co. ❿ A glass case displays rates for Wash This Way Auto Detail. ⓫ Limo license plates sport messages such as 2FAST4U and H8TRFFC. ⓬ The disc jockey heard on the car radio is longtime Los Angeles rock jock Uncle Joe Benson. ⓭ As you leave the ride, the Aerosmith concert video loop shown in front of you occasionally shows Tyler screaming "Rock 'n' Roller Coaster!!!"

Hidden Mickeys. ❶ Mickey hides twice on a sign for the ride on the building: Tyler's shirt has Mickey silhouettes and a boy wears mouse ears. ❷ The three-circle shape also appears as tile pieces in a beige section of the foyer's floor mosaic, ❸ as a distorted carpet pattern in the first display room, ❹ as cables on the recording-studio floor, ❺ on the registration stickers of the limos' rear license plates and ❻ as the "O" in the phrase "Box #15" on an exitway trunk.

Key facts. *Duration:* 1 min. 22 sec. *Capacity:* 120; 5 24-seat vehicles seated 2 across. *Queue:* Indoor; overflows into shaded outdoor area. *Single Rider line:* Often available. *Fear factor:* Very fast start, darkness. *Restraint:* Shoulder harness. *Top speed:* 57 mph (92 kph). *Track:* Standard steel, 3,403 ft (1037 meters), max height 80 ft (24 meters). *Debuted:* 1999. *Health advisory:* Disney suggests you skip this ride if you have problems with your heart, back or neck, have high blood pressure, are prone to motion sickness, or are pregnant. *Access:* Height min 48 in (122 cm); wheelchair and ECV users must transfer. *Location:* Sunset Blvd.

The Twilight Zone Tower of Terror features a high-speed drop into the dark mysterious realm of the Twilight Zone.

WARNING!

For safety, you should be in good health and free from high blood pressure, heart, back or neck problems, motion sickness, or other conditions that could be aggravated by this adventure.

Expectant mothers should not ride.

Supervise children at all times.

Persons who do not meet the minimum height requirement may not ride.

Must transfer

40"

KEEP OUT

Tower of Terror entrance.

The Twilight Zone Tower of Terror
Disney's best thrill ride randomizes drops, psychs you out

★★★★★ ✔ FP+ You plummet—and soar—up to 130 feet (40 meters) aboard a pitch-black freight elevator in this fully realized thrill ride. The falls, the lifts, the effects... they're all unpredictable, as a computer randomly freestyles each ride individually. Loaded with special effects and superb detailing, the dark, creepy experience appeals to nearly everyone except those with an intense fear of falling.

From the moment you walk through its entranceway, Disney has designed the attraction to freak you out. It's set in what appears to be an abandoned hotel, its lobby covered in cobwebs. You stop in a spooky library, then head to an unwelcoming basement where a rusty service elevator creaks as its doors shut... only to open a moment later as the elevator stops at a floor with ghosts, then close again as it heads up to a nonexistent 13th floor where things really start to get creepy. And then, just when you

realize you're about to fall, there's just the right amount of perfectly timed... silence.

A 'somewhat unique' story. According to Disney lore, the extravagant 12-story Hollywood Tower Hotel opened in 1917 as a gathering place for Tinseltown elite. Two decades later, on Oct. 31, 1939, the hotel hosted a Halloween party in its rooftop lounge. But at precisely 8:05 p.m. a huge lightning bolt hit the building, dematerializing two elevator shafts and the wings they supported. Among the victims were five people riding in an elevator — a child actress with her nanny, a young Hollywood couple and a bellhop.

The hotel stood deserted for decades, and now has mysteriously reopened, just in time for your visit. As you arrive to check in, a bellhop asks you to wait in the library, where immediately the power goes out but a black-and-white TV comes on, showing the start of the 1960s television show, "The Twilight

Average wait times (standby line)

9a	10a	11a	12p	1p	2p	3p	4p	5p	6p	7p	8p	9p	10p	11p
20m	55m	50m	60m	35m	35m	35m	30m	25m	20m	30m	25m	10m	10m	---

Zone." As host Rod Serling describes a "somewhat unique" story about a maintenance service elevator, he adds, "we invite you, if you dare, to step aboard. Because in tonight's episode, you are the star."

Boarding the hotel's service elevator, you enter that episode yourself, traveling past strange images as you journey to a mysterious 13th floor. Once there, your cab unexpectedly moves forward, its doors slam shut and soon you're tossed — violently — up, down — down, up — up, up, down. Every ride is different. Occasionally other doors open, revealing the open sky and the theme park down below. Those five victims from 1939 may appear again, or rain may fall, or an odd smell may waft around you. Finally the madness stops, and you calmly arrive in the basement. "The next time you check into a deserted hotel," Serling intones, "make sure you know just what kind of vacancy you're filling. Or you may find yourself a permanent resident of… 'The Twilight Zone.'"

Tips. *Where to sit:* For the most unobstructed view of the effects, ask to sit in the center of the elevator's front row. As you line up at the boarding area, tell the attendant you'd like the last spot in Row 2. *Uneasy about the drops?* Ask to sit at the end of a row. In the boarding area, that corresponds to the first spot in any of the six rows. Your seat will be against a side wall and have a handle to hold onto.

Fun facts. ❶ When Serling speaks on the television, you're actually watching him introduce a 1961 "Twilight Zone" episode, "It's a Good Life." He originally said "This, as you may recognize, is a map of the United States," though on the video the camera cuts away as he pronounces the word "map" and you hear him say "maintenance service elevator." ❷ The cast members' break room is between the drop shafts. When you scream, they hear you. "It's very difficult to relax," one tells us. ❸ In 1993 as it was being built, the Tower was struck by lightning.

Fun finds. ❶ To the right of the lobby's reception desk, an American Automobile Association plaque gives the hotel a "13-diamond" ranking. A tongue-in-cheek honor, it was presented to Disney by the AAA when the ride opened in 1994. ❷ A poster at the concierge desk promotes a show by Anthony Freemont, the name of a 6-year-old boy in a 1961 "Twilight Zone" episode ("It's a Good Life") who uses telepathic powers to terrorize his neighbors. ❸ In the boiler

room, though the service elevators' tracking dials only go to "12," their arrows go to an unmarked "13." ❹ As your elevator doors close in front of you, a hint at your destination—a "1" on the left door and a "3" on the right—disguises itself as a "B," the elevator's letter. ❺ A small inspection certificate on the interior wall of the elevator is signed by "Cadwallader," a jovial character in the 1959 episode "Escape Clause" who secretly is the devil. Dated Oct. 31, 1939 (the day of the hotel's lightning strike), the certificate has the number 10259, a reference to the date "The Twilight Zone" series premiered: Oct. 2, 1959. ❻ In the basement, the clock in the office is stuck on the time 8:05, the moment of the lightning strike. ❼ The hotel gift shop's outdoor display windows are still decorated for the Halloween of 1939, the night of the mythical lightning strike.

Hidden Mickeys. ❶ The three circles appear as a pair of folded wire-rim glasses on the concierge desk (the temples form Mickey's face, the eye rims make his ears). ❷ The sheet music to the 1932 ditty "What! No Mickey Mouse?" is in the left library, on a bookcase directly in front of the entrance door. ❸ The little girl in the TV video is holding a 1930s Mickey Mouse doll. ❹ In the boiler room, the shape appears as large, round ash doors beneath a fire box on a brick furnace (on your right just after you've entered the room), and ❺ as water stains just to the left of a fuse box on the boiler room's left wall, just past the spot where the queue divides. ❻ Mickey also hides up on the 13th floor, in the center of the star field as it comes together to form a pinpoint.

Key facts. *Duration:* 4 min. *Capacity:* 84 (4 21-seat elevators). *Queue:* Indoor, air-conditioned; overflows into shaded outdoor queue. *Fear factor:* This is one scary ride; although its ascents and drops are smooth, Disney's mind games are intense, especially for younger riders who have never been in such a believable artificial environment; when the dim elevator shaft turns dark and silent even some adults find the tension hard to bear. *Restraint:* Seat belt. *Debuted:* 1994, revised 2002. *Health advisory:* Disney suggests you skip this ride if you have problems with your heart, back or neck, have high blood pressure, are prone to motion sickness, or are pregnant. *Access:* Height min 40 in (102 cm); wheelchair and ECV users must transfer. *Disability services:* Handheld captioning. *Location:* Sunset Blvd.

Fireworks and more.

Star Wars: A Galactic Spectacular

High-tech extravaganza celebrates saga

NEW! ★★★★★ ✔ You'll cheer at the end of this show. It will remind you why you liked Star Wars in the first place. It's not a fireworks show, but rather a near-perfect melding of different media and technology—flames, lasers, pyro and projected video—one that consumes you with delight.

Who knew? The Chinese Theatre makes a great movie screen—projected images are crystal clear and compelling. Adjacent buildings also get into the act; the spectacle fills your field of vision.

The show incorporates scenes from every film in the saga. You'll see the twin suns of Tattooine, dive into the trenches of the Death Star, visit the swamps of Dagobah and scavenge desolate Jakku with Rey. Darth Vader strides toward you with his raspy scuba-tank breath. TIE fighters fly straight at you and seem to explode next to you. Towering flames shoot up 140 feet (43 meters) into the air; their heat palpable on your skin.

Key moments stand out as particularly delightful. A laser-beam lightsaber fight in the sky is so spot-on with the show's subject matter that it's hard not to grin. Emperor Palpatine seems to make the palm trees in front of the theater crackle with electricity; it's a startling effect. A nice touch: projections at the end of the show include posters from the series, including some for the original film.

A pricey dessert party ($69 adults, $39 children) includes Star Wars-themed treats and beverages, including alcoholic options. You nosh inside Star Wars Launch Bay, then watch the show from a reserved VIP area. To make reservations call 407-939-3463.

Tips. *When to arrive:* 30–45 minutes before showtime for a prime spot. *Where to stand:* Prime viewing is near Center Stage, directly in front of the Chinese Theatre in the center of the street, in front of two new production towers along Hollywood Boulevard. If you watch from further back, storefronts will obscure your view of much of the show.

Key facts. *Duration:* 12 min. *Showtime:* Once nightly, time varies. *Fear factor:* Real and simulated fire, lasers, explosions. *Weather issues:* Canceled by rain or thunderstorm. *Access:* Wheelchairs, ECVs OK. *Location:* On, next to and behind the Chinese Theatre, viewed from Hollywood Blvd.

Photo: © Disney

Mickey slays Maleficent.

Fantasmic

Kitschy spectacle offers a Disney way to cap your day

★★★ **FP+** Held in an open-air amphitheater, this lavish evening spectacle includes boats, cannons, characters, fireworks, fountains, laser beams, music, smoke, water screens and before you can say "great balls of fire!" one of those, too. It tells a story of good versus evil, as Mickey Mouse dreams of animals and princesses but also of scheming villains. Most of it takes place on a 60-foot-tall (18-meter) mountain that's ringed by a narrow lagoon.

Though confusing, the show is a visual delight. It begins as Mickey, dressed as the Sorcerer's Apprentice from the 1940 movie "Fantasia," conducts water fountains like instruments in an orchestra. As his powers increase, he imagines flowers and animals that perform a version of "I Just Can't Wait to be King" from the 1994 film "The Lion King."

The mouse's dream becomes a nightmare as a video version of Monstro the whale (1940's "Pinocchio") lunges at the audience and the amphitheater turns dark. Live-action villains include Gov. Ratcliffe (1995's "Pocahontas"), the Evil Queen (1937's "Snow White and the Seven Dwarfs"), Jafar (1992's "Aladdin") and Maleficent (1959's "Sleeping

Beauty"), who transforms into a dragon and ignites the lagoon with her fiery breath.

All ends well, of course. A boat parade includes Ariel (1989's "The Little Mermaid"), Belle (1991's "Beauty and the Beast") and Snow White. The finale is a now-you-see-him, now-you-don't, now-you-do Mickey farewell.

A snack bar sells hot dogs and other snacks. Souvenir hawkers roam the stands.

Tips. *When to go:* If there are two shows see the second one; it will be much less crowded. Arrive an hour early for the first show, 30 minutes early for the second. *Where to sit:* As close to front row center as possible. If you get a FastPass you'll sit just left of center. Front rows can get misted with water.

Hidden Mickey. Pinocchio's water bubble forms Mickey's head; two others his ears.

Key facts. *Duration:* 25 min. *Capacity:* 9,900 (6,900 seats). *Queue:* Outdoor, uncovered. *Fear factor:* Loud noises, bright flashes, fiery water. *Weather issues:* Cancelled during rain. *Debuted:* 1998 (Disneyland 1992). *Access:* Wheelchairs, ECVs OK. *Disability services:* Assistive listening, reflective captioning. *Location:* Sunset Blvd.

Pixar Place.

Studios area

Most buildings at the rear of the park resemble the 1940s campus of the Walt Disney Studios in California. Pixar Place is styled after the headquarters of that animation studio in Emeryville, Calif.

Hidden Mickeys. ➊ Drips of purple paint on a recessed light hide his silhouette, on a recessed light outside the Stage 1 Co. Store, under a bronze lion head. ➋ It also appears twice inside Mama Melrose's Ristorante Italiano, as spots on a vine leaf at the bottom right of a lattice fence to the right of the check-in desk and ➌ as a spot on the right shoulder of a nearby dalmatian statue.

Live entertainment

Entertaining for adults, exciting for children, the former Jedi Training Academy has been updated with new characters and action:

UPDATED! ★★★ Jedi Training: Trials of the Temple. Kids volunteer to learn lightsaber techniques, duel villains. Adversaries include Darth Vader, Kylo Ren and the Seventh Sister, a character from the animated series "Star Wars Rebels." *25-min. shows every 30 min. 10:10a–7:40p. Next to Star Tours, near Echo Lake.*

Restaurants and food

Want to relax in a regular restaurant? You can do it back here, in an Italian one.

★★★★ ✔ $34 DDP Mama Melrose's Ristorante Italiano. Traditional Italian cuisine gets a California twist at this comfortable eatery, which is hidden in a back corner of the park. It's so relaxing you may need a nap afterward. Mama's is best for families and couples who need a break and want comfort food. The signature dish is chicken alla parmigiana; other choices include seasonal pastas, brick-oven flatbreads, even a steak. Portions are generous. Resembling a converted warehouse, the dining room has open ceilings strung with Christmas lights, brick walls covered with Californian and Italian pop-culture relics, and wood floors. Mismatched light fixtures add to the eclectic look. *11:30a–9:30p; $14–$33 (children $10–$11). Seats 250. Muppets Courtyard.*

★★★ **$33 DDP Sci-Fi Dine-In Theater.** This starlit indoor dining room channels a 1950s drive-in theater, with a huge silver screen that shows trailers from kitschy sci-fi flicks such as "The Devil Girl from Mars," "Plan 9 from Outer Space" and "Attack of the 50-Foot Woman" as well as odd newsreels, intermission bumpers and space-age cartoons. Diners sit two abreast in miniature versions of 1950s Chevy and Pontiac convertibles. Unfortunately, the tight row seating makes it tough for families to talk. A pricey menu overhypes its food; if you go stick to the hamburgers and milkshakes. Make sure you ask for a car when you check in; otherwise you may get a plain-Jane patio table at the back of the room. Don't expect a car to yourself without a reservation. *11a–9:30p; $14–$32 (children $10–$12). Seats 252. Commissary Way.*

★★★ ✔ **$15 DDPq ABC Commissary.** Live palms, cushioned booths and chairs, unobtrusive lighting and soft carpet make this the park's most comfortable fast-food spot. The only downside: Ceiling-mounted televisions play ABC-TV promos on a short loop, over and over, ad infinitum. Food is mostly fine but often forgettable—burgers, sandwiches, occasionally a good specialty. *10:30a–8:30p; $8–$12 (children $6–$7). Seats 690, including 128 outdoors. Commissary Lane.*

★★ **$17 DDPq Backlot Express.** This faux prop warehouse offers mostly lackluster burgers, hot dogs, chicken, grilled sandwiches and salads. Some choices are themed to Star Wars, such as the Dark Side Chicken and Waffles. Open ceilings and concrete floors add to the "warehouse" feel of the place, which almost always has at least a few empty tables. Refills come free at the self-serve soft-drink station. Real Hollywood clutter crowds the walls and corners—thousands of authentic movie and television props, gadgets and trivial-but-fascinating down-and-dirty junk (for example, call sheets from the "Cheers" television series and Bennie the Cab stunt car from 1988's "Who Framed Roger Rabbit"). Outside seating is mostly under umbrellas; several tables offer good viewing of the adjacent Jedi Training shows. *11a–9p; $10–$14 (children $6–$8). Seats 600, including 270 outdoors on mostly-covered tables. Echo Lake.*

★★★ **$11 DDPs Hey Howdy Hey Take Away.** Hot dogs, frozen drinks. *10:30a–9p; $6–$9. Pixar Place.*

Animation Courtyard.

Commissary Way.

NEW! DDPq PizzeRizzo. This fast-food pizza spot, owned by Muppet Rizzo the Rat, replaces Toy Story Pizza Planet. Opening fall 2016. *Muppets Courtyard.*

★★★ **$11 DDPs The Writer's Stop.** This former early-morning bakery now serves more as the waiting area for the adjacent Sci-Fi Dine-In. It serves pretzels, a cheese and sausage plate, spiced nuts and alcoholic drinks. *11a–9:30p; $5–$7. Seats 8 at 4 small tables; 2 stand-up tables. Commissary Lane, next to the Sci-Fi Dine-In.*

Shops and merchandise

A first-rate Star Wars shop stands out among the shopping choices in these areas.

In Character. Princess costumes (Ariel, Rapunzel, Merida, Elsa, Anna); also Minnie Mouse costumes. Princess plushies, dolls, toys, children's wear. Many Minnie-ear headbands. Outdoor stand. *Animation Courtyard.*

It's a Wonderful Shop. Oddly, this Christmas shop doesn't have a Christmas theme. Instead, it looks like a prop warehouse, with all sorts of gewgaws on the walls.

Merchandise includes ornaments, stockings and nutcrackers. *Muppets Courtyard.*

NEW! Launch Bay Cargo. This large store has more high-end, expensive Star Wars stuff than Tatooine Traders. It doesn't really have apparel, nor make-your-own lightsaber/droid stations like that store does, but it does have nice, large action figures of a wide variety of Star Wars characters; toy/remote-control/replica Star Wars spaceships; nice light-up lightsabers; toy BB-8 robots; CDs of the Star Wars film soundtracks; books; a wide variety of Star Wars character maquettes; replica costumes, helmets; even some life-size character statues. Fine art, oil paintings, lithographs, signed photographs, prints. Also a D-Tech on Demand station where you can customize your own MagicBand or phone/tablet case—in Aurabesh, of course. *At the exit of Star Wars Launch Bay, Animation Courtyard.*

Stage 1 Company Store. Muppet stuff; toys; also arty stuff; Disney art and design books. The front is a children's shop, with infantwear, children's wear and costumes that will transform your little girl into Minnie Mouse or Tinker Bell. *Muppets Courtyard.*

The Studio Store. Merchandise from Disney Junior shows; infantwear; plushies; toys for toddlers; Duffy bears (and outfits); sundries. *Animation Courtyard.*

Tatooine Traders. Drool you will over this store's Star Wars stuff—from its Yoda backpacks to its Droid Factory to its Stormtrooper helmets. Star Tours souvenirs include toy Starspeeders and action figures. *At the exit of Star Tours, Echo Lake.*

Toy Story Dept. "Toy Story" toys, children's apparel. ●utdoor stand. *Pixar Place.*

The Writer's Stop. Disney books and movies; kitchen supplies; packaged food. *Commissary Lane.*

A closer look

Embracing the concept that ●rlando was "Hollywood East," at first the park produced many movies and television shows. In 1988 (a year before it opened to the pubic) it shot the films "Ernest Saves Christmas" and "Newsies" on its backlot. In 1990 Warren Beatty and Madonna chewed the park scenery in "Dick Tracy." A 10-year-old Britney Spears competed in the television series "Ed McMahon's Star Search," as did an 11-year-old Justin Timberlake. They both lost, but soon appeared together on the Disney Channel program "The New Mickey Mouse Club." Also in the cast: fellow pre-teens Christina Aguilera, Ryan Gosling and Keri Russell (all shown below). Both shows were produced in the building that today houses Toy Story Mania.

Meanwhile, the building that today is the Star Wars Launch Bay housed Walt Disney Feature Animation Florida. Initially a "second unit" for the company, it produced sequences of 1991's "Beauty and the Beast." Later it expanded, creating entire films such as 1998's "Mulan" and 2002's "Lilo & Stitch." After its 2004 movie "Home on the Range" bombed at the box office, Disney management downsized and eventually closed the studio, and soon shuttered all of the park's movie and television operations. Today, the Studios has no studios and does no production work.

The cast of "The New Mickey Mouse Club," 1993.

Maintenance bay queue room.

Star Tours

High-tech 3-D simulator randomizes thrills, adventures

UPDATED! ★★★★★ ✔ FP+ Taking off on a tourist trip where everything goes wrong, you'll be immersed in the Star Wars universe by this 3-D motion simulator. Even the line is fun. You'll want to go on it multiple times, as its scenes and destinations change with each flight. You might head to Tatooine, Coruscant, Naboo, or even a Death Star, may be stopped by Darth Vader or receive a hologrammed message from Princess Leia ("Help me, Star Tours, you're my only hope!"). A newly-added scene takes you to Jakku, the heroine's home planet in "The Force Awakens." Also new is a hologram message from BB-8.

Tips. *When to go:* Early, then again after lunch. *Where to sit:* In the middle of a center row for the best 3-D experience and to avoid nausea. Avoid the front row (the visuals may be skewed) and the back (you may knock your head against the back wall). *To understand the story:* Watch the queue and boarding videos;

they set it up. *For families:* Pose your kids on a Speeder bike across from the ride entrance.

Fun finds. ❶ Ewoks chatter in their outdoor village at night. They play music, too. ❷ The cipher JK0966, on a circular plate on the wall on your right just before you reach the arrivals and departures screen, is a nod to character James Kirk and the month and year his "Star Trek" TV series debuted—September 1966. ❸ Just below that mark, N1C7C01 jumbles the registration number of that show's Enterprise, NCC-1701. ❹ IG0088 on that plate is a cryptic call-out to bounty hunter IG88 from 1980's "Episode V: The Empire Strikes Back." ❺ On the screen, news regarding "Flight 1138 to Chandrila" pops up on the bottom left. That's a reference to the first movie directed by George Lucas, 1971's "THX1138." ❻ Aurebesh type under R2-D2's Starspeeder port reads "Astromech Droid Socket." ❼ The number of your flight—"1401"—is a selfie shout-out to

Average wait times (standby line)

9a	10a	11a	12p	1p	2p	3p	4p	5p	6p	7p	8p	9p	10p	11p
10m	40m	40m	50m	55m	30m	30m	35m	25m	20m	15m	10m	10m	5m	---

Illustration © Disney

Jakku.

Walt Disney Imagineering, which is headquartered at 1401 Flower St. in Glendale, Calif. ⑧ The page "Will the owner of a red and black landspeeder, vehicle ID THX1138, please return to your craft?" is another nod to the first Lucas film. ⑨ "Departing Tatooine passenger Sacul, Mr. Egroeg Sacul, please see a Star Tours agent at gate 2D." Egroeg Sacul is "George Lucas" spelled backward. ⑩ "Paging Star Tours passenger Mot Worrom, please pick up the nearest flight courtesy comlink" refers to Tom Morrow, a pun of a name with a long Disney history. Initially, Tom was the Audio-Animatronic operations director of Mission Control in the 1970s Tomorrowland attraction Flight to the Moon (today's Stitch's Great Escape). In the 2000s, a tiny transparent Tom Morrow 2.0 hosted the Innoventions area of Epcot. ⑪ As you enter a second queue room Rex, the pilot of the Starspeeder in the original Star Tours ride, sits to your left in an open crate. Every now and then a power surge causes him to burst out a line of his old dialogue: "Welcome-welcome-welcome-welcome aboard!" He sometimes sparks. ⑫ "Reubens Robotics" is the name of the factory Rex is being returned to—a nod to his voice talent Paul Reubens (best known as childlike comedian Pee-wee Herman). ⑬ The Aurebesh at the top of his shipping label translates to "Boyd's Be There In A Minute Delivery Service." ⑭ To the left of Rex, the type SWD77808399020508 breaks down as "Star Wars dates" and the year each of the first six Star Wars movies debuted (i.e., the first one came out in 1977). The "08" refers to the television series "Star Wars: The Clone Wars." ⑮ Just past Rex, some bird-like robots sit in cages. In Star Tours 1.0 they sat above the entrance to the boarding area, squawking at riders beneath them. ⑯ "This job is a lot better than, say, fixing broken droids all day" chatty luggage scanning droid G2-9T may proclaim—an inside joke, as his job in the original Star Tours queue was exactly that. Among the items his scanner reveals in the luggage for your flight are ⑰ the white gloves of Mickey Mouse, ⑱ WALL-E, ⑲ Madame Leota's crystal ball from Magic Kingdom's Haunted Mansion; ⑳ the whip and fedora of Indiana Jones and ㉑ Wally B, the insect star of the ground-breaking 1984 cartoon "The Adventures of André and Wally B" created by the Graphics Group, later re-named Pixar. ㉒ "Everything's perfectly all right now. We're fine. We're all fine here now, thank you. How are you?" G2-9T reassures a supervisor on an intercom after some alarms go off. In Episode IV of the Star Wars saga, Han Solo said the same thing to a Death Star supervisor on an intercom. ㉓ "Boring conversation anyway," the droid adds, hanging up on his

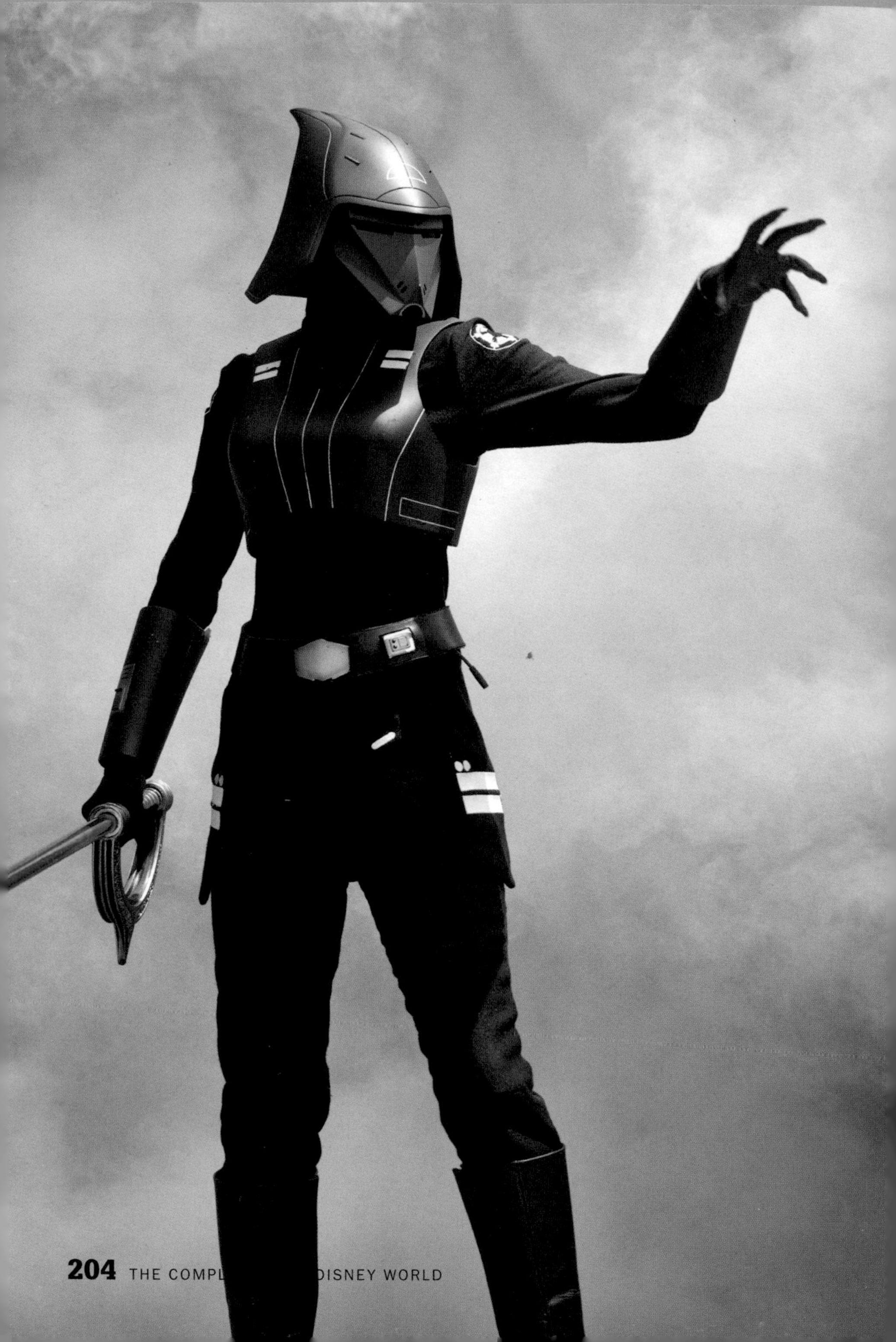

Outside Star Tours. Ordinary weapons withdrawn, Jedi Training Padawans use the Force to push the Seventh Sister (at left) back into her temple. Children ages 4–12 sign up for the training at the nearby Indiana Jones Adventure Outpost anytime after the park opens.

supervisor with the phrase Solo muttered after blasting his intercom. ㉔ ●ccasionally the droid breaks out into song. *"Star Tours! Nothing but Star Tours!"* he sings to the Star Wars theme, parroting the performance of lounge singer Nick Winters (Bill Murray) in a 1978 skit on "Saturday Night Live." ㉕ When he sings *"I've been looking at the same bags, all my livelong day…"* he's hinting at his first job at Disney—as a goose in America Sings, a musical show at California's Disneyland. In it he warbled "I've Been Working on the Railroad." Other hints he was once a goose: his yellow beak, webbed feet and wagging tail (the upcoming passenger-scanning droid has the same history). ㉖ Figures passing behind a window include Jar Jar Binks, encased in carbonite. ㉗ Voiced by deadpan actor Patrick Warburton, passenger scanner G2-4T sometimes compliments a passerby with "Nice work, pal"—the same praise Warburton gives a small boy in the pre-flight video of Epcot's Soarin' Around the World. ㉘ In the safety video, the flight attendant's coy tone of voice and wagging finger match those of the host of a Delta Airlines safety video that went viral in 2008. ㉙ On the ride itself, holograms always use the correct pronoun for the Rebel spy(s) on your ship: "him," "her" or "them."

Hidden Mickeys. ❶ ●utside the building the shape hides as moss high on a tree trunk below the Ewoks. ❷ In a silhouette window in the queue, an R2 droid adjusts two satellite dishes on its head to make it briefly appear to have Mickey ears. ❸ Three planets occasionally align to form the shape on the passenger scanning screen behind droid G2-4T. They come together on the lower left of the screen. The ears the planets form are small. ❹ City spotlights form the shape in the Coruscant segment of the ride, in the lower-right corner of your view. ❺ It shows up again at the end of that segment, as a row of door hatches along a back wall.

Key facts. *Duration:* 7 min. *Capacity:* 240 (6 40-seat simulators) *Queue:* Indoor, overflows into partially-covered outdoor area. *Fear factor:* Skittish children may be startled by some effects. *Restraint:* Seat belt. *Debuted:* 1989 (Disneyland 1987), revised 2015. *Health advisory:* Disney suggests you skip this ride if you have problems with your heart, back or neck, have high blood pressure, are prone to motion sickness, or are pregnant. *Access:* Height min 40 in (102 cm); wheelchair, ECV users must transfer. *Disability services:* Assistive listening, handheld captioning. *Location:* Near Echo Lake.

Launch Bay entrance.

Star Wars Launch Bay

There's plenty here if you take time to find it

★★★★ ✓ You can trade with a Jawa, meet Chewbacca and see full-scale movie props at this Star Wars-focused spot. No matter how much (or little) you know about the saga, you're sure to find something here that's worth checking out.

A 10-minute behind-the-scenes film kicks things off, a collection of interviews with the directors, producers and writers behind the Star Wars films. Four galleries display Star Wars concept art, maquettes, full-size models and movie props; plaques offer background information. A window dedicated to "The Force Awakens" has full-size replicas of Rey's Speeder and BB-8. In a recessed area are two character greeting spots. Chewbacca awaits you in an ancient Jedi temple; Kylo Ren accepts your presence on an Imperial command ship. At a nearby Game Center you can play Disney Infinity 3.0 using a Star Wars character as your avatar.

The best part of the Launch Bay is the Cantina, a faux bar and casino that channels the infamous Mos Eisley Cantina; details include a Dejarik holographic chessboard and glasses of (plastic) blue bantha milk.

A pair of Jawas wander the room. The hooded, bright-eyed merchants don't speak; instead they mime actions to get their points across. What makes them so special is that you can actually trade with them—just show them a trinket and if they like it they'll eagerly offer something in return. No character from the Star Wars universe signs autographs, but they will pose for pictures if you ask nicely.

Be sure to catch the Stormtroopers patrolling the area. Armed with blasters, the pair hassles you, asks for your identification and reassures you that "the First Order is here for your protection." They typically patrol through the building, then out to the Chinese Theatre and back.

Average wait times

9a	10a	11a	12p	1p	2p	3p	4p	5p	6p	7p	8p	9p	10p	11p
10m	10m	15m	20m	15m	10m	10m	10m	10m	10m	10m	10m	10m	---	---

© Disney

Meeting Chewbacca.

As you exit you walk through Launch Bay Cargo, a shop that's well-stocked with quality merchandise, including elaborate costumes.

Tips. *Want to skip the movie?* Go through the gift shop and you'll get right into the main building, skipping the wait to see the film. *How to trade with the Jawas:* You'll have no problem making a trade if you offer something shiny or that lights up; glow sticks and plastic-bead necklaces are perfect. Anything with BB 8 on it really catches their eye. Food, money and sharp objects don't.

Fun finds. ❶ Cast member nametags list their home planet (i.e., Alderaan) instead of their hometown. ❷ Trash cans are marked with Aurebesh writing that translates to "Waste Please." ❸ On the wall of the Game Center, Aurebesh writing translates to "Let the Wookiee win." ❹ In the Cantina, the house rules for playing Sabacc (a card game) are detailed in Aurebesh above a glowing blue table. ❺ An Aurebesh ad on the Cantina wall translates to "Binary sunset drink specials; Twice the suns, half the price." ❻ If you're wearing a baseball cap, a Jawa may come up to you and flip it upside-down. ❼ Near the Cantina, droid parts and other junk are stored behind a gated-off door labeled "Lost and Found" in Aurebesh. Among the junk are the heads of G2-9T and G2-4T, two droids from the queue of the Star Tours attraction.

Key facts. *Duration:* Allow 1 hr, plus 30 min to meet characters. *Operating hours:* 9a–9p; the Stormtroopers patrol for 20 min every 30 min. *Queue:* Outdoor, covered. *Weather issues:* Not exactly troopers when it comes to weather, Stormtroopers stay indoors during rain. *Debuted:* 2015. *Access:* Wheelchairs, ECVs OK. *Location:* Animation Courtyard.

Captain Phasma's helmet.

Helmet photo © Disney

Shooting at targets.

Toy Story Mania

Quick 3-D midway games are easy to play, tough to master

UPDATED! ★★★★★ ✔ FP+ You don 3-D glasses and then sit side-by-side with a partner in a moving vehicle, stopping in front of each game for about 45 seconds to (virtually) pitch baseballs at flying plates, shoot darts at dinosaur balloons, even hurl eggs at scurrying animals.

The games are easy to play and rewarding whether you score high or low; when you hit an object, the illusion is often enhanced by a real blast of air or spritz of water. The games are hosted by an assortment of "Toy Story" characters, including Woody and Buzz Lightyear. The ride was updated in 2016 with an additional track and boarding area (which should reduce wait times), as well as a few new targets.

The standby queue winds past a huge robotic Mr. Potato Head, who interacts with people in line thanks to a wealth of phrases pre-recorded by the voice of the character,

comedian Don Rickles. He occasionally sings a song, or takes off his hat or ear.

Tips. *When to go:* Immediately after the park opens or anytime with a FastPass. *For families:* A small child can ride on your lap as long as his or her legs fit under the lap bar.

Hidden Mickey. In the boarding area on a wall mural, as frames on the box this "toy"—a Toy Story Midway Games Playset—came in.

Key facts. *Duration:* 7 min (game play 5 min). *Capacity:* 108 (2 per vehicle). *Queue:* Indoor, overflows into uncovered outdoor area. *Restraint:* Lap bar. *Debuted:* 2008, revised 2016. *Health advisory:* Vehicles spin and move in a jerky, funhouse fashion between game screens. *Access:* Offline loading area for disabled guests, into vehicles equipped with guns that have buttons as well as pull strings; ECV users must transfer. *Disability services:* Closed captioning. *Location:* Pixar Place.

Average wait times (standby line)

9a	10a	11a	12p	1p	2p	3p	4p	5p	6p	7p	8p	9p	10p	11p
25m	40m	50m	45m	40m	30m	45m	50m	40m	40m	40m	35m	15m	5m	---

You've got a friend in... your partner!

BY MICAELA NEAL There are three keys to getting a high score on Toy Story Mania: Shoot constantly (your cannon can fire six objects per second), know where the high-value targets are, and... teamwork! To get a top score, work together with the person sitting next to you. That way, the two of you can hit multiple targets simultaneously, which will reveal hidden levels of the game.

GAME BOOTH	HIGH-VALUE INITIAL TARGETS	HOW TO REVEAL BONUS TARGETS
HAMM AND EGGS	① A 500-pt horse is in the barn doorway. ② Green ducks in the lake are 500 pts. ③ A 500-pt squirrel runs up both sides of the screen. ④ Three gophers repeatedly pop up along the bottom. The brown ones are 500 pts; the grays 1000. ⑤ Animals in the tree are 1000 pts each. A 1000-pt goat peers out of the barn window. A 1000-pt mouse skitters along its roof.	① Hit the mouse (see Tip 5 at left) and the barn will rotate to reveal its interior, which is filled with 2000-pt rats. Hit every rat and 1000-point rats appear in the grass. ② Hit the fox on the henhouse (in the bottom left corner) and three hens will scurry out of it. The first is worth 1000 pts; the second 2000 pts; the third 1000 pts. ③ Hit the 500-pt donkey that walks along the hills and the animal will turn and run the other way as a 2000-pt target.
REX AND TRIXIE'S DINO DARTS	① 500-pt targets are in the lava, on eggs at the bottom left, held by two red dinos at the bottom center and tied to a blue stegosaurus and red raptors in back. ② A blue dino on the right chews 1000-pt targets, others tie to a back pink bronto. ③ Pterodactyls hang from the sky with 500- and 1000-pt targets.	**Team up with your partner** to hit the lava flows until the volcano erupts. Then hit the two meteors on the left and right of the volcano three times each (the last two meteors, worth 500 pts each, must be hit within one second of each other). This will cause three large comets (spheres formed by 1000-pt balloons) to crash into the screen.
GREEN ARMY MEN SHOOT CAMP	① Helicopters hover with plates worth 1000 pts. More 1000-pt plates appear within the mass of plates and are carried by trucks along the bottom. ② Airplanes tow plates worth 2000 pts. Others are tossed up on either side of the mountain.	**Team up with your partner** to simultaneously hit the two 1000-pt plates that are tossed up from the sides of the mountain (see note at left) at the same time. Doing so will open the mountain and reveal a tank that shoots plates toward you worth 5000 pts each.
BUZZ LIGHTYEAR'S FLYING TOSSERS	① Meteors near the sides are 500 pts. ② Rockets are 1000 pts. ③ Jetpack aliens are worth 2000 pts. ④ Aliens at the top corners of the screen are 5000 pts.	**Team up with your partner** to simultaneously hoop all of the aliens in the central rocket to launch it and reveal a huge robot. When its mouth opens, toss rings into it to score, if you reveal it early enough, up to 2000 pts per toss.
WOODY'S ROOTIN' TOOTIN' SHOOTIN' GALLERY	All initial targets are worth 100 pts each.	① Each 100-pt target triggers a series of bonus targets worth up to 1000 pts each. ② As your vehicle moves from screen 1 to 2 (or from screen 2 to Woody's Bonus Roundup), hit two 100-pt or 500-pt targets close together to reveal a 2000-pt target.
WOODY'S BONUS ROUNDUP	The second-to-last mine cart on each track is always worth 2000 points.	① Hit 1000-pt targets above the carts by 2 bats to wake them and reveal 5000-pt targets. ② Hit all of the carts on a track and the last one will be worth 5000 pts. ③ The final target is worth 2000 pts if you hit it often enough.

© Disney

Casey and Jake.

Disney Junior Live on Stage

Quality preschooler puppet show delights families

★★★★★ FP+ Mickey Mouse and other stars of Disney Junior television shows teach children how to solve everyday problems in this lively puppet show, doing it in a way that has kids bouncing, dancing and singing along. Updated in 2013, the current version features characters from the programs "Mickey Mouse Clubhouse," "Doc McStuffins," "Jake and the Never Land Pirates" and "Sofia the First."

Production values are the equal of any Disney show. The puppets are articulated, the sound is crisp, and hundreds of tiny overhead spotlights ensure everything is lit. Human host Casey addresses her young audience as equals, and bounces into it to meet some children face-to-face. Kids sit on a flat, carpeted floor, which makes it easy for them to be part of things. The semicircular stage curves into the seating area, so even if you arrive at the last minute you'll still be close to the action.

Tips. *When to go:* See the first show of the day. The crowd will be small and the performers fresh. *Where to sit:* In the middle of the theater, where young ones are close to the stage but can still see onto it. Avoid the first three rows; since the stage is elevated, little ones who sit that close often can't see the characters. If you have a FastPass you enter the theater first and get your choice of places to sit. A couple of benches in the back of the theater can hold leftover grandparents. *Need a bathroom?* Doors at the right of the theater lead to the restrooms of the Hollywood Brown Derby.

Key facts. *Duration:* 22 min. *Capacity:* 600. *Queue:* Outdoor, shaded. *Showtimes:* Scheduled performances, see below. *Debuted:* 2001, last revision 2013. *Access:* Wheelchairs, ECVs OK. *Disability services:* Assistive listening; handheld and reflective captioning. *Location:* Animation Courtyard.

Typical show times

9a	10a	11a	12p	1p	2p	3p	4p		5p	6p	7p	8p	9p	10p
9:40	10:30	11:20	12:10	1:30	2:20	3:10	4:00	4:50	5:40	---	---	---	---	---

"I want more..."

Voyage of the Little Mermaid

Grainy video mars stage show with lively singer, puppets

★★★ FP+ Sweet but not sappy, this indoor stage show tells an abridged version of Disney's 1989 movie "The Little Mermaid" with live performers, puppets and video clips. A misty high-tech theater creates the sensation of being underwater, as you watch a rollicking blacklight rendition of "Under the Sea," a Broadway-quality Ariel longing to be "Part of Your World" and Ursula the Sea Witch singing "Poor Unfortunate Souls." At the end the mermaid grows her gams and hugs her honey. The only downer: an abundance of large-screen video that is distinctly low-res.

Tips. *When to go:* Before noon or after dark, when there's the smallest crowd. *Where to sit:* In the center, two-thirds back; you'll see many cool effects on the theater's ceiling and walls. Avoid the front three rows if you have small children; they won't be able to see all the action on the elevated stage.

Fun fact. One of the show's original Ariels was Leanza Cornett, who went on to become the 1992 Miss Florida, the 1993 Miss America and a host of many television shows.

Fun find. A wooden replica of huckster P.T. Barnum's 1842 "FeeJee Mermaid" hides in the lobby, on the wall above the theater's right entrance door as one of Ariel's treasures. Half dead monkey, half dried fish tail, Barnum's creation toured the country, convincing many that mermaids were real.

Key facts. *Duration:* 17 min. *Capacity:* 600. *Queue:* Outdoor, shaded; indoor lobby. *Fear factor:* Some little ones cry when they see Ursula, a 12-foot-tall (4-meter) robotic octopus with glowing eyes. *Showtimes:* Continuous shows; first one typically before 10a. *Debuted:* 1992. *Access:* Wheelchairs, ECVs OK. *Disability services:* Assistive listening, reflective captioning. *Location:* Animation Courtyard.

Average wait times (standby line)

9a	10a	11a	12p	1p	2p	3p	4p	5p	6p	7p	8p	9p	10p	11p
5m	5m	5m	5m	5m	5m	5m	5m	5m	5m	5m	5m	5m	5m	---

Jungle Cruise model.

Walt Disney: One Man's Dream

Vintage artifacts bring the world of Walt Disney to life

★★★★ ✔ A salute to the life and dreams of Walt Disney, this multimedia gallery combines memorabilia exhibits with a short film. The attraction has 400 artifacts in its collection, though many are rotated on and off display. One of the most interesting is the robotic Abraham Lincoln figure that starred in the 1964-65 New York World's Fair. Here shown without clothing (or even skin!) Honest Abe has a control board next to him with buttons that read "elbow" and "finger."

Other pieces include the desk Disney used as a Missouri second-grader (with his initials "WD" carved into it) and his studio desk from the 1930s. His hand in theme-park history is well represented. Built by Disney himself in 1949, a hand-wired wooden diorama displays early ideas for multiple-room attractions such as Snow White's Scary Adventures. Nearby, a "Dancing Man" electronic marionette tested figure-movement techniques that led to the development of Audio-Animatronic figures.

Display cases hold tabletop models used to create the first Jungle Cruise and Peter Pan's Flight rides. Another display portrays the creation of It's a Small World. A simulated TV studio shows Disney filming a video he used to interest investors in his ultimate, unfulfilled dream: the Experimental Prototype Community of Tomorrow, or EPCOT.

A 200-seat theater shows a moving biographical film. Narrated by Disney himself through audio clips, the inspirational 16-minute movie is surprisingly straightforward. (When a new Disney movie is about to premiere, the theater previews it instead.)

Tips. *When to go:* Stop by during the hottest part of the day, when this calm, cool spot is especially refreshing. It's also a great spot to get out of the rain. *For young adults:* Watch the movie. Walt Disney offers some good insight about the importance of failing when you're young.

Key facts. *Duration:* Unlimited, allow 35 min total, the movie is 16 min. *Capacity:* 200. *Showtimes:* The movie plays continuously. *Debuted:* 2001, revised 2010. *Access:* Wheelchairs, ECVs OK. *Disability services:* Assistive listening, reflective and handheld captioning, Audio Description. *Location:* Behind the Great Movie Ride, just to the left of the Animation Courtyard.

Photo illustration © Disney

"No cheap 3-D tricks."

Jim Henson's MuppetVision 3-D

Silly, gentle film is a park classic

★★★★ ✔ FP+ Chaos reigns as Kermit the Frog attempts to demonstrate the latest invention of Dr. Bunsen Honeydew in this 3-D movie, which showcases the inspired humor and attention to detail of the late Jim Henson. Miss Piggy stars in two musical numbers, both of which go haywire. In the process, you get squirted with water, showered with bubbles and caught in a crossfire of cannonballs. The attraction has a timeless charm. Digitally restored in 2010, the film and its pre-show video are bright and clear. The pre-show takes place in a prop warehouse filled with real Muppet memorabilia.

Tips. *When to go.* In the middle of the day, when the lines are long at other attractions, and the cool theater will feel especially refreshing. There's no need for a FastPass except on the most crowded days. *Where to sit:* In the center of a middle or back row. The film will be in great focus, and the 3-D effects will really pop. Avoid the first few rows. The film will seem blurry as the red and green images separate when viewed too closely, and some effects won't make sense without an audience in front of you. *For families:* Don't be afraid that your young children could be startled by the 3-D effects. Unlike some 3-D films, this one uses the technology to make you smile, not jump.

Fun fact. Created when digital animation was in its infancy, the Waldo character was the world's first digitized puppet, and, thanks to this film, the first digital 3-D character.

Key facts. *Duration:* 25 min. *including* pre-show. *Capacity:* 584. *Queue:* Indoor, air-conditioned; also rarely used shaded outdoor area. *Debuted:* 1991, restored 2010. *Access:* Wheelchairs, ECVs OK. *Disability services:* Assistive listening, reflective and activated video captioning, Audio Description. *Location:* Muppets Courtyard.

Average wait times (standby line)

9a	10a	11a	12p	1p	2p	3p	4p	5p	6p	7p	8p	9p	10p	11p
5m	5m	5m	5m	5m	5m	5m	5m	5m	5m	5m	5m	5m	5m	---

Disney's Animal Kingdom

Discovery River.

NATURE LOVERS WILL ADORE this sophisticated, fully realized theme park. Focused on animals and their environments in lands that include Africa and Asia, its attractions include a roller coaster through the Himalayas, indoor stage shows based on two of Disney's best animal-themed movies and a truck ride into a wildlife savanna. The park is also a zoo, with 250 species of exotic animals displayed in lush natural habitats. Many are rare, endangered or the biggest, smallest or most colorful of their kind. Accredited by the Association of Zoos and Aquariums, Animal Kingdom conducts animal research and breeds endangered species. As a zoo, it's the most popular one in the United States.

Six lands make up the theme park:

The Oasis. Bordered by tropical animal habitats, two shaded walkways calmly lead to the core of the park.

Discovery Island. The park's central hub is home to its icon, the massive Tree of Life. Trails wind around the surrounding Tree of Life Garden, passing animal enclosures that are often nearly hidden. Also here are the park's biggest shops and a 3-D movie.

Africa. With its architecture, artisans, dancers, musicians and native African staffers, Disney's village of Harambe is the most fully-realized section of the park. The mythical town struggles to convert its economy to ecotourism. Attractions include a realistic Kilimanjaro Safaris truck ride, which takes you through a forest and savanna filled with roaming elephants, giraffes and lions. You'll see a family of gorillas on the Gorilla Falls wildlife trail. The Festival of the Lion King musical revue show is a park classic, full of energy and a joyous spirit.

Rafiki's Planet Watch. You board a train to get to this straightforward zoological area, an offshoot of Africa. It combines an indoor veterinary and research facility—which includes a number of smaller exhibits and presentations—with an outdoor petting zoo.

Asia. Looking for a roller coaster? Here you go. As an angry Yeti chases you, you'll take a tea train forward, backward, up and down on Expedition Everest. The land also includes a bird show, raft ride, Asian wildlife trail and a new nighttime spectacle. Two rural areas create Disney's Asia—the riverside kingdom of Anandapur and the mountainside village of Serka Zong.

DinoLand U.S.A. This tongue-in-cheek land celebrates the public's curiosity with all things dinosaur. Attractions include an indoor thrill ride that takes you back to the age of dinosaurs and a cheesy roller coaster that does the same thing. Young families will like its flying-dinosaur hub-and-spoke ride. Meanwhile, an incongruent indoor theater presents a "Finding Nemo" stage musical.

Nightlife. The park transformed itself in 2016 to add unique nighttime experiences. Kilimanjaro Safaris now has rides after dark, with strategic lighting and a faux sunset. Fixed animal carvings appear to move in the new Tree of Life Awakens show, which animates the trunk of the tree. A new Jungle Book stage show takes place on and above the Discovery River. Street parties in Discovery Island and Africa offer nearly non-stop music and dancing.

Two major additions are on the horizon for the park in 2017.

Rivers of Light. The theme of this upcoming nighttime spectacle is how water and light connect us with the natural world. Each illuminated from within, elaborate floats of four animal spirits—the Tiger, the Elephant, the Turtle and the Owl—will continually change colors.

"Rivers of Light pays homage to traditional Asian lantern festivals and this beautiful myth about the Aurora Borealis," says Imagineer Michael Jung. "There's an ancient belief that when animals passed from one world to another, they danced in the sky and became these beautiful rivers of light." Water screens display clips of live-action animals, which will appear to fly through the air and turn into glittering constellations. This long-delayed water pageant is scheduled to open sometime between September 2016 and the spring of 2017. Originally planned to debut in early 2016, technical snafus have delayed it. In the meantime, "The Jungle Book: Alive with Magic" holds its place on the Discovery River Lagoon.

The Tree of Life.

Pandora – The World of Avatar. The lush, alien world of Pandora comes to life in the park in the spring of 2017. Based on James Cameron's "Avatar" movie series, the 12-acre (5 ha) land will have elements from the original 2009 film as well as its upcoming sequels. The area will have two attractions. You'll fly on the back of a banshee in Avatar Flight of Passage, a flight simulator similar to Epcot's Soarin' Around the World. The Na'vi River Journey will be a tranquil boat ride past glowing plants, alien creatures and an Audio-Animatronic Na'vi shaman as it winds through a bioluminescent rainforest. Rock faces of the floating Hallelujah Mountains will tower over the land, which consumes the space that once held Camp Minnie-Mickey.

Best of the park. The only Walt Disney World theme park that's less than 25 years old, Animal Kingdom has no wide expanses of concrete, no cheesy fast-food spots, no aging restrooms or embarrassingly dated attractions. On a beautiful day, just wandering around it can be fun. Particular highlights include: ❶ A giraffe—or a rhino, or an ostrich—may come right up to your truck on the open-air truck ride Kilimanjaro Safaris, as you meander through 110 acres of simulated African habitat brimming with free-roaming animals; new after-dark trips offer a different perspective. ❷ Just a few feet away from you, two groups of gorillas examine you with eyes and expressions that are oh-so-human on the Gorilla Falls Exploration Trail. ❶ne group's a family, with a massive silverback, motherly females and wrestling youngsters; the other a bachelor troupe. ❸ The self-guided nature of the park's animal attractions gives it a slower pace and invites you to relax. ❹ The park has two great live indoor shows: Festival of the Lion King invigorates you with acrobats, a fire dancer, creative costumes and great music; Finding Nemo: The Musical re-imagines its film using huge puppets and live singers. ❺ With a backward plunge followed by an 80-foot (24-meter) drop, the Expedition Everest roller coaster takes you on a unique high-speed adventure.

Worst of the park. Some traditional theme-park fans hate this park, and their most common complaints are worth noting. ❶ First, there's the walking. It's a half-mile from the front of the park to the back of it, and a half-mile from the left side to the right. Attractions are often far apart, with large gaps of open space between them. Altogether the park covers 500 acres (202 ha), five times the space of the Magic Kingdom. ❷ You spend a lot of time outside in the heat, which can be challenging between April and October when the Central Florida weather is unusually hot and humid.

Harambe Village.

Patterson's eland.

If it rains. With its large size and many outdoor attractions, Disney's Animal Kingdom makes it tough to ignore the weather. No ride or show closes due to rain alone, but the Flights of Wonder bird show can be changed and shortened. Roller coasters Expedition Everest and Primeval Whirl temporarily close when lightning is in the area, as does The Boneyard playground, Kali River Rapids, TriceraTop Spin and the wildlife trails in Africa and Asia. Nearby lightning also cancels Flights of Wonder and scheduled street performances. Ironically, Kilimanjaro Safaris trips are actually better in the rain after hours of hot sun, as its savanna animals are usually more active.

Family matters. All of the thrill rides at Animal Kingdom have height minimums—40 inches (102 cm) for Dinosaur, 44 inches (112 cm) for Expedition Everest, 38 inches (97 cm) for Kali River Rapids and 48 inches (122 cm) for Primeval Whirl. The park offers one character meal, available for all three meals: Donald's Safari Dining at Africa's Tusker House, which stars Donald Duck, Daisy Duck, Mickey Mouse and Goofy. An excellent Wilderness Explorers program offers hands-on activities that are especially fun for children, who can earn badges at 31 stations spread throughout the park.

Where to meet characters. The park is the only place at Disney World to meet Flik, Russell and Dug, or Tarzan. Tusker House in Africa hosts character meals.

Baloo. Upcountry Landing, off the walkway between Asia and Africa.

Chip 'n Dale. Conservation Station, Rafiki's Planet Watch.

Daisy Duck. Tusker House meals.

Donald Duck. Cretaceous Trail, DinoLand U.S.A; Tusker House meals.

Flik. Between Pizzafari and the Creature Comforts Starbucks, Discovery Island.

Goofy. DinoLand U.S.A. Service Station; Tusker House meals.

King Louie. Upcountry Landing, off the walkway between Asia and Africa.

Mickey Mouse. Adventurers Outpost, Discovery Island; Tusker House meals.

Minnie Mouse. Adventurers Outpost, Discovery Island.

Pluto. DinoLand U.S.A. Service Station.

Pocahontas. Character Landing, between Discovery Island and DinoLand U.S.A.

Rafiki. Conservation Station, Rafiki's Planet Watch.

Russell and Dug. Wilderness Explorers Club House, near the entrance to It's Tough to Be a Bug, Discovery Island.

Tarzan. Between Island Mercantile and Pizzafari, Discovery Island.

Tam Tam Drummers of Harambe.

Adventurers Outpost.

Know before you go. Need a stroller? Cash? A Fastpass fix? Here's where to find it:

ATMs. Park entrance, on the right; outside the Dinosaur Treasures gift shop.

Baby Care Center. Changing rooms, nursing areas, microwave, playroom. Sells diapers, formula, pacifiers, over-the-counter meds. Next to Starbucks, Discovery Island.

FastPass+ kiosks. Cast members help you with FastPasses at these walk-up touch-screens. Look for them inside the Oasis Guest Relations building, on Discovery Island outside the Island Mercantile shop and in Asia at the entrance to Kali River Rapids. You can also get help from designated cast members stationed on Discovery Island outside the Discovery Trading Co. shop and in Africa to the right of Tamu Tamu Refreshments (under the Dawa Bar if it's raining).

First aid. Registered nurses treat minor emergencies, call EMTs for serious issues. Next to the Creature Comforts Starbucks, Discovery Island.

Guest Relations. Cast members answer questions, reserve restaurants, exchange currency, have maps and times guides for all parks, store items found in the park that day. Walk-up windows outside park entrance (far left); adjacent walk-in lobby inside the park.

Locker rentals. $7 a day, $5 deposit. Inside the park entrance, next to Guest Relations.

Package pickup. Disney will send anything you buy in the park to the park entrance to pick up later at no charge. Allow three hours. Packages can also be delivered to Disney hotels or shipped nationally.

Parking. Cars $20 a day. Preferred parking ($15) gives everyone in car a bottle of water.

Stroller rentals. At Garden Gate Gifts, inside the park entrance on the right. Single strollers are $15 a day ($13 length of stay), doubles $31 ($27 length of stay). Get replacements at Mombasa Marketplace, Africa.

Disney transportation. Buses serve all Disney resorts and theme parks as well as the Blizzard Beach water park; there's no direct service to Disney Springs, Typhoon Lagoon or ESPN Wide World of Sports.

Wheelchair and scooter rentals. Garden Gate Gifts, at the park entrance, rents wheelchairs for $12 a day ($10 length of stay). EVCs are $50 ($20 deposit).

Harambe Street Parti.

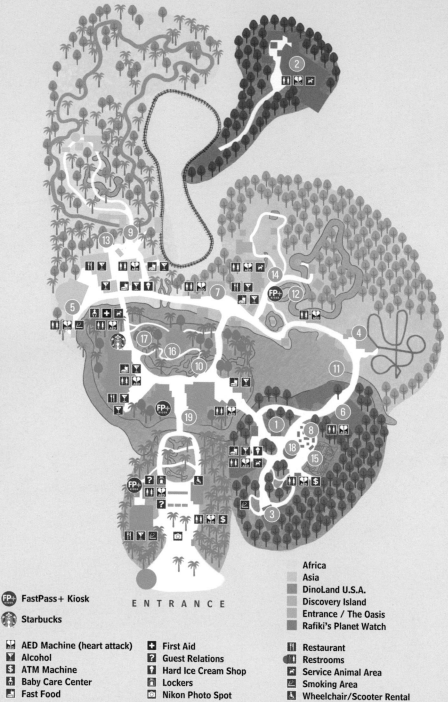

FP+ FastPass+ Kiosk

Starbucks

ENTRANCE

Africa
Asia
DinoLand U.S.A.
Discovery Island
Entrance / The Oasis
Rafiki's Planet Watch

AED Machine (heart attack)
Alcohol
ATM Machine
Baby Care Center
Fast Food

First Aid
Guest Relations
Hard Ice Cream Shop
Lockers
Nikon Photo Spot

Restaurant
Restrooms
Service Animal Area
Smoking Area
Wheelchair/Scooter Rental

Art: Micaela Neal

Attractions at a glance

Here's a look at the attractions at Disney's Animal Kingdom, each of which is reviewed in detail later in this chapter. Each is rated from one to five stars (★); a checkmark (✔) indicates an author favorite. The FastPass+ logo (FP+) appears if it can be reserved in advance. Numbers in green circles correspond to those shown on the map at the left.

❶ The Boneyard. ★★★★★ Dig-site playground has climbing zone, slides, sand pit and tunnels. Kids can trigger dinosaur roars, other special effects. *DinoLand U.S.A.*

❷ Conservation Station. ★★★ ✔ Serious animal-care facility has exhibits, presentations, vet center with viewable procedures. Petting zoo holds domesticated animals, brushes provided. Inconvenient, accessible only by train. *Rafiki's Planet Watch.*

❸ Dinosaur. UPDATED! ★★★ ✔ FP+ You search for dinos on this dark jerky ride, and barely miss a meteor shower. An intense, loud experience now with new effects, creatures. Threatening dinosaurs chase you. *Min. height 40 in. (102 cm). DinoLand U.S.A.*

❹ Expedition Everest. ★★★★★ ✔ FP+ This indoor-outdoor roller coaster is a runaway train which speeds into and out of a mountain, goes backward and zooms past an angry Yeti. Smooth ride, high lift, one curving steep drop. *Min. height 44 in. (112 cm). Asia.*

❺ Festival of the Lion King. ★★★★★ ✔ FP+ Rousing in-the-round musical revue includes acrobats, fire-baton twirler, flying ballerina, many stilt walkers and talented live singers. A park classic. *Africa.*

❻ Finding Nemo The Musical. ★★★★★ ✔ FP+ Broadway-quality stage musical retells 2003's "Finding Nemo" with huge puppets and live singers. Dory is a hoot. *DinoLand U.S.A.*

❼ Flights of Wonder. ★★★★ ✔ Live bird show presents a conservation message in a humorous, lightweight way. Includes about 20 species; some fly over the audience. New top over seating area doesn't drip. *Asia.*

❽ Fossil Fun Games. ★★★ ✔ Winners of these midway games get stuffed-animal prizes. $4 to $5 per game. *DinoLand U.S.A.*

❾ Gorilla Falls Exploration Trail. ★★★★★ ✔ Shady walkway roams past unusual African species; has a beautiful aviary and large gorilla habitat. Other animals include okapi, meerkats, monkeys. *Africa.*

❿ It's Tough to Be a Bug. REFURBISHED! ★★★ FP+ Playfully sadistic 3-D movie displays insect survival skills. Stars characters from 1989's "A Bug's Life." Intense for preschoolers. *Discovery Island.*

⓫ The Jungle Book: Alive with Magic. NEW! ★★★★ FP+ Bollywood-style tribute to "The Jungle Book" celebrates musical numbers from the 1967 Disney movie with performances by live singers and dancers. Huge water screens in the background are lit with colorful, music-synched patterns and clips from the 2016 film. Nightly shows take place on Indian-inspired water floats in the open-air Discovery River Theater. *Asia.*

⓬ Kali River Rapids. ★★★★ ✔ FP+ Jerky, wet raft ride travels down a threatened rainforest river; riders often get soaked. *Min. height 38 in. (97 cm). Asia.*

⓭ Kilimanjaro Safaris. EXPANDED! ★★★★★ ✔ FP+ Bouncy open-air truck wanders 100-acre forest and savanna; passes elephants, giraffes, lions, rhinos and many other rare species, all of which appear to be roaming freely. Now with night trips. *Africa.*

⓮ Maharajah Jungle Trek. ★★★★★ ✔ Pathway around and through a crumbling palace passes bats, tigers and other Asian animals, meanders through an aviary full of rare and exotic birds. *Asia.*

⓯ Primeval Whirl. ★★★ FP+ Kitschy roller coaster takes you back in time, as cartoon-cutout dinosaurs along its track warn "The End is Near." Jerky, with spinning cars and one slight but steep drop. *Min. height 48 in. (122 cm). DinoLand U.S.A.*

⓰ The Tree of Life Awakens. NEW! ★★★★★ ✔ Colorful projected light brings the park icon to life after dark. Evocative stories begin every 12–20 minutes, but something is always happening. *Discovery Island.*

⓱ Tree of Life Garden. UPDATED! ★★★ Narrow pathways wind through a lush tropical garden, alongside massive Tree of Life roots and waterfalls, past kangaroos, flamingos and other exotic creatures. A new, engaging presentation in front of the Tree features 21 free-flying macaws; brief shows are hourly until 3 p.m. *Discovery Island.*

⓲ TriceraTop Spin. ★★★★★ Dumbo with four-seat dinosaurs, cheesy roadside carnival theme. *DinoLand U.S.A.*

⓳ Wilderness Explorers. ★★★★ ✔ Children earn badges doing nature activities with docents. Based on Russell's scouting experiences in the 2009 movie "Up." Well done; includes elaborate booklet. *Park-wide.*

DiVine.

Posing for fans. A macaw in the Oasis.

The Oasis

What's this? An entrance to a theme park, but with no stores or souvenir stands in sight? That's not a wide walkway, but a series of small trails? An entrance where you can't spend money, can't ride anything, but are still supposed to do... something?

What a heavenly idea.

Walt Disney touched on it with his Main Street U.S.A., a wistful walkway that's post-card-perfect and filled with life. Tugging on your heartstrings, it needs no "attractions."

It had you at hello.

Still, Main Street U.S.A. is an illusion. Its faux storefronts hide very real shops. Its vintage bakery is really Starbucks. When you enter the street, the first things you see are a popcorn stand and an ice cream cart.

When you enter the Oasis, the first things you see are spoonbills. Pink, orange and white. Living, breathing, swishing their spatulas back and forth. From there you go left. Or right. Whichever you decide,

flowering flora from throughout the world—eucalyptus, jacarandas, orchids —combine with towering bamboo and swaying palms to create a beautiful natural canopy.

Tucked underneath it, a haven of pools and streams forms a small zoo, its animals in natural habitats. Wandering down side trails, you might see a swamp wallaby, or step on a footbridge, or come upon what at first seems to be just leaves and vines, but is really DiVine, a performance artist concealing herself in the foliage.

Animal Kingdom has stores, of course, and carts and stands and a Starbucks. But they're still to come, after this purely thematic introduction.

Disney originally planned to call the Oasis "Genesis Gardens" until the company realized the religious connotations of that phrase might not go over that well with some visitors. Early concept art included a walk-through version of Noah's Ark.

Swamp wallaby.

The Oasis Animal Guide

By **Micaela Neal.** Dart straight through the park's entranceway and you won't see a thing. Slow down and look around a bit and you'll spot some unique creatures, including:

Anteater. The world's largest anteater at 9 feet (3 meters) long, the southern giant anteater can slurp up 30,000 ants a day with its 2-foot-long (1-meter-long) tongue. It has the largest claws of any mammal, and uses its huge bushy tail as a blanket.

Babirusa. Although its name means "pig-deer," genetically this boar-like mammal is closer to a hippo than a pig. The male's strange antler-like tusks grow up through his muzzle and curl back toward his face.

Military macaw. This parrot's olive-green feathers resemble Spanish army fatigues. It eats clay from riverbanks for nutrients.

Patagonian cavy. Looking like a giant guinea pig on stilts, this gentle long-legged rodent can run 28 miles per hour (45 kph) and leap 6 feet (2 meters).

Reeve's muntjac. The small, shy deer is known as the "barking deer" for its danger-signaling call. Males have short antlers and large canine teeth for fighting off enemies.

Southern giant anteater.   Cavy.

Black swan, black-necked swan, roseate spoonbills.

Rhinoceros iguana. Named for the horn-like scales on its nose, this 3-foot (1-meter) long reptile lays some of the largest lizard eggs. A group of iguanas is called a "mess."

Scarlet macaw. The national bird of Honduras, this noisy, beautiful bird has the longest tail feathers of any macaw.

Spoonbills. These large wading birds filter food out of the water by shaking their flat, paddle-shaped bills back and forth. When courting, a male hunts sticks for a female's nest and presents them to her one at a time; she often shakes her head in dismissal. Disney lets its spoonbills breed and raise young in front of guests, sometimes extremely close to fences. Often mistaken for a flamingo from a distance, the roseate spoonbill has vivid pink plumage that's tinged with red and orange. The African spoonbill has white feathers.

Swamp wallaby. Normally timid, this nocturnal kangaroo relative will defensively kick and scratch the face of a predator. It can drink salt water when fresh isn't available.

Swans. With the longest neck of any swan, the black swan is featured on the flag and coat of arms of Western Australia. The mostly white black-necked swan is the largest waterfowl in South America.

Babirusa.

Rhinoceros iguana.

Pizzafari.

Discovery Island

A tropical circle wrapped by a river. That's Discovery Island, the most traditional area of Disney's Animal Kingdom, the home of most of its restaurants and shops. Buildings display whimsical Caribbean architecture. Disney recently redid them, replacing their bright colors with more subtle earth tones. Interiors are just as attractive, with fanciful animals adorning the ceilings, columns, shelves and walls. Floors mix textured concrete with inlaid stone and broken-tile mosaics.

Nightlife. Discovery Island turns festive after dark. The Tree of Life transforms in ways you may not believe even after you see them. A nightly Carnivale street party fills the area with life, channeling the animalistic abandon of Caribbean and Brazilian festivals.

Fun finds. Each interior has an animal theme. ❶ Migrating and working animals highlight the Island Mercantile shop. Wooden birds and butterflies resemble airplanes; nearby beavers look like saws. ❷ Animals from the north, south, east and west embellish the four corners of the Discovery Trading Co. shop. ❸ Bright murals in each Pizzafari dining room focus on different type of animals—those that carry their homes with them, live their lives at night or hang upside down. More than 500 carved animals from Oaxaca, Mexico, hang from walls and ceilings. ❹ Flame Tree Barbecue has a predators-and-prey decor. Each structure has its own motif: mongooses eat geckos on the order building, seven patio huts have alligators eating fish, anteaters ants, eagles snakes, eels crabs, owls rabbits, snakes mice, spiders butterflies.

Hidden Mickeys. ❶ In Pizzafari, as orange spots on the lower left side of a spotted shell of a painted turtle. ❷ As black spots on a leopard, and as gray spots underneath it. ❸ At the Adventurers Outpost character-greeting spot, as the center of radiating rays of orange and brown in the bottom left corner of the giant-postcard photo backdrop.

Live entertainment

During the day, free-flying birds catch you off-guard. At night the land throbs with joyful music and dancing.

NEW! ★★★★★ ✔ Discovery Island Carnivale. Vividly feathered dancers and stilt-walkers move, shake and gyrate everything mama gave them, leading park visitors in a free-spirited frenzy under flashing black lights. Live band Viva Gaia provides the music, a joyful explosion of dance tunes that's hard to resist; the blood-pumping atmosphere is contagious. Twenty-somethings make up most of the mob, though families and children also join in. Young girls love it. So do cast members. Look around and you'll see store clerks twirling and whirling in their open doorways, order takers at the nearby Flame Tree Barbecue grooving at their cash registers. The parties liven up as the night goes on and the crowd grows; the liveliest party is usually the last one. Before the first show of the night, the dancers parade through Discovery Island from a spot between Pizzafari and the Creature Comforts Starbucks, urging the crowd to follow them to the party. *Typically four 20-min shows hourly 6:30p–10p. Across from Flame Tree Barbecue.*

NEW! ★★★★★ ✔ Sunset Serenatas. Children twirl with joy as Víctor Espínola plays a Paraguayan harp. His rhythmic, haunting music sounds almost like a piano or guitar. Espínola has played with Yanni on tour. *Typically five 20-min shows 5p–9:30p. Across from Flame Tree Barbecue.*

NEW! ★★★★★ ✔ Viva Gaia Street Band. This colorful five-piece band plays upbeat Caribbean-flavored tunes while dancers encourage audience members to boogie along. At night the band is accompanied by the Discovery Island Carnivale. *Typically three 20-min shows hourly 3:45p–5:30p.; at night four 20-min shows hourly 6:30p–10p with the Discovery Island Carnivale. Across from Flame Tree Barbecue.*

★★★★ ✔ Winged Encounters. A flock of 21 endangered macaws fly freely over the island, landing on a perch in front of the Tree of Life. Docents feed the birds while answering questions and talking about the species on display. *Unannounced flights are hourly 9 a.m. to 3 p.m., dependent on weather and if the macaws are in the right mood. Docent presentation in front of the Tree of Life; birds visible throughout the island. 5–10 min.*

Restaurants and food

You'll find terrific food in Discovery Island, including a new Disney Signature Restaurant filled with fascinating artifacts.

Pizzafari mural.

Discovery Island Carnivale.

NEW! ★★★★★ ✔ $54 DDP2 Tiffins. Stepping into this serene, sophisticated restaurant is like entering a museum, filled as it is with authentic art and artifacts presented on walls and in display cases. The fascinating items tell the story of how Imagineer Joe Rohde and his team created Disney's Animal Kingdom, including notes, journals and sketches from their travels collecting inspiration for the park. One display shows a fanciful costume from the Festival of the Lion King next to photos of the real-life African apparel that inspired it. The food is outstanding—lovingly crafted and beautifully presented. Especially delicious is the marinated octopus appetizer, with its crispy charred skin contrasting with its tender meat; the whole-fried sustainable fish served head-on; and the hoisin-glazed halibut with forbidden rice. *11:30a–3:30p, 4p–9:30p; $29–$53 (children $10–$15). Seats 287 (145 in the Grand Gallery, 78 in the Trek Gallery, 64 in the Safari Gallery). No same-day reservations. Discovery Island, behind Pizzafari on the walkway toward Pandora. A Disney Signature Restaurant.*

★★★★★ ✔ $20 DDPq Flame Tree BBQ. Four o'clock in the morning. That's when the cooks arrive to smoke pork for the pulled-pork sandwich at this outdoor counter-service spot. Also prepared daily: St. Louis ribs and roasted chicken. Looking for a bargain? Get the chicken and rib combo meal, $16 but big enough for two. Tables sit alongside a stream or in covered pavilions. A waterside pavilion overlooks the Discovery River amphitheater. *On walkway to DinoLand U.S.A. 11a–10p. $11–$20 (children $5–$6). Seats 500.*

UPDATED! ★★★★★ ✔ $16 DDPq Pizzafari. This counter-service pizza spot went through several changes in 2016—its back end was converted into Tiffins and the Nomad Lounge; its menu was refreshed. It now serves flatbreads and pasta as well as individual pies. Pizzas are now hand-crafted and made in-house as opposed to being pre-made and heated up. *On the walkway to Africa. 11a–9:30p. $10–$12 (children $5–$6). Seats 580.*

NEW! ★★★★★ ✔ $23 Nomad Lounge. Multiple windows at this elegant bar offer expansive views of the Discovery River. A wraparound covered patio offers cushy seating and a relaxed rustic atmosphere of a treehouse. A large drink menu features many specialty cocktails; beers include choices from Ethiopia, Laos and Vietnam. *11:30a–9:30p, $7–$21. Seats 124 inside, 88 outside. Adjacent to Tiffins, Discovery Island.*

★★★ **$9 DDPs Eight Spoon Café.** Cheese pasta, Mickey pretzels. *11a–10p; $5. In front of It's Tough to be a Bug.*

★★★ **$10 DDPs The Feeding Ground.** Popcorn, rum drinks, punch, beer. *11a–10p; $4–$8. In front of It's Tough to be a Bug.*

★★★★ **$9 DDPs Isle of Java.** Cookies, pastries; coffees, rum drinks. *9a–11p; $3–$6. On walkway to DinoLand U.S.A.*

★★★★ **$10 DDPs The Smiling Crocodile.** Cheese grits with pulled pork; chicken drumsticks, beer. *11a–10p; $5–$6. Alongside the walkway to Asia.*

★★★ **$10 DDPs Starbucks Creature Comforts.** Standard Starbucks menu. Large indoor ordering area, but no indoor seats. *9a–11p; $5–$6. On walkway to Africa.*

★★★ **$9 DDPs Terra Treats.** Gluten-free pastries, hummus, rice chips, beer. *10a–7p; $3–$7. Next to the entrance to Africa.*

Shops and merchandise

A shopping mecca, Discovery Island offers distinctive items as well as typical Disney souvenirs. All of its stores stay open up to an hour after the park closes.

Discovery Trading Company. Previously named Disney Outfitters, this calm spot with its wood shelving, carved wooden animal statues and tile floors provides an appropriate setting for its high-end merchandise. You'll find fashionable apparel and graphic tees for men, women, juniors and children; quality brands include Vera Bradley. A nice selection of Pandora jewelry has its own featured display. *Across from Flame Tree Barbecue.*

Island Mercantile. The shelves of this large store are stocked with merchandise from locations throughout the park, including a wide range of Animal Kingdom apparel, backpacks, hats and souvenirs from specific attractions. Fine artwork is worth a look; the assortment varies throughout the year. *Next to the Oasis bridge.*

Riverside Depot. This place has a little of everything—everything you can find everywhere else at Disney. It's this park's version of The Emporium at Magic Kingdom, though it's much smaller. The main, largest room is jam-packed with Disney merchandise; another section has dozens of Disney plushies; a final area stocks infant wear and novelty hats. A clock tower marks the main entrance to the store, a 2016 expansion of the Discovery Trading Co. *Across from Island Mercantile.*

Viva Gaia.

The Tree of Life Awakens.

Photo © Disney

The Tree of Life

Park icon has hidden gardens, wildlife, amazing evening shows

UPDATED! ★★★★ ✓ The park centerpiece, this fantastical African baobab symbolizes the grandeur of nature and embodies the idea that all life is interconnected. Sculpted into its gnarled roots, trunk and branches is a tapestry of more than 400 animals.

Tree of Life Gardens. A lush area filled with exotic wildlife surrounds the tree, with grottos, streams and waterfalls weaving through tropical hills. An open spot in front of the tree offers a good view of flamingos, crowned cranes and whistling ducks. To the right are lemurs resting in a patch of trees; to the left a shady otter habitat with an underwater viewing area.

Two walking trails are rarely crowded; wander down one and you'll have its peaceful environment almost all to yourself. One trail snakes past parrot, porcupine, stork and Galapagos tortoise habitats; it runs between the entrances to Africa and Asia, along the Discovery River. The second trail leads to an up-close look at the kangaroo enclosure; it starts off at the walkway to Africa and exits behind the Wilderness Explorer Club House, near the entrance to It's Tough to be a Bug.

NEW! Tree of Life Awakens. At night, the tree "awakens" with crisp light projections that read so well they look nearly three-dimensional. Four short, randomized shows play on the tree's trunk, branches and canopy, depicting scenes of animals and nature rendered in a vibrant art style that's almost like stained glass come to life. It's all set to a moving orchestral score.

The longest show is a tribute to nature-themed movies including "The Lion King," "Finding Nemo," even "Avatar." Others tell stories of animal spirits, including a curious doe, an adventurous fox and a pair of lovestruck hummingbirds. In the future, Disney will add more sequences to the lineup.

Between shows, seamless effects and constantly-shifting lights add a bit more magic to the park icon. Watch the sculpted creatures carefully to see them move; each animal has three different actions. There are hundreds of effects in total, including a cardinal landing on a branch, clouds of glowing fireflies, and representations of each of the four seasons.

Tips. *When to go:* Early in the morning to see the animals at their liveliest; after the sun sets to watch the nighttime light projections. *For families:* If you have small children, give them a hand spotting the kangaroos from the walking trail; their viewing spot sits behind a concrete wall about 4 feet (1.2 meters) tall.

Fun facts. ① The tree stands 145 feet (44 meters) high; 50 feet (15 meters) wide at its middle; 170 feet (52 meters) wide at its base. Its leafy canopy spreads 160 feet (49 meters). ③ Designer Zsolt Hormay also created the rockwork at Magic Kingdom's Big Thunder Mountain Railroad and the snow and rockwork at Blizzard Beach.

Fun finds. The front viewing area is framed by animals emerging from its roots. They include ① an armadillo, ② big-horned sheep, ③ buffalo, ④ crocodile, ⑤ deer, ⑥ elephant, ⑦ Komodo dragon ⑧ and otter. The front of the tree includes ⑨ a bald eagle, ⑩ buffalo, ⑪ deer, ⑫ rhino, ⑬ roadrunner, ⑭ songbird taking flight, ⑮ seahorse and ⑯ tiger. Seen from the kangaroo trail, carvings on the left side include ⑰ an ant, ⑱ cheetah, ⑲ platypus, ⑳ egret, ㉑ gorilla, ㉒ moose, ㉓ sable antelope, ㉔ squid, ㉕ tortoise ㉖ walrus as well as ㉗ some flying ducks. From the Discovery Trail you can make out ㉘ a beaver, ㉙ beetle, ㉚ bittern, ㉛ camel, ㉜ chimp, ㉝ climbing elephant, ㉞ fish, ㉟ fox, ㊱ giraffe, ㊲ orca, ㊳ peacock, ㊴ porcupine, ㊵ rabbit, ㊶ shrew, ㊷ snapping turtle, ㊸ tapir and ㊹ a wolf. The back side of the tree, visible from the path along the Discovery River as well as the walkway between Africa and Asia, includes ㊺ a barn owl, ㊻ bat with wings outstretched, ㊼ bear, ㊽ gibbon, ㊾ hippo, ㊿ rearing horse (51) humpback whale, (52) meerkat, (53) octopus, (54) scorpion, (55) snail (56) and a herd of wildebeest running up the trunk.

Hidden Mickey. The three-circle shape is formed by grayish-green moss on the front of the tree, just to the left of a buffalo's face.

Tree of Life Gardens key facts. *Duration:* Allow 25 min. *Specs:* 2 trails, length 1,680 ft (512 m), 12 viewing areas, 20 species. *Debuted:* 1998. *Access:* Wheelchairs, ECVs OK.

Tree of Life Awakens key facts. *Duration:* 3-5 min per show. *Operating hours:* Shows every 10-15 min starting at nightfall; effects continuously. *Debuted:* 2016. *Access:* Wheelchairs, ECVs OK. *Location:* Shows take place on the front of the Tree of Life.

Red kangaroo.

Tree of Life Garden Animal Guide

By Micaela Neal. The new macaws are easy to see; they fly right over your head. But you'll see many more creatures if you wander down into the trails of the Tree of Life Garden.

NEW! Blue-and-gold macaw. Pairs of these parrots mate for life and aggressively defend their nest from predators. They fly close together, their wings nearly touching.

NEW! Blue-throated macaw. Discovered in 1921, only about 250 of this critically-endangered bird remain in the wild. A patch of blue feathers under its beak distinguishes it from the blue-and-gold macaw.

Cotton-top tamarin. With a puffy crest of fur on its head, this tiny, endangered primate lives in family groups and mates for life. Its sophisticated sounds resemble bird chirps.

Flamingo. The smallest, pinkest and most common flamingo, the lesser flamingo performs ritualized group displays of marching, head-flagging and wing salutes.

Galapagos tortoise. The world's largest tortoise at 5 feet (2 meters) long, this boulder-like reptile can live 150 years. Males "fight" by stretching their necks up as far as possible; the highest stretch wins.

Asian small-clawed otter.

Cotton-top tamarin.

Lesser flamingo.

Painted stork.

Green-winged macaw. The second largest macaw, this red parrot is twice the size of the similar-looking scarlet macaw.

NEW! Hyacinth macaw. The largest flying parrot, this vibrant blue macaw has a 4-foot (1-meter) wingspan. Its huge hooked beak is strong enough to crack coconuts.

Kangaroos. A kangaroo can jump 9 feet (3 meters) in the air, leap 40 feet (12 meters) and reach speeds of 30 mph (48 kph). It licks its forearms to stay cool. The red kangaroo stands 7 feet (2 meters) tall. The least common kangaroo in United States zoos, the Western grey kangaroo has a face like a donkey. When threatened, it growls like a dog.

Lappet-faced vulture. The most powerful, aggressive and widespread African vulture, this fierce-looking bird will eat live prey. Skin folds—lappets—hang off its head.

Lemurs. To remove toxins the collared lemur spits on poisonous millipedes and rolls them between its hands before eating them. The ring-tailed lemur uses its tail to signal its location and warn of danger.

Military macaw. See Oasis Animal Guide.

Otter. The world's smallest otter, the Asian small-clawed otter can stay underwater eight minutes. Very social, it loves to play tag and tug-of-war, and can juggle pebbles.

Painted stork. This yellow-billed bird is named for the patch of delicate pink feathers above its tail. Though a young stork can loudly call to attract its parents, by 18 months it's practically voiceless.

Paroon shark-catfish. At up to 10 feet (3 meters) long and 650 pounds (300 kg), this is the largest scaleless freshwater fish.

Porcupine. The largest African rodent, the African crested porcupine has a crown of erect quills. Hundreds of other quills rise when alarmed; their barbed tips imbed themselves easily in would-be predators.

Red-fronted macaw. This powerful flyer mates for life; pairs sometimes sing duets. Couples affectionately nibble each other's face feathers and grasp beaks.

Saddle-billed stork. See Kilimanjaro Safaris Animal Guide.

Scarlet macaw. See Oasis Animal Guide.

Tambaqui. This chubby, herbivorous fish looks like the smaller carnivorous piranha.

West African crowned crane. See our Kilimanjaro Safaris Animal Guide.

White stork. The legend of storks bringing human babies to homes comes from the migration of this bird from Africa to Germany every spring, a common time for human births. It nests on German chimneys.

A winding walkway leads to the indoor theater for It's Tough to Be a Bug.

It's Tough to Be a Bug!

Gleefully sadistic 3-D film delights some kids, scares others

★★★ FP+ "It was awesome!" said the 8-year-old girl, leaving the theater with her parents. "I hated it!" cried the 7-year-old boy next to her. Different children have different reactions to this impish 3-D movie, which tortures its audience by using characters from the 1998 movie "A Bug's Life" to demonstrate how insects defend themselves. Special effects make it seem like you're sprayed with acid and attacked by poison quills. Two robotic characters appear: easygoing ant Flik (your host) and grasshopper villain Hopper. Once state-of-the-art, the show is blurry compared to modern 3-D films. The theater tucks inside the base of the Tree of Life.

Tips. *When to go:* Anytime. There's no need to get a Fastpass; the show rarely fills to capacity. Fastpass holders take a more direct route to the theater, but do not get in early or get special seating. *Where to sit:* In the center of a back row. Lean back to feel all the effects.

Fun fact. "A Bug's Life" voice actors repeat their roles as Flik (Dave Foley), Chili (Cheech Marin) and Hopper (Kevin Spacey).

Fun finds. ❶ Outside the lobby a plaque honors Dr. Jane Goodall's work with chimpanzees. ❷ Lobby posters and ambient music recall previous theater shows such as "Beauty and the Bees" and "Little Shop of Hoppers." ❸ The theater is an ant burrow; its projection booth a wasp nest. ❹ As the show ends, fireflies swarm to exit signs.

Hidden Mickey. ❶ He appears as a tiny dark splotch on a tree in the queue to the right of a door reading "Cast Members Only."

Key facts. *Duration:* 8 min. *Capacity:* 430. *Queue:* Outdoor, shaded. *Showtimes:* Continuous. *Fear factor:* Menacing bugs. *Debuted:* 1998. *Access:* Wheelchairs, ECVs OK. *Disability services:* Assistive listening, reflective captioning, Audio Description. *Location:* Entrance is off the walkway that leads to Asia.

Average wait times (standby line)

9a	10a	11a	12p	1p	2p	3p	4p	5p	6p	7p	8p	9p	10p	11p
5m	5m	5m	5m	5m	5m	5m	5m	5m	5m	5m	5m	5m	5m	---

A troop leader teaches a brother and sister the "W" sign of the Wilderness Explorers.

Wilderness Explorers

All ages will enjoy this hands-on scavenger hunt

★★★★ ✔ First you learn the Wilderness Explorer call: "The wilderness must be explored! Caw! Caw! Roar!" Then off you (or you and your child) head to earn "badges" (stickers) at 31 stations scattered throughout the park. Activities teach you about animals, nature and world cultures.

Every challenge is different. To earn a Veterinary Badge you help diagnose the health of a sea turtle. To get a Dinosaur Badge you join in a search for dino fossils. An Animal-Find Badge has you check off the animals you see, like a birder does with a life list. Play a rhythm on an African drum to receive a Music Badge. Find artifacts and learn folklore about the mythical "abominable snowman" to collect a Yeti Badge.

Yes it can take forever. In fact, Disney assumes you'll take more than one day to complete everything. But if you've got that time there's no rush. Another good thing: if your child is interested in these subjects participating in Wilderness Explorers can be a terrific bonding experience.

It's all wonderfully low-tech. There are no video screens, no hand-held gizmos, no special effects. Instead Disney hands you a surprisingly nice handbook (a wonderful souvenir) and you and your child discover, sketch, explore and occasionally chat with real live people. Earning even a few badges is a great way to enhance your day.

Wilderness Explorers was earnest young Russell's scout troop in the 2009 Pixar movie "Up." The counselors who run this program are part of his troop; their uniforms look just like his and the call they teach is his.

Tip *How to do it:* Get your handbook as soon as you enter the park, and earn your badges as you take in whatever rides, shows and animal exhibits you were already planning to see. For example, as you view the Gorilla Falls animals you can earn a Ham Radio Badge, a Hiking Badge, a Birding Badge, a Tracking Badge and a Gorilla Badge.

Key facts. *Duration:* Allow 20 min per badge. *Operating hours:* Typically 10a–7:30p. *Weather issues:* Closed in thunderstorms. *Debuted:* 2014. *Access:* Players may stay in wheelchairs, ECVs. *Location:* Sign up for the game at a stand at the footbridge between The Oasis and Discovery Island.

Harambe Village waterfront.

Africa

The most fully realized of any Walt Disney World land, the Africa section of Animal Kingdom re-creates an East African port village with a passionate attention to both detail and, unusual for a theme park, economic realities. The area depicts Harambe, a former trading post for gold and ivory. Based on real towns in Africa, it's worn and weathered by decades of rain and sand storms and poverty, yet starting to prosper today by embracing a new idea: building an economy based not on the destruction of natural resources but rather the protection of them. In other words, ecotourism. Various tours through its wildlife reserve generate most of this new revenue, though various hotels, shops, markets and other small enterprises have also popped up. A new Harambe Theater has recently taken over an old fort, hosting a version of Disney's hit musical, "The Lion King."

Typical of Swahili construction techniques, Harambe buildings have coral-rock substructures covered with decaying plaster and topped with thatch or rusting corrugated metal roofs. Strung wires carry electricity throughout the town, energized by old transformers mounted on wooden poles.

Foundations of former buildings still sit within the main streets, while lampposts bear the phrase "Harambe 1961," a reference to the year the village gained independence from Great Britain. Authentic East African canned goods and camping paraphernalia decorate shop interiors.

Nightlife. The Harambe Street Parti isn't as wild as Discovery Island's Carnivale. And that's a good thing, as it gives you a distinct choice in after-dark celebrations. While Carnivale is geared toward young adults but welcomes families, this one's just the opposite, primarily for families yet somehow still perfect for any age. Tinged with a sweet soul, house band Burudika offers softer rhythms; its dancers defined more by their smiles than their costumes. Here there are no flashing black lights, just soft colored spotlights. You'll still want to dance, though—the atmosphere demands it. The Parti differs in another way too: it's more varied. Between Burudika's set are shows by the Harambe Village Acrobats, which always include audience volunteers.

Fun facts. ① The coral rock you see is really volcanic rock from California. ② The village has seven thatch huts, each built on-site by Zulu craftsmen Disney brought over from South Africa, using berg grass harvested by relatives back home. ③ In Swahili, the word "Harambee" refers to an East African tradition of community self-help events. ④ "Tamu Tamu" translates to "very sweet." ⑤ "Dawa" is Swahili for "strong medicine."

Fun finds. Though posted warnings clearly state that "Affixing of Advertisements is Forbidden" on Harambe walls and buildings, hundreds of plastered posters appear throughout the village. ① Some have serious messages, such as "Ivory Poachers Beware!" ② Some promote local businesses such as the Harambe Theater, home of the Festival of the Lion King attraction or ③ Harambe Fish & Crustacea ("We Also Offer Fishing Tours!"), which has its office above restrooms near the theater, alongside a waterway walkway. Two posters refer to the design chief of the Animal Kingdom theme park, Disney Imagineer Joe Rohde. ④ One for Cap'n Bob's Super Safaris includes a sketch of the captain, who looks remarkably like Rohde. ⑤ Another plugs Jorodi Masks & Beads, a small workshop on the second floor of the faux open-air market that forms the serving area of the Tusker House buffet restaurant (a sign at the shop promotes its earrings, a reference to Rohde's signature earlobe adornments). Spiritual messages appear, most of them painted by hand. ⑥ "It does not matter who you are or where you are from, we are all children of the world" states one on the side of the Malimwengu ("Worldly") Guest House, a facade across from the Harambe Market. ⑦ Two Swahili proverbs appear in the market's dining area. "Kila mlango na ufunguo wake" (every door has its own key) and ⑧ "Kupoteya njia ndiyo kujua njia" ("to get lost is to learn the way"). ⑨ "You Are Most Beautiful" reads a message hidden in a market alley. Other posters and signs display a sly sense of humor. ⑩ "Did You Ever Think You May Enjoy a Sausage?" awkwardly asks a poster promoting the Famous Sausages stand at the Harambe Food Market. ⑪ Backaches, bad debts, bad luck, troubled marriages and "all diseases" are among the ailments cured by traditional herbalist healer Dr. Jomo, according to a hanging sign on the market's

Independence lamppost.

Harambe Village Acrobats.

side wall. ⑫ "The Plumber Tel 50716" reads a nearby wooden plank, adding "If plumber not available call her sister—50716." Yes, the same number. ⑬ "Baboons Are Not to be Fed!" warn signs throughout the market. ⑭ As for interesting finds that aren't posters or signs, there's at least one. ⓪n a metal cart in front of the guest house, a patch on a large gray backpack reads "Mousketeer Mountaineer Expeditions." The pack itself travels, most often to the Expedition Everest area of the park's adjacent land of Asia.

Hidden Mickeys. Various forms of Disney's signature character appear throughout its African village. Look closely and you'll find him portrayed: ① As a drain cover and two groupings of pebbles in the side walkway that leads to Asia, in front of the Tamu Tamu ice-cream stand. The letter "S" marks the cover. ② As a second drain cover and pebble grouping, this one in the main walkway just to the left of the Mombasa Marketplace gift shop, marked by the letter "D." ③ As three large gray circles in the pavement behind the nearby Harambe Fruit Market. ④ Waving, in a poorly painted portrait of the mouse on the

outside wall of the Harambe Food Market. Though this image of Mickey is easy to see (it's more than 2 feet (0.6 meters) tall and directly alongside a busy walkway) most Disney fans consider it a Hidden Mickey because of the ironic—and to most people indecipherable—phrase underneath it: "Fichwa! Fellow." In Swahili, "fichwa" means hidden. ⑤ Sipping a huge cup of coffee, Mickey appears in another amateur portrait that's so poorly drawn he looks somewhat like the 1960s television character Mighty Mouse. Titled "Mister Mouse," it's on the back of the food market's front wall. ⑥ As a pattern on a white shirt at the back of the food market, a silhouetted figure wearing Mickey ears that's part of a metallic silver design. A clothes hanger supports the shirt, one of many for sale at a market stand. ⑦ As three circles on a tribal shield, just to the left of that shirt. The shield leans against a fence, behind a table with shells on it.

Live entertainment

Authentic African street performers and musicians liven the village of Harambe.

Photo: Micaela Neal

★★★★★ ✔ **Burudika.** This Afropop band performs engaging rhythmic music that's subtly complex, and irresistibly toe-tapping. Dancers encourage audience members of all ages to join in the fun. The group performs in the evening as part of the Harambe Wildlife Parti. *Five 30-min shows 5p–10p. Old Square, in front of Tusker House.*

NEW! ★★★★★ ✔ **Harambe Soccer Meerkats.** The local soccer team enlists volunteers—children and adults—for this unique and entertaining show, which resembles one of those soccer warmups you had as a kid—with the friendly African coaches who sometimes did handstands and juggled soccer balls with their feet. Your coaches were like that, right? Whenever a volunteer does anything—passes the ball, headbutts it—the troupe cheers. *Two 20-min shows 3p–5p. In front of the Festival of the Lion King theater; moved to the Dawa Bar during rain.*

NEW! ★★★★★ ✔ **Harambe Village Acrobats.** Beads, bells, feathers and grass decorate the costumes of this skilled troupe, which drums and dances as it tumbles and forms pyramids. *Four 20-min shows hourly 6p–10p. Old Square, in front of Tusker House.*

NEW! ★★★★★ ✔ **Karibu Sisters.** Three women singing in Swahili harmonize beautifully, their hypnotic music almost sounding like chanting as they perform acoustic renditions of African songs, one focused on the traditional roles of women. They encourage crowd members to dance along and play simple musical instruments. *Seven 20-min shows hourly 2:30p–8:30p. Across from Harambe Market; later shows are in the Old Square, across from Tusker House.*

NEW! ★★★★★ ✔ **Kora Tinga Tinga.** As he meanders through Harambe Market, this friendly, talented musician plays a handcrafted kora, a harp-like instrument made from a hollowed-out African gourd, cowskin and fishing line. He'll happily answer questions, encourage children to dance and even let you pluck at the kora's strings if you ask. His music pipes through Harambe Market's speakers, seamlessly replacing the normal ambient tunes. He made his kora himself; he's been playing since he was 8 years old. *Six 20-min shows hourly noon–6p. Throughout Harambe Market; later shows are in the Old Square, in front of Tusker House.*

NEW! ★★★★ ✔ **Muziki.** This stilt-walking musician invites kids to join him in a drum circle, where he has them follow his rhythm. While dancing and playing his handheld wooden xylophone, he encourages the children to play as fast as possible. He high-fives each volunteer individually at the end of the performance. *Seven 15-min shows hourly 10a–4p. Near Tamu Tamu Refreshments.*

Karibu Sisters.

Advertisements are forbidden.

★★★★★ ✔ **Tam Tam Drummers of Harambe.** Every show's a delight as this rousing percussion quintet gives visitors of all ages lessons in hip-shaking West African dances. About a dozen volunteers follow its leader's whistled cues, some skillfully, all gleefully. *Seven 15-min shows 9a–1p. Old Square, in front of Tusker House.*

Restaurants and food

Places to eat include a buffet with character meals and a terrific outdoor food market.

★★★★ ✔ **$52 DDP Tusker House.** Decked out in safari gear, Donald and Daisy Duck, Goofy and Mickey Mouse roam among the tables and greet diners at this African-American buffet restaurant. Once an hour the characters dance and lead kids around the tables in a mini-parade. Breakfast offers standard fare; standouts at lunch and dinner include couscous, tabbouleh, salmon and salads; spit-roasted carved meats and stews are also pretty good. The children's buffet doesn't have any African choices. The buffet area resembles an open-air market, with draped fabric shading food stations and what appears to be shops on the second floor. The "Safari Orientation Centre" of the mythical Harambe Village, the dining rooms are lined with real African artifacts, faux maps and notices. *Breakfast 8a–10:55a; $30–$33 (children $18–$20). Lunch and dinner 11a–3:30p, 4p–9:30p; $37–$43 (children $22–$26). Seats 1,206; outdoor bar seats 256. Africa.*

★★★★★ ✔ **$16 DDPq Harambe Market.** You'll feel like you're actually in an African market here, surrounded by weathered art, hand-lettered signs and hanging baskets. The Wildlife Express train chugs by every few minutes. You sit outside under umbrellas as you listen to ambient African music, sometimes from live musicians who wander through the market or play nearby. You order from walk-up windows though the food is table-service quality—best is the masala chicken, battered beef and pork sausage and the coconut custard milk tart. Instead of a regular soft drink try the fruity African Bibo; ask for half Bibo, half Sprite. *11a–10p; $9–$13 (children $6–$7). Seats 200 outdoors, mostly covered. Africa.*

Mister Mouse

Tusker House.

★★★ **$9 Dawa Bar.** Specialty drinks, African beer. Outdoor stand. *10a–10p; $7–$11.*

★★★★ **$8 Harambe Fruit Market.** Fresh fruit, Mickey Mouse pretzels. Outdoor stand. *11a–dusk. $2–$5. Seats 36 behind stand.*

★★★★ **$11 Kusafiri Coffee Shop and Bakery.** Freshly baked pastries, a breakfast sandwich, panini sandwiches for lunch, desserts, coffee and hot chocolate from a window adjacent to Tusker House. There's also the Amarula Schokoleti—hot chocolate with Amarula. *9a–10p, $3–$11.*

★★★ **$12 Mahindi.** Popcorn, glazed nuts, slushies. Outdoor stand. *11a–11p; $4–$16. Across from Tusker House.*

★★★★★ ✔ **$10 Tamu Tamu.** This shady outdoor window couldn't be more unassuming; you'll have to look twice to find it. Earlier a sandwich shop, in 2016 the stand reverted back to its original incarnation to offer hard ice cream treats. Also here: A Dole Whip-like pineapple soft-serve topped with either dark or coconut rum; it's not real ice cream but you won't care. You'll have to look three times to find the seating area. It's behind the window, in a patio-like setting that's covered but not protected from rain. *11a–10p. $5–$7. Seats 92 in outdoor covered seating behind the window. Across from Tusker House.*

★★★ **$9 Zuri's Sweets Shop.** Bulk and packaged candy; cookies and other baked sweets. *9a–11p; $2–$8. An extension of the Mombasa Marketplace store.*

Shops and merchandise

Harambe Village stocks plenty of African merchandise as well as Disney souvenirs.

Mombasa Marketplace. For a real taste of Africa, check out this eclectic shop. Merchandise includes African books and cookbooks, batik caftans made in Kenya, bamboo plants and braided "money trees," musical instruments and serious safari hats. Fans of "The Lion King" can find Simba plushies and hard-to-find puzzles. The store's dark woods, plaster walls and authentic African table displays transport you to a different place. Outside the shop, an African artist carves figurines, canes and other works. There's a henna artist, too. *Across from Tusker House.*

Ziwani Traders. With slightly higher-end merchandise than the adjacent Mombasa Marketplace, this spot stocks beaded animal figurines, original oil paintings and hand-painted ostrich eggs. Decorated like a trading post and outfitting shop, the store has authentic safari gear on its out-of-reach high shelves and ceiling, including heavy-duty backpacks, canteens and lanterns. *Next to Mombasa Marketplace.*

Harambe Soccer Meerkats.

The savanna during the day...

Kilimanjaro Safaris

Disney's largest attraction makes you forget you're in Florida

★★★★★ ✔ FP+ An excellent zoological attraction, this open-air truck ride takes you through a seamless re-creation of an African jungle and savanna. Filled with free-roaming animals, it's a wildlife preserve being used by Disney's mythical Harambe village to replace its timbering economy with eco-tourism. There are few visible fences, and many animals can come up to your vehicle. Creatures include crocodiles, elephants, giraffes, hippos, lions, rhinos, warthogs and many species of antelope. Rutted roads, creaky bridges and blind corners lend to the sense of adventure. Though drivers say the journey will take two weeks and cover 800 square miles (1250 square km), it's actually a 20–25 minute trip through about 100 acres (40 ha).

NEW! Nighttime safaris began in 2016, adding nocturnal hyenas, ambient sounds of animal calls, and strategically-placed lights that illuminate some habitats. A bright orange glow shines through the trees of the savanna, representing the setting sun. Later, soft blue beams simulate moonlight. Overall these trips offer more adventurous experiences, as you often have to actively search for wildlife by seeking out their shadowed silhouettes. The usual animated commentary from your truck driver is quieter and less frequent, allowing you to fully appreciate the peaceful atmosphere. While some animals are asleep, many are more lively after dark; the male lion sometimes stands up and roars. Disney veterans will notice that the night safaris take a slight detour from the regular path, skipping Monkey Point and the rickety bridge.

Other animals are new too. Painted dogs appear during the day. The last habitat is now home to a scimitar-horned oryx. Recent births include three Masai giraffes, a bongo, two white rhinos and two warthogs.

Average wait times (standby line)

9a	10a	11a	12p	1p	2p	3p	4p	5p	6p	7p	8p	9p	10p	11p
20m	40m	60m	35m	30m	35m	40m	35m	30m	30m	20m	30m	10m	5m	---

© Disney

...the savanna at night.

Tips. *When to go:* First thing in the morning through the standby line, when crowds are light and the animals are feeding. Another good time: during a shower, especially after a hot morning or afternoon. The animals will be especially active; elephants sometimes play in their pool when it rains. *Where to sit:* On the left of the truck for the best views, in front for the smoothest ride, in back to take photos because you can turn around and shoot behind you. Hold on tight to your camera, though—the back of the truck gets especially bouncy. *For families:* Ask for the front row. If your boy or girl asks the driver questions about animals, the driver will often answer them directly. Ask the cast member in the boarding area (the one who asks "How many?") to let you sit in the row you prefer. You'll almost always get to.

A closer look. The ride used to tell a story. Flying overhead, a warden would radio your truck to report that poachers had shot the preserve's famous elephant Big Red and that offspring Little Red was missing. Leaving the preserve to hunt for the bad guys, you sped off on a wild chase, finding the poachers' campfire and swerving to avoid the gunfire of their fleeing Jeep. Then you found them, hands in the air, the warden's plane on the ground and his rifle aimed at them, with Little Red safe and sound in a preserve truck.

Fun facts. ❶ Disney created the "muddy" road by coloring concrete to look like soil, then while it was still wet rolling truck tires through it and tossing in dirt, stones and twigs. ❷ The first hippo pool contains all males; the second females. ❸ There's a reason your driver says the termite mounds are "as hard as concrete." ❹ Kilimanjaro Safaris has the largest collection of Nile hippos and African elephants in North America. ❺ It's the largest Disney attraction in the world. The entire Magic Kingdom would fit inside it.

Fun finds. ❶ Posters for Big Red still appear in the queue office. ❷ Prehistoric drawings are on a gate past the flamingos and on rocks to your right as you pass the lions.

Hidden Mickeys. ❶ Just beyond the clay pits past a baobab tree, the three circles appear as a puffy spot between a split branch, opposite the main elephant area. ❷ They form the flamingo island ❸ as well as an indentation in a boulder on the right, just past that island but before the next gate.

Key facts. *Duration:* 22 min. *Capacity:* 36 riders per truck, 4 per row. *Queue:* ●utdoor, covered. *Debuted:* 1998, revised 2016. *Health advisory:* Avoid if pregnant. *Access:* ECV users transfer. *Disability services:* Assistive listening, handheld captioning. *Restrictions:* No flash photography after sunset. *Location:* Behind Harambe Village.

Cheetah.

Kilimanjaro Safaris Animal Guide

By Micaela Neal. It's impossible to spot every species in Disney's Harambe Wildlife Preserve on just one trip through it, as they're never all out at the same time. But here's a list of animals you might see, along with some interesting facts about them:

Addax. Domesticated by Egyptians as early as 2500 BC, this antelope is critically endangered today. Its spiraling horns grow up to 2 feet long (0.6 meters).

Ankole cattle. The horns of these bodacious bovines (also known as Watusi cattle) have a circumference of 28 inches (71 cm),
thicker than the horns of any other animal. Full of blood vessels, they keep the cows cool.

Bongo. The shy "Ghost of the Forest" is the largest forest antelope; the Western bongo's height can reach 8 feet (2.5 meters). Swahili for "thirteen," the name "bongo" comes from the 13 white stripes on its sides.

Bontebok. Extinct in the wild, this antelope has a chocolate-brown coat with a purplish sheen. Both sexes have horns.

Cheetah. The world's fastest land animal, this large feline can accelerate from 0 to 70 mph (113 kph) in just three seconds—the

Addax.

Ankole cattle.

Addax: Micaela Neal

African elephants.

same rate as those Cadillac convertibles at the Rock 'n' Roller Coaster at Disney's Hollywood Studios. The cheetah hunts by day, primarily by sight. While chasing prey, it uses its long tail to stay balanced; its dog-like semi-retractable claws provide traction.

Cormorant. A skilled fisher, the white-breasted cormorant is also known for its unusual mating ritual: a male and female court by wrapping their necks around each other. A group of cormorants is called a gulp.

Elephant. The largest living land animal, the African elephant can reach 20 feet tall (6 meters) and weigh 14,000 pounds (6,400 kg). Its vocalizations include low-frequency rumbles that are inaudible to people but other elephants can hear from miles away. It lives in a matriarchal group. During a mating, the entire herd takes part in a noisy "mating pandemonium"—females and calves circle the couple, mill, wave their trunks and trumpet for up to an hour. Unlike Asian elephants, both sexes of African elephants have tusks.

Flamingo. The world's largest flamingo, the greater flamingo can live up to 75 years. Overall it's also the palest flamingo, though feathers under its wings are bright orange.

Giraffe. The firm kick of the tallest land animal can crush a lion's skull. Males fight violently by slamming their long necks into each another. Disney has two giraffe subspecies: the Masai, the largest giraffe with jagged spots on its coat; and the reticulated, with smooth spots separated by a reticulated

Bontebok.

Greater flamingos.

Spotted hyena.

(net-like) grid of white lines. Reticulated giraffes are the most common in zoos.

Hippopotamus. The most aggressive African animal, the Nile hippopotamus can outrun a man. It grows up to 15 feet long (5 meters) and can weigh 8,000 pounds (3,600 kg). During the day it rests underwater; it can hold its breath for 12 minutes. A pinkish, moisturizing oil oozes from its skin to act as a sunscreen. At night, it grazes on land. Its closest relatives are dolphins and whales.

NEW! Hyena. It has the strongest bite of any mammal; its jaws crush bones with ease. It eats fast, and a lot. It can devour a third of its body weight—in other words, the equivalent of a large lamb—in 30 minutes. It eats practically everything from a kill, including its prey's bones, hooves, skin and teeth. Though known for living off of scavenged carcasses left by other predators, hyenas are the dominant predator in Africa, responsible for a quarter of all game animals killed. Hyenas and lions steal kills from each other. Female hyenas are larger, more aggressive, and more dominant than males. They lead clans of up to 80 individuals. Cubs are usually born as twins; one will often kill the other to establish dominance. The most vocal African mammal, the hyena can make at least 11 distinct sounds. A human-like "laugh" is really a sign of submission to clan superiors. The hyena whoops to communicate over long distances. Disney has two spotted hyenas, the largest species. They appear in the same habitat as its painted

Nile crocodile.

Nile hippopotamus.

African lion.

dogs (not at the same time), but often hide from the safari trucks behind rocks.

Kudu. Topped with twisting 5-foot (1.5-meter) horns, clashing greater kudu males can get stuck together and starve to death. Their horns are used to make Jewish shofars, blown at Rosh Hashanah.

Lion. The most social big cat, the lion form prides of five to 10 individuals; females hunt while the dominant male defends the group. The roar of the African lion can be heard 5 miles (8 km) away. The largest African predator, it can run 37 mph (60 kph) and leap 40 feet (12 meters). It sleeps 20 hours a day.

Mandrill. This social, non-aggressive monkey bares its massive canine teeth as a greeting, not a threat. It beats its hands against the ground when upset. The male mandrill, the largest and most colorful of all the monkeys, becomes more brilliant the more times he has mated. Disney's 1994 film "The Lion King" featured the wise mandrill shaman Rafiki.

Nile crocodile. The most prolific wild predator of humans, the 20-foot (6-meter) long, 2,200-pound (1,000 kg) Nile crocodile can kill thousands a year. It also takes on giraffes, young hippos, elephants, even lions.

Okapi. With a giraffe's body, face and horn-like ossicones mixed with what appears to be the striped legs and rear end of a zebra, the forest-dwelling okapi is the closest giraffe relative. It sleeps just five minutes a day. The species wasn't identified until 1900.

Okapi.

Mandrill.

Painted dogs.

Ostrich. The world's largest bird can stand 8 feet (2.4 meters). Capable of running 45 mph (72 kph), it is the fastest two-legged land animal. A kick from its legs can kill a lion. Contrary to popular belief, it doesn't "hide" by sticking its head in sand; instead it simply lays its head on the ground.

NEW! Painted dog. Give me a "P"! Give me an "A"! Give me an "I-N-T"! Give me an "E"! Give me a "D"! Give me a "D-O-G"! Before a hunt, a pack of 6 to 30 of the world's most sociable canines holds an energetic "pep rally," running, jumping, wagging their tails and bumping noses with every other member in the pack while "singing" in a way that resembles the tweets of songbirds. The rallies apparently do their job—the painted dog is the most successful African predator, its hunts ending in success 80 percent of the time. By comparison, lions catch their intended prey 20 percent of the time. The carnivores hunt during the day in a relay style, taking turns chasing an animal until it drops from exhaustion. Also known as the African wild dog, the painted dog can run 37 mph (60 kph) for up to 3 miles (5 km). It can eat 9 pounds (4 kg) of meat per day. When not hunting, pack members play with each other, care for and share food with pups as well as sick or elderly members, and mourn their dead. Named for its beautiful multicolored coat, which features patches of red, black, brown, white and yellow fur, the painted dog is more closely related to a fox

Ostrich.

Pink-backed pelican.

Micaela Neal

Micaela Neal

Patterson's eland.

than a domestic dog, or even a wolf. The most endangered large carnivore in Africa; there are less than 3,000 left in the wild.

Patterson's eland. The world's largest antelope can weigh 2,000 pounds (900 kg) and stand 6 feet tall (2 meters). South African farmers raise the species like cattle. Its sweet milk takes months rather than days to expire.

Pink-backed pelican. This social bird will reuse the same nest for years. The back of the male turns pink during mating season.

Rhinoceros. Poached for its horns—which are nothing more than large masses of keratin, the worthless protein of human fingernails—the rhinoceros is endangered. Actually gray, the black rhinoceros has a triangular upper lip used for grasping leaves

and a horn up to 4 feet (1.2 meters) long. It can charge at 35 mph (56 kph). The largest, most social, and most numerous rhino species, the white rhinoceros weighs up to 5,000 pounds (2,300 kg). Its name is a mistranslation of the Afrikaans "wijt" ("wide"), a reference to its broad, grazing mouth.

Sable antelope. Only older males are black ("sable"); females and young are reddish-brown. Both sexes have scimitar-shaped horns that can kill lions. Adults rest in a ring around their young, horns out.

Sacred ibis. Worshipped as the god Thoth in ancient Egypt, the sacred ibis supposedly protected the country from plagues and serpents. They were often mummified and put into pharaohs' tombs. You walk past the

Black rhinoceros.

White rhinoceros.

Scimitar-horned oryx (left), sable antelope (above).

habitat for the sacred ibis in the Kilimanjaro Safaris queue; the attraction's Fastpass entrance walkway is right next to it.

Saddle-billed stork. Depicted in ancient Egyptian hieroglyphics, this large wading bird was named for its bill, which is topped with a yellow saddle-like growth.

NEW! Scimitar-horned oryx. "Unicorn!" If a child shouts out that word when spotting this desert antelope, he or she isn't completely wrong—it's likely the animal that spawned the unicorn myth. Egyptians used to bind its long, curved horns together and often the two horns would grow into one. Even in the wild sightings of a one-horned oryx were common for thousands of years, as its thin horns broke off easily and when one did it did not grow back. Today the creature is extinct in the wild, having been hunted for its horns literally to death in the year 2000. It's the largest mammal to have gone extinct in the wild this century. Before that happened it gathered in a nomadic herd of up to 70 individuals, and when traveling was led by a female in a single-file march. It could survive for up to 10 months without water. Both males and females have horns, which curve backward in a shape similar to an Arabian sword called a scimitar. Horns of females can grow over 3 feet long (1 meter).

Springbok. The national animal of South Africa can run 60 mph (97 kph) and leap 13 feet (4 meters). The antelope is the most common prey of the lion, making up 70 percent of its caught meals.

Tortoise. A mediator between man and the gods according to some African cultures, the African spurred tortoise is named for its spurred back legs. You walk past its habitat in the Safaris queue; the attraction's Fastpass entrance walkway is right next to it.

Warthog. Named for the male's warty facial growths, this hairy grassland pig defends itself with sharp 6-inch (15-cm) lower tusks and curved 2-foot (0.6-meter) upper tusks. Warthog Pumbaa provides pungent comic relief in Disney's 1994 film "The Lion King."

Waterbuck. Despite its name, this shaggy antelope doesn't spend much time in water; it just hides there to escape predators. Like the feathers of a duck, its coat repels water.

West African crowned crane. This stately bird trumpets loudly at sunrise. It has a red cheek with a white top, unlike its cousin the East African crowned crane which has a white cheek with a red top. You walk past it in the queue; the Fastpass entrance is next to it.

White-bearded wildebeest. An inspiration for the Beast's face in Disney's 1991 movie

Micaela Neal

Grant's zebra.

"Beauty and the Beast," this odd antelope looks like a striped, hairy horse that has the horns of a cow. In Africa, 1.2 million wildebeest migrate annually up and down the Serengeti ecosystem in Tanzania and Kenya, an 8-month circular journey that covers 10,000 square miles (1,000 square meters) and is the world's largest wildlife movement.

Yellow-backed duiker. Named for its habit of diving into underbrush when startled ("duiker" means "diver" in Afrikaans), this antelope has a yellow patch on its rump that erects when alarmed.

Yellow-billed stork. Look, up in the sky! It's diving! It's flipping over on its side! This African wood stork loves to perform aerial stunts, which apparently it does just for fun.

It feeds by following crocodiles and hippos in the water and gobbling up the small fish, frogs and insects that get stirred up in their wake. It's related to the painted stork on Discovery Island and the wood stork found in Florida.

Zebra. White with black stripes, the Grant's zebra "barks" instead of neighs. Members of a herd take turns sleeping.

Sources for animal guides in this chapter include ARKive, the National Geographic Society, the San Diego and Woodland Park zoos, Disney's Animal Kingdom, "Animal: The Definitive Visual Guide to the World's Wildlife" by the Smithsonian Institution and "The Book of Animal Ignorance" by John Lloyd and John Mitchinson.

White-bearded wildebeest.

Warthog.

Beware the bovine. Even if it isn't there.

Gorilla Falls Exploration Trail

Enchanting walking trail passes gorillas, meerkats, more

★★★★★ ✔ Formerly known as the Pangani Forest Exploration Trail, this wooded walkway crosses streams and passes waterfalls as it leads you past African animals in natural settings. Presented as a string of research areas, the path combines a scientific theme with a playful sense of humor. Exhibits shed light on subjects as diverse as bushmeat and baobab trees, while a sign along the path warns "Beware of Buffalo!" and later, just past the gorilla viewing area, a large rock bears a striking resemblance to Jafar, the villain of Disney's 1992 movie "Aladdin." A research station features naked mole rats, interactive displays and child-level cages and tanks that hold creatures kids find fascinating, such as plate-sized giant African bullfrogs and hissing cockroaches. A 40-foot (12-meter) glass wall lets you view hippos underwater.

A suspension bridge and viewing island divide two large gorilla habitats. One holds a family; the other a bachelor troupe.

New! Creatures debuting in the past year include the flamboyant flower beetle, the Cairo spiny mouse and two birds: the blue-headed dove and southern carmine bee-eater. No longer on display: the four-striped grass mouse and hedgehog tenrec.

Tips. *When to go:* In the morning, when the hippo water is clear (stay quiet and they may come up to the window) and the gorillas are active. *For families:* Know that the bushmeat exhibit (just past the colobus monkeys) shows animals killed for their meat.

Hidden Mickeys. ① As tiny beads on the tile counter of a cart near the entrance to the trail. Mickey's head is a white-and-blue bead; his ears are black beads. **②** Twice in the trail's research station, first on a backpack to the left of the naked mole rats **③** and second on a small ledge behind a desk lamp, as the combination of the letter "O" in the word "Asepco" on a box of soap.

Key facts. *Duration:* Allow 30–45 min. *Specs:* 1 trail (2,100ft, 640m), 9 viewing areas, 10 species plus others in aviary and indoor exhibits. *Operating hours:* Park open–dusk. *Weather issues:* Closed during thunderstorms. *Debuted:* 1998. *Access:* Wheelchairs, ECVs OK, benches are scattered throughout. *Disability services:* Audio Description. *Location:* To the right of Kilimanjaro Safaris.

Micaela Neal

Western lowland gorilla.

Gorilla Falls Exploration Trail Animal Guide

By **Micaela Neal.** The new name of this trail makes it obvious it has gorillas. But it has other interesting animals too, including an amazing collection of African birds.

African green pigeon. Rare in zoos, this colorful bird has a high-pitched call of *"Thweeeloo thweeeoo!"* It eats figs, but also carrion and dried antelope blood.

Bearded barbet. Named for the thick bristles under its bill, this red-and-black bird has a call that's a growling *"scraahhk."*

NEW! Bee-eater. Watermelon red with a teal forehead, the carmine bee-eater—the largest bee-eater in southern Africa—will also devour dragonflies, butterflies and grasshoppers. After catching an insect, it beats its prey against its perch before swallowing it whole. Very social, the bird gathers in large colonies that can number in the thousands. Some flocks are larger than 10,000. In 2004 Disney housed a pair of the birds backstage that fledged a chick, making the park the only facility in North America to successfully rear a newborn with its parents.

Black crake. The long, spindly toes of this small wading bird allow it to walk on

Bearded barbet.

African green pigeon.

Micaela Neal

African bullfrog.

floating plants. It uses its neon-yellow bill to pick parasites off of hippos and warthogs.

Blue-bellied roller. Known for doing acrobatic somersaults as it flies, this beautiful blue-and-tan bird hunts from high in trees, dive-bombing on prey. It has a forked tail.

NEW! Blue-headed dove. How to pick up girls, according to this cute little rainforest pigeon: First, face a girl, then stand still, coo, bow a few times so that your mouth touches your stomach, and then chase her around and around and around. A couple mates for life and works together to raise its young.

Boa. The Kenyan sand boa spends 80 percent of its life buried, with its face poking out; it suffocates prey by dragging it under the sand. Its diet includes naked mole rats.

Bullfrog. An inspiration for Star Wars character Jabba the Hutt, the plump African bullfrog is the largest amphibian in southern Africa, reaching a length of up to 9 inches (23 cm). It has a painful bite and will eat anything it can swallow; a male will munch on his own offspring as he "guards" them against threats.

NEW! Cairo spiny mouse. Spine-like bristles pop up on the back of this ancient rodent, which first appeared 5 million years ago. Females are super maternal; an expecting mom will steal another's baby to practice nursing and grooming. If she can't find a newborn, she'll treat an adult like one.

Cichlid. The African cichlid fish feeds on hippo waste. A mother protects her young by hiding them in her mouth.

Black crake.

Greater blue turaco.

Micaela Neal

Micaela Neal

Angolan black-and-white colobus monkey.

Colobus monkey. It has no thumbs. That's why this tree-dwelling primate is named "colobus"—the Greek word for "mutilated." The Angolan black-and-white colobus monkey uses branches as trampolines to leap 50 feet (15 meters) in the air; its long fur and tail act as a parachute as it falls back to earth.

Dung beetle. The god of the rising sun. Khepri. That's who this scarab beetle represented to ancient Egyptians, who felt its act of rolling a ball of dung across the ground was a sacred symbol of Khepri rolling the sun across the sky. And yet they built pyramids.

Emperor scorpion. This docile arachnid is one of the largest scorpions, up to 8 inches (20 cm) long. Like other scorpions, it glows bright blue-green under ultraviolet light.

NEW! Flamboyant flower beetle. Size matters with this scarab beetle—the larger the male's horn, the healthier he is. He uses the Y-shaped projection to fight other males for mating rights with particular females. An important flower-pollinator, the insect feeds on flower pollen and nectar. Also known as the striped love beetle, it has a green and yellow shell with a bright rainbow-like tint.

Gorilla. At up to 450 pounds (204 kg), the Western lowland gorilla is the largest and most powerful primate; however it doesn't eat meat and is the least aggressive primate—its iconic chest-beating is just a display. It's intelligent, able to learn sign language and can make and use tools. Like humans, gorillas have fingernails and fingerprints, 32 teeth and can stand upright. They also have the same sexual cycle—females menstruate about every 28 days, births happen at 9 months, juveniles typically go through puberty when they're about 11 or 12 years old. A mature male has a silver back and is twice the size of a female. The Western lowland gorilla is the most populous gorilla species.

Great blue turaco. The world's largest turaco, this shy, beautiful bird grows over two and a half feet (1 meter) long. It rarely comes down from the treetops, where it eats leaves and fruit. Some cultures prize its tail feathers as good-luck charms.

Hammerkop stork. Named after the German word "hammerkopf" ("hammerhead") because of its odd-shaped head, this strange bird is not a stork at all, but rather closely related to pelicans. It compulsively builds tree nests, using thousands of sticks for each one. The result can be up to 4 feet (1 meter) across and strong enough that a full-grown human man could sit in it and it wouldn't break. The bird decorates the nest with berries, flower petals and other colorful trinkets.

Hippopotamus. See Kilimanjaro Safaris Animal Guide.

Hoopoe. A relative of kingfishers, the green wood hoopoe climbs trees like a woodpecker. It probes for insects under tree bark using its curved red bill.

Micaela Neal

Slender-tailed meerkat.

Jacana. Jesus! It walks on water! Well sorta, as the African jacana's oversized feet allow it to step across streams and ponds by standing on the tops of aquatic plants. The dominant female leads a harem of males, a rare situation in the bird world.

Kingfisher. "Hey, if you're not doing anything Friday night, how about we go out for lizard? My treat!" A male blue-breasted kingfisher woos a female by catching the scaly reptile and feeding it to her. When not courting, the bird uses its large red and black bill to excavate nests in termite mounds.

Lungfish. With its primitive lungs, this eel-like fish can breathe air. During a dry season the African lungfish plods through mud using its long, fleshy fins. Its ancestors developed true limbs and evolved into land animals. Some evidence shows a link to humans. The species was discovered by a fisherman in 1938.

Madagascar hissing cockroach. This wingless roach hisses by forcing air through its abdominal breathing pores. Its docile nature makes it a common stand-in for more familiar species in films and television.

Meerkat. A type of mongoose, the slender-tailed meerkat can kill a snake, including a striking cobra. It lives and works with others in shared, multifamily community burrows of up to 30 individuals. The animals divide communal duties such as babysitting, food finding and sentry duty, the last of which is shared by rotating guards. A meerkat often stands and gazes at its surroundings; females

African jacana.

Blue-breasted kingfisher.

Jacana: Micaela Neal

Micaela Neal

Taveta golden weaver.

sometimes nurse upright. A famous fictional meerkat is Timon of "Lion King" fame.

Naked mole rat. Neither mole nor rat, this pink, blind rodent uses teeth on the outside of its mouth to dig without swallowing dirt. It's the only mammal that organizes itself into ant-like colonies led by a queen. A colony can live 25 years and produce over 1,000 offspring. They don't feel pain, as they lack the necessary neurotransmitter.

Okapi. Our Kilimanjaro Safaris Animal Guide has information on this creature.

Ornate spiny-tailed lizard. This foot-long (30 cm) desert herbivore is named for its thick, armored tail and the pattern of striking colors on its back. A gland around its nose excretes salt.

Pancake tortoise. This reptile's flat shell makes it look like a pancake with legs. Thanks to its lightweight skeletal structure, it's the fastest and most agile tortoise. When threatened, it doesn't withdraw into its thin pliable shell. Instead, it dashes for cover, squeezing into tight rock crevices where it hides until the coast is clear.

Pygmy goose. The smallest African waterfowl, the African pygmy goose is in truth a misnamed duck. It eats water lilies. The male is more colorful than the female, with chestnut, metallic-green and white feathers and a bright yellow bill.

Snowy-headed robin-chat. A type of flycatcher, this orange-and-black songbird

hunts insects on the wing. It's named for the streak of white feathers on top of its head.

Spider tortoise. Named for the web-like pattern on its shell, this tiny tortoise is critically endangered due to the illegal pet trade.

Tarantula. Named for the distinctive star-shaped pattern on its abdomen, the aggressive Mombasa starburst tarantula has a painful bite that can rush you to an emergency room.

Weaver birds. To compete for females, male taveta golden weavers build grapefruit-sized nests over water; a female chooses her mate based on how impressed she is by his nest-building skills. The larger, quieter white-headed buffalo weaver is named for its tendency to follow African buffalo and eat the insects that creature disturbs.

White-bellied go-away bird. Named for its call, which sounds like "g'away," this odd bird has a tall gray crest and a long tail. It climbs like a squirrel, moving noisily from tree to tree. Its favorite food is plantains.

Yellow-backed duiker. See Kilimanjaro Safaris Animal Guide.

Zebra. The rarest and largest zebra, the Grevy's zebra is twice the size of the Grant's zebra seen on Kilimanjaro Safaris. The species brays like a donkey, and is white with black stripes with a white belly. Ancient Romans used it in circuses. A herd's foals are left in male-led care centers while their mothers get water.

Micaela Neal

Wild animals. Dancers perform within a few feet of their audience.

Festival of the Lion King

In-the-round musical spectacle is Disney's best show

★★★★★ ✔ FP+ Fans of Disney's 1994 movie "The Lion King" will love this rousing musical spectacle. Filled with energized renditions of the best songs from the film, it combines the pageantry of a parade, the wit of a Catskills comedy revue and the emotions of a gospel revival. The show is presented in-the-round in an air-conditioned theater.

It begins with an evocative take on the film's opening scene, as animal-costumed dancers create an abstract sunrise to "The Circle of Life." Four singers bring in nearly 50 more performers, including Timon, the revue's wisecracking emcee. Parade floats roll in too. On one is Simba, another Pumbaa.

From then on, singers, dancers, acrobats, stilt-walkers and giant puppets fill your field of vision. "Tumble Monkey" acrobats fly through the air, a fire-baton twirler performs to "Be Prepared," a ballerina soars overhead to "Can You Feel the Love Tonight?"

A twirling finale reprises all the songs as it transforms into a kaleidoscopic circle of life.

Tips. *When to go:* Anytime with a Fastpass. You'll enter the theater before the rest of the crowd and easily get a good seat. *For families:* Since the bleachers are shallow, children often can't see if they sit behind someone tall.

Fun find. After the show, Timon's back-stage microphone picks up his aside, "Could somebody hose down those Tumble Monkeys? They're starting to smell a little gamey."

Key facts. *Duration:* 28 min. *Capacity:* 1,375. *Queue:* Indoor area spills into outdoor covered line. *Showtimes:* Scheduled, typically hourly mid-morning to evening. *Weather issues:* During a rain, the audience is held in the theater until the floats move backstage. *Debuted:* 1998. *Access:* Wheelchairs, ECVs OK. *Disability services:* Assistive listening, hand-held captioning. *Location:* Harambe Theater, behind Tusker House on the Discovery River.

Typical show times

9a	10a	11a	12p	1p	2p	3p	4p	5p	6p	7p	8p	9p	10p	11p
---	10:00	11:00	12:00	1:00	---	3:00	4:00	5:00	6:00	7:00	8:00	---	---	---

Julie Neal

Vets examine animals in front of you at the veterinary care center.

Conservation Station

Offshoot of Africa has petting zoo, educational exhibits

★★★ ✔ This indoor pavilion houses straightforward exhibits, a veterinary care center and a few character-greeting spots. A petting zoo sits next to it. Though the area is inconveniently located, it's well done. Its best feature: a glass-walled operating room that lets you watch animals undergo medical procedures. Vets explain what's going on while overhead cameras offer up-close views. To get to the area you take a train—the Wildlife Express—from Africa to an offshoot area called Rafiki's Planet Watch. Despite its name the train offers no wildlife views, just a glimpse of a few backstage animal-care areas.

Tips. *When to go.* Arrive first thing in the morning to see the vet procedures. About three animals are treated each morning.

Fun facts. ❶ Complete with a corrugated-metal water tank, the train's African depot is patterned after British structures built in East Africa during the early 1900s. Next to the formal station is a local plaster-and-thatch addition. ❷ Why such a fancy train? Because it was originally meant to take you on a safari of its own through the Harambe Wildlife Preserve, before Disney's animal care facilities grew larger than anticipated. ❸ The thatched-roof huts along the train track were made by hand in Indonesia.

Hidden Mickeys. ❶ As overlapping circles in tree grates. ❷ Throughout the entrance mural and the Song of the Rainforest display. ❸ As orange spots on an outdoor stage wall. ❹ Often as a pattern on a sheared sheep.

Key facts. *Duration.* Allow 90 min–2 hr. *Species:* 49. *Operating hours:* 9:30a–5:50p. *Weather issues:* The train does not run during thunderstorms. *Debuted:* 1998. *Access:* Wheelchairs, ECVs OK; ECV users transfer to wheelchairs to enter the petting zoo. *Location:* At the end of the Rafiki's Planet Watch walkway.

Average wait times (Wildlife Express train)

9a	10a	11a	12p	1p	2p	3p	4p	5p	6p	7p	8p	9p	10p	11p
---	10m	10m	10m	10m	10m	10m	10m	10m	---	---	---	---	---	---

Micaela Neal

Pineywoods cow.

Rafiki's Planet Watch Animal Guide

By Micaela Neal. Some of the cutest critters in all of Disney live out in this remote area of Animal Kingdom, many in aquariums. Look around to find the following:

NEW! **Aardvark.** This living fossil has been around for 54 million years. It has a nose like an anteater, ears like a donkey, feet like a rabbit and a tail like a giant rat. Once it has opened a termite mound, it can eat up to 500,000 termites in one sitting with its thin, foot-long tongue. Hunted for meat and leather, its name is Afrikaans for "earth-pig." It sometimes stars in presentations on a stage next to Affection Section.

African bullfrog. For details see the Gorilla Falls Exploration Trail Animal Guide.

NEW! **Alpaca.** This gentle, curious cousin of the llama is bred for its soft, durable fur, which comes in 22 colors. It hums, or shrieks if in danger. Fighting males warble like birds.

American alligator. Growing up to 16 feet (5 meters) long, this reptile has 80 teeth, but usually won't eat animals larger than raccoons. Chirping, yellow-striped young—used for presentations—grow to be solid gray-black. Adults bellow, unique for crocodilians.

Annam leaf turtle. Found in the wild only in a small area of central Vietnam, this rare reptile is also known as the Vietnamese pond turtle. It loves to bask in the sun to kill off parasites such as leeches.

Asian brown tortoise. This primitive reptile (AKA the Burmese black tortoise) provides more parental care than any other tortoise.

Bearded dragon. Covered with spiky scales, a dewlap (fold of skin) creates the "beard" of the inland bearded dragon. During courtship and aggression displays, it inflates and turns black. The reptile waves its arm in a slow circle to show submission.

NEW! **Beetles.** One of the largest beetles at up to 5 inches (13 cm) long, the park's new Atlas beetle gets airborne by launching itself from a tree. A male can lift 850 times its own weight. To help it stay underwater, the sunburst diving beetle uses a bubble of air like a scuba tank. Its larva is the only known animal with bifocal vision; each of two eyes has two retinas and two focal planes; it switches its vision between the two to capture prey. Also here: the flamboyant flower beetle. For details on it see the Gorilla Falls Animal Guide.

Caiman lizard. Raised scutes (scales) on the back of this 4-foot (1-meter) lime-green reptile resemble those of the caiman crocodile. The more colorful male has a red head.

NEW! **Chinese crocodile lizard.** The large, bony scales that run down its back make this

Micaela Neal

South African hedgehog.

lizard look like a small crocodile, although it's really related to monitor lizards and Gila monsters. It's known as "the lizard of great sleepiness" and is believed to be a cure for insomnia in its native China.

NEW! Chinese three-striped box turtle. Unlike other turtles, which are worth about $7 each, this endangered reptile goes for around $1,800 in China, due to the mistaken rumor that its shell can cure cancer. It's also known as the golden coin turtle.

Egyptian tortoise. This cute, tiny tortoise is only 5 inches (13 cm) long.

Emperor scorpion. See Gorilla Falls Exploration Trail Animal Guide.

Goats. The long floppy ears of the Anglo-Nubian goat earn it the nickname "Rabbit Goat." With less than 300 remaining in the wild, the Arapawa goat descends from two goats released on Arapawa Island by Captain James Cook in 1773. The gentle Nigerian dwarf goat can be trained to use a leash; its milk is used for cheese and making soap.

Gopher tortoise. Native to the southeast United States, this endangered reptile digs deep burrows that it shares with other animals. These burrows can be 50 feet (13 meters) long and 10 feet (3 meters) deep.

Hedgehog. Seen in Conservation Station presentations, the nocturnal South African hedgehog rolls into a ball when threatened, exposing only its spiny back. Hedgehogs fight by butting heads.

Katydid. At up to 6 inches (15 cm) with a 10-inch (25-cm) wingspan, the Malaysian giant katydid is the world's largest katydid. It's bright green, camouflaged to look like a leaf.

Komodo dragon. See Maharajah Jungle Trek Animal Guide.

Kunekune pig. The world's smallest and most sociable pig, the kunekune is as smart as a dog. Its name, pronounced "cooney cooney," means "fat and round."

Madagascar hissing cockroach. See Gorilla Falls Exploration Trail Animal Guide.

Mantids. Camouflaged to look like a decaying leaf, the Malaysian dead-leaf mantis displays colorful wings when threatened. Named for its slender, violin-shaped prothorax, the violin mantis hunts flying insects.

NEW! Oman spiny-tailed lizard. Looking like a small tortoise without a shell, this desert native digs burrows. When fleeing a predator, it dives into its burrow and plugs the entrance with its stocky tail.

NEW! Ornate horned frog. This plump frog has a huge mouth that appears to take up the entire front half of its body. As a result, it is sometimes called "mouth with legs" or "Pac-Man frog." It will eat nearly anything that will fit inside its mouth.

Pineywoods cow. Descended from original Spanish stock left in the southern United States in the early 16th century, this rare cow has since bred without interference along the Gulf Coast.

Axolotl.

NEW! Poison dart frogs. Discovered in 1968, the blue poison dart frog will chase and wrestle intruders into its territory. Considered one of the most toxic animals on the planet, the 2-inch (5 cm) golden poison dart frog has enough poison to kill 10 grown men. The green-and-black poison dart frog has a toxin, epibatidine, that is being researched for its potential as a powerful new painkiller that is 200 times more effective than morphine but without any negative side effects. The male frog carries tadpoles on his back to a pool of water.

Prehensile-tailed skink. The largest skink species, this tree-dweller uses its long tail to maneuver from branch to branch.

Puerto Rican boa. This large snake hangs in front of cave entrances to catch flying bats.

Pythons. Named for its tendency to curl into a ball when frightened, the ball python—used for presentations—is revered by the Nigerian Igbo people. If one is accidentally killed, the community will build it a coffin and have a funeral. The large, angular snout of the green tree python has heat-sensing pits. The yellow hatchling turns green and nocturnal as an adult; the change may be overnight or take months.

Salamanders. Cute as a button, the endangered, aquatic axolotl ("ACK-suh-LAH-tuhl"), which unlike other salamanders can't breathe air, was a staple in the diet of Aztecs. The colored glands of the European fire salamander exude samandarin, a neurotoxin that causes muscle convulsions, hypertension and hyperventilation. With no hind legs, the eel-like greater siren is the most primitive salamander alive today. Its duckling-like cheeps intimidate predators. At 4 feet (1.5 meter) long, the aquatic, snake-like two-toed amphiuma is the longest salamander in the United States. It has two rows of teeth.

Sheep. The rare babydoll sheep, just 2 feet (1 meter) tall, originated in the United States in the 1980s. Its fine wool resembles cashmere. The oldest North American sheep breed, the Gulf Coast native sheep was brought to the United States by Spanish colonists in the 1500s; it's now indigenous to portions of all Gulf Coast states. A breed of hair sheep, the Katahdin has a woolless, smooth coat that doesn't need to be sheared.

Sicilian miniature donkey. According to Christian lore, Mary rode one of these docile mammals the night Jesus was born. A cross-shaped stripe lays over its back and shoulders. Brother and sister Jack and Jill have been at Animal Kingdom since the park opened in 1998.

Stick insects. Camouflaged to look like a prickly twig, the giant spiny stick insect travels in groups at night. Ten inches (25 cm) long and quite aggressive, the female Malayan jungle nymph lays the largest eggs in the insect world. She snaps her spiny back legs together like scissors.

Micaela Neal

Caiman lizard.

NEW! Tailless whip scorpion. Measuring 8 inches (20 cm) across, the Tanzanian giant tailless whip scorpion looks like a huge, spindly cross between a spider and a scorpion. Its two front legs have adapted to be long and whiplike, and are used not for walking but as antennae-like sensory organs. It is one of the few arachnids that shows social behavior; a mother communicates with her young by caressing them with her whiplike front legs, and the young do the same with her and with their siblings.

NEW! Tamarins and marmosets. Named for its resemblance to German emperor Wilhelm II, the park's new emperor tamarin sports a long, white, regal mustache. Endangered due to habitat loss and illegal pet trading, the golden lion tamarin is named for its mane of fur. Only the dominant male and female in a group of Geoffroy's marmosets reproduce; subordinate females cease ovulating due to pheromones produced by the dominant female. Also here: the cotton-top tamarin. For details on it see the Discovery Island Animal Guide.

Tarantulas. The burrow of the Arizona blond tarantula goes 2 feet (1 meter) straight down. The third largest tarantula, the Brazilian salmon pink tarantula is also known (correctly) as the "birdeater." The aggressive brown baboon tarantula rears itself up and strikes down repeatedly when provoked. It is eaten by baboons. The agile Indian ornamental tarantula can catch flying insects in midair. The Mexican fireleg tarantula doesn't build a web to catch prey (which includes geckos); instead it hunts down its victim, injecting it with venom that both paralyzes and begins to liquify it. A Mexican red rump tarantula stars in the 1955 sci-fi movie "Tarantula," in which a giant one terrorizes a desert. Also here: the Mombasa starburst tarantula. For details on it see the Gorilla Falls Animal Guide.

Toads. The biggest native toad in the United States, the Colorado river toad is the archetypal "psychedelic toad"—its hallucinogenic venom is illegal to possess. The endangered Puerto Rican crested toad was thought to be extinct until 1967. The flat, aquatic Surinam toad looks like a mottled brown leaf. Its odd face has a triangular head and beady eyes, but no tongue or teeth. Young toads develop in pockets on a mother's back; 60-100 emerge as miniature adults.

NEW! Tonkin bug-eyed frog. Sitting still and camouflaged right at the water's edge, this rough-textured frog can project its voice like a ventriloquist. When frightened, it curls into a ball and plays dead. It's also known as the Vietnamese mossy frog.

Tree monitor. The slender black tree monitor can sense movement 800 feet (240 meters) away. It climbs trees with the help of its semi-prehensile tail, which is two-thirds the lizard's full length.

Chakranadi sitarist.

Asia

Like Disney's African village of Harambe, its mythical Asian kingdom of Anandapur also wrestles with economic issues. A collage of architectural and landscaping themes from throughout Southeast Asia portray another decaying community trying to move out of poverty by preserving and promoting its environment. In this story, locals have turned an ancient royal forest and its crumbling hunting lodge into a wildlife preserve and conservation area, while a river-rafting business battles loggers for control of a once-pristine river. Meanwhile, in the nearby mountainside village of Serka Zong, an American entrepreneur is offering mountain climbers a tea-train shortcut to Mount Everest, ignoring warnings from villagers about a Yeti who protects the area from just such souless ventures.

Fun facts. ❶ Walkways look like dried mud but are actually brown concrete. Bicycle tracks and footprints press into them, made by Disney cast members and their children.

❷ "Place of delight" in Sanskrit, a sacred language of Hinduism, the word "Anandapur" is also the name of a real town in East India that's home to 35,000 people. ❸ "Chakranadi" translates to "river that runs in circles." It's the name of an actual river near the west coast of India. ❹ "Serka Zong" is Tibetan for "fortress of the chasm."

Fun finds. ❶ Authentic Asian rickshaws and rusty bicycles sit alongside some walkways. Disney purchased the bicycles at garage sales. ❷ Dried yak dung. That's the Himalayan building material the plaster simulates on buildings around Expedition Everest. ❸ Near the gibbons exhibit, a crumbling Indian tiger shrine has scarf and garland offerings and bells that celebrate answered prayers. ❹ Each Anandapur business in the land displays a tax license featuring a formal portrait of the kingdom's king and queen. The bigger the license, the more taxes the business pays. Small stands have small licenses; the Yak & Yeti restaurant has a huge one. ⑤ Walls and drain covers shoot water at a small play area just past the entrance to Kali River Rapids. ⑥ Like in Disney's African town of Harambe, some of the best details in its Asian kingdom are the many rusted signs and aged murals that seem to show up everywhere. Few are authentic, but all look to be. "Remember young travelers, no night lodging," reads a sign at the tiny Drinkwallah bar and snack stand near the main entrance to the land. ⑦ Asian Coca-Cola signs surround Drinkwallah. ⑧ A note on a bulletin board on the wall of Gupta's Gear (a faux shop near Expedition Everest) reads "Billy—it's a small world after all! Met your brother on the trail... Mikey."

Hidden Mickey. The three circles hide inside the Drinkwallah snack stand, as a small golden crown on a carved cermonial mask on the wall.

Live entertainment

Two unique acts bring a sense of Asian music to the park. I especially like the sitar player—he really gets into it.

★★★★★ ✔ **Chakranadi.** This sitar-tabla duo performs haunting original instrumentals, an evocative style of music you rarely hear live, if at all. *30-min shows hourly 2p–5p Sun.–Mon., Fri.–Sat. In front of Yak & Yeti.*

★★★★ ✔ **DJ Anaan.** A disc jockey spins catchy Asian pop tunes while two young women in colorful saris dance and encourage onlookers to join them. Channels the dance-fest finale of the movie "Slumdog Millionaire." *20-min shows intermittently 2p–4p, 4p–6p Tue.–Thr. In front of Yak & Yeti.*

Restaurants and food

Want to get out of the heat when you eat? You've got one choice in Asia.

★★★★ ✔ **$32 DDP Yak & Yeti.** Except for Disney's expensive new Tiffins restaurant, this is the only place inside Animal Kingdom where servers bring you your food. Highlights include a crispy Mahi Mahi that doesn't taste a bit fishy; its sweet and sour sauce is the best I've had. Infused with flavor, mango iced tea is a perfect accompaniment. For an appetizer try the mild Ahi tuna, served with hot dipping sauce and sweet slaw. For dessert go for the pineapple and cream cheese wontons—two honey-sauced skewers which you dip into vanilla ice cream—then resist the urge to lick your plate like a dog. Other good food choices: pork egg rolls and seafood curry. Kids pick from a mini burger, vegetable lo mein, chicken tenders or an egg

Serka Zong Bazaar.

Siamang, with newborn, in front of Kali River Rapids.

roll. Portions are generous, and the service rivals that of a Disney-owned restaurant. Relaxed dining areas offer lots to look at. Supposedly a converted home, the restaurant has a plethora of authentic Asian artifacts on its walls and ceilings; chairs, drapes and light fixtures are totally mismatched, just as they should be. You can usually be seated immediately without a reservation during the first half-hour the restaurant is open; ask to sit upstairs by the windows to people-watch the walkway below. *11a–8p; $18–$29 (children $9). Seats 250, 8 at the bar. In front of the Discovery Island walkway. Run by Landry's; direct reservations at 407-824-9384.*

★★★ **$5 DDPs Anandapur Ice Cream Truck.** Soft-serve floats and waffle cones from an authentic Polynesian jitney. *$4–$5. Outside stand; near Expedition Everest.*

★★★★ **$6 DDPs Caravan Road.** Asian vegetarian dishes, teriyaki beef sliders. Formerly the Bradley Falls kiosk. ●pen seasonally. *$4–$7. Kiosk; Africa walkway.*

★★★ **$6 DDPs Chakranadi.** Mickey Mouse and other pretzels, glazed nuts, beer. *$4–$7. Cart; near the exit to Kali River Rapids.*

★★★ **$7 DDPs Drinkwallah.** Noodle salads, frozen and rum drinks. *$7. Seats 34 in waterside area. Discovery Island walkway.*

★★★★ **$6 DDPs Mister Kamal's.** Nice vegetarian and Indian snacks. Samosas, falafel, hummus. *$5–$6. Africa walkway.*

★★★★★ ✔ **$11 DDPs Royal Anandapur Tea Co.** Oh the teas! There are 22 of them, enough to find just what you want (my daughter loves this place). Also coffees; pastries. *9a–11p; $7–$16. In front of Yak & Yeti.*

★★★★ **$8 Thirsty River Bar.** This stand sells frozen and specialty drinks; Asian and African beer and wine. Disney lore says the walls are covered with travelers' mementos because this is the former home of a popular Everest sherpa family. Actually it's the old FastPass building for Expedition Everest, from back when a FastPass was a ticket issued from a machine. *11a–park close. Drinks $4–$10. Next to Expedition Everest, convenient to the Discovery River theater.*

★★★★ ✔ **$13 DDPq Trek Snacks.** Newer stand changes its menu each day. Early on it's pastries and fresh fruit; at 11 a.m. a new board goes up featuring sandwiches, salads,

Photo: Micaela Neal

edamame. *9a–park close; $2–$9. Adjacent to the Thirsty River Bar.*

★★★ **$8 DDPs Warung Outpost.** Pretzels, specialty margaritas, beer. *$2–$9. Adjacent to the Thirsty River Bar.*

★★ **$12 DDPq Yak & Yeti Local Food Cafés.** Asian food court staples served from walk-up windows. Beer, sangria. *$2–$9. In front of Yak & Yeti.*

★★ **$7 Yak & Yeti Quality Beverages.** Beer, frozen specialty drinks, sangria. *$2–$9. To the side of Yak & Yeti.*

Shops and merchandise

Disney merchandise? There's not much of it here. But there are plenty of things you won't find anywhere else, including some cuddly baby Yeti plushies guaranteed to make your friends say "Oh, he's so cute!"

Bhaktapur Market. Amazingly cramped, this small, open-air boutique sells authentic merchandise from Asia, much of it exotic kitsch. Run by the adjacent Yak & Yeti Restaurant, it also offers Yak & Yeti souvenirs. *In front of Yak & Yeti.*

Mandala Gifts. This teeny open-air store sells junior apparel and accessories, much of it nature-themed, with only some of it having anything to do with Disney. Included are colorful sundresses, short-shorts, scarves,

costume jewelry and some cute straw hats. *In front of Yak & Yeti.*

Serka Zong Bazaar. The high shelves of this shop are jam-packed with authentic Asian artifacts and mountaineering gear; an immense clawed Yeti figure rises from the center. Things you can buy include Expedition Everest souvenirs (don't miss the adorable Yeti plush and knit hats) and ride photos, as well as prayer flags from Tibet and books about the real Mt. Everest. Sometimes it has lovely Christmas ornaments created from air cylinders left behind on the actual Mt. Everest. *At the exit to Expedition Everest.*

Animal guide

Two monument areas, one Thai and one Nepalese, provide homes for hooting gibbons. Supposedly built in 637 AD, the temples are covered in bamboo scaffolding as cash-starved villagers slowly restore them.

Siamang. This largest, loudest gibbon inflates its throat sac and produces a "hoot" that reaches 113 decibels, nearly as loud as jet aircraft at 100 yards (91 meters).

White-cheeked gibbon. The territorial call of this small ape is a crescendo of siren-like "whoops." Males and juveniles are black with white cheeks; females and newborns are blond.

Yak & Yeti.

Micaela Neal

Giving back. A pied crow returns a dollar to an audience volunteer.

Flights of Wonder

Educational, comedic show has flying birds, green message

★★★★ ✔ Birds fly inches over your head in this entertaining live show, which demonstrates natural behaviors as it promotes the intrinsic value of these animals and the need to protect them. Altogether you'll see about 20 birds, including a bald eagle.

Though the subject is serious, the presentation is anything but. Just as it gets started, it's interrupted by a loony lost tour guide who wanders up onstage, flag in hand, in search of his group. You soon learn that he suffers from "FOB"—Fear of Birds. As the show's host urges him to face his fears, you witness various up-close-and-personal flight and behavior demonstrations. The grassy natural stage features a backdrop of a crumbling stone building set in a shady grove.

A brief preshow in front of the theater stars a great horned owl. When the show is over, handlers often bring out a bird or two for a brief meet-and-greet session.

NEW! A 2016 update replaced hanging fabric above the seating area with a metal roof, so you'll no longer get dripped on after a rain.

Tips. *Where to sit:* In the center, at the end of a front row. Birds will fly over your head (arrive 25 minutes early to be among the first people in the theater). *For families:* Since the seating area is flat, small children should sit close to the stage. Want your child to be in the show? Sit front and center and have her wave wildly when the trainer asks for volunteers.

Key facts. *Duration:* 25 min. *Capacity:* 1,150. *Queue:* ●utdoor, shady. *Showtimes:* Scheduled performances mid-morning through mid-afternoon. *Weather issues:* Changed and shortened during rain, cancelled during lightning and thunderstorms. *Debuted:* 1998. *Access:* Wheelchairs, ECVs ●K. *Disability services:* Assistive listening. *Location:* On the walkway to Africa, to the left of the Yak & Yeti restaurant.

Typical show times

9a	10a	11a	12p	1p	2p	3p	4p	5p	6p	7p	8p	9p	10p	11p
---	10:30	11:30	12:30	---	2:30	3:30	4:30	---	---	---	---	---	---	---

Churning waters splash riders on Kali River Rapids.

Kali River Rapids

Wet, exhilarating raft ride condemns rainforest destruction

★★★★ FP+ This raft ride takes you down a twisting, turning jungle river that has a 25-foot (8-meter) drop. Erupting springs, spraying water jugs and squirting statues ensure you get wet, maybe soaked. At night, lights along the waterway add color. Each raft holds 12 people; nearby lockers (free to use while you're on the ride) keep valuables dry.

The ride carries a strong conservation message, as it depicts the process of deforestation. Though it begins in a lush jungle, at the river's headwaters it shows the illegal operations of a logging business, clear-cutting a pristine section of a rainforest to harvest tropical hardwoods, setting ablaze wood that doesn't have commercial value.

Tips. *For families:* Talk to your children about the ecological issues raised in this attraction. Deforestation and habitat loss are worthwhile topics, especially when you are surrounded by species being threatened.

Animal guide. In the queue, a large cage holds a red-billed blue magpie. Excellent at mimicking voices, the bird will rob nests for eggs and chicks.

Fun finds. ❶ Mr. Panika's Shop sells "Antiks Made to Order." ❷ King of Pop Michael Jackson is among the raft riders in a mural in the last queue room; he's at the top right of a raft with his hands raised. ❸ On the exitway, push a button on a footbridge to shoot sprays of water on unsuspecting riders.

Key facts. *Duration:* 6 min. *Capacity:* 240 (20 12-person rafts). *Queue:* Outdoor, shaded. *Fear factor:* 1 steep drop. *Restraint:* Seat belt. *Weather issues:* Closed during thunderstorms. *Debuted:* 1999. *Health advisory:* Avoid if pregnant or have back, blood pressure, heart, motion sickness or neck problems. *Access:* Height min 38 in (97 cm), ECV users transfer. *Location:* On the walkway to the Maharajah Jungle Trek.

Average wait times (standby line)

9a	10a	11a	12p	1p	2p	3p	4p	5p	6p	7p	8p	9p	10p	11p
10m	25m	35m	40m	55m	75m	65m	60m	30m	30m	20m	25m	10m	5m	---

You walk through the overrun grounds of a mythical ancient hunting lodge.

Maharajah Jungle Trek

Exotic trail has captivating bats, tigers, a Komodo dragon

★★★★★ ✔ Tigers, giant fruit bats and other exotic Asian animals line this shady winding walkway. A lush aviary is filled with beautiful birds. Docents are stationed at key viewing spots. Overhead fans help keep you cool in the bat pavilion, the attraction's only indoor area. Some people are afraid of the bats, but there is no need to be. They're *fruit* bats.

The circular walkway winds through the ruins of a mythical hunting lodge, which, in one of Disney's best architectural efforts, has been taken over by the forces of nature. Trees have taken root within towers, bursting their seams from within. Birds have moved into the grand ballroom, which has lost its roof. Eventually, the story goes, the lodge was given to the local village, which uses it today as a wildlife refuge.

NEW! Lion-tailed macaque monkeys, water buffalo, prehensile-tailed skink, blue-crowned laughingthrush and Goldie's lorikeet.

Tips. *When to go:* First thing (the bats are fed at 9:15 a.m., and the rest of the animals are lively) or during a light shower (the tigers get playful). *For families:* Kids will like spotting the shed antlers past the tiger area. Eli, a male deer, grows new ones every four months.

Fun finds. ① Giant painted bat kites hang over the entrance to the bat house. ② Just before the aviary, an environmental history of mankind is depicted in a sequence of carvings on a stone wall. Man emerges out of the water; comes to a paradise rich with wildlife; chops down its tree; faces floods, death and chaos; and finally gains happiness when he learns to respect nature. ③ An actual fertility urn sits in the small aviary entrance building, which in Disney's story is the tomb of Anantah, the first ruler of Anandapur. Anantah's ashes are said to be in the urn, which shows an abstract couple engaging in... um, fertility activity.

Hidden Mickeys. ① At the second tiger viewing area, in the first mural on the right as swirls of water under a tiger. ② As a maharajah's earring in the first mural on your left.

Key facts. *Duration:* Allow 30 min. *Specs:* 1,500-ft trail (460 meters), 7 viewing areas. *Species:* 14 plus aviary. *Hours:* 9a–dusk. *Weather issues:* Closed in thunderstorms. *Debuted:* 1998. *Access:* Wheelchairs, ECVs OK. *Disability services:* Audio Description. *Location:* Just beyond Kali River Rapids.

Tiger.

Maharajah Jungle Trek Animal Guide

By Micaela Neal. Bats, tigers, a monkey and unusual birds highlight these Asian habitats.

Bar-headed goose. With seasonal migrations over the Himalayas, this is one of the highest-flying birds.

Bartlett's bleeding-heart dove. The crimson patch on its breast—which looks like a bloody wound—gave this bird its name.

Bats. With a 6-foot (2-meter) wingspan, the Malayan flying fox is the world's largest bat. It can eat its body weight in fruit and vegetation daily. The Rodrigues fruit bat struggles to survive on the Indian Ocean's tiny Rodrigues Island, with only a few hundred of its kind left in the wild.

Blackbuck. In Hindu mythology, this antelope transports the moon goddess Chandrama. It can run 50 miles per hour (80 kph). Males have ringed, spiraling horns; females smooth curved ones.

Black-collared starling. This songbird feeds by blindly probing dense vegetation with an open bill.

NEW! Blue-crowned laughingthrush. Only 200 of these critically endangered songbirds remain in the wild, in a tiny area in

Blackbuck.

Komodo dragon.

Micaela Neal

Rodrigues fruit bat, Victoria crowned pigeon, Mandarin duck.

China. Its distinctive cry resembles laughter. Living in close-knit family groups, young birds help their parents feed and raise chicks.

Crane. The tallest flying bird, the sarus crane stands 6 feet (2 meters) tall and has an 8-foot (2.4-meter) wingspan. It's revered and considered a symbol of marital fidelity in India.

Crested wood partridge. This rotund, grapefruit-sized bird uses its feet to probe for insects and seeds.

Cuckoo. Unlike most cuckoos, the chestnut-breasted malkoha builds its own nest and raises its own young.

Deer. Hunted throughout history for its hide, meat, and impressive antlers, only a few thousand Eld's deer remain in a 15-square-mile (24 sq-km) Indian marsh. Its wide, spreadable hooves are perfect for wetland living.

Emerald tree monitor. This bright green tree-dweller is one of the few social monitor lizards. It removes the legs of stick insects before swallowing the bodies.

Fairy bluebird. This beautiful songbird has piercing red eyes; the male is iridescent blue and black. Its call is a liquid, two-note *"glue-it."*

Great argus pheasant. One of the largest pheasants at up to 6 feet (2 meters) long, it was named after the mythological Argus, the Greek hundred-eyed giant, for the eye-like pattern on its flight feathers.

Green-winged dove. Common in rainforests, the male courts females by dancing and bobbing his head.

Hooded pitta. This tiny black-and-green bird is about the size of a baseball. Though it's usually timid, it displays excitement by bowing, bobbing its head, flicking its wings and fanning its tail.

Junglefowl. The shy green junglefowl looks like a chicken with the plumage of a peacock. Its multicolored feathers are mainly metallic green and bronze; its comb and wattles are pastel blue, pink and purple.

Komodo dragon. At 10 feet (3 meters) long and 250 pounds (115 kg), this beast is the world's largest lizard. Its venom, combined with 57 types of dangerous bacteria that thrive in its mouth, makes its bite deadly. A tenacious predator, it hunts monkeys, horses, smaller Komodo dragons and other animals; in 20 minutes it can swallow a goat whole. It will also eat dead animals; it can smell them from six miles (10 km) away. Sometimes, it digs up human bodies from graves and devours them. Intelligent and curious, it plays by sticking its head into boxes and shoes.

Micaela Neal

Nicobar pigeon.

Mandarin duck. A pair of these colorful birds are a traditional wedding gift in Korea. A mother duck coaxes her ducklings to jump to the ground from their tree hollow nest; she then leads the youngsters to water.

Masked plover. Named for its distinctive yellow mask, this skittish wading bird sleeps for only a few minutes each day. It has a small yellow claw hidden in each wing; a false myth says the claws inject venom.

NEW! Monkey. With fewer than 2,500 animals remaining in the wild, the lion-tailed macaque is one of the rarest and most threatened primates. Its long tufted tail inspired its name; a silver-white mane is also lion-like. Males defend their territory with loud, whooping calls. The animal should debut along the walkway in late 2016.

Nicobar pigeon. This blue-green relative of the extinct dodo has long hackles that look like dreadlocks.

NEW! Parakeets. Bright yellow-green with a red head, the newly added Goldie's lorikeet looks like a tiny watermelon. Sometimes it sleeps on its back, legs sticking up in the air. The plum-headed parakeet likes to mimic electronic tones. Only the male's head is purple; the female's is gray.

Peacock. Also known as the dragonbird, the Java green peafowl hunts venomous snakes. Both the male and female are lavishly colored, but only the male has the iconic 6-foot (2-meter) train of feathers.

Pied imperial pigeon. This large black and white pigeon swallows fruits whole; its favorite food is figs. The male courts by inflating his neck and hopping in place.

Prehensile-tailed skink. See Rafiki's Planet Watch Animal Guide.

Shama thrush. A recording of this bird was one of the first of a bird song, in 1889 on an Edison wax cylinder.

Tiger. This endangered, 660-pound (300-kg) predator is the world's largest cat. Its unique stripe pattern is on both its fur and its skin. It can walk silently, leap 30 feet (9 meters), and drag 3,000 pounds (1,360 kg). A group of tigers is called an "ambush."

Victoria crowned pigeon. The world's largest pigeon, this blue turkey-sized bird is named after Queen Victoria. It has an unusual booming call, and sports a lacy white-tipped crest.

NEW! Water buffalo. The world's largest bovine, this ox relative has wide-splayed hooves to distribute its weight and keep it from sinking into the mud. Blanche, Dorothy and Rose, the trio of female water buffalo at the Maharajah Jungle Trek, were named after the three stars of the sitcom "The Golden Girls." Less than 4,000 water buffalo are left in the wild.

Julie Neal

Climbing a mountain.

Expedition Everest

Thrilling mountain coaster goes backward, angers Yeti

★★★★★ ✔ FP+ This smooth high-speed roller coaster climbs forward, zooms backward in the dark and takes some steep sweeping turns. What appears to be an old tea train zips you around, into and through a snow-capped mountain and narrowly escapes a snarling beast. Though you don't go upside down, your 4,000-foot (1,219-meter) journey climbs 200 feet (61 meters), stops twice, takes an 80-foot (24-meter) drop and hits 60 miles (97 km) per hour. It's a rush.

After dark the mountain glows with eerie oranges and purples. The completely dark track makes for a much scarier experience, as you can't see where you're going as you speed along; as you plummet down the big drop, you feel as if you're falling off the edge of the mountain into a black void. The illusion of the mountain's towering height is also enhanced, as the darkness makes it difficult to get a sense of scale by looking out at the rest of the park.

A monster myth. The coaster is more fun if you know its story, which—if you look for it—is told by props in the standby queue. The tale starts in the 1920s, as tea plantations begin to flourish along the mountains of the mythical Asian kingdom of Anandapur. A steam train line is established to carry the tea to villages, where it ships to distant markets. Soon, however, strange track snaps appear, which force the trains to shut down. Locals blame the British, claiming their attempts to reach the summit of nearby Mt. Everest has angered the Yeti, a creature they say guards the mountains. But today the rail line has reopened. Despite local protests, a bohemian American (known only as Bob) has restored the old tea trains for his Himalayan Escapes Tours and Expeditions, a new business that

Average wait times (standby line)

9a	10a	11a	12p	1p	2p	3p	4p	5p	6p	7p	8p	9p	10p	11p
15m	20m	45m	45m	35m	35m	35m	30m	30m	25m	25m	15m	10m	5m	---

Julie Neal

End of the line.

makes it easy for trekkers to get to Everest quickly. You're on his first train.

What could possibly go wrong?

Tips. *When to go:* At night. *Where to sit:* In the front seat for the best view and mildest ride; in back for the wildest experience. *How to save time:* Use the Single Rider line if you arrive at a busy time, don't have a FastPass, don't mind going by yourself and don't care where you sit; you'll get on right away.

Fun finds. ❶ Posters and other warnings from villagers urge you to cancel your trip. ❷ The height-minimum bar is a vertical Yeti footprint. A bar above it reads "You must be one Yeti foot tall to ride." ❸ In the queue, ringable bells hang from the red structure (a mandir) just past the first building. ❹ Each train pulls out with a "toot-toot!" ❺ On the lift hill, eerie music fills a small temple. ❻ As the track comes to an end, Yeti claw marks and footprints appear in snow to your right. ❼ Steam rises from each train's boiler after it pulls back into the boarding area.

Hidden Mickeys. In the queue ❶ as a hat on a Yeti doll in the Tashi's Trek and Tongba Shop, ❷ light switches in a nearby display of patches, ❸ a dent and holes in a tea kettle in the Yeti Museum, ❹ a black mark mixed with animal tracks in a Documenting Bio-Diversity display, under a Small Mammal Tracks sign and ❺ with a sorcerer's hat as stains in a photo of a woman with a walkie-talkie. ❻ In the gift shop, as carved yellow spheres at the bottom of both sides of a merchandise display across from the photo-pickup area.

A closer look. Yetis are not real; scientists agree there is no credible evidence they exist. The Yeti legend, however, indeed exists. For centuries, Himalayans have told stories about a humanoid monster that fiercely guards the area around Mt. Everest. Reports increased in the 20th century when Westerners began seeing an "Abominable Snowman." Interest peaked in 1960, when Sir Edmund Hillary's fact-finding trip to the peak brought trip-wire and time-lapse cameras but found nothing. The villain of 1964's stop-motion classic "Rudolph the Red-Nosed Reindeer" is a Yeti named Bumbles. The 2001 Disney/Pixar film "Monsters, Inc." includes an Abominable Snowman voiced by John Ratzenberger.

Key facts. *Duration:* 3 min. *Capacity:* 34 per train (5 cars seat 6, one 4). *Queue:* Indoor, outdoor, mostly covered. *Fear factor:* High lift, often dark, threatening monster, 1 steep drop. *Restraint:* Lap bar. *Top speed:* 60 mph (97 kph). *Weather issues:* Closed during thunderstorms. *Health advisory:* Avoid if pregnant or have back, blood pressure, heart, motion sickness or neck problems. *Access:* Height min 44 in (112 cm); wheelchair, ECV users must transfer. *Debuted:* 2006. *Location:* Serka Zong.

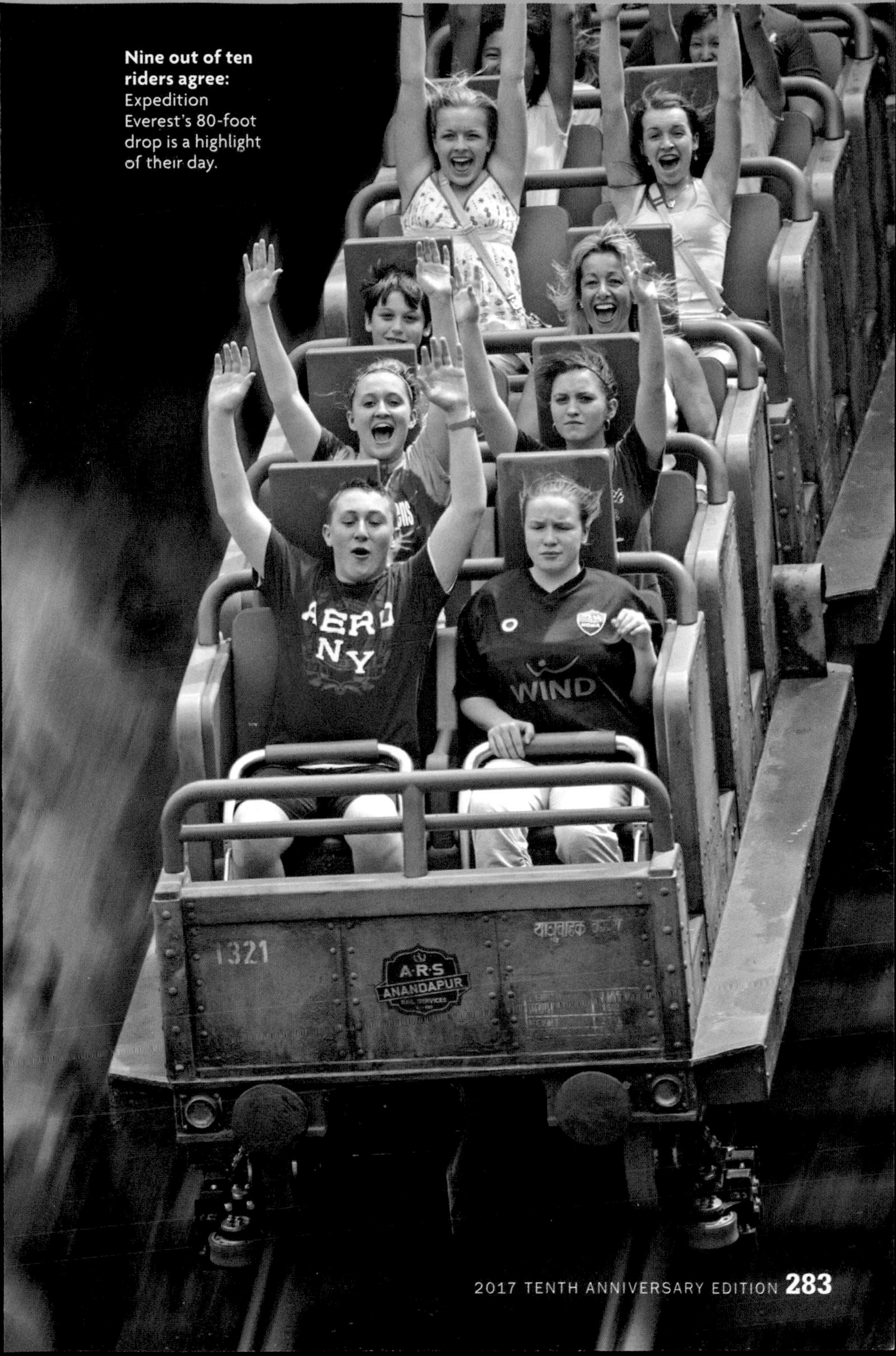
AERO
NY
WIND
1321
A·R·S
ANANDAPUR
RAIL SERVICES

Nine out of ten riders agree: Expedition Everest's 80-foot drop is a highlight of their day.

Peacock dancer.

The Jungle Book: Alive with Magic

Hooray for Bollywood! And this flashy, splashy placeholder.

★★★★ ✔ FP+ Think of it as a Broadway musical spectacular, but on water. With singers and dancers and costumes and lights, musicians and fire and drama and frights.

And water screens. Of course.

Spiced with an Indian sense of showmanship, the show freely mixes melodramatic moments with catchy song-and-dance numbers and a sacred-cowful of eye candy.

Dancers perform right in front of you, on four floating stages that line the shore. Musicians sit at the sides of the stages, banging drums, playing flutes, ringing bells. Out in the lake, singers channel Baloo, King Louie and Kaa as dancers near and far interpret their words. Moving floats bring the heat: bare-chested guys twirling fire batons. Water screens add drama, as do, in a surprising moment, some trees on the far side of the lake.

Songs are familiar yet inventive. In "Trust in Me," a sultry female singer and multiple sinuous dancers portray Kaa, the snake. Shuffling hoofers twirl parasols to "I Wanna Be Like You," which keeps its Dixieland swing. Costumes are elaborate; lighting is subtle yet ever-changing. And then there are all these little extras: handheld candles, tiny dots of makeup, fans that turn dancers into peacocks.

On the downside, the show relies on foggy water screens and echoing audio to tell its story. If you don't know it when you arrive, you still won't when you leave.

When last-minute snafus delayed the debut of the Rivers of Light spectacle, Disney created this one in just 30 days. It's scheduled to run only until Rivers of Light is ready to go.

Tips. *To get a good seat:* Get in the Standby line two hours early; if you have a FastPass or dining package (disneyworld.com, 407-939-3463) an hour early. Standby and dining viewers line up in DinoLand U.S.A. and sit on the left side of the theater. FastPass holders queue in Asia and sit on the right. *To avoid a huge crowd:* If there are two shows on your night, see the second one.

Key facts. *Duration:* 25 min. *Capacity:* 5,000. *Fear factor:* Real and simulated fire. *Weather issues:* Shortened by mist, canceled by rain or thunderstorm. *Access:* Wheelchairs, ECVs OK. *Disability services:* Assistive listening. *Location:* Discovery River Theater, in front of Expedition Everest.

Kaa, the snake charmer.

Cementosaurus.

Primeval Whirl. Chester & Hester's Dino-Rama.

DinoLand U.S.A.

A love letter to all things dinosaur. That's what DinoLand U.S.A is, or at least what it appears to be at first glance. But look again and you'll see it's also something else: a sly parody of stuffy science centers, tacky tourist traps, and corny country carnivals. Places that once flourished throughout the U.S.A. until the mighty mouse stepped in and, for the most part, squashed them like bugs.

In other words, here Disney is mocking its old small-time rivals. Pointing out how inferior they were. Showing off what Disney was not, is not and has no plans ever to be. By being exactly that.

Confusing? You betcha. Especially since no map, times guide or cast member ever points any of this out to you. Like so much else at Disney's Animal Kingdom, you're supposed to discover it on your own.

Disney intends that you wander the land, and slowly notice how nothing seems to be like a Disney park at all. The lobby of the Dino Institute is dusty, its dioramas plastic. Zoo animals live in plain-Jane habitats. Food stands have names such as Dino-Bite Snacks.

You chat with a carny. The woman tells you that the cracked, striped asphalt you're standing on really is an old parking lot, one she used years ago. You believe her.

And then suddenly it hits you. "Aha! I see what they're up to here! It's supposed to be old-fashioned! It's meant to be cheap! This parking lot was designed to boil my feet! Those Disney devils! What a crafty bunch!"

Diggin' up bones. The story begins in 1947, when an amateur fossil-hunter named Chester discovered dinosaur bones near his Diggs County gas station. Realizing the importance of his find, he and some scientist friends banded together to buy the site as well as an old fishing lodge—creating the Dino Institute, a non-profit organization dedicated to the "Exploration, Excavation and Exultation" of dinosaur fossils.

During the 1970s the Institute received a generous grant from McDonald's (yes, product placement even in a fictional story), which enabled it to build a formal museum and research center, and develop a new archeological technique: time travel. It turned its old building into a cafeteria for its graduate students; adjacent structures became a dorm and garage. Soon the entire area opened to the public as DinoLand U.S.A., a "dinosaur discovery park." Visitors poured in.

But then Chester developed a new interest: money. Teaming up with his wife Hester, he transformed his gas station into a souvenir stand. Grotesquely gaudy, Chester & Hester's Dinosaur Treasures was an "Emporium of Extinction," selling trinkets small in value but high in profit potential. Tourists packed the place, so much so that soon Chester built a large parking lot in front of it. As the couple's fortunes grew, the embarrassed Dino Institute pressured it to sell its station and move away.

But Chester and Hester refused. Not only that, they retaliated, turning their parking lot into Chester & Hester's Dino-Rama (a play on "diorama"), a cheesy carnival that mocked the scientists' time-travel efforts. Today the Institute still welcomes visitors, and Chester & Hester's cousins run the Dino-Rama.

A paper trail of notes and scribbles tells an additional story about three grad students.

Like pieces of a puzzle, its details hide on bulletin boards, clipboards and whiteboards around and inside the Boneyard playground and Restaurantosaurus eatery.

It's not all a joke. According to Imagineer Joe Rohde, in a subtle way DinoLand U.S.A. represents the conflict between order and chaos, authority and disobedience.

Nightlife. DJ Dino-Mite stands on top of a pickup truck; music includes the Chicken Dance, Disney songs (i.e., "I Wanna Be Like You"), "Party Rock Anthem." A crowd gathers, but there's a problem: Unlike the live bands in Discovery Island and Africa, the DJ has no entourage of dancers to encourage his group to dance. Children play with hula hoops. Parents tap their toes. Everyone is dying to get up and boogie but no one is willing to go first. All this needs is some dancing dino dames (hey, I'm female, I can say "dame") showing everyone how to wiggle their tails and— voila!—party rock is in the house tonight! The DJ performs intermittently typically from 7:30 to 10 p.m. in front of Chester & Hester's Dinosaur Treasures gift shop.

Fun finds. ❶ "Lost—My Tail" reads a note on a bulletin board across from the Boneyard. It's from the apatosaurus cast over the land's entrance, which has a disconnected tailbone. ❷ A folk-art Cementosaurus stands across from the Dino-Rama. Two baby dinos hide

♦

Coke cart Cementosaurus art.

The Dino Institute.

underneath it. ❶ne is hatching. ❸ At Restaurantosaurus, ambient music includes the 1988 Was Not Was hit "Walk the Dinosaur," proto-punk icon Jonathan Richman's "I'm a Little Dinosaur" and "Ugga Bugga," a Springsteen-like tune by Barnes and Barnes, a band led by one-time child television star Bill Mumy. ❹ Chester and Hester appear on a poster in the main dining hall. ❺ Greasy hand prints form dinosaur shapes on the walls of the Quonset hut garage, as do ❻ cans of Sinclair Litholine Multi-Purpose Grease and Dynoil ("keep your old dinosaur running"). ❼ A hangout for grad students, a rec room includes posters for bands Dinosaur Jr. and T Rex ❽ and a juke box filled with songs such as "Dust in the Wind." ❾ ❶utside the room, students have rearranged the letters in the word AIRSTREAM on the back of its converted travel trailer to read I ARE SMART. ❿ Four sketches for "The Rite of Spring" sequence in Disney's 1940 film "Fantasia" hang by the restrooms. ⓫ Gas is 29.9 cents a gallon on rusty pumps in front of Dinosaur Treasures as well as on a painted-over sign on its rear roof. ⓬ "Rough scaly skin... Making you groan?... Don't despair... Use Fossil Foam" read four sequential signs hanging above the shop's entrance from one direction; "When in Florida... Be sure to... Visit... Epcot" from the other. ⓭ Boxes above garage doors read "Chester's dig '47," "Chester's pet rocks 1966" and "Train Parts. ⓮ Items turned into dinosaurs on the walls include an oil funnel and ⓯ gas-pump nozzle. ⓰ Above the main room, tiny plastic dinos ride trains, snow ski and flee lava flows. ⓱ Chester and Hester appear in a photo on a wall. ⓲ Ambient music in the shop and its restrooms includes The Hoosier Hot Shots' 1935 ditty "I Like Bananas Because They Have No Bones" (*"I don't like your peaches; they are full of stones. I like bananas because they have no bones."*) ⓳ A road sign identifies the main walkway as U.S. 498, a reference to the park's opening in April, 1998.

Hidden Mickeys. ❶ As cracks in the asphalt next to the Cementosaurus. ❷ On the back of the statue, on a Steamboat Willie cast-member pin on its fourth hump. ❸ As a half-dollar sized orange rock in the concrete, to the right of the leftmost post in front of Dinosaur Treasures, near the restrooms.

Restaurants and food

Sadly, DinoLand U.S.A. has the least inspired food in the park—or perhaps that's the idea: **★★ $15 DDPq Restaurantosaurus.** It's such a shame—matching the park's most memorably wacky decor with its most forgettable food. Burgers, chicken and hot dogs. *11a–11p; $9–$13 (children $7–$8). Seats 750, including 104 outside in mostly shady areas.* **★★ $10 DDPs Corn-Ivores.** Popcorn stand. *11a–10p; $4–$8. Dino-Rama.* **★★★ ✔ $9 DDPs Dino-Bite Snacks.** Hand-scooped Häagen-Dazs waffle cones and other ice cream treats, including a Bug Sundae with gummy worms and cookie crumbles. *11a–11p; $5. 50 seats on a covered outdoor deck. In front of Restaurantosaurus.* **★★ $11 DDPs Dino Diner.** Vintage travel trailer sells nachos, glazed nuts, frozen drinks. *11a–10p; $5–$8. Dino-Rama.* **★★★ $10 DDPs Trilo-Bites.** Buffalo chicken waffle sliders, waffle sundaes, beer. *11a–10p; $5–$6. Across from the Boneyard.*

Shops and merchandise

Two shops offer loads of dinosaur merchandise, mostly toys but some apparel.

Chester & Hester's Dinosaur Treasures. Toy dinos as well as plenty of other things for kids—Disney games, novelty hats, plushies and candy. *Across from Primeval Whirl.*

The Dino Institute Gift Shop. Fossils and paintings of dinosaur skeletons lit with track lighting decorate this classy store, which resembles a museum gift shop. A giant sea turtle skeleton hangs from the ceiling. Dinosaur items dominate the store, from apparel to plush, books to puppets. Souvenir ride photos. *At the exit to the Dinosaur ride.*

Animal guide

Fittingly, DinoLand U.S.A.'s animal habitats are straight out of the 1970s, uninspired with lots of concrete. They hold three creatures.

Abdim's stork. Named for Turkish Governor Bey El-Arnaut Abdim, this wading bird is seen as a harbinger of rain and good luck to native Africans.

American crocodile. Growing up to 18 feet (5.5 meters) and 2,000 pounds (907 kg), this large predator cannot survive extreme low temperatures. A 2009 cold spell killed off 150 American crocs in Florida, including Wilma, a famous female on Sanibel Island, the author's hometown.

Asian brown tortoise. This primitive reptile, also known as the Burmese black tortoise, provides more parental care than any other tortoise.

Restaurantosaurus Airstream trailer.

Swinging into a slide. Atop the Boneyard playground.

The Boneyard

Disney's best playground is themed to an archaeological dig

★★★★★ ✔ Geared for toddlers through elementary-school kids, this large outdoor playground is themed to be a dinosaur dig site. Two distinct areas are connected by an overhead footbridge. Highlights include a three-story tower of nets and slides and a sandy pit where kids dig for mammoth bones.

Extras include a maze of tunnels, walls embedded with dinosaur skeletons, climb-on bones and rocks, steep net and rope-climbing ramps and waterfalls just right to drench a young head. Mesh canopies filter the sun, and the flooring is a spongy material that stays cool and won't harm tumbling youngsters. Overhead fans keep things breezy. An abundance of nooks and crannies makes it easy to lose sight of your child, but there's only one exit and its gate is always monitored.

Tips. *When to go:* Anytime, though cooler periods are always more comfortable. *Where to sit:* There are many places for parents to get off their feet and relax, including multiple picnic tables and a ledge that surrounds the sandy dig area.

Fun finds. ❶ Notes sound when kids bang a "xylobone" in a wall near a Jeep. ❷ Nearby dino tracks trigger roars when children step on them. ❸ On a whiteboard along the top back wall, the dig site's three fictional grad students and their professors have posted their findings and work schedules. ❹ As heard on pirate radio station W-DINO, the playground's ambient music includes "Brontosaurus," an obscure 1970 tune by The Move, the British band that would later become classical-pop fusion hitmakers The Electric Light Orchestra, and the 1977 hit "Godzilla" (*"Oh no! There goes Tokyo! Go go Godzilla!"*) by Blue Oyster Cult.

Hidden Mickeys. ❶ Mickey's three circles appear at the entrance as a big stain under a drinking fountain, ❷ as a quarter and two pennies on a table in a fenced-off area on the second level by the slides ❸ and as a fan and two hardhats in a fenced-off area at the back of the mammoth-bone pit.

Key facts. *Duration:* Allow 15–30 min. *Capacity:* 500. *Operating hours:* May open 1 hour after park open. *Weather issues:* Closed during thunderstorms. *Debuted:* 1998. *Access:* Wheelchairs, ECVs OK. *Location:* Dino Institute, near Discovery Island.

© Disney

An angry carnotaurus threatens you on Dinosaur.

Dinosaur!

A carnotaurus stalks you in this bumpy, dark, scary ride

UPDATED! ★★★★ ✔ FP+ Ferocious dinosaurs chase you in this tense dark ride. As your vehicle (a motion simulator on a track) careens through a primeval forest, asteroids rain from the sky, raptors threaten you, a carnotaurus chases you. Smoke cannons, strobe lights and loud sounds ratchet up the thrills.

The adventure begins at the stuffy Dino Institute Discovery Center, a 1970s-style museum. After a multimedia show explains that an asteroid shower wiped out dinosaurs long ago, the museum's director announces that, thanks to a new time-traveling vehicle, you can safely go back to that time yourself. But when her sneaky assistant Grant Seeker reprograms your ride, all heck breaks loose

A recent update added a smoky tunnel of green spiraling light to a time-machine portal at the beginning of the ride, and a few additional raptors to the first dinosaur scene.

Tips. *Where to sit:* Ask for the front seat for the best view and most legroom.

Fun finds. ① A cast of the largest, most complete T-Rex ever found (Sue, 1990) stands in front of the ride. ② In the boarding area, red, yellow and white pipes are marked with the chemical makeups of ketchup, mustard and mayonnaise—a nod to McDonald's, the ride's original sponsor.

Hidden Mickey. His shape hides in a mural in the first lobby, as marks on a tree trunk.

Key facts. *Duration:* 3 min, 30 sec. *Capacity:* 144 per hour. *Queue:* Indoor. *Fear factor:* Intense, loud, jerky, dark. *Restraint:* Seat belt. *Debuted:* 1998. *Health advisory:* You should be free from motion sickness; pregnancy; high blood pressure; heart, back or neck problems. *Access:* Height min 40 in (102 cm); wheelchair and ECV users must transfer. *Disability services:* Assistive listening, video captioning.

Average wait times (standby line)

9a	10a	11a	12p	1p	2p	3p	4p	5p	6p	7p	8p	9p	10p	11p
10m	35m	40m	50m	35m	30m	30m	20m	10m	10m	10m	10m	10m	5m	---

© Disrey

A time machine spins as it zig-zags down a narrow track on Primeval Whirl.

Primeval Whirl

Silly spinning coaster is twice the fun after dark

★★★ FP+ A kitschy journey back to the moment when dinosaurs became extinct, this quirky roller coaster combines the thrills of an old-school Wild Mouse with the spins of a Disney tea cup. You'll often feel like you're about to fall off its narrow track, as its wide cars whip around turns as they build speed.

According to Disney lore, Primeval Whirl is the work of local low-brow gasoline station owners Chester and Hester; their dime-store Dino-Rama dupe of the real time machine at the nearby Dino Institute.

Tips. *When to go:* At night. Its cartoon clocks, spinning vortices, dinosaur cut-outs warning "The End is Near" and hundreds of little white lights stand out way more after dark. *How to spin fast:* Put the heaviest person in your group at one side. *For families:* If you have a child who's nervous about roller coasters, have them sit in the middle. *For couples:* You're jerked and thrown together throughout the ride, as the seats form two cozy couple spots. *Queasy?* Stare at the center of the dash to keep your dizziness at bay.

Fun finds. ❶ In the queue, hub caps and egg beaters decorate a cartoonish time portal. ❷ Each candy-colored "Time Machine" ride vehicle includes the fins and chrome of a 1950s car and the huge reflectors of a retro bicycle. ❸ On its dash sits an old alarm clock, clock radio, egg timer and table radio.

Key facts. *Duration:* 2 min, 30 sec. *Capacity:* 104 on 2 tracks (4 per car). *Queue:* Outdoor, covered. *Fear factor:* Jerky, spins, 1 steep drop. *Restraint:* Lap bar. *Top speed:* 29 mph (47 kph). *Weather issues:* Closed during thunderstorms. *Debuted:* 2002. *Health advisory:* Avoid if pregnant or have back, blood pressure, heart, motion sickness or neck problems. *Access:* Height min 48 in (122 cm); wheelchair and ECV users transfer. *Location:* Chester & Hester's Dino-Rama.

Average wait times (standby line)

9a	10a	11a	12p	1p	2p	3p	4p	5p	6p	7p	8p	9p	10p	11p
10m	35m	35m	35m	40m	40m	40m	30m	30m	25m	25m	20m	10m	5m	---

Double Dumbo. Unlike the Flying Elephants, TriceraTop Spin dinos seat four.

TriceraTop Spin

An underrated hub-and-spoker perfect for young families

★★★★★ ✔ Circling around a colorful spinning-top tin toy, you and up to three other passengers ride in a chubby triceratops that climbs, dips and dives at your command. Eye candy includes playful dinosaurs that pop out of the spinning top, flying cartoon comets that circle around it and, at night, small white bulbs that line the hub and spokes and light everything up. Manic banjo and fiddle music adds a wacky cornpone touch.

Though the ride lacks the classic charm of Magic Kingdom's similar Dumbo the Flying Elephant, it's easier to enjoy. There's never a long wait; in fact there's often no wait at all, especially first thing in the morning. And since each vehicle seats four, small families can ride together. Though Disney purists dismiss the ride as too cheesy, younger children will love it. And after all, cheesy is the whole point of the Dino-Rama area, which is Disney's riff on a cheap roadside carnival.

Tips. *When to go:* Anytime except the hottest part of the day, when the asphalt "parking lot" of this carnival reflects just too much heat. *Where to sit:* In the front seat for the most legroom, in back to control the height of your dino. *For families:* TriceraTop Spin is the only ride at the park that is completely toddler friendly, with nothing scary and no height minimum. *For couples:* Ride this to give you an excuse to touch; the cozy seats force you to squeeze together.

Fun fact. The vehicles circle every 13 seconds. That's the same speed as Dumbo and Aladdin's Magic Carpets, half the pace of the rockets of Astro Orbiter.

Key facts. *Duration:* 90 sec. *Capacity:* 64 (4 per car, seated two across). *Queue:* Outdoor, covered. *Weather issues:* Closed during thunderstorms. *Debuted:* 2001. *Access:* ECV users must transfer. *Location:* Chester & Hester's Dino-Rama.

Average wait times

9a	10a	11a	12p	1p	2p	3p	4p	5p	6p	7p	8p	9p	10p	11p
5m	5m	5m	5m	5m	5m	15m	10m	10m	10m	10m	10m	10m	5m	---

Step right up. Dino-Rama's Fossil Fun Games cost a few bucks to play, but aren't rigged.

Fossil Fun Games

Fair midway games that children can beat

★★★ ✔ The centerpiece of the tongue-in-cheek Chester & Hester's Dino-Rama carnival, these five midway games reward winners with prizes. Compared to actual carnival games they're easy. In fact, three are designed specifically for kids: the watergun-powered Fossil Fueler, ball-rolling racing derby Mammoth Marathon and frenetic mallet-striker Whac-A-Pachycephalosaur ("Whacky Packy" for short). Two others, a ball toss and a basketball throw, require serious skills to win.

Tips. *Fossil Fueler:* To increase your odds of winning the game, use your free hand to cradle your gun barrel and shoot straight. *Mammoth Marathon:* Ask for a practice ball beforehand. Roll your balls slowly. *Whac-A-Pachycephalosaur:*

Wait until you see a dino head pop up before you swing at it; don't try to anticipate.

Key facts. *Duration:* 1 min. *Cost:* $3–4. *Players:* 1–10. *Weather issues:* Closed during thunderstorms. *Debuted:* 2002. *Access:* Players may remain in wheelchairs, ECVs. *Location:* Chester & Hester's Dino-Rama.

Bruce.

Nemo and Marlin.

Finding Nemo—The Musical

The movie as a song-and-dance puppet show. And it works.

★★★★★ ✔ FP+ Shimmying sharks, body-surfing turtles and a bicycle-riding stingray star in this colorful, whimsical stage show, which re-creates the 2003 Pixar movie "Finding Nemo" as a musical. Nine songs tell the story with help from acrobats, dancers and huge mechanical puppets. Broadway-quality but for its length, the show is funny, touching and a visual treat.

Main characters are represented by live performers, who act out their roles while operating large puppet versions of themselves. Others are portrayed using a variety of puppetry styles, including bunraku, a Japanese form in which one huge puppet is operated by multiple puppeteers. The production takes place in the enclosed Theater in the Wild.

Tips. *When to go:* Get a Fastpass; holders get to enter the theater 20 to 30 minutes early. If you can't, arrive at least 30 minutes early; the last show of the day is usually the least crowded. Food is allowed in line but not inside the theater. *Where to sit:* In the middle of the auditorium to see the full spectacle; along the center catwalk to be immersed in it.

Fun finds. ❶ Before the show begins, Nemo swims back and forth through oversized bubbles on the sides of the stage. ❷ As you leave, the movie's gulls ("Mine?... Mine?") bid you goodbye ("Bye?... Bye?"). Just like the film's birds, they're voiced by "Finding Nemo" director Andrew Stanton.

Hidden Mickey. Mickey's shape appears as three blue bubbles, two lit and one drawn, at the bottom left of the stage wall.

Key facts. *Duration:* 30 min. *Capacity:* 1,500. *Queue:* Outdoor, uncovered. *Showtimes:* Mid-morning to early evening. *Debuted:* 2007. *Access:* Wheelchairs, ECVs OK. *Disability services:* Reflective captioning. *Location:* Along the walkway to Asia, past Chester & Hester's Dino-Rama.

Typical show times

9a	10a	11a	12p	1p	2p	3p	4p	5p	6p	7p	8p	9p	10p	11p
---	---	---	12:00	1:00	2:00	---	4:00	5:00	---	7:00	---	---	---	---

Mayday Falls.

Water Parks

GIGGLES, LAUGHS AND SQUEALS fill the air at Blizzard Beach and Typhoon Lagoon, Walt Disney World's two water parks. Close your eyes and you'll hear a unique serenade of happy people enjoying life. Why? Because it's just so much fun to play in water, especially with people you care about.

The United States has more than a thousand water parks, but few offer such an immersive experience as these two. Plastic culverts appear to be streams and rivers, their steel supports hidden under forested hills. Offbeat pop songs provide a fun back beat. Everywhere you look is spic-and-span.

How do the parks compare? Sunny and spacious, Blizzard Beach has longer and faster slides with many height minimums, a better preteen spot and a wackier theme. Shady and intimate, Typhoon Lagoon offers bigger waves, a better toddler spot and a wider variety of attractions, only two of which restrict visitors by their height.

Highs. ❶ Whether it's a multi-person tube slide, a side-by-side mat race or simply a makeshift Monkey in the Middle game in a pool, Disney's water parks offer many ways for you to interact with your partner, children or friends. ❷ Disney's lazy rivers let you drift away in dappled shade, and there's hardly ever a wait. ❸ The scariest attraction in all of Walt Disney World is Summit Plummet at Blizzard Beach. The most fun? For many, it's the wave pool at Typhoon Lagoon. ❹ Unlike the passive "here we are now entertain us" attractions common in theme parks, water-park experiences often demand you get off your rear end and actually do something. Such as swim, slide, splash, snorkel or surf.

Lows. ❶ The food. Except for some creative snacks, the food at Disney water parks is overpriced and uninspired. ❷ The lines. If you don't plan your day right, long waits for the waterslides can definitely put a damper on your fun. ❸ The stairs. Tummy not toned? Butt not buff? You'll be huffin' and puffin' as you climb many hot, sunny stairways.

Planning your day. Regardless of whether you visit Blizzard Beach or Typhoon Lagoon, be prepared for a workout. Though both parks are smaller than any of the Disney theme parks and require less walking, their attractions are more physical. Queues often wind up stairs in direct sun. And you'll be outside all day; the only indoor spots are the restrooms and the main gift shops.

Cooler days. Colder days can be enjoyable. Except for the 70-degree (21° Celsius) pools of Typhoon Lagoon's Shark Reef, all of Disney's water-park water is heated to 80 degrees (27° Celsius).

Tickets. As of July 2016, an adult ticket good for admission to both parks in the same day costs $55 for most of the year, $60 during the summer (the end of May through the end of August). Tickets for children ages 3–9 are $49 and $54. Those under 3 are admitted free.

If you already have a ticket to a Disney theme park, you can add to it what Disney calls the Water Park Fun & More option. It gives you one admission per day of your ticket to either a water park, miniature golf course (before 4 p.m.), ESPN or a round of golf at the 9-hole Oak Trail golf course. It adds $64 to the cost of a one-day Magic Kingdom ticket, $72 to a longer Magic Kingdom ticket, and $72 to any other theme-park ticket regardless of length. Water park annual passes cost $115 for adults and children. Water-park annual passes that are good only after 2 p.m. are $69. Most prices are discounted for Florida residents and members of the U.S. military.

What to bring with you. We say travel light—just a cap or hat, wallet or purse, sunscreen and swimsuit (Disney does not allow suits with rivets, buckles or exposed metal; or string-back or thong suits). Consider rash guards to protect skin from burns and scrapes, especially for children. A towel is a must, but you can rent one for $2. Want to bring more? Disney will let you haul in a cooler, food, small toys, strollers, towels and wheelchairs, but not alcohol, boogie boards, glass containers, tubes or water toys.

How to avoid the crowd. The two most popular water parks in the world, Blizzard Beach and Typhoon Lagoon each attract about 8,000 visitors a day. Such crowds often make empty beach chairs tough to find, and create lines for slides that are just ridiculous. At a theme park few people would wait in line 40 minutes for a 10-second ride, but at a water park people do it every day. To avoid these crowds, follow these four steps:

Arrive at the park before it opens. Get there 45 minutes before it officially opens, which is typically 9 or 10 a.m. This gives you time to park, walk to the entrance, scan your ticket or MagicBand, and rent a locker and towels at a relaxed pace, while still staying ahead of the masses (at both water parks, the entrance usually opens 15 minutes early).

Snare your chairs, then hit the slides. You'll have your choice of chairs, including some by the pool and others back in the shade. Waiting lines at the slides will be short or nonexistent, so you can do them all before noon.

Do pools and rivers after lunch. Same for playgrounds. They all get crowded on busy days, but none of them ever have lines.

If there's a storm, wait it out. Most guests will leave, unaware that in Florida a thunderstorm usually lasts about an hour, and is followed by a clear sky. Once it is over you'll have the park almost all to yourself.

Sitting down. Each park has hundreds of beach chairs and their use is complimentary. But those in good spots get taken very early.

Reserved seats. Both parks rent reserved covered patios or decks but they cost a pretty penny—$345 a day for up to 6 people ($200 after 2 p.m.) with additional users (up to 10) $25 each. For that you get 6 cushioned chairs including 2 lounge chairs, a table, a cooler stocked with water, a locker rental, towels, refillable soft-drink mugs and an attendant who stops by every 20 minutes. Handy for families with very young or elderly members, the spots often sell out in the summer. Reserve one at 407-939-7529 up to 90 days early.

Best seats. The best spot at Blizzard Beach is patio No. 4, a secluded, shady alcove near the chairlift, preteen area and toddler zone. The best spots at Typhoon Lagoon are cabanas No. 2 (very shady, next to a large strangler fig, overlooks the lazy river) and No. 3 (a wood deck under a large umbrella on the bank of the river, with a nice view of the surf pool). For $55 you can reserve a smaller spot, with two lounge chairs, a small table and a beach umbrella. It probably won't be conveniently located or offer any real views.

Drinking up. A refillable soft-drink mug is $10.75. It's good for one day but can be renewed

Melt-Away Bay.

for $6.50. Both parks sell beer and mixed drinks with, alas, no all-you-can-drink option.

Seasonal closures. Both parks close for maintenance. Typhoon Lagoon usually shuts down in November and December, Blizzard Beach in January and February.

What if it rains? If lightning strikes within five miles of a water park Disney will close its rides and clear its pools. If the attractions close for 30 minutes or more, if you've been in a park less than four hours you can get a rain check (from Guest Relations stands and ticket booths) good for a future entry anytime within one year; all members of your party then have to leave. You can't get a rain check on a day you've used a previous one to get in.

Family matters. Almost nowhere offers a better place for families to bond than a Disney water park. There are, however, a few issues parents should be aware of.

Age restriction. To enter a park, visitors under age 14 must be with someone at least 18.

Life jackets. Disney offers use of standard life jackets at no charge. The parks do permit guests to bring in water wings, even though those swimming aids are easy to puncture.

Lost children. Easy to identify by their distinctive uniforms and name tags, Disney cast members take lost children to marked areas at the front of each park. To avoid losing their kids, some families arrange ahead of time to meet in a specific spot at a specific time in case if they lose track of each other.

Rafts and toys. Disney doesn't let you bring in rafts or air-filled toys. It provide rafts, tubes and mats at rides made for them.

Swim diapers. Infants and toddlers who are not potty-trained are required to wear plastic swim diapers. Gift shops sell them.

Blizzard Beach

A towering ski jump. Snow-covered ski slopes. A mountainside chairlift. They all combine to create the illusion that this 60-acre (24-ha) water park is a really a melting snow-ski resort. But in reality, of course, it's a whimsical hot-weather haven. Carved out of a forest of pine trees, it's the second-most-popular water park in the world, attracting nearly 2 million visitors a year. Disney's Winter Summerland miniature golf course sits in front of it.

Attractions. Below, each attraction is rated from one to five stars (★) based on how well it lives up to its promise. A checkmark (✓) indicates an author favorite.

★★★★ ✓ **Cross Country Creek.** Lined with evergreens, this shady floating stream circles the park as it flows under bridges, over springs, past a squirting snowmaking machine and through a cave with ice-cold dripping water. Seven entry points offer complimentary tubes. *25 min (round trip). 3,000 ft (914 m), 15 ft (5 m) wide, 2.5 ft (1 m) deep, max speed 2 mph (3 kph). Fear factor: None.*

★★★ **Downhill Double Dipper.** You'll drop down a short tunnel, drop down again, then shoot through a curtain of water... all as you race against someone next to you in these steep, enclosed tube slides. Alpine cowbells cheer you on as you leave the gate just like at a real slalom race; a finish-line scoreboard flashes your time. Thrill-seeking youngsters love it. Pull up on your tube handles just before the catch pool to fly across the water. *6 sec. 230 ft (70 m), 50 ft (15 m) drop, max speed 25 mph (40 kph). Fear factor: You feel out of control. Height min 48 in (122 cm).*

★★★ ✔ **Melt-Away Bay.** Nestled against the base of Mt. Gushmore, a 90-foot (27-meter) snow-capped peak, this swimming pool appears to be created by streams of melting snow. Bobbing waves wash through the pool for 45 minutes of every hour; a sandy sunbathing beach lines one side. The pool's shallow beachside entry makes it easy for young children to enter it. *Unlimited time. 1 ac (.5 ha). Fear factor: None.*

★★★★ ✔ **Runoff Rapids.** Banked curves make you feel like a bobsledder on these three banked tube slides. Two open ones allow two-person tubes perfect for a young couple or parent and child; an enclosed one-person slide is a dark plastic pipe lit by pin lights which give it a weird Space Mountain effect. Reached by a back-of-Mount-Gushmore climb up 127 steps, Runoff Rapids is worth every huff and puff. *600 ft (183 m). Fear factor: Enclosed tube may feel claustrophobic.*

★★★★★ ✔ **Ski Patrol Training Camp.** This inventive collection of experiences for preteens is a gem. At Fahrenheit Drop, kids hold on to a sliding T-bar that drops them into an 8-foot (2-meter) pool; the ride has two bars, which move over the water at different heights. At the Thin Ice Training Course, overhead rope grids help kids hang on as they walk over slippery floating icebergs. As for tube slides, Snow Falls has wide ones for the timid, Cool Runners has the brief bumpy kind. A short enclosed body slide, Frozen Pipe Springs plops riders out a few inches above its pool. Children can see each ride before choosing it. *Unlimited time. Fear factor: None.*

★★★★ ✔ **Slush Gusher.** Looking like a gully covered in slushy snow, this steep body slide starts off slow but gives fully grown riders some airtime off its second drop; the heavier the rider, the wilder the flight. A viewing area at the end has covered bleachers. Visible from most of the park, Slush Gusher

Downhill Double Dipper.

Toboggan Racers.

is easy for kids to evaluate ("I am definitely doing that!") before they get in line. *2 drops. 11–13 sec. 250 ft (76 m), 90 ft (27 m) drop, max speed 50 mph (80 kph). Fear factor: Scary second drop. Height minimum 48 in (122 cm).*

★★★★ ✔ **Snow Stormers.** You lie face-first and speed down S-curves on these fast high-banked mat slides, three side-by-side courses that make it easy for family or friends to race each other. To win, keep your elbows on your mat and your feet up. As you careen up corners water splashing in your face makes it tough to see; a horizontal line on the wall helps you keep your bearings. *15–20 sec. 350 ft (107 m). Fear factor: Fast, disorienting.*

★★★★★ ✔ **Summit Plummet.** The scari-est ride in all of Walt Disney World, this very steep 12-story body slide is Disney's true tower of terror. Lying down at the top of what looks like a ski jump, you cross your arms and feet then push yourself over the edge. The sky and scenery blur as you fall; the water around you roars as you splash down. The impact can send much of your swimsuit where the sun never shines; wear a T-shirt or rash guard to avoid stinging your skin.

One of the tallest and fastest slides in the United States, Summit Plummet has no exit stairway; those who chicken out squeeze back down the crowded entrance steps in what cast members privately refer to as the "walk of shame." The launch tower rises only 30 feet (9 meters) above Mt. Gushmore and just 120 feet (37 meters) over the park, but it seems much taller. The fall is so intense even some of its designers don't care for it. Disney Imagineer Kathy Rogers told me that during its construction "I made the mistake of going up the stairs and looking down. I thought, 'There's no way I'd put my body in there!' I did it once and said, 'Done!'"

It's easy to determine if Summit Plummet is a ride you can handle, as it's viewable from throughout the park. Is your child going, but you're not? There's a viewing area at the end of the slide. *9–10 sec. 360 ft (110 m), 66-degree 120 ft (37 m) drop, max speed 60 mph (97 kph). Fear factor: All of it. Height min: 48 in (122 cm).*

★★★★★ ✔ **Teamboat Springs.** Nowhere else at Disney do so many families have such a good time together—all ages laugh and smile on this, the world's longest family raft ride. Sitting in a raft the size of a plastic kiddie pool, up to 8 people slide down a high-banked course together, spinning on tight curves which toss them up on steep walls. Thirty holes in each raft's bottom edge make sure derrieres get soaked; a 200-foot (61-meter) ride-out area passes under a dilapidated roof that's dripping cold water. There's often a minimum of four riders per tube, so smaller groups sometimes ride together. *2 minutes.*

1,200 ft (366 m). Fear factor: Rough ride; unavoidable water sprays.

★★ **Tikes Peak.** Gentle slides, rideable baby alligators and an ankle-deep squirting ice pond highlight this unshaded preschooler playground. There's a fountain play area, a little waterfall and a scattering of sand boxes, as well as lawn chairs, chaise lounges and picnic tables. Children should wear water shoes; the concrete pavement can get very hot. *Unlimited time. Fear factor: None. Height maximum: 48 in (122cm) for slides.*

★★★★ ✔ **Toboggan Racers.** Inspired by amusement-park gunnysack slides, this straight, 8-lane mat slide races guests down its two dips face first. Since multiple riders go at once, whole families and large groups of friends can compete against each other. More joyful than scary, Toboggan Racers is fun for all ages. To go really fast, push off the starting line quickly then slightly lift the front of your mat so it doesn't plow in the water. Regardless of technique, the heaviest rider usually wins. *10–20 sec. 250 ft (76 m). Fear factor: None.*

Characters. Wearing his vintage swimsuit, Goofy often greets guests next to the park's Lottawatta Lodge fast-food spot and sometimes wanders nearby walkways. He's usually out for 30 minutes at a time. Expect the shortest lines late in the afternoon.

Food. Three Blizzard Beach fast-food spots and two seasonal ones offer hamburgers, hot dogs, sandwiches, salads and personal pizzas ($8–$11). Snack stands sell hot mini donuts, cotton candy, funnel cakes, ice cream treats, nachos and snow cones. Other spots have coffee, tea, pastries, beer and rum drinks. Have a sweet tooth? If they're fresh, get the hot mini-donuts. Disney will let you bring a cooler and food into the park, but not glass containers or alcohol.

Shopping. Located in the park's Alpine Village entrance area, the Beach Haus stocks a decent selection of beachwear, swimwear and sportswear from Billabong, Oakley, O'Neill, Quiksilver, Roxy and Speedo. Across from the park's changing rooms, the Shade Shack sells beach towels and sundries while North Pearl offers Japanese akoya pearls in their oysters (5–10 millimeters, $16), pearl settings and pearl jewelry.

Fun finds. ❶ The park's eclectic ambient music mixes summertime tunes with Christmas ditties. It includes "Day-O" (Harry Belafonte, 1956), "Joy to the World" (Three Dog Night, 1975), "Hot Dog Buddy Buddy" (Bill Haley & His Comets, 1956), as well as "Frosty the Snowman" (the Beach Boys version, 1964). ❷ "Caution: Low Flying Gator"

Hidden Mickey.

Surf pool.

reads a sign behind the women's dressing room, the roof of which has ski tracks from park mascot Ice Gator, on its roof. ❸ Barrels of "Instant Snow" from the Joe Blow Snow Co. line the walkways to Slush Gusher, Summit Plummet and Teamboat Springs. ❹ Actual snow-making equipment (from the fictional Sunshine State Snow Making Co.) sits alongside Cross Country Creek and the Toboggan Racers queue. ❺ A beach chair with an umbrella and a skier with a leg cast appear in ancient drawings inside the cave that the Cross Country Creek travels through. ❻ The Northern Lights shine through its ceiling.

Key facts. *ATM:* At the Guest Relations kiosk at the park entrance. *Cooler policy:* Coolers with up to two wheels are allowed. Blizzard Beach does not store medication coolers. *First aid:* To the right of the Beach Haus gift shop, Alpine Village. *Guest Relations:* A kiosk just outside the park entrance. *Life jacket use:* Complimentary at Snowless Joe's, Alpine Village. *Lockers:* Costing $10–$15 per day with no deposit, keyless lockers are located next to Snowless Joe's, near the Ski Patrol Training Camp and alongside the Downhill Double Dipper. Nearby self-service kiosks give you a 4-digit PIN good for unlimited access all day. *Lost children:* Taken to a marked, staffed table in

Alpine Village, on the walkway between the changing rooms and Lottawatta Lodge food spot. *Lost and Found:* At the Guest Relations kiosk, outside the park entrance. *Parking:* Free. *Phone number:* 407-560-3400. *Strollers and wheelchairs:* Allowed but not rented. The park's sandy areas are tough to wheel through. *Towel rentals:* At the Beach Haus and Snowless Joe's, Alpine Village ($2 each). *Disney transportation:* Disney buses shuttle guests to Blizzard Beach from all Disney-owned hotels, the Walt Disney World Swan and Dolphin and Disney's Animal Kingdom theme park. Officially there is no Disney bus service from Blizzard Beach to other parks or Disney Springs, but most buses that stop at Animal Kingdom also stop at Blizzard Beach.

A closer look. Disney's history books tell of a freak snowstorm that hit central Florida in the mid-1990s. And of how, mesmerized by the snow, the company's imagineers had a brainstorm—"Let's build a ski resort!"

Within a few days, they had done just that. They built a small mountain and topped it with a ski jump. They created bobsled, slalom and sledding runs. They made an Alpine Village, complete with a hotel and gift shop.

When the snow stopped they realized the foolishness of their efforts—they were, you know, in the Sunshine State—but before the imagineers could go drown their sorrows they spotted a lone alligator, still blue from the cold, which had somehow strapped on a pair of skis and was careening down their ski jump. Flying wildly through the air, this giddy "Ice Gator" landed on their restrooms, crashed into their gift shop, and emerged with a smile.

Watching him, the imagineers realized that their failed ski resort would make a great water park. They quickly reconfigured the ski jump as a body slide, redid the ski runs into mat and tube slides, and turned a convenient creek into a lazy river. Naming their new creation Blizzard Beach, they opened it to the public. On April Fools Day, 1995.

Typhoon Lagoon

With an atmosphere that's one part Hawaii and two parts "Gilligan's Island," this shady, silly escape immerses you in a tropical environment. The 61-acre (25-ha) park is located down the street from Disney Springs, within easy access of Interstate 4. Typhoon Lagoon is the most popular water park in the world, drawing more than 2 million visitors a year.

Attractions. Below, each attraction is rated from one to five stars (★) based on how well it lives up to its promise. A checkmark (✔) indicates an author favorite.

★★ **Bay Slides.** These two short children's body slides are in the calm left corner of the surf pool, an area called Blustery Bay. One slide is uncovered with a few gentle bumps; the other has a 4-foot (1-meter) tunnel. Though kids disappear on the walkway up to the slides parents have no need for concern; its 10 steps lead only to the slides. *10 sec. 35 ft (11 m), max speed 7 mph (11 kph). Fear factor: None. Height max: 60 in (152 cm).*

★★★★★ ✔ **Castaway Creek.** Lined with palms, this shady lazy river circles the surf pool. Expect to get misted, drizzled on and, as you float into a cave, maybe completely drenched. Shoreline sights include three crashed boats and the Ketchakiddee Creek playground; the Mt. Mayday Trail suspension bridge crosses high above you. The creek splits in two for a short distance. There's never a wait, though the creek gets crowded on summer afternoons. *25 min (round trip). 2,100 ft (640 m), 15 ft (5 m) wide, 3 ft (1 m) deep, max speed 2 mph (3 kph). Fear factor: None.*

★★★★★ ✔ **Crush 'n' Gusher.** Powered by water jets as well as gravity, these three flumes have both lifts and dips, just like roller coasters. The wildest one, Pineapple Plunger has three short tunnels and two peaks. Coconut Crusher has three tunnels of various lengths. A slightly longer track, Banana Blaster includes one long and two

Surf pool.

Castaway Creek.

medium-length tunnels, but only has two-person rafts. To stay in control, push your feet down into the front of your tube. For a wilder time, lift your feet up. Riding Pineapple Plunger? Lean back to catch some air. Ride together if there are no more than three people in your group; in general the more people on a tube, the faster and more fun it is.

According to its backstory, the ride is the hurricane-ravaged remains of the Tropical Amity (say it slowly) fruit-packing plant. The flumes were its spillways, which once cleaned fruit. Aptly named Hideaway Bay, the ride's 5-acre (25-ha) setting tucks behind the park's main locker area and includes a shallow gradual-entry pool lined with chairs and chaise lounges, a perfect place for toddlers to play. *30 sec. 420 ft (128 m), max speed 18 mph (29 kph). 2-, 3-person tubes. Covered queue. Fear factor: Chaotic, disorienting; few visual reference points. Height min 48 in (122 cm).*

★★ **Gangplank Falls.** Though it doesn't last long, this big-tube slide has its moments, as riders go under waterfalls and through a small cave. To make it worthwhile ride it early or late in the day, when there's little or no wait. *30 sec. 300 ft (91 m), avg speed 7mph (11 kph). 4-person rafts. Fear factor: Rough ride; unavoidable water sprays.*

★★ **Humunga Kowabunga.** Did Bart Simpson name these tubes? Maybe so; these three identical enclosed body slides are his type of thing: short, steep, straight dark drops. A shady viewing area lets Homer and Marge types watch their wayward offspring whoosh into the run-out lanes. *7 sec. 214 ft (65 m), 60-degree 50 ft (15 m)drop, max speed 30 mph (48 kph). Fear factor: Scary but brief. Height min 48 in (122 cm).*

★★★ **Keelhaul Falls.** Tubes slowly build speed on this short gentle C-curve, the park's tamest full-size tube slide. Heavier guests glide up the side of the slide just before it ends. *50 sec. 400 ft (122 m), avg speed 6 mph (10 kph). Fear factor: None.*

★★★★★ ✔ **Ketchakiddee Creek.** This large and elaborate geyser-and-volcano area is a kiddie water park all its own. For tiny tots a 100-foot palm-lined tube slide has three little dips; a surrounding area offers bubbly small fountains and ankle-deep streams and pools. More adventurous toddlers hurl themselves down two slip 'n' slides (cushy 20-foot (6-meter) mats with 20-degree drops) while older kids battle each other at the S.S. Squirt, an oversized sand sculpture with swiveling water cannons. Nearby water hoses shake, shimmy and squirt atop a 12-foot (4-meter) tall Blow Me Down boiler. The area has shady chairs and picnic tables; many families build sandcastles. Crowds often pack Ketchakiddee Creek in the afternoon, as Disney doesn't enforce its posted rule that children who play here be shorter than 48 in (122 cm). *Unlimited time. 18 activity spots. Fear factor: None. Height max 48 in (122 cm) for slides.*

★ **Mayday Falls.** A triple vortex, this swervy "white water" tube slide triple vortex can spin you around, but it's not as much fun as it should be. Since its water is just an inch or two deep and its bottom is rippled concrete, the ride pounds your rear end like some sadistic fitness machine. There's one small waterfall. *30 seconds. 460 ft (140 m), average speed 10 mph (16 kph). Fear factor: Rough ride.*

★★★ **Mount Mayday Trail.** Hidden at the back of the park, this fern-and-hibiscus-lined scenic walkway goes over a suspension bridge high above Castaway Creek, then winds up Mount Mayday to the impaled Miss Tilly shrimp boat. There's nothing to do, but it is pretty. Tiny streams splash over the walkway, which begins at the entrance to the Gangplank Falls tube slide (look for the sign) and ends at the top of the Humunga Kowabunga body slide. The trail is usually vacant even on the most crowded days, as few visitors know it's here. *Fear factor: None.*

★★★★★ ✔ **Shark Reef.** You look down on tropical fish as you snorkel over an artificial reef in this chilly saltwater pool. Sights include "smiling" rainbow parrotfish, Dory-esque blue tangs, rays and passive little leopard and bonnethead sharks. Hold still as you float to have the fish come close to you. For the most time above the reef take the scenic route, in the uncrowded water away from the overturned tanker. A resting area sits in the middle of the pool. Want to watch someone else snorkel? Do it underwater, through the windows of a real capsized tanker. *Unlimited, though swimmers are not allowed to reverse their course. Fear factor: Cold saltwater. Complimentary use of masks, snorkels, life vests, changing areas and outdoor showers.*

An optional Supplied Air Snorkeling experience (Reef Adventure, ★★★★★ ✔) includes use of an air tank, regulator, flippers and instruction and usually takes place away from the crowd. It's run by the National Association of Underwater Instructors. Fees go to a conservation program. *30 minutes. Ages 5 and up, $20. Late April to late August.*

★★★★ ✔ **Storm Slides.** Winding down a steep wooded hill, these shady, high-banked body slides are long and curvy. Each of the three offers a different experience: Jib Jammer is totally open to the sky; Rudder Buster has a small tunnel; Stern Burner includes a longer, dark tunnel. Don't want to ride? You can wait for those who do on unshaded bleachers at the catch pool. *25 seconds. 300 ft (91 m), maximum speed 20 mph (32 kph). Fear factor: May frighten toddlers.*

Gangplank Falls.

Shark Reef.

★★★★★ ✔ **Surf Pool.** Body-surfable waves sweep down this large pool, making it a popular teen hangout as well as a fun spot for families. Few people body surf but many gather to be knocked around by the waves, the height of which varies throughout the day. A chalkboard in the front of the pool shows the daily schedule. *Unlimited time. Waves 2–6 ft (1–2 m). Fear factor: Waves intimidate, can topple you even in shallow areas. Young children should stay with parents.*

The 2.5-acre (1-ha) area resembles a tropical cove, with a real sandy beach, bubbling tide pools and a sand bar about 50 feet (15 meters) out. The 115-by-395-foot (35-by-120-meter) wave pool is the largest in North America in terms of capacity, water volume and wave height. Waves are created in the closed-off deep end, as 12 backstage chambers repeatedly push 80,000 gallons (300,000 liters) of water through two underwater doors.

Characters. Lilo and Stitch greet parkgoers until 4 p.m. in front of the Singapore Sal's gift shop. They do not appear together, but rather alternate for 20 minutes at a time. Expect the shortest lines after 3 p.m.

Food. Typhoon Lagoon fast-food spots sell fish, hamburgers, hot dogs, small pizzas, salads, sandwiches, fried shrimp and turkey legs ($8–$11). The Leaning Palms fast-food counter has the greatest variety.

Snack stands have cotton candy, funnel cakes, hot mini donuts, nachos, pretzels, smoothies and soft-serve ice cream. The donuts are an indulgent treat. Other stands offer coffee, tea and pastries; a converted scooter truck serves beer and mixed drinks.

The park has two picnic areas, though you can set up a meal virtually anywhere. Disney will let you bring a cooler and food into the park, but not glass containers or alcohol.

Shopping. Near the entrance, Singapore Sal's has beach towels, sundries, swimwear and young-adult apparel from Billabong, ●akley, ●'Neill, Quiksilver and Roxy. At Shark Reef, a Pearl Factory stand sells Japanese akoya pearls in their oysters (5–10 mm, $16), pearl settings and jewelry.

Fun finds. ❶ Nautical flags hanging above the park entranceway spell out a friendly message: "WELCOME TO TYPHOON LAGOON." ❷ Discreetly hanging to their right, another row of flags spells out the more ominous "PIRANHA IN POOL." ❸ Feel sadistic? In front of the Happy Landings snack bar, aim the props of outboard motors waiting to being serviced at passing floaters on Castaway Creek and squirt them with water. ❹ Long-forgotten

Typhoon Lagoon mascot Lagoona Gator lives in the Board Room, a shack in front of the surf pool. Look inside to find a poster for the movie "Bikini Beach Blanket Muscle Party Bingo," a flyer for a concert by The Beach Gators ("So cold blooded, they're hot!").

Key facts. *ATM:* At Singapore Sal's gift shop, near the park entrance. *Cooler policy:* Coolers with up to two wheels are allowed. Typhoon Lagoon does not store medication coolers. *First aid:* Behind the Leaning Palms fast-food restaurant. *Guest Relations:* A kiosk just outside the park entrance. *Life jacket use:* Complimentary. At Singapore Sal's and High 'N Dry Towels, both near the park entrance. *Lockers:* Costing $10–$15 per day with no deposit, lockers are located next to Snowless Joe's, near the Singapore Sal's gift shop and Shark Reef. Nearby self-service kiosks give you a 4-digit PIN good for unlimited access all day. *Lost children:* Taken to Safe Harbor, a staffed area outside of Singapore Sal's gift shop, near the park entrance. There's sometimes a sandwich board there that reads "Lost Children." *Lost and Found:* At the Guest Relations kiosk, outside the park entrance. *Parking:* Free. *Phone number:* 407-560-7223. *Strollers and wheelchairs:* Allowed but not available for rent. The park's sandy areas are tough to wheel through. *Towel rentals:* At Singapore Sal's, near the park entrance ($2 each). *Disney transportation:* Disney buses shuttle guests to Typhoon Lagoon from all Disney resort hotels. Before 10 a.m. the buses drop off guests at Typhoon Lagoon and then continue to Disney Springs; after 10 a.m. they stop first at Disney Springs. There is no direct bus service between Typhoon Lagoon and any Walt Disney World theme park.

A closer look. According to Disney lore, the Placid Palms resort was built on Florida's volcanic Atlantic coastline, in a tranquil Florida valley alongside a Florida mountain. Right. Anyway, over the years the valley experienced a few tremors and rumblings but overall remained, well, placid. Then in 1955, Hurricane Connie struck the Placid Palms head-on. The storm impaled a shrimp boat on the volcano, destroyed an adjacent fruit processing plant, blew in crates of fireworks from a nearby island (where at the time a Mr. Merriweather Pleasure put on a nightly fireworks show) and cut off the harbor from the Atlantic, trapping saltwater fish at a reef. Despite these setbacks, Placid Palm managers remained totally cool. Grabbing some sign paint, they renamed their place the Leaning Palms and re-opened it as a topsy-turvy playground: a water park. Typhoon Lagoon opened on June 1, 1989.

Shark Reef sign.

Jock Lindsey's Hangar Bar.

Disney Springs

EIGHTEEN MILLION A YEAR. That's how many visitors Disney is hoping come each year to this reimagined and greatly expanded dining, shopping and entertainment complex, which for the last few decades was known as Downtown Disney. Eighteen million. That's 50,000 a day. Project managers say it's costing the company $350 million, for which it's getting a million-square-foot development with its own dedicated highways, bus lanes, pedestrian bridges and parking garages that finally end the problem of finding an open space. When finished—the official done-date is August 16, 2016, though at press time that was starting to look iffy—Disney Springs will have 150 retailers and restaurants, the latter of which will include 10,000 dining seats.

Decidedly more refined than other Disney shopping efforts, the new complex offers a diverse mix of what Disney describes as "premium, affordable luxury and fast fashion" retailers and "sophisticated dining diversions" designed to appeal to young singles and conventioneers as well as the traditional Disney family crowd.

Four neighborhoods. Basically a huge outdoor mall, Disney Springs has four areas.

Town Center. The heart of the project, this area looks like a Florida town from the 1920s, its buildings reflecting the period's Mediterranean Revival, Craftsman and industrial architecture. Streams flowing through the area form convincing artificial springs and beautiful blue water, which at night are lit by floating lights. Set behind a large central depot for Disney buses, Town Center includes a small open-sided mall and 10 performance stages, allowing for lots of live entertainment.

Totally new from the ground up, Town Center was built on a chunk of land last used for bus stops and parking lots, stretching from Planet Hollywood to the World of Disney.

The Landing. This new section is behind Town Center, on the site of the former Pleasure Island. It completely reimagines the space as the active waterfront of Disney's 1920s town, its walkways embedded with sea shells and lined with shops and restaurants. Yet there's still nightlife here, most notably at The Edison but also at restaurants such as STK Orlando and Morimoto Asia that turn clubby at night. Electronic ambient music is shared with the adjacent West Side.

The Marketplace. When it opened in 1975 as the Lake Buena Vista Shopping Village, this 48-acre (19 ha) open-air shopping mall was intended to connect to the rest of Walt Disney World only by monorail. Charming for its day, its architecture recalled a Swiss village, with buildings covered in naturally stained rough-hewn beams and cedar-shake shingles—a trendy look in '70s California, where Disney's design team was based. As its name changed over the years—to the Walt Disney World Village, then the Disney Village Marketplace and finally just the Marketplace—the area lost some of its charm; its planned monorail beams replaced by highways, its stained wood painted over in bright shades of orange, red and green. For its Disney Springs incarnation the Marketplace hasn't changed much. Disney has expanded its signature World of Disney store, added a walkway over its end of Village Lake that makes it easier to get around, built pedestrian bridges over adjacent roadways that make the area easier to reach from nearby hotels, and updated its ambient music. Its woodwork now has a natural color scheme, and its bus depot has closed.

West Side. Chunks of abandoned elevated railways stand over the walkway, the most obvious of very few changes to this area. The shady platforms provide a respite from the Florida sun; they were going to be perches for guests to look down on the area until budget and safety issues killed off that idea.

Highways, bridges and parking. Out front, once gridlocked Buena Vista Drive is all new, with central bus lanes and 10 lanes for car traffic. Pedestrian bridges span the road, as does a bridge for a highway that leads directly to the area from Interstate 4. Replacing parking lots that held 1,500 cars, two parking garages hold four times that many.

Best of the Springs. ❶ Disney Springs is the most creative and entertaining shopping area in Central Florida, perhaps in the entire state. ❷ By design, every new restaurant serves good food and every new shop is a good one—either an unusual one-of-a-kind place, the flagship location of a chain, or a chain that offers something different from others like it elsewhere. ❸ Young adults will love the area, with its modern stores such as Uniqlo, lively street entertainment and spirited nightspots such as STK Orlando and the Edison.

Worst of the Springs. ❶ *"I'm melting! I'm melllting!"* You'll feel like the Wicked Witch of the West if you're here on a summer afternoon, as yet again Disney's California designers have created an area ideal for their state but so wrong for Florida. You'll broil on these sun-soaked walkways every sunny day from May through September. ❸ Most of the new places offer only pricey goods and grub, as Disney continues to skew upscale. ❹ Except for a still-to-come Walt Disney restaurant in the Landing, new areas lack a Disney feel, as nearly every eatery and shop comes from an outside business. ❺ Finally, it may be simply too big. Too exhausting to fully enjoy in one visit, too impossible to track down all the spots that would most appeal to you, too easy to get lost in its meandering design.

Know before you go. The following information is accurate as of July, 2016:

ATMs. The Marketplace has three ATMs: at Marketplace Snacks, near Once Upon a Toy and inside World of Disney. The West Side has two: at the House of Blues Co. Store and at Starbucks. The Disney Springs Welcome Center holds a Town Center ATM.

First aid. At the Marketplace, aspirin and Band-Aids are sold at World of Disney; at Town Center at Sundries; in the West Side at DisneyQuest Emporium and the Cirque du Soleil box office. There is no first aid office.

Guest Relations. Called the Welcome Center, it's in Town Center next to D-Luxe Burger, near the Lime Garage. 9a–11p.

Hours. In general 10a–midnight, though hours can vary by venue.

Mailbox. In the Marketplace, next to the fountain in front of World of Disney.

Parking. It's free. Two garages hold 6,000 vehicles. Open spaces are remarkably easy to find, thanks to a series of electronic signs. One at the entrance of each garage shows you the number of open spots by floor; signs and lights inside lead you to them. There's a parking lot at the west end, near the Cirque du Soleil theater and the House of Blues complex.

© Coca-Cola Co. / Macbeth Photo

Coca-Cola Store Orlando.

Valet parking. In front of the Cirque du Soleil theater and at the entrance to the bus stop, between Town Center and the West Side ($10 2 hrs, $20 day, after 1:30p).

Stroller rentals. At Town Center at the Sundries shop behind the Coca-Cola Store (single $15/day, double $31, plus $100 dep).

Disney transportation. Buses serve all Disney hotels (8a–2a from Town Center). Boats (9a–1:30a) shuttle guests from Old Key West, Port Orleans and Saratoga Springs to The Landing (docking between Jock Lindsey's Hangar Bar and Paradiso 37), and from one side of Disney Springs to the other. The Marketplace dock is hidden behind Rainforest Cafe on a walkway to Saratoga Springs.

Wheelchair and scooter rentals. At Town Center at the Sundries shop behind the Coca-Cola Store (wheelchairs $12 day, ECVs $50 day, each w/ $100 deposit).

Town Center

Shops and merchandise. The dominant retail area, Town Center has many large stores and some international brands.

NEW! Alex and Ani. This eco-friendly jewelry boutique features wire bracelets decorated with hanging bangles, with a collection of Disney-themed bangles exclusive to this location.

NEW! American Threads. Trendy women's apparel with lots of floaty tops and sundresses at prices typically half that of comparable shops. Inside open-air mall.

NEW! Anthropologie. Womenswear, including shoes and accessories.

NEW! Coca-Cola Store Orlando. The world's most famous soft drink gets the royal treatment at this three-story complex, which celebrates its history, taste and cultural significance. There's a huge collection of Coke memorabilia, a bottling line, a chance to taste-test over a hundred soft drinks from around the world... and a ton of Coke merchandise. A rooftop patio serves alcoholic beverages.

NEW! Edward Beiner. Prescription eyeglasses and sunglasses from brands such as Cartier, Chanel, Ray-Ban and Tom Ford.

NEW! Columbia Sportswear. Casual outdoor clothing. Inside open-air mall.

NEW! Everything But Water. Tops and bottoms are sold separately at this pricey swimwear shop, with price tags in the neighborhood of $60 to $90 for each piece. Tops come in sizes up to F. Also a few cover-ups and men's trunks. Inside open-air mall.

NEW! Francesca's. It's not chic, but does sell womenswear and accessories at good prices.

NEW! Free People. Bohemian apparel, shoes and underthings for young women, from the Urban Outfitters family.

NEW! Johnny Was. This Los Angeles-based womenswear boutique sells hippie-style apparel, much of it with embroidery.

NEW! Johnston & Murphy. Classic old school men's and women's shoes and resort wear. Inside open-air mall.

NEW! Kate Spade. Quirky, sophisticated women's apparel, shoes, handbags and accessories featuring graphic designs.

NEW! Kipling. Colorful nylon backpacks, bags and luggage that can be personalized with letters or patches. Every item comes with a key fob adorned with the shop's mascot monkey. An in-store photo booth lets you don Mickey Mouse ears and take a selfie to post.

NEW! Lacoste. Alligator shirts make a rainbow along one wall of this shop, which also sells other sportswear and accessories.

NEW! Levis. Jeans, casual apparel.

NEW! Lilly Pulitzer. Colorful Palm Beach beachwear and resort wear from this popular designer name. Inside open-air mall.

NEW! L'Occitane en Provence. This South-of-France shop sells French body, face, fragrance and home products. Try out all-natural scrubs at the sink station, or get a complimentary mini-facial or hand massage. The aroma is intoxicating.

NEW! Lucky Brand. Known for their stylish jeans and too-cute-for-words cotton tops, Lucky Brand clothing is expensive—but for a good reason. Much of it is handmade, with tears and washes and aging done by hand. This location is twice the size of a regular Lucky Brand store. Inside open-air mall.

NEW! Luxury of Time. Breitling, Bremont, Bulgari, Mont Blanc, Movado, Tag Heuer watches. A Diamonds International shop.

NEW! MAC Cosmetics. The official line of this cosmetics shop is "professional makeup for anyone at a moderate price." Walk-in makeup demos are complimentary; express makeovers available with $30 purchase. Hour-long makeovers, private lessons and nighttime makeup classes offered.

NEW! Melissa Shoes. Every pair of boots, sandals and shoes sold here is made from eco-friendly, hypoallergenic materials.

NEW! Na Hoku. "Hawaii's Finest Jewelers Since 1924," this shop sells jewelry the old-school way: under glass in a wraparound counter. Island-inspired pieces showcase birds of paradise, palm trees, starfish.

NEW! Oakley. Upscale sunglasses.

NEW! Origins. Launched by Estee Lauder, this all-natural skin-care shop offers products especially for those with sensitive skin.

NEW! Pandora. Quality charm and bead bracelets; fine, costume jewelry; creative, colorful Disney items.

NEW! Sephora. Packed with women young and old, this cosmetics and fragrance shop has a secret—samplers. There are literally hundreds of products to sample, along with complimentary classes and mini makeovers. The bustling shop has a distinctly un-chic vibe, welcoming to everyone.

NEW! Shore. This beach-themed boutique stocks casual vacation clothes for men, women and children, including cotton T-shirts and swimwear.

NEW! Sperry. Besides the ubiquitous boat shoe, this shop sells sandals and apparel, including swimsuits. Inside open-air mall.

NEW! Sugaroo. This artsy family-owned shop features handmade jewelry, art prints and toys. Inside open-air mall.

NEW! Superdry. Vintage Americana and kitschy Japanese-inspired graphics adorn the flip-flops, hoodies, jackets and T-shirts of this British brand.

NEW! Tommy Bahama. Island-inspired sportswear and swimwear for men and women, often in eclectic prints. Look up to see a beautiful skylight. Inside open-air mall.

NEW! Trophy Room. NBA legend Michael Jordan's son Marcus offers high-end sneakers, sportswear and memorabilia.

NEW! UGG. U.S. producer of Australian-style boots that became trendy in the '90s due to their comfy twin-faced sheepskin. Today's brand also includes slippers, shoes, blankets, apparel, home furnishings and handbags. Inside open-air mall.

NEW! Under Armour Brand House. Clothes that wick sweat, of course, but also footwear and fitness devices are sold at this sprawling two-story store. A video station tests your jumping, sprinting and other athletic skills, and shows you how they measure up against world records. A curving staircase spells out "Following in the footsteps of greatness takes passion, dedication and will."

NEW! Uniqlo. The flagship store of this fast-growing Japanese clothier. Uniqlo ("YOU-nee-klo") sells low-cost but "highly finished" quality-fabric shirts, jeans and other basics that come in few styles but a stunning array of colors.

NEW! UNOde50. Sophisticated hand-crafted jewelry from Spain.

NEW! Vera Bradley. Iconic colorful quilted travel bags and accessories include the Disney Collection, which features the head

© Sprinkles

Sprinkles.

of Mickey Mouse; it's only sold on Disney property. Inside open-air mall.

NEW! Vince Camuto. Chic women's bags, hats, jewelry and shoes, most incorporating beautiful soft leather.

NEW! Volcom. Board shorts, hats, jeans, swimsuits, T-shirts and other surf and skateboard apparel for men, women and children. The newest Volcom items come to this location first, then go out to other stores.

NEW! Zara. Expect racks and racks and racks of clothes at eye-popping low prices at the flagship store of this popular bargain-store chic clothing shop, which specializes in cute knockoffs of the absolute-latest designer styles. The Spanish-based chain is known for needing just one week to develop an item, produce it and get it into its stores, as well as pulling it one week later if it doesn't sell.

Restaurants and food. Several good eateries have opened at this all-new area.

NEW! ★★★★ $32 Frontera Cocina. Whoa! Flavors burst from the food at this casual, convivial Mexican restaurant. The basic ingredients are outstanding—the house-made chips, the rice, the plantains. Entrees include make-your-own soft tacos, crispy tortas, enchiladas, chicken, shrimp and pork. Celebrity Chef Rick Bayless has a home in Mexico and travels throughout the country,

looking for authentic dishes; he melds those regional flavors into the offerings here. The bar offers 50 different tequila, mezcal and sotol choices. A walk-up outdoor window sells tacos, guacamole, margaritas and beer. The tall ceiling raises the noise level in the dining room, which is in one big open space, but that seems to add to the relaxing family-friendly ambience. A few quibbles— the signature Oaxacan Red Chile Chicken is tasty but almost impossible to figure out how to eat, as it is a connected half-chicken smothered with thick red-brown mole sauce. Also, this is the rare Mexican eatery that charges for chips and salsa. *11a–11p; $14–$34 (children $9). Seats 280, 40 at outdoor patio.*

NEW! Planet Hollywood Observatory. On the drawing board for years, a major makeover of the world's most popular Planet Hollywood is finally here, and promises to bring this oh-so-'90s icon into the modern world. Oddly, it'll do that by going back in time, becoming a 1920s observatory straight out of the machine-age of star travelers such as Buck Rogers and Flash Gordon. Outdoor changes include a dining terrace, a bar and live entertainment; inside the open dining room will take on the look of a planetarium, with stars and constellations on its ceiling. Remaining will be Planet Hollywood's displays of movie memorabilia, including the blue gingham dress worn by Judy Garland in 1939's "The Wizard of Oz." As for the food, it will probably stay under-rated and pretty good. On board for sure will be the signature Chicken Crunch appetizer, a recipe from cofounder Demi Moore that uses Cap'n Crunch cereal. The restaurant should re-open in late 2016. *11a–mid; $14–$30 (children $8). Seats 720.*

NEW! ★★★★ ✔ $12 Amorette's Patisserie. Almost too pretty to eat, this bakery's light pastries are delicate delights. Quality ingredients include green tea crumble, caramelized bacon pieces. Also coffee, champagne, whole cakes. Alas there's only one indoor table, along with several stand-up spots. *$8. Seats 4.*

NEW! ★★★★ ✔ $12 Blaze Fast-Fire'd Pizza. Three minutes is all it takes to cook a pizza at this eatery. Just like at a Subway or Moe's Southwest Grill, you direct your meal makers as they move down an assembly line, building your thin-crust pie to your specifications. It's then flash-fired in an open-flame oven. Other offerings include salads, blood-orange lemonade and s'mores pies. This Blaze is larger than others, the chain's 5,000-square-foot (1,500-square-meter) flagship. *11-inch pies $5–$10; 40 toppings. Seats 200. Opens late 2016.*

NEW! ★★★ $16 DDPq D-Luxe Burger. Ranch-themed burger joint has a small indoor seating area, but on cool days (or at night) you can eat on its patio overlooking a pond. The menu features, you guessed it, burgers—mostly smothered in toppings. A ground chicken patty and veggie burger round out the menu. Each sandwich is almost too thick to fit in your mouth, and is served in a messy paper sleeve. Artisanal gelato shakes come with or without alcohol. Outstanding fries come with dipping sauce; ask for one of each. The rustic interior has exposed beams and a farmhouse vibe. *11a–11p; $10–$13 (children $7). Seats 100, inc 8 at bar, 48 on outside covered patio.*

NEW! ★★★★★ ✔ $9 Sprinkles. The signature red velvet cupcake is to die for, and actually tastes homemade; it's soft on the inside, and has a dense heft to it. Other offerings include cookies, shakes and slow-churned ice cream in 13 flavors. A Sprinkles Sundae gives you a scoop of ice cream with a cupcake for just $8. In front of the shop, a Cupcake ATM dispenses boxed treats 24 hours a day. *10a–11p. $4–$10. No seating inside, 68 outside, mostly covered.*

Entertainment. Take you higher, then dance to the music. (Sly Stone, you kids you.)

★★★★★ ✔ Street performers. Bands and musicians perform throughout Town Center; Living Statues appear in the fountain plaza in front of Uniqlo. Show times vary.

The Landing

Shops and merchandise. Small boutique shops fill these retail spaces, which are meant to complement the surrounding restaurants and nightlife.

NEW! America's Game-Day Gear. Hats, jerseys, T-shirts with sports team logos. Outdoor stand.

NEW! APEX by Sunglass Hut. This modern sunglass store has an environmental simulator that lets you compare polarized to non-polarized lenses and check out a pair of glasses in different light conditions and wind speeds; standing in front of it is a great way to cool off from the heat. A Build-Your-Own-Oakleys station lets you mix and match lenses, frames, icon and ear socks. Brands include Oakley, Ray-Ban, Maui Jim.

NEW! The Art of Shaving. Started by a husband and wife, later bought by Proctor & Gamble, this shop sells high-end shaving supplies, fragances and grooming products. Barber Spa indulgences include the Royal Shave, which starts off with a hot towel and protective oil; follows with hot shaving cream, a traditional straight razor, a shave with the grain then against, a second hot towel with lemon oil, an after-shave mask of minerals and oils to deep-clean your pores, a cold towel with lavender oil, a hydrating toner and after-shave balm. *Haircut $40. Shave $35–$55. Both $55–$80. Appts: 407-560-8320.*

NEW! Chapel Hats. Cute fashion-forward yet retro hats for women, men and children— beanies, berets, cadets, cloches, drifters, fedoras, fascinators, Steampunk top hats and furry Spirit Hoods with ears and pockets in built-in scarves. Ideal for cosplay at The Edison. The tin ceiling is vintage. Around the corner is a Chapel Hats open-air stand.

Duncan Yo-Yos. Also juggling diablos, from an outdoor stand.

NEW! Erwin Pearl. It's not just pearls; this lovely shop (the biggest of 30 nationwide) sells quality enamel and semi-precious fashion jewelry and accessories marked by style, creativity, sometimes whimsy. Exclusive Van Gogh collection includes beautiful purses, scarves, watches. Many pieces feature blooming flowers. Founder 98-year-old Erwin Pearl calls manager Stephanie twice a week.

© The Edison / Bling Divas Entertainment

The Edison, Los Angeles location.

Eyecatchers. Reflective metal wind spinners; some Disney designs. Outdoor stand.

NEW! Filthy Rich. Costume jewelry inspired by pieces worn by celebrities such as Kate Middleton, Marilyn Monroe. Outdoor stand.

NEW! Havaianas. This Brazilian brand is the original rubber flip-flop. Colorful, sometimes pricey styles for both sexes, all ages. Includes a make-your-own station.

NEW! Sanuk. Lightweight casual shoes and squishy comfortable flip-flops, some made from the same foam as yoga mats. Funky but functional; adored by wearers. The only other Sanuk is in Hawaii.

NEW! The Ship's Store. Nautical-themed apparel, mugs, board games, sunglasses, watches. Boat, outboard-motor models; cute rubber ducks are priced beyond retail. Blue-blood vibe. At The Boathouse restaurant.

Shop for Ireland. Small store has unusual mix of Irish apparel, cookbooks, infantwear, mugs, music. At Raglan Road.

NEW! Sound Lion. Hi-tech headphones, docking stations, ear buds, speakers as well as "education in digital music applications that improve the listening lifestyle." Included is a Skull Candy store-within-a-store; other brands include Beats by Dre, Sennheiser. Everything can be tested, clerks are willing to open any box. Known for its customer service and matching the prices of its competitors.

Restaurants and food. My top picks: the new Homecoming, Raglan Road and the latter's fast-food spin-off Cookes of Dublin.

NEW! ★★★ $50 DDP2 The Boathouse. A first-class decor and friendly servers can't overcome the sinking feeling you get at this lakeside tourist trap. Though its dining areas are filled with antique outboard motors and other eclectic and fascinating nautical items, you pay through the nose to sit by them. Its $50 steaks come with nothing—no salads, no sides. An ear of corn is $8; a kids fruit cup $10. High-quality seafood and ambitious finishes are wasted in entrees that are often too salty, too small or too bland. If you go, afterward take a walk out on the dock; the historic boats back there are beautifully restored. *11a–11p; $19–$62 (children $10); meals for two $60–$135; raw bar $4–$100; bar menu to 2a $15–$29. Seats 600. Direct reservations at 407-939-2628 (939-BOAT).*

NEW! ★★★★★ ✓ $35 DDP Chef Art Smith's Homecoming. Don't think it's just about the fried chicken. Quality and authenticity suffuse everything here—the drinks, the appetizers, the entrees, the desserts. You could take a dart and throw it at the menu and not have a bad meal. Only the peas and carrots for the kid's meals and the french fries start out frozen; the kitchen creates everything else from scratch, including the no-label hot sauce that sits on the table. Although Art Smith is a celebrity chef—James Beard Award winner, Top Chef Masters, Oprah Winfrey's personal chef for 10 years—he was born and raised on a family farm in North Florida. Homecoming is a celebration of rural Florida food, from someone who knows and understands it. Smith, a former cast member of the Disney College Program from Florida State University, built the restaurant using Florida cypress, camphor and eucalyptus woods, commissioned a Tampa artist to paint a mural over the open kitchen and displays a huge portrait of a Florida farmer on the wall. *11a–mid Sun–Thr, 11a–1a Fri–Sat; $15–$41 (children $9–$15). Seats 200, inc 20 at the bar, 35 on covered outside porch and 10 outside the porch at a grab 'n' go spot by the water.*

NEW! ★★ $50 DDP Morimoto Asia. Stick to the signature dishes at this sophisticated eatery from "Iron Chef" star Masaharu Morimoto: Peking duck or St. Louis spare ribs. Both are delicious, the duck with perfect crisp skin. Other choices, however, are just… meh. Some sushi is made with "krab," imitation crab meat. So sad! The place is lovely, all in black and white with the walls decorated with oversized portraits of Japanese people. A two-story layout includes terraces, a grand hall, private rooms and waterside seating. Roasting ducks hang from the exhibition kitchen. The cuisine is Pan-Asian, with Chinese, Korean and Thai influences. The kid's menu comes complete with origami paper and instructions. *Lunch 11:30a–5p $14–$28 (children $12), dinner 5p–10p, Sun–Thr, to 11p Fri, Sat $16–$54 (children $12); late-night menu to mid. Seats 626, inc 26 at two bars, 44 on outside patio, mostly covered. Uses one Disney Dining Plan credit at lunch, two at dinner. Direct reservations: 407-939-6686.*

NEW! Paddlefish. At presstime the old Fulton's Crab House was undergoing a complete re-do, transforming into the Paddlefish. Some things won't change—it will still sit inside a big steamship, serve seafood, lots of crab and lobster corn dogs. A rooftop lounge will stay open until 2 a.m. offering expansive views over the water. *Opens fall 2016.*

★★★★ $32 DDP Paradiso 37. A loud yet laid-back vibe combines with good burgers, fries, burritos and guacamole to make this waterside spot a better value than the nearby Boathouse, and a better choice than STK Orlando or Morimoto Asia unless you're just out to go big. Its menu represents the street food of the 37 countries of the Americas—in other words the street food of Miami, where the owner is from. Options include Chilean salmon and an outstanding little appetizer: Central American "crazy corn," roasted on the cob and covered in cheese. A bar reps 37 tequilas including some at $50 a shot. Paradiso doubled its seating in 2015, adding more outdoor dining, a second level and a new outdoor stage. *11:30a–12p, to 1a Thr–Sat; $16–$30 (children $8). Seats 500 (inc 200 outside, 20 at bar). Live entertainment nightly 5p–11p. Direct reservations: 407-934-3700.*

★★ $28 DDP Portobello. This lovely little hideaway doesn't totally disappoint, though you'll find better Italian spots in the theme parks. OK entrees sound better than they taste; many lack flavor, sandwiches have lots of bread. Service is sometimes sharp, sometimes sloppy. Decor is very Italian; seating is comfortable and spacious. *Lunch 11:30a–3:45p $11–$15 (children $5–$11); dinner 4–11p $11–$29 (children $5–$11). Seats 414, inc 86 outside. Direct reservations: 407-934-8888.*

★★★★★ ✔ $31 DDP Raglan Road. It's everything you'd hope for at a vacation restaurant—unique food, memorable atmosphere, fine service, welcoming to children—at a price less than nearly all of the new places surrounding it. This isn't an aspiring lifestyle-oriented-upscale-concept tourist trap, this is the real thing, a real Irish restaurant run by real Irish people who know Irish food and drink and know how to serve it. Its master chef is Kevin Dundon, the proprietor of Ireland's Dunbrody Country House Hotel and Restaurant, where he also runs a cooking school. He's cooked for many celebrities in his career, including Queen Elizabeth and singer Bono. His experience shows: Raglan Road's food is a step beyond tradition—pub classics have distinctly gourmet touches. The decadent bread pudding—big enough to share—comes with creamers of butterscotch and creme anglaise. Guinness is on tap; other choices include an ample selection of other beers and ales, and a mead that tastes like warm alcoholic honey. The antique decor includes two 130-year-old bars from Ireland with traditional leaded-glass dividers. Ask to sit in the loud main room to see the Irish dancers and band. *Lunch 11a–3p $15–$26; dinner 3–11p $15–$29 (children $8–$14). Live band, table step-dancers evenings Mon–Sat; two outdoor bars. Seats 600, inc 300 outside. Direct reservations: 407-938-0300.*

NEW! ★★★★ $62 DDP2 STK Orlando. This clubby chophouse chain is known for

© Disney

Erin McKenna's Bakery NYC.

its sleek and sexy atmosphere, loud music, knowledgeable servers and exorbitant prices. Expect superior steaks, salads and sides, from menus where everything is a la carte, even sauces and toppings; steaks come in small, medium and large. A DJ plays 70s, 80s and 90s music nightly; many people dress up. An upstairs patio offers a quieter experience with great views. *Lunch 11:30a–3:30p $15–$92; dinner 5–11p $28–$92 (children $10); DJ at night. Seats 352, inc 124 outside. Direct reservations: 407-917-7440.*

★★★★★ ✔ **$12 DDPq Cookes of Dublin.** Flaky and hot. That's what you'll get at this authentic Irish hole-in-the-wall, whether you order the hand-battered fish and chips (actually more like thick fries) or the comforting beef and lamb pie. Other choices include battered sausages, burgers and salads. Everything's "almost-to-order" so expect a short wait. None of the fried food is the least bit greasy. The tiny spot is run by Raglan Road, which it butts up against. Stop by during an off time to have a shot at a table. *11a–11p; $7–$12 (children $7–$8). Seats 33, addl stand-up tables, 24 outside, mostly covered.*

NEW! ★★★★ ✔ **$3 DDPs The Ganachery.** Exquisite premium chocolates made on-site, often in view. Milk or dark chocolate is sold by the piece, or in beautifully packaged boxes of six, nine or 12. *10a–11p; $3–$27. No seating.*

NEW! ★★★★ ✔ **$4 DDPs Erin McKenna's Bakery NYC.** This place is a dream for people with dietary restrictions. Everything is gluten-free, soy-free, dairy-free and egg-free, and sweetened with unprocessed sugar or agave. Staff gleefully meet your particular needs as they bake cookies, cupcakes, doughnuts and other goodies throughout the day. Unfortunately the only place to sit is outside on a nearby bench. *10a–11p; $2–$5. No seating.*

NEW! ★★★★ ✔ **$13 DDPq Morimoto Asia Street Food.** Tucked up next to the Morimoto Asia restaurant, this small spot offers good people-watching and a nice juxtaposition of flavors. You won't find this unusual, flavorful food at typical fast-food outlets. Best are the noodles and small bao sandwiches with super-soft buns. Soda refills are free; just ask. *11a–10p; $6–$12. 53 seats on a covered patio next to a walkway.*

NEW! ★★★★ ✔ **$9 Tea Traders Café.** Tea lovers will feel like kids in a candy store here. Unusual selections include frozen teas as thick as milkshakes, spiked teas and baked treats made with tea leaves. Brews use ingredients from gardens around the world, hand-blended and freshly prepared. Daily hands-on brewing demonstrations and traditional Chinese tea ceremonies entertain; if you're a tea novice helpful staff will offer suggestions and free samples. Teas are served at the counter or to go. Also packaged teas, teapots, accessories. *10a–11p Sun–Thr, 10a–11:30p Fri–Sat; teas $4–$9, pastries $1–$2. Seats 6 at bar.*

NEW! ★★★★ ✔ **$11 Vivoli il Gelato.** A real Italian family runs this gelataria, the manager does not speak English. The family's Florence store has been selling gelato since 1932; today it's a landmark in Italy. The family's recipes have been passed down through the years. Quality gelato is made using real Florida fruit and cocoa powder, hazelnuts and pistachios imported from Italy. The best flavor is the creamy riso (rice pudding), the owner's favorite. On hot days there's a long line to order, but it moves quickly. *10a–mid; gelato and sorbetto $5–$7; sundaes, floats, shakes $10; other snacks $5–$8; 20 flavors; servings come in 3 cup sizes or a cone. No seating.*

Bars, clubs and entertainment. A highlight: nightlife unlike anything else at Disney.

NEW! ★★★ **Boathouse boat tours.** It's a car! It's a boat! Oh my God it's sinking! With you riding shotgun and up to two of your friends or family members in the back seat, a trained captain splashes a rare Amphicar into the lake behind Disney Springs, then putts you through the water for 20 minutes as he tells you the history of this bizarro 1960s German convertible. Similar tours are available on replicas of a 40-foot 1969 Italian water taxi and an itsy-bitsy 19th-century steamboat. The Amphicar tour is the most authentic; the steamboat tour romantic, but all are pricey for what you get. *10a-10p weather permitting; Amphicar $125 for up to 3 adults or 2 adults and 2 small children; water taxi $75 per person (children under age 13 $50); steamboat tour for 2 $150; taxi, steamboat tours inc chocolate-covered strawberries, champagne toast, live music. Walk-up reservations avail. 407-939-2628. The Boathouse restaurant.*

NEW! The Edison. Dames and daddies will wreck their credit cards at what promises to be a swell take on a power plant in the 1920s. Stunningly swanky, the speakeasy-themed club should flicker filament lamps and silent films on very dark walls, and have cabaret girls, contortionists, DJs, jazz combos and palm readers. Further reasons why it might seem like everyone in Orlando has gotten there ahead of you: its many nooks, crannies and long leather sofas; its friendly gangsters and busy flappers who fix up and hand over fancy hootch and giggle water as well as over-styled yet nifty nibbles (you may need

your flashlight app to read the menus); and, wheeling a trolley of absinthe, a roving Green Fairy who will definitely not be Tinker Bell. Similar to The Edison nightclub in Los Angeles, this one will have the same dim lighting and Industrial Gothic mechanics, but with additional themed areas such as a Telegraph Lounge, Patent Office and waterfront patio and perhaps more emphasis on food. Sure it'll cost you a few clams, and there are sure to be long waits for saps and Dumb Doras who don't make reservations, but if you want to have a drink or two at a place you'll remember, this joint should be the bee's knees. Dieselpunk cosplayers may get dolled up for the occasion; nearby Chapel Hats has perfect fedoras and fascinators. *Opens spring 2017.*

NEW! ★★★★ ✔ **$20 Jock Lindsey's Hangar Bar.** You can enjoy this relaxing lounge whether you understand its story or not. It's jam-packed with interesting stuff, from an old-fashioned diving suit above a diving bell booth to a map crisscrossed with the markings of journeys to a machine that silently makes balls of ice used in one of the signature drinks. Pay attention (especially to the menu) and you'll learn the story from hundreds of references. It's about how Jock Lindsey, the pilot who flew Indiana Jones to safety at the beginning of the 1981 film "Raiders of the Lost Ark," ended up in Central Florida with his pet snake Reggie and turned a hangar into a dive bar. Jock's total time onscreen: about a minute. But no matter. Beyond the teeming Indy references, the lounge includes many homages to the still-beloved Adventurers Club that was once nearby. But wait, there's more. Comb over this place and you'll find nods to 1993's "Jurassic Park" (yes, though that world's at Universal), Marvel Comics, Pixar movies, 1991's "The Rocketeer." Need a Star Wars fix? Look on a plane fuselage that holds some booths to find "RTO-D2" stenciled at eye-level. Though the Hangar Bar just opened in 2016, it's already revamped its menu to include a couple of small meals beyond signature small plates—waitresses tell me too many people were coming in asking "Where are the french fries?" Specialty drinks are strong and generous with fun souvenir glasses. Visit at night; during the day the sun blazes in from the top windows. *11:30a–mid Sun–Thr, 11:30a–1a Fri–Sat; $9–$17. Seats 188, inc 50 on covered outside patio.*

★★★★★ ✔ **Raglan Road.** Definitely not the place for a quiet evening out, this

© Disney

Splitsville.

dyed-in-the-wool Irish pub is busy, loud and awesome at night. A lively house band plays ballads, jigs and reels early, late sets get rowdy; energetic step dancers perform in front of the band and atop an old parson's pulpit in the middle of the room, occasionally with children from the audience. An ever-changing variety of Irish and European beers and whiskeys satisfies nearly everyone, though some of us go for the mead, an ancient sweet drink made from fermented honey. Make a reservation ahead of time to ensure a table; to get one that views the stage specifically ask for that when you check in and be willing to wait. *Main stage band 4p–1:30a Mon–Thurs, 7:30p–1:30a Fri–Sat, noon–4p and 7:30p–1:30a Sun; dancers on the hour 5p–10p, Sun noon–4p; outdoor band on patio nightly. No cover. Restaurant seats 600; all ages. Direct reservations: 407-938-0300.*

NEW! ★★★ **STK Orlando.** Forget the meat. After dark it's beefcake, cheesecake, booze and booty-shaking as the bar of this steakhouse becomes a youthful mecca of loud, laissez-faire extravagance. A DJ drops driving beats every night after 6:30 or so, friendly bartenders keep you hydrated, elevated dance areas urge you to show your stuff. Contrasts nicely with the retro Edison club right across the walkway. *Seats 352, inc 124 outside. Direct reservations: 407-917-7440.*

NEW! Walt Disney restaurant. This three-story eatery will celebrate Walt Disney, the man. Expect fascinating memorabilia everywhere. Known by Disney execs as "The Walt," it was awaiting its official name from Imagineering as this book went to press, just as it was this time last year. You'll find it left of the Edison, near the balloon. It's now planned to open in early 2017, but may be delayed.

★★★★★ ✓ **Street performers.** Bands and musicians perform near the Boathouse and the Edison. Show times vary.

West Side

Shops and merchandise. Mostly budget-friendly shops offering a mix of odd items, with the occasional awesome shop tossed in.

Bongos Gift Shop. Cuban apparel, books, margarita glasses, mugs, CDs autographed by Bongos Cuban Cafe owner Gloria Estefan. A small shop inside the restaurant that sadly rarely seems to have customers.

Cirque du Soleil Boutique. Stunning circus caps, apparel, figurines, masks, purses and scarves hide among more-routine T-shirts and La Nouba souvenirs. Crowded after shows. Next to the box office.

Curl by Sammy Duvall. Junior and adult beachwear, fashion apparel, hats, jewelry, purses, shoes, sunglasses, swimwear.

Billabong, Hurley, Oakley, Roxy brands. Watches by Nixon, G-Shock. Often an artist at a table outside the shop will hand-paint Toms canvas shoes to order. **DisneyQuest Emporium.** Disney souvenirs, sundries.

Fit2Run. Florida shop stocks athletic walking and running shoes, tech running apparel and accessories such as performance eyewear, tech socks, personal-training devices. Official running retailer of RunDisney.

House of Blues Company Store. This laid-back shop's eclectic items at first glance seem unrelated to each other. But the blues CDs, cornbread mix, folk art, hot sauce and incense all share a through-the-roof quotient of cool. Funky skull-head T-shirts fit right in.

Memory Lanes. The Splitsville gift shop.

Orlando Harley-Davidson. Here's a motorcycle shop that's no bike, all shop. Heavy metal thunder? Only on display, for the kiddies to climb on.

Pop Gallery. Signed paintings, three-dimensional wall art, wild glass sculptures. Champagne bar. Next to Splitsville, right next to the Orange parking garage.

Something Silver. Silver jewelry your 'tween can afford, in many styles from around the world. A jewelry store that is neither upscale nor empty. Odd little knick-knacks, too.

Sosa Family Cigars. This Miami-based shop offers cigars, for now mainly from the Dominican Republic that use Dominican and Nicaraguan tobacco. Hand-rolling demonstrations are authentic. Adults can smoke.

NEW! Star Wars Galactic Outpost. Star Wars apparel, collectibles, toys, video games, Vinylmation inspired by the Star Wars saga.

Sunglass Icon. Quality sunglasses from brands such as Chanel, Gucci, Oakley.

Super Hero Headquarters. Toys, apparel and collectibles based on Disney's Marvel characters and movies.

United World of Soccer. Cleats, team club jerseys, including Orlando City items; other sports gear. Jerseys customized on-site.

Restaurants and food. Best bets: The House of Blues restaurant and the Disney food trucks. There's a good Starbucks, too.

★★ **$40 DDP Bongos Cuban Cafe.** Pop singer Gloria Estefan created this Cuban restaurant, but it hasn't held up nearly as well as "The Rhythm is Gonna Get You" or her other classic hits. If you've ever eaten Cuban food in Miami (or Havana) you won't be impressed with these bland dishes. Aside from the food, however, there is much to like. The architecture is unique—maybe the only building anywhere that's built around a three-story adobe pineapple. An evocative decor recalls Cuba during the 1940s and 1950s. A second-story patio is a great place to watch the dancing and enjoy the view over the lake and well as crowds down on the walkway below. The star of a pricey drink menu is a refreshing mojito. Gloria, come out of the dark, cook up some ropa vieja and save this place! *11a–11p, 'til 12p Fri, Sat; $16–$45 (children $6–$9). Seats 560 (60 outside, 87 bar). No reservations. 407-828-0999.*

★★★★ ✔ **$29 DDP Crossroads at House of Blues.** Colorful folk art adds a funky, artistic vibe to the walls, ceilings, even the bathrooms at this quirky, casual spot, a bluesy bayou take on a Hard Rock Cafe. The food stands on its own, authentic Southern fare served up in generous portions—everything from voodoo shrimp to spicy jambalaya to a melt-in-your-mouth jalapeño cornbread. Service is especially attentive and engaging. Dining rooms get louder at night as more young adults show up. Weekends have live music. *11:30a–11p Sun–Mon; 'til 12p Tue–Wed, 1:30a Thr–Sat; $12–$29 (children $7). Seats 578 (158 outside, 36 outside bar). Brunch Sun 10:30a, 1p in Music Hall; $34 (children $17); 250 seats. No reservations. 407-934-2583.*

★★★ **$27 DDP Splitsville Luxury Lanes.** It's time to re-think bowling alley food. The fare at this retro spot is surprisingly high-quality, with huge portions and an extensive menu. Good choices include the juicy hamburgers, creative sliders and fresh sushi. Draft beer comes in an ice-cold goblet glass; cocktails are generous with alcohol. Servers are friendly and attentive. There are three distinct seating areas: indoors by the bowling, outside in front of the building and upstairs on a second-floor balcony. All three offer great people-watching, and usually live music to boot. *Mon–Wed 10:30a–1a, Thr–Fri 10:30a–2a, Sat 10a–2a, Sun 10a–1a. $12–$25 (children $7–$8). Seats 450, including 50 outside.*

★★★ **$30 DDP Wolfgang Puck Grand Café.** Wolfgang Puck fans will be disappointed by this one-time standout; over the years its small offerings have turned too bland and pedestrian. Epcot's Via Napoli has much better pizza. Disney's Puck eateries have suffered since their namesake's 2002 split from his wife and business partner, Barbara Lazarof, and his sale of them to

Levy's Restaurants, which also owns nearby Portobello and Paddlefish. Lazarof personally decorated the Puck restaurants, giving them their eye-catching (if now dated) look. *Lunch 11:30a–4p $13–$29 (children $8–$9); dinner 4p–10:30p Sun–Mon, to 11p Tue–Thr, to 11:30p Fri, Sat $13–$31 (children $8–$9); weekend lunch serves dinner menu; takeout window; private room for groups. Seats 586, inc 30 at sushi bar. Direct res: 407-938-9653.*

★★★ **$45 DDP2 Wolfgang Puck Dining Room.** It's past its prime. What used to be a special fine-dining experience is now less than memorable. The menu has a little of everything but nothing especially creative. Best choices are the steak and salmon, which are cooked spot-on. Portions are on the small side. The wait staff can be aloof, and isn't always attentive, although the hostesses are friendly. The ambience is quiet and relaxing, with lovely views of the lake. *6–9p Sun–Thr, 6–10p Fri–Sat; $25–$45 (children $10–$16). Seats 120. Direct reservations: 407-938-9653.*

★★★ **$7 DDPs Disney's Candy Cauldron.** Candied and caramel apples, chocolate-covered strawberries made in view; other treats. The decor recalls the dungeon of Disney's 1937 movie "Snow White and the Seven Dwarfs." *10a–11p; $4–$12. No seating.*

★★★★ ✔ **$15 DDPq Disney food trucks.** Four trucks serve dishes influenced by recipes from particular Disney theme parks. Best bets include hand-dipped corn dogs in the spirit of those at Disneyland and butter chicken inspired by Disney's Animal Kingdom. At least two trucks can always be found in Exposition Park, where a small stage offers nightly entertainment. *12:30p–11p, $8–$14 (no kids menu); hours vary based on crowds, weather. Seating varies by location. Exposition Park next to Bongos Cuban Cafe.*

★★★ **$7 Häagen-Dazs.** This is just a typical Häagen-Dazs stand; the ice cream is as good as ever but it definitely isn't unique. There's no real seating anywhere nearby; it can be tricky to find a nice spot to enjoy your treat before it starts to melt. *10:30a–11p. Ice cream $6–$7 (children $5); shakes $8; sundaes $7–$9 (children $6). 14 flavors. No seating.*

★★★★ ✔ **$ DDPq The Smokehouse at House of Blues.** You'll have a magical experience for an affordable price if you stop by this take-out window at the right time. In the evenings, talented musicians play classic rock and blues from a patio nearby; lights strung over tables provide mood lighting. If you eat in the afternoon, it can be downright unpleasant: there's no entertainment, you sit out in the heat, and your only shade is from a few trees. The menu is Southern barbecue with sweet sauce; meats are smoked in the main House of Blues kitchen. Food comes

AMC Dine-In Theatre.

Disney food truck.

in little cardboard boxes; it can be messy. *11:30a–10p; $7–$13 (children $7). Seats 100 outdoors, at uncovered tables nearby.*

★★★★★ ✓ **$10 DDPq Starbucks.** The food is a cut above standard coffee-shop fare at this special Starbucks. Creative and tasty small plates, draft beers and a nice wine selection are available on the evening menu; the best bet here is the creamy truffle macaroni and cheese, which is topped with a light crunchy breading. The building's design has a lot of thought and detail put into it; eco-friendly touches include tables made from salvaged trees and a green roof made up of hundreds of living lemongrass plants. An interactive touchscreen "chalkboard" shows a live feed of guests; touch the screen and it switches to a live view of the Disneyland Starbucks. The building uses Disney's Wi-Fi service, though for some reason it always seems a lot faster here. Crowded after 10 a.m., often everyone seems to be under 30. *8a–mid, coffee beverages $3–$5; evening menu starting 4p, $3–$8 (no kids meals); also pastries, all-day breakfast items; rare coffee blends available from Reserve bar in dining area. Seats 60, inc 25 on patio.*

Bars, clubs and entertainment. This is where the authors go for movies; the parking is so convenient now for the Fork & Screen.

★★★ ✓ **AMC 24 Theaters.** Arrive early at the traditional multiplex of this modern movie palace; latecomers are forced into seats that are stupidly close to the screens. Auditorium No. 1 offers an Enhanced Theater Experience, with a 20-percent larger floor-to-ceiling screen and 12-channel audio. A self-service concession area can slow you down as you enter. Separate Fork & Screen Dine-In Theatres offer a nicer way to catch a flick: in an comfortable reserved recliner, with a waiter who brings you food and drinks that are nothing to brag about but decent. Assume you'll be ordering during the previews, get your food in the opening minutes of the film, get the check halfway through and pay your bill before it ends. Servers aren't disruptive and never stand in front of you. Note: The FFork & Screen Dine-In entrance is far removed from the main one, close to the main entrance to the Orange (west) parking garage. *Multiplex $7–12 based on time of day (children ages 2–12 $9), 3-D movies $5–$6 addl; 16 theaters w stadium seating, 2 3-story theaters w balconies; Fork & Screen $10–$19 (children $10–$11); 6 theaters; patrons must be 18 years or older or accompanied by someone over 21; tiny bar. Total seats 5,390. THX Surround Sound, Sony Dynamic Digital Sound. Listings: 888-262-4386. Box office: 407-827-1308.*

La Nouba B-Boy trio.

★★★ **Bongos Cuban Cafe.** This spacious Gloria Estefan-owned spot channels Havana (or at least Miami) on Friday and Saturday evenings, when its live band and dance floor attract a spirited crowd. Drinks are pricey, service sound. *11:30p–2a; restaurant capacity 560; all ages admitted; no cover. 407-828-0999.*

★★★ ✔ **Characters in Flight.** This 10-minute tethered balloon ride is pricey for what it is; a trip on the nearby Orlando Eye giant wheel is twice as long and costs as little as $2 more. This one's at Disney though, which means you get a 400-foot-high (122-meter) birds-eye view of Disney Springs and in the distance the rest of Walt Disney World; though you're stuck where you stand and can't move around. The balloon sways a little, but otherwise moves so slowly you barely feel it. Afternoon and evening flights are often cancelled by winds and weather. *8:30a–mid; $18 (children ages 3–9 $12); all ages $10 before 10a; 9 min; children less than 12 years of age must fly with adult; capacity: 30 when winds 0–3 mph (0–5 kph), 20 3–12 mph (5–19 kph), 10 12–22 mph (19–35 kph); does not fly in winds above 22 mph; weather refunds given on the day of purchase only.*

★ **DisneyQuest.** Badly dated "high-tech" adventures from the 1990s lose out to purposefully retro arcade games from the 1980s inside this depressing 5-story building, where Disney is letting something that used to be great waste away. Wear-and-tear is everywhere; a once-Genie-hosted Cybrolator (all custom-voiced by the late Robin Williams) has been an ordinary elevator for years. If it's already included in your Disney tickets you can still have a blast with the right attitude, especially during bad weather, but if you have to pay extra for it you'll regret it; the games you can play at home have now surpassed nearly everything here. If you do go look for one great recent addition: pseudo-vintage Fix-It Felix cabinets (from the 2012 movie "Wreck-It Ralph") that are addicting to play. Closing soon, to be replaced by the NBA Experience (see below). *Noon–9p; $45 (children ages 3–9 $39), includes unlimited play. Height min (in/cm): 51/130 CyberSpace Mountain, Buzz Lightyear's AstroBlaster; 48/122 Mighty Ducks Pinball Slam; 35/89 Pirates of the Caribbean. Children under 10 must be with an adult. No strollers. 2 counter cafes. Free coat check. Capacity 3,689. 407-828-4600.*

★★★★ **House of Blues Music Hall.** You might get squished like a sardine on the main floor, but there are no bad views from the balcony of this intimate two-story music venue, which offers great acoustics, good service and pricey drinks at a wraparound bar. It books a range of mainly blues and rock acts;

both local wannabes and major stars perform close to the audience. A folk-art decor, hardwood floors and quality lighting add to the experience. A fun Gospel Brunch raises the roof on Sundays. The adjacent Crossroads restaurant (see above) has acoustic acts at its outdoor bar, plugged-in shows late Thursday–Saturday. *Showtimes typically 7p–9:30p; doors open 60 min early weekdays, 90 min weekends; $8–$95; all ages; capacity 2,000 (tables, stools 150; standing room 1,850). General admission; diners at the restaurant get priority. Outdoor bar shows 6p–11p, until 2a Thr–Sat. 407-934-2583 or hob.com.*

★★★★★ ✔ **La Nouba.** Amazing, beautiful, classy, cute, elegant, fantastic, funny, quirky and getting just a little dated, this European-style (i.e., animal-free) circus suffers only from its opening act's 1990s World Wide Web backdrop. Otherwise it's exactly what a modern circus should be: a sophisticated collection of highly skilled acrobats and jugglers presented in a purpose-built, acoustically superb arena. Most any seat offers a fine view; sitting in the front row helps you appreciate the complexity and skill of the acts. Though veteran Cirque du Soleil patrons may expect a bit less comedy and a bit more variety, for Cirque newcomers it's superb. Movie buffs will find references to 1997's "The Fifth Element" in La Nouba's odd music and warbling diva, and influences of 1998's "Dark City" in its looming cityscapes and unexpected moving floors. New acts include a B-Boy trio's acrobatic tricks, flips and spins. Art lovers will note homages to Calder and Matisse. Front-row center is Row A, Section 103, Seat 6. The highest prices are in the "Golden Circle": Rows E and F, Section 103, Seats 1 through 20. Designed specifically for a Disney audience, it's appropriate for children of any age who can sit still and appreciate it. *6p, 9p Tue–Sat; $59–$162 (children $48–$137). Seats 1671. 90m show, no intermission; arrive 30m early. Snack stand. Tickets avail 6 months early at cirquedusoleil.com or the box office (11a–11p, until 9p Sun–Mon, 407-939-7600).*

NEW! NBA Experience. Interactive experiences, "immersive video productions," a restaurant and a store will make up this 2017 attraction, the replacement for DisneyQuest.

★★★ ✔ **Splitsville.** Despite its name and retro red-white-and-black color scheme, this impressive boutique bowling alley is definitely not your daddio's. Its 30 lanes aren't all side-by-side but rather are clustered in groups of four and six, spread out over two floors and surrounded by bars, dining tables, pool tables, a sushi bar and on some nights live entertainment. Short lanes and approaches wreck the games of serious bowlers, but others find the setup neat. Days skew to families, nights to adults, as a DJ spins upstairs and the five bars are often packed; business groups have loads of fun. A window runs the length of the first four lanes downstairs, putting those bowlers on display to outsiders. Prices are crazy—you pay by time, not by game, and the amount per person varies by the size of your group as well as the time you play. On average if everyone in your group is a fast bowler and doesn't take extra time to eat or drink, you'll spend about $20 per person for two games—about what adults pay at a standard bowling alley. If anyone takes their time, however, that price can easily double, and that's before factoring in food, drinks and a tip. Enticing servers take you to your lane and eagerly deliver anything you'd like. *10:30a–1a Mon–Wed; 10:30a–2a Thr, Fri; 10a–2a Sat; 10a–1a Sun. $12–$20 per person per session; sessions 60–90m based on size of party (children age 9 and under $7). 407-938-7467.*

★★★★★ ✔ **Street performers.** Live bands and solo musicians perform in front of the West Side Starbucks and in the Food Truck plaza; Living Statues appear in front of the Cirque du Soleil theater. Show times vary.

Marketplace

Shops and merchandise. Unlike the other Disney Springs areas, the Marketplace is dominated by Disney shops. Also different: the many carts and kiosks on its walkways, tempting you with everything from flowers to yo-yos. It's anchored by the World of Disney, Walt Disney World's largest store.

Arribas Brothers. Hand-cut crystal, hand-blown glass and engraving. Artisans work in front of guests. A huge blown-glass wall sculpture from St. Augustine artist Thomas Long is not for sale.

The Art of Disney. Collectible animation cels, attraction posters, Lenox china figurines, lithographs, paintings and more.

Basin. The aroma intoxicates you inside this lovely shop, which offers items for the "shower, tub, sink and soul." Try out the salt and sugar scrubs in the handy sinks; shelves teem with all-natural massage and shampoo bars, bath bombs, body butters and lotions.

Made in Orlando, fresh soaps come in many colors and scents.

Bibbidi Bobbidi Boutique. A child's makeover salon similar to the one inside Cinderella Castle at Magic Kingdom. Now in its own spot near Once Upon a Toy. *Salon: 8:45a–7:30p; girls $65–$195 and up, boys $20; ages 3–12; allow 30–60 min. Reservations: 407-939-7895 available 6 months in advance.*

NEW! Curl's Bungalow. Hats, sandals, sunglasses. An offshoot of the Curl by Sammy Duvall store at the West Side. Outdoor stand.

Disney Design-A-Tee. Design a Hanes T-shirt using a touchscreen. Choose from hundreds of Disney graphics; add three or four lines of text. Results look amateur.

Disney's Days of Christmas. Huge holiday shop has dated ornaments, figurines, Mickey-eared Santa hats, stockings; most with a stale 1990s design. Embroidery and engraving available.

Disney's Pin Traders. Small open-air shop filled with collectible pins. Limited variety.

Disney's Wonderful World of Memories. Scrapbooks, photo albums, frames. Small selection of good Disney books.

Ghirardelli. Candy, cocoa, fudge sauce, hot-chocolate mix. Free chocolate samples.

Happy Hound. Outdoor kiosk with custom collars and tags, outfits, toys; spills over onto the walls of a nearby store.

NEW! Icon Jewelry by Bico. Based on universal symbols, the pewter jewelry at this outdoor stand is from Australia and enhanced with crystal, leather and rosewood. You can customize it, too.

NEW! Just Plumerias. Plants and cuttings of this Hawaiian flower. Outdoor stand.

NEW! Kate & Leo. Charming child-focused cart has games, toys and art supplies, none of which need batteries. Outdoor stand.

Lefty's. Outdoor kiosk has products for left-handers, much like those at the original Lefty's on San Francisco's Fisherman's Wharf.

The Lego Store. Part store, part playground, this crowded shop boasts the world's largest Pick-A-Brick wall, with 320 bins sorted by color and size. There's a huge variety of Lego collections, priced as little as $7. Indoor-outdoor play areas include tracks for kids to race the vehicles they build. Giant creations outside the shop make good photo backdrops.

Little Miss Matched. For 'tween girls: cute, affordable, cheaply made mismatched socks in many colors, styles and lengths—liners, anklets, knee highs. Colorful clothing, accessories. One of 7 stores in the chain.

Marketplace Co-Op. Six boutiques make up this spot, which looks like a cooperative of small independent merchants but is actually a Disney testing lab for retail-shop concepts and products. None of the stores are necessarily permanent; Disney "reimagines" them whenever it sees fit. The current line-up: **Cherry Tree Lane** sells sophisticated women's accessories such as bags, jewelry, scarves, shoes; **D-Tech on Demand** offers personalized electronic accessories; **Disney Centerpiece** (the second best spot, in my opinion) sells odd home furnishings and housewares based on theme-park art, such as salt-and-pepper shakers that look like Adventureland trash cans; **Disney Tag** sells Disney-flavored luggage, travel accessories and gear; **Twenty Eight & Main** (ding ding ding… numero uno!) uses vintage Disney art to adorn shirts, accessories and wall art in unusual ways, lately using Star Wars characters to re-imagine 1970s posters for classic Magic Kingdom attractions; **WonderGround Gallery** stocks commissioned, original and limited-edition artwork inspired by Disney/ Pixar films, characters and icons.

Marketplace Fun Finds. Cheap Disney souvenirs sold under big letters that spell out "F-U-N." Not a must.

Mickey's Pantry. Mickey Mouse-styled housewares; non-Disney cookware, food, tableware, wine. A Spice and Tea Exchange area blends salts, sugars, spices and teas.

Once Upon a Toy. Hasbro store has theme-park items, Build-Your-Own Mr. Potato Head station. In the back room a giant toy train circles the ceiling.

Pearl Factory. Outdoor stand offers Japanese akoya pearls in their oysters (6–9 mm, $16); settings, pearl jewelry.

Rainforest Cafe Retail Village. Every bit as inspired as its name, this restaurant shop has forgettable animal-themed apparel, plush, toys; some cute sundresses. The animated decor is impressive in a 1990s way.

Savannah Bee Company. This outdoor stand sells products and foods made from all-natural honey. Yum.

Set the Bar. Outdoor stand offers funny, whimsical bar-inspired items, including drinking games, flasks and wine toppers.

Sublime Gifts and Finds. Yet another outdoor stand, this one with journals, inspirational signs and books.

T-Rex Dino-Store. Dinosaur-themed children's apparel, toys; Build-A-Dino area. Outdoor play pit has faux fossils, sluice.

Tren-D.

Dockside Margaritas.

Tren-D. Interesting junior apparel from Disney, Billabong, Hurley, Roxy. Easy to overlook, but always worth a stop.

EXPANDED! World of Disney. Enlarged in 2016 to include four new rooms, this department store has areas for Girls, Ladies and Juniors, Boys, Men, Infants, Hats and T-shirts, Housewares, Home Decor, Jewelry and Pins, Candy and Snacks, Souvenirs. It's still often too crowded for quality service; many items are also in park gift shops.

Restaurants and food. Of the plethora of table-service restaurants at Disney Springs, know how many are in the Marketplace? Two. Just two. And in a way they're the same place.

★★ **$34 DDP Rainforest Café.** Robotic animals come to life every 22 minutes in the faux jungle of this 1990s eatery, created by the same group that later did T-Rex. Young kids love it, but it gets old quickly for parents. A vast menu offers standard chain food that is neither exceptional nor awful. An outdoor volcano erupts every half hour from the roof; you can see its propane fire throughout Disney Springs. A quiet Lava Lounge behind the restaurant has its own menu as well as the full one. It doesn't require a reservation, has no robotic elephants and provides nice views of the lake. *11a–10:30p; $15–$34 (children $9). Seats 575, inc 30 at outdoor bar. Direct reservations: 407-827-8500. No same-day reservations.*

★★★ **$34 DDP T-Rex.** Dinos and prehistoric beasts roar and move every 22 minutes at this lively eatery, reminiscent of its sister restaurant Rainforest Cafe. You choose from four distinct environments: a fiery volcano area, a glowing Ice Age cave, a jungle habitat and a calm ocean area (which comes complete with large aquariums that house saltwater fish and a bar that changes colors). No matter where you sit, it's loud and difficult to have a quiet conversation. Expect generous portions of typical American food from the extensive menu. A standout is an over-the-top dessert, Chocolate Extinction, which will feed the table. A Dino Dig area for kids includes a place to store shoes and clean up. *11a–10:30p; $16–$34 (children $9). Seats 626, inc 26 at bar. Direct reservations: 407-828-8739.*

NEW! ★★★ **DDPq $12 AristoCrepes.** Disney's 1970 movie "The Aristocats" gives this stand its name. Savory and sweet crepes, wine, beer. *4p–11p; $7–$9. No seating.*

NEW! ★★★★ ✔ **DDPq $13 B.B. Wolf's Sausage Co.** Get it? Big Bad Wolf. Apparently the villain in Disney's 1933 cartoon "The Three Little Pigs" has finally caught his prey; he's serving up a sampler of three pork sausages at this stand. Who's afraid of the Big Bad Wolf? Well, now we know who should have been. Other sausages too, including a veggie. Draft beer. *11a–11p; $8–$10. No seating.*

★★★★ ✔ **$10 Dockside Margaritas.** Florida rum, fruit and sugar cane make the potent potables at this shady spot special. Despite its name most of its options aren't margaritas; mojitos, rum runners, fruit wine and local beers dominate. Don't overlook its long waterside bar; you can't see it from the front. Drinks *$7–$14 (non-alcoholic $5–$6); nuts $4. 50 covered outdoor seats inc 12 at bar.*

★★★★★ ✔ **$11 DDPq Earl of Sandwich.** We know exactly one person who hates Earl of Sandwich. And a hundred who love it. Hot crusty sandwiches and soothing soups make this fast-food spot the most popular at Disney Springs; its roast beef sandwich and tomato soup are legendary among Disney regulars. On the downside it's always crowded and finding an open table is sometimes a chore. Don't let the long line discourage you; it moves quickly. Prices are comparable to a Subway but here you get what signs claim is, only with a slight exaggeration, "the best hot sandwich in the world." The holiday sandwich, with turkey and dressing, is to die for. The original restaurant in the small Earl of Sandwich chain, this one is owned by the ancestors of John Montagu, the fourth Earl of Sandwich who in 1762 invented the sandwich. Breakfast items are cheaper than those at the nearby Wolfgang Puck Express but not as good. *Breakfast 8:30a–10:30a $3–$8; lunch, dinner 10:30a–11p $6–$8 (children $4). Seats 190, inc 65 outside.*

★★★ **$5 DDPs Joffrey's.** Along with Wetzel's Pretzels (see below), this little coffee, tea and smoothie stand sits right next to the Waterside Stage. *$4–$6.*

★★★★ **$11 Ghirardelli Soda Fountain.** Rich, house-made Ghirardelli chocolate is used to make the decadent desserts served at this ice cream parlor. It's hard to finish the massive sundaes, so plan to share. People flock here, so also be prepared to wait awhile to order. The interior looks like an old-fashioned ice cream counter and smells of heavenly chocolate. Finding a seat is a challenge. Inside tables are stalked by families trying to nab a spot, while outside areas are often hot enough to instantly melt your treat. *10:30a–11p Sun–Thu, 10:30a–mid Fri–Sat; ice cream $5–$7, sundaes $10–$11, shakes $7–$9 (children $3–$7); 13 flavors of ice cream. Seats 88, inc 22 outside.*

★★★ **$7 DDPs Goofy's Candy Company.** Fresh and create-your-own apples, cookies,

other treats. Coffees, smoothies. *10a–11p; $4–$12. No seating.*

★★★ **$12 Marketplace Snacks.** Easy to overlook, this small stand's main benefit is its location—right next to the shady tables of Dockside Margaritas. Go ahead, sit there. Blame it on me. Hot dogs, nachos. *10a–11p; $8–$10; beer, wine $7–$9. No seating.*

NEW! ★★★★ **$9 DDPs Starbucks.** There's only one thing wrong with this walk-up stand—it's a walk-up stand. As such it pales to the Starbucks on the West Side. *8a–mid; breakfast sandwiches $4–$5, lunch $5–$6; in front of World of Disney. No seating.*

★★★ **$9 Wetzel's Pretzels.** This small stand sells hand-rolled pretzels, hot dogs, and lemonade. Stick to the pretzels. Next to the Waterside Stage. *9:30a–11p; $4–$7.*

★★★★ ✔ **$24 DDPq Wolfgang Puck Express.** Here's the Puck place you'll prefer—its food is at least as good as the other Puck locations but less expensive, prepared faster and there's never a wait to get seated. Best bets include the breakfast pizza, the barbecue chicken pizza, the salads and the chicken and butternut-squash soups. Everything's made-to-order, and it all comes with real cutlery on real plates. Bring cash for a tip; though you order at a counter a server brings you your food and refills your drinks. *Breakfast 9a–11a, $10–$15 (no kids meals); lunch, dinner 8:30a–10:30p $11–$20 (children $7–$8). Seats 184.*

Entertainment. Yes! Some things for your 2-year-old! Don't overlook the fountain.

★★★★★ ✔ **Street performers.** On many evenings a DJ hosts a kids or adult dance party across from World of Disney, musicians perform near T-Rex. Show times vary.

★★★★ **Kiddie rides.** Hand crafted in Italy, the Marketplace Carousel is a small antique merry-go-round that has 19 horses (originally with real horse hair) and two carriages. Painted murals above the horses depict the nearby landscape, a plain mural with red roses hides the three-circle shape of Mickey Mouse. Nearby is the Marketplace Express kiddie train, and also another kid's favorite, a splash fountain made of three rings that forms a Hidden Mickey. *Carousel next to Earl of Sandwich, train across from Tren-D next to Disney Pin Traders. Fountain at entrance to pedestrian bridge to Hotel Plaza Blvd. Both 10a–11p, until 11:30p Fri, Sat; $2, children less than 42 in (107 cm) tall must be accompanied by adult who rides free; cash, credit cards.*

Jostens Center.

A real SportsCenter

One of the few places on Disney property that is not a tourist spot, the 230-acre (93-ha) ESPN Wide World of Sports complex (700 S Victory Lane, Lake Buena Vista FL 34747. 407-828-3267, live operator 407-939-1500, youth group information 407-939-4263; espnwwos.com) is the top youth sports center in the United States. Each year it hosts more than 100 events and attracts about 330,000 athletes and 1.5 million total visitors. Facilities include a baseball stadium, two field houses, 18 multipurpose fields, 16 baseball/softball fields, a track-and-field area and a 10-court tennis center.

Popularity. As of 2016 over 3.4 million athletes have competed at the complex, representing more than 231,000 teams. Larger events include the annual Disney Soccer Showcase, which draws more than 11,000 athletes and 660 teams. The complex is also a recruiting ground for colleges, as high school competitions such as the Disney Field Hockey Showcase attract hundreds of coaches.

Design. Built in 1996, ESPN Wide World of Sports features what Disney calls "Florida Picturesque" architecture—yellow Spanish-style buildings offset by blue and green accents. Its field area has shady walkways landscaped with palms and hardwoods on its left side, thanks to the triangular shapes of its baseball and softball fields, but few trees on its right side, where rectangular multi-purpose fields often leave little extra space.

Video coverage. Roving ESPN production crews, robotic cameras and a 20-zone audio system capture the action at most events. About a dozen highlight and interview clips are produced daily, which air on video screens throughout the complex as well as on Disney hotel-room televisions. Major events are covered with up to seven cameras, two more than most ESPN college-football telecasts. Hidden within the grounds of the baseball stadium, a 2,500-square-foot (760-square-meter) production center includes two studios and eight edit bays. One of five ESPN distribution hubs in the United States, the complex is the anchor point for more fiber-optic cable than AT&T Stadium in Dallas. **National coverage.** Over the past decade various ESPN cable networks have aired over 2,000 hours of coverage from the Wide World of Sports complex. Streaming service ESPN3 airs over 600 hours of events each year. **ESPN Innovation Lab.** Located in a small building between the tennis center and Hess Convertible Fields 7 and 9, ESPN staffers develop broadcast technologies by using the sports complex as a real-world testing ground for the ESPN Emerging Technology Group. So far the results have included Ball Track, a Doppler-radar system that can continuously update the distance and height of a baseball in flight; ESPN Snap Zoom, a freeze-frame technology that zooms in on an area of a football play to provide more insight on the action; and the EA Virtual Playbook, which allows studio analysts to bring to life key match-ups, formations and game action with multi-dimensional animation. Unfortunately, the lab is closed to the public.

Venues. Consisting of eight distinct venues, the complex has an array of courts and fields. **Baseball Quadraplex.** For baseball this is Disney's nicest place to play. It features four manicured fields, a half field for infield drills and various bullpens, batting tunnels and pitching machines. Center fields have batter's-eye backdrops. Field 3 has lights. A separate pitching area has 10 enclosed bullpens. The quad is used by pro players during Atlanta Braves Spring Training, Gulf Coast League and Fall Instructional League seasons. *340 ft (104 m) right- and left-field lines, 385 ft (117 m) power alleys, 400 ft (122 m) center field. Fields 2, 4 and 5 have small covered infield bleachers, Field 3 has small covered bleachers behind home plate. No concession stand. Restrooms, pay phones, souvenir kiosk.* **Champion Stadium.** This double-decker ballpark hosts amateur competitions as well as Atlanta Braves Spring Training games. Wide concourses create a pleasant atmosphere, but the stadium lacks the intimate feel found at other Florida Spring Training sites. Most seats are in direct sun. A general-admission grass berm beyond left field seats 2,000. Concession stands offer sandwiches, hot dogs, soft drinks and beer. *340 ft (104 m) right- and left-field lines, 385 ft (117 m) power alleys, 400 ft (122 m) center field. 9,500 seats,*

80 percent behind infield. 4 sky boxes; 2 open-air suites with patios. Gift shop. **Hess Sports Baseball Fields.** Four large diamonds (Fields 21–24) sit at the far right of the complex. A lack of landscaping creates a sunny environment for spectators. All fields have lights and bullpens, with batting tunnels nearby. *355 ft (108 m) maximum right- and left-field lines, 489 ft (149 m) maximum center field. Small 3-row infield bleachers may be tented. No concession stand, snack tents may be set up. Soft-drink machine. Restrooms nearby.* **Hess Sports Convertible Fields.** Spread throughout the complex, these 13 huge rectangles can host football, lacrosse, soccer and similar sports. Features vary. *Specs:* Next to the Baseball Quadraplex, Fields 7 and 9 lack scoreboards, though Field 7 has a coaching tower. Behind the HP Field House, Fields 16 and 17 include lights for night play, as do adjacent Fields 18 and 19. Next to the Jostens Center, Field 20 has no scoreboard. Note: Because of their proximity to the complex entrance plaza, Fields 19 and 20 have ambient music: a soundtrack of upbeat pop tunes. Most fields are crowned with 1-degree slopes. *Fields 7 and 9 lack spectator seating; share a concession stand, restrooms. Field 16 has a small shaded bleacher area. Fields 17 and 18 have large sections of covered stadium seats; have concession stands and restrooms nearby. Field 19 lacks spectator seating; has concession stands and restrooms nearby. Field 20 has no spectator amenities.* **HP Field House.** With high arches and trusses reminiscent of a 1950s field house, the main arena at this 165,000-square-foot (50,300-square-meter) facility can host a variety of multi-court events. Two auxiliary courts sit upstairs. The bottom floor has locker rooms, a workout area and pro memorabilia cases. *Next to Champion Stadium. 5,500 stadium seats; top row 35 ft (11 m) high. Auxiliary courts have 6-row bleachers. Concession stands sell sandwiches, hot dogs, snacks, soft drinks, no beer. Wetzel's Pretzels stand at aux. courts. Restrooms. No gift shop. Back patio overlooks Hess Field 17.* **Jostens Center.** This indoor arena has all of its competition area in one space. It can be divided into two inline hockey rinks, six basketball courts or a dozen volleyball courts. Locker rooms are available. *5-row bleachers line two sides. Concession stand, Wetzel's Pretzels stand on second level. Restrooms on both levels. Adjacent to souvenir shop, ESPN Wide World of Sports Grill.*

"Now let's try a silly one."

Diamondplex Softball Complex. Six fields can accommodate fast-pitch softball, slow-pitch softball or youth baseball. A central tower at the main quad has a concession stand, as well as areas for scorekeepers and officials. All fields have lights and bullpens, with batting tunnels nearby. *Fields 10 and 11 maximum dimensions: 275 ft (84 m) right-, left- and center-field lines. Quad fields (12, 13, 14 and 15) maximum dimensions: 305 ft (93 m) right-, left- and center-field lines. Fields 10 and 11 have small covered bleachers behind their home plates. Quad fields have small covered infield bleachers. Concession stand sells sandwiches, hot dogs, snacks, soft drinks, beer. Restrooms, pay phones. Souvenir kiosk nearby.*

Tennis Center. These 10 clay courts, which include a stadium court, once hosted the U.S. Men's Clay Court Championships as well as matches in the 2016 Invictus Games hosted by Prince Harry of Great Britain. All courts are in direct sun; seven have lights. *Stadium court elevated bleachers seat 1,000. No amenities, though food and souvenir carts may be set up for events. The back side of the adjacent ESPN Innovation Lab has a concession stand that, if open, sells sandwiches, hot dogs, snacks and soft drinks; nearby are soft-drink machines, restrooms, pay phones.*

New Balance Track and Field Complex. This polyurethane area meets the standards of the International Association of Athletics Federation, the sport's governing body. Its 1,312-ft (400-m) track has nine 48-inch (122-cm) lanes, double straightaways, three shot-put rings, two discus/hammer rings, a javelin runway, two high-jump pits, two interior horizontal-jump runways and two pole-vault zones. An adaptable cross-country course is adjacent. *Large covered bleachers. No concession stand. Adjacent restrooms.*

Policies and resources. The complex includes food spots, gift shops, a Welcome Center and some procedures and practices:

Admission. Though courts and fields are open only to participating groups, the public is welcome as spectators. Admission for amateur events is $17.50 for ages 10 and above, $12.50 for ages 3–9. Length-of-event tickets are often available. Walt Disney World annual passholders get in free. Professional events are ticketed separately.

ATM. There's one, outside the gates by the ESPN Clubhouse store. A portable ATM is set up in Champion Stadium for Braves games.

Coolers. You can bring in a cooler of up to one gallon for personal use. Coaches can bring in coolers up to five gallons. No coolers are allowed in the Jostens Center.

Credentials. Athlete and coach credentials are distributed to teams at registration. To get them, each team must have paid its tournament entry fee and submitted waivers for each athlete and coach. A coach can pick up credentials for an entire team.

Family matters. Parents wanting to watch their child compete will find shaded bleachers at most outdoor venues, and either bleachers or stadium seats at most indoor spots. Nursing mothers will find the best indoor options to be various nooks and crannies in the HP Field House and Jostens Center, or, on uncrowded days, a back table at the ESPN Wide World of Sports Grill (although none of these three spots allow strollers). Moms might find it tough to nurse in Champion Stadium; the baseball park has few private spots beyond restrooms, especially out of the heat.

First Aid. Trainers in marked tents aid injured athletes. The entrance gift shop stocks over-the-counter pain medications, bandages and other basic supplies.

Food. Concession stands dot the grounds; temporary carts offer snacks and beverages on event days. You can place advance orders for boxed meals, bulk beverages and snacks to be delivered to particular fields; items range from $8 sandwiches to $20 pizzas. Officially only visitors with special dietary needs (i.e., medical conditions, religious doctrines) may bring food into the complex, however this rule is often not enforced. No glass bottles or alcoholic beverages can be brought into the complex, though many concession stands sell beer. Indoor American fast-food spot **ESPN Wide World of Sports Grill (★★★ $)** has you order at a counter but delivers your food to your table. The menu has chicken wings, individual pizzas, salads and sandwiches; best bets are the BLT and barbecued-pork sandwiches. Soft drinks are refillable. A photo prop looks like a "SportsCenter" set. Seven huge high-def screens show popular sports channels as well as, sometimes, events going on within the complex. More TVs are at the separate bar, which serves liquor as well as beer and wine. *Across from Champion Stadium, next to the Jostens Center. 10:30a–7p; on slow days will close early or have limited menu. Lunch, dinner: $8–$14, Seats 350, 48 in bar.*

ESPN Production Center.

Getting around. Larger than most Disney theme parks, the complex requires a lot of walking to get around. The hike from the parking lot to the Softball Complex is seven-tenths of a mile (1 km), which at a leisurely pace takes about 15 minutes.

Parking. General parking is free; valet parking is available during some events for $10 to $20, depending on the event. Though expanded recently the parking lot still often fills to capacity. Overflow parking is available on grassy areas behind the lot and on the median of Victory Way, the road that leads to the complex. Late arrivals for Atlanta Braves Spring Training games often park alongside the road, and then have to walk almost a mile (1.6 km) to Champion Stadium.

Park tickets. The Welcome Center sells all types of Disney World park tickets, including a specially priced ticket that's available only to complex visitors. A "1-Day After 2 p.m." ticket provides admission to any one theme park for $74; a similar "1-Day After 1 p.m." for water parks is $32. The tickets are valid only on the day of purchase. (Prices as of July 2016.)

Pets. Except for service animals, no animals are allowed on the grounds.

Restrooms. Facilities are available at, or near, all competition venues.

Shops. The ESPN Clubhouse Shop offers ESPN, sports-team and complex apparel, as well as a small selection of collapsible chairs, sunglasses and umbrellas. The shop has two locations: at the complex entrance and inside Champion Stadium. Next to the ESPN Wide World of Sports Grill, a Custom Tee Center booth customizes event T-shirts. Souvenir kiosks are often set up at event venues.

Strollers. Strollers are allowed in most areas of the complex, but prohibited inside the HP Field House, Jostens Center and ESPN Wide World of Sports Grill. Stroller parking is available outside of those venues.

Transportation. Complimentary Disney bus service is usually available from Disney's All-Star, Caribbean Beach and Pop Century Resorts. Buses typically run from an hour before the complex opens to 11 p.m. or closing time on event days, as well as every Thursday through Monday from 5 p.m. to 11 p.m. The buses arrive at ESPN on the hour and the half-hour. Buses may not be able to accommodate all teams and equipment.

Welcome Center. Located between the HP Field House and Jostens Center, a small Welcome Center offers event schedules and provides general Disney World information. It also sells theme-park, water-park and La Nouba tickets; makes Disney dining reservations; and helps with transportation issues.

Wheelchairs. Complimentary wheelchairs are available at the Welcome Center.

Invictus Games.

Art of Animation. Cars area.

Accommodations

AS THE MOST POPULAR vacation destination on the planet, Walt Disney World has no shortage of places to stay. Disney itself owns 20 resort hotels, all with architecture, decor and landscaping that immerse you in a unique experience. Combined, these places can hold 126,000 people. More than a dozen other hotels at Disney are managed by outside companies, such as Hilton and Marriott. This chapter reviews all of them, and includes details you won't find anywhere else.

Why stay at a Disney hotel? Staying anywhere on Disney property is convenient. It's easy to get to a park early in the morning and to return to your hotel for a midday break. Benefits of a Disney-owned hotel include:

Extra Magic Hours. Each day, at least one theme park offers extended hours for guests of Disney-owned hotels, opening either one hour early or staying open up to two hours late. Water parks also participate.

Complimentary transportation. Disney boats, buses and monorail trains take you to its parks, Disney Springs and, in some cases, the ESPN Wide World of Sports complex.

Children's activities. The hotels have complimentary swimming-pool games and other activities for kids, and provide life jackets. Some host Movies Under the Stars nights, which show Disney films on outdoor screens.

Magical Express. This complimentary bus service shuttles you between the Orlando International Airport and your Disney-owned hotel. In most cases you bypass baggage claim, as Disney itself picks up your luggage from your airline. In addition, you can often check your baggage for your return flight at your resort. Magical Express is available to guests using particular airlines.

MagicBand. This wristband acts as a room key, park ticket and charge card. Each Disney hotel guest, including each child, gets one with their reservation packet or at check-in.

Package delivery. Anything a Disney hotel guest buys at a Disney theme park can be delivered to their hotel free of charge.

Guaranteed admission. If they have tickets, Disney resort guests are guaranteed entry into Disney theme parks, even, in most cases, when those parks are officially filled to capacity. Visiting at Christmas, the Fourth of July or another peak period? This matters.

Special deals. Disney resort guests can prepay for their meals through the Disney Dining Plan and get preferred tee times and discounts at Disney's four golf courses.

Disney hotel categories.
Disney groups its 20 hotels into four groups by room rate—and therefore by their amenities, room size and how many people those rooms will hold.

Value resorts. (Disney's All-Star, Art of Animation, Pop Century). These huge complexes hold Disney's least expensive rooms. Most rooms sleep four. Amenities are limited, but do include swimming pools, playgrounds and food courts. Luggage service is hourly. Oddly, the Values are the only Disney hotels with obvious Disney themes; many are trimmed with props that recall Disney movies.

Moderate resorts. (Disney's Caribbean Beach, Coronado Springs, Fort Wilderness, Port Orleans). These large complexes have geographical themes, larger rooms, elaborate pools and in most cases table-service restaurants. Most rooms have queen beds. Amenities include on-site recreation.

Deluxe resorts. (Disney's Animal Kingdom Lodge, BoardWalk Inn, Contemporary, Grand Floridian, Polynesian Village, Wilderness Lodge, Yacht and Beach Club). Serious architecture and lush landscaping distinguish these top-of-the-line hotels. Rooms are large; most sleep five. Amenities include fine restaurants, club levels and valet parking.

Deluxe Villas. (Disney's Old Key West and Saratoga Springs; sections of Animal Kingdom Lodge, Beach Club, BoardWalk, Contemporary, Grand Floridian, Polynesian Village, Wilderness Lodge). These Disney Vacation Club (DVC) timeshare units are available nightly as owner usage permits.

Family suites.
Large family? Small family, but want more than one bedroom? Disney gives you two choices. Connecting rooms have a door that opens between them that locks from both sides. The trouble is, they're not that common. For example, of the 2,800 rooms at Disney's Pop Century Resort, only 700 connect. Worse, Disney will let you request connecting rooms but often won't guarantee them. Connecting rooms have fallen out of favor lately in the hotel industry, as their nature makes stays less safe.

Disney's other option? Family suites. These lack the privacy of connecting rooms, and during peak periods can cost more that two standard rooms. They're available at two Disney hotels, the All-Star Music Resort and the Art of Animation Resort. The All-Star suites have recently been refurbished and are often relative bargains. Still, a quick glance at TripAdvisor shows most visitors say that Disney's Art of Animation suites are better. In a nutshell, that's because it specializes in family suites. They make up most of its places to stay, and their buildings consume 75 percent of its grounds. Unlike those at All-Star Music, Art of Animation suites are accessed from indoor hallways in buildings that require MagicBands (or key cards) to enter.

Moderate or Deluxe?
Trying to decide between these two hotel types? If you're traveling with children and money is an issue, we say go Moderate. Deluxe resorts, of course, are nicer. Most go all out with their theme, their restaurants are better, their rooms usually larger and their linens more plush. But they're not as casual, and have smaller fast-food spots and fewer swimming pools. Equally important: if you're driving a car you can park close or sometimes right next to your room at a Moderate resort, a big deal when you're trying to get going in the morning or coming back at night after an exhausting day at the parks carrying sleeping toddlers in your arms. At Deluxe resorts, however, the "self-parking" lot can be a literal half-mile from the hotel entrance, and then you've still got an indoor hike through lobbies, up elevators and down what can be very long halls. And, of course, Deluxe rates are higher than Moderate rates.

How about no room at all?
Seeking a truly memorable stay? Have a sense of adventure? Consider camping at Fort Wilderness.

About these reviews.
We rate hotels from one to five stars (★) based on their quality and value; a checkmark (✔) indicates an author favorite. Room rates don't include resort tax (13.5 percent at the All-Star Resorts; 12.5 percent elsewhere). All hotel addresses are in the city of Lake Buena Vista, Florida.

All-Star Sports.

Happiness is a cheap room

IF YOU'RE ON A TIGHT BUDGET, Disney's least-expensive places to stay—its Value Resorts and the campsites at its Fort Wilderness Resort—may be just what you're looking for. All have rack rates as low as $150 a night. Campsites start at less than $80.

A cursory glance at Disney's website could make you think that its Value Resorts are basically the same, identical except for their themes and possible inclusion of higher-priced family suites. To some extent, that's true. Built to compete with a rash of discount motels on nearby U.S. 192 (most of which have since fallen into disrepair), each Value Resort is laid out like a typical motel complex, but on a giant scale. An entrance building holds check-in and concierge counters, a food court, gift shop and bus stop; behind it is the main swimming pool. Multi-story lodging buildings spread out from there, with hundreds and sometimes thousands of rooms accessed from outdoor walkways. Stairwells and elevators hide behind massive re-creations of Disney film characters or other cultural icons.

In truth, however, the Value Resorts have many differences, important ones you should know about. I'll break them down in just a

minute. But first I think you should know that my husband, daughter and I spend a lot of time at these places.

For Mike, photographing them is a never-ending job. At the Value Resorts nearly every building has a different look, so to visually represent the area each structure demands its own shot. Photographing Fort Wilderness is also quite an assignment, as the light there is so dappled by its trees and the place is filled with unusual details that cry out to be illustrated—its stables, pony ranch, the many people putting around in electric carts. Most of these images don't make it into our print books, but they do in our digital versions, especially the ones for Apple devices. We also use them in our social media posts.

Ten questions. I wondered: if you were sitting here with me at my kitchen table as I write this, what might you ask me about these spots? I came up with these questions:

1. What's the food situation? The hotels have food courts. The campground has a table-service restaurant (with buffets for breakfast and dinner, a regular menu at lunch), two dinner shows, a to-go menu and a general store with groceries. The food courts vary. We like the ones at All-Star Music and All-Star Sports; we could eat their roast beef and fish sandwiches for days. We love the specialty entrees at Art of Animation even though they take awhile to prepare and can get pretty expensive. But we've never had a good meal at the All-Star Movies food court (though to be fair, it is scheduled to be renovated soon), and lately the one at Pop Century has been bland. It used to serve retro TV dinners and a cheesecake that looked to be tie-dyed, but today there's nothing that's all that special.

When you think of country food, do you think KFC, or maybe Cracker Barrel? If so you'll be shocked by Trail's End, the restaurant at Fort Wilderness. Its lunch is a hidden treasure; its breakfast and dinner buffets have some unique specialty items. The fried chicken is first-rate at the campground's take-out window after 4 p.m. and at the Hoop-Dee-Doo Musical Revue dinner show.

2. How are the pools? Not bad. Our daughter *lived* in the Disney pools as an adolescent, a benefit of her mom working at the resorts. And though she preferred the ones at the more expensive hotels, since they had slides and other features, she liked the ones at the Value Resorts just fine. Their main pools are big, with lots of space to play in, and the small ones are often empty, especially in the middle of the day. Some have unusual shapes. Seen from above, the main pool at All-Star Music is a guitar, the pool behind it a piano. A Pop Century pool is a bowling pin. Want a slide at this price? Camp at Fort Wilderness. Its main pool has a big curved one.

3. Where are these places? The three All-Star Resorts are in the western part of Disney property, near the Animal Kingdom theme park and Blizzard Beach water park. Art of Animation and Pop Century are more centrally located, close to Disney's Hollywood Studios and the ESPN Wide World of Sports complex, near Interstate 4. Fort Wilderness lines Bay Lake near Disney's northern border, a few miles from Magic Kingdom.

4. Are these the REAL room rates? Yes and no. To its credit, Disney never tacks on a "resort fee" or "self-parking fee" or any other such nonsense to any of its hotel rates. However, the state of Florida does. It adds a sales tax (6.5 percent) and a Tourist Development Tax (another 6 percent). If you stay at one of the All-Star Resorts you'll also pay a local sales tax (0.5 percent) because unlike most of Walt Disney World they're located in Osceola County, Fla., not Orange County. So a $100-a-night room will actually cost you $113 at an All-Star Resort, $112.50 at Art of Animation or Pop Century. Likewise, a $60-a-night camping space at Fort

Art of Animation. Little Mermaid pool.

Fort Wilderness pony ride.

Wilderness will in truth cost $67.50. (The hidden costs of renting a car at the Orlando International Airport are even worse. In June 2016, the Hertz website quoted us a rate of $495 for a one-week rental of a Chevy Camaro convertible. The actual cost: $636. Because it included an Airport Concession Fee ($51), a Customer Facility Charge ($32), a Vehicle Licensing Cost ($18), an Energy Surcharge ($1) and various state and local taxes ($39). It would have been even higher if we had needed a Child Seat ($91) or purchased a Loss Damage Waiver ($220).

5. Do the rooms have free Wi-Fi service? Yes. So do the campsites. In most cases the bus stops and swimming pools have it too.

6. How hard is it to get to your car? Fifty feet. That's how close some Value Resort rooms are to their parking lots, as lodging buildings often butt right up against them. Parking lots wrap around the sides of each All-Star Resort and Pop Century, and clock three sides of the Little Mermaid section of Art of Animation. At Fort Wilderness you park right next to your tent.

7. How hard is it to get your luggage to your room? Not too tough. Some Value Resort lodging buildings are distant from parking lots, but all have elevators, and each resort's check-in area has bellhops ready to wheel your bags to your room on a hand trolley. If you're getting to your hotel through Disney's Magical Express bus service, Disney delivers your luggage to the room. If you're using the service to get to Fort Wilderness, your bags will be dropped off at your campsite.

8. Are these places better than budget spots just outside Disney? If you lived here like I do, and were familiar with the areas around Walt Disney World, you probably wouldn't even ask this question. Because for the most part, the area around Disney is a dump. An exception is Celebration, a large planned community developed by Disney that's right next to it. But there's only one hotel within Celebration itself (the Bohemian), and its rates start at about $175.

There are some decent places just east of Disney, a spattering of indoor-hall chains such as Courtyard by Marriott and Hilton Garden Inn that start at about $90 a night, a rate that may include a free basic breakfast. However, since these hotels are located on the busy service roads along Interstate 4, staying at one can add 30 minutes to your drive to any Disney theme park. And when you get there you'll pay a $20 parking fee.

Driving back might take you even longer. Afternoon and after-dark post-Wishes traffic jams get so thick on I-4's eastbound lanes that cars on them often simply come to a halt. And you'll probably need to stop somewhere on the way back to have dinner, as properties such as Courtyard by Marriott typically don't have restaurants or food courts and aren't within walking distance to any.

And, of course, if you stay off-site you won't get those other benefits of staying at a Disney spot, such as early park admission. So why even consider these off-property hotels? Maybe because you're headed to Universal as well as Disney, and want to stay between the two. Or because you have loads of loyalty points with Hilton or Marriott, so your room won't cost you anything. Note: If you stay near the Orange County Convention Center (4 miles east of Disney) the taxes you pay will be higher: 13.63 percent. Because they'll also include a convention tax. Whether or not you go to a convention.

9. How nice are the grounds? Frankly, we're impressed. Check our photos. You'll see some nice landscaping, and few if any dead plants, trees or splotches of grass. Ironically, the nicest looking of Disney's Value Resorts are its cheapest—its All-Star Resorts. Naturally wooded spaces surround many of their buildings. Tree-lined boulevards shade the Broadway and Country Fair sections of All-Star Music. At Pop Century, tall trees outline a long entranceway.

10. How do these places differ from each another? Five differences stand out to me—what they look like, their food choices, what they offer for children, their bus service, and the crowds they attract.

Facades, food and family fun. As for looks, the All-Stars can be garish, Pop Century and Art of Animation less so. Fort Wilderness looks like what it is—a swath of Florida wilderness overlaid with an Old West theme. The campground has the most for children to do by far, everything from archery lessons to horseback riding.

Bus service. You'll love it at the Art of Animation Resort. When buses pull up there they're always empty, so you're almost guaranteed to get a seat. The other Values have buses too; Fort Wilderness also has water taxis that take you to Magic Kingdom. They're not the quickest trip, but they are special.

Crowds. The other big difference between Disney's budget hotel choices are their crowds. This distinction doesn't get talked about much, but in our opinion it really matters. Because when you're sharing a hotel with thousands of other people, how they act and what type of mood they're in can't help but affect your adventure.

In our experience, the happiest people are at the All-Star Resorts. Yes, they offer relatively little regarding amenities, and their simple rooms clearly reflect that they're Disney's cheapest places to stay. But despite

Pop Century parking.

All-Star Music.

© Disney

All-Star Sports.

that, or maybe because of it, adolescents, young adults, young families... nearly everyone we see at the All-Stars is in good spirits and has a spring in their step. Perhaps they're just delighted to be at Disney. Or maybe the fact that they're not spending a fortune on their hotel room makes them pleased as punch, and keeps them focused on the fun of their vacations.

As I've mentioned before, I also see more dads with inappropriate tattoos and sleeveless shirts here, but thinking that they symbolize the crowds is completely off base. Because for every one of those guys there are many who don't look like that, and for every dad there seems to be a marching band or lacrosse team or gaggle of Brazilian girls celebrating their 15th birthdays. Yes, it's a younger crowd here. And it's happy.

Grumpy. He's more than just a Dwarf. Somehow, his spirit dominates Pop Century. Slumping when they walk, guests who trudge past us on its walkways seem resigned to be there, as if they couldn't afford to stay somewhere better and for some reason can't, to quote a song we've heard once or twice, Let It Go. Pop Century has youth groups too, but for the most part only those involved in events at the ESPN Wide World of Sports complex. So one week it's filled with 12-year-old cheerleaders, the next week... not a sea of

matching uniforms or hair bows anywhere. To be fair, we should point out that Pop Century also has its fans—families who stay at the resort every year. Like similar All-Star guests, they decorate the windows of their rooms with soaped sayings and character plushies and other fun stuff, and worship at the altar of Happy. Not Grumpy.

The Little Mermaid section of Art of Animation has—usually—the calmest crowd of any of the Value hotels. It gets youth groups just like Pop Century, but on other days when I walk through it, the people I see are relaxed young couples and families. And why wouldn't they be? The Mermaid area has its own pool, the resort's food court is Disney's best, and then there's that great bus service.

Calm, content, peaceful... those feelings come with the territory at Fort Wilderness. Our daughter, who is now 22, has loved the campground her entire life, and she's far from the only one. Tent camping attracts all ages of those who love the outdoors, mostly families with an adventurous streak but also some young adults. And trust us, you'll fit right in. There's a whole Disney camping cult that does exactly this. Don't have a tent? Disney will rent you one and set it up. RV camping skews toward seniors, often grandparents reforming bonds with their adult children and grandchildren.

All-Star Movies.

Disney resort hotels

All-Star Resorts

★★★ ✔ Bad, bad, bad. For years that's been my conclusion about All-Star Movies, All-Star Music, and All-Star Sports, three side-by-side resorts that were Disney's first Value Resorts and still today offer the company's cheapest room rates. I said the rooms were too small. I said the food was bad. I said the architecture was hideous.

But I've changed my mind.

Because last year my husband and I suddenly had some medical problems, and found ourselves without a place to live. The timing couldn't have been worse. It was March. The pinnacle of Spring Break. When hotel rates throughout Orlando were sky high, and for the most part rooms were sold out.

So, cellphones in hand, we logged onto the Disney website, navigated to the All-Star Resorts page and hit refresh, refresh, refresh. After literally an hour a room opened up at All-Star Sports. We nabbed it.

We stayed at the resort for a week, all day every day. Working out of our room, we had no problem with its small size (there were only two of us, as our daughter was in college). We appreciated that everything worked—the Wi-Fi, the outlets, the sinks, the air conditioner. We ate at the food courts morning, noon and night. They had a new look about them, and their entrees were delicious, at least at lunch and dinner. (For more on our adventure see my accompanying sidebar, "Spring Break at the All-Star.")

For one night Disney moved us to a family suite at All-Star Music (at no extra charge, as a high-school class needed our room) and that larger space was as comfortable as a nicely furnished apartment. But after the seventh day we had to leave. All of the All-Stars were so overbooked that even when we waited until after midnight and went to the front desk... nothing was available.

So we moved. To a similarly-priced motel less than a mile from Disney. One on U.S. 192 that, according to the reviews on TripAdvisor, was the best of the bunch out there.

And that's when I learned how good the All-Stars are. Because this non-Disney place sucked. The air conditioner worked—at least a few hours every day. There was no restaurant, so for food we tiptoed down a broken-beer-bottled sidewalk to a McDonald's.

The trashiest McDonald's I have ever been to with food that left both of us ill. And that's when it hit me. Taken for what they are, Disney's All-Star Resorts are pretty darn good. Especially All-Star Movies and Sports, because of their food courts.

As for the look of the All-Stars, the old art major in me still recoils at the sheer horror of it, though I've learned that most guests don't share that reaction, especially children. To me, All-Star Movies and All-Star Music have the best-looking lodging areas (Toy Story, Calypso) and some of the ugliest (Love Bug, Mighty Ducks, Rock Inn, Country Fair). At All-Star Sports the tennis-themed Center Court is OK; the B-ball-based Hoops Hotel just weird.

Highs. ❶ It's cheap. Cheaper than any other Disney spot, and about the same price as places just outside of Disney that suffer some serious maintenance issues. Many were hit hard by the opening of the All-Stars, then took another hit when Hurricane Charley passed through the area in 2004 and have never recovered. ❷ Though your third-grader may have better taste, the abundance of little details on each building makes it easy to find your room ("Remember Mike, we're just left of the pink tennis racket, under the big blue flag and giant '30–15' score"). ❸ Landscaping is generous. Many buildings sit in a native palm-and-pine forest that thankfully wasn't clear-cut for construction, and the walkways between them are trimmed out with healthy planted trees and shrubs. ❹ Pools are nice for the price; some have fountains. ❺ Many rooms are near parking lots. ❻ Empty tables are often easy to find at the All-Star Music and All-Star Sports food courts, as their dining areas are never that packed except during the morning breakfast rush (in our experience, that's about 7:30 a.m. to 9 a.m.). Though the breakfasts at those two food courts won't give much to write home about, their lunches and dinners are surprisingly good.

Lows. ❶ Architecture and exterior details are often garish, sometimes cheap. ❷ Rooms are small, most have double beds. ❸ There's no restaurant; food courts handle ordering and checkout poorly. For example, if you order a waffle, then get your drink, then stand in line to pay, then get your utensils and napkins and such and then find a table just like you're supposed to do—your waffle will absolutely be cold when you sit down to eat it. (A solution: have one person in your party get everything but your food while another person simultaneously gets only your food

Spring break at the All-Star. Testing the theory that Disney's Value Resorts are awful places to stay when they're filled with young people, my husband and I stayed at the All-Star Sports Resort during the peak of a recent Spring Break, the week before Easter in 2015.

And by stay, I mean *stay*.

For seven straight days we never left, remaining at the resort all day long, every day, walking through the grounds and both pool decks every morning, noon and night to eat every one of our meals at the All-Star Sports food court.

And here's what it was like: Yes, the entire place was full of high schoolers and college kids. Cheerleaders. Lacrosse teams. Marching bands. Spring breakers.

And yes, they did clash, visually at least, with the families there. And some of those families did have that deer-in-the-headlights look as they roamed the grounds, wondering where the other families had disappeared to in this supposed family mecca.

But it wasn't loud. The food court was often dominated by young people but they were always in such a hurry to get somewhere—to the parks, to their games, to their buses—that they never stayed in the dining areas very long, and never had any loud conversations.

And it wasn't rowdy. At the pools a few pale girls in bikinis laid out nervously on chaise lounges as a few pasty guys pretended not to look at them. But the pools themselves were filled with Disney lifeguards hosting kiddie games. We witnessed nothing even slightly wild or crazy.

However, we did hear the high schoolers who filled the rooms around ours outside it every morning at nine ("All right then! Everyone to Epcot!!!"). And thanks to the four chatty girls staying next to us, as the week went on we couldn't help but hear which guys in their class were totally hot and totally not in vivid giggly detail. (Hey Tyler R., if you would just shave that stupid mustache...)

But we were only paying $120 a night, half the rate of anywhere else. Our room was clean and easy to work in; we wrote much of this chapter there. The food at breakfast was fair, but the lunch and dinner items were really good. Overall it suited our needs perfectly.

All-Star Music.

while a third person finds and holds your table. And if one of you gets a waffle, all of you should get something from that same order counter.) ❹ The All-Star Movies food court serves lackluster food. ❺ Since Disney uses the All-Star Resorts as its main lodging area for its many youth-group visitors, the resulting adolescent atmosphere may irritate some families. ❻ Some teens can lack decorum, as can some adults. ❼ Bus stops face a blinding sun on most mornings and offer little protection during inclement weather.

Rooms. Colorful walls and classy fabric accents create a calm atmosphere. A curtain closes off the bedroom from the vanity; a door divides the vanity from the toilet and tub. Adjoining rooms have connecting doors. Looking for a family suite? Consider the ones at All-Star Music. They're not as nice as those at Art of Animation and have outdoor entrances, but calmer looks and lower rates. *Rooms: 260 sq ft (24 sq meters); 2 double beds or 1 king, sleep 4. Family suites: 520 sq ft (48 sq meters); king, sleeper double and 2 twins, kitchenette; 2 baths; sleep 6. Last renovated: 2015. Access: Outdoor.*

Swimming pools. Each All-Star resort has two themed pools. Behind its central hall is a large pool with an adjacent kiddie pool; a second smaller pool anchors an outlying lodging area. None of the pools have slides.

Restaurants and food. Each All-Star resort has a food court, bakery and small bar open to its main swimming pool. Disney redid the Sports and Music food courts a few years ago; they've gotten much better. The Movies food court missed out on that update. Today it cries out for one, and may get one soon, perhaps as early as 2017.

Key facts. *Resort type:* Disney Value Resorts with clustered lodging buildings. *Size:* 5,740 rooms, 298 suites, 246 ac (99 ha). *Built:* 1994 (All-Star Music, Sports), 1999 (Movies). *Location:* Western Disney near Animal Kingdom; Movies 1901 W Buena Vista Dr 32830; Music 1801 W Buena Vista Dr; Sports 1701 W Buena Vista Dr. *Miles to:* Animal Kingdom 1 (2 km); Blizzard Beach 1 (2 km); Disney Springs 4 (6 km); Epcot 5 (8 km); ESPN 3 (5 km); Hollywood Studios 3 (5 km); Magic Kingdom 5 (8 km); Typhoon Lagoon 4 (6 km). *Other amenities:* Each resort: Laundromat, laundry service, shop; 1 mi (3 km) fitness trail; arcade, playground, pool games. *Phone:* All-Star Movies 407-938-7000 (fax 407-938-7111); Music 407-938-6000 (fax 407-938-7222); Sports 407-938-5000 (fax 407-938-7333). *Disney transportation:* Buses (often dedicated to each individual resort, sometimes shared); Disney parks, Disney Springs, ESPN. *Rates:* Rooms $89–$194, discounts to $77; suites $216–$396, discounts to $194.

All-Star Movies.

Animal Kingdom Lodge.

Animal Kingdom Lodge

★★★★★ ✔ A giraffe may wander behind your balcony at this resort, which is basically a classy, engaging tribute to the animals and peoples of Africa. The resort's lobbies are filled with African artifacts, its decor uses African designs and themes, its restaurants use recipes inspired by African cuisine. Its headline attraction, though, is its collection of wildlife. Giraffes, zebras, exotic antelope... they all roam freely behind the buildings. Many rooms overlook their savannas.

The resort has two distinct halves: Jambo House, its original lodge, and Kidani Village, a newer, smaller timeshare complex. At Jambo House, 19 interconnected buildings arc around an open savanna. At Kidani Village, one very long building does the same thing.

Which should you pick? Jambo House, definitely. It's fully realized, with many restaurants, a large, pretty swimming pool and loads of other amenities. Kidani Village pales in comparison. It doesn't serve breakfast, has a much smaller savanna, and when you arrive at the resort you park in a parking garage, breaking the mood.

Highs. ❶ Roaming wildlife. **❷** Superb restaurants. **❸** Good pools. **❹** Unique children's programs. **❺** A breathtaking lobby. **❻** The larger suites are stunning. **❼** Interesting African cast members.

Lows. ❶ Pricey. **❷** Most standard rooms sleep four, not five. **❸** A distant location.

Rooms. Multicolored fabrics complement dark wood furniture handcrafted in Africa. Ground-level rooms have patios; others have balconies which extend 4 feet (1.2 meters). Most overlook wildlife, though some face the pool or parking lot. Jambo House suites hog prime locations at the end of animal trails; some have pool tables. Kidani Village has 492 Disney Vacation Club (DVC, or timeshare) villas; Jambo House has 109. *Rooms: 340 sq ft (104 sq meters), 1 king bed, 2 queens or 1 queen plus bunk beds, small refrigerator; sleep 4. Suites sleep 4–9, timeshare villas 4–12. Accessed from indoor halls.*

Swimming pools. Open 24 hours, the large Jambo House pool has a nice water slide and a gradual ramp. Nearby are a kiddie pool, two hot tubs, a shady playground and a flamingo habitat. The Kidani pool area has a winding slide, one hot tub and large water play area.

Restaurants. A wonderful buffet, Boma combines American comfort food with non-threatening African options. Serving areas resemble market stands, each in its own hut or makeshift stand. Several dining areas sit under thatched ceilings with light fixtures made from hand-cut glass and tin. Relaxing and romantic, Jiko is a Disney Signature Restaurant, a African-fusion jewel. Hanging from its ceiling, sculpted kanu birds fly over you to bring you luck. Representing a sunset, a back wall slowly changes color. Offering Indian-inspired East African cuisine, Sanaa serves dishes both spicy and mild. Its colorful dining room comes with a bonus: if you sit near a window exotic animals will roam right by you. Hanging from abstract acacia trees, the room's lights look like ripe fruit.

Key facts. *Resort type:* Disney Deluxe resort with two lodges, animal savannas. *Size:* 762 rooms, 19 suites, 708 villas, 74 acres (29 ha). *Built:* Jambo House 2001, Kidani Village 2009. *Location:* Southwest Disney, near Animal Kingdom. *Address:* 2901 Osceola Parkway 32830. *Miles to:* Animal Kingdom 1 (oo km); Blizzard Beach 1 (oo km); Disney Springs 5 (8 km); Epcot 5 (8 km); ESPN 5 (8 km); Hollywood Studios 3 (5 km); Magic Kingdom 6 (10 km); Typhoon Lagoon 5 (8 km). *Other amenities:* 24-hour animal viewing, night-vision animal spotting, arcade, nightly campfire, culinary tours and wine tastings, playground, poolside crafts; afternoon, after-dark truck safaris into savannas (extra charge); business center; laundromat, laundry service, massages, shops. *Children's activities:* Organized African cultural programs, arts and crafts, cookie decorating; face painting, pool games; Kidani Village has basketball, shuffleboard, tennis courts. *Phone:* 407-938-3000. *Fax:* 407-938-4799. *Disney transportation:* Buses serve Disney parks and Disney Springs and shuttle back and forth between the two sides of the resort. *Rates:* Rooms $308–$724, discounted to $199; suites and villas: $318–$2806, discounted to $231.

Art of Animation Resort

★★★★ ✔ Disney. That's the theme of this hotel. Seems obvious, right? I mean, right about now I totally understand if you're thinking "I paid $25 for a book to tell me a Disney hotel is themed to Disney? Coulda guessed that, Julie. Hmm... where's that return slip?"

But hold on, I'm making a point here. Because believe it or not, the Art of the Animation Resort is the only hotel at Walt Disney World where the subject is Disney, or at least nothing but Disney. The All-Star

Art of Animation. Cars area.

Resorts include some Disney cues; Pop Century has a few too. But if you're looking for all Disney all the time, this is your spot.

Laid out in a semicircle, the resort consists of a central amenities center that's bordered by three distinct suite sections, each one devoted to a particular Disney or Pixar animated movie—1994's "The Lion King," 2003's "Finding Nemo" and the 2006 film "Cars." Off to the side a grouping of standard rooms recall the 1989 movie "The Little Mermaid."

Each landscape reflects its movie's locale and includes representations of characters and items seen in its film. Lodging buildings look as if they're covered with drawing paper, each piece a rough sketch of a character. Thirty-foot sketchpads lean against the sides of the structures, discreetly hiding their outdoor stairwells. Disney did these areas well. Filled with creative touches, they're just loud enough to satisfy children yet never too tacky to turn off their parents.

Somewhat removed from the rest of the resort, its "U"-shaped Little Mermaid compound consists solely of standard rooms. Constructed to be part of the adjacent Pop Century Resort, its buildings look just like the ones at that complex: four-story rectangles wrapped in outdoor walkways and fronted by huge fiberglass icons. In this case that means an astronomical Ariel, a king-sized King Triton, and an enormous evil Ursula. It can take 10 minutes to walk from the area to the resort's food court or bus stops. But it has its own pool, is right next to a parking lot and its room rates are low, less than half that of a suite.

Art of Animation backs up to Pop Century. A stone footbridge, jogging trail and circular roadway connect the areas.

Highs. ❶ Richly detailed landscaping, especially in the Cars area. Roaming through a respectable take on an Arizona desert, its central walkway is lined with convincing full-size versions of most of that movie's automobile characters. ❷ Dedicated bus service. Disney buses arrive empty and head straight to their destination. And since they load from only one station (a covered one, in front of the amenities center) if you're in line when your bus pulls in you'll probably get a seat. ❸ It's the closest Disney hotel to the ESPN complex and Interstate 4. ❹ It has the best food court of any Disney hotel, with quality items available throughout the day. ❺ Only the Little Mermaid section gets youth groups.

Lows. ❶ You don't get a restaurant, or a swimming pool with a slide, even though you're paying, in most cases, hundreds of dollars a night. ❷ All standard rooms are in the Little Mermaid section, which compared to the rest of the resort is done on the cheap.

❸ Staying in one of those rooms? Though they have their own parking lot and swimming pool, they're quite a hike to the amenities center, up to a 10-minute walk each way.

Rooms and suites. Subtle they're not. But the family suites aren't nearly as garish as they could be and include many creative touches. Their furnishings, however, can be cheap; sometimes the fiberboard is obvious.

"Look at this stuff! Isn't it neat?" If you're a fan of the movie you just might say that as you enter one of the resort's standard rooms. Its dresser and nightstand look like furniture the Little Mermaid has found in a shipwreck. A wall mirror is circled in shells, some of them light up. A small table and vanity appear to be stone; the floor in the toilet and bathtub area actually is. In terms of size and layout the rooms are identical to those at the All-Star Resorts and Pop Century. *Suites 565 sq ft (172 sq meters), sleep 6; 1 queen bed, 1 sleeper-sofa double bed, 1 dining-table double bed, kitchenette, 2 full baths; accessed from indoor halls. Rooms: 260 sq ft (24 sq meters), 2 double beds or 1 king, small refrigerator; sleep 4; accessed from outdoor walkways.*

Swimming pools. Hey! I hear Dory! Dip your head under the surface of the main Big Blue pool to hear the voices of Finding Nemo characters. A zero-entry side makes the pool easy for toddlers and disabled guests to enjoy;

a kiddie pool, splash pad and pool bar stand are nearby. A smaller Cars pool has a memorable Cozy Cone Motel look; a small one in the Little Mermaid is surprisingly plain. Both smaller pools have kiddie pools next to them.

Restaurants and food. Really good. Made to order, tasty, unique… some of the items at the Landscape of Flavors food court rival those at Disney's better table-service restaurants. The only problem with these dishes: they take forever to make, about 10 minutes each. If everyone in your party gets one there's no problem, but if someone orders pancakes or a bacon cheeseburger heaven help you. They'll get their food immediately, and stand around watching it get cold while your fancy thing is prepared. Disney will probably fix this flaw someday (most table-service spots figured it out long ago), but right now it's a frustrating flaw in what otherwise is a first-class food court. Concept art from the hotel's featured films lines the dining areas; the nicest one is the Circle of Life dining room to the left of the ordering area. Featuring, of course, a Lion King decor, it's round.

You'll sing along, or at least hum along, to the food court's ambient music—it's just too good to ignore. A surprising mix, it includes "He Lives in You" from the Broadway version of "The Lion King" and from "Cars," Sheryl Crow's "Real Gone" and Rascal Flatts' cover of

Art of Animation. Little Mermaid area.

Art of Animation. Finding Nemo area.

"Life is a Highway." The loop also plays in the nearby shop, restrooms and registration area.

NEW! Autographs of Disney and Pixar animators are slowly starting to dot the lobby's sketchpad-like chandelier. Signed in person by the artists when they visit Walt Disney World, the signatures join the one of Disney animation chief John Lasseter, which has been on the fixture since opening day.

A closer look. When it broke ground in 2010, the Art of Animation complex was planned to be part of the Pop Century Resort, its "Legendary Years" half celebrating the culture of the 1910s, 1920s, 1930s and 1940s. Work stopped after the tragic events of 9/11, when the crowds at Disney plummeted. Only the resort's amenities center and one lodging area were under roof, the only big prop in place a Buck Rogers toy rocket. Letting the complex sit there unfinished for nine years, Disney eventually changed its plans, in part due to the popularity of its new family suites at All-Star Music, in part because it realized that early American pop culture ("23 Skidoo!") no longer held much interest. Pop Century's remaining Classic Years section opened in 2003, Art of Animation in 2012.

Key facts. *Resort type:* Disney Value Plus resort with clustered buildings. *Size:* 864 rooms, 1120 suites, 65 acres (23 ha). *Built:* 2012. *Location:* South Disney close to Interstate 4, near Hollywood Studios and the ESPN Wide World of Sports complex. *Address:* 1850 Century Dr 32830. *Miles to:* Animal Kingdom 4 (6 km); Blizzard Beach 4 (6 km); Disney Springs 3 (5 km); Epcot 5 (8 km); ESPN 2 (3 km); Hollywood Studios 3 (5 km); Magic Kingdom 6 (10 km); Typhoon Lagoon 2 (3 km). *Other amenities:* Arcade, nightly campfire, playground, poolside crafts; laundry service, massages, shops. *Children's programs:* Organized activities include pool games. *Phone:* 407-938-7000. *Fax:* 407-938-7070. *Disney transportation:* Buses run to Disney parks and Disney Springs. *Rates:* Rooms $114–$203, discounted to $90; suites $277–$474, discounted to $249.

BoardWalk Inn and Villas

★★★★★ ✔ OK, let's add this up. Among Disney's Deluxe hotels, this one is… nope, not the most practical. That's the Polynesian. Best value? No way. That's Animal Kingdom Lodge. Fanciest-shmanciest? Grand Floridian. Yet somehow, if you judge a Disney hotel solely on its ability to deliver relaxation—deluxe relaxation, the thing you're supposedly going on vacation and spending these big bucks to achieve, the BoardWalk comes out on top.

Disney cut no corners with this complex, which re-creates a mythical Atlantic City boardwalk of the 1940s. Everything has the look of a small waterfront community of the era, one that grew as time went on. Lining a wide wooden walkway, mom-and-pop shops tuck under apartments and small hotels, newer buildings appear unrelated to older ones next door. Surrounded by water on three sides, the BoardWalk also includes a dance hall, dueling-piano bar and, discreetly hidden from everyone who doesn't need to find it, a conference center. Spread out among interconnected buildings, some rooms overlook the boardwalk and lake, though most face lawns or swimming pools.

Highs. ❶ Pitch-perfect charm, with a real boardwalk on a manicured lake. ❷ Unusual entertainment options. ❸ A variety of places to eat, with more nearby. ❹ Within walking distance to Disney's Hollywood Studios as well as the back entrance to Epcot.

Lows. ❶ Hungry? If you want more than a snack you'll have to go outside, even in bad weather. Every restaurant at the resort is on the boardwalk. ❷ Want to go to the front entrance of Epcot? Disney won't take you there unless the weather's bad.

Rooms. For 2017 all BoardWalk rooms have new color schemes and updated bathrooms. Ahh... period-perfect pastels take you back in time. Bathrooms have marble sinks. Perfect for couples, garden suites

have private front lawns with white picket fences outside, a loft bedroom inside. *Rooms: 385 sq ft (117 sq meters), 2 queen beds, sleeper sofa, small refrigerator; sleep 5. Suites and villas sleep up to 12. Accessed from indoor halls.*

Swimming pools. It's either creepy or cool—the giant clown face at the Luna Park swimming pool. We say cool. Because the pool's red slide forms the clown's tongue. And the sight of little kids popping out of the mouth of a crazy old guy covered with greasepaint is... um... OK creepy. Really creepy. Screaming Stephen King Pennywise Universal Halloween Horror Nights creepy. Still, Disney meant well. Overall the 200-foot (61-meter) slide looks, and feels, like a 1920s roller coaster, with white wooden trim, small dips and sweeping turns. On the hotel side of the resort a quiet pool is pretty but skimps on landscaping. On the villas side, a second small pool has more trees and a large grill.

Restaurants and food. Stay here and you'll have plenty of choices for dinner: the classy little Big River Grille & Brewing Works, homey Trattoria al Forno, noisy ESPN Club sports bar or the Flying Fish Café, a Disney Signature Restaurant that closed for several months in 2016 to create an airier decor and new menu, though its famous potato-wrapped snapper remains. Next door, portraits of every Miss America line an ice-cream shop.

BoardWalk Inn and Villas.

Key facts. *Resort type:* Disney Deluxe resort with interconnected buildings. *Size:* 378 rooms, 20 suites, 533 villas, 45 acres (18 ha). *Built:* 1996. *Location:* Central Disney, between Hollywood Studios and Epcot. *Address:* 92101 N Epcot Resorts Blvd 32830. *Miles to:* Magic Kingdom 4 (6 km), Epcot <1 (2 km), Hollywood Studios <1 (2 km), Animal Kingdom 4 (6 km), Blizzard Beach 4 (6 km), Typhoon Lagoon 4 (6 km), Disney Springs 2 (3 km), ESPN 4 (6 km). *Other amenities:* Arcade, BBQ grill, bike and surrey rentals, fitness center, lighted tennis courts; 2 nightclubs; laundromat, laundry service; shop with groceries; conference center, business center. *Children's programs:* Organized activities include arts and crafts, pool games. *Phone:* 407-939-5100. *Fax:* 407-939-5150. *Disney transportation:* Buses serve Magic Kingdom, Animal Kingdom, water parks and Disney Springs; boats serve Hollywood Studios and the back entrance of Epcot and Hollywood Studios unless lightning is in the area; if so buses take you to the Studios and the front entrance of Epcot. *Rates:* Rooms $408–$1,130, discounted to $256; suites and villas $369–$3,396, discounted to $256.

Caribbean Beach Resort

★★★ ✔ This is the Caribbean? Sorry mon. Except for some architectural details, neither Capt. Jack Sparrow nor Bob Marley would recognize this place. Where are the mountains? The cookie-cutter Sandals resorts? There's nothing truly Caribbean here, but look beyond that and there's a lot to like. It certainly looks tropical, with leaning palms and little white beaches dotting the shores of its central lake. Colorful metal-roofed lodging buildings cluster into six villages, each of which has its own parking lot. In the center of it all is Old Port Royale, a dining, shopping and recreation center. Footbridges over the lake lead to Caribbean Cay, a flowery acre of isle dotted with benches and hammocks.

A rewarding mix of value and convenience, Caribbean Beach is a good choice for those who want a resort-hotel experience but don't want to bust their bank account. Stay here and you'll certainly feel like you're on vacation, even before you get to a theme park. Disney's second largest hotel complex, it sits in the middle of Walt Disney World, a short drive to anywhere you want to go.

Highs. ❶ Decent rates. ❷ Convenient to all Disney parks, Disney Springs, ESPN and Interstate 4. ❸ Comfortable rooms are near parking lots. ❹ Tropical landscaping lends a distinct vacation feel.

Lows. ❶ Dining facilities are weak and too limited, especially at breakfast. ❷ Check-in counters are at the Custom House, a building along the entranceway far from other areas.

Rooms. Aaaargh! Cheesy be the pirate rooms! These high-price options have plastic furniture—molded beds that look like ships, dressers that resemble crates—and double beds instead of queens. Most rooms, though, look pretty good, thanks to a 2015 makeover. It gave the rooms a subtle tropical decor, included an upgrade to queen beds and, in most cases, added a bunk-sized mattress that flips out from a bench. *Rooms: 314 sq ft (96 sq meters), 1 king or 2 queen beds, some flip-out bunk beds, small refrigerator; sleep 4–5. Pirate rooms have 2 double beds; sleep 4. Accessed from outdoor walkways.*

Swimming pools. A scandal it be! The main swimming pool looks like the Castillo San Felipe del Morro citadel in San Juan, P.R.—the same building that inspired the look of the Pirates of the Caribbean exterior at the Magic Kingdom. As floating pretend pirates invade, pseudo conquistadors fend them off with water cannons and water slides. One slide is 102 feet long (31 meters); a shorter one has a 90-degree turn. A pirate-themed splash zone dumps water onto the heads of giggling toddlers. Two big hot tubs bubble nearby. Quiet pools nestle into each of the resort's six lodging villages.

Restaurants and food. For breakfast and lunch it's a food court. For dinner there's also Shutters, a comfortable spot where many Disney chefs get their start, which can be both a good thing and a bad one. Of course, there's always a food court.

Key facts. *Resort type:* Disney Moderate Resort with lodging villages. *Size:* 1,877 rooms, 45 suites, 125 ac (50 ha). *Built:* 1997. *Location:* Central Disney between Disney's Hollywood Studios and Disney Springs. *Address:* 9900 Cayman Way 32830. *Miles to:* Animal Kingdom 5 (8 km); Blizzard Beach 3 (5 km); Disney Springs 2 (3 km); Epcot 4 (6 km); ESPN (5 km); Hollywood Studios 3 (5 km); Magic Kingdom 5 (8 km); Typhoon Lagoon 1 (2 km). *Other amenities:* Bike, surrey, boat rentals; campfire, fishing trips, hammocks, picnic area, sand volleyball court; 1 mi (2 km) fitness trail; laundry service, laundromat, shop. *Children's activities:* Arcade; playgrounds; arts and crafts, pool activities; dance

Caribbean Beach.

Contemporary Resort.

party; Pirate Adventure Cruise ($40). *Phone:* 407-934-1000. *Fax:* 407-934-3288. *Disney transportation:* Buses serve Disney parks, Disney Springs, ESPN; a separate bus circles within Caribbean Beach as a hotel shuttle. *Rates:* $166–$340, discounts to $136.

Contemporary Resort

★★★ Large comfortable rooms and an indoor monorail station can't overcome the cold feel of this large lakefront hotel. Channeling a corporate complex from the 1970s, it displays an abundance of thin convention carpet and lots of sprayed concrete; ceilings are often acoustical tile. A 15-story A-frame connects to a nondescript wing of cheaper rooms and a restricted timeshare tower. A large convention center consumes a few floors and spills over into a second building. A Disney Vacation Club property, Bay Lake Tower looks more modern and has its own recreation area and rooftop lounge.

Highs. ❶ On the monorail line. ❷ A short walk from the Magic Kingdom. ❸ Spacious, classy rooms. ❹ Extensive water recreation. ❺ A-frame room balconies offer great views.

Lows. ❶ Packed, noisy character meals. ❷ Expensive restaurants. ❸ Weak fast food.

Rooms. Spacious, most have an attractive Asian decor, some have amazing views from breezy balconies. *Rooms: 394 sq ft (120 sq meters), 1 king or 2 queen beds, daybed, small refrigerator; sleep 5. Suites sleep 4–8, timeshare villas 4–12. Accessed from indoor halls.*

Swimming pools. The main pool has a 17-foot-high (5-meter) spiraling slide, a large fountain and a row of smaller sprays. A second pool sits right next to the lake; it's round and gets deep in its center. A Bay Lake Tower pool includes a 20-foot-high (6-meter) spiraling slide wrapped in a glass block. Near it are a Mickey-shaped kids fountain, shuffleboard and bocce ball courts and a BBQ pavilion with shaded picnic tables.

Restaurants and food. You want it, you got it. Superb New American and Japanese fare served with a stunning view, from the truly contemporary California Grill perched atop the hotel's A-frame, a Disney Signature Restaurant. Blended flavors at The Wave, an upscale American eatery serving fresh food in a sophisticated decor for breakfast, lunch and dinner. A character meal at Chef Mickey's, though Mickey stays mighty busy as his restaurant stays busy constantly.

Key facts. *Resort type:* Disney Deluxe resort with A-frame, wing and timeshare wing. *Size:* 632 rooms, 23 suites, 295 villas, 55 acres (22 ha). *Built:* 1971. *Location:* Northwest Disney near Magic Kingdom. *Address:* 4600 N World Dr 32830. *Miles to:* Magic Kingdom <1

(2 km), Epcot 4 (6 km), Hollywood Studios 4 (6 km), Animal Kingdom 7 (11 km), Blizzard Beach 5 (8 km), Typhoon Lagoon 6 (10 km), Disney Springs 7 (11 km), ESPN 7 (11 km). *Other amenities:* Arcades; beer tastings, boat rentals; campfire; guided fishing trips; tennis, beach volleyball courts; watersports; fitness center, hair salon, laundromat, laundry service; convention center, business center. *Children's activities:* Arts and crafts, beach and pool activities; the Electrical Water Pageant passes behind the hotel between 10:05p and 10:25p. *Phone:* 407-824-1000. *Fax* 407-824-3539. *Disney transportation:* Monorail trains serve Magic Kingdom, Epcot, the Grand Floridian and Polynesian Village; boats head to Wilderness Lodge and Fort Wilderness; buses run to Hollywood Studios, Animal Kingdom, water parks and Disney Springs. *Rates:* Rooms $356–$1,035, discounted to $269; suites and villas $582–$3,622, discounted to $370.

Coronado Springs Resort

★★★ ✔ Circling a 15-acre (6-ha) lake, this sprawling convention complex offers a quality place to stay at a decent price, even if you're not there on business. Shady walkways weave through three distinct lodging areas. Thick Canary Island date palms, swaying hammocks and a white-sand beach give the resort's Cabanas section a look of Mexico's Gulf Coast. Next to the convention center are the Casitas ("small homes"), which despite their name are no different inside than the rooms everywhere else. Interconnected multistory buildings form an urban-like complex; fountains and small gardens dot small plazas.

Ever lived in Arizona? If so you'll feel right at home at the back of the resort, where its Ranchos landscape uses cactus, gravel and sagebrush to recall the American Southwest. It does that well; let your mind wander and you'll swear you're in a retirement village outside Tucson. "Hey, Mabel! Where's my Just for Men?" All kidding aside, the area gives you a sense of a unique part of United States that most of us Easterners rarely see.

Highs. ❶ *¡Ay caramba!* The food is good! Long-known for its lame dining choices, today Coronado Springs has the best, and best variety, of dining options of any Disney Moderate hotel. **❷** A top-notch recreation center is far from the business buzz. **❸** All rooms are near parking lots. **❹** It's Disney's most affordable, family-friendly conference hotel.

Lows. ❶ Love to hike in high heels? Yeah, me neither. That's why if you're here on business you should stay in the Casitas (men too, at least those who don't care to hike in hard oxfords). Your feet will thank you. **❷** Where's

Coronado Springs.

Fort Wilderness. Campsite with Disney tent.

Mickey? Not here. If it didn't have its Three Caballeros gift shop you'd never know this was a Disney hotel. There's no character meal, no pirate or princess rooms, no monorail.

Rooms. A modern Mexican look combines dark woods with orange and turquiose accents. A few business suites hide in the complex, some the size of two rooms, some as big as three. *Rooms: 314 sq ft (29 sq meters), 2 queen beds or 1 king, small refrigerator; sleep 4. Accessed from outdoor walkways.*

Swimming pools. He spits! The jaguar hiding in the grass is never in a good mood, aiming his drool at everyone who passes by him on the pool's winding waterslide. That's one of many nice touches at the Dig Site, a large outdoor recreation area that claims to be excavating the Lost City of Cibola. A 50-foot (15-meter) pyramid stands next to the pool. Nearby are buried treasures in the sand, a kiddie pool, a sand volleyball court, old-time swing sets and a 22-person hot tub. Quiet pools snuggle into each lodging area.

Restaurants and food. Breakfast! This hotel serves it so many good ways. Stylish hole-in-the-wall Las Ventanas offers creative dishes with copies of USA Today. Food court Pepper Market serves Disney's best Mexican fast food in a comfortable setting. Grab-and-go Café Rix lets you munch its pastries in the classy confines of a sophisticated lounge. And then there's the pool! Its Siestas Cantina snack counter serves breakfast too, including egg sandwiches and decent oatmeal. Las Ventanas and Pepper Market and are also open for lunch and dinner; the main evening spot is the traditional Maya Grill.

Key facts. *Resort type:* Disney Moderate Resort with lodging villages. *Size:* 125 ac (50 ha), 1,877 rooms, 45 suites. *Built:* 1997. *Location:* Western Disney between Hollywood Studios and Animal Kingdom, next to Disney's Western Way entrance. *Address:* 1000 W Buena Vista Dr 32830. *Miles to:* Animal Kingdom 2 (3 km); Blizzard Beach <1 (1 km); Disney Springs 4 (6 km); Epcot 3 (5 km); ESPN 5 (8 km); Hollywood Studios 1 (2 km); Magic Kingdom 4 (6 km); Typhoon Lagoon 3 (5 km). *Other amenities:* Bike, surrey, boat rentals; campfire, fishing trips, hammocks; Fitness center, fitness trail; hair salon with hand, facial, foot treatments; nail salon, laundry service, laundromat, shop, convention center, business center. *Children's amenities:* Arcade, arts and crafts, playgrounds, pool activities. *Phone:* 407-939-1000. *Fax:* 407-939-1001. *Disney transportation:* Buses serve Disney parks, Disney Springs. *Rates:* $170–$341, discounts to $140; suites $409–$1378, discounts to $351.

Fort Wilderness Resort

★★★★ ✔ Pitch a tent and you'll feel totally removed from civilization at this large old-fashioned campground. The longer you stay, the more you'll bond with your family, friends or partner. It may be a touch too much Frontierland and more expensive than most places to camp, but it offers most everything you could want in a campground, and if you let yourself get into it you're almost guaranteed to have an enjoyable, memorable experience.

Cabins, RVs, tents. You can stay in any of them. You can bring a tent or rent one from Disney. You can bring an RV, one you own or one you borrow from someone else. Though shuttle buses loop through the area, many campers rent electric carts to get around.

The campground's 700 acres (280 ha) are for the most part a dense palm-and-pine forest which hugs a 450-acre (180-ha) lake. Man-made 1960s canals cut through the grounds, and what was once a cypress wetland is now dry as a bone, but otherwise Disney has left this chunk of native Florida relatively unscathed. Expect to spot rabbits, squirrels, woodpeckers, and the occasional deer. Cabins and campsites line 28 paved loops, which branch off from a trio of two-lane roads. In back is a lakeside amenities complex, the Old West-styled "Settlement." It includes a beach, general store, marina, music hall, petting zoo and stables, a restaurant and barbecue pavilion. Playgrounds dot the campground. A central recreational area includes the larger of two swimming pools.

Some families have made a stay at Fort Wilderness a yearly tradition. During the Spring Break, Halloween or Christmas seasons they put together elaborate makeshift homes strewn with colorful overhead lights, decorated with flags and other paraphernalia and dotted with pup tents for each of their children. The result is a series of charming little neighborhoods where everyone knows everyone else, where the evening air fills with the aroma of sizzling steaks and the squeaks and squeals of playing children.

Highs. ❶ The casual, peaceful, wooded setting. ❷ The variety of outdoor recreation, everything from archery lessons to horseback rides. ❸ It's a unique experience, unlike anything else at Disney World. ❹ Tent camping is the cheapest way to stay at Disney, especially if you have a large group. ❺ Don't know how to camp? Disney will rent you a tent and set it up for you. ❻ It's possible to bring your pet.

Lows. ❶ Cabins are expensive. Though they sleep six, on average cabins cost about $100 a night more than the family suites at All-Star Music and Art of Animation, which also sleep 6. ❷ Dining options are limited. There's one restaurant. ❸ And then there's the elephant in the room: the campground is in Central Florida. The mecca of muggy weather, a place where few people even lived before the invention of air conditioning. Between May and September, the afternoon heat index at Disney exceeds 105 degrees nearly every single day. And it rains. Often in downpours and thunderstorms, an average of 33 inches (84 cm) during those months alone.

Tent sites. These slim rectangles can hold two tents or one tent and a pop-up van, and allow up to 10 people. They're 10 feet wide, 60 feet deep (3 meters wide, 18 meters deep). A large field, Creekside Meadow hosts groups of 20 or more, can hold 160 and has no hookups.

RV sites. Disney sorts its recreation-vehicle sites into three categories. Full-Hookup sites can hold one RV and one tent. Preferred sites allow one RV and two tents and are within walking distance of the Settlement; some are next to the dog park. Designed for big rigs, Premium Sites are larger but allow only an RV. *Sizes: Full-Hookup and Preferred sites 10 by 60 ft (3 by 18 meters); Premium sites 18 by 60 ft (5 by 18 meters).*

Campsite amenities. All sites except those at Creekside Meadow include a paved pad, picnic table, charcoal grill and hookups for cable TV, electric, the Internet, water and sewage. All are near air-conditioned 24-hour comfort stations, which have private bathrooms, showers, ice dispensers, laundromats and vending machines. Disney locks these buildings at night, though you can always get into one with your MagicBand or key card. Paved walkways connect your spot to recreation areas and bus stops.

Cabins. Recently refurbished, these faux log cabins include a living room, kitchen, dining area, bedroom, bathroom and rough-hewn furniture. New storage drawers in the living room and counter space in the kitchen help keep your stuff organized. Outside there's a wood deck, BBQ grill, and picnic table. Most cabins sit in a pine and palm forest in the front half of the campground. Some are in a cypress wetland that Disney drained in the 1960s. Its trees are still there, but not their undergrowth. Thirteen cabins are handicapped-accessible. *Cabins: 504 sq ft (154 sq meters), sleep 6. Queen bed, bunk* bed, queen sleeper sofa, 54-inch (137 cm) TV, refrigerator, dishwasher, convection/microwave oven, 2 countertop burners, cookware, daily housekeeping and dishwashing. **Swimming pools.** A 67-foot (20 meter) corkscrew slide marks the main Meadow pool. A smaller quiet pool—the "Wilderness Swimmin' Pool" sits in the camping area. **Restaurants and food.** The very good Trail's End offers breakfast and dinner buffets as well as a standard (and outstanding) lunch. Hankerin' for some singin' with your ˜eatin'? Consider the cowboy corn of the Hoop-Dee-Doo Musical Revue or the all-American county charm of Mickey's Backyard Barbecue, which includes a live country band, a trick roper and a big ol' dollop of 1950s-style patriotism.

Policies and resources. *Campfires:* You can have one if it's in an enclosed fire pit with a solid top and stands off the ground. Open-air fires are not allowed. If you don't have firewood, Disney will sell you a half bin for $25, a full bin for $50. *Electric carts:* Rent one or bring your own. Reserve one up to a year in advance at 407-824-2742. *Pets:* You can have up to four if you're staying in a designated cabin or a climate-controlled RV. Leashed dogs can ride on carts and run free at the dog park. Bringing a pet costs $5 a day. *Tent and cot rentals:* Disney rents tent for $30 a night, which includes set-up and breakdown. You can book one as late as an hour before sundown if a tent is available at 407-939-7807, option 4. Disney rents cots for $5 a day.

Key facts. *Resort type:* Disney Moderate Resort with campsites and cabins. *Size:* 409 cabins, 784 campsites, 740 ac (299 ha). *Created:* 1971, cabins 1986. *Location:* Northwest Disney, a few miles from Magic Kingdom. *Address:* 4510 N Fort Wilderness Trail 32830. *Miles to:* Animal Kingdom 6 (10 km); Blizzard Beach 4 (6 km); Disney Springs 9 (10 km); Epcot 4 (6 km); ESPN 6 (10 km); Hollywood Studios 4 (6 km); Magic Kingdom 2 (3 km); Typhoon Lagoon 6 (10 km); Other amenities: Arcade; archery lessons; bike, cart, surrey, boat rentals; dog park; picnic areas; Segway tours; stables; walking trail; basketball, horseshoes, tennis, tetherball, volleyball courts; cane-pole fishing, fishing trips; carriage, wagon, trail, pony, horseback rides; Laundromat; 2 stores with groceries, camping supplies. *Children's activities:* Arts and crafts, pool activities, playgrounds, nightly outdoor marshmallow roast and movie with live entertainer and Chip 'n Dale; the Electrical Water Pageant passes behind the campground between 9:45 and 10:05 p.m. *Phone:* 407-824-2900. *Fax* 407-824-3508. *Disney transportation:* Buses serve Disney parks, Disney Springs, shuttle within grounds; boats go to the Magic Kingdom, Contemporary Resort, Wilderness Lodge. *Rates:* Cabins: 309–$505, discounts to $246. Tent sites $50–$107. RV sites $69–$129 *(full hook-up), $79–$140 (preferred), $85–$145 (premium). Group camping:* $10 per person, min 20 people; info at 407-939-7807. Note: Campsites are rarely on booking sites and therefore rarely discounted. To book one go to disneyworld.com or call 407-939-7429.

Grand Floridian Resort

★★★★★ The signature Disney resort lives up to its promise, even if its grandness seems out of place next to the world's most popular theme park. With gabled roofs and miles of moldings, scrolls, and turn posts, its genteel buildings bring back the Victorian era of the Sunshine State. Canary palms and Southern magnolias highlight a stately landscape. At night a grand pianist and small orchestra entertain in the lobby's five-story atrium.

Highs. ❶ Comfortable rooms. ❷ Fine dining. ❸ On the monorail loop. ❹ Unique experiences for children.

Lows. ❶ Very expensive. ❷ More formal than fun. ❸ The self-parking lot is in Tampa. Or at least it seems to be. Man, what a walk!

Rooms. Light woods and fabrics, ceiling fans and marble sinks recall the turn of the 20th century. *Rooms:* 440 sq ft (134 sq meters), 2 queen beds or 1 king, some daybeds, small refrigerator; sleep 5. Suites sleep 4–8, villas 5–12. Accessed from indoor halls.

Swimming pools. A calm pool sits in a central courtyard, surrounded by a kiddie pool and hot tub. Kids love the beachside pool. Its swerving slide takes 12 seconds to travel; a 20-foot (6-meter)waterfall splashes you. A zero-entry side welcomes toddlers and wheelchair visitors; a water play area imagines Disney's 1951 movie "Alice in Wonderland."

Restaurants and food. Sophisticated options highlight the menus of four restaurants. Cítricos is a Mediterranean Disney Signature Restaurant. Narcoossee's is a Disney Signature seafood spot, a circular building over the Seven Seas Lagoon. The Grand Floridian Café is classy but casual, with floral wallpaper and thick carpeting. Cinderella stars at the character dinner at 1900 Park Fare, though she's upstaged by

Grand Floridian.

what amounts to a comedy troupe: her bickering stepsisters Anastasia and Drizella and stepmom Lady Tremaine. Prince Charming's on hand too, gallantly kissing the hand of any female who offers it. A breakfast buffet has Mary Poppins, Winnie the Pooh and a character who despite Disney's best efforts many children still don't recognize, Alice of "Alice in Wonderland" fame ("Little kids call me Alison," she tells me). And then there's Victoria & Albert's, a AAA 5-Diamond restaurant that doesn't admit children under age 10.
Key facts. *Resort type:* Disney Deluxe resort. *Size:* 842 rooms, 25 suites, 147 villas, 40 acres (16 ha). *Built:* 1988. *Location:* Northwest Disney, near Magic Kingdom. *Address:* 4401 Grand Floridian Way 32830. *Miles to:* Magic Kingdom 1 (2 km), Epcot 4 (6 km), Hollywood Studios 4 (6 km), Animal Kingdom 7 (11 km), Blizzard Beach 5 (8 km), Typhoon Lagoon 7 (11 km), Disney Springs 7 (11 km), ESPN 7 (11 km). *Other amenities:* Arcade, beach, boat rentals, fireworks cruise, nightly campfire, guided fishing trips, tea parties, tennis courts and clinics, walking trail; hair salon, laundromat, laundry service; spa; wedding chapel; shop with groceries; convention center, business center. *Children's programs:* Pontoon-boat pirate adventure; pool activities; the Electrical Water Pageant passes behind the hotel between 9:15p and 9:35p. *Phone:* 407-824-3000.

Fax: 407-824-3186. *Disney transportation:* Monorail trains serve Magic Kingdom, Epcot, the Contemporary Resort, Polynesian Village; buses Hollywood Studios, Animal Kingdom, water parks, Disney Springs; boats Magic Kingdom, Wilderness Lodge, Fort Wilderness. *Rates:* Rooms $569–$1499, discounted to $342; suites and villas $569–$3804, discounted to $449.

Old Key West Resort

★★★★ Visitors from Southwest Florida and perhaps the Keys will feel right at home amid the Olde Florida facades, swaying palms and falling pine needles at this timeshare village, the original Disney Vacation Club community. Lodging buildings combine clapboard siding with shuttered windows, gingerbread accents and tin roofs, clustering into villages along three roadways. Spacious villas view woods, canals and the Lake Buena Vista golf course. Near the entrance is Conch Flats, a food, shopping and recreation center.
Highs. ❶ Good restaurant. ❷ Spacious villas, big closets. ❸ You park within steps of your villa. ❹ Palm-packed landscaping.
Lows. ❶ Pools are too scarce, simple and small. ❷ There's no indoor fast-food spot.
Villas. Most have tropical color schemes with hardwood floors, granite countertops,

a balcony or patio. The units are notable for their size; some bedrooms are so big that even with two queen beds they look empty. *Sleep 4–12. Accessed from outdoor walkways.*

Swimming pools. The slide at the Conch Flats pool hides in a giant sandcastle. A lighthouse is nearby, also a kiddie pool, playground and hot tub. Three villages have quiet pools.

Restaurants and food. Jimmy Buffett might feel at home at Olivia's Cafe; its menu focused on regional dishes using shrimp, conch and accents such as mango glazes. A tin ceiling highlights a homey decor.

Key facts. *Resort type:* Disney Deluxe Villas resort with clustered buildings. *Size:* 761 villas, 74 acres (30 ha). *Built:* 1991. *Location:* East Disney, between Disney Springs and Port Orleans. *Address:* 1510 N Cove Rd 32830. *Miles to:* Magic Kingdom 4 (6 km), Epcot 2 (3 km), Hollywood Studios 3 (5 km), Animal Kingdom 5 (8 km), Blizzard Beach 4 (6 km), Typhoon Lagoon 2 (3 km), Disney Springs 2 (3 km), ESPN 3 (5 km). *Other amenities:* Arcade; bike, boat and surrey rentals; campfire; fitness center; guided fishing trips; marina; playground; basketball, shuffleboard, volleyball courts; 3 tennis courts, 2 lighted; laundromat, laundry service; shop with groceries. *Children's programs:* Arts and crafts, pool activities, sandcastle building. *Phone:* 407-827-7700. *Fax* 407-827-7710. *Disney transportation:* Buses serve Disney parks, Disney Springs, a separate shuttle circles within the resort; boats go to Disney Springs; Port Orleans, Saratoga Springs. *Rates:* Studios $327–$489, discounted to $229; Villas $452–$1978, discounted to $316.

Polynesian Village Resort

★★★★★ ✔ Walt Disney World's first family resort, the Polynesian offers a definitive Disney experience: a room at a themed, world-of-its-own hotel that's just a short glide on a monorail from its most popular theme park. The South Seas complex has 12 buildings, the spaces between them filled with palms, waterfalls, and torch-lit walkways. A central building holds the resort's front desk and concierge, restaurants, bar, shops and monorail station. Disney redid the resort in 2015, restoring the word "Village" to its name; giving it a new parking lot, motor lobby, indoor lobby, bar and swimming pool complex; redoing its rooms; turning some of them into timeshare units and building more. The Poly has a sad claim to fame: it's where John Lennon signed the documents that officially dissolved The Beatles in 1974.

Highs. ❶ Distinctive laid-back and child-friendly. ❷ Beautiful rooms and tropical landscaping. ❸ Fully embraces its American Tiki culture. ❹ Its unique, spirited bar.

Old Key West.

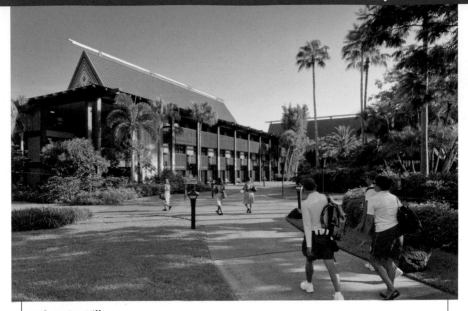

Polynesian Village.

Lows. ❶ It's expensive. ❷ Its confusing grounds make it easy to get lost.

Rooms. Hand-carved furniture, batik-print fabrics, and dim lighting create a unique decor. Twenty offshore bungalows each include a deck with a small plunge pool and speakers that pipe in the audio of Magic Kingdom's fireworks show. *Rooms: 415 sq ft (00 sq meters), 2 queen beds or 1 king, some daybeds, small refrigerator; sleep 5. Suites and villas 4–9. Accessed from indoor halls.*

Swimming pools. Completely redone in 2015, a central Lava pool nestles against a volcano slightly shorter that it used to be so diners behind it can see Cinderella Castle. A zero-entry gradual ramp provides access for toddlers and physically challenged guests. Nearby is a hot tub and a new Kiki Tikis Splash Play area, a water playground for children 48 inches (122 cm) and under. Larger and more elaborate than other Disney water playgrounds, it includes buckets that dump water on kids and playful tikis that spit and spout. A smaller East pool rarely has a crowd.

Restaurants and food. OK, this will take awhile. There's so much to pick from: A one-time coffee shop, Kona Café has its tables and booths in a subdued, carpeted area that's open to the lobby, though it's evolved into serving fine Pan-Pacific American meals. Skewers of Polynesian-flavored meats and seafood are grilled over open fires and continually delivered to your dinner table at 'Ohana, a restaurant that for dinner offers Lilo, Stitch and Mickey Mouse in a maraca-shaking character meal. There's moving, there's shaking, and certainly no surplus of fabric at the memorable Spirit of Aloha dinner show, which does its dances while somehow also workng in a sitcom skit, a hula lesson for kids and oh yeah—a dinner, some salty something you won't remember. And then there's Trader Sam's Grog Grotto, an extremely Disneyfied little rum bar owned by the "head salesman" seen on Magic Kingdom's Jungle Cruise ride. Its decor includes a giant clam named Shelly; Uh-Oa, the Audio-Animatronic "tiki goddess of disaster" who once lorded over the Enchanted Tiki Room; and of course, shrunken heads. Best of all, these items all come to life when patrons order certain drinks, and with the place nearly always full that means every few minutes. Servers are skippers, of course, and add to the fun. One might suddenly open fire at "the hippos in the trees" or don a snorkel and start swimming around the tables or suddenly shout out a joke: Why are pirates called pirates? They just arrgh!" Disneyphiles should search the walls for the hidden Orange Bird, or the reference to Rosita, the mysterious Tiki Room bird that no one knows what happened to.

Key facts. *Resort type:* Disney Deluxe resort. *Size:* 497 rooms, 5 suites, 380 villas, 39 acres (16 ha). *Built:* 1971, updated 2015. *Location:* Near Magic Kingdom. *Address:* 600 Seven Seas Dr 32830. *Miles to:* Magic Kingdom 1 (2 km), Epcot 4 (6 km); Hollywood Studios 4 (6 km); Animal Kingdom 6 (10 km), Blizzard Beach 5 (8 km), Typhoon Lagoon 6 (10 km), Disney Springs 6 (10 km), ESPN 7 (11 km). *Other amenities:* Arcade; beach; boat and surrey rentals; campfire; guided fishing trips; hula-dancing lessons; walking trail; laundromat, laundry service; Evening torch-lighting ceremony has a fire-baton twirler; a musician often entertains in the lobby. *Children's amenities:* Playground; arts and crafts, beach and pool activities; Lilo's Playhouse childcare center (ages 3-9) offers dress-up, crafts, storytelling; decor inspired by the art of Little Golden Books; the Electrical Water Pageant passes behind the hotel between 9p and 9:20p. *Phone:* 407-824-2000. *Fax* 407-824-3174. *Disney transportation:* Monorail trains serve Magic Kingdom, Epcot, Contemporary, Grand Floridian resorts; buses serve other parks, Disney Springs; boats serve Magic Kingdom. *Rates:* Rooms $452–$1213, discounted to $310; suites and villas $439–$3,698, discounted to $230; villas $439–$878, discounted to $230; Bungalows $2272–$3659, discounted to $1,184.

Pop Century Resort

★★★ ✓ OK man, dig this. The other day I was getting jiggy with surfing the Web, and came across a site for Florida's Citrus County school district. Dullsville? No way. Because on it were study aids and yada yada yada I came across one titled "Slang of the 1960s." Since I was, like, totally buggin' for ways to liven up this review and thought tossing in some far-out phrases might float your boat, I looked at it. And under the letter "M" I found this: "Mickey Mouse: Out of touch with styles and trends." And I thought "Whoomp, there it is! That's what Disney is doing with this resort! Yes, offering triggers of nostalgic memories we're supposed to have so we can share them with our kids, but also playing against that old stereotype of the company by celebrating styles and trends that are so totally over today.

Visually the idea works, and there's a reason it should. Catchphrases, dance crazes, a progression of tech from tabletop jukeboxes to cellphones the size of bricks… in many ways what defines the American 20th century is its popular culture. And so much comes and goes so quickly that what once was a gas gas gas is soon, like, nowhere.

Like the All-Star Resorts, Pop Century uses huge props to disguise motel-like structures and groups them together. In this case, each

Pop Century. 1970s courtyard.

Pop Century. 1950s pool.

group recalls a particular decade of American pop culture, from the 1950s to the 1990s (yes just the second half the century, but... well see the Art of Animation review). The buildings nail their themes with rooftop catchphrases, everything from "Crazy Man" to "Do The Funky Chicken!" If you like, you can stroll through the ages, as the resort plays out chronologically. At the far right are the 1950s; moving left you travel through the 1960s, 1970s, 1980s and finally the 1990s. Intense colors reflect each age; a swirl of tie-dyed hues for the '60s, primary colors for the '80s.

Super-sized sock-hoppers be-bop to tunes from a 40-foot-tall (12-meter) tabletop jukebox in the 1950s area, where the stars of Disney's 1955 movie "Lady and the Tramp" gaze at each other across the courtyard. Nine giant bowling pins mark the corners of the building; a tenth one forms the shape of the pool.

Giant Duncan yo-yos bookend two 1960s structures. A whoop-ass can of Play-Doh creates the centerpiece of one building; characters from Disney's 1967 version of "The Jungle Book" become the other.

Huge foosball players compete in the 1970s courtyard. A giant Mickey Mouse rotary telephone and the biggest of all Big Wheels add to the wow factor, as do huge eight-track tapes.

Inky, Blinky, Pinky and Clyde chase Pac-Man across the walls of Pop Century's 1980s

buildings, Roger Rabbit (from 1988's "Who Framed Roger Rabbit") anchors one; a huge 1988 Sony Walkman another. Colossal Rubik's Cubes corner these structures, in various stages of completion.

And then finally, what a blast! Fifty-five-foot cellphones mark the ends of the single 1990s building, recalling the large mobile phones of that decade.

Highs. ❶ It's fun. For me at least, it's almost impossible not to smile as I walk past a huge yo-yo or 8-track tape. ❷ It's cheap, its rooms only slightly more expensive than those at the All-Star Resorts. ❸ Walking around won't wear you out, since the resort using four-story buildings to compress the space its rooms take up (All-Star buildings are three stories). Parking lots hug the sides of the resort, its rooms are around its amenities complex. ❹ Driving a car? Pop is two stops from Interstate 4. ❺ The Art of Animation resort is next door, across a small lake. ❻ Some icons hide humor. In the 1970s area, the back of the 8-track "Country Highway: Seventies Greatest Hits" reveals its tunes, which include "Energy Crisis of Love," "Kung Fu Convoy" and "It's The Me Decade, But I Still Love You." The screens of the cellphones on the 1990s building show a call going out to "407-938-4000"—the phone number of the Pop Century Resort.

Port Orleans Riverside.

Lows. ❶ "Note: Buses may arrive full due to guest demand. If so, please wait for next bus." That's what a sign reads at the Pop Century bus stop. Because for some reason, this 2,880-room resort shares its buses with other Disney hotels, and the buses often stop at them first. Bogus! ❶ Bus stops face a blinding sun on most mornings and offer little protection in bad weather. ❷ Though the chow court won't cost you much bread, lately its choices have been grody to the max.

Rooms. The decades disappear when you step into your pad, which will have only the slightest of period references. Instead, there's a calm sense of colors and fabrics. *Rooms: 260 sq ft (24 sq meters), 2 double or 1 king bed, sleep 4. Accessed from outdoor walkways.*

Swimming pools. Wicked! Four giant spraying flowers attract dudes and dudettes from throughout the resort to the central Hippy Dippy pool, often leaving the others relatively empty. A kiddie pool has a flower shower. Nearby Goofy stands watch over a pop jet playground; behind him is an actual 1960s Little Red Corvette. Of those other pools the best one is the 1950s Bowling Pin pool, which itself forms the shape of a pin. Its deck sports those triangular lane markings you see on bowling lanes everywhere.

Restaurants and food. Totally tubular when it opened, the Everything Pop food court embraced the 20th century with a Fluffernutter sandwich, tie-dyed cheesecake, and a TV dinner of fried chicken and whipped potatoes in a tray made of aluminum foil. Lately however it's become a total drag. Those items are gone, and nothing retro has replaced them. A refrigerated version of the cheesecake hides in a back case. Can you dig it? No. The food court still looks hip, but the Man ruined it man! As I'm writing this I'm eating breakfast at the food court, its chicken fried chicken. How is it? Like, barf me out! Tough, tasteless and cold. Like other Value Resorts, Pop Century lacks a full-service restaurant. Ain't that a bite?

Key facts. *Resort type:* Disney Value Resort with clustered lodging buildings. *Size:* 177 ac (71 ha), 2,880 rooms. *Built:* 2003. *Location:* South Disney near the ESPN Wide World of Sports complex and Interstate 4, not far from Disney's Hollywood Studios, adjacent to and within walking distance to Disney's Art of Animation Resort. *Address:* 1050 Century Dr 32830. *Miles to:* Animal Kingdom 4 (6 km); Blizzard Beach 4 (6 km); Disney Springs 3 (5 km); ESPN 2 (3 km); Hollywood Studios 3 (5 km); Magic Kingdom 6 (10 km); Typhoon Lagoon 2 (3 km). *Other amenities:* Fitness trail lined with signs tracking 1950–1999 pop culture events, circles over to the Art of Animation Resort, laundry service, laundromat, shop. *Children's activities:* Arcade, playground, poolside activities; food-court or lobby dancing with Disney cast members daily (to "The Twist" 8a; "The Mickey Mouse Club March" 2p; "The Hustle" 6p). *Phone:* 407-938-4000. *Fax* 407-938-4040. *Disney transportation:* Buses serve Disney parks, Disney Springs, often the ESPN complex. *Rates:* $99–$212, discounts to $85.

Port Orleans Resorts

★★★ ✔ Though Disney lumps them together as if they're similar, in many ways these two side-by-side resorts are quite different. Representing New Orleans, the smaller French Quarter has tree-lined walkways that look like narrow streets, lots of wrought-iron railings and some intimate gardens. Its swimming pool area recalls a Mardi Gras parade; its food court a warehouse of parade props. Representing the plantation country of the Old South, the sprawling Riverside has four distinct areas. Three recall Southern plantations, their white-columned buildings set within shady live oaks, magnolias and other hardwoods. The other symbolizes more primitive areas, with walkways that meander through unkempt palmettos and pines. Riverside also has a restaurant, though it's only open for dinner.

Highs. ❶ The French Quarter is intimate, easy to get around. **❷** Riverside is spacious, and in good weather relaxing. **❸** Rooms are close to parking lots. **❹** Rooms are often heavily discounted online, as the complex is usually the last one at Disney to fill up.

Lows. ❶ French Quarter's theme can look cheap. **❷** At Riverside, getting to your room can be a hike if you don't have a car.

Rooms. French Quarter rooms have cherry woods and purple and gold fabrics. Riverside rooms vary. Those in its Alligator Bayou have hickory furnishings and quilt-like duvets; its Royal Guest Rooms have fiber-optic-fireworks headboards and Disney character decor. *Rooms: 314 sq ft (96 sq meters), 2 queen beds or 1 king, small refrigerator; sleep 4. Alligator Bend rooms add trundle beds; sleep 5. Accessed from outdoor walkways.*

Swimming pools. A fiberglass dragon slide winds through the French Quarter pool; a fiberglass alligator jazz band dances through its grounds. At Riverside, a swerving slide dribbles water on riders at the recently refurbished Ol' Man Island pool. Tired swimmers rock away their cares on a nearby covered porch. Five little peaceful pools tuck into Riverside's lodging areas.

Restaurants and food. Port Orleans has one restaurant, Riverside's Southern-inspired

Port Orleans French Quarter.

Saratoga Springs.

Boatwright's Dining Hall. Wood tables sit on tile floors; a back room has a fireplace. The French Quarter has the best snack: made-to-order beignets coated in powdered sugar. **Key facts.** *Resort type:* Disney Moderate resorts. *Size:* French Quarter 1,008 rooms, 90 acres (36 ha); Riverside 2,048 rooms, 235 acres (95 ha). *Built:* French Quarter 1991, Riverside 1992. *Location:* Northeast Disney, near Disney Springs. *Addresses:* French Quarter 2201 Orleans Dr 32830; Riverside 1251 Riverside Dr 32830. *Miles to:* Magic Kingdom 4 (6 km), Epcot 2 (3 km), Hollywood Studios 4 (6 km), Animal Kingdom 6 (10 km), Blizzard Beach 4 (6 km), Typhoon Lagoon 2 (3 km), Disney Springs 2 (3 km), ESPN 4 (6 km). *Other amenities:* Arcade, campfire, playground; bike, boat, surrey rentals; guided fishing trips, cane-pole fishing; carriage rides (same-day reservations 407-824-2832); laundromat, laundry service; shop with groceries. *Children's programs:* Pontoon-boat pirate adventure; pool activities. *Phone:* French Quarter 407-934-5000, Riverside 407-934-6000. *Fax:* French Quarter 407-934-5353, Riverside 407-934-5777. *Disney transportation:* Buses head to Disney parks, Disney Springs; boats serve Disney Springs; Old Key West, Saratoga Springs; shuttle between French Quarter, Riverside. *Rates:* $175–$336, discounted to $147.

Saratoga Springs Resort

★★★★ This DVC complex is the only Disney resort hotel with a golf course. Lodging buildings horseshoe (ha!) around a recreation center. Located behind Disney Springs, Saratoga Springs is as far away as you can get from a Disney theme park and still be at a Disney resort. Despite its name, there's nothing New York, no springs, no horses. Considered part of Saratoga Springs because it's right next door, unrelated Treehouse Villas nestles into a pine forest. Its 60 octagons stand 10 feet (3 meters) off the ground.

Highs. ❶ Tranquil. ❷ Direct golf course access. ❸ Fine fitness center, spa. ❹ Villas are adjacent to parking lots.

Lows. ❶ Children may mistake its understated look for that of an apartment complex. ❷ The main pool is small and often crowded.

Villas. Saratoga Springs residences have large masculine furniture; larger ones add whirlpool tubs, Grand Villas have two-story living rooms. Rustic-chic Treehouse Villas have cathedral ceilings, granite countertops. *Sleep 4–12. Accessed from outdoor walkways.*

Swimming pools. Cascading waterfalls brace a long slide at the main pool; a Donald Duck fountain spouts off unpredictably. Each lodging area has a quiet pool; the Treehouse Villas one is really quiet.

Restaurants and food. Manly steak place the Turf Club Bar & Grill feels like a country club spot; you can shoot billiards while you wait for your table. Balcony tables overlook the golf course and Disney Springs. **Key facts.** *Resort type:* Disney Deluxe Villas resort with clustered buildings. *Size:* 828 villas, 65 acres (26 ha). *Built:* 2004. *Location:* East Disney, across a lake from Disney Springs. *Address:* 1960 Broadway 32830. *Miles to:* Magic Kingdom 5 (8 km), Epcot 3, Hollywood Studios 4 (6 km), Animal Kingdom 6 (10 km), Blizzard Beach 4 (6 km), Typhoon Lagoon 2 (3 km), Disney Springs 2 (3 km), ESPN 4 (6 km). *Other amenities:* Arcades, bike rentals, nightly campfire, fitness center, guided fishing trips, surrey rentals; basketball, shuffleboard courts, spa, 2 lighted tennis courts, 2 walking trails; golf course; laundromat, laundry service; shop with groceries. *Children's programs:* Arts and crafts; ceramic, canvas, plaster painting activities; pool activities. *Phone:* 407-827-1100. *Fax:* 407-827-1151. *Disney transportation:* Buses serve Disney parks, Disney Springs, a separate shuttle circles within the resort, Treehousers transfer at the Springs and Grandstand stops; boats head to Disney Springs, Old Key West, Port Orleans. *Rates:* Studios $327–$489, discounted to $229; Other villas $452–$1978, discounted to $316.

Wilderness Lodge

★★★★★ ✔ A dead ringer for an old park-service lodge of the American West, this rustic resort hides behind a small forest alongside Bay Lake. Highlighted by a three-sided stone fireplace, its layers of rock illustrating the geological history of the Grand Canyon, an eight-story lobby branches off into three wings. An indoor hot spring flows into an outdoor mountain stream. You'll swear it does.

A fourth-floor indoor balcony has cozy sitting areas and front and back porches; the fifth floor has a small back balcony.

Highs. ❶ Stunning lobby. **❷** Quality dining and amenities. **❸** Comfortable, easily accessible rooms. **❹** A pleasant boat ride takes you to the Magic Kingdom.

Lows. ❶ Most rooms sleep 4, unlike most Disney hotels at this price point.

Rooms. Vibrant quilts, plaid drapes, Mission-style furniture and handcrafted embellishments recall the best of the West. Carved panels top padded headboards. *Rooms: 344 sq ft (104 sq meters), 2 queen beds or 1 king, small refrigerator; sleep 4. Suites, villas sleep 4–12. Accessed from indoor halls.*

Swimming pools. A part of that mountain stream, a large pool features a curving slide that sprays riders with mist. Nearby are two tubs (one hot, one cold), a kiddie pool, a new

Wilderness Lodge.

Yacht Club.

water play area and a geyser that faithfully goes off hourly. A Villas quiet pool has four bubbling springs and a 15-person whirlpool. **Restaurants and food.** "I said, WHAT. WILL. IT. BE. BUCK. A. ROOS!" Brusque servers spill the beans of the Whispering Canyon Cafe, a tasty barbecue spot where no one whispers. Don't ask for ketchup. Serious foodies head to Artist Point, a Disney Signature Restaurant focused on the Pacific-Northwest. **Key facts.** *Resort type:* Disney Deluxe resort with lodge, two wings, DVC building. *Size:* 701 rooms, 27 suites, 136 villas, 65 acres (26 ha). *Built:* 1994. *Location:* Northwest Disney, southeast of Magic Kingdom. *Address:* 901 Timberland Dr 32830. *Miles to:* Magic Kingdom 1 (2 km), Epcot 3 (5 km), Hollywood Studios 4 (6 km), Animal Kingdom 6 (10 km), Blizzard Beach 5 (8 km), Typhoon Lagoon 5 (8 km), Disney Springs 5 (8 km), ESPN 7 (11 km). *Other amenities:* Arcade; beach, bike, boat and surrey rentals; nightly campfire, movie at main pool; fitness center, guided fishing trips, lobby tour; paved trail leads to Fort Wilderness; Segway tour; childcare center; laundromat, laundry service. *Children's programs:* Free organized activities 2:30p-4p; the Electrical Water Pageant passes behind the hotel between 9:35p and 9:55p. *Phone:* 407-824-3200; villas 407-938-4300. *Fax:* 407-824-3232. *Disney transportation:* Buses serve Disney parks, Disney Springs, boats head to Magic Kingdom; the Contemporary Resort, Fort Wilderness. *Rates:* Rooms $289–$1,025, discounted to $202; suites and villas $515–$1,529, discounted to $319.

Yacht and Beach Club

★★★★ ✔ These side-by-side resorts share Disney's best hotel swimming complex. Their comfortable rooms are easy to get to and they have good food at all price levels. The oyster-gray clapboard of the Yacht Club recalls formal oceanfront hotels common in New England in the 19th century. The pale-blue-and-white Beach Club strikes a more whimsical look, its stick-style buildings capturing the look of vintage seaside cottages.

Highs. ❶ An outstanding pool complex. ❷ Good food. ❸ Within walking distance of Epcot (the Beach Club is just a few hundred feet from its World Showcase), and Hollywood Studios if you don't mind a longer walk.

Lows. ❶ Expensive rates. ❷ Little fast food. ❸ No fair-weather transport to the front of Epcot.

Rooms. Nautical motifs feature white furniture. *Rooms: 381 sq ft (116 sq meters), 2 queen beds or 1 king, some daybeds, small refrigerator; sleep 5. Suites sleep 4–8, villas 4–8. Accessed from indoor halls.*

Swimming pools. A Nantucket lagoon that's really a miniature water park, sprawling Stormalong Bay includes a meandering pool, a lazy river, a shallow inlet with a real sandbar, a shady hot tub and an assortment of bridges, fountains and waterfalls. The spiral staircase of a life-sized shipwreck leads to a slide that's 300 feet (91 m) long. Starting off in a dark tunnel (the inside of the ship's fallen mast), it enters daylight at a rocky outcropping where waterfalls shower riders just before they splash into the pool. A large kiddie pool has overhead sprinklers and a sandy play spot; a small one on the pirate ship has a tiny slide.

Restaurants and food. Decisions, decisions. Will it be a gigantic sundae at Beaches & Cream, a retro soda shop that's next to impossible to get into? A pleasant meal at the Captain's Grille, perhaps Disney's most underrated place to eat? A character buffet with Donald Duck, Goofy and Minnie Mouse at the surprisingly relaxed Cape May Cafe? Or a serious steak at the seriously expensive Yachtsman Steakhouse, a Disney Signature Restaurant that everyone seems to love? If it's me I'm headed to Beaches & Cream, getting there about 30 minutes or so before it opens so I'll be sure to get a table. And when it does—peanut butter sundae baby!

Key facts. *Resort type:* Disney Deluxe resort with adjoining buildings. *Size:* 1,197 rooms, 112 suites, 208 villas, 30 acres (12 ha). *Built:* 1990. *Location:* Central Disney, next to Epcot. *Addresses:* Beach Club 1800 Epcot Resorts Blvd 32830, Yacht Club 1700 Epcot Resorts Blvd 32830. *Miles to:* Magic Kingdom 5 (8 km), Epcot back entrance <1 front entrance 4 (6 km), Hollywood Studios 2, Animal Kingdom 5 (8 km), Blizzard Beach 3 (5 km), Typhoon Lagoon 3 (5 km), Disney Springs 3 (5 km), ESPN 5 (8 km). *Other amenities:* Arcades, beach, bike and boat rentals, boat rides, nightly campfire, fireworks cruises, guided fishing trips, walking trail; Changing of the Guard each afternoonn; volleyball, croquet, tennis courts; hair salon, health club, laundromat, laundry service; shop with groceries; conference center, business center. *Children's programs:* Pontoon-boat albatross adventure; complimentary arts and crafts, ceramics (extra charge), beach and pool activities. *Phone:* Beach Club 407-934-8000, villas 407-934-2175, Yacht Club 407-934-7000. *Fax:* Beach Club 407-934-3850; Yacht Club 407-934-3450. *Disney transportation:* Buses serve Magic Kingdom, Animal Kingdom, water parks, Disney Springs; boats serve the back entrance of Epcot and Hollywood Studios except when lightning is in the area, then buses run to the front of those parks. *Rates:* Rooms $356–$1,004, discounted to $249; suites and villas $414–$3,637, discounted to $390.

Beach Club.

Walt Disney World Dolphin.

Not Disney, but at Disney

One of the world's most popular Marriott-owned hotels, the most popular U.S. Armed Forces Recreation Center, a stunning Four Seasons resort... they're all on Disney property. And then there's the Disney Springs Resort Area, a tree-lined boulevard of choices.

Walt Disney World Swan and Dolphin. Giant swans, huge fish, a towering triangle—the architecture is one-of-a-kind at these convention resorts, which sit right in the middle of Walt Disney World and use Disney's bus system. Now owned by Marriott, they were the signature properties of Starwood Resorts until 2016. Highlights include an elaborate swimming area, nine classy restaurants and Disney World's only karaoke bar. The smaller Swan is quiet and intimate, the Dolphin boisterous and bubbly. Interiors are modern; rooms feature Westin Heavenly Beds. Designed by architect Michael Graves, the two buildings feature abstract entertainment architecture. Surrounded by huge banana palms, the Dolphin is a tropical mountain, its waterfall splashing into the lagoon between the structures and then onto the Swan, a huge sand dune. *Location:* Central Disney next to Disney's Yacht and Beach Club, near Hollywood Studios. *Phone:* Swan 407-934-4499; fax 407-934-4710; Dolphin 407-934-4000; fax 407-934-4884. *Rates:* $299–$594, discounts to $149; suites: $390–$1440, discounts to $190. Additional $25 nightly resort fee.

Four Seasons Orlando. Far from the crowds in a remote Disney area, this uber-luxe Spanish Revival resort sits amid mature live oaks, cypress stands and nearly a thousand palms. Oranges and teals accent white furnishings. *Location:* Northeast Disney property, beyond Port Orleans. *Phone:* 407-313-7777, fax 407-313-8500. *Rates:* $549–$830, discounts to $366; suites $695–$12,000, discounts to $545.

Shades of Green. Exclusively for active and retired members of the U.S. military and their families and friends, this relaxed resort is the only Armed Forces Recreation Center in the continental United States. Built as the Disney Golf Resort, it sits next to Disney's Palm, Magnolia and Oak Trail golf courses. Light woods trim huge rooms. *Location:* Across from Disney's Polynesian Village Resort. *Phone:* 407-824-3400, fax 407-824-3665. *Rates (based on rank, the higher one, the higher the other):* Rooms $98–$148, suites $262–$394.

Disney Springs area hotels. You'll pay less for your room at one of these older hotels, and often be able to book one at the last minute when Disney properties are full. *Miles to:* Animal Kingdom 7 (11 km); Blizzard Beach 5 (8 km); Disney Springs <1 (1 km); Epcot 4 (6 km); ESPN 5 (8 km); Hollywood Studios 5 (8 km); Magic Kingdom 5 (8 km); Typhoon Lagoon 3 (5 km).

B Resort & Spa. Heavily damaged by 2004's Hurricane Charley, this 17-story tower was closed for a decade, gutted to the walls and rebuilt as a stylish hotel with a playful theme. Imaginative ingredients create contemporary "farm-to-table" comfort food at the new American Kitchen Bar & Grill, run by chef Justin Leo. *Size:* 32 ac (13 ha); 370 rooms, 24 suites. *Built:* 1972. *Rooms:* 2 double beds or 1 king bed, double sleeper sofa, ceiling fans; 20 rooms have bunk beds; sleep 3–5. *Address:* 1905 Hotel Plaza Blvd 32830. *Amenities:* Restaurant, poolside café; zero-entry swimming pool; fitness center, full-service spa; business center, conference center; laundromat; mini-mart. *Phone:* 407-828-2828, fax 407-827-6338. *Rates:* $105–$195, discounts to $90; suites $185-$205, discounts to $149; additional $24 daily resort fee, $18 daily self-parking fee.

Best Western Lake Buena Vista. Originally a Travelodge, this 18-story lakefront tower became a Best Western in the year 2000. *Size:* 12 ac (5 ha); 321 rooms, 4 suites. *Built:* 1972. *Rooms:* 2 queen beds, refrigerator, balcony or patio, sleeps 4–5; accessed via indoor halls. *Address:* 2000 Hotel Plaza Blvd 32830. *Amenities:* 2 restaurants, Pizza Hut Express, swimming pool, kiddie pool; tennis courts; fitness center; arcade, childcare service; playground; business center, meeting and event space; car rental counter, laundromat. *Phone:* 407-828-2424, fax 407-827-6390. *Rates:* $85–$149, discounts to $66; additional $14 daily resort fee.

Buena Vista Palace. Finishing a two-year makeover in 2016, this 27-story tower is now part of the Hilton group. *Size:* 27 ac (11 ha); 890 rooms, 124 suites. *Built:* 1972. *Rooms:* 2 queen beds, small refrigerator, most have balcony or patio, sleep 4; accessed via indoor halls. *Address:* 1900 Hotel Plaza Blvd 32830. *Amenities:* 2 restaurants, Disney character breakfast; 3 swimming pools, pool concierge, hot tub; basketball, tennis, volleyball courts; fitness center, salon, sauna, spa; arcade, child-care service, children's scavenger hunt; business center, convention center; car rental counter, concierge; laundromat, laundry services; mini-mart. *Phone:* 407-827-2727, fax 407-827-3136. *Rates:* $89–$170, discounts to $74; suites $145–$499, discounts to $109; additional $20 daily resort fee.

Doubletree Guest Suites. The only all-suite hotel at Disney; a Hilton brand. *Size:* 7 ac (3 ha); 229 suites. *Built:* 1972. *Suites:* 1 or 2 bedrooms, queen beds, small refrigerator, microwave, sleeps 6; accessed via indoor halls. *Address:* 2305 Hotel Plaza Blvd 32830. *Amenities:* Restaurant, swimming pool, kiddie pool, hot tub; fitness center, playground, pool table, tennis courts, business center, car rental counter, child-care service, laundromat, laundry services, meeting rooms, mini-mart. *Phone:* 407-934-1000, fax 407-934-1015. *Rates:* Suites $115–$429, discounts to $99.

Hilton. The most upscale Disney Springs hotel. *Size:* 23 ac (9 ha); 704 rooms, 110 suites. *Built:* 1972. *Rooms:* 2 double beds, mini-bar, sleeps 5; accessed via indoor halls. *Address:* 1751 Hotel Plaza Blvd 32830. *Amenities:* Seven restaurants, Disney character breakfast; 2 swimming pools, kiddie pool with spray area, arcade, fitness center, golf pro shop, pool table, business center, car rental counter, child-care services, laundromat, meeting rooms, mini-mart, salon. *Phone:* 407-827-4000, fax 407-827-3890. *Rates:* $95–$340, discounts to $79; suites $155–$360, discounts to $119.

Holiday Inn. *Size:* 10 ac (4 ha); 323 rooms, 1 suite. *Built:* 1972. *Rooms:* 2 queen beds, sleeper, small refrigerator, work desk, balcony or patio, sleeps 4–5; accessed via indoor halls; suite available. *Address:* 1805 Hotel Plaza Blvd 32830. *Amenities:* One restaurant, zero-entry swimming pool with whirlpool, business center, health club, laundromat, laundry services. *Phone:* 407-828-8888, fax 407-827-4623. *Rates:* $109–$205, discounts to $89.

Wyndham Lake Buena Vista. A favorite of British guests, formerly the Regal Sun and the Grosvenor. *Size:* 13 ac (5 ha); 619 rooms, 7 suites. *Built:* 1972. *Rooms:* 2 queen beds, sleep 4–6; accessed via indoor halls; suites available. *Address:* 1850 Hotel Plaza Blvd 32830. *Amenities:* Restaurant, pub, Disney character breakfast, 2 swimming pools, kiddie pool, water playground, fitness center, playground; basketball, shuffleboard, tennis, volleyball courts; business center, car rental counter, currency exchange, laundromat, laundry services, meeting rooms. *Phone:* 407-828-4444, fax 407-828-8192. *Rates:* $75–$155, discounts to $64; suites $435–$529, discounts to $349.

A Disney entrance.

Planning Your Trip

With just a little bit of preparation, it's easy to put together a terrific Walt Disney World vacation. Planning one isn't brain surgery—all you need is this book, access to the Internet and a phone; a Disney telephone directory appears at the back of this book. Ideally you should start putting your plan together a year in advance. For basic planning, here's a simple 12-step plan:

❶ **Decide when to go.** You can have a good time at Disney any day of the year, but if you've got the flexibility, the first two weeks of December is the best time to go. It's not terribly crowded, and there's more to see and do than any other time, thanks to the holiday decor and entertainment. Crowds are light and hotel rooms less expensive from mid-January to Valentine's Day, the first half of May and between Labor Day and mid-November. The least crowded, least expensive week of the year is the one after Labor Day. The worst times to visit? July and early August, when crowds are thick and the air thicker; and the week between Christmas and New Year's, when crowds are horrid and temperatures can be near freezing.

❷ **Decide how long to stay.** Want to see the best of everything Disney has to offer? You'll need at least a week.

❸ **Build your budget.** Add up your estimated daily expenses, including less-obvious spending like spur-of-the-moment snacks, souvenirs and gifts for the folks back home.

❹ **Decide where to stay.** Disney operates 20 resorts, and nearly every hotel chain known to man has at least one property within 10 miles. Disney hotels are most convenient, of course, and offer other benefits such as Extra Magic Hours (time in the parks before or after closing time), free transportation and packaged dining and recreation options.

❺ **Buy your airline tickets.** The Orlando International Airport is 19 miles east of Walt Disney World, about a 30-minute drive.

Driving to Disney? It's smack dab in the middle of Florida alongside Interstate 4, 15 miles southwest of downtown Orlando, 70 miles northeast of Tampa.

❻ Decide what you want to do. Thumb through this book and check out the official Disney website disneyworld.com. If you have children, let them pick out their favorites.

❼ Choose your park tickets. Disney offers a variety of options, including packages with pre-paid dining and recreation if you stay at a Disney resort hotel. Tickets are priced by the number of days they are good for; the more days the better the value.

❽ Make a plan. Check the calendar at disneyworld.com for park hours, fireworks schedules and special events. Talk with your family about having a day or two when you don't visit a park and instead do something else. If you will be staying at a Disney hotel, check Extra Magic Hours at disneyworld.com.

❾ Book it. Purchase your park tickets and reserve your Disney room through Disney at 407-934-7639 or disneyworld.com. Call between 7 a.m. and 10 p.m. Eastern time.

❿ Reserve your restaurants. Character meals, dinner shows and key dining times for regular restaurants fill up months in advance. The restaurant that books the quickest is Cinderella's Royal Table, inside Cinderella Castle. You can book a Disney table as early as 190 days out if you're staying at a Disney hotel, 180 days if you're not (407-939-3463, disneyworld.com). Many entertainment and recreation choices require reservations, too.

⓫ Reserve your rides. Choose your Fastpass+ times on the very first day you can, so you'll have the most variety to pick from. Disney hotel guests can reserve Fastpasses 60 days in advance; others can do so 30 days out. Be obsessive with this; key times for popular rides, shows and character greetings often go on the first day they're available.

⓬ Rent a car, maybe. Disney has such an extensive transportation system that you may not want to rent a car. Its complimentary Magical Express buses shuttle Disney hotel guests from the Orlando airport, and its boats, buses and monorails move guests around Disney property free of charge. However, guests with cars get around faster, and have the option to visit areas outside Disney. You can rent a car at the airport or at most hotels on Disney property.

We say get a car, specifically a Ford Mustang convertible, from either Hertz at the airport or a Hertz Local Edition (HLE) location. The Mustang has room for two adults and two children, a driving position that's pretty easy to see out from, not a lot of room in the trunk (in other words, pack light) and most importantly, a top that's amazingly easy to put up and down. Drop your top as you leave the airport and you will instantly feel like you are officially on vacation. You'll feel the warmth of Florida air, really notice the rows of palms that line local interstate exchanges, and once you're at Disney you'll smell all the freshly cut grass. It's a splurge, yes, but one that you'll enjoy every day of your trip and your kids will long remember.

What to pack. Disney World visitors often underestimate the heat and humidity of Central Florida, and are unprepared for the outdoor exposure a Disney vacation includes.

For all ages. Musts include T-shirts, loose-fitting cotton tops, capris and shorts with large pockets, baseball caps and swimsuits, and broken-in walking shoes (pack two pair per person, so if it rains everyone still has a dry pair). Flip-flop sandals with a strap between the toes are a bad idea; they create blisters when used this intensely. In the winter you'll need clothes to layer, such as jackets, sweaters and sweatshirts, as days start off cool but warm quickly. January mornings can be below freezing at 9 a.m. but 60 degrees by noon. Temperatures at 7 p.m. should be no higher than the 50s through March. From May through August, the heat index is usually at least 105 degrees by noon. For detailed weather data log on to weather.com and type in the ZIP code 32830.

Other essentials include an umbrella or rain poncho, sunglasses and sunscreen. Keep your hands free on your trip by using a backpack instead of a purse. Don't forget tickets, reservation confirmations and all the various battery chargers a modern life requires. And don't splurge on those speed -sunglasses are the No. 1 item guests lose at Disney. Cast members find hundreds of pairs a day.

For children. Dress your children like you dress yourself—casually, comfortably—but with more protection from the sun (i.e., wide-brimmed hats). Bring snacks (granola bars, raisin boxes) and, for autographs, a Sharpie (a thick one so far characters can hold it easily).

Most forgotten item. The most common item Disney World visitors mistakenly leave at home—and at the end of the trip the one they most often leave in their hotel rooms—is the charger for their phone.

© Disney

MagicBand, with MagicBandits.

Charming chips: MyMagic+

Developed by Disney at a cost of reportedly close to $1 billion, MyMagic+ is a high-tech "vacation management system" that can help you make the most of your Disney stay. You can use it to schedule attractions days in advance, make dining reservations, buy food and merchandise, even open the door to your hotel room. It consists of three things: a wristband, an app, and a new FastPass+ system that lets you book your attraction times before you leave home. All three debuted in 2014, and Disney has been tweaking them since. Here's how they worked as of July 2016:

What is a MagicBand? A high-tech device that appears to be a simple rubber wristband, it's your ticket, room key, charge card, FastPass ticket and more. A radio-frequency identification (RFID) chip inside it stores a randomly assigned code that identifies you to an encrypted database, which itself stores information such as your park and FastPass+ privileges, room access and credit card data. You decide how much information to give it, and still provide your PIN for purchases that come to more than $50.

MagicBands come in seven colors: red, blue, green, pink, yellow, orange and gray;

replacement bands are gray by default. You can customize yours with trinkets called MagicBandits, which Disney sells throughout Walt Disney World. The bands can withstand hot and cold temperatures, are waterproof but don't float, and have three-year embedded batteries.

One noticeable change brought about by MagicBands is that Disney no longer has turnstiles at its park entrances. Now there are poles. Waist-high posts, each with a glowing "touch point" that scans your fingerprint and checks to make sure your MagicBand (or plastic park ticket) is valid. When the touch point turns green, you're good to go.

Why should I wear one? Two reasons: Because it can make your Disney stay more efficient, as it replaces cards and papers that you'd otherwise have to carry, and it can make your visit more fun. As Disney adds to its technology, its theme-park experiences are already becoming more personalized. Many advances went live in 2016. Now, as you scan your pass at an attraction's FastPass touch point, screens discreetly flash nearby cast members information about you ("Julie. Day 1 of stay.") which lets them greet you in a surprisingly personal manner ("Hi Julie. How's your first day going?"). Some attractions acknowledge you by themselves. Screens in front of you bid you goodbye at the end of It's a Small World ("Adios, Julie and Mike"). Your name appears on a postcard from Mars as you leave Space Mountain. At Epcot's Mission Space, after you finish your flight training you're greeted with the news that you passed your test: your astronaut ID badge, complete with your name and your "recruitment center"—your hometown.

In the future, some Audio-Animatronic figures may greet you by name, as will live characters such as Cinderella ("So Maddie, isn't this your first visit to my castle?")

What are its drawbacks? The biggest downside is that the system tracks you in ways you may not care for, as it lets Disney monitor nearly everything you do. The characters you meet. The souvenirs you buy. The attractions you visit and the time you see them. The restaurant you went to for lunch, the entree you ordered and the size of the tip you left your waitress. At its best, this information helps the company respond to shifts in crowd patterns, sending out additional staff and entertainment to busy areas, adding ride vehicles to overwhelmed attractions and learning which servers diners like most. However it's possible—perhaps inevitable—that Disney will also collect data about you for commercial reasons. Disney says that it does not use information collected with MyMagic+ to personalize or target advertising to children under age 13.

How do I get a one? MagicBands are free for Disney hotel guests and annual passholders. Other visitors can buy them for $12.95. If you live in the United States, are booked into a Disney resort hotel and reserve your bands at least 10 days before your trip, Disney ships them to you; otherwise they send them when you check in. Disney sells MagicBands in all of its theme parks and at Disney Springs.

What if I lose it? If you misplace your MagicBand, someone else could use it to get into your hotel room or make small purchases under your name, but as soon as you report it as missing Disney deactivates it. Replacement bands are free for Disney hotel guests; others pay $12.95.

What is My Disney Experience? It's a free app for iPhones, iPads and Android devices. Using it lets you view attraction wait times, use GPS park maps, make and modify FastPass+ reservations, schedule restaurant reservations, and access your other Disney information. To use it, you create a Disney account and link your park ticket to it.

What if I don't have a smartphone? You need one (or a tablet) to use the app, but not to use MyMagic+. The system's planning and reservation tools also appear on touchscreen kiosks at each theme park and online at mydisneyexperience.com.

What if I don't want this 'magic'? If you aren't comfortable using MyMagic+ don't worry; you aren't required to use it to visit Walt Disney World. As for that viewpoint, however, you may just want to, as they say in these parts, let it go. Disney has made the system so convenient, efficient and widespread that you'll probably feel compelled to be part of it. You don't need a MagicBand to get into a theme park or to use the FastPass+ system, as Disney also offers hard plastic tickets.

My Disney Experience app.

© Disney

FastPass+ touch point.

Sleep late, no wait: FastPass+

FOR YEARS AN OLD COLLEGE FRIEND would ask me "How do I show up at Disney at noon, not wait in a line, and still see the big things I want to see?" I never had an answer. In fact, in my 10 years of writing this book, hers was the one question that always left me stumped. Until now. Because though it's not perfect, Disney's FastPass+ gives you the freedom to put together days however you want to, days that include showing up at a park when it's already crowded and still doing exactly what you want. Here's a primer on the service, updated as of July 2016:

What is FastPass+? It's an attraction reservation system. You use it book admission to theme-park rides in advance, so you won't have to wait in long lines for them when you're on your vacation. You can also reserve good viewing spots for shows and parades. Each FastPass assigns you a specific window of time when you can enter the ride or show's FastPass+ entrance. Most rides give you a one-hour window. Shows and parades require you to show up between 15 or 30 minutes early; most either let you in their theaters early or let you see their shows from their best viewing areas.

You reserve attractions by using the My Disney Experience app, or at the Disney website (disney.com) or in person at theme-park kiosks. When you arrive at an attraction, you enter its FastPass line by tapping your MagicBand or park ticket against a waist-high scanner, which Disney calls a touch point.

You can make your reservations way in advance; before you leave home. Everything is digital. Nothing is on paper.

The system updates Disney's former Fastpass (lowercase "P", no "plus") scheme. It used paper tickets, which you could only get at the attractions they were good for, use only on the day you got them, and couldn't change. As part of the upgrade, more than twice as many attractions accept FastPasses.

Does it cost money? No. It's free of charge, included with your park ticket.

Is it like a restaurant reservation? Yes. Except it usually has a one-hour window and doesn't charge you a penalty if you don't use it.

How many FastPasses can I get? You can make three reservations per day in advance, for each person in your party, for each day your park tickets are valid. If you've booked a room at a Disney resort hotel, you can start scheduling your FastPasses up to 60 days before you check in. If you're staying somewhere else, you can book them 30 days out, for up to seven days. Annual passholders can book up to 10 days of FastPasses at a time. Once you use your three FastPasses for a day (or after they expire or you cancel them) you can get another one, and then continue to book more one-at-a-time.

Do I have to get the same passes for everyone in my group? No. You can reserve a ride or show only for particular members of your party, leaving the others free to get passes for something else.

Can I change my mind? Yes. You can always reschedule a FastPass reservation, add or remove people from it, or cancel it altogether and book a different one.

Are there limits? Yes. For each day your park ticket is valid, you can book three FastPasses in advance. Magic Kingdom and Disney's Animal Kingdom let you freely choose any attractions you want, but the other parks don't: Epcot and Disney's Hollywood Studios divide your choices into two tiers and restrict you to one from column A (in general, the most popular attractions) and two from column B. You can only reserve a ride or show once per day; you can't book a FastPass for Soarin' Around the World at 9 a.m. and then get another one at 10 a.m. You can't overlap your FastPasses; if the window for one is 9:50 a.m. to 10:50 a.m., you can't book another one that's good from 10:40 a.m. to 11:40 a.m.

And then there's the greatest limit: availability. Every attraction has a limited number of FastPasses available, and the most popular rides and shows can "sell out" way in advance. However, that availability is constantly changing, as whenever you're online booking or canceling passes thousands of other vacationers are too. Sometimes even attractions that have been booked solid for months suddenly will have FastPasses available just moments before they're valid, although these often get snapped up literally within seconds.

What are these kiosks? They're touchscreens, which are usually clustered together in groups of three or four. Each theme park has a few of these clusters, with trained cast members standing by to assist you. They let you add, change or cancel FastPass reservations for that day in that park.

What if I show up late? Though Disney doesn't publicize it, each 1-hour FastPass window has a grace period. Typically, you can arrive at a ride up to 5 minutes early or

15 minutes late. If you miss your designated FastPass window due to circumstances beyond your control (weather, Disney transportation delays), cast members will usually try to accommodate you. The later you are, however, the less helpful they'll be.

What if I don't use the service? You'll face long Standby waits at many attractions, spend more time on your feet, go on fewer rides, see less shows, and get much less for your Disney dollar. Flip through our attraction pages to see how long some Standby wait times have become. Since the new service began, many are much longer than many visitors expect. On peak days, some wait times have reached six hours.

How do I take advantage of it? First, buy your park tickets. Then download the app, create your Disney account, and link into it the members of your family or group that will be visiting the parks together.

Next, flip through this book's pages on attractions. Jot down those you most want to experience and note their Standby wait times, so you don't waste a pass on something that doesn't need one. Book your FastPasses as soon as you can, far in advance of your trip so you can create days that best suit your needs. Passes for the more popular and newest attractions go quickly, as do those for parades.

Once you're at a park, use the FastPass kiosks when they're convenient. Doing so not only gets you the help of someone who knows what they're doing, it lets you avoid any Wi-Fi reception problems. Though it employs an innovative AT&T system, Disney's service isn't always reliable, especially inside buildings and during heavy-use times such as right before a parade. Kiosks near park entrances tend to be the most crowded.

At the start of a park day, take a screen shot of your FastPasses and text it to the other people in your party. Doing so makes it easy for everyone to remember what reservations they have, and gives them proof that they do indeed have a FastPass for an attraction if Disney's internal system breaks down.

Ready... get set... plan. Needless to say, using FastPass+ makes your Disney visit much less spontaneous, and the advanced planning can be a real pain. But overall it can help give you a much better vacation. If you use it correctly, it gives you the freedom to visit the parks on your terms (say, by arriving at noon instead of the break of dawn), and guarantees that you can do the things you most want to do without waiting in long lines.

Epcot Flower & Garden Festival.

Festive fêtes, flowers, food

Yes you can wear a costume at Walt Disney World—at its Halloween Party. But that's just one of many things that make Disney's seasonal events worth considering.

Epcot Flower & Garden Festival. This 75- to 90-day garden party includes seminars, demonstrations and celebrity guest speakers, as well as character topiaries, a butterfly house with a live caterpillar and chrysalis exhibit and 30 million flowers. Themed weekends celebrate art, insects and Mother's Day. Concerts feature 1960s and 1970s acts. Vendor booths line walkways. *The first week in March through mid-late May. Included in park admission. 407-934-7639.*

Epcot Food & Wine Festival. This two-month festival celebrates international food and drink. More than two dozen World Showcase booths sell small portions of ethnic and regional dishes. Each booth typically offers three food items and an alcoholic beverage. Events include cooking demonstrations, pricey dinners and wine seminars. Free Eat to the Beat concerts feature vintage pop acts such as Rick Springfield and Wilson Phillips. Included in park admission. *Mid-Sep–mid-Nov. Details at disneyworld.com/ foodandwine or 407-939-3378.*

Mickey's Not-So-Scary Party. Disney's most festive event, this series of Halloween parties are perfect for children, teens, young adults... people of any age who can appreciate clean campy fun. Focused on themes such as "The Nightmare Before Christmas" and The Haunted Mansion, the Magic Kingdom bash includes a unique parade, a special fireworks show, a new stage show, two dance parties and many character meet-and-greets. Dressed as candy makers, cast members hand out goodies throughout the park. Attendance is limited to 25,000 people—a third of the park's capacity. Most rides are open, and few have long lines. Viewing areas for the first parade are crowded, though. So are greeting spots for some characters, as many wear Halloween costumes or are rarely seen at other times.

Dates. The parties are held several nights a week throughout September and October. Each one runs from 7 p.m. until midnight.

Tickets. Adults $72–$105, children ages 3–9 $67–$100. Parties closest to Halloween cost more, children under age 3 admitted free. Admission is not included in any other Disney ticket; small discounts may be available for annual passholders and Disney Vacation Club members. Sold at 407-939-5277, disneyworld. com and Walt Disney World Guest Relations and Guest Services counters.

Costume rules. In 2016 Disney changed its rules regarding the type of costume you can wear at the event. In general, it cannot be "inappropriate, offensive, objectionable or violent," "obstructive" or "detract from the experience of other guests." It can't contain a pretend weapon that resembles or could easily be mistaken for an actual weapon, or a pointed or sharp object that could strike another visitor. However, plastic light sabers and toy swords are OK. You can dress as a Disney character, but can't pose for pictures or sign autographs as if you are an actual one.

If you're over 14 years of age, you can't wear a mask, a cape that extends below your waist, or a full-length princess dress or other clothing that reaches or drags on the ground. You can, however, adorn yourself with headwear that doesn't cover your face, transparent wings or a tutu. You may be subject to additional security screenings if you wear a layered costume or one that forms a prop that surrounds your body. A child age 13 and under can wear a mask, as long as his

or her eyes are visible and the mask doesn't cover the child's entire face. Disney may modify these costume rules in the future.

Tips. *When to buy tickets:* Early, especially for weekend nights in October, which often sell out. *When to arrive:* At 4 p.m. Your party ticket is good at that time, so you'll have three hours to explore the park before the party starts. Some partygoers come early just to get in line to meet popular characters such as Jack and Sally or the Seven Dwarfs, each of whose lines start to form about 5:30 p.m. Once the party begins, the wait to meet these stars can be two or three hours. *Should you wear a costume?* Yes! Many people do, adults and children alike. Young adults and families often go all out. Many outfits are homemade and elaborate; some are bizarre. Once I spotted a group of younger men dressed as masculine versions of Disney princesses, then a group of older men who had transformed themselves into dolls from It's a Small World. *How long to stay:* Until midnight. Much of the crowd leaves after the fireworks show. Lines for rides dwindle down to nothing, and good viewing spots for the second parade are easy to find even right before it starts. During the last hour of the party, cast members handing out candy get more generous and the character dance parties get more fun, as teens and young adults show up as well as families.

Independence Day.

© Disney

Halloween partygoers dressed as Giselle and Raggedy Ann pose with the park's Anastasia.

Mickey's Very Merry Party. On many evenings Magic Kingdom hosts this festive Christmas event, which is worth its additional fee. There's a lot to see and do, including exclusive shows and parades, a "Jingle Cruise" version of the Jungle Cruise ride, a Christmas-themed fireworks display, two character dance parties and over two dozen character meet-and-greets. Many regular park attractions are also open, and Disney hands out complimentary hot chocolate and cookies throughout the park. Attendance is limited to 25,000 people.

Dates and hours. The parties are held several nights a week from early November until the week before Christmas. Each one runs from 7 p.m. until midnight.

Tickets. Adults $86–$99, children ages 3–9 $81–$94. Parties closest to Christmas cost more, children under age 3 are admitted free. Admission is not included in any other Disney ticket; small discounts may be available for annual passholders and Disney Vacation Club members. Sold at 407-939-5277, disneyworld. com and Walt Disney World Guest Relations and Guest Services counters.

Tips. *When to buy tickets:* Early. Many parties sell out, sometimes even the first one. *When to arrive:* At 4 p.m. Your ticket is good at that time, so you'll have three hours to explore the park before the party starts.

How long to stay: Until midnight. During the last two hours of the party, the lines for its attractions, characters and complimentary hot chocolate and cookies nearly go away, but the dance parties get more crowded, and therefore more fun. *When to ride Jingle Cruise:* Late, after its lines die down. It's very popular, especially right at 7 p.m.

Other events. Disney World hosts unique festivals and parties year-round.

St. Patrick's Day. Events mark this Irish holiday at two locations: Raglan Road at Disney Springs and the United Kingdom pavilion at Epcot's World Showcase. *Epcot events included in standard park admission.*

Easter Weekend. Outfitted in colorful homemade gowns straight out of the Old South, the teenage Azalea Trail Maids of Mobile, Ala., greet guests on Magic Kingdom's Main Street U.S.A. and lead its parade. At Epcot, children hunt for Easter eggs. Some Disney hotels offer egg decorating, egg hunts and characters in costumes.

Gay Days. Gay and lesbian adults of all ages congregate at Disney during the first week in June; many wear red shirts in solidarity. Groups gather at each park on a particular day. Disney does not sponsor the event but condones it; its bakery cases have offered rainbow cupcakes. Once controversial, the event has become more accepted lately. Details at gaydays.com or 407-896-8431.

Sounds Like Summer Concert Series. Cover bands perform tunes from stars such as Elton John and The Supremes nightly at Epcot's America Gardens amphitheater.

Independence Day Weekend. A spectacular Magic Kingdom fireworks show surrounds you if you're on Main Street U.S.A. Disney's Hollywood Studios has fireworks too. Historic characters share their stories at Epcot's American Adventure pavilion.

Night of Joy. Live concerts by contemporary Christian artists highlight this Magic Kingdom event. Most rides are open. Early Sept. $39 1 night; $78 2 nights. nightofjoy.com.

Christmas in general. Even the most diehard Scrooge will warm up to Disney in November and December. Most parks offers special entertainment and elaborate decor. *Magic Kingdom:* Hands down this park has the most Christmas spirit; its Main Street U.S.A. decorations are so iconically American you'll swear they're straight from your childhood. Santa Claus meets guests just inside the park entrance. At night, Cinderella Castle appears to be covered in glowing icicles. Christmas fireworks, parades and shows become part of the regular Magic Kingdom schedule during the last two weeks of December. *Epcot:* Forget Future World, the holiday mood here is all at World Showcase. Each pavilion has at least one holiday storyteller; most are excellent. The American Adventure pavilion also hosts the Candlelight Processional, a first-rate (and extremely popular) retelling of the birth of Jesus. *Disney's Hollywood Studios:* The park brings back the look of an Old Hollywood Christmas, with tinsel-heavy decorations and witty Citizens of Hollywood skits. *Disney's Animal Kingdom:* Traditionally there's not much spirit here, though recent evening additions to the park could change that. Some characters wear seasonal outfits.

New Year's Eve. Magic Kingdom, Epcot and Disney's Hollywood Studios ring in the new year with special fireworks, complimentary party hats and noise makers. Disney's Animal Kingdom also celebrates. Many restaurants have celebratory menus. New Year's Eve is extremely crowded in all theme parks, the busiest night of the year. Park events are included with standard park admission.

Holiday costs. During the days surrounding Easter, Independence Day, Thanksgiving, Christmas and New Year's, hotel rates and one-day park tickets are at their most expensive. So is food, as Disney charges a premium for its dining plan and often increases the prices at buffets.

Christmas parade.

Mickey Mouse pancakes.

Involving your children

Like looking forward to Christmas morning, anticipating your Disney vacation can be nearly as much fun as the trip itself. Build your family's excitement with these ideas:

"We're going to Disney World!" Spring that good news in a fun way. For example:

A backpack. As a present, fill a new backpack with Disney World items such as an autograph book or a T-shirt. Your child will quickly figure out what it means.

A hunt. Create a scavenger hunt that uses clues about Disney characters or quotes from Disney movies. Make each "find" a Disney trinket that has a card attached with the next clue. Attach the final card (announcing the trip) to a helium-filled Mickey balloon tucked inside a new suitcase. When the suitcase is opened, the balloon floats up.

A letter. Mail your child a letter or post-card that appears to be from Mickey Mouse, Cinderella or another Disney character and reads "can't wait to meet you at Disney World!" Mickey could add "See ya real soon!"

Puzzle. Create one that when assembled announces your trip. Use paint or markers to write "We're going to Walt Disney World

tomorrow!" ("next week!" etc.) on the pieces. Give it to your child as a surprise present.

Quiz. Create a quiz about Disney characters, movies or Disney World itself. Each question is on the front of a card laid face up on a table; its answer is on the back with one letter written larger, with a thick marker. When a child answers a question correctly, he or she turns over that card. When all the cards are revealed, they spell out a message such as: "We Are Going to Disney World on Tuesday!" For help coming up with questions see this book's theme park chapters.

Sources for these materials. Disney items for these ideas are available at disneystore. com or at 407-363-6200. Uninflated Disney Mylar balloons are sold on Amazon.com; the balloons can be inflated at most any florist or card shop for a token fee. Dick Blick Art Supplies (800-828-4548, dickblick.com) sells pre-cut Create-A-Puzzle kits.

Saving for your trip. Want to teach your kids the value of a dollar? Your Disney trip can help. The more involved they are in the budgeting for it, the more they'll learn the benefits of saving and wise spending. Once your trip is in the works, create a "Disney Fund" to help pay for it or perhaps just special extras, such as a character meal, backstage tour or horseback ride. Start with a large bowl (a Tupperware one will do), then decorate it and label it "Disney Fund." Put the bowl in a visible spot in your kitchen, so it's easy for everyone in your family to toss in extra money and change. Another idea: Use the fund to save up some spending money for your kids.

Anticipating your trip. Unusual meals, arts and crafts, family movie nights—they all offer easy ways to make the wait special:

Countdown meals. Count down the days to your trip by creating Disney-themed meals and snacks that you enjoy at regular intervals (90 days before your trip, 60 days before, etc.).

Mickey Mouse pancakes are easy to make. Start by spooning some pancake batter into the center of a wide pan, leaving lots of room on the sides and top of the pan. Then dollop out two smaller blobs, each an inch or two away from the first one so as they bake they spread out and touch it. Later, use a wide spatula to lift and flip your Mickey with one confident twist of your wrist.

Other ideas: ❶ Setting your dining table Beauty and the Beast style, with a single red rose. ❷ A Lion King meal of ants on logs: celery strips topped with raisins and filled with peanut butter. ❸ Little Mermaid Ursula cupcakes, with purple frosting and eight gummy worms for tentacles. ❹ Pirates of the Caribbean fruit swords on wooden skewers, perhaps with an accompanying treasure hunt.

Countdown chain. "How long 'til Disney?" Making one of these is a fun way to answer that question, especially if everyone pitches in.

Using construction paper, create a chain that has the same number of links as the number of days until your trip. Number the links consecutively on one side; decorate the other side with glitter, markers, paint and stickers. Perhaps give each link its own theme, such as a particular Disney character or attraction. Make special links for countdown milestones such as "One Month To Go" and "One Week To Go." Hang the chain in a conspicuous spot, then tear off one of its links at the same time each day, perhaps first thing in the morning or just before bedtime. Remove the last link just before you set off on your trip.

Disney movie nights. Watching films that form the basis of the attractions you're about to experience will help everyone get psyched for your vacation, and make the trip itself more fun. To make your nights special, schedule them when the whole family can relax together. Before you hit play, have everyone get all of their distractions out of the way: no emails, no chores, no homework, no texting!

Disney Fund.

Magical Express bus.

Disney Planning A–Z

Alcohol. Guests cannot bring alcoholic beverages into any Walt Disney World theme or water park, though those of legal age can carry open containers of purchased alcoholic beverages (drinks served in restaurants, however, cannot be taken elsewhere). All Disney theme parks serve alcohol, though the Magic Kingdom only offers it on the dinner menu of its Be Our Guest restaurant. There are no liquor stores on Disney property, though hotels and theme-park gift shops sell beer, wine and liquor. It is illegal to carry open containers of alcohol in a car or public area in Central Florida. The legal age to purchase and consume alcohol in Florida is 21.

AA meetings. Friends of Bill W. Orlando (Alcoholics Anonymous) meet Monday through Saturday at 8 a.m. at the Community Presbyterian Church at 511 Celebration Ave. in Celebration, a community right next to Walt Disney World across Interstate 4. Meetings are also offered at 7 p.m. Wednesdays and Saturdays at 215a Celebration Blvd., in the North Village Meeting Room by the pool.

Birthdays. Walt Disney World offers many ways to help celebrate a birthday:

Balloons and buttons. Disney hotel concierge will deliver balloons to a room or a restaurant. Available free at theme-park Guest Relations offices, personalized Happy Birthday buttons cue cast members to recognize celebrants.

Cakes. Disney table-service restaurants offer a 6-inch (15-centimeter) birthday cake ($23, chocolate or vanilla, serves 5). Plan ahead and Disney's Cake Hotline will let you choose your filling, icing and personalized decorations (407-827-2253, $32 and up, 72 business hrs. notice). Most hotel restaurants offer Mickey Mouse cake (in his shape, with his face) through room service or concierge with 72 business hours notice ($54, serves 12). Restaurants will add candles on request.

Cruises. You can watch Magic Kingdom's Wishes fireworks or Epcot's IllumiNations from a pontoon boat. One-hour trips include snacks and drinks ($318 for up to 8 people on a 21-foot [6-meter] boat, decorative banner and balloons $25 additional; $371 for up to 10 people on a 25-foot [8-meter] boat including banner and balloons). Cakes are available through Disney's Cake Hotline (see above). You can reserve a cruise 180 days in advance at 407-827-2253. It requires a credit card to book and there's a 24-hour cancellation policy.

Flowers and gifts. Disney Floral & Gifts (407-827-3505, disneyflorist.com) delivers adult and child arrangements, baskets and other presents throughout Disney property.

Goodie bags. Standard bags contain a party hat, game, coloring book and crayons; deluxe bags add a magnet activity set and Mickey-shaped straw (407-939-3463).

Goofy telephone call. Goofy will call your Disney room with a birthday greeting (no charge, arrange at 407-824-2222).

Parties. At Disney Springs, the Goofy's Candy Company store offers kids celebrations themed to Goofy or Cinderella. They include balloons, favors, treats, drinks and games, and extra goodies for the birthday child. ($350 for up to 12 guests; $25 for additional guests up to 20. Ages 3 and up. 90 minutes. Reservations available 90 days in advance at 407-939-2329.)

Room decorations. Disney Floral & Gifts will decorate your Disney room in a personalized birthday theme (407-827-3505).

Children's services. As you might guess, Disney offers many special services for kids.

Baby Care Centers. Located in each theme park, these quiet, air-conditioned spots are designed for parents with infants or toddlers. They have private nursing rooms with rocking chairs; changing rooms with tables and unisex bathrooms; feeding areas with high chairs and kitchens with microwaves, ovens and sinks; lounges with televisions, chairs and sofas; and playrooms. The centers sell baby food, diapers, formula, juice, pacifiers and over-the-counter medications.

Magic Kingdom's Baby Care Center is next to the Crystal Palace restaurant. Epcot's is in the Odyssey Center building, between Test Track and the World Showcase. The Hollywood Studios Baby Care Center is next to that park's Guest Relations office; the one at Animal Kingdom is tucked behind the Starbucks on Discovery Island.

Babysitters. In-room provider Kids Nite Out (407-828-0920, kidsniteout.com) supplies babysitting and childcare for kids 6 weeks to 12 years, including those with special needs. Caregivers bring toys, activities, books and games. Rates start at $18 per hour with a 4-hour minimum plus a $10 transportation fee.

Childcare centers. Five Disney-owned hotels offer an evening childcare center: Disney's Animal Kingdom Lodge, Beach Club, Polynesian Village and Wilderness Lodge. Each has a secure room staffed by adults and stocked with arts and crafts, books, games, toys and videos. Children must be toilet trained (no pull-ups) and between 4 and 12 years old Reservations are required. *Animal Kingdom Lodge, Wilderness Lodge:* 4–4:30p to mid.; $15/hr per child, 2-hr min.; includes dinner 6–8p; 407-939-3463. *Beach Club, Polynesian Village:* 4–4:30p to mid.; $55 per evening per child; includes dinner 6–8p. 407-939-3463. *Walt Disney World Dolphin:* $15/hr per child, 2-hr min., includes dinner 6:30p–7:30p. 5:30p–mid. 407-934-4241.

Child swap. Also known as Rider Swap, this complimentary service allows you and your partner to enjoy a ride even if you have a child who can't ride it (or doesn't want to) who you don't want to leave unattended. To use it, arrange it with a cast member at the ride's entrance. At FastPass attractions, you get in line while your partner gets a FastPass-like ticket to ride later. At non-FastPass attractions, you, your partner and your child wait in line together. You ride while your partner stays with your child, then your partner rides.

Discounts for children. Disney World offers reduced prices for children ages 3 to 9 for park tickets (slightly), food and dining plans and paid-recreation options. Older children are charged adult rates. Children younger than age 3 are admitted free into Disney theme and water parks. Children are also charged less for the Disney Dining Plan.

Equipment rentals. Disney has the basics, such as cribs, rollaway beds and strollers. Outside companies rent these items and more, and often handle delivery and pickup. *Cribs and rollaway beds:* Disney resort hotels offer free use of cribs; request one when you make a reservation. Rollaway beds typically incur an extra fee ($15). Baby's Away (888-376-0084, 407-334-0232, babysaway.com) rents standard cribs. *Strollers:* You can rent strollers at each theme park and at Disney Springs. Single strollers rent for $15 a day; double strollers $31 a day. For multiple-day rentals consider a length-of-stay rental. You pay once, wait in line less and save some money (you save $2 a day on single strollers, $4 on doubles). Disney Springs requires a $100 credit-card deposit. Made of molded plastic, Disney's strollers are not designed for infants. For an infant stroller, contact Baby's Away (407-334-0232), Kingdom Strollers (407-674-1866), Magic Strollers (866-866-6177)

© Disney

Bibbidi Bobbidi Boutique, Cinderella Castle.

or Orlando Stroller Rentals (800-281-0884). *Other equipment:* Baby's Away rents car seats, high chairs and playpens. Most car-rental companies offer infant or child seats ($7–$15 per day) with advance notice.

Portrait and facial artists. *Caricaturists:* These artists offer their services in all parks, at most Disney hotels and at Disney Springs. Finished portraits come with storage tubes. Prices range from $18 to $99, based on the number of people in the work and whether it includes color. *Face painters:* You or your child can get your face painted for $12 to $18 at all Disney theme parks, Disney Springs and at Disney's BoardWalk Resort. Some stands offer themed designs (animal ones at Disney's Animal Kingdom, Star Wars at Disney's Hollywood Studios). Painters will touch up your face free of charge the same day if you show your receipt. *Silhouette artists:* Artists cut profiles out of paper in Magic Kingdom (Main Street U.S.A., Liberty Square), Epcot (France pavilion) and at Disney Springs (Marketplace). Prices start at $9.

Infant care. Diaper-changing stations are in men's and women's restrooms throughout Disney World. Moms can nurse babies anywhere on Disney property without hassle.

Lost children. Lose your child? Tell the closest Disney cast member. They'll instantly spread the news throughout the park, and advise you on what to do next. Typically cast members who encounter lost children take them to the park's Baby Care Center. Some parents introduce their children to a cast member first thing when they arrive at a theme park, and point out the worker's distinctive name tag. Other parents use a permanent marker to write their cell-phone number on the child's arm.

Bibbidi Bobbidi Boutiques. Little girls turn into princesses and pop stars at these female-focused salons. There are two of them: in Magic Kingdom inside Cinderella Castle and at Disney Springs next to the Once Upon a Toy store. Three basic princess packages are available: Crown ($60 for a hairstyle, shimmering makeup, nail polish, sash and purse), Courtyard ($100, adds a sparkling Bibbidi Boutique T-shirt and tutu to the Crown package) and Castle ($200 and up, adds a princess costume, wand and crown to the Courtyard package). Frozen packages (Anna or Elsa) include a hairstyle, shimmering makeup and face gems, sash, nail polish, cinch sack and 12-inch Olaf plush ($115). An optional gown adds $50. There's also a Knight Package for boys ($20 for hair gel, hair confetti and a toy sword and shield). All packages can add an Imaging Package ($33 for five prints of an image). Ages 3 and up. Reservations can be made up to 180 days in advance: 407-939-7895.

Pirates League. This Magic Kingdom salon transforms adults and children into swashbucklers, swashbucklerettes and mermaids. Packages ($30–$75) include facial effects, a reversible bandana, a false earring and eye patch, a sword, a temporary tattoo, a pirate coin necklace, an official pirate name and a personalized oath. Costumes, headwear and photo packages are also available. Participants can join an Adventureland Pirate Parade daily at 4 p.m. (Ages 3 and up. At the exit of Pirates of the Caribbean. Reservations up to 180 days in advance: 407-939-2739.)

Restaurants. Most Disney eateries offer kids' menus and high chairs. Only one excludes children: Victoria & Albert's at the Grand Floridian. Expense-account spots outside Disney often aren't child-friendly.

Convention facilities. Six hotels at Disney—the BoardWalk, Contemporary, Coronado Springs, Grand Floridian and Yacht Club and the Walt Disney World Swan and Dolphin—have convention and conference centers. The largest convention facility is at the Dolphin; its Atlantic Hall consumes 60,000 square feet [18,300 square meters]. Attendees get discounted rooms, deals on golf and theme-park tickets.

See also **Tickets.**

Disability services. Disney offers a variety of services for guests with hearing, mobility, visual or other disabilities.

Disability Access Service. An update of Disney's Disability Access Card, this service offers the same benefits but now does it all electronically, though the My Disney Experience app. If you have a nonapparent medical disability that makes it hard on you to stand for extended periods, showing your MagicBand or plastic ticket at a ride or show lets you schedule a return time comparable to its current Standby wait and then enter its Fastpass line, and if you run late it's OK. At least that's the official policy. Unofficially, cast members often have the ability to let the most seriously impaired visitors enter their FastPass+ line immediately, which lets them treat everyone with the proper compassion.

Available at Guest Relations offices, the service is valid for up to 14 days, but can be renewed. You don't need a doctor's note, but you do have your photo taken.

Cognitive services. Disney publishes a free pamphlet—Disney's Guide for Guests with Cognitive Disabilities—that's filled with tips. It's available online (at disneyworld. disney.go.com/guest-services/guests-with-disabilities) and at Guest Relations locations.

Hearing services. *Disney's Handheld Device:* The size of a thick smartphone, this gadget amplifies the audio at attractions, turns on captions on pre-show video screens (single-button activators also do this) and displays captions at narrated moving attractions. Available at Guest Relations locations, it costs nothing to borrow but requires a $25 daily deposit. captions from an LED display on a back wall. *Guest Assistance Packets:* Available at many attractions, these binders holds a script of the ride or show and a flashlight, as well as a pen and small pad of paper for cast members to use to communicate with a guest who has trouble hearing. *Reflective captioning:* At many theatrical attractions, cast members can supply handheld acrylic panels that reflect captions from a back wall. *Sign language interpreters:* These animated performers typically translate live shows at Magic Kingdom on Mondays and Thursdays, Epcot on Fridays, Disney's Hollywood Studios on Sundays and Wednesdays and Disney's Animal Kingdom on Tuesdays and Saturdays. Signing cast members wear identifying pins. For a schedule of interpreted shows call 407-824-4321. *TTY telephones:* Pay phones with amplified handsets and Text Typewriters are located throughout the parks.

Mobility services. Disney theme parks rent mobility scooters (Electric Conveyance Vehicles, or ECVs) and wheelchairs on a first-come, first-served basis; neither requires proof of need. They can't be transferred from park to park, but the deposit ticket from one rental is good for others on the same day. *Mobility scooters:* Disney rents ECVs for $70 a day which includes a $20 deposit. Arrive early to rent one, popular with obese as well as disabled guests they sell out quickly. The maximum weight allowed is 450 pounds (204 kg). You can bring your own scooter into any park. *Wheelchairs:* These rent for $12 a day ($10 a day for multiple-day rentals). The maximum weight is 350 pounds (159 kg). Identified by blue flags, parking-lot wheelchairs are free to use. Personal wheelchairs can be used anywhere on Disney property. *Off-property rental companies:* You can't reserve a chair or ECV in advance from Disney, but you can from Apple Scooter (800-701-1971), Best

Price Scooters and Strollers (866-866-3434), Buena Vista Scooter Rentals (866-484-4797), CARE Scooter Rentals (800-741-2282) or Scooterbug (800-726-8284). *Strollers as wheelchairs:* Disabled children in strollers can get wheelchair benefits if their parents pick up a special tag at Guest Relations. *Transferring:* Some attractions require wheelchair and ECV users to transfer to a ride vehicle. Disney cast members are not allowed to lift guests. *Zero-entry swimming pools:* Nine Disney hotels have pools designed with a side that gradually slopes into the water, so visitors in appropriate wheelchairs can roll into it—the Art of Animation, Caribbean Beach, Contemporary (behind Bay Lake Tower), Grand Floridian, Polynesian Village, Saratoga Springs and Yacht and Beach Club resorts, and both the Jambo House and Kidani Village areas of Animal Kingdom Lodge.

Visual services. *Audio Description:* Details and descriptions of some attractions are provided by Disney's Handheld Device (see Hearing Services, above). *Audiotape guides and tours:* Tapes orient guests to a park; tours offer routes and provide distances between attractions and recommend stopping spots. Free at Guest Relations with a $25 deposit. *Braille guide:* Each park has handheld braille guides which describe attractions, restaurants and shops. Free at Guest Relations locations with a $25 deposit. *Braille maps:* Each park has a stationary braille map with raised graphics.

Parking. Each park has a designated handicapped parking area. Courtesy trams do not serve this area, as they do not accommodate wheelchairs or ECVs.

Restrooms. All Disney restrooms have wheelchair-accessible stalls. Companion restrooms are throughout Disney property.

Service animals. Trained and leashed (or harnessed) service animals are welcome throughout Disney property, and can go on most attractions with their owners. Each park has designated potty break spots. If you have a service animal, you will most likely enter attractions through an alternate entrance, usually the FastPass+ entrance.

Transportation. Most Disney buses and all monorail trains accommodate wheelchairs and mobility scooters. Buses use a 30-by-48-inch (76-by-122 centimeter) lift; trains use portable ramps. Some boats accept chairs and scooters depending on water conditions.

Theme park guides. For each of its parks Disney publishes a complimentary Guide for Guests with Disabilities, which has in-depth information and a detailed map. All Guest Relations locations stock all four guides.

Disney Dining Plan. Disney hotel guests and Disney Vacation Club members can add this prepaid meal plan (and sometimes, recreation plan) to their park-ticket purchase. About 100 restaurants participate. Five packages are available; prices below are as of July, 2016 and may fluctate:

Quick-Service Plan. Provides two fast food meals and one snack per day, again with a refillable drink mug. *Adults $44 per day, children ages 3–9 $19.*

Standard Plan. Provides a table-service meal, a fast food (quick-service) meal and a snack per each nightly stay and a refillable drink mug for use at your resort. *Adults $64 per day, children ages 3–9 $23.*

Deluxe Plan. Provides three daily table-service (or fast food) meals, two snacks and a refillable drink mug. *Adults $115 per day, children ages 3–9 $35.*

Premium Plan. Provides three daily table-service (or fast food) meals, two snacks and a refillable drink mug for use at your resort. Other perks include unlimited use of many recreation options, vouchers to the Cirque du Soleil show La Nouba, unlimited use of child-care facilities and select theme-park tours. Requires purchase of at least a one-day park ticket. Buy it six months early to cherry-pick your recreation times. *Adults $208 per day, children ages 3–9 $153.*

Platinum Plan. Add to the Premium Plan an itinerary planning service, a spa treatment, a fireworks cruise and other extras. *Adults $260 per day, children ages 3–9 $202.*

How the plans work. You can use Disney Dining Plan meal and snack credits in any combination during your stay. For example, you can eat all table-service meals one day, all fast-food meals the next, and nothing but snacks the day after that. If one person in your party uses up his or her plan, others can continue to use theirs. Disney defines a breakfast meal as one entrée and one beverage; or a combo meal and a beverage or juice. Lunch and dinner are defined as one entree, one dessert and one beverage; or a combo meal, dessert and beverage.

To use the plan, present your MagicBand to a cashier or server. Food usage is tracked electronically; balances are available on each food receipt. Nearly every Disney-owned restaurant participates in the Dining Plan, as do snack locations such as food carts and sweet shops. Tips are not included; neither are alcoholic beverages, some bottled drinks, souvenir mugs, or snacks and beverages from recreation-rental counters.

Key conditions. Each Dining Plan has four important conditions: ❶ It is sold per party, not per person. If one person in your group buys a Dining Plan, everyone else in your group must too. The only exception: children under age 3. They can eat from an adult's plate. ❷ Kids are kids. When their parents are using a Dining Plan, children 3–9 must order from a kid's menu when one is available. Likewise, those children over 9 years of age must order from adult menus. ❸ Some restaurants take two credits. These include Disney Signature restaurants, dinner shows and Cinderella's Royal Table at Magic Kingdom. There's a very good new Signature Restaurant on the plan for 2017: Tiffins, at Disney's Animal Kingdom, which serves lunch and dinner. Room-service meals at Disney Deluxe Resorts charge two credits, too. ❹ Leftover credits have no value. Just like those magical accoutrements of Cinderella, unused Dining Plan meals and snacks expire at midnight on your check-out date.

Getting your money's worth. If you take advantage of it the Dining Plan will give you memorable meals. Handle it poorly, however, and your magical vacation can include a frustrating waste of time and resources. Here are four keys to getting the most for your money: ❶ Don't overestimate your hunger. When determining which plan to buy, keep in mind that it's tough to eat enough food to justify buyng three table-service meals a day. ❷ Use your credits efficiently. Except for those at Disney Signature restaurants, the plan considers nearly all table-service meals equal. In most cases, dining with a princess, Mickey Mouse or Lilo and Stitch at an all-you-can-eat feast uses no more credits than getting a hamburger and fries at Disney's cheapest table-service spot, the Plaza Restaurant at Magic Kingdom. ❸ Know where the deals are. Though your plans will charge you the same amount—one credit—for most meals, some restaurants give you more for it. Use this book to note their average meal prices before you decide where to eat. ❹ Make your reservations early. Disney restaurants book to capacity sometimes months in advance, especially for the most popular dining times such as 7 p.m. for dinner. Book your tables as early as possible.

Extra Magic Hours. Each day at least one Walt Disney World theme or water park opens an hour early, or stays open two hours late, for those guests staying at Disney-owned resorts, the Walt Disney World Swan and Dolphin, Shades of Green or the Disney Springs Hilton. To take advantage of an extra morning hour, simply arrive at the designated park's entrance with a valid park ticket or MagicBand wristband. During evening hours, you'll be asked to scan your MagicBand at each attraction. Note: On a day when a park offers an Extra Magic Hour in the morning, that park will be more crowded than usual later, during its regular hours.

Floral services. Disney Floral & Gifts (407-939-4438, 8a–6p daily, disneyflorist.com) sells floral arrangements, gift baskets, balloons, fruit, liquor and plants, each with as much or as little Disney theming as desired. Delivery is available at theme parks, resorts and Disney Springs. A Disney Dream Makers division can decorate your room before you arrive or for special occasions. The Disney Event Group has business arrangements (407-939-7129, disneymeetings.com); Disney's wedding planners help with bridal displays (407-939-4610, disneyweddings.com).

Gasoline stations. Three Speedway stations sit on Disney property, all are open 24 hours with self-serve pumps and a convenience store. Gas prices are in line with stations other stations in Central Florida. *Near Magic Kingdom:* On the park exitway, next to the Walt Disney World Car Care Center (1000 W. Car Care Drive, 32801; 407-938-0143). *Near Disney's Hollywood Studios:* Corner of Buena Vista Drive and Epcot Resorts Boulevard. Car wash available (300 East Buena Vista Drive, 32801; 407-938-0151). *Near Disney Springs:* Across the street from the Lime parking garage (1475 Buena Vista Drive, 32801; 407-938-0160).

For Orlando-area gasoline prices over the past 24 hours see orlandogasprices.com.

Guest Relations. Each Disney theme and water park—and Disney Springs—has at least one Guest Relations office. Disney staffers make dining reservations, upgrade park tickets, sell annual passes, check on lost items (for items lost the same day) and provide answers to general questions. Free guidemaps and Times Guides for all the Disney World parks are available. Disabled guests can pick up park-specific guides for guests with disabilities, arrange Disability Access Service or borrow Disney's Handheld Device. International visitors can pick up complimentary Attraction Translation Devices, park maps in German, Japanese, Spanish and Portuguese and exchange currency. Many staffers are multilingual.

Each theme park has a walk-up Guest Relations window outside its entrance, and at least one location inside. Magic Kingdom's Guest Relations spot is at City Hall. Epcot has an indoor office to the left of Spaceship Earth. Guest Relations at Disney's Hollywood Studios sits beside Sid Cahuenga's shop. Disney's Animal Kingdom's location is just inside the entrance on the left. Disney Springs' Guest Relations office is its new Welcome Center in its Town Center area.

International travelers. Wireless "Ears to the World" headsets ($100 deposit) provide translation of attraction audio into French, German, Japanese, Portuguese or Spanish. Other services include multilingual park maps, menus and tours. Multilingual cast members have nametags with gold badges.

Kennel. Located on Disney property across from the Port Orleans Resorts, Best Friends Pet Care Kennel is well maintained yet expensive. Billing itself as a "luxury pet resort," it refers to many of its 200-plus spaces as "suites" and "condos" since they are divided into multiple spaces, even though many are no larger than a cage. Some include controlled access to small outdoor areas. Dog facilities include 14 "vacation villas," 6-by-7-foot (2x2-meter) rooms with raised bedding and flat-screen televisions, as well as four larger "VIP suites." Dog owners can stop by and spend time with their unleashed pet in a grassy backyard with water-play area. Dogs and cats must be at least 4 months old. Birds house in an area with hamsters, guinea pigs, rabbits, ferrets and other pocket pets (owners supply cages, supplies and food). No primates or venomous pets are allowed. Optional services include daytime boarding; activities such as nature walks, grooming and playgroups; and pampering such as ice-cream treats and bedtime stories. The 50,000-square-foot (4,600-square-meter) facility is well maintained. (Dogs: overnight $41–$89, daycare $34–$89; optional services $5–$22. Cats: overnight $28–$40, daycare $26–$35; optional services $3–$8. Small

animals: overnight $11–$25. Across from Disney's Port Orleans Resort at 2510 Bonnet Creek Parkway, Lake Buena Vista 32830; 407-209-3126; wdw.bestfriendspetcare.com).

Lockers. You can rent a multi-use, key-operated locker to store belongings at each theme park, inside the entrance. You pay $7 a day plus a $5 deposit, for a locker 11 inches tall (28 cm) by 9 inches wide (23 cm) by 16 inches deep (41 cm). For a larger locker, 17.5 inches tall by 12 inches wide by 16 inches deep (45 by 31 by 41 cm), you pay $9 a day. When visiting more than one park in one day, return your locker key to get your deposit back, then present your receipt (and another deposit) at any subsequent park to get a locker there at no charge. You can rent single-use lockers at the bus booths at Epcot, Disney's Hollywood Studios and Disney's Animal Kingdom. These cost $1; and only take quarters.

Lost and found. At Disney parks and Disney Springs, you can check on items lost that same day at Guest Relations. Disney hotels have internal lost and found offices via concierge. ESPN Wide World of Sports holds lost items at its Welcome Center. After one day items move to the Theme Park Lost and Found office (407-824-4245, 9a–7 p.m. daily, shipping no charge) next to the Transportation and Ticket Center. It keeps most items 30 days; cameras, credit cards, eyeglasses, purses and wallets 90 days; hats, strollers and sunglasses one week. If you've lost your purse and it had, say, a wallet and iPhone inside, ask Lost and Found to check for all three items. Sometimes only one item is found—for example, your iPhone but not the purse it was in. (Magic Kingdom 407-824-4521, Epcot 407-560-6646, Disney's Hollywood Studios 407-560-3720, Disney's Animal Kingdom 407-938-2785, Blizzard Beach 407-560-5408, Typhoon Lagoon 407-560-6296, Disney Springs 407-828-3150, ESPN Wide World of Sports 407-541-5600.)

Magical Express. This bus transportation and luggage delivery service is complimentary if you are staying at a Walt Disney World resort. To be more specific, if you are bound for a Disney-owned hotel traveling via commercial airline to the Orlando International Airport you can skip the airport's baggage claim area and take a shuttle bus to your hotel, where your bags then "magically" appear. When it's time to return home, if you are traveling on a participating airline you can check your bags for your flight at your hotel. Then you simply board a bus back to the airport. If you're spending your entire vacation at Disney, Magical Express makes traveling to Walt Disney World cheaper, and eliminates the need to rent a car. The service carries over 2.2 million passengers a year.

Eligibility. You can use the service if you are staying at any Disney-owned resort. If you're book into the Walt Disney World Swan and Dolphin, Shades of Green or any Disney Springs hotel you're not eligible.

Booking. Reserve the service when booking your hotel accommodations, or anytime up to 10 days before your trip at 866-599-0951.

Arrivals. Upon landing, go directly to the Magical Express Welcome Center (on Level 1 at the B side of the terminal) to check in and board your shuttle bus. Luggage is delivered to your hotel within three hours after resort check-in for flights arriving between 5 a.m. and 10 p.m. daily. For later arrivals you collect your luggage at baggage claim, bring it to the Welcome Center yourself and carry it into the resort with you. International guests always claim their own baggage.

Departures. As your vacation draws to a close, you'll receive a Magical Express Transportation Notice advising you of the time of your bus ride back to the airport. With some airlines—Alaska, American, Delta, JetBlue, Southwest and United—you check your bags and get boarding passes at your hotel, eliminating those chores at the airport. You'll need to stop by your hotel's Resort Airline Check-In Desk three hours prior to your flight time and show a government-issued photo I.D. and your Disney MagicBand.

Money. Nearly every Disney restaurant, snack stand and shop accepts credit and debit cards as well as cash. You'll need cash for tips, highway tolls, pressed-coin machines, single-use lockers, some taxi and limo services and parking fees at themo parks.

ATMs. Chase Bank automated teller machines are located in each Disney theme and water park, at Disney Springs, at the ESPN Wide World of Sports complex and at all Disney resort hotels. The machines accept cards from the Cirrus and Plus systems. Withdrawals using out-of-state cards, or cards from a bank other than Chase, incur surcharges of $1.50 to $2.50. *Magic Kingdom:* By the lockers at the main entrance, City Hall, the Adventureland/Frontierland breezeway,

near the Pinocchio Village Haus restrooms. *Epcot:* Both entrances, at the American Adventure restrooms and the Future World bridge. *Disney's Hollywood Studios:* ATMs are located outside the entranceway and outside the Keystone Clothiers shop. *Disney's Animal Kingdom:* At the park entrance and outside the Dinosaur Treasures gift shop in DinoLand U.S.A. *Transportation and Ticket Center:* At the far right near the bus depot. *Blizzard Beach:* Outside the park entrance. *Typhoon Lagoon:* Singapore Sal's. *Disney Springs:* In the Welcome Center at Town Center; in the Marketplace near the Tren-D store, next to the Ghirardelli shop and inside the World of Disney; and on the West Side outside Starbucks and the House of Blues Co. Store. *ESPN Wide of World of Sports:* There's one, outside the gates by the ESPN Clubhouse store. A portable ATM is set up in Champion Stadium for Braves games.

Credit and debit cards. Disney accepts American Express, Diners Club, Discover, Japan Credit Bureau (JCB), MasterCard and Visa cards, even at snack stands.

Currency exchange. Foreign currency can be exchanged for U.S. dollars at the Orlando International Airport, main bank branches, theme park Guest Relations locations and Disney resort hotel concierge desks.

Disney Dollars. This whimsical scrip is no longer sold, but still accepted at all Disney World theme parks and Disney-owned resorts and gift shops.

Gift cards. Disney gift cards can be used for purchases throughout Disney World. The cards have no fees and don't expire. They can be ordered online in $25 increments up to $150 plus denominations of $200, $250, $300 and $500. Choose from hundreds of designs, or personalize a card using a photograph (disneygiftcard.com).

Gratuities. Tips often will be refused by Disney concierge staff and other cast members; guests can express appreciation for cast-member service by emailing wdw. guest.communications@disneyworld.com; comments can boost a career. Gratuities are accepted by Magical Express bus drivers, housekeeping staff, restaurant servers, valets and the non-Disney concierge staff at the Walt Disney World Swan and Dolphin Resort and Disney Springs hotels. An 18 percent tip is automatically added to the bill on room-service orders at Disney hotels, with use of a Tables in Wonderland discount card, for restaurant parties of six or more and at prepaid eateries and dinner shows. Gratuities are not included in the Disney Dining Plan.

Rental cars. Renting a car requires a major credit card or debit card with major-credit-card backing. Using a debit card will require a deposit (usually $200–$300) that will be credited back to the user's account a week or so after the car is returned.

Traveler's checks. Nearly any Disney expense can be paid for with traveler's checks. The Disney Springs SunTrust Bank (1675 E Buena Vista Dr, 32830; Mon–Fri 8a–5p; 407-828-6103) is the closest full-service bank that sells, replaces and redeems them. For refunds on lost or stolen checks call American Express (800-992-3404). Thomas Cook sells Prepaid Currency Cards (800-287-7362).

Wire transfers. The Disney Springs SunTrust Bank handles these, too.

Park policies. Walt Disney World theme and water parks have specific rules and policies, though many aren't heavily publicized.

Age restrictions. Children under the age of 14 must be accompanied by someone older than 14 to enter a park. Children under the age of 7 must be with someone older than 14 to go on a ride or see a show.

Dress codes. As family-oriented areas, the Disney parks have long had a policy of refusing, or revoking, admission to anyone who their managers deem is dressed inappropriately, especially if another visitor complains about it and the offender refuses suggestions to comply. In the case of an offensive T-shirt, a wearer may only be asked to turn it inside-out. In general, you have to wear "proper attire," including shoes and a shirt at theme parks, and your clothing can't drag the ground. Visible tattoos can't include "objectionable language or designs." If you are older than 14 years of age you can't wear a costume or a mask, unless you need the mask for medical reasons. A child's mask can't obstruct his or her peripheral vision and has to have eyeholes large enough to fully reveal the child's eyes. Note: Mickey's Not-So-Scary Halloween Party has its own costume rules. They appear in this chapter's Seasonal Events article.

Allowed items. ❶ You can bring most any type of food or drinks into any Walt Disney World theme or water park—any snack, food item or non-alcoholic beverage that doesn't require heating and is not in a glass container. ❷ You can bring medications too, and store a drug cooler in a locker or at Guest Relations. ❸ You can bring an umbrella.

Prohibited items. Selfie sticks? Drones? No way. Other restrictions: ❶ You can't bring in devices such as remote-control toys, skateboards, scooters, inline skates or shoes with built-in wheels. ❷ You can't bring in alcohol or any illegal substance. ❸ Strollers larger than 36 by 53 inches (92 by 132 cm) are taboo, as are backpacks, coolers or suitcases bigger than 24 inches long by 15 inches wide by 18 inches high (61 by 38 by 46 cm). ❹ Don't bring a wagon, or any other trailer-like object that's pulled by a person or pushed or towed by stroller, wheelchair or ECV. ❺ A mobility device such as a wheelchair or scooter must be manually or electrically powered, have only one rider, and travel no faster than a walking pace. ❻ And it can't be huge—no bigger than 36 inches (92 cm) wide and 52 inches (132 cm) long. ❼ You can't bring in a mobility device that has less than three wheels or can't stay balanced when stopped, unpowered or unoccupied, even if it has training wheels. ❽ You can't possess a weapon of any kind, or an object that appears to be one, including a toy gun, toy blaster or squirt gun. ❾ Forget Fido unless he's an approved service dog or miniature horse. ❿ Disney forbids folding chairs, glass containers except small ones like baby-food jars, and large tripods. ⓫ You can't bring a balloon into Animal Kingdom, or a plastic straw.

Prohibited behaviors. Disney may kick you out of a park if you: ❶ Alter, sell or transfer your park ticket, FastPass or other entitlement. ❷ Create photographs, videos or recordings in the park for commercial purposes. ❸ Distribute printed or recorded materials. ❹ "Engage in an unsafe act." ❺ Feed animals, including birds. ❻ Use a demonstration, speech, banner, flag or sign for commercial purposes or to incite a crowd. ❼ Impede in the park's operation. ❽ Portray yourself to other visitors as an actual Disney park character, or pose for photos or sign autographs as one. ❾ Sell goods or services or display them for sale. ❿ Smoke tobacco, e-cigarettes or other substances or products that produce smoke or a vapor except in designated smoking areas. ⓫ Use profanity or engage in disruptive, illegal, offensive or unsafe behavior, including running.

Security policies. To enter a park, you agree that your person and your bags, clothing, parcels and other items can all be subject to security inspections, hand-held scanners, metal detectors and other screenings at entrances to the park and within it. You

Parking tram. Designed in 1971, its driver shade and mirrors earned it the nickname "Flying Nun."

agree that you won't bring any particular item into a park that Disney says you can't, and if you leave something unattended, you understand that Disney will deal with it in any way it considers appropriate.

Operating hours. Park operating hours vary throughout the year; the hours listed here are the most common. *Magic Kingdom:* The world's most popular theme park is typically open 9 a.m.–10 p.m. It can, however, open as early as 7 a.m. and close as late as 4 a.m. Magic Kingdom's operating hours have the greatest variance of any Disney World theme park. *Epcot:* 9 a.m.–9 p.m. Future World is open 9 a.m.–9 p.m., though some minor attractions may close at 7 p.m. World Showcase is officially open 11 a.m.–9 p.m., though its International Gateway entrance opens at 9 a.m. and its Norway pavilion, and perhaps Mexico pavilion may open at 9 a.m. *Disney's Hollywood Studios:* 9 a.m.–7 p.m. *Disney's Animal Kingdom:* 9 a.m.–11 p.m. *Water parks:* 10 a.m.–5 p.m. Details are at 407-824-4321 and disneyworld.com.

Park closures. During peak periods the Disney theme parks can fill to capacity and close as early as 10 a.m. to additional visitors, even to those who have valid tickets. Closures for capacity are easy to predict—they typically occur only on obviously busy days such as Independence Day and the week between

Christmas Eve and New Year's Eve. Disney closes its parks in five distinct phases:

Phase 1. The park stays open to any additional guest who has purchased a park ticket, though Disney stops ticket sales at that park.

Phase 2. Open to only those additional guests who have multi-day park passes or are staying at a Disney-owned resort.

Phase 3. Open to only those additional guests who are using the last day of a multi-day pass or staying at a Disney-owned resort.

Phase 4. Open to only those additional guests who are staying at a Disney resort.

Phase 5. No additional entry available.

Before employing the steps above, occasionally the Magic Kingdom will first close its parking lot to new cars, then stop using Disney transportation (monorail, buses, boats) to shuttle in new guests.

If you are already in a Disney theme park when it closes for capacity, you are not asked to leave. But if you leave one park to head to another one, you're taking a risk that you'll get locked out of both. Because of its expansive lawns and other open areas, Epcot rarely closes. To learn if a Disney theme park is currently closed, call 407-824-2222.

Parking. Disney charges a fee to park at its theme parks. Daily rates are $20 for cars, motorcycles or taxis; $22 for campers; $25

for buses and tractor-trailers. Disney resort hotel guests and annual passholders get free parking. If you are a Tables in Wonderland cardholder you can park free, too; you receive a parking refund at a Guest Relations location with a table-service dining receipt. New preferred parking puts you closer and gives everyone in your vehicle a bottle of water for a $15 surcharge. All park parking is just outside its main entrance except at Magic Kingdom. Its lot is a mile away at the Transportation and Ticket Center; after parking guests take either a monorail or a ferry to that park.

Parking is free at water parks and Disney Springs. Most parking is free at the ESPN complex; premium spots may cost $5.

Hotel parking. Every Disney-owned hotel provides complimentary parking to guests staying at it or coming to shop or dine. Valet parking is available at all Disney Deluxe Resorts (and Disney Springs) for $20 daily not including gratuity; your hangtag gives you free valet parking at any other Disney hotel that same day. Valet parking is complimentary for Tables in Wonderland cardholders with dining reservations and guests with a current handicap license plate or tag. Shades of Green charges $5 for parking, the Walt Disney World Swan and Dolphin Resort charges $18 for overnight self-parking, $26 for overnight valet parking, $18 per exit for day self-parking, $26 per exit for day valet parking.

Photographic services. Disney offers various photo services in its parks, hotels, restaurants and at Disney Springs:

PhotoPass. With this service Disney photographers take shots of your group throughout Walt Disney World, but you pay for only those images you choose, if any. Photographers are stationed many places, including most park icons and character spots, linking images to your MyMagic+ account. You can view and buy each shot on the My Disney Experience app, at park Camera Centers or online, up to 45 days from when it was taken. Any Disney cast member will take a photo of your group with your own camera free of charge. (Single downloads $15, Memory Maker Unlimited photo-and-video package $169 if arranged in advance, archive disc $199. 407-560-4300; disneyphotopass.com).

Disney Fine Art Photography & Video. You choose the locations, themes and wardrobe, then pose at picturesque settings in professional packaged portrait sessions. Each one lasts 20 minutes to an hour, and includes

a disc with 60 to 100 images. (Sessions: $180–$400; print packages $75–$285; book up to 30 days in advance; 407-934-4004).

Restaurant souvenirs. If you eat at the following spots you can (but don't have to) buy photos Disney will take of you either before you enter the dining area or while you eat: 1900 Park Fare (Grand Floridian Resort), Chef Mickey's (Contemporary Resort), Cinderella's Royal Table (Cinderella Castle, Magic Kingdom, where the photos are included in your meal price), the Hoop-Dee-Doo Revue Dinner Show and Mickey's Backyard Barbecue (Fort Wilderness Resort & Campground), 'Ohana (Polynesian Village Resort), the Princess Storybook Dining (Akershus, Norway pavilion, Epcot, photos included), the Spirit of Aloha Dinner Show (Polynesian Village Resort), and the Tusker House character meals (Harambe Village, Disney's Animal Kingdom).

Ride souvenirs. Some attractions take photos of you riding them. Prints cost about $20; digital images are included in the PhotoPass Memory Maker package. *Magic Kingdom:* Buzz Lightyear's Space Ranger Spin, Space Mountain, Splash Mountain. *Epcot:* Frozen Ever After, Test Track. *Disney's Hollywood Studios:* Rock 'n' Roller Coaster, Tower of Terror. *Disney's Animal Kingdom:* Dinosaur, Expedition Everest.

Photography. Whether it's one in your phone or a fancy DSLR, a camera can capture spontaneous moments that create treasured memories. Consider giving your children their own cameras and perhaps bringing waterproof models for swimming pools and water parks. Whatever shots you snap, take turns being the photographer; if mom takes all the pictures none will include mom.

Nikon picture spots. These marked locations offer photogenic, iconic backdrops for your shot, such as Magic Kingdom's Cinderella Castle or Epcot's Spaceship Earth.

Selfie sticks. They're not allowed in any Walt Disney World theme or water park.

Pin trading. In 1999 Disney began the tradition of collectible-pin trading. Many visitors exchange pins, but most trading is with cast members who wear pin-filled lanyards; those with green ones trade only with kids. Each park sells pins, which range from $8 to $35.

Postal services. You can access the U.S. Postal Service throughout Disney World.

Sending mail. *Magic Kingdom:* Guests can drop stamped mail in old-fashioned letter boxes at the park entrance next to the Newsstand gift shop and on Main Street U.S.A. (postmarks read "Lake Buena Vista" not "Walt Disney World"). *Epcot:* Camera Center, Spaceship Earth, Future World; also in an old mailbox in front of the American Adventure pavilion in the World Showcase. *Disney's Hollywood Studios:* Oscar's Super Service, entrance plaza. *Disney's Animal Kingdom:* Garden Gate Gifts, entrance plaza. **Stamps.** *Magic Kingdom:* Newsstand, entrance plaza. *Epcot:* Camera Center, under Spaceship Earth. *Disney's Hollywood Studios:* Oscar's Super Service, entrance plaza. *Disney's Animal Kingdom:* Garden Gate Gifts, entrance plaza. *Disney hotels:* Main gift shops. *Disney Springs:* Welcome Center, Town Center. **Receiving mail.** *Disney resort hotels:* You can receive letters, packages and postcards if you are staying at any Disney resort. Mail should include your arrival date if the item will be received before you check-in. *Non-Disney hotels:* Nearly all convention hotels in the area accept mail for guests, as do some other properties. Contact the particular hotel.

Quinceañera. Disney offers teen Latinas ways to mark their 15th birthdays. Packages and prices vary (321-939-4555).

Refurbishments and rehabs. Disney makes public its schedule of attraction operational updates and refurbishments (407-824-4321, disneyworld.com).

Restaurant policies. Disney-operated eateries share many policies and procedures. **Children's meals.** Available throughout Disney theme parks and hotels, Disney Kids' Picks meals come with unsweetened applesauce, baby carrots or fresh fruit (your choice of two) and a beverage of low-fat milk, juice or water (french fries, a cookie and soft drinks can be substituted). Less than 35 percent of a Kids' Picks meal's calories come from fat. **Discounts.** Disney's Tables in Wonderland discount card ($150–$175 annually, available to annual passholders, Disney Vacation Club members and Florida residents, 407-566-5858, weekdays 9a–5p) saves its holder and up to nine guests 20 percent off food and beverage during non-holiday periods at most Disney table-service restaurants, Value Resort food courts and some other spots. An 18 percent gratuity is added. Visitors with annual passes to Walt Disney World typically save 10–20 percent off lunch or dinner at these locations. **Dress codes.** Most Disney restaurants have a dress code equal to that of the theme parks. With the exceptions of Cinderella's Royal Table, the Hollywood Brown Derby, Le Cellier and Tiffins, Disney Signature Restaurants have a business casual dress code—for men jeans, dress shorts, dress slacks or trousers and a shirt with a collar or T-shirt underneath; for women jeans, dress shorts or a skirt with a blouse or sweater, or a dress; not permitted are cut-offs, men's caps or hats, swimsuits, swimsuit cover-ups, tank tops or torn clothing. Victoria & Albert's requires jackets for men; dresses or dressy pants suits for women. **Gastric-bypass surgery guests.** These guests can present a weight-loss-surgery card (issued by their doctor or hospital) to a server to pay the child price for an adult meal at buffets, or to possibly order from a kids menu at non-buffet meals. **Gratuities.** Disney adds an automatic 18 percent gratuity to dining bills for parties of 8 or more. In general, tip 15–20 percent for good service; 10 percent for mediocre. **Reservations.** Having a dining reservation is often a must at Disney, even for restaurants in your hotel. The best eateries often book to capacity far in advance, especially for popular dining times. During peak periods many don't accept walk-up diners regardless of how long a guest is willing to wait.

You can make reservations 180 days in advance, 190 days if you'll be staying at a Disney resort hotel (My Disney Experience app, disneyworld.com, 407-939-3463). Dinner shows and dining at Cinderella's Royal Table require payment up front; refunds are possible if bookings are cancelled 24 hours in advance. All Disney restaurants require a credit or debit card to hold a reservation; you may be charged a $10-per-person fee if you don't show up or cancel your reservation less than 24 hours in advance. Some hotel concierge desks and restaurant check-in counters can also book reservations.

Plan to arrive at least 5 minutes early. Your party will be seated at the first available table that can hold it. Most Disney restaurants will hold your reservation for 15 minutes.

Cinderella's Royal Table inside Magic Kingdom's Cinderella Castle is the toughest reservation to nab. It often books in full on the first day of availability. Other hot spots: Be Our Guest (Magic Kingdom), California Grill and Chef Mickey's (Contemporary Resort), Le Cellier (Epcot) and Victoria & Albert's (Grand Floridian Resort). The most popular reservation time is 7 p.m. to 8 p.m. To eat during that hour book your table at least a week early, especially for a party of six or more.

Special diets. No-sugar, low-fat, low-sodium, vegetarian or vegan diets can be met at table-service restaurants by telling a reservation clerk, host or server. Dinner shows need 24 hours notice. With three days notice, Disney restaurants can meet needs such as allergies to gluten or wheat, shellfish, soy, lactose or milk, peanuts, tree nuts, fish or eggs. Many counter-service restaurants offer gluten-free, low-fat and vegetarian options. No Disney restaurant serves food with added trans fats or partially hydrogenated oils.

Glatt kosher meals are available at most full-service restaurants with 24 hours notice at 407-939-3463. Requests require a credit-card guarantee and have a 24-hour cancellation policy. You can get kosher fast-food without advance notice at Cosmic Ray's Starlight Café (Magic Kingdom), Liberty Inn (Epcot), ABC Commissary (Hollywood Studios), Pizzafari (Animal Kingdom) and the food courts at the All-Star, Caribbean Beach, Pop Century and Port Orleans Riverside resorts.

Shipping services. Some resorts have a business center or desk with shipping supplies. Expect to pay a handling fee. Shipping luggage to a hotel can be cheaper than checking it as airline baggage; send them so they arrive a couple of days early. To be sure the hotel holds your packages, address your shipping labels as follows:

Guest's name (same as on reservation)
c/o Name of hotel
Hold for guest arrival on (date)
Reservation (number)
Hotel street address
City, FL ZIP Code

At theme parks. Package Pickup can deliver purchases made in that park to any Disney-owned hotel or, via UPS or FedEx, any domestic or international address.

At Disney Springs. Stores can deliver purchases to Disney resort hotels or ship items via UPS or FedEx.

Shopping. Disney World has hundreds of stores, selling everything from hand-rolled cigars to the largest selection of Mickey Mouse merchandise in the world. Order it at disneystore.com or at 800-328-0368.

Disney return policy. Disney-owned stores will accept returns on merchandise within 90 days of purchase with a valid receipt. Items that cannot be returned include those marked "as is" or "all sales final," original artwork, fine jewelry and special orders. If you return an item without a receipt you'll receive credit based on the item's selling price at the time of the return. Some stores on Disney property—including many in Epcot's World Showcase and at Disney Springs—are not run by Disney; return policies at these shops vary. In most cases, Disney Stores across the U.S. accept returns of items bought at Disney-owned Disney World stores with a valid receipt.

Single Rider Lines. If you don't mind experiencing a ride by yourself, a Single Rider line is an easy way to lessen the time you have to wait. During peak periods, using one can cut your wait time by at least 30 minutes. You'll find Single Rider lines at Test Track in Epcot, Rock 'n' Roller Coaster Starring Aerosmith at Disney's Hollywood Studios and Expedition Everest at Disney's Animal Kingdom. There's also one at the Blizzard Beach chair lift. *How they work:* When ride operators can't fill a vehicle from the regular line without breaking up a group, they take a person from a Single Rider line. Groups can wait in that line together but will be split up. Single Riders cannot specify where they sit.

Smoking. Florida law requires that all restaurants in the state be smoke-free. Smoking is allowed in freestanding bars that earn less than 10 percent of their income from food.

Disney theme parks have designated smoking areas. All Disney hotel rooms, balconies and patios are smoke-free (a $250–$500 "room recovery fee" is charged to guests who smoke); smoking is permitted at Fort Wilderness campsites and on cabin porches. All shops are non-smoking except the Disney Springs cigar shop. No tobacco products are sold in the parks, but are available (but not displayed) at hotel gift shops and Disney Springs. Speedway stations sell them openly.

Spas. Disney has three full-service spas. All offer aromatherapy, exercise facilities, facials, manicures and pedicures, massages and child services. Robes and slippers are provided for body treatments.

Mandara Spa. At the Walt Disney World Dolphin, this Asian-inspired spa has two indoor gardens. Services include cellulite treatments, stone therapies (407-934-4772). **Senses Spa.** This Grand Floridian spa offers a massage followed by a cocoon-like body wrap, a lavender facial and a pedicure with a hot-stone massage that uses honey lavender botanical oils. A second Senses at Saratoga Springs offers bamboo fusion massages, blueberry facials and a pedicure with a blueberry sugar scrub, hydrating masque and warm paraffin treatment (407-939-7727).

Sports and recreation. Archery lessons? Surfing lessons? You have many choices here, including some you wouldn't expect. **Archery.** Fort Wilderness offers lessons followed by target practice. Children's bows are small; left-handed bows are available; arrows have rounded tips. *Check in at Bike Barn. $39, 90 min, Thurs–Sat 2:45p. Ages 7 and up. 10 students per class. Reservations taken 90 days early at 407-939-7529.*
Bicycle and surrey rentals. Nine Disney hotels rent bikes and/or multi-seat surreys: BoardWalk, Caribbean Beach, Coronado Springs, Fort Wilderness, Old Key West, Port Orleans, Saratoga Springs, Wilderness Lodge and Yacht and Beach Club (bikes only) *Bikes $9 hr, $18 day; surreys $20–$22 30 min.*
Boat charters. *Pirates and Pals Fireworks Voyage:* View Magic Kingdom's Wishes from a pontoon boat helmed by a pirate; greet characters afterward ($59 adults, $34 children; Fri–Mon, nightly at holidays; Contemporary Resort marina; 407-939-7529). *Fireworks Charters:* A guide takes you and your friends out to see Wishes or IllumiNations ($275–$325; 1 hr, up to 10 people, snacks; Wishes boats leave from Contemporary, Grand Floridian, Polynesian Village, Wilderness Lodge marinas; Illuminations boat leaves from Yacht Club; 407-939-7529). *Yacht charter:* Cruise the Seven Seas Lagoon and Bay Lake on the Grand 1, a 52-foot (16 m) Sea Ray yacht ($744 for 1 hr, $1,116 90 min, $1,488 2 hrs, up to 18 people; includes captain, deckhand; food, butler optional; Grand Floridian; 407-824-2682).
Boat rentals. Disney has the world's largest fleet of rental boats. Boats vary by marina; for details call 407-939-7529. *Two-seat canoes and kayaks:* $7 30 min, $11 hr. *Two-seat Sea Raycer outboards:* $32 30 min, $45 hr; ages 12–15 may drive with a licensed driver; height min 60 in (152 cm), weight max per boat 320 lbs (145 kg). *Center-console Boston Whaler Montauk outboards:* $45 30 min; capacity 6. *Pedal boats:* $7 30 min. *Swan pedal boats:*

$12–$14 30 min; Walt Disney World Swan and Dolphin only. *Three-seat Sea-Doo personal watercraft:* $80 30 min, $135 hr; max 3 riders per vehicle, max combined weight 400 lbs (181 kg); at Sammy Duvall's Watersports Centre, 407-939-0754, Contemporary Resort. *Sea-Doo tour:* $135 1-hr morning group ride on Seven Seas Lagoon, also at Sammy Duvall's. *SunTracker pontoon boats:* $45 30 min; capacity 10. *Sunfish sailboats:* $20 hr; operator must be at least 16 with a valid driver's license; renters 18. *Hobie Cat sailboats:* $25 hr; same policies as Sunfish.
Campfires. Held often at a small outdoor amphitheater at the Fort Wilderness Resort and Campground, Chip 'n Dale's Campfire Sing-a-Long is a charming, throwback event that doesn't even cost anything. It includes a marshmallow roast, 30-minute sing-a-long with the two chipmunks (sit on the benches down front to meet one up close and personal) and a movie. A snack bar sells s'mores kits, marshmallows and sticks (Free. Schedule: 407-824-2727). Port Orleans Riverside offers a campfire sing-a-long (without a movie) seasonally. Other campfire activities are held seasonally at 11 resorts—Animal Kingdom Lodge Jambo House, Animal Kingdom Lodge Kidani Village, the Beach Club, BoardWalk, Caribbean Beach, Contemporary, Coronado Springs, Old Key West, Polynesian Village, Port Orleans French Quarter, Saratoga Springs and Wilderness Lodge.
Carriage and wagon rides. Available at the Fort Wilderness, Port Orleans Riverside and Saratoga Springs resorts, horse-drawn carriages hold four adults or a small family. *$45 per carriage. 25 min 5:30–10p, those under 18 must ride with adult; reservations accepted 90 days in adv at 407-939-7529; same-day bookings at 407-824-2832.* Fort Wilderness has 32-passenger wagons. Firework-view rides available. Pioneer Hall. *$8 adults, $5 children 3–9, under 3 free. 45 min 7, 9:30p Children under 11 must ride with adult. Walk-ups only. Group rides with 24 hrs notice at 407-824-2734.*
Diving and snorkeling. If you're open-water certified, you can scuba dive in a 5.7-million-gallon saltwater aquarium as part of Disney's DiveQuest experience, held at Epcot's The Seas pavilion. The tank has more than 65 species, including sharks, rays and sea turtles. The Epcot Seas Aqua Tour puts you in the tank with scuba-assisted snorkel (SAS) equipment. Proceeds from both experiences go to the Disney Worldwide Conservation Fund. *DiveQuest: $175, 40 min.*

in water, 3-hr experience. Includes gear, lockers, showers, mini tour. Park admission not required. Optional video. Up to 12 divers per group. Ages 10 and up; those under 12 must dive with adult. Open-water certification req. Information at 407-939-8687. Aqua Tour: $140, 30 min in water, 2.5 hrs total. Inc. instruction. Park admission not required. Ages 10 and up; under 18 must dive with adult. 407-939-8687.

Dolphins in Depth. You'll spend about a half-hour in knee-deep water with Epcot's bottlenose dolphins, learn about their anatomy and behavior and watch biologists do research. Individual instruction; interaction not guaranteed. No swimming. *$199; 3 hrs; includes T-shirt, photo with dolphin, refreshments, use of wetsuit; ages 13 and up, those under 18 must be with an adult; 407-939-8687.*

Fishing from boats. Catching a fish is almost a certainty on these guided pontoon boat trips, as their waters are stocked with largemouth bass, bluegill and catfish, all fish must be released and only a handful of anglers are fishing at any one time. Most trips catch five to 10 fish; anglers average a few per hour. Bay Lake and Seven Seas Lagoon are teeming with bass ($240–$275 2 hrs, $460 4 hrs, addl hrs $115; trips leave early and mid-morning and early afternoon; up to 5 people; includes bait, guide, equipment, refreshments; trips on Bay Lake, Seven Seas Lagoon, Crescent Lake, Village Lake and the Coronado Resort's Lago Dorado; no license required; reservations taken 2 weeks in advance; 407-939-2277).

Fishing from shore. At Fort Wilderness and Port Orleans Riverside (cane poles $4 30 min, $9 day, 4–6 pole package $14 30 min, $28 day; rods $6 30 min, $13 a day; 7a–3p, includes bait, no license required, Fort Wilderness 407-824-2900, Riverside 407-934-6000).

Horseback trail rides. Guides lead small groups down shady pine and palmetto trails at the Fort Wilderness Resort & Campground. Excursions start at the Tri-Circle D Livery at the resort's entrance. Early birds see wildlife such as snakes and deer ($46; 45 min.; 8:30a–3:30p daily; closed-toe shoes required, no sandals or flip-flops; no trotting; ages 9 and up; height min 48 in (122 cm), max weight 250 lbs (113 kg); required reservations available 30 days in advance; 407-939-7529).

Marathons. A pair of running events—a 26.2-mile full marathon and a 13.1-mile half marathon—highlight Disney's Marathon Weekend (the first weekend in January). The full route goes through all four theme parks. Typically more than 30,000 athletes compete.

Some runners dress as princesses in the Princess Half Marathon (mid-February) which winds through Magic Kingdom and Epcot. Many other races are held throughout the year (407-938-3398; rundisney.com).

Miniature golf. Two themed complexes make it easy to take a break from theme-park activities ($14 adults, $12 children 3–9; second rounds half-price if same day or next day; 10a–11p, last tee time 30 min before close; in-person same-day reservations accepted at 407-939-7529). *Fantasia Gardens:* Across the street from the Walt Disney World Swan and Dolphin, this two-course complex is busy at night, when tee-time waits can be an hour. Splashing brooms and dancing-ostrich topiaries line a Gardens course themed to Disney's 1940 movie "Fantasia." A Fairways course replicates real links with long fairways, sandy bunkers, roughs and undulating hills (407-560-4753; Gardens course closes at 10:30p). *Winter Summerland:* Next to Blizzard Beach, these two courses are often deserted at night. Themed to the activities of elves who vacation here (Santa bought them the course as a respite from their duties at the North Pole), the courses are dotted with tiny trailers and Christmas decor. Getting a hole-in-one is easy; greens often funnel into cups. Way more fun than Fantasia Gardens (407-560-7161).

Pony rides. Smaller children can take a short pony ride at Fort Wilderness petting farm; a parent walks the pony along a path ($5, cash only; 10a–5p daily; ages 2 and up; maximum height 45 in (114 cm); maximum weight 80 lbs (36 kg); 407-824-2788).

Surfing lessons. Know how to swim? Fit? If so, then you are almost guaranteed to learn how to ride the crest of a wave at a Typhoon Lagoon surfing lesson. It holds instruction at dawn in the surf pool of Typhoon Lagoon, before the water park opens to the public. Conducted on dry land, a step-by-step introduction teaches you the basics, then you get in the surf pool with a soft-sided surfboard and attempt to ride wave after wave after wave. Instructors critique and advise you throughout the lesson. Waves average about 5 feet (1.5 meters) for adults; half that for children. ($165; 2.5-hr lesson; includes 30 mins on land, 2 hrs in water, surfboards provided; must be 8 yrs or older, strong swimmer; days, hours vary with season; spectators permitted; max 12 students per class; reservations accepted 90 days in advance; 407-939-7529).

Surfing parties. Typhoon Lagoon can host a private surfing party for up to 25 people

Golf courses and lessons

Grouped into three facilities, Walt Disney World's five golf courses offer different experiences. There's the long course, the short course, the flat course, the water course, and the child-friendly 9-hole. Home to alligators, deer, egrets, herons, otters and the occasional bald eagle, each is designated as a wildlife sanctuary by the Audubon Cooperative Sanctuary System. All but the Lake Buena Vista course roam away from civilization. Greens have ultra-dwarf TifEagle Bermuda grass, which offers a true, fast roll. Build extra time into your round, as the pace may be slower than you expect. Arnold Palmer Golf Management runs all Disney courses.

Lake Buena Vista course. Disney's least forgiving links have narrow, tree-lined fairways and small greens. Your play will demand accuracy on tee shots and approaches. Errant shots can hit windows. Signature hole No. 7 has an island green; No. 18 is a 438-yard dogleg to the right. Ten holes have water hazards. You tee off at the Saratoga Springs Resort then weave through Old Key West. *Yardage:* 5,204–6,802. *Par:* 72. *Course rating:* 68.6–73.0. *Slope rating:* 122–133. *Designer:* Joe Lee. *Built:* 1972. *Location:* Pro shop at Saratoga Springs.

Magnolia course. How's that shoulder turn? It needs to be efficient on this long-game course, which is set in a rolling terrain amid 1,500 magnolia trees. The Magnolia has elevated tees and greens and 97 bunkers, the most of any Disney course. Greens are quick. Host to the final round of a PGA Tour stop for four decades, it's tested most top-name pros. *Yardage:* 5,232–7,516. *Par:* 72. *Course rating:* 69.4–76.5. *Slope rating:* 125–140. *Designer:* Joe Lee. *Built:* 1971. *Location:* Across from Disney's Polynesian Village Resort.

Oak Trail course. A walking course, this 9-hole is nice for a quick game, getting some practice, or introducing a child to the sport. With small greens and two good par 5s, the course requires accuracy with short irons. The longest hole, the 517-yard No. 5, has a double dogleg. Water hazards cross three fairways. Most greens and tees are elevated. Scorecards list separate pars for children 11 and under and for those over 12. Golf shoes must be spikeless; tennis shoes are permitted. *Yardage:* 2,532–2,913. *Par:* 36. *Course rating:* 64.6–68.2. *Slope rating:* 107–123. *Designer:* Ron Garl. *Built:* 1980. *Location:* Next to Shades of Green, across from Disney's Polynesian Village Resort.

Tranquilo. Once Disney's Osprey Ridge course, these links today are part of the Four Seasons resort hotel. The challenging course winds through dense vegetation, oak forests and moss hammocks. More than 70 bunkers, mounds and a meandering ridge provide obstacles, banking and elevation changes. Some tees and greens are 20 feet (6 meters) above their fairways. Another challenge: the course often has swirling winds. A bit of relief: fairway waste bunkers have hard sand, so you can play out of one with a normal swing. The clubhouse has a restaurant. *Yardage:* 5,402–7,101. *Par:* 72. *Course rating:* 69.5–74.4. *Slope rating:* 123–131. *Designer:* Tom Fazio. *Built:* 1992. *Location:* Clubhouse is just east of Disney's Fort Wilderness campground.

Palm course. Pretty palms. Ugly hazards. This course has both. Water hazards line seven holes and cross six. Shorter and tighter than the nearby Magnolia, the Palm has a few long par 4s and a couple of par 5s that can be reached in two using a fairway wood. The large, elevated greens can be maneuvered with good lag putting. Save a sprinkle of pixie dust for hole No. 18; a long par 4 that was rated as high as fourth toughest hole on the PGA Tour. The Palm is rated one of Golf Digest's Top 25 Resort Courses. *Yardage:* 5,311–6,957. *Par:* 72. *Course rating:* 69.5–73.9. *Slope rating:* 126–138. *Designer:* Joe Lee. *Built:* 1971. *Location:* Next to Shades of Green, across from Disney's Polynesian Village Resort.

All 18-hole courses have putting greens and driving ranges. Transportation is provided to and from all Disney-owned resorts. Proper golf attire is required. (Green fees for 18-hole courses: $70–$195, cart included. 9-hole Oak Trail course: $15–$38, $15–$20 for under 18. Reservations available 90 days in advance for Disney resort guests, 60 days other players; cancellations require 48 hours notice).

Lessons. Choose from 30-minute tune-ups, 1-hour lessons, half-day or full-day golf schools, video analysis, group lessons, on-course playing lessons and club fittings. ($75–$175; juniors 17 and under starting at $50; Palm/Magnolia facility, run by PGA pros; all ages and skill levels; 407-454-5096).

Golf equipment is available for rent: (clubs for men and women $15–$50; shoes $10 per pair, free for resort guests; range balls $7 per basket; Oak Trail pull carts $6; 407-939-4653; disneygolf.com).

either before the park opens or after it closes. Each party gets up to 150 waves, broken into sets of 25; you choose the direction of the waves, whether left or right breaks. Party-goers need to bring their own boards and towels. ($1,100 for morning parties Thur, Sat, Sun; $1,200 for evening parties Sun–Thur, $1,500 for 125 waves, $1,800 for 150 waves; $1,400 Fri, Sat., $1,750 for 125 waves, $2,100 for 150 waves; 407-939-7529).

Tennis. Disney has 34 lighted courts for recreational use, all at hotels. Use is complimentary for hotel guests, from 8 a.m. to 10 p.m. on a first-come, first-served basis. Courts are at Bay Lake Tower at Disney's Contemporary Resort, Kidani Village at Disney's Animal Kingdom Lodge, BoardWalk Inn and Villas, Old Key West Resort, Saratoga Springs Resort, the Yacht and Beach Club Resorts and the Walt Disney World Swan and Dolphin. Group and private lessons available at Bay Lake Tower, Kidani Village, BoardWalk, Saratoga Springs and the Yacht and Beach Club Resorts ($90 per hour, 321-228-1146).

Watersports. At Disney's Contemporary Resort at Sammy Duvall's Watersports Centre. A legend himself among waterskiers, Duvall has won 80 pro championships (407-939-0754). *Parasailing:* Soaring hundreds of feet above the 450-acre (182 ha) Bay Lake beneath an open parachute, you get a birds eye view of Disney World. You don't get wet; you take off and land on the boat (single riders $95 for 8–10 min at 450 ft [137 meters], $130 for 10–12 min at 600 ft [183 meters]; tandem riders $170 for 8–10 min at 450 ft, $195 for 10–12 min at 600 ft; weight per flight 130–330 lbs [59–150 kg]). *Other watersports:* Kneeboard, tube, wakeboard or water-ski behind an inboard. Instructors are patient, especially with kids. ($85 30 min, $165 1 hr, $135 per addl hr; Skiing adds about $20, up to 5 skiers; includes equipment, driver; extra charge if picked up from Fort Wilderness, Grand Floridian, Polynesian or Wilderness Lodge).

Taxes. Two types of taxes are relevant to most visitors: *Hotel taxes:* All hotels charge sales tax and a 6-percent resort tax on rooms. *Sales taxes:* Nearly all of Disney sits in Orange County, where the sales tax rate is 6.5 percent. A portion of it is in Osceola County, which has a sales tax of 7 percent. This area includes the All-Star Resorts and the ESPN complex.

Telephone services. Although no cell-phone towers stand on Disney property, recent technology from AT&T has enhanced the network at the resort. Miniature concealed antennas both indoors and out have greatly boosted cellular coverage. The distributed-antenna system (DAS) is the largest network of its kind in a single location in the world. All parks still have weak service on their most crowded days; reception can be especially spotty before or after parades or fireworks, when usage is at its peak. A particularly bad area is The Seas pavilion in Epcot.

Disabled guests. Telecommunications Devices for the Deaf (TDD) are available at Guest Relations offices in the theme parks and Disney Springs. Many pay phones are equipped with amplifying headsets.

Local calls. Callers must include the area code—"407" for all Disney numbers—in all local calls. It is not necessary to dial "1" first.

Hotels. Area hotels often add a hefty service charge on telephone calls made from a room phone. Check the information card near the phone for a list of costs involved.

Pay phones. Pay telephones are still found in all Walt Disney World theme parks, Disney Springs and Disney hotels. Local calls, including calls within Disney, cost 50 cents.

Prepaid phone cards. Private prepaid phone cards are sold at Disney World gift shops and Guest Relations offices. Outside Disney they're available at convenience stores, supermarkets and pharmacies.

Tickets. Though Disney's Magic Your Way ticketing concept is promoted as a way to let you create a ticket that matches your particular needs, it's also complicated. At first glance, it can seem impossible to understand. In a nutshell, Disney's plan lets you tailor tickets to include from one to 10 days of theme-park visits, and then add options such as the ability to visit more than one park a day or spend time at Disney's water parks. Disney also offers annual passes. Florida residents get discounts and monthly-payment plans. The more days the ticket includes, the cheaper it is on a per-day basis. Disney raises its ticket prices at least once a year; the following prices were those as of July 2016.

Single-day tickets for Magic Kingdom. *Value season (late Feb–early March, late Aug–Sept):* $112 adults, $105 children ages 3–9. *Regular season (mid March–May excluding peak Spring Break periods, late July–mid Aug, Oct–mid Nov, Dec until Christmas weeks):* $117 adults, $111 children ages 3–9. *Peak season (peak Spring Break periods,* *late May–July, Thanksgiving and Christmas weeks):* $132 adults, $126 children ages 3–9.

Single-day tickets for other parks. *Value season:* $103 adults, $97 children. *Regular season:* $109 adults, $102 children. *Peak season:* $121 adults, $115 children.

Multi-day tickets. *Two days:* $215 adults, $202 children. *Three days:* $309 adults, $290 children. *Four days:* $346 adults, $325 children. *Five days:* $362 adults, $341 children. *Six days:* $378 adults, $357 children. *Seven days:* $394 adults, $373 children. *Eight days:* $404 adults, $383 children. *Nine days:* $415 adults, $395 children. *Ten days:* $426 adults, $404 children.

A "base ticket"—the prices quoted above—provides admission to one Disney theme park per day, and is good for up to 10 days. The days the ticket is used do not need to be consecutive, but it expires 14 days after its first use. Base tickets have two options:

Park Hopper. This option lets you visit more than one theme park in the same day. A downside: FastPass+ policies make it tough to book FastPasses at more than one park a day. The price ranges from $61 to $74, depending on the number of days on your ticket.

Water Park Fun & More. This adds admission to Disney World's two water parks, the ESPN Wide World of Sports complex and/ or rounds of golf at Disney's 9-hole Oak Trail golf course or Disney's two miniature golf courses. The Water Parks Fun & More surcharge is $68 to $77, depending on the number of days on your ticket. Regardless of how long you stay, if you use this option at least twice during your visit it pays for itself.

Annual passes. These tickets ($798) admit you to the four theme parks, plus give you free parking and discounts on dining, entertainment and merchandise. A Platinum Plus option ($883) adds water parks and the ESPN complex and can include use of the PhotoPass service. Florida residents, U.S. military members and DVC members pay less. Seasonal passes are available.

Discounts and upgrades. Disney offers discounts for Florida residents and members of the U.S. military. Purchased tickets can always be upgraded, but not downgraded.

Water park tickets. One-day tickets to either Blizzard Beach or Typhoon Lagoon are $62 for an adult, $53 for a child. Annual passes good at both water parks are $117 for an adult, $105 for a child. A 1-day ticket can be upgraded to an annual pass on the same day.

Buy tickets at disneyworld.com or call 407-934-7639 from 7 a.m. to 10 p.m. Eastern time.

Tours. Guided tours offer a closer look at Disney World. Those that go backstage don't allow photography there. Unless indicated, tourgoers younger than 18 must be with an adult. To book a tour call 407-939-8687. Arrive 15 min. early, with a photo ID.

Backstage Magic. View creative and tech operations at Magic Kingdom and Epcot, plus visit Disney's departments for Creative Costuming and Central Shops. Check in outside Epcot's main entrance at the far right ($255–$270; 7 hrs, 9a Mon–Fri; includes bus transportation, bottled water, gift, barbecue lunch at Wilderness Lodge; ages 12 and up).

Backstage Tales. Visit the behind-the-scenes animal-care areas at Disney's Animal Kingdom. A portion of proceeds goes to the Disney Conservation Fund. Check in at the park entrance ($90, valid park ticket required; 3 hr 45 min, 7:30a; ages 12 and up).

Behind the Seeds. Walk through the greenhouses of the Living with the Land boat ride. Check in at the Soarin' gift counter ($20 adults, $16 children, valid park ticket required; 1 hr, 9 tours 10:30a–4:30p; all ages).

BoardWalk Ballyhoo. Learn the architecture and history of Disney's BoardWalk Inn. Check in at the Belle Vue Lounge (free; 45 min, 9a Wed–Sat; all ages).

ESPN Wide World of Sports Tour. Take an inside look at this vast athletic complex (free; 1 hr, on busy days only; all ages).

Family Magic. Capture a dastardly villain as you skip through Magic Kingdom on a scavenger hunt. Best suited for groups with children age 4–10. Check in at the Town Square Theater, on Main Street ($39, valid park ticket required; 2 hr, 10a; same-day reservations available by walk-up only; all ages, those under 16 must be with an adult).

Holiday D-Lights. Tour the backstage decorations shop, view the holidays trimmings on Magic Kingdom's Main Street U.S.A., see Epcot's Candlelight Processional. Check in at Epcot's main entrance ($260; 5 hrs, 4p select nights late Nov–Dec; includes light buffet, a limited-edition keepsake pin; shoes must have closed toes, heels; ages 16 and up).

Keys to the Kingdom. Learn the history and guiding philosophies of the Magic Kingdom on Disney's most popular tour, which takes you into the park's underground Utilidor. Check in at the Town Square Theater, on Main Street ($79, valid park ticket required; 5 hrs, 8:30a 9a 9:30a; includes an exclusive keepsake, lunch at Columbia Harbour House; photography strictly prohibited; same-day reservations available by walk-up only; ages 16 and up). **The Magic Behind Our Steam Trains.** See how Magic Kingdom preps its antique trains for daily operation, discuss Walt Disney's love of trains. Photography is encouraged. Check in outside the park entrance ($54, valid park ticket required; 3 hrs, 7:30a; ages 10 and up). **NEW! Savor the Savanna.** Take a night trip through the Animal Kingdom savanna in a private truck, with a stop for African-inspired snacks, beers and wines at an open stand in the middle of the reserve. Check in at the entrance to Kilimanjaro Safaris ($169, valid park ticket required; 4:30p, 5:30p 6:30p; includes a commemorative keepsake, food, drinks; cancelled by severe storms or lightning, but not by rain; ages 8 and up). **NEW! Sense of Africa.** Get an insightful look at the art and architecture of Disney's Animal Kingdom Lodge, as well as its animals and animal-care facility. Check in at the Sunset Lounge, in Jambo House ($249; 3 hrs 30 min, 7a Tue, Sat; includes Boma breakfast buffet; cancelled by severe storms or lightning, but not by rain; reservations required, no same-day reservations; ages 10 and up). **NEW! Starlight Safari.** Take a nighttime trip through the savannas of Disney's Animal Kingdom Lodge aboard an open-sided truck. You're provided with a pair of night-vision goggles to observe freely-roaming animals such as giraffes, flamingos and zebras. A portion of proceeds goes to the Disney Conservation Fund. Check in at Sanaa ($70; 1 hr, 10p; cancelled by severe storms or lightning, but not by rain; ages 8 and up). **The Ultimate Day for Young Families.** A VIP tour of Disney's most family-friendly attractions in Magic Kingdom, Hollywood Studios and Animal Kingdom. Designed for parents with children younger than 10 years old ($299, valid park ticket required; 7 hrs, 8:10a Tue, Fri, Sun; includes table-service lunch; reservations available 180 days in advance; all ages; details at 407-560-4033). **The Ultimate Day of Thrills.** A VIP tour of Disney thrill rides throughout Magic Kingdom, Hollywood Studios and Animal Kingdom ($299, valid park ticket required; 7 hrs, 8:15a Tue, Fri, Sun; includes shorter waits at FastPass+ attractions, table-service lunch; tourgoers must be at least 48 inches tall (122 cm); reservations available 180 days in advance; all ages; details at 407-560-4033). **The UnDISCOVERed Future World.** Go backstage at Epcot's Future World

pavilions, learn about Walt Disney's planned Experimental Prototype Community of Tomorrow. Check in inside Innoventions, across from the Storm Struck exhibit ($69, valid park ticket required; 4 hrs, 8:30a 9a; includes pin; ages 16 and up). **VIP tours.** A theme-park day led by a guide for your individual group, using your custom itinerary ($315–$380 per hr, min 7 continuous hrs, valid park ticket required; includes door-to-door transportation, preferred seating at shows, shorter waits at FastPass+ attractions; up to 10 people per group including infants; reservations available 90 days in advance; all ages; details at 407-560-4033). **Walt Disney: From Marceline to the Magic Kingdom.** Explore Magic Kingdom attractions that had their start at the 1964 World's Fair, learn what motivated Disney to achieve his dreams. Check in at the Town Square Theater ($35, valid park ticket required; 3 hrs, 8a; ages 12 and up). **Wild Africa Trek.** A swaying footbridge high over Nile crocodiles and a life-line lean over hippos highlights this hike through the Harambe Wildlife Preserve at Disney's Animal Kingdom. An open-air private pickup takes you through the savanna, where a covered viewing stand has superb snacks. Check in at the entrance to Kilimanjaro Safaris ($190–$250, valid park ticket required; 3 hrs, eight tours 8a–2:30p; includes photographer, keepsake water bottle, food, refreshments; cancelled by severe storms or lightning; height min 48 in [122 cm]; weight min 45 lbs [20 kg], max 300 lbs [136 kg] while wearing safety harness; shoes must have closed toes and a back strap; ages 8 and up). **Wilderness Back Trail Adventure.** Ride a rugged Segway X2 down shady trails at the Fort Wilderness Resort and Campground. Check in at the Bike Barn ($95; 2 hrs, 8:30a 11:30a Tue–Sat; second portion cancelled by rain; first portion moved under covered pavilion; weight min 100 lbs [45 kg], max 250 lbs [113 kg]; same-day walk-up reservations at the marina; ages 16 and up). **NEW! World Showcase: DestiNations Discovered.** Take a tour of World Showcase pavilions that includes backstage access. Check in inside Innoventions, across from the Storm Struck exhibit ($109, valid park ticket required; 5 hrs, 9:30a; includes lunch at Restaurant Marrakesh in Morocco; all ages). **Yuletide Fantasy.** Explore the holiday decor of Magic Kingdom, Epcot and Disney hotels. Check in at Epcot's main entrance at the far right ($99; 3 hrs, late Nov–Dec; includes keepsake and treat; ages 16 and up).

Transportation. Though many visitors get around Disney in cars, other options abound.

Disney buses. A huge fleet of diesel buses connects Disney's resorts with all theme and water parks and Disney Springs, and also between some parks. Buses typically arrive every 20 to 30 minutes, from one hour before park opening until one hour after closing. Though the buses run from theme park to theme park, they do not go from all theme parks to Blizzard Beach, Disney Springs or Typhoon Lagoon, and serve ESPN Wide World of Sports usually only from Disney's All-Star, Caribbean Beach and Pop Century resorts. There's no official bus service between hotels, though hotels in the same area often share the same buses.

Disney monorails. These electric trains connect the Transportation and Ticket Center (TTC) with Magic Kingdom and the Contemporary, Grand Floridian and Polynesian Village resorts; monorails typically arrive every 5–10 minutes. A separate line runs to Epcot. Operating hours vary.

Disney boats. Ferries connect Magic Kingdom with the TTC and the hotels on Seven Seas Lagoon and Bay Lake; Epcot and Hollywood Studios with hotels in between those parks; and Disney Springs with Port Orleans, Old Key West and Saratoga Springs. For transportation details call 407-939-7433.

Rental cars. If you're already at Disney, the most convenient place to rent a car may be Disney's Car Care Center at the exit of the Magic Kingdom parking lot. A counter (407-824-3470) offers Alamo and National vehicles and provides shuttle service to all Disney hotels. Satellite desks are at the Walt Disney World Dolphin (407-934-4930) and the Buena Vista Palace (407-827-6363). Four other hotels at Disney have car-rental counters: the Disney Springs Hilton (Avis, 407-827-2847), Doubletree Guest Suites (Budget, 407-827-6089), Wyndham (Dollar, 407-583-8000) and Shades of Green (Hertz, 407-938-0600).

Taxicabs and town cars. Taxicabs, town cars and other vehicles are available for travel around Disney and the surrounding area. Mears Transportation—the largest transportation operator in the area, and the only contracted provider for Disney—has the most choices (non-Mears "gypsy" cabs lurk in the area; some have unpredictable rates and take only cash). Mears taxis (pickup 407-422-2222 or 407-699-9999, 24-hr reservations 407-423-5566) operate under the Yellow Cab, Checker Cab and City Cab brands. Transportation within Disney should cost $15–$30; the fare to the Orlando International Airport is typically $65–$75. For groups of 5 to 8 people, vans charge $90–$100 (24-hr reservations 407-423-5566, current fares available at mearstransportation.com; vehicles with child seats available on request).

Weather. Florida's subtropical climate creates mild winters but summers that are hot and humid. Between May and August Disney guests can get exhausted with little effort, as the sun rises almost straight up in the sky. Temperatures in that direct heat usually are about 12 degrees warmer than those in the shade, and can easily reach 100 degrees. Afternoon heat indexes usually exceed 105 degrees. Brief afternoon thunderstorms are common. Overall, July is the hottest month at Disney, January the coolest. August is the wettest month, December the driest.

Hurricanes. Though hurricanes often strike the Florida coast, the risk of one hitting Disney is low, as the resort sits in the middle of the state—since the power of a hurricane is generated by being over water, its intensity lessens upon landfall and usually dissipates quickly. Three hurricanes, however, came close to Disney World in 2004. Disney closed its parks and golf courses for those storms, but kept its hotels open. The eye of Hurricane Charley passed just a few miles south. Florida's hurricane season is June through November. Disney allows you to cancel hotel reservations without penalty whenever the National Hurricane Center issues a hurricane

WALT DISNEY WORLD WEATHER

MONTH	AVG HIGH	AVG LOW	RAIN
Jan	72	48	2.4 in.
Feb	73	49	2.7 in.
Mar	77	53	3.3 in.
April	82	58	3.0 in.
May	87	64	3.8 in.
June	90	70	6.0 in.
July	93	72	6.6 in.
Aug	92	72	7.3 in.
Sept	90	71	6.0 in.
Oct	84	65	3.2 in.
Nov	79	57	2.4 in.
Dec	73	50	2.2 in.

warning for the Orlando area (or a guest's place of residence) within seven days of your scheduled arrival date. If you're at Disney when a hurricane approaches, take it seriously and follow Disney's advice.

Rain gear. Disney sells clear plastic ponchos throughout its property; children and adult sizes cost about $8.50. Umbrellas are also available. Small collapsible ones go for about $15; large golf umbrellas are $43.

Weather refunds. There are no refunds at Disney World for bad weather. Disney theme parks stay open, rain or shine; water parks offer rain checks in some circumstances.

Weddings. Up to a dozen couples tie the knot at Walt Disney World every day. Sound strange? Actually, there's a lot to recommend it. Disney has unrivaled facilities for a family gathering, good year-round weather, a quality honeymoon spot and a one-stop Fairy Tale Weddings division. Most weddings are performed at Disney's Wedding Pavilion next to the Grand Floridian Resort and Spa. Several hotels—including the BoardWalk, Polynesian Village, Wilderness Lodge and Yacht Club—also host ceremonies.

Planning. Named after funnyman Martin Short's wedding planner in Disney's 1991 movie "Father of the Bride," Franck's Bridal Studio can arrange accommodations, cakes, flowers, music, photography and rehearsal dinners. It's next to the wedding pavilion.

Costs. Disney offers three packages, which vary based on the number of guests and level of services. The average Disney wedding costs $31,000 and includes 100 people. Prices start at $2,495. For details call 321-939-4610 or visit disneyweddings.com.

Honeymoons. Disney planning services includes an online registry (858-433-1506, disney.honeymoonwishes.com), which lets couples create a wish list for their trip and have family and friends contribute. More honeymoon help is available at 321-939-4610 and at disneyweddings.com.

Wi-Fi. Disney provides complimentary wireless Internet access throughout its property, though it's often slow on crowded days and reception can be poor. For answers to technical issues, call Disney for assistance at 407-827-2732.

Youth groups. Disney World offers various activities and competitions for youth groups of 10 or more. Participants get discounted group rates for both accommodations and theme-park tickets. Opportunities include:

Disney Performing Arts OnStage. This audition-based program invites community groups and middle- and high-school students to perform at Disney year-round. Instrumental and vocal groups participate, as do dance ensembles (instrumental groups 866-242-3617, vocal 866-578-4823, dance 866-578-4827). Optional performance workshops are available (866-578-4830). More information is available at disneyyouth.com/our-programs/performing-arts.

Festival Disney. Held each spring, this educational experience is open to middle-school, junior- and senior-high school concert bands, jazz ensembles, marching bands, orchestras, vocal ensembles, show choirs and auxiliary units. No audition is required; directors choose either competitive or non-competitive adjudication options. Performances take place at Saratoga Springs and Disney's Hollywood Studios (800-872-3378).

Disney Youth Education Series (YES). These programs give elementary through high school students real-world learning experiences at Disney theme parks. Hands-on courses focus on Applied Sciences, Environmental Studies, Liberal Arts and Leadership Development.

Finally, about alligators. A quick lesson: Stay out of the ponds, lakes and lagoons at Walt Disney World. And if you see an alligator, don't feed it. In 2016, a 2-year-old boy was attacked by one in the water behind Disney's Grand Floridian resort hotel and later found dead. He and his family were at an outdoor movie event when he waded into about a foot of water. Trappers later caught the reptile. Like many other ponds and lakes, the Seven Seas Lagoon connects into a network of canals that flow through the Disney property. Hundreds of alligators roam freely.

The likelihood of being injured by one in Florida is low. Since 1973 the reptiles have attacked about 375 people in the state, about nine per year. Of those, two-thirds required medical care and 23 died. Until this incident, none of those deaths were at Disney World. Typically alligators only approach people if they have been fed by someone earlier, which unfortunately is common. Alligators usually hunt for food from dusk until dawn.

Florida has 20 million residents and more than a million alligators, according to its Fish and Wildlife Conservation Commission.

Telephone Directory

Area Code 407 unless indicated

AUTOMOBILE RENTALS
Alamo Car Care Center............................... 824-3470
  Buena Vista Palace 827-6363
Avis Disney Springs Hilton 827-2847
Budget Doubletree Guest Suites.................... 827-6089
Dollar Wyndham 827-8324
Thrifty WDW Dolphin.................................... 934-4930

AUTOMOBILE SERVICES
Car Care Center 824-0976
  After hours.. 824-4777

BANKING SERVICES
Suntrust Disney Springs 828-6103

BUSINESS SERVICES
Disney Event Group Bus. gatherings.......... 939-7129
Disney Institute 566-2620
Disney Professional Seminars 824-7997

CONVENTION PLANNING
Disney convention centers 321 939-7129
WDW Swan and Dolphin 934-4290

DISABILITY SERVICES
Sign-language show schedule 824-4321
  Special requests 939-7807
TDD numbers Disney information 827-5141

ENTERTAINMENT
AMC Theater Disney Springs 827-1308
  Movie listings.. 888 262-4386
Atlantic Dance Hall BoardWalk Resort 939-2444
Cirque du Soleil Disney Springs 939-7600
House of Blues Disney Springs 934-2583
Jellyrolls BoardWalk Resort......................... 560-8770

FLORISTS
Disney Floral & Gifts 827-3505
  Disney Dream Makers 939-4438
  Convention services.................................... 827-1266
  Wedding services.............................. 321 939-4610

GASOLINE STATIONS
Speedway Disney Springs............................ 938-0160
  Epcot Resort Area....................................... 938-0151
  Magic Kingdom... 938-0143

GENERAL INFORMATION
Disney Springs 939-6244
Poison Control Center 800 222-1222

Time and temperature 646-3131
Walt Disney World Community relations.... 828-3453
  Customer service (live operator)................... 824-2222
  Hotel reservations 939-7429
  Merchandise guest services................. 877 560-6477
  Recreation reservations 939-7529
  Technical support... 939-7765
  Theme-park ticket sales 939-7429
  Vacation package booking 939-7675
  Walt Disney World Travel Co........................ 939-6244
  For United Kingdom visitors 939-7718
  If calling from the U.K........................... 087 0242 4908
Weather Three-day Disney forecast.............. 824-4104

HAIR SALONS AND BARBER SHOPS
Bibbidi Bobbidi Boutique 939-7895
Harmony Barber Shop Magic Kingdom...... 824-6550
Ivy Trellis Salon Grand Floridian Resort...... 824-1679
Periwig's Yacht Club Resort...................... 934-3260
The Salon WDW Dolphin.............................. 934-4772

HOTELS AND RESORTS
B Resort and Spa Disney Springs............... 828-2828
Best Western Disney Springs....................... 828-2424
Buena Vista Palace Disney Springs........... 827-2727
Disney's All-Star Resorts
  All-Star Movies.. 939-7000
  All-Star Music.. 939-6000
  All-Star Sports... 939-5000
  Lost and found... 939-6882
Disney's Animal Kingdom Lodge 938-3000
  Lost and found... 938-4778
Disney's Art of Animation Resort 938-7000
Disney's BoardWalk Inn and Villas 939-5100
  Lost and found... 939-5116
Disney's Caribbean Beach Resort 934-3400
  Lost and found... 934-3090
Disney's Contemporary Resort 824-1000
  Lost and found... 283-3659
Disney's Coronado Springs Resort 939-1000
  Lost and found... 939-3070
Disney's Fort Wilderness Resort 824-2900
  Campfire movie schedule............................. 824-2727
  Electric cart rental 824-2742
  Group camping... 938-3398
  Horseback riding... 824-2900
  Lost and found... 824-2726
  Pony rides 824-2788
Disney's Grand Floridian Resort 824-3000
  Lost and found... 824-2988
Disney's Old Key West Resort 827-7700
Disney's Polynesian Village Resort 824-2000
  Lost and found... 824-2192

Disney's Pop Century Resort 938-4000
Lost and found... 934-3090
Disney's Port Orleans Resorts
French Quarter.. 934-5000
Riverside 934-6000
Disney's Saratoga Springs Resort 827-1100
Lost and found.. 827-4942
Disney Vacation Club 800 800-9100
Sales information... 566-3100
Disney's Wilderness Lodge Resort 824-3200
Lost and found.. 824-4751
Wilderness Lodge Villas 938-4300
Disney's Yacht and Beach Club Resort
Beach Club 934-8000
Beach Club Villas... 934-2175
Yacht Club 934-7000
Doubletree Guest Suites Disney Springs.. 934-1000
Four Seasons Orlando 877 970-8117
Hilton Disney Springs 827-4000
Holiday Inn Disney Springs........................ 828-8888
Shades of Green 824-3600
Walt Disney World Swan & Dolphin ... 934-4000
Wyndham Disney Springs............................ 828-4444

KENNELS
Best Friends Pet Care Center........877 493-9738

LOST AND FOUND
Disney Central Lost and Found 824-4245
Disney parks Animal Kingdom 938-2785
Disney's Blizzard Beach 560-5408
Epcot.. 560-6646
Magic Kingdom.. 824-4521
Disney's Typhoon Lagoon 560-6296
Disney's Hollywood Studios.......................... 560-3720
Disney Springs 828-3150
ESPN Wide World of Sports 541-5600

PHOTOGRAPHY SERVICES
Disney Photographic Services 827-5099
PhotoPass 560-4300

POLICE
Orange County Sheriff 254-7000
Osceola County Sheriff 348-2222
Walt Disney World Security 560-7959
Urgent matters... 560-1990

RECREATION
Boat rentals 939-7529
Camping Groups 938-3398
Carriage rides 939-7529
Characters in Flight Disney Springs.......... 938-9433

ESPN Wide World of Sports 828-3267
Live operator... 939-1500
runDisney... 938-3398
Youth group information............................... 939-4263
Fishing Disney excursions 939-2277
Golf Disney tee-time reservations................. 939-4653
Horseback riding Fort Wilderness 824-2900
Marathons and foot races 938-3398
Miniature golf Fantasia Gardens................. 560-4753
Winter Summerland...................................... 560-7161
Pony rides Fort Wilderness 824-2788
Reservations Disney recreation 939-7529
Splitsville Disney Springs............................ 938-7467
Surfing lessons Typhoon Lagoon 939-7873
Tennis Reservations, lessons........................ 621-1991
Wagon rides 939-7529
Watersports Sammy Duvall's....................... 939-0754

SPECIAL OCCASIONS
Cake Hotline Ordering 827-2253
Floral arrangements 321 939-4610
Honeymoons 800 370-6009
Quinceañera events 321 939-4555
Weddings 321 939-4610

THEME PARKS
Blizzard Beach Blizzard Beach Dr 560-3400
Capacity closures 939-4636
Disney's Animal Kingdom Osceola Pkwy . 939-5277
Disney's Hollywood Studios S Studio Dr . 939-5277
Epcot Epcot Center Dr 824-4321
Extra Magic Hours Schedule 824-4321
Magic Kingdom Seven Seas Dr.................... 939-5277
Refurbishments Schedule 824-4321
Ticket inquiries 566-4985
Annual Passholder Hotline 827-7200
Ticket sales General 566-4985
Convention attendees.................................. 939-4686
Tours 939-8687
VIP Tours 560-4033
Typhoon Lagoon E Buena Vista Blvd 560-4120

TRANSPORTATION SERVICES
Disney's Magical Express 866 599-0951
Mears Transportation Luxury sedans 423-5566
Airport shuttles.. 423-5566
Group transportation sales........................... 839-1570
Taxicabs (Checker, City, Yellow Cabs)........... 422-2222
Walt Disney World Transportation 939-7433

YOUTH GROUPS
Disney Youth Programs 866 842-3340
Disney Performing Arts 800 359-0509

Index

1900 Park Fare..315
50's Prime Time Cafe............................172

A
AA meetings...348
AAU Boys Natl Basketball Chmpnshp..............292
ABC Commissary.....................................173
Adventurers Outpost...............................215
Agent P's World Showcase Adventure............158
Akershus Royal Banquet Hall.................112, 156
Alcohol..348
AMC 24 Theater......................................285
America Gardens Theater..........................146
American Adventure, The....................146-149
American Music Machine..........................149
Archery...371
Ariel's Grotto.. 37
Artist Point..326
Astro Orbiter.. 89
ATMs..358

B
B Resort and Spa....................................332
Baby Care Centers..................................349
Babysitters..349
Backlot Express......................................173
Banks...358
Barnstormer, The.................................... 84
Baseball Quadraplex...............................289
Bay Slides...264
Be Our Guest.....................................37, 46
Beaches & Cream...................................328
Beauty and the Beast Live on Stage........186-187
Best Western Lake Buena Vista.................333
Bibbidi Bobbidi Boutique.................... 50, 351
Bicycle and surrey rentals........................371
Biergarten......................................112, 151
Big River Grille & Brewing Works..............306
Big Thunder Mountain Railroad.................. 72
Birthdays...348
Blaze..274
Blizzard Beach.................................258-263
Bluezoo..330
Boat charters...371
Boathouse, The................................276, 278
Boat rentals...372
Boatwright's Dining Hall..........................324
Boma—Flavors of Africa..........................303
Boneyard, The..234
Bongos Cuban Cafe...........................285, 286
Braves Spring Training.............................292
British Revolution...................................142
Buena Vista Palace and Spa.....................333

Burudika...203
Buzz Lightyear's Space Ranger Spin..........90-91

C
California Grill.......................................310
Campfires..372
Canada pavilion................................138-139
Cape May Café.......................................328
Captain Jack Sparrow's Pirate Tutorial......36, 37
Captain's Grille......................................329
Carriage and wagon rides........................373
Casey Junior Splash 'n' Soak Station......... 85
Casey's Corner....................................... 47
Casey's Corner pianist............................ 36
Castaway Creek......................................264
Celebrate the Magic................................100
Chakranadi..203
Champion Stadium..................................289
Characters in Flight................................286
Chef Mickey's..310
Chefs de France...............................112, 143
Childcare centers...................................349
Child swap...349
Children..349
China pavilion..152
Christmas..370
Cinderella's Royal Table.......................37, 46
Circle of Life, The..................................129
Citizens of Hollywood.............................176
Citizens of Main Street........................... 36
Cítricos...316
Columbia Harbour House......................... 48
Conservation Station...............................223
Convention facilities...............................351
Cookes of Dublin....................................277
Coral Reef Restaurant.............................113
Cosmic Ray's Starlight Cafe..................... 48
Country Bear Jamboree........................... 68
Cross Country Creek................................258
Crossroads at House of Blues...................285
Crush 'n' Gusher....................................264
Crystal Palace....................................37, 47

D
Dapper Dans... 36
Diamondplex Softball Complex..................291
Dinosaur...230
Disability services..................................352
Disney Dining Plan..................................353
Disney Dollars.......................................358
Disney Junior Live on Stage.....................195
Disney Spring Training.............................291
Disney's All-Star Resorts.........................301

Disney's Animal Kingdom Lodge.........................302
Disney's Art of Animation Resort.....................304
Disney's BoardWalk Inn and Villas..................305
Disney's Candy Cauldron 285
Disney's Caribbean Beach Resort...................308
Disney's Contemporary Resort 309
Disney's Coronado Springs Resort..................311
Disney's Fort Wilderness Resort 312
Disney's Grand Floridian Resort......................315
Disney's Old Key West Resort 317
Disney's Polynesian Village Resort.................318
Disney's Pop Century Resort...........................321
Disney's Port Orleans Resorts.........................323
Disney's Saratoga Springs Resort....................324
Disney's Wilderness Lodge 326
Disney's Yacht and Beach Club 327
DisneyQuest..286
DiVine 204
Diving and snorkeling 373
DJ Anaan..204
Dockside Margaritas..282
Dolphins in Depth..373
Doubletree Guest Suites 333
Downhill Double Dipper...................................258
Dumbo the Flying Elephant............................. 83

E
Earl of Sandwich...282
Easter Weekend 367
Edison, The..278
Electrical Water Pageant................................. 40
Electric Umbrella...117
Ellen's Energy Adventure................................132
Enchanted Tales with Belle........................37, 80
Epcot Intl Flower & Garden Festival...............367
Epcot Intl Food & Wine Festival......................368
Equipment rentals, children 350
Erin McKenna's Bakery NYC............................277
ESPN Club 306
ESPN Wide World of Sports Grill.....................294
Expedition Everest.........................201, 227-229
Extra Magic Hours..354

F
Face art 350
Fantasia Gardens 375
Fantasmic 197
FastPass+ 22-26
Festival of Fantasy Parade.........................37, 98
Festival of the Lion King 201, 219
Festival of the Masters....................................368
Finding Nemo—The Musical 201, 235
Fishing 373

Flag Retreat... 36
Flame Tree Barbecue.......................................209
Flights of Wonder...224
Floral services..354
Flying Fish Cafe..307
Food trucks..285
For the First Time in Forever 178
Forty Thirst Street..282
Fossil Fun Games..233
Fountain, The...330
Four Seasons Orlando......................................331
France pavilion...142-143
Fresh Mediterranean Market...........................330
Friar's Nook 48
Frontierland Hoedown..................................... 36
Frozen Ever After.......................................154-155
Funnel Cakes..119, 149

G
Gangplank Falls...265
Garden Grill 113
Garden Grove Café...330
Gasoline stations...355
Gaston's Tavern... 48
Gay Days...367
Germany pavilion...151
Gift cards 358
Golf...373
Goofy's Candy Company...................................282
Gran Fiesta Tour...157
Grand Floridian Café 316
Gratuities 358
Great Movie Ride, The 177
Groceries 355
Guest Relations..355

H
Haagen-Dazs..285
Hall of Presidents, The 64-65
Harambe Market...209
Harmony Barber Shop...................................... 51
Haunted Mansion, The...................................... 67
Height minimums 351
Hess Sports Fields...290
Highways...356
Hilton at Disney Springs..................................333
Holiday Inn at Disney Springs 333
Holidays..356
Hollywood & Vine 172
Hollywood Brown Derby, The...........................172
Honey, I Shrunk the Kids Playground..............182
Honeymoons...381
Hoop-Dee-Doo Musical Revue.........................314

Horseback riding................................374
House of Blues Music Hall.......................287
HP Field House.................................290
Humunga Kowabunga..............................265

I

IllumiNations..................................159
Il Mulino......................................331
Imagination pavilion...........................130
Impressions de France......................142-143
Independence Day Weekend.......................368
Indiana Jones Epic Stunt Spectacular...........179
Innoventions...................................125
International travelers.........................356
it's a small world...........................76-77
It's Tough to Be a Bug.........................216
Italy pavilion.............................149-151

J

Jammitors......................................131
Japan pavilion.............................144-146
Jeweled Dragon Acrobats........................152
Jiko—The Cooking Place.........................303
Jim Henson's MuppetVision 3-D..................181
Jock Lindsey's Hangar Bar......................279
Jostens Center.................................290
Journey into Imagination with Figment..........130
Jungle Cruise...................................58

K

Kali River Rapids..............................225
Karamell-Kuche.................................119
Katsura Grill..............................117, 146
Keelhaul Falls.................................265
Kennel...361
Ketchakiddee Creek.............................265
Kilimanjaro Safaris........................220-221
Kimonos..331
Kona Café......................................319
Kringla Bakeri Og Kafe.....................117, 156

L

La Cantina de San Angel....................117, 156
La Cava del Tequila........................117, 156
La Hacienda de San Angel..............113-114, 156
Landing, The...................................275
La Nouba.......................................287
L'Artisan Des Glaces.......................117, 143
Le Cellier.................................114, 139
Les Halles Boulangerie Paitisserie.........118, 143
Liberty Inn....................................118
Liberty Square Riverboat........................66
Liberty Tree Tavern.............................47

Lights, Motors, Action Extreme Stunt Show...183
Living with the Land...........................129
L'Occitane en Provence.........................273
Lockers..357
Lost and found.................................357
Lost children..................................351
Lotus Blossom Cafe.........................118, 152
Lunching Pad, The...............................48

M

Mad Tea Party...................................79
Magic Carpets of Aladdin........................59
Magical Express................................357
MagicBand....................................22-23
Maharajah Jungle Trek..........................226
Main Street Bakery..............................48
Main Street Electrical Parade..............37, 99
Main Street Philharmonic........................36
Main Street Trolley Parade......................36
Main Street Vehicles............................55
Mama Melrose's Ristorante Italiano.............173
Many Adventures of Winnie the Pooh, The........78
Marathons......................................374
Mariachi Cobre.................................156
Marketplace, The...............................280
Marketplace Snacks.............................282
Matsuriza......................................146
Maya Grill.....................................312
Mayday Falls...................................266
Medical services...............................358
Melt-Away Bay..................................258
Mexico pavilion............................156-157
Mickey's Backyard Barbecue.....................314
Mickey's Not-So-Scary Halloween Party..........368
Mickey's PhilharMagic...........................74
Mickey's Very Merry Christmas Party............370
Min and Bill's Dockside Diner..................173
Miniature golf.................................375
Mission Space..................................133
Money..358
Monsieur Paul..............................114, 143
Monsters Inc. Laugh Floor.......................87
Morimoto Asia..................................276
Morocco pavilion...........................143-144
Mount Mayday Trail.............................266
Move It! Shake It! Dance & Play It!........37, 97
Mulch, Sweat and Shears........................176
My Disney Experience.........................23-24
My Magic+....................................22-26

N

Narcoossee's...................................316
NBA Experience.................................287

New Balance Track and Field Complex 291
New Year's Eve 371
Night of Joy 368
Nine Dragons Restaurant 114, 152
Norway pavilion 152-156
Notorious Banjo Brothers and Bob, The 36

O
O Canada 139
'Ohana 320
Olivia's Cafe 318

P
Pangani Forest Exploration Trail 222
Paradiso 37 276
Parasailing 375
Parking 360
Pecos Bill Cafe 49
PeopleMover 88
Pete's Silly Sideshow 37
Peter Pan's Flight 75
Pets 361
Photography 361
PhotoPass 361
Pin trading 362
Pinocchio Village Haus 49
Pirate's Adventure, A 56
Pirates League 51, 351
Pirates of the Caribbean 62-63
Pizzafari 209
Planet Hollywood Observatory 274
Plaza, The 47
Polynesian Village Resort 318
Portobello Country Italian Trattoria 276
Postal services 363
Primeval Whirl 231
Princess Fairytale Hall 37
Prince Charming Regal Carrousel 73

Q
Queues 363
Quinceañera celebrations 364

R
Raglan Road 277, 279
Rainforest Café 208, 282
Reflections of China 152
Refurbishments and rehabs 364
Rental cars 29, 379
Restaurant Marrakesh 115, 144
Restaurant policies 364
Restaurantosaurus 209
Rock 'n' Roller Coaster Str Aerosmith 188-189

Rose & Crown Dining Room & Pub 115, 142
Royal Majesty Makers 36
Runoff Rapids 259

S
San Angel Inn 115, 156
Sanaa 303
Sbandieratori Di Sansepolcro 150
Sci-Fi Dine-In Theater Restaurant 173
Seas with Nemo & Friends, The 126-127
Selfie sticks 356
Sergio 150
Serveur Amusant 142
Seven Dwarfs Mine Train 81
Shades of Green 332
Shark Reef 266
Shipping 365
Shopping 365
Shula's 331
Shutters 308
Single Rider lines 363
Ski Patrol Training Camp 259
Skipper Canteen 47
Slush Gusher 259
Smokehouse at House of Blues, The 285
Smoking 366
Snow Stormers 259
Soarin' Around the World 128
Sommerfest 118, 151
Sorcerers of the Magic Kingdom 56
Sounds Like Summer Concert Series 368
Space Mountain 94-95
Spaceship Earth 123-124
Spas 366
Special events 367
Spice Road Table 115-116, 144
Spirit of Aloha 321
Splash Mountain 70-71
Splitsville Luxury Lanes 285, 287
Sports and recreation 371
Sprinkles 274
St. Patrick's Day 367
Star Tours 180
Star Wars land 19
Star Wars Launch Bay 171, 176
Star Wars: Jedi Training Academy 176
Starbucks 117, 173, 211, 282, 285
Starring Rolls Cafe 173
Stitch's Great Escape 86
STK Orlando 277, 279
Storm Slides 266
Studio Catering Co. 174
Summit Plummet 259

Sum of all Thrills, The............131
Sunset Ranch Market............174
Sunshine Seasons............118
Super Hero Headquarters............284
Surf Pool............267
Surfing lessons............375
Sweet Spells............176
Swiss Family Treehouse............57

T

Tam Tam Drummers of Harambe............204
Tamu Tamu............211
Tangierine Cafe............118, 119
Taste Track............118
Tatooine Traders............176
Taxes............375
Taxicabs and towncars............379
Teamboat Springs............260
Tea Traders Cafe............278
Telephone services............375
Tennis Center............291
Tennis............375
Teppan Edo............116, 146
Test Track............134-135
Theme park policies............376
Tickets............377
Tikes Peak............260
Toboggan Racers............261
Tokyo Dining............116, 146
Tommy Bahama............273
Tom Sawyer Island............69
Tomorrowland Speedway............96
Tomorrowland Terrace............49
Tony's Town Square............47
Tortuga Tavern............49
Tours............378
Tower Gifts............176
Town Center............273
Town Square Theater............37
Toy Story Land............19
Toy Story Mania 184-185
Toy Story Pizza Planet Arcade............174
Trader Sam's Grog Grotto............320
Trail's End Restaurant............313
Transportation............379
Trattoria al Forno............307
Tree of Life Garden............217
Tren-D............281
T-REX............282
TriceraTop Spin............232
Turf Club Bar & Grill............325
Turtle Talk with Crush............126
Tusker House............208, 215

Tutto Gusto Wine Cellar............118, 151
Tutto Italia............116-117, 150
Twilight Zone Tower of Terror, The............190-193
Typhoon Lagoon............264-269

U

UGG............273
Under the Sea............82
Uniqlo............273
United Kingdom pavilion............139-142
United World of Soccer............284

V

Via Napoli............117, 150
Victoria & Albert's............316
Vivoli Gelateria............278
Voices of Liberty............149
Voyage of the Little Mermaid............194

W

Walt Disney: One Man's Dream............196
Walt Disney restaurant (Disney Springs)............279
Walt Disney World Railroad............54
Walt Disney World Swan and Dolphin............330
Walt Disney's Carousel of Progress............92-93
Walt Disney's Enchanted Tiki Room............60-61
Water sports............375
Wave, The............310
Weather............380
Weddings............381
Wetzel's Pretzels............282
Wheelchairs............352
Whispering Canyon Cafe............327
Wi-Fi............381
Wilderness Explorers............218
Winged Encounters............205
Winter Summerland............375
Wire transfers............358
Wishes............101
Wolfgang Puck Dining Room............285
Wolfgang Puck Express............282
Wolfgang Puck Grand Cafe............285
World of Disney............281
Writer's Stop, The............174
Wyndham Lake Buena Vista............333

Y

Yachtsman Steakhouse............329
Yak & Yeti............208
Yak & Yeti Local Food Cafés............211
Ye Olde Christmas Shoppe............51
Yorkshire County Fish Shop............118, 142
Youth groups............381

About the authors

A FORMER WALT DISNEY WORLD concierge supervisor, Julie Neal is the author of "The Complete Walt Disney World" series of travel guides. As such she's spent over 2,500 days at Disney World not counting her time behind the desk. A roller coaster freak and a wildlife enthusiast, she lists Expedition Everest and the Gorilla Falls Exploration Trail as her favorite Disney attractions. Her passions outside the world of theme parks include animal rights, reading and old movies.

Julie's husband Mike designed the book and took most of the photos for it. As it's been since he first rode it in high school, his favorite Disney attraction is Space Mountain, from the front seat. Outside of work his interests include cheeses, filmmaking and palm trees.

Julie and Mike live in Orlando with their daughter Micaela, who helps out in the family business when she's not scuba diving or going to school at Florida State. Her favorite Disney ride: Big Thunder Mountain Railroad.

For years the Neals have shared their home with the most important members of their family, their dogs. Bear was a farmer, a chocolate lab who actually cultivated fields of mushrooms in his neighborhood, checking on them nightly until they were just right to gulp. Next was the world's most cuddly 85-pound rescue dog, Oliver. As diverse in his lineage as he was in his lizard tracking, Ollie left his forever home in 2015, heading off to that great lizard hunting ground in the sky.

He got a second chance.

When you want a pet, consider one from A Better Life Pet Rescue, an all-volunteer organization based in Central Florida. Since 2005 we've rescued over 2,000 animals from unfortunate environments, provided them with medical and hands-on care, and placed them with loving foster parents until we found their forever homes.

We always have animals in need. Check them out at betterlifepets.com. Only 20 percent of people adopt their pets from shelters or rescues. Be one of them. Or donate, or be a foster parent. Because every animal deserves a second chance.

www.betterlifepets.com

A Better Life Pet Rescue

OPEN YOUR HEART TO A RESCUED PET